ESSAYS
IN STYLISTIC
ANALYSIS

ESSAYS IN STYLISTIC ANALYSIS

Edited by Howard S. Babb
UNIVERSITY OF CALIFORNIA, IRVINE

 HARCOURT BRACE JOVANOVICH, INC.
NEW YORK   CHICAGO   SAN FRANCISCO   ATLANTA

Upsala College
Library
East Orange, N. J. 07019

FOR CORINNA

COVER ART: Georges Braque, *Helios I,* 1946. Lithograph.
Permission ADAGP 1971 by French Reproduction Rights, Inc.

© 1972 BY HARCOURT BRACE JOVANOVICH, INC.

All rights reserved. No part of this publication may be reproduced or transmitted in any form or by any means, electronic or mechanical, including photocopy, recording, or any information storage and retrieval system, without permission in writing from the publisher.

ISBN: 0-15-522902-8

Library of Congress Catalog Card Number: 78-169066

Printed in the United States of America

Preface

THE purpose of this anthology is to present a group of essays that reveal the variety of assumptions on which stylistic critics proceed, the variety of ways in which they interpret style. Most of the essays, whatever their theoretical orientation, involve specific, often intensive, verbal analysis, and all of them seem to me exciting pieces of criticism. While I have aimed primarily at illustrating a broad spectrum of approaches to the study of style, I have also chosen essays which, taken together, treat a wide variety of literary texts. The texts discussed range in genre through poetry, prose, and drama; in time, from the Middle Ages to the present; and in language, from English and French to Spanish, German, and Czech. And I have sought after variety of another sort in selecting pieces that analyze different features of style, such as diction, syntax, imagery, and metrics. Finally, in addition to essays that have already appeared in England and America, this anthology includes three pieces of European criticism published in translation for the first time.

My own interest in stylistics was kindled some years ago through an argument, which I lost, with three fellow graduate students, David Ferry, Philip Finkelpearl, and Robert O'Clair. In 1961–62, with the kind backing of my chairman, Robert M. Estrich, I was granted two quarters of assigned research duty by Ohio State University, for which I am deeply grateful, since they enabled me to begin exploring stylistics systematically. For part of that time I lived in Zurich, where Mrs. Elisabeth Brock-Sulzer most generously met with me periodically to direct and discuss my reading in French and German stylistic criticism. Without her wisdom and guidance then, I would not have come to imagine the present anthology.

I owe thanks to the University of California at Irvine for underwriting some of the expenses involved in readying materials for the anthology, and to a number of my colleagues who willingly translated snatches of Old French and Italian for me. I am especially obliged to several persons associated with Harcourt Brace Jovanovich: to Merton Rapp and Everett Sims, for believing in the anthology; to Martha Lowenstine, for the translations from Spanish; and to Karen Kirtley, for a most extraordinary job of editing.

But my greatest debt is to my wife. She has provided translations not only of the three essays from German and of their quotations, but of the passages in French and Latin that appear in the essays by Croll and Riffaterre. And her own interest in style, her experience with languages, her knowledge of comparative literature have been constant aids in our preparing of this volume.

Contents

INTRODUCTION 3

GEORGES LOUIS LECLERC, COMTE DE BUFFON
    Discourse on Style: An Address Delivered Before the French Academy 11

HEINRICH WÖLFFLIN
    Introduction to *Principles of Art History* 18

RICHARD M. OHMANN
    Prolegomena to the Analysis of Prose Style 35

DAVID LODGE
    FROM The Novelist's Medium and the Novelist's Art 50

THEOPHIL SPOERRI
    Style of Distance, Style of Nearness 62

ROY HARVEY PEARCE
    On the Continuity of American Poetry 79

MORRIS W. CROLL
    The Baroque Style in Prose 97

JOSEPHINE MILES
    FROM The Primary Language of Poetry in the 1540's and 1640's 118

FRITZ STRICH
    FROM Language 138

LEO SPITZER
    Linguistic Perspectivism in the *Don Quijote* 148

ERICH AUERBACH
    Roland Against Ganelon 182

W. K. WIMSATT, JR.
    Diction 206

JAN MUKAŘOVSKÝ
    K. Čapek's Prose as Lyrical Melody and as Dialogue 218

SIGURD BURCKHARDT
    King Lear: The Quality of Nothing 235

vii

ELISABETH BROCK-SULZER
    The Poet at War with His Language: Remarks on the Newer French Lyric   250
IAN WATT
    The First Paragraph of *The Ambassadors:* An Explication   275
JOHN HOLLOWAY
    Matthew Arnold   293
HARRY LEVIN
    FROM Observations on the Style of Ernest Hemingway   321
MARK SCHORER
    Fiction and the "Analogical Matrix"   338
RICHARD M. OHMANN
    Literature as Sentences   353
MICHAEL RIFFATERRE
    Describing Poetic Structures: Two Approaches to Baudelaire's "Les Chats"   362

ESSAYS IN STYLISTIC ANALYSIS

Introduction

Since this anthology is intended to represent the diversity of approaches to stylistic interpretation, it would be folly to attempt any rigorous definition of *style* here. Suffice it to say that in most of the essays that make up this volume, the critics examine literary texts intensively to seize on verbal traits that they regard as somehow characteristic of the authors' varying linguistic modes. In order to highlight some of the issues involved in stylistic criticism, however, four pieces of a more theoretical cast have been included at the beginning of the anthology.

All the essays except the first, the Comte de Buffon's "Discourse on Style" (1753), are drawn from the twentieth century, for this is the period in which detailed concern with the verbal procedures of individual authors has really burgeoned and in which various approaches to the study of style have manifested themselves most fully. Certainly I do not mean to suggest that all the contemporary interest in language may be classified as stylistic or that critics of earlier periods were uninterested in the workings of words and the linguistic procedures of particular writers. But it seems fair to say that a cluster of ideas associated with rhetoric dominates most of the commentary on specifically verbal matters prior to the twentieth century. These ideas are discernible in Aristotle's authoritative *Rhetoric* and were reinforced by such books as Cicero's *Orator*, so it is little wonder that they should have powerfully affected critics of times earlier than our own—or indeed that they should retain some influence today. In this tradition, rhetoric is conceived of as essentially persuasive, oriented toward moving an audience rather than toward revealing the private experience of the speaker. Language, in turn, is imagined as the "dress" of thought and thus to some degree distinct from thought, with the speaker first deciding what he wants to express and then seeking, among alternative possibilities, the most effective way in which to express it. Since this tradition assumes that there are different ways of saying much the same thing, judgments of good and bad style may arise and the study of rhetoric may become normative.

Clearly, ideas like these minimize the personal component in verbal expression. As might be expected, in the treatments of rhetoric that have derived over the years from Aristotle and Cicero, the authors often provide us, when they come to consider language specifically, with more or less elaborate lists of verbal figures—categorized according to some principle and illustrated by quotations from a number of authors—which may be viewed as models. Classical antiquity did of course originate a somewhat different set of criteria that bore heavily on considerations of style in literary texts through many centuries: the doctrine of the separation of styles (touched on in this anthology by Erich Auerbach in his essay on the *Chanson de Roland*), which distinguished among several stylistic levels, each appropriate to a different type of material. But to illustrate a typically rhetorical attitude toward style, Buffon's "Discourse on Style" has been included in the anthology: his "Discourse" takes for granted the primacy of thought, seems to assume the separability of thought and words, which may be more or less effectively disposed, and is imbued with the consciousness of language as working on an audience. Not only does Buffon's essay exemplify in some respects a whole tradition of stylistic criticism, but it also makes what must be the most famous statement about style—"le style est l'homme même" (style is the man himself)—a statement that has frequently been taken out of context to become a central tenet in a kind of stylistic criticism vastly different from Buffon's.

Before going on to consider some of the directions twentieth-century stylistic analysis has taken, and thus some of the emphases to be found in the various essays, we would do well to look briefly at several concepts and terms that are likely to crop up in any piece of stylistic criticism, if only to remind ourselves of how problematic the concepts may prove and how ambiguously the terms may be used. For instance, the concept of *choice*, which appears normally to mean deciding on one among alternative ways of saying the same thing, is frequently invoked, perhaps partly as an acknowledgment of the literary artist's freedom, but mainly in the belief that the artist definitively reveals his individuality in his style through the particular choices he makes. Yet to talk in this fashion about choosing among alternatives often seems to imply that there are alternative ways of saying precisely the same thing, an implication which runs counter to the doctrine that content and form are inseparable, that to say something in different ways is in fact to say different things. The doctrine of inseparability, then, may be felt to undermine the idea of choice as it is ordinarily entertained. (This general area of theory is sensitively explored by Richard M. Ohmann in his "Prolegomena to the Analysis of Prose Style," the third essay in this collection.) More than that, the very notion may deflect our attention from the operative stylistic fact, the word or phrase on the page, to some creative process that we try to imagine the artist as having gone through, frequently a dead end in criticism—unless we are willing to understand references to choice mainly as a kind of shorthand for claims that words other than those selected would have meant something different to an audience, would have affected it differently.

Another recurrent idea in the study of style is *deviation from the norm*, again a criterion that would pay tribute to the artist's originality yet ends by raising questions of its own. Given the extensiveness of linguistic systems and their constant modification, one may ask whether it is always possible to obtain and define norms with assurance and thus to determine the context which would confer unique significance, as a deviation, on a particular verbal form. Still other questions arise when this idea is examined closely. Is it always possible to differentiate securely, in verbal materials, between the component of convention and the deviant element, given the fact that even deviations must somehow make use of linguistic convention if they are to be comprehended? If the criterion of deviation from the norm is to be applied, whose sense of the norm is to be taken as the standard? Is the artist's consciousness of the convention from which he deviates a factor? Are readers confined to making do with whatever awareness of linguistic norms they themselves may possess? In any case, to build an analysis of style primarily on a writer's deviations would appear to ignore a host of material that is stylistically relevant. (Michael Riffaterre discusses the problem of deviation at length in "Criteria for Style Analysis," *Word*, XV [1959], 154–74, where he redefines *norm* to designate local verbal contexts in relation to which stylistic devices strike readers as unpredictable and therefore deviant. This position informs his "Describing Poetic Structures: Two Approaches to Baudelaire's *Les Chats*," reprinted in the present anthology. Among other essays included here, Elisabeth Brock-Sulzer's "The Poet at War with His Language" examines deviations from "normal" French in the poems of Verlaine and Mallarmé.)

Of the specific terms that keep turning up in stylistic criticism, *expression* and its variants are undoubtedly the most ambiguous. These terms may refer to what the work expresses—that is, reflects—of its author, period, culture; or to what the work *expresses*, realizes in its forms, which act to detach the work as an esthetic object from all the elements that have gone into its making; or to the expressive power of a work, its ability to affect and move its audience; or to various amalgams of these senses. (Wolfgang Kayser discusses comparable ambiguities attending the term *Ausdruck* in his *Das Sprachliche Kunstwerk* [Bern, 1948].) Similarly, *meaning* may be employed to stress what the author intends to say, what the work articulates in itself as an esthetic whole, or what it conveys to its readers.

Such ambiguities arise, of course, because of the indigenous complexity in any use of language. For every utterance, in the most general sense, involves by definition a speaker attempting to convey something, the utterance itself, and the audience implicitly brought into being by the fact that the utterance consists of words, which are inevitably public forms in that their reason for being is communication. And even when the critic, in his particular approach to style, determines to emphasize one of these aspects above others, he may find himself hard put to control the multiple implications with which the basic vocabulary of stylistic criticism reverberates. To complicate matters further, in many essays dealing with literary style, the critic is simply out to analyze a specific text, either proceeding intuitively, on the basis of his own assumptions about the significance of style, or utilizing some theoretical framework that is never clearly set forth. It therefore seems best, as I suggested earlier, to begin the present collection with several essays that explicitly discuss significant theoretical questions. Among these more theoretical selections are the piece by Ohmann already mentioned, "Prolegomena to the Analysis of Prose Style"; Heinrich Wölfflin's Introduction to his *Principles of Art History*, where he indicates a number of ways in which style—albeit style in painting and architecture—may be interpreted, differentiating between expression and representation and, in the case of the latter, between imitation and decoration; and excerpts from David Lodge's *Language of Fiction*, in which the critic explores the problem of translation and argues for the uniqueness of the world realized verbally in fiction as well as in poetry. In order to clarify theoretical distinctions I have sought, in the individual introductions provided for each piece of practical stylistic analysis, to highlight what seem to me to be the critic's assumptions about stylistic interpretation, whether he articulates them or not, and to indicate whether his analysis is oriented toward discovering the external cultural and individual factors that lie behind and manifest themselves in the literary work, or toward treating the work as a relatively self-contained entity, or toward considering the work in terms of its effects on an audience.

Although the essays in practical analysis anthologized here reveal much of the range of twentieth-century stylistic criticism, it has not been possible to illustrate every modern approach. One approach not represented, for instance, derives from Ferdinand de Saussure, who distinguished between *la parole*, the individual utterance, and *la langue*, the set of conventions that make up a given language, concentrating on the latter as an intellectual, psychic, and social system. Saussure's position was modified by Charles Bally, who continued to regard language as a system but emphasized its expressive values (as a vehicle of communication that moves an audience) and so conceived of *la stylistique* as a study of the affective content of the verbal structures that constitute the system. Bally, however, excluded literary style from the domain of *la stylistique* on the grounds that the proper materials for the latter are spontaneous expressions, whereas the words of the artist are more consciously chosen and subserve an esthetic intention. Marcel Cressot, in *Le Style et ses techniques* (Paris, 1947), goes a step further than Bally, employing literary as well as non-literary materials to survey the expressive possibilities of the French language. But plainly this sort of approach illuminates the qualities of a linguistic system in its entirety rather than the particular configuration of procedures which individualizes a writer's verbal manner; and, even when the approach is used in dealing with a single author, it tends to eventuate in a catalogue of his expressive resources rather than a pointed analysis of his style.

Another mode of contemporary stylistic criticism omitted from this anthology is the sort of statistical analysis that depends upon processing large amounts of verbal material through computers. Despite the interesting explorations of this area by Gustav Herdan, among others, and despite Louis T. Milic's application of such a method in his book *A Quantitative Approach to the Style of Jonathan Swift* (The Hague, 1967), the results to date are disappointing for anyone interested in reasonably inclusive characterization of an artist's style. For many of the features identified by computers are typical of the given language itself rather than peculiar to the writer in question. And other features isolated as distinctive of an individual's style may often lie below the reader's threshold of perception: although they are discernible by computers working with large amounts of data, they seem not to have definable effects upon the reader as he encounters the writer's words. While data of this sort may serve as valuable evidence in determining the author of an unacknowledged text, they are less helpful if one is attempting to describe the salient qualities of a writer's style.

Although some areas of twentieth-century stylistic investigation have been excluded from this anthology, then, many more have been included. And the essays selected are roughly grouped in three broad categories. As I have already noted, one group of verbal analysts interprets style as a manifestation of something lying behind the work—of the nation or culture to which the artist belongs, of his literary period, or of the particular individual. In "Style of Distance, Style of Nearness," Theophil Spoerri describes two basic styles as characteristic of man himself, of the potentialities of the human spirit. In "On the Continuity of American Poetry," Roy Harvey Pearce calls attention to a national characteristic, to the strain of self-consciousness in American literature, citing poems by Poe, Emerson, Whitman, and Emily Dickinson. Morris Croll, in "The Baroque Style in Prose," details some stylistic features of anti-Ciceronianism, a European intellectual movement of the Renaissance. In excerpts from "The Primary Language of Poetry in the 1540's and 1640's" Josephine Miles seeks to define a period style in English literature, and she remains constantly aware of the difficulty inherent in any such venture—the difficulty of differentiating, for any specific piece of language, between what is assignable to the period and what to the writer. An extract from Fritz Strich's *Deutsche Klassik und Romantik*, which exhibits something of the mode of *Geistesgeschichte*, distinguishes between certain Classical and Romantic verbal usages in German through references to texts by Goethe, Novalis, and Kleist.

No doubt the best-known interpreter of style as a revelation of the man is Leo Spitzer, whose position derives in some measure from Benedetto Croce's philosophy. For Croce in his *Æsthetic*, the primary spiritual activity is "intuition," which is "the undifferentiated unity of the perception of the real and of the simple image of the possible"; and "intuition" is identical with "expression": "Every true intuition or representation is also *expression*. That which does not objectify itself in expression is not intuition or representation, but sensation and mere natural fact. The spirit only intuites in making, forming, expressing." Since Croce so emphasizes the objectification indigenous to expression, which is definitively characterized by the form it achieves, one may wonder how one may reliably project himself back through that form to regain the artist's original "point of view" and then recreate for himself "the whole process" of expression that the artist has gone through—as Croce declares that the proper reader must. Nevertheless, it remains true for Croce and his followers that the forms of expression—presumably because expression and intuition are identical—serve as windows through which the spiritual activity that enabled the expression can be glimpsed. Thus Karl Vossler, in *Frankreichs Kultur im Spiegel seiner Sprachentwicklung* (Heidelberg, 1913), relates the development of the French language to a collective mentality, to a national psychology. And thus Spitzer, in his "Linguistic Perspectivism in the *Don Quijote*," reprinted in this collection, explores a cluster of verbal traits to discover Cervantes the artist in his style.

A second group of critics, some of them especially sensitive to the status of the literary work as an esthetic object, leans toward interpreting style as it functions within the text itself. In "Roland Against Ganelon," Erich Auerbach, though referring to different conceptions of reality, concerns himself primarily with examining the modes of representing reality in the *Chanson de Roland*. W. K. Wimsatt, Jr., investigates the patterns of emphasis incorporated in Johnson's diction and syntax in an extract from *The Prose Style of Samuel Johnson*. Jan Mukařovský, a member of the formalist Prague School, studies Karel Čapek's management of intonation in "K. Čapek's Prose as

Lyrical Melody and as Dialogue." In "*King Lear:* The Quality of Nothing," Sigurd Burckhardt explores Shakespeare's language to suggest that it becomes an embodiment of meaning. Elisabeth Brock-Sulzer shows how both Verlaine and Mallarmé work against the grain of the French language to create their poems, with Mallarmé in particular using words as virtual substances. And the very title of Ian Watt's essay—"The First Paragraph of *The Ambassadors:* An Explication"—implies his attentiveness to the text. It may also remind us, though Watt himself concentrates on James's style, how frequently explication, even when undertaken for different purposes, yields insights into an author's style.

There is, finally, a body of stylistic criticism which treats words as essentially transitive, interpreting a writer's style in terms of its effects on an audience. Whenever a critic speaks of verbal effects, of course, he is presuming the response of an audience. But the most developed example in this anthology of interpretation oriented toward an audience is the essay by John Holloway entitled "Matthew Arnold." Here Holloway is concerned with Arnold's modes of persuasion—both the ways in which Arnold encourages readers to adopt the qualities of mind he advocates, and the devices by which at times Arnold creates a dramatic version of himself as possessing the qualities in question. Though Harry Levin describes an image that Ernest Hemingway cultivated of himself through his life and his pronouncements, Levin's analysis of Hemingway's literary prose reveals how, at its best, it fabricates for readers the illusion that they are participating directly in experience. In "Fiction and the 'Analogical Matrix'," Mark Schorer interprets the imagery of three novels in different ways: as it reflects the conceptions of the author, as it functions structurally in the work, and as it "evaluates theme" for the reader. A second essay by Richard M. Ohmann, "Literature as Sentences," represents an approach to interpretation grounded in fairly technical linguistic analysis (though Ohmann employs his technical knowledge to serve a keen literary awareness): distinguishing between a sentence's surface structure and deep structure, he indicates that the latter not only testifies to the vision of the artist but also makes particular claims on the attention of the audience. The final essay, even more fundamentally concerned with the reader's response, is Michael Riffaterre's "Describing Poetic Structures: Two Approaches to Baudelaire's *Les Chats.*" Here the critic defines a stylistic device (or a deviation from the norm) as any verbal procedure that strikes the reader as unpredictable in its local context. The article is of added interest, however, because it illustrates, in Riffaterre's examination of "Les Chats" and in his review of another reading of the poem offered by Roman Jakobson and Claude Lévi-Strauss, a structuralist approach to stylistic analysis—an approach that is somewhat differently exhibited in Mukařovský's essay on Čapek and that is becoming prominent in contemporary stylistic criticism.

Considerations of variety, then, have governed the selection of essays for this anthology: variety in approaches to the study of style as well as in the goals pursued by the analysts; variety in the texts analyzed, which are drawn from different literary periods, genres, and languages; variety, finally, in the kinds of verbal materials and patterns which claim the interest of the critics. Some deal primarily with diction, directing their attention perhaps to abstract terms, perhaps to newly coined words;

others deal with syntax, with the form of the verbal period, for instance, or with the use of direct discourse; still others are concerned with modes of argument, which may involve irony or ways of defining terms. One of the selections examines imagery; others treat such matters as prose rhythm, stanzaic structure, meter, rhyme, and the handling of the caesura.

A number of pieces in this anthology are already well known, but many others are, I think, less well known than they should be. And three of the essays—those by Fritz Strich, Theophil Spoerri, and Elisabeth Brock-Sulzer—appear in English here for the first time. Whether the given essay is familiar or not, I must hope that the separate introduction provided for each piece will aid the reader to place it in an appropriate intellectual context, to perceive how the particular critic works, and so to compare his procedure with others represented in this volume. In any case, the essays themselves are eminently worth reading and re-reading, if merely for the sake of the illumination they bring to the literary texts discussed.

BIBLIOGRAPHY

The student of style will find some bibliographical aid in books such as *Style in Prose Fiction*, edited by H. Martin (New York, 1959), Wolfgang Kayser's *Das Sprachliche Kunstwerk* (Bern, 1948), and R. Wellek and A. Warren's *Theory of Literature* (New York, 1949). But the major bibliographies of stylistics are:

BAILEY, RICHARD W., and DOLORES M. BURTON, *English Stylistics: A Bibliography* (Cambridge, Mass., 1967)

HATZFELD, HELMUT A., *A Critical Bibliography of the New Stylistics Applied to the Romance Literatures, 1900–1952* (Chapel Hill, N.C., 1953). Reprinted (New York, 1966)

―――, *A Critical Bibliography of the New Stylistics Applied to the Romance Literatures, 1953–1965* (Chapel Hill, N.C., 1966)

MILIC, LOUIS T., *Style and Stylistics: An Analytical Bibliography* (New York, 1967)

Discourse on Style: An Address Delivered Before the French Academy

❧ GEORGES LOUIS LECLERC, COMTE DE BUFFON ☙

Georges Louis Leclerc, Comte de Buffon (1707–1788), occupies an important position in intellectual history as the author of *Histoire naturelle, générale et particulière* (1749–1804), one of the first attempts to survey the various facts of natural history and place them within a comprehensive structure. In relation to literary history, Buffon is known as the originator of the phrase "le style est l'homme même" (style is the man himself), which appeared in his "Discours sur le style," delivered to the French Royal Academy of Sciences in 1753. Inasmuch as the phrase has haunted a good deal of the talk about style since then, I should add immediately that its sense in Buffon's essay is somewhat different from the sense that the phrase has come to bear as an isolated aphorism, one commonly taken to mean that style is peculiarly expressive of an artist's individuality and so may provide access to his inner self.

Buffon's view of writing, as the "Discourse" reveals, is extremely conventional, grounded in certain standard assumptions of rhetorical criticism and related to several classical tenets. The foundation of style, according to him, is the ordering of one's thoughts before putting pen to paper. Once the arrangement of ideas and their interrelationships have been settled, the writer seeks out an appropriate verbal expression for them. The conception implies a split between thought and expression as separable activities—the same sort of split implied by the recurrent claim of rhetorical criticism that language is the "dress" of thought—and Buffon's phrasing often testifies to such a separation, as in his slighting reference to those who invent "new combinations of syllables, merely to say what everybody else has said already." If thought and expression are imagined as to some degree distinct, it follows that the writer may choose more or less fitting expressions for his ideas. Thus Buffon makes a number of normative judgments about style in his essay, castigating those who "desire to be everywhere striking" and as a result play wittily with words at the expense of the thoughts represented or those who "express ordinary, everyday matters with an air of singularity or pretense." Again in accordance with rhetorical doctrine, Buffon regards the aim of style as persuasion (rather than self-expression) and holds that writing will be especially effective if the writer is himself sincere (an echo, perhaps, of the traditional notion that the good orator must be a good man): "If he writes as he thinks, if he is himself convinced of what he wishes to prove, this good faith with himself, which is the foundation of propriety toward others and of sincerity in style, will make him accomplish his whole purpose."

In the course of his essay Buffon reveals his allegiance to still other dicta with long histories in literary theory: the desirability of imitating nature's forms, the inherent superiority of "the most general terms" and "the most inclusive ideas," the pre-eminent status of the sublime. The implications of Buffon's "Discourse" and of his concern with the sublime are examined by Theophil Spoerri in "Style of Distance, Style of Nearness" (reprinted on pages 63–78), where Spoerri takes off from Buffon to construct two archetypal stylistic modes. Yet the more immediate value of Buffon's essay for this anthology is that it represents an approach to matters of style which prevailed for many years—and which still survives to some extent in many handbooks for courses in composition.

GENTLEMEN, in calling me to join your number you have bestowed on me a great honor; yet glory is a good only in so far as the recipient is worthy of it, and I am not convinced that certain essays written without art, and devoid of other orna-

---

"Discourse on Style: An Address Delivered Before the French Academy," by Georges Louis Leclerc, Comte de Buffon, translated by Lane Cooper, is reprinted from *Theories of Style in Literature*, edited by Lane Cooper (New York, 1968), pp. 170–79. I have omitted several of Cooper's footnotes and identified those that remain by naming the author of each in brackets.

ment than nature's own, are adequate title to make me dare assume a place among the masters of art—among the eminent men[1] who here represent the literary splendor of France, and whose names, celebrated to-day among the nations, will resound on the lips of our remotest posterity. Gentlemen, in fixing your choice on me you have had other motives: you have wished to give the illustrious body to which I have for many years had the honor of belonging a new mark of respect. Though shared by others, my gratitude is not the less lively. Yet how shall I fulfill the duty which it lays on me to-day? I have nothing to offer you, Gentlemen, but what is yours already: some ideas on Style, which I have gathered from your works—which I have conceived in reading and admiring you. Submitted to your intelligence, they will not fail of proper recognition.

In all times there have been men with the ability to rule their fellows by the power of speech. Yet only in enlightened times have men written and spoken well. True eloquence supposes the exercise of genius, and a cultivated mind. It is far different from that natural facility in speaking which is simply a talent, a gift accorded those whose passions are strong, whose voices are flexible, whose imaginations are naturally quick. Such men perceive vividly, are affected vividly, and display their emotions with force; and by an impression purely mechanical they transmit their own enthusiasm and feelings to others. It is body speaking to body; all movements and all gestures combine equally for service. What, indeed, is requisite in order to arouse and draw on the crowd? What do we need if we would agitate and persuade even the more intelligent? A vehement and affecting tone, expressive and frequent gestures, rapid and ringing words. But for the limited number of those whose heads are steady, whose taste is delicate, whose sense is refined, and who, like you, Gentlemen, set little value on cadence, gestures, and the empty sound of words, one must have substance, thoughts, arguments; and one must know how to present them and shade them and arrange them. It is not enough to strike the ear and hold the eye; one must work on the soul, and touch the sensibilities by addressing the mind.

Style is simply the order and movement one gives to one's thoughts. If these are connected closely, and rigorously compressed, the style will be firm, nervous, and concise. If they are allowed to follow one another loosely and merely at the lead of the diction, however choice this be, the style will be diffuse, nerveless, and languid.

However, before seeking the particular order in which actually to present his thoughts, the writer must first form another more general and more absolute order, where only primary aspects and fundamental ideas shall enter. It is in fixing their places in this prior plan that he sees his subject growing circumscribed, and comes to realize its true extent; and it is by keeping these first outlines continually before him that he is able to determine the proper intervals between the main ideas, and develops the accessory and intermediary ideas that shall serve to fill in. By sheer force of genius he will grasp the sum of these general and particular ideas in their true perspective; by a great delicacy of discernment he will distinguish thoughts that are fertile

---

[1] For example, Voltaire, Marivaux, Montesquieu, Maupertuis. Most of the others are now forgotten; that, however, is no sure ground for a belief that Buffon is here ironical. [Cooper]

from such as are sterile; by a sagacity born of long experience in writing he will perceive in advance the ultimate result of all these mental operations. If a subject be at all vast or complex, very seldom can it be taken in at a glance, or penetrated in its entirety by a single and initial effort of genius; and seldom even after much reflection will all its relations be comprehended. Accordingly, one cannot give this matter too much attention; it is, indeed, the sole way to consolidate, develop, and elevate one's thoughts. The more substance and force they receive through meditation, the more easily will they afterward pass into concrete expression.

This plan, though not the resultant style, is nevertheless its basis, supporting it, directing it, regulating its movement, subjecting it to law. Without that basis the best of writers will wander; his pen running on unguided will form haphazard, irregular strokes and incongruous figures. However brilliant the colors he employs, whatever the beauties of detail he introduces, since the ensemble jars or else makes no adequate impression, the work will not really be a construction; hence, though admiring the brilliancy of the author, we may suspect him of lacking true genius. Here is the reason why those who write as they speak, though they may speak excellently, write badly; that those who abandon themselves to the first flashes of their imagination assume a tone which they cannot sustain; that those who are in fear of losing their isolated and fugitive thoughts and who at separate times write in detached fragments, cannot unite these save by forced transitions; that, in a word, there are so many works made up by assemblage of pieces, and so few cast in a single mould.

Every subject, however, is a unit and, no matter how vast it be, can be comprised in a single treatise; hence, interruptions, pauses, sections, and the like, should be employed only when different subjects are under consideration, or when, having to discuss great, thorny, and disparate questions, genius finds its march broken by a multiplicity of obstacles and is constrained by the force of circumstances.[2] Otherwise a great number of divisions, far from rendering a work more solid, destroy its coherence. To the eye the book seems clearer; but the author's design remains obscure. You cannot make an impression on your reader's mind, or even on his feelings, but by continuity of the thread, by harmonious interdependence of the ideas, by a successive development, a sustained gradation, a uniform movement, which every interruption enfeebles or destroys.

Why is it that the works of nature are so perfect? Because each work is a whole, and because nature follows an eternal plan from which she never departs. She prepares in silence the germs of her productions. She sketches the original form of each living being in a single effort. This form she develops and perfects by a continuous movement and in a time prescribed. The result is wonderful; yet what should strike us is the divine imprint that it bears. The human spirit can *create* nothing, nor can it bring forth at all until fertilized by experience and meditation; in its acquired knowledge lie the germs of its productions. But if it imitates nature in its procedure and labor; if it exalts itself by contemplation to the sublimest truths; if it unites these; if it

---

[2] In what I said here I had in mind *L'Esprit des Lois*, in its substance an excellent work, and to be criticized solely on the score of its too frequent sections. [Buffon]

forms of them an entirety systematized by reflection: it will build upon unshakable foundations monuments that cannot pass away.

It is for want of plan, for want of sufficient preliminary reflection on his subject, that a man of intelligence finds himself embarrassed with uncertainty at what point to begin writing. Ideas come to him from many directions at a time; and since he has neither compared nor subordinated them, nothing determines him to prefer one set to another; hence he remains perplexed. When, however, he has made a plan, when he has collected and put in order all the essential thoughts on his subject, he recognizes without difficulty the instant when he ought to take up his pen; he is aware of the critical point when his mind is ready to bring forth; it is urgent with him to come to the birth; nay, he has now only pleasure in writing: his ideas follow one another easily, and the style is natural and smooth. A certain warmth born of that pleasure diffuses itself throughout, giving life to every phrase; there is a gradual increase of animation; the tone grows elevated; individual objects take on color; and a glow of feeling joins with the light of intellect to increase it and carry it on, making it spread from what one is saying to what one is about to say; and the style becomes interesting and luminous.

Nothing is more inimical to this warmth than the desire to be everywhere striking; nothing is more contrary to the light which should be at the center of a work, and which should be diffused uniformly in any composition, than those sparks which are struck only at the cost of a violent collision between words, and which dazzle us for a moment or two, only to leave us in subsequent darkness. These are thoughts that shine only by contrast, when but one aspect of an object is presented, while the remaining sides are put in shadow; and ordinarily the aspect chosen is a point or angle whereon the writer exercises his wit with the greater ease in proportion as he departs farther from the important sides on which good common sense is accustomed to view things.

Again, nothing is more opposed to true eloquence than the employment of superfine thoughts and the anxious search for such ideas as are slender, delicate, and without substance; ideas that, like leaves of beaten metal, acquire brilliancy only as they lose solidity. The more of this attenuated and shining wit there is in a composition, the less will there be of muscle, real illumination, warmth, and style; unless perchance this wit is the mainspring of the subject, and the writer has no other purpose than mere pleasantry. In that case the art of saying trifles will be found more difficult, perhaps, than that of saying things substantial.

Nothing is more opposed to the beauty of naturalness than the pains people take to express ordinary, every-day matters with an air of singularity or pretense; nor is there anything more degrading to the writer. Far from admiring him for this, we may pity him for having spent so much time in making new combinations of syllables, merely to say what everybody else has said already. This is the fault of minds that are cultivated but sterile; they have words in abundance but no ideas. Accordingly they juggle with diction, and fancy that they have put together ideas, because they have been arranging phrases, and that they have refined the language, when they have really corrupted it by warping the accepted forms. Such writers have no style; or, if you wish, they have only its shadow. A style ought to mean the engraving of thoughts; whereas they only know how to trace out words.

To write well, then, an author must be in full possession of his subject; he must reflect on it enough to see clearly the order of his thoughts, and to put them in proper sequence—in a continuous chain, each of whose links represents a unified idea; and when he has taken up his pen, he must direct it successively from one main point to the next, not letting it stray therefrom, nor yet allowing it to dwell immoderately on any, nor, in fact, giving it other movement than that determined by the space to be traversed. Herein consists the rigor of style; and herein lies that which gives it unity and regulates its speed. It is this, too, and this alone, which suffices to render a style precise and simple, even and clear, lively and coherent. If to obedience to this principle—a principle dictated by genius—an author joins delicacy and taste, caution in the choice of phraseology, care in the matter of expressing things only in the most general terms, his style will have positive nobility. If he has, further, a certain distrust of his first impulses, a contempt for what is superficially brilliant, and a steady aversion for what is equivocal and trifling, his style will be not simply grave, but even majestic. In fine, if he writes as he thinks, if he is himself convinced of what he wishes to prove, this good faith with himself, which is the foundation of propriety toward others and of sincerity in style, will make him accomplish his whole purpose; provided always that his inner conviction is not expressed with too violent enthusiasm, and that he shows throughout more candor than confidence and more light than heat.

Gentlemen, it is thus—as it seems to me when I read you—that you would speak to me for my instruction: my soul eagerly receiving such oracles of wisdom would fain take flight and mount on a level with you. How vain the effort! Rules, I hear you add, can never take the place of genius. If that be lacking, they are useless. To write well—it is at once to think deeply, to feel vividly, and to express clearly; it is to have at once intelligence, sensibility, and taste. Style supposes the united exercise of all the intellectual faculties. Ideas and they alone are its foundation. Well-sounding words are a mere accessory, dependent simply upon the possession of an external sense. One needs only to possess something of an ear for avoiding awkwardness in sound, and to have trained and bettered it by reading the poets and orators, and one is mechanically led to imitate poetical cadence and the turns of oratory. Now imitation never created anything; hence this euphony of words forms neither the basis nor the tone of style. It is, in fact, often found in writings devoid of ideas.

The tone, which is simply an agreement of the style with the nature of the subject, should never be forced, but should arise naturally from the very essence of the material, depending to a large extent upon the generalization one has in mind. If the author rises to the most inclusive ideas, and if his subject itself is lofty, his tone will apparently rise to the same height; and if while sustaining the tone at that altitude his genius proves copious enough to surround each particular object with a brilliant light, if the author can unite beauty of color with vigor of design, if he can, in a word, represent each idea by a lively and well-defined image, and make of each sequence of ideas a picture that is harmonious and energetic, the tone will be not simply elevated but sublime. Here, Gentlemen, the application would avail more than the rule, and illustration be more instructive than precept; but since I am not permitted to cite the sublime passages that have so often transported me in reading your works, I am forced to limit myself simply to reflections. The well-written works are the only ones that will go down to posterity: the amount of knowledge in a book, the peculiarity of the facts, the novelty even of the discoveries, are not sure warrants of immortality. If the works that contain these are concerned with only minor objects; if they are written without taste, without nobility, without inspiration, they will perish; since the knowledge, facts, and discoveries, being easily detached, are passed on to others, and even gain intrinsically when appropriated by more gifted hands. These things are external to the man; the style is the man himself.[3] Style, then, can be neither detached, nor transferred, nor altered by time: if it is elevated, noble, sublime, the author will be admired equally in all ages. For it is truth alone that is permanent, that is even eternal. Now a beautiful style is such in fact only by the infinite number of truths that it presents. All the intellectual graces residing in it, all the interdependences of which it is composed, are truths not less useful, and for the human spirit possibly more precious, than those, whatsoever they be, that form the core of the subject.

The sublime is to be found only in lofty subjects. Poetry, history, and philosophy all deal with the same material, and a most lofty material, namely, man and nature. Philosophy describes and portrays nature; poetry paints and embellishes it; poetry paints men also, enlarges them, intensifies them, creates heroes and divinities. History represents man only, and represents him as he is. Accordingly, the tone of the historian will become sublime only when he draws a picture of the greatest men, when he exhibits the greatest actions, the greatest movements, and the greatest revolutions; under other circumstances it will suffice if he be always majestic and grave. The tone of the philosopher might become sublime whenever he is to speak of the laws of nature, of creatures in general, of space, of matter, of time and motion, of the soul, of the human intellect, of the sentiments, and of the passions; elsewhere it will suffice if he be noble and elevated. But the tone of the orator and the poet, so soon as the subject is lofty, should be ever sublime, because they have the right to bring to the grandeur of their subject just as much color, as much movement, and as much illusion as they please; and because, having at all times to paint and enlarge the objects of their representation, they must at every point employ all the force and display all the extent of their genius.

---

[3] "Ces choses sont hors de l'homme, le style est l'homme même." Some of the earlier editions read: "le style est *de* l'homme même." The expression did not occur in the original version which Buffon submitted to President de Ruffey. Its exact wording has been a matter of fruitless discussion in America. Buffon's thought is perfectly clear: whereas the subject-matter of a scientific treatise, say, is external to the man, and would exist whether the man existed or not, the style, or the order in which the man arranges his thoughts on the subject-matter, springs from the man himself; the style is so much of the man as exists in the ordering of his thoughts. See M. Nollet's edition of the *Discours*, p. 22, and the *Nation*, January 25, 1906 ("Notes"). Compare Ben Jonson, *Timber*, edited by F. E. Schelling, p. 64. [Cooper]

Introduction to *Principles of Art History*

❧ HEINRICH WÖLFFLIN ❧

Heinrich Wölfflin's *Principles of Art History: The Problem of the Development of Style in Later Art*—originally published as *Kunstgeschichtliche Grundbegriffe* in 1915—has not only established itself as a classic in art criticism but has deeply influenced a number of literary studies as well. Such outstanding later scholars as Erich Gombrich, in *Art and Illusion* (1960), and Meyer Schapiro, in "Style," from *Anthropology Today: An Encyclopedic Inventory* (1953), have paid tribute to Wölfflin's work even when taking issue with it in one way or another. And his differentiations between the renaissance and the baroque underlie books of literary analysis so diverse as Fritz Strich's *Deutsche Klassik und Romantik* (1922)—a portion of which is reprinted on pages 139–47; Theophil Spoerri's *Renaissance und Barock bei Ariost und Tasso* (1922); and Wylie Sypher's *Four Stages of Renaissance Style* (1955).

Despite the fact that later art historians have distinguished a "Mannerist" style intervening between the High Renaissance and baroque styles described by Wölfflin in his *Principles*, and despite the fact that Wölfflin is concerned here with an art whose medium is not language, I have thought it worth while to include Wölfflin's introductory chapter in the present anthology: in part because of his influence on some analysts of verbal style, but in the main because his chapter outlines so clearly a variety of directions in which stylistic studies have proceeded, whatever the medium in question. In a given creation, Wölfflin acknowledges elements of a personal style (reflecting the artist's private temperament), of a national style (conditioned by racial characteristics), and of a period style (determined by the forms favored in the particular epoch). And he categorizes all these elements as "expressive" in the sense that they are related to the man, the nation, and the age behind the creation. But his emphasis in the *Principles* falls elsewhere—on "the mode[s] of representation as such" manifested within the created works, modes to which artists are "bound" by virtue of occupying different points in time in the history and development of art; and Wölfflin's main purpose is to characterize two such modes, High Renaissance and baroque, through delineating five major contrasts between them. In thus dealing with "representational possibilities," he makes a further distinction relevant to stylistic analysis, a distinction between the mimetic and decorative aspects of representation, between its allegiance to the thing imitated and its allegiance to an ideal of beauty (shared by the artist and his audience).

Through the course of his book, Wölfflin touches on all these matters again and again as he seeks to validate the contrasts he has defined by exploring a wealth of examples drawn from painting, sculpture, and architecture. In his final chapter he sketches an explanation for the development from mode to mode, claims a certain periodicity in discerning the recurrence of the modes through much of Western art, and suggests finally some correlations between the specific modes and "permanent differences of national types," with the "German imagination" disposed to realize itself in one mode and the Italian in the other. But the chief value of Wölfflin's *Principles* resides in the author's efforts to identify the two modes of representation descriptively through the most delicate analysis of many works of art.

The Double Root of Style

Ludwig Richter relates in his reminiscences how once, when he was in Tivoli as a young man, he and three friends set out to paint part of the landscape, all four firmly resolved not to deviate from nature by a hair's-breadth; and although

---

"Introduction to *Principles of Art History*," by Heinrich Wölfflin, is reprinted from *Principles of Art History: The Problem of the Development of Style in Later Art*, translated by M. D. Hottinger (New York, 1950), pp. 1–17, by permission of G. Bell & Sons, Ltd., publishers. Published in the United States by Dover Publications, Inc.

the subject was the same, and each quite creditably reproduced what his eyes had seen, the result was four totally different pictures, as different from each other as the personalities of the four painters. Whence the narrator drew the conclusion that there is no such thing as objective vision, and that form and colour are always apprehended differently according to temperament.

For the art historian, there is nothing surprising in this observation. It has long been realised that every painter paints "with his blood." All the distinction between individual masters and their "hand" is ultimately based on the fact that we recognise such types of individual creation. With taste set in the same direction (*we* should probably find the four Tivoli landscapes rather similar, of a pre-Raphaelite type), the line will be in one case more angular, in another rounder, its movement here rather halting and slow, there more streaming and urgent. And, just as proportions tend now to the slender, now to the broad, so the modelling of the human body appeals to the one as something rather full and fleshy, while the same curves and hollows will be seen by another with more reticence, with much more economy. It is the same with light and colour. The sincerest intention to observe accurately cannot prevent

BOTTICELLI, *Birth of Venus* (detail). Uffizi. Scala Florence / New York.

Lorenzo di Credi, *Venus*.
Uffizi. Alinari.

a colour looking now warmer, now cooler, a shadow now softer, now harder, a light now more languid, now more vivid and glancing.

If we are no longer bound by a common subject from nature, these *individual styles* become, of course, much more distinct. Botticelli and Lorenzo di Credi are two painters related by epoch and race, both Florentines of the later Quattrocento. But when Botticelli*[1] draws a female body, its stature and shape is perceived in a way peculiar to him, and as radically and unmistakably different from any female nude of Lorenzo's* as an oak from a lime. The impetuosity of Botticelli's drawing endows every form with a peculiar verve and animation. In Lorenzo's deliberate modelling, vision is essentially fulfilled by the object in repose. Nothing is more illuminating than to compare the similar curve of the arm in the two pictures. The sharp elbow, the spirited line of the forearm, the radiant spread of the fingers on the breast, the energy which charges every line—that is Botticelli. Credi, on the other hand, produces a more flaccid effect. Though very convincingly modelled, that is, conceived

---

[1] Asterisks behind the names of artists or works mentioned in the text refer to reproductions in the book. . . .

in volumes, his form still does not possess the impetus of Botticelli's contours. That is a difference of temperament, and that difference penetrates throughout, whether we compare the whole or the details. In the drawing of a mere nostril, we have to recognise the essential character of a style.

For Credi, a definite person posed. That is not the case with Botticelli, yet it is not difficult to see that the conception of form in the two artists is bound up with a definite notion of beautiful form and beautiful movement, and if Botticelli has given full play to his ideal of form in the slender erectness of his figure, even with Credi we feel that the special case of reality has in no way prevented him from expressing *his* temperament in the pose and proportions of his figure.

The psychologist of style finds a particularly rich booty in the stylised drapery of this epoch. With relatively few elements, an enormous variety of widely differing individual expression has here come to birth. Hundreds of artists have depicted the Virgin seated with the drapery pouched between the knees, and every time a form has been found which reveals a whole man. And yet it is not only in the great line of Italian renaissance art, but even in the painterly[2] style of the Dutch genre painters of the seventeenth century that drapery has this psychological significance.

As is well known, satin was a favourite subject of Terborch's,* and he painted it specially well. It seems as if the fine material could not look otherwise than it is shown here, yet it is only the artist's innate distinction which speaks to us in his forms, and even Metsu* saw the phenomenon of these fold-formations essentially differently. The fabric is apprehended as something rather weighty in fall and fold, the ridge of the fold is less delicate, each of its curves lacks elegance, and from the whole sequence of folds, the pleasing ease, the brio has vanished. It is still satin, and painted by a master, but seen beside Terborch's, Metsu's fabric looks almost dull.

And now, in our picture, that is not merely the result of a chance off-day. The spectacle is repeated, and so characteristic is it that we can continue on the same lines if we proceed to the analysis of figures and grouping. Consider the bare arm of the music-making lady in Terborch's picture—how finely it is felt in joint and movement, and how much heavier Metsu's figure seems—not because it is less skilfully drawn, but because it is felt differently. In Terborch, the grouping is light and the figures are bathed in air. Metsu gives something more massive and compact. An accumulation such as the bundled folds of the thick table-cloth with the writing materials could not be found in Terborch.

And so on. And if, in our reproduction, there is little trace of the shimmering lightness of Terborch's tonal gradations, the rhythm of the whole still speaks an audible language, and it requires no special persuasion to see in the equipoise of the parts an art inwardly related to the drawing of the folds.

The problem remains identical in the trees of landscape painters. A bough, a fragment of a bough, and we can say whether Ruysdael or Hobbema is the painter,

---

[2] *Malerisch*. This word has, in the German, two distinct meanings, one objective, a quality residing in the object, the other subjective, a mode of apprehension and creation. To avoid confusion, they have been distinguished in English as "picturesque" and "painterly" respectively. [Translator's note]

TERBORCH, *Chamber Music*. Louvre.

not from isolated external features of the "manner," but because all the essentials of the sense of form exist even in the smallest fragment. Hobbema's* trees, even when he paints the same species as Ruysdael,* will always seem lighter, their outlines are freer, they rise more airily in space. Ruysdael's graver style charges the line with a peculiar ponderous emphasis, he loves the slowly undulating outline, he holds the masses of foliage more compactly together, and thoroughly characteristic of his pictures is the way in which he prevents any separation of the individual forms, but gives a close-knit weft. Trees and mountain contours meet in sombre contact. While Hobbema, on the other hand, loves the graceful, bounding line, the diffused

Metsu, *The Music Lesson*. Copyrights John Maurits van Nassau Mauritshuis.

Hobbema, *Landscape with Windmill*. Buckingham Palace. Copyrights reserved.

Ruysdael, *Marsh in a Wood*. Staatsgemäldesammlungen.

mass, the variegated terrain, and charming vignettes and vistas—every part seems like a picture within a picture.

With ever-increasing subtlety, we must try in this way to reveal the connection of the part with the whole, so that we may arrive at the definition of individual types of style, not only in design, but in lighting and colour. We shall realise that a certain conception of form is necessarily bound up with a certain tonality and shall gradually come to understand the whole complex of personal characteristics of style as the expression of a certain temperament. For descriptive art history there is much to be done here.

The course of the development of art, however, cannot simply be reduced to a series of separate points. Individuals fall into larger groups. Botticelli and Lorenzo di Credi, for all their differences, have still, as Florentines, a certain resemblance when compared with any Venetian, and Hobbema and Ruysdael, however divergent they may be, are immediately homogeneous as soon as to them, as Dutchmen, a Fleming like Rubens is opposed. That is to say: to the personal style must be added *the style of the school, the country, the race.*

Let us define Dutch art by contrasting it with Flemish art. The flat meadows round Antwerp present in themselves no other scene than the Dutch pastures to which native artists have given the expression of the most widespread tranquillity. But when Rubens* handles these themes, the subject looks totally different: the earth rolls in vigorous waves, tree-trunks writhe passionately upwards, and their foliage is handled so completely in closed masses that Ruysdael and Hobbema in comparison appear as equally delicate silhouettists. Dutch subtlety beside Flemish massiveness. In comparison with the energy of movement in Rubens' design, Dutch design in general is restful, whether it be the rise of a hill or the curve of a petal. No Dutch tree-trunk has the dramatic force of the Flemish movement, and even Ruysdael's mighty oaks look slender beside Rubens' trees. Rubens raises the horizon high and makes the picture heavy, the Dutch relation of sky and earth is radically different: the horizon lies low, and it even happens that four-fifths of the picture is given up to air.

These are considerations which only become valuable when they can be generalised. The subtlety of Dutch landscape must be linked up with allied phenomena and pursued into the domain of the tectonic. The courses of a brick wall or the weaving of a basket are felt in Holland as peculiarly as the foliage of the trees. It is characteristic that not only a miniaturist like Dow but even a narrator like Jan Steen has time, in the midst of the most boisterous scene, for the accurate drawing of a wicker work. And the network of whitened joints on a brick wall, the pattern of neatly set flagstones, all these small details are really enjoyed by the architectural painters. As to Dutch architecture proper, however, we may say that stone seems here to have achieved a quite specific lightness. A typical building such as the Rathaus of Amsterdam avoids everything which, had it been conceived by a Flemish imagination, might have invested the great mass of stone with an appearance of weight.

We encounter here at all points the bases of national feeling, where the sense of form comes into immediate contact with spiritual and moral elements, and art history has grateful tasks before it as soon as it takes up systematically this question of the

RUBENS, *Landscape with Cattle*. Buckingham Palace. Copyrights reserved.

national psychology of form. Everything hangs together. The still poses of the Dutch figure pictures also form the bases of the objects of the architectural world. But if we bring Rembrandt into the matter, with his feeling for the living quality of light which, withdrawing from every substantial form, moves mysteriously in infinite spaces, we might easily be tempted to develop the observation into an analysis of Germanic art in contrast to Romanesque art in general.

But here the problem already branches. Although in the seventeenth century Dutchman and Fleming are still clearly distinguishable, we cannot forthwith base a general judgment of a national type on one single epoch. Different times give birth to different art. Epoch and race interact. We must first establish how many general traits a style contains before we can give it the name of a national style in a special sense. However profoundly Rubens may impress his personality on his landscape, and however many talents may veer to his pole, we cannot admit that he was an expression of "permanent" national character to the same extent as contemporary Dutch art. The colour of time is stronger with him. His art is powerfully affected by a particular cultural current, the mode of feeling of Roman baroque, and so it is he, rather than the "timeless" Dutch artists, who challenges us to form an idea of what we must call *period style*.

This idea is best to be obtained in Italy, because the development there fulfilled itself independently of outside influences and the general nature of the Italian character remains fully recognisable throughout. The transition from renaissance to baroque is a classic example of how a new *zeitgeist* enforces a new form.

Here we enter upon much-trodden paths. Nothing is more natural to art history than to draw parallels between periods of culture and periods of style. The columns and arches of the High Renaissance speak as intelligibly of the spirit of the time as the figures of Raphael, and a baroque building represents the transformation of ideals no less clearly than a comparison between the sweeping gestures of Guido Reni and the noble restraint and dignity of the Sistine Madonna.

Let us this time remain on strictly architectural ground. The central idea of the Italian Renaissance is that of perfect proportion. In the human figure as in the edifice, this epoch strove to achieve the image of perfection at rest within itself. Every form developed to self-existent being, the whole freely co-ordinated: nothing but independently living parts. The column, the panel, the volume of a single element of a space as of a whole space—nothing here but forms in which the human being may find an existence satisfied in itself, extending beyond human measure, but always accessible to the imagination. With infinite content, the mind apprehends this art as the image of a higher, free existence in which it may participate.

The baroque uses the same system of forms, but in place of the perfect, the completed, gives the restless, the becoming, in place of the limited, the conceivable, gives the limitless, the colossal. The ideal of beautiful proportion vanishes, interest concentrates not on being, but on happening. The masses, heavy and thickset, come into movement. Architecture ceases to be what it was in the Renaissance, an art of articulation, and the composition of the building, which once raised the impression of freedom to its highest pitch, yields to a conglomeration of parts without true independence.

This analysis is certainly not exhaustive, but it will serve to show in what way styles express their epoch. It is obviously a new ideal of life which speaks to us from Italian baroque, and although we have placed architecture first as being the most express embodiment of that ideal, the contemporary painters and sculptors say the same thing in their own language, and whoever tries to reduce the psychic bases of style to abstract principles will probably find the decisive word here more readily than with the architects. The relationship of the individual to the world has changed, a new domain of feeling has opened, the soul aspires to dissolution in the sublimity of the huge, the infinite. "Emotion and movement at all costs." Thus does the Cicerone formulate the nature of this art.

We have, in thus sketching three examples of individual style, national style, and period style, illustrated the aims of an art history which conceives style primarily as expression, expression of the temper of an age and a nation as well as expression of the individual temperament. It is obvious that with all that, the quality of the work of art is not touched: temperament certainly makes no work of art, but it is what we might call the material element of style taken in the broad sense that the particular ideal of beauty (of the individual as of the community) is included in it too. Works of art history of this kind are still far from the perfection they might attain, but the task is inviting and grateful.

Artists are certainly not readily interested in historical questions of style. They take work exclusively from the standpoint of quality—is it good, is it self-sufficing, has nature found a vigorous and clear presentment? Everything else is more or less indifferent. We have but to read Hans van Marées when he writes that he is learning to attach less and less value to schools and personalities in order only to keep in view the solution of the artistic problem, which is ultimately the same for Michelangelo as for Bartholomew van der Helst. Art historians who, on the other hand, take the differences between the finished products as their point of departure have always been exposed to the scorn of the artists: they have taken the detail for the essence; they cling just to the non-artistic side in man in wishing to understand art as expression only. We can very well analyse the temperament of an artist and still not explain how the work came into being, and the description of all the differences between Raphael and Rembrandt is merely an evasion of the main problem, because the important point is not to show the difference between the two but how both, in different ways, produced the same thing—namely, great art.

It is hardly necessary here to take up the cudgels for the art historian and defend his work before a dubious public. The artist quite naturally places the general canon of art in the foreground, but we must not carp at the historical observer with his interest in the variety of forms in which art appears, and it remains no mean problem to discover the conditions which, as material element—call it temperament, *zeitgeist*, or racial character—determine the style of individuals, periods, and peoples.

Yet an analysis with quality and expression as its objects by no means exhausts the facts. There is a third factor—and here we arrive at the crux of this enquiry—the mode of representation as such. Every artist finds certain visual possibilities before him, to which he is bound. Not everything is possible at all times. Vision itself has its history, and the revelation of these visual strata must be regarded as the primary task of art history.

Let us try to make the matter clear by examples. There are hardly two artists who, although contemporaries, are more widely divergent by temperament than the baroque master Bernini and the Dutch painter Terborch. Confronted with the turbulent figures of Bernini, who will think of the peaceful, delicate little pictures of Terborch? And yet, if we were to lay drawings by the two masters side by side and compare the general features of the technique, we should have to admit that there is here a perfect kinship. In both, there is that manner of seeing in patches instead of lines, something which we can call painterly, which is the distinguishing feature of the seventeenth century in comparison with the sixteenth. We encounter here a kind of vision in which the most heterogeneous artists can participate because it obviously does not bind them to a special mode of expression. Certainly an artist like Bernini needed the painterly style to say what he had to say, and it is absurd to wonder how he would have expressed himself in the draughtsmanly style of the sixteenth century. But we are clearly dealing with other concepts here than when we speak, for instance, of the energy of the baroque handling of masses in contrast to the repose and reserve of the High Renaissance. Greater or less movement are expressional factors which can be measured by one and the same standard: painterly and draughtsmanly, on the other hand, are like two languages, in which everything can be said, although each has its strength in a different direction and may have proceeded to visibility from a different angle.

Another example. We can analyse Raphael's line from the point of view of expression, describe its great noble gait in contrast to the pettier fussiness of Quattrocento outlines: we can feel in the movement of the line in Giorgione's Venus the kinship with the Sistine Madonna and, turning to sculpture, discover in Sansovino's youthful Bacchus the new, long, continuous line, and nobody will deny that we feel in this great creation the breath of the new sixteenth century feeling: it is no mere superficial history-writing to connect in this way form and spirit. But the phenomenon has another side. By explaining great line, we have not explained line. It is by no means a matter of course that Raphael and Giorgione and Sansovino sought expressive force and formal beauty in line. But it is again a question of international connections. The same period is for the north, too, a period of line, and two artists who, as personalities, have little in common, Michelangelo and Hans Holbein the Younger, resemble each other in that they both represent the type of quite strictly linear design. In other words, there can be discovered in the history of style a substratum of concepts referring to representation as such, and one could envisage a history of the development of occidental seeing, for which the variations in individual and national characteristics would cease to have any importance. It is certainly no easy task to reveal this inward visual development, because the representational possibilities of an epoch are never shown in abstract purity but, as is natural, are always bound to a certain expressional content, and the observer is then generally inclined to seek in the expression the explanation of the whole artistic product.

When Raphael erects his pictorial edifices and, by strict observance of rules, achieves the impression of reserve and dignity to an unprecedented degree, we can find in his special problem the impulse and the goal, and yet the tectonics of Raphael are not entirely to be attributed to an intention born of a state of mind: it is rather a question of a representational form of his epoch which he only perfected in a certain way and used for his own ends. Similar solemn ambitions were not lacking later, but it was impossible to revert to his formulas. French classicism of the seventeenth century rests on another visual basis, and hence, with a similar intention, necessarily arrives at other results. By attributing everything to expression alone, we make the false assumption that for every state of mind the same expressional methods were always available.

And when we speak of the progress of imitation, of the new impressions of nature which an epoch produced, that is also a material element which is bound to *a priori* forms of representation. The observations of the seventeenth century were not merely woven into the fabric of Cinquecento art. The whole groundwork changed. It is a mistake for art history to work with the clumsy notion of the imitation of nature, as though it were a homogeneous process of increasing perfection. All the increase in the "surrender to nature" does not explain how a landscape by Ruysdael differs from one by Patenir, and by the "progressive conquest of reality" we have still not explained the contrast between a head by Frans Hals and one by Dürer. The imitative content, the subject matter, may be as different in itself as possible, the decisive point remains that the conception in each case is based on a different visual schema—a schema which, however, is far more deeply rooted than in mere questions of the progress of imitation. It conditions the architectural work as well as the work of representative art, and a Roman baroque façade has the same visual denominator as a landscape by Van Goyen.

The Most General Representational Forms

THIS VOLUME is occupied with the discussion of these universal forms of representation. It does not analyse the beauty of Leonardo but the element in which that beauty became manifest. It does not analyse the representation of nature according to its imitational content, and how, for instance, the naturalism of the sixteenth century may be distinguished from that of the seventeenth, but the mode of perception which lies at the root of the representative arts in the various centuries.

Let us try to sift out these basic forms in the domain of more modern art. We denote the series of periods with the names Early Renaissance, High Renaissance, and Baroque, names which mean little and must lead to misunderstanding in their application to south and north, but are hardly to be ousted now. Unfortunately, the symbolic analogy bud, bloom, decay, plays a secondary and misleading part. If there is in fact a qualitative difference between the fifteenth and sixteenth centuries, in the sense that the fifteenth had gradually to acquire by labour the insight into effects which was at the free disposal of the sixteenth, the (classic) art of the Cinquecento and the (baroque) art of the Seicento are equal in point of value. The word *classic* here denotes no judgment of value, for baroque has its classicism too. Baroque (or, let us say, modern art) is neither a rise nor a decline from classic, but a totally different art. The occidental development of modern times cannot simply be reduced to a curve with rise, height, and decline: it has two culminating points. We can turn our sympathy to one or to the other, but we must realise that that is an arbitrary judgment, just as it is an arbitrary judgment to say that the rose-bush lives its supreme moment in the formation of the flower, the apple-tree in that of the fruit.

For the sake of simplicity, we must speak of the sixteenth and seventeenth centuries as units of style, although these periods signify no homogeneous production, and, in particular, the features of the Seicento had begun to take shape long before the year 1600, just as, on the other hand, they long continued to affect the appearance of the eighteenth century. Our object is to compare type with type, the finished with the finished. Of course, in the strictest sense of the word, there is nothing "finished": all historical material is subject to continual transformation; but we must make up our minds to establish the distinctions at a fruitful point, and there to let them speak as contrasts, if we are not to let the whole development slip through our fingers. The preliminary stages of the High Renaissance are not to be ignored, but they represent an archaic form of art, an art of primitives, for whom established pictorial form does not yet exist. But to expose the individual differences which lead from the style of the sixteenth century to that of the seventeenth must be left to a detailed historical survey which will, to tell the truth, only do justice to its task when it has the determining concepts at its disposal.

If we are not mistaken, the development can be reduced, as a provisional formulation, to the following five pairs of concepts:

1. The development from the linear to the painterly, *i.e.* the development of line as the path of vision and guide of the eye, and the gradual depreciation of line: in more general terms, the perception of the object by its tangible character—in outline and surfaces—on the one hand, and on the other, a perception which is by way of surrendering itself to the mere visual appearance and can abandon "tangible" design. In the former case the stress is laid on the limits of things; in the other the work tends to look limitless. Seeing by volumes and outlines isolates objects: for the painterly eye, they merge. In the one case interest lies more in the perception of individual material objects as solid, tangible bodies; in the other, in the apprehension of the world as a shifting semblance.

2. The development from plane to recession. Classic[3] art reduces the parts of a total form to a sequence of planes, the baroque emphasises depth. Plane is the element of line, extension in one plane the form of the greatest explicitness: with the discounting of the contour comes the discounting of the plane, and the eye relates objects essentially in the direction of forwards and backwards. This is no qualitative difference: with a greater power of representing spatial depths, the innovation has nothing directly to do: it signifies rather a radically different mode of representation, just as "plane style" in our sense is not the style of primitive art, but makes its appearance only at the moment at which foreshortening and spatial illusion are completely mastered.

3. The development from closed to open form. Every work of art must be a finite whole, and it is a defect if we do not feel that it is self-contained, but the interpretation of this demand in the sixteenth and seventeenth centuries is so different that, in comparison with the loose form of the baroque, classic design may be taken as *the* form of closed composition. The relaxation of rules, the yielding of tectonic strength, or whatever name we may give to the process, does not merely signify an enhancement of interest, but is a new mode of representation consistently carried out, and hence this factor is to be adopted among the basic forms of representation.

4. The development from multiplicity to unity. In the system of a classic composition, the single parts, however firmly they may be rooted in the whole, maintain a certain independence. It is not the anarchy of primitive art: the part is conditioned by the whole, and yet does not cease to have its own life. For the spectator, that presupposes an articulation, a progress from part to part, which is a very different operation from perception as a whole, such as the seventeenth century applies and demands. In both styles unity is the chief aim (in contrast to the pre-classic period which did not yet understand the idea in its true sense), but in the one case unity is achieved by a harmony of free parts, in the other, by a union of parts in a single theme, or by the subordination, to one unconditioned dominant, of all other elements.

[3] *Klassisch.* The word *classic*... refers to the art of the High Renaissance. It implies, however, not only a historical phase of art, but a special mode of creation of which that art is an instance. [Translator's note]

5. *The absolute and the relative clarity of the subject.* This is a contrast which at first borders on the contrast between linear and painterly. The representation of things as they are, taken singly and accessible to plastic feeling, and the representation of things as they look, seen as a whole, and rather by their non-plastic qualities. But it is a special feature of the classic age that it developed an ideal of perfect clarity which the fifteenth century only vaguely suspected, and which the seventeenth voluntarily sacrificed. Not that artistic form had become confused, for that always produces an unpleasing effect, but the explicitness of the subject is no longer the sole purpose of the presentment. Composition, light, and colour no longer merely serve to define form, but have their own life. There are cases in which absolute clarity has been partly abandoned merely to enhance effect, but "relative" clarity, as a great all-embracing mode of representation, first entered the history of art at the moment at which reality is beheld with an eye to other effects. Even here it is not a difference of quality if the baroque departed from the ideals of the age of Dürer and Raphael, but, as we have said, a different attitude to the world.

Imitation and Decoration

THE REPRESENTATIONAL FORMS here described are of such general significance that even widely divergent natures such as Terborch and Bernini—to repeat an example already used—can find room within one and the same type. The community of style in these two painters rests on what, for people of the seventeenth century, was a matter of course—certain basic conditions to which the impression of living form is bound without a more special expressional value being attached to them.

They can be treated as forms of representation or forms of beholding: in these forms nature is seen, and in these forms art manifests its contents. But it is dangerous to speak only of certain "states of the eye" by which conception is determined: every artistic conception is, of its very nature, organised according to certain notions of pleasure. Hence our five pairs of concepts have an imitative and a decorative significance. Every kind of reproduction of nature moves within a definite decorative schema. Linear vision is permanently bound up with a certain idea of beauty and so is painterly vision. If an advanced type of art dissolves the line and replaces it by the restless mass, that happens not only in the interests of a new verisimilitude, but in the interests of a new beauty too. And in the same way we must say that representation in a plane type certainly corresponds to a certain stage of observation, but even here the schema has obviously a decorative side. The schema certainly yields nothing of itself, but it contains the possibility of developing beauties in the arrangement of planes which the recessional style no longer possesses and can no longer possess. And we can continue in the same way with the whole series.

But then, if these more general concepts also envisage a special type of beauty, do we not come back to the beginning, where style was conceived as the direct expression of temperament, be it the temperament of a time, of a people, or of an individual? And in that case, would not the only new factor be that the section was cut lower down, the phenomena, to a certain extent, reduced to a greater common denominator?

In speaking thus, we should fail to realize that the second terms of our pairs of concepts belong of their very nature to a different species, in so far as these concepts, in their transformations, obey an inward necessity. They represent a rational psychological process. The transition from tangible, plastic, to purely visual, painterly perception follows a natural logic, and could not be reversed. Nor could the transition from tectonic to a-tectonic, from the rigid to the free conformity to law.

To use a parable. The stone, rolling down the mountain side, can assume quite different motions according to the gradient of the slope, the hardness or softness of the ground, etc., but all possibilities are subject to one and the same law of gravity. So, in human psychology, there are certain developments which can be regarded as subject to natural law in the same way as physical growth. They can undergo the most manifold variations, they can be totally or partially checked, but, once the rolling has started, the operation of certain laws may be observed throughout.

Nobody is going to maintain that the "eye" passes through developments on its own account. Conditioned and conditioning, it always impinges on other spiritual spheres. There is certainly no visual schema which, arising only from its own premisses, could be imposed on the world as a stereotyped pattern. But although men have at all times seen what they wanted to see, that does not exclude the possibility that a law remains operative throughout all change. To determine this law would be a central problem, the central problem of a history of art.

Prolegomena to the Analysis of Prose Style

RICHARD M. OHMANN

Surely Richard Ohmann is among the most intelligent and provocative of the younger critics who have come to deal with matters of style during the last few years. Trained in both literature and linguistics (as is clear in "Literature as Sentences," a second essay by Ohmann in the present anthology, pages 353–61), he has also concerned himself with questions of stylistic theory, as his "Prolegomena to the Analysis of Prose Style" amply demonstrates. One measure of the interest of this essay is its frequent republication since it originally appeared in 1959.

Ohmann begins his essay by formulating a fundamental theoretical problem in stylistic analysis: the belief that form and content are identical —that each statement is the unique expression of a thought—is incompatible, he proposes, with the very idea of style, which presumes that there are different "*ways* of saying *something*" and that a writer reveals his individuality through the particular way he chooses. The rest of the essay is essentially devoted to validating this concept of choice and implementing it for stylistic analysis. Ohmann rejects a theory involving constant "forms of thought" offered by I. A. Richards, partly on the ground that Richards' theory does not allow one ultimately to distinguish firmly between the number of forms of thought and the number of sentences (so that thought and expression become identical again), and partly on the ground that "neither the external world ... nor our 'experience' of it offers any ready-made forms of thought." Rather, Ohmann argues, man is confronted with a formless, "chaotic world-stuff" (an equivalent of "content"), and he himself "shapes the world by choosing from it whatever perceptual forms are most useful to him." Thus man endows experience with form through the exercise of choice—even if, as Ohmann admits, this choice is "most often ... unconscious and inevitable." Ohmann places the writer's engagement with his language on a level above the individual's experience of the world: although the artist's freedom is limited by the very structures of the given language, still he makes a host of significant choices. And Ohmann goes still farther in seeking to establish the component of individuality in a writer's style: he defines *proposition* in such a way that a single proposition can be expressed by many different sentences, thus allowing once more for variant formulations of a roughly constant content. Finally, he takes up Susanne Langer's notion of "presentational symbolism" as an element of style, insisting that "the configurations of feeling which accompany any [verbal] argument" should be viewed not simply as modes of persuading the reader but as "sheer expression" of the artist's "self."

One may be tempted to feel that this whole argument weights too heavily the concept of choice—a concept which seems implicitly to direct attention to the decision-making of the artist rather than to the created world of his prose—especially since Ohmann reverts again and again to the idea of style as meaning (which involves communication to an audience). But he has put the sort of theory outlined in this essay to good use in his *Shaw: The Style and the Man* (1962), where he examines Shaw's verbal traits and rhetoric to indicate their correlations with the artist's particular being, his "most confirmed epistemic stances."

THE CONSIDERATIONS of this essay are of a very primitive sort. If they are prolegomena to the study of style, they are preliminary by several stages to the study of style in the novel. What is more, a few decades ago they would have seemed utterly superfluous to most rhetoricians, who were quite content to think of style as the verbal dress of disembodied thought. Yet now comes a school of criticism which

---

"Prolegomena to the Analysis of Prose Style," by Richard M. Ohmann, is reprinted from *Style in Prose Fiction*, edited by H. Martin (New York, 1959), pp. 1–24, by permission of Columbia University Press.

aims to discredit the split between form and content, a school which argues that no two different utterances mean the same thing, and, more radically that, "every statement is a unique style of its own."[1] This organicist position, in spite of its stringency, has appealed increasingly to critic and linguist alike.[2] In fact it has nearly attained the status of dogma, of an official motto, voiced in the triumphant tones of reason annihilating error. Appealing as the idea is, commonplace though it has lately become in criticism, semantics, and linguistics, it would seem to render futile most extant stylistic analysis, if not to undercut the whole idea of style. For if style does not have to do with *ways* of saying *something*,[3] just as style in tennis has to do with ways of hitting a ball, is there anything at all which is worth naming "style"? If not, most critics of style have really given us judgments about what writers mean, masquerading as judgments about manner. The critic can talk about what the writer says, but talk about style he cannot, for his neat identity—one thought, one form—allows no margin for individual variation, which is what we ordinarily mean by style. Style, then, becomes a useless hypothetical construct half way between meaning and the person who means, and the study of style would seem to be the moribund offspring of a prolific reification: the assumption that because there is a word "style," there must be a thing to match.

Confronted with this dilemma, the conscientious critic can only say, with Wittgenstein, "Whereof one cannot speak, thereof one must be silent," and rejoice at the elimination of another pseudo-discipline. The trouble with this ascetic solution is that the critic may still feel it useful to speak of style. If he *is* unwilling to see stylistics tossed into the positivist's scrap-heap, along with ethics and metaphysics, he may work out a compromise: the most common is to say that style is part of what we ordinarily call meaning,[4] that it is peripheral meaning, or subterranean meaning, or connotative meaning. Such a solution is fruitful, I think, but it leads to a new problem. If style exists, by courtesy of this redefinition, where are its boundaries? Which part of meaning is to be called style, and which is really meaning? In short, how can we tell style from not-style?

These difficulties are not, I hope, mere compliant straw men to be handily blown down. They are real, and they are crucial, for on their resolution depend answers to these questions: What is style? What kind of scrutiny will it reward? What can it show about the writer?

---

[1] Andrews Wanning, "Some Changes in the Prose Style of the Seventeenth Century" (Ph.D. dissertation, University of Cambridge, 1938), p. 20.

[2] An example of the linguist's position: "It is a well-tried hypothesis of linguistics that formally different utterances always differ in meaning...." Leonard Bloomfield, "Linguistic Aspects of Science," *International Encyclopedia of Unified Science*, I (Chicago, 1955), 253.

[3] Here, as with too many pseudo-philosophical problems, ordinary language seems to have been the villain. Our speech makes a separation between saying and thing said: one *says it*. And if expressing is an action that one performs on an idea, just as hitting is an action performed on a tennis ball, why not different *ways* of expressing an idea? The distinction works with vocal speech, for the same words can be spoken with different stress, pitch, tone, and so forth; but a moment's reflection shows that it does not apply to the written word, and that any approach to stylistics empowered by a split between form and content is in serious theoretical trouble.

[4] This is Mr. Wanning's theoretical justification for proceeding with his study.

LET ME BEGIN the argument, unabashedly, where so many critical arguments begin—with I. A. Richards.

> Socrates is wise.
> Wisdom belongs to Socrates.

Mr. Richards offers these two sentences as a capsule demonstration of the way in which we "can put one thought form into many different word patterns."[5] He does not, as he may seem to do, neatly sever form and content; he is arguing a more subtle case, and one which ends by leaving form and content neither quite joined nor totally separated—a happy compromise, seemingly, for the beleaguered would-be critic of style. Let us examine it.

Mr. Richards uses the example concerning the wisdom of Socrates in a discussion calculated to refute J. S. Mill's contention that "the principles and rules of grammar are the means by which the forms of language are made to correspond with the universal forms of thought."[6] On the contrary, argues Mr. Richards, anyone who wishes to predicate wisdom of Socrates may cast his thought in one of several molds. Conversely, in English, thoughts of incompatible forms often take the same syntactical shape: for example, "I see a tiger" and "I kick a tiger." It is obvious that to kick a tiger is to act on it, whereas to see a tiger is to be affected in a complicated way by it. Mr. Richards submits that the tiger would no doubt administer a terminal lesson in logic to the man who confused sentence forms with forms of thought in this disastrous fashion.

His contention that the two sentences about Socrates express *congruent* thoughts is not, however, a contention that they express the *same idea*, or mean the *same thing*, or are *equivalent*. In one statement Socrates is the given quantity; in the other, wisdom. One sentence works by limiting the denotation of "Socrates," by eliminating possible statements such as "Socrates is stupid," and "Socrates is foolish." The other sentence focuses on a set of attributes and ways of behaving called "wisdom," and tells of one point in space-time where we can find it, namely in Socrates. One sentence belongs in a context of curiosity about Socrates; it might come in answer to the question, "What sort of mind had Socrates?" The other might satisfy someone who is looking, not for an honest, but for a wise man. The two sentences differ in the type of information given, in pattern of emphasis, in the sort of expectation they satisfy. In short, they say different things.

Rather than artificially separating idea from expression, Mr. Richards suggests that ideas fall into a finite set of categories, according to logical shape or form. His medial position between a dualism of manner and matter which is currently heretical, and a monism which is orthodox but fatal, allows to style a tenuous existence as the manner of clothing ethereal forms of thought in neatly tailored word patterns.[7]

---

[5] *Interpretation in Teaching* (New York, 1938), p. 285.
[6] *Inaugural Lecture at St. Andrews*, quoted by Richards, p. 280.
[7] This rescue maneuver is my inference from Mr. Richards's position; *his* main aim is to debunk the monism of Mill's grammar.

Under the aegis of this theory the study of a writer's style becomes the examination of the formal changes he works on each group of ideas, of the metamorphoses through which he puts each form of thought.

Attractive as this theory may seem to the critic who wishes to talk about style, but is hard put to see what style is, I think it must be rejected, even at the cost, possibly, of a final lesson in logic from Mr. Richards's tiger. For one thing, these shadowy forms of thought are so indistinguishable from each other, so nearly hidden by overlapping word patterns, that, rather than implementing a rigorous criticism, they would make it inhumanly difficult. Mr. Richards's distinction between seeing and kicking a tiger is easy enough to follow; one idea is of the form "*a* receives sense data from *b*," and the other is of the form "*a* acts on *b*." But what of the sentence "I feel a tiger"? To which form of thought does it belong? A new form of thought must no doubt be established to contain this sentence. But the process is endless; as rapidly as the forms multiply, borderline sentences will rise up to plague the classifier, who may eventually find, as a result of his labors, that the number of forms precisely equals the number of sentences.

In raising this objection I have tentatively accepted the notion of "forms of thought," and merely questioned the practicability of their use by a critic. But the disconcerting proliferation of thought forms calls the whole theory into question. If there is a separate form for every thought, then the concept of "form" is identical with that of "thought," and we can dispense with one or the other. To look at the matter from another angle, let me press somewhat further the hypothetical meeting of man and tiger, attending to forms of thought. To an observer the tiger consists of certain sense data—color, texture, odor, shape, motion, sound—data related to each other in extremely complex ways, however simple and primitive an object the tiger may seem to the adult's highly integrated mind. The man is a similar complex. Both tiger and man are capable of receiving sensations from, say, the jungle around them, as well as from each other. And the jungle, like man and tiger, is a welter of surfaces, glints of light, disorderly movements, unmusical noises. In this tangle of sensation the man sees trees, plants, a tiger; but these *Gestalten* are not inherently *there;* they are arbitrary ways of breaking up the flux; arbitrary, that is, except that the man has in the past been rewarded for using them, to the extent that parts of his environment (e.g., the tiger) demand, with special persistence, recognition as separate things.[8] When the man kicks the tiger, an exceedingly intricate shift takes place in the arrangement of sense data, a shift which is indistinguishable *in type* from the shifts which are occurring every millionth of a second. There has been a change; something has happened, but something is always happening, and it is man who separates one phenomenon from another, both by seeing and by naming. Our habits of sorting and classifying are so ingrained that we cannot describe or imagine things as they appear

---

[8] This view is, to the best of my knowledge, in accord with current perception theory. For instance: "perception is never a sure thing, never an absolute revelation of 'what is.' Rather, what we see is a prediction—our own personal construction designed to give us the best possible bet for carrying out our purposes in action. We make these bets on the basis of our past experience." W. H. Ittelson and F. P. Kilpatrick, "Experiments in Perception," *Scientific American Reader* (New York, 1953), p. 581.

to the tiger, or in the infant's "blooming, buzzing confusion." The world in itself, the infant's world, is barren of form, without order, mere raw material for man's perceptual and verbal manipulation. The forms of thought, then, are not inherent in things as they are. There is no logical or ontological reason why, on some tiger-infested tropical island, a people could not see man and tiger as one entity, and give a single name to this "object." Then "I kick the tiger" might run, "The tigerman coalesces footwise," and "I see the tiger" could read, "The tigerman coalesces eyewise." Surely the two ideas are now of the same form, as are the two sentences.

In another section of *Interpretation in Teaching*,[9] Mr. Richards argues that communication depends on a sameness of experience—a uniformity offered from without and a uniformity as organized from within. His acceptance of "forms of thought" must depend on this "sameness," on a belief that experience affords common elements to all men. But if my analysis is correct, experience is not molded from without, except in so far as nature rewards certain of man's sorting responses to the passing show and punishes others. It is interesting to note that we may be led into a misconception partly by the very word "experience." A logician points out that "'experience' itself is a relational term masquerading as a thing-name; x is an experience if and only if there is some y (the experiencer) which stands in the experience relation to x."[10] Ordinary language urges us to think of experience as a constant, offered with impartial sameness to all experiencers, rather than as an infinite series of relations of which no two need be alike.

The conception of experience as a series of relations is damaging also to Mr. Richards's claim that experience has "uniformity as organized from within," for it seems extremely improbable that any experiencer should ever stand in exactly the same relation to a field of perception as any other experiencer, or, indeed, that any man should see the same way twice. I do not wish to peddle a crippling subjectivism; communication does take place, and we must act most of the time as if there were uniformity of experience. At the same time it seems more accurate to speak behavioristically and say that men often respond similarly to similar fields of perception—respond similarly, that is, either in words or in action.

Neither the external world, then, nor our "experience" of it offers any ready-made forms of thought to the analyst who wishes to see style as the way in which ideas get into words. What nature does offer to experience, however, and experience to language, is a constant *formlessness*. Just as, in the existentialist view, man is confronted in his search for ethical order by the indifference of the universe, man in his search for perceptual order faces a chaotic world-stuff which gives no hints as to the proper method of sorting. But Camus calls the world's moral anarchy benign, in that it allows us to consider man the maker of his own morality, and the chaos pictured by modern psychologists has a parallel advantage: the perceiver, according to this theory, shapes the world by choosing from it whatever perceptual forms are most useful to him—though most often the choice is unconscious and inevitable. The

---

[9] P. 68.
[10] Charles W. Morris, "Foundations of the Theory of Signs," *International Encyclopedia of Unified Science*, I, 123.

unfriendly behavior of tigers may, to be sure, coerce him in his perceptual sorting, and his choice of perceptual forms largely governs his choice of linguistic categories, but the selections are initially free, in an important sense.

In these multifarious *ur*-choices, these preverbal and verbal pigeon-holings, style has its beginnings. If the critic is able to isolate and examine the most primitive choices which lie behind a work of prose, they can reveal to him the very roots of a writer's epistemology, the way in which he breaks up for manipulation the refractory surge of sensations which challenges all writers and all perceivers. In this Heraclitean flux, and not in the elusive forms of thought, is the common source of all perceptions, all sentences, all prose. The stream of experience is the background against which "choice" is a meaningful concept, in terms of which the phrase "*way* of saying *it*" makes sense, though "it" is no longer a variable. Form and content are truly separate if "content" is not bodiless ideas, but the formless world-stuff. And if such a hypothesis carries forward the analysis of style only a comfortless millimeter or so, at least it offers to that discipline a firm theoretical base, and a justification as well, inasmuch as it establishes an accessible and interesting connection between style and epistemology.

BEFORE THIS HYPOTHESIS can be of use, however, it requires major refinement. The most obvious barrier to a fruitful consideration of these fundamental epistemic choices is the fact that most of them are irrevocably made for any given writer by the particular language he writes in. A James Joyce or a Gertrude Stein may reshuffle linguistic forms in an attempt to draw aside the curtain that English places between us and the world of psychic and physical phenomena, but most conventional writers permit English to govern their epistemologies, as do all who merely speak the language. In other words, writers in English deal with bare experience only as it is censored by their language; they manipulate linguistically a world which is already highly organized for them.

Take, for example, the question of grammatical case. In English, a language which, compared to its neighbors, is syntactically rigid and very slightly inflected, most contemporary linguists recognize two cases[11] (as opposed to the four, five, or six of earlier grammarians). Of these two, genitives are relatively uncommon, so that nearly all occurrences of nouns are in one case. This limitation of cases means that a noun standing by itself, say "dog," calls attention merely to the animal of that name, and tells us nothing about it, not even that it is *not* a dog seen in an attitude of possession, since we have many constructions such as "hair of the dog" which express the genitive idea without recourse to the genitive case. The isolated word "dog's" names an animal *seen as owning something;* that is, it conveys a somewhat different idea. It also

[11] "Contemporary" in a loose sense: Otto Jespersen, whose semi-notional approach to grammar has made him seem old-fashioned to many later linguists, is one who argues against more than two cases in English; *The Philosophy of Grammar* (London, 1924), pp. 173–86. Writers of the Fries-Trager-Smith era also favor a two-case system, as for example, Paul Roberts in *Understanding Grammar* (New York, 1954), pp. 39–40, and Donald Lloyd and Harry Warfel in *American English in Its Cultural Setting* (New York, 1956), pp. 241–42.

creates a different set of expectations; to say "dog" is probably to stimulate the question "What about a dog?"; but the word "dog's" leads to the question "Dog's what, and what about it?" Thus English offers the speaker or writer two different notions of a certain four-footed animal; it sees the canine beast in two different ways.

In French, by contrast, there is only one form of *chien*. That word in isolation tells nothing about the dog at all. At the atomic level of meaning English has two things where French has but one. When we turn to Latin, with its six cases, the difference becomes more obvious. To translate *canis* properly, we would have to use a term such as "dog-doing-something-or-having-something-predicated-of-it" (actually, a full translation would be much more complex even than this). *Canem* might be partially rendered "dog-being-acted-upon-or-seen-as-the-goal-of-action." In Latin there is no conceivable way of expressing the English idea of "dog," untrammeled by ideas of position, agency, attitude, possession, mode of being perceived, and so forth. There is in Latin no symbol which is so free to be manipulated syntactically.

The writer in English, therefore, sees the universe through a verbal screen which divides it up less finely; classes are larger in English, because less subtly distinguished. What we conceive of as one thing, the writer of Latin must have conceived of, in some unquestioning, preverbal way, as six different things. These are the epistemic implications of case. The implications for style are equally significant: the importance of word order in English, the many possibilities of achieving emphasis in Latin by placement of a word, the greater dependence of the English writer on "function words." Epistemic differences of this sort run through the whole Indo-European family of languages, but within that family the similarities are more noticeable than the differences, and one must examine languages of other groups to find out how radically verbal environments can differ.

Benjamin Lee Whorf, a pioneer in metalinguistics, studied Western languages in juxtaposition with esoteric languages such as Hopi, and found that we treat the cosmos as much more segmented than do they—often artificially so.[12] We objectify time into a thing with boundaries and divisions instead of seeing it in terms of relations in lateness as Hopi does. We have "distributed nouns," such as "meat," "water," and "butter," whereas Hopi has none; nor does Hopi have abstract nouns. Evidently the Hopi language is in some sense closer to the raw material of perception than English is, with its complex and sophisticated system of categories.

It is notorious that Korzybski, Hayakawa, and other semanticists go further than Whorf, attacking Western languages for making inaccurate distinctions and concealing the functional relationships of nature.[13] Supposedly, Indo-European language structure was responsible for our long slavery to Aristotelian philosophy and Newtonian physics[14] and is to blame for a good share of our present neuroses

---

[12] *Language, Thought, and Reality* (Cambridge, Mass., and New York, 1956), especially "The Relation of Habitual Thought and Behavior to Language" and "Languages and Logic."

[13] See, for example, "What Is Meant by Aristotelian Structure of Language?," in *Language, Meaning, and Maturity*, edited by S. I. Hayakawa (New York, 1954).

[14] According to this view it is not surprising that the Hopi have produced no Newton, but it is surprising that no Einstein has risen among the Pueblos.

to boot. This criticism of ordinary language seems to me even more utopian than that leveled against it by the early positivists, and logically faulty as well. The semanticists use the very language which, according to them, hoodwinks us so severely to point out the fallacies of thought which it induces. Certainly a language which permits analysis of its own artificialities—which in effect transcends its own limitations—will suffice for most ordinary thinking.

Thus I find attacks on the cosmological limitations of English beside the point. What *is* relevant to the study of style is the fact that any language persuades its speakers to see the universe in certain set ways, to the exclusion of other ways. It thereby limits the possibilities of choice for any writer, and the student of style must be careful not to ascribe to an individual the epistemic bias of his language. A writer cannot escape the boundaries set by his tongue, except by creating new words, by uprooting normal syntax, or by building metaphors, each of which is a new ontological discovery. Yet, even short of these radical linguistic activities, an infinite number of meaningful choices remain to be made by the writer. A heavy dependence on abstraction, a peculiar use of the present tense, a habitual evocation of similarities through parallel structure, a tendency to place feelings in syntactical positions of agency, a trick of underplaying causal words: any of these patterns of expression, when repeated with unusual frequency, is the sign of a habit of meaning, and thus of a persistent way of sorting out the phenomena of experience. And even single occurrences of linguistic oddities, especially in crucial places, can point to what might be called temporary epistemologies.

Here, then, is one way in which the term "style" is meaningful, one kind of *choice* which really exists for the author. This view does not, of course, represent an entirely new departure from conventional stylistics, even though my formulation has been elicited by the chaos of past criticism. Style as epistemic choice may be what John Middleton Murry has in mind when he says that "a true idiosyncrasy of style [is] the result of an author's success in compelling language to conform to his mode of experience." [15] It probably is what W. K. Wimsatt refers to when he calls style "the last and most detailed elaboration of meaning." [16] New or not, this approach to style has the advantage of being philosophically defensible, as well as the advantage of yielding results that have to do with the literary work as a whole, not merely with its (nonexistent) window dressing. Finally, the method which I suggest saves the study of style from having to rely *only* on those impressionistic, metaphorical judgments which have too often substituted for analysis: dignified, grand, plain, decorative, placid, exuberant, restrained, hard, and the whole tired assortment of epithets which name without explaining.[17]

Yet this account of style is not complete. The naive, commonsense feeling that

---

[15] *The Problem of Style* (London, 1922), p. 23.

[16] *The Prose Style of Samuel Johnson* (New Haven, 1941), p. 63. Mr. Wimsatt is one critic who has fruitfully approached style in this way, both in this book and in *Philosophic Words* (New Haven, 1948).

[17] Such terms may be legitimately used to name habits of meaning which have been described specifically; see, for instance, Mr. Wimsatt's discussion of "plain" and its opposite, *Prose Style of Johnson*, p. 101. The more usual procedure, however, is to use them as if they had clear a priori meaning.

style is a *way* of saying *something* demands more than a cursory dismissal. For one thing, a discussion of style as epistemic choice can operate effectively only over wide areas of prose, where habitual kinds of choice become evident. There is little sense in comparing the epistemic decisions of a writer who is discussing a rowing match with those of a writer on Christian ideas of teleology. The very choice of subject matter precludes a large number of stylistic decisions: it can force the writer to be concrete or abstract, for instance. Thus the criticism of style requires a more manageable backdrop than the entire panorama of the world. If, as Wittgenstein says, "the world is the totality of facts, not of things,"[18] perhaps individual facts, or combinations of them, will serve the purpose.

This position is the one that I propose to take, and I shall use the term "proposition" to describe what is expressed by sentences. As before, Mr. Richards's remarks will provide a convenient starting place for the argument. During a discussion of logic[19] he lists these three sentences:

> Mussolini is mortal.
> Voltaire is witty.
> Havelock Ellis is old.

A logician, he says, would claim that these sentences "express propositions of the same form," a contention which "is flagrantly not so." The first sentence, Mr. Richards says, means "Mussolini will die sometime"; the second means "Voltaire makes remarks which cause in certain people a peculiar pleasure, and in others a peculiar annoyance"; the third, "Havelock Ellis has lived through many years." These sentences show that "the similar adjectives stand for very different forms." Mr. Richards's analysis is revealing, and the particular logician he has in mind[20] *had* made the error of assuming that syntactical structure is a key to the structure of propositions. But Mr. Richards makes precisely the same error in implying that his *translations* of the first three sentences reveal the structure of the propositions they express, for he takes the translations as showing that the propositions are of different forms. And by what superior right is the sentence "Mussolini will die sometime" a better indication of propositional form than the sentence "Mussolini is mortal"? Or for that matter, why not other sentences, such as "Mussolini's life will end," or "Mussolini will not live forever"? If the first two sentences express the same proposition, then there are many other sentences which do so, and these sentences are of many syntactical forms. I see no way of picking one of such a group of sentences as *the* mirror of the proposition it expresses.[21]

The difficulty, of course, is that a "proposition," as Mr. Richards uses the term and as I wish to use it, has no form at all. The form of a proposition, like the forms of

---

[18] Ludwig Wittgenstein, *Tractatus Logico-Philosophicus*, translated by C. K. Ogden (London, 1922), p. 31.
[19] *Interpretation in Teaching*, p. 370.
[20] Susan Stebbing, *A Modern Introduction to Logic* (London, 1930), p. 51.
[21] The truth is, I think, that most logicians would say that Mr. Richards's *sentences* are of the same form, and not the propositions they express.

thought, is illusory, if I am right in what I take a proposition to be. It is the class of all sentences which are related to a fact or a cluster of facts in this way: if the fact (or cluster) exists, the sentences are all true; if the fact does not exist, the sentences are all false. In other words, they contain no parts which will not stand or fall with the fact. The process of determining, by observing facts, whether a sentence is true or false, is called "verification."[22] What may have led Mr. Richards to claim that his translations revealed the propositional forms which had been concealed by the original versions, is the fact that the restatements are more nearly descriptions of the facts which would go to *verify* the propositions involved.

Thus, for a sentence to express a proposition is for it to be a member of a group of sentences. But this class membership does not imply that a given sentence is one subform of a main propositional form. Rather, all members of the class have a most general form: the form "x is the case," or $f(x)$. And this form they have in common with *all* sentences, and with all propositions, for "the general propositional form is a variable."[23] This form distinguishes propositions from expletives, isolated words, commands, and so forth, none of which state that anything is the case, but it does not distinguish one proposition from another.

Propositions, then, offer a second locus for the analyst of style. Many sentences can express the same proposition; that is, they can be jointly verifiable by reference to the same fact. This is Bloomfield's contention when he states that "formally different utterances," though they always differ in meaning, may be equivalent "as to some partial phase of meaning." Equivalence covers "the phase of meaning which is observable indifferently by all persons," and "it is only the accompanying personal and social adjustments which differ."[24] These "adjustments" in language I would call "style," but it is worth noting again that they, as well as the root idea, are *meanings*, and not merely embellishment. Style is the hidden thoughts which accompany overt propositions; it is the highly general meanings which are implied by a writer's

---

[22] See A. J. Ayer, *Language, Truth and Logic*, revised edition (New York, 1946), pp. 13, 35, for a positivist's account of the criterion of verifiability. See also Alfred Tarski, "The Semantic Conception of Truth and the Foundations of Semantics," *Semantics and the Philosophy of Language* (Urbana, Ill., 1952), especially pp. 15–17. According to Tarski, whose article is a classic in the field, the general definition of "truth" is a logical conjunction of all equivalences of the form "x is true, if and only if p," where "p" is any "true" sentence and "x" is the name of that sentence (i.e., that sentence in quotation marks). Tarski's definition seems to bypass propositions altogether by applying the term "true" to sentences only; and in view of the long dispute over propositions among logicians and philosophers, Tarski's move may be a wise application of Occam's razor. But it has the disadvantage of throwing out a term which is in common use by both philosophers and laymen, and the more severe disadvantage of leaving no term at all to describe that which sentences express. For these reasons I follow Ayer, *The Foundations of Empirical Knowledge* (London, 1940), pp. 100–1, in retaining the term. But I am made uncomfortable by an identification of "proposition" and "sentences which are true or false" (as in Wittgenstein, *Tractatus*, pp. 61–103), and more uncomfortable by a gentleman's agreement to use the term "proposition" while confessing ignorance as to its meaning. My own definition (which I have not seen elsewhere) is somewhat odd in that it requires us to think of a *class* of sentences as being true or false. But it jibes reasonably well with most technical usage, and has notable advantages for the study of style, the main one being that it places something between sentences and the facts, thus allowing meaningful talk of what sentences express (propositions) as well as of what they describe (facts).

[23] Wittgenstein, *Tractatus*, p. 103.   [24] *International Encyclopedia of Unified Science*, I, 253.

habitual methods of expressing propositions. Thus, as an aid to analyzing a writer's dissection of the entire universe, the critic may examine what the writer does with modest corners of that universe—that is, with particular facts and particular propositions.

Some theory such as the one I have been suggesting must be held by the modern critic who looks to style for insight into meaning, who believes that "the consideration of style is a consideration of complete meanings, and there is little of any importance that can be studied that is not a consideration of meanings."[25]

So FAR I have been outlining a theory of style which describes choices that I have called epistemic. These choices are important, for they are the critic's key to a writer's mode of experience. They show what sort of place the world is for him, what parts of it are significant or trivial. They show how he thinks, how he comes to know, how he imposes order on the ephemeral pandemonium of experience. These insights into a writer's world view are well worth pursuing, to whatever extent style can yield them. But an account of style which focuses on discursive content alone is only partial; style as it appears, for example, in the novel, I have left largely untouched. For the limits of speakable thought are not the boundaries of experience, or even of rational experience, and thoughts not included in the totality of verifiable propositions are nonetheless an integral part of style, as of knowledge. Thus argues Susanne Langer, who finds post-positivist man on "a tiny grammar-bound island" of human thought, in "the midst of a sea of feeling."[26] He wants to talk of good and evil, substance, beauty, and so forth, but whenever he does, he lapses into nonsense (according to the positivists). Mrs. Langer's method of egress from the narrow cage is well known. She calls symbolism of the sort tolerated by radical empiricists "discursive," and claims that even beyond its limits there is a possibility of genuine semantic. This semantic she calls "presentational symbolism," because its symbols "are involved in a simultaneous, integral presentation."[27] Of this sort is the symbolism of single words, or cries, or music and the visual arts. It is a symbolism of emotional configurations, Mrs. Langer contends, for feelings have contours just as do thoughts, though of a different kind. They are static, grasped in sudden gestalts, rather than formed by gradual accretions of meaning. And to presentational symbolism belongs a large part of what we call "style," a part with which I have yet to deal.

Mrs. Langer says elsewhere,[28] "A statement is always a formulation of an idea, and every known fact or hypothesis or fancy takes its emotional value largely from the way it is presented and entertained." For "idea" my term is "proposition," and this substitution brings Mrs. Langer's statement into close parallelism with my analysis of varying descriptions of facts—but with this exception: her point is that one proposition may be expressed in many different *emotional* forms. The claim is incontestable; a large portion of the submerged meaning in prose is presentational, and the constant shaping of emotions is an always audible counterpoint to the melodic line of discursive

---

[25] Wanning, "Some Changes," p. 20.   [26] *Philosophy in a New Key* (New York: Mentor edition, 1948), pp. 70–71.   [27] *Ibid.*, p. 79.   [28] *Feeling and Form* (New York, 1953), p. 258.

thought. The presentational part of prose does not, of course, get communicated by a special set of symbols or by a code of emotive punctuation marks. It is buried in an exceedingly complex set of relationships among the same symbols which transmit the discursive meaning. These relationships are what Bloomfield referred to as accompanying personal and social adjustments."

Many critics see the emotional freight of literature as of primary importance, even in prose that is mainly discursive. Hence epigrams such as "Style is the man himself," or "Style is ingratiation."[29] Certainly the configurations of feeling which accompany any argument are vital in governing its reception by the reader. The writer must observe the amenities common to all human relationships, by "saying the right thing," as Kenneth Burke puts it, by showing himself a particular human being in a certain social relationship with his auditor.[30] Style adds the force of personality to the impersonal forces of logic and evidence, and is thus deeply involved in the business of persuasion. Students of rhetoric since Plato have been largely concerned, at one or another level of sophistication, with analyzing the role of emotion in inducing agreement, and with the methods of embodying it in writing.

But an analysis of tone, distance, dramatic situation, and the rest, solely as ways of persuading, is only a partial analysis, and one which can lead to the damaging distrust of rhetoric as tricky and insidious. Emotion enters prose not only as disguises for slipping into the reader's confidence, but as sheer expression of self. Complete honesty demands that the writer not only state his ideas accurately, but also take an emotional stance. A proposition is never held altogether dispassionately, nor can it be expressed without some indication of feeling (except in the artificial languages of logic and mathematics, where symbols and structural patterns have no connotations, no psychic contexts). This being so, the writer must either recreate in prose the emotional concomitants of his thinking, or be in some degree unfaithful to himself. To acknowledge the expressive value of tone, however, is not to say that it is isolated from the persuasive value. When a writer such as Newman creates a full picture of the frame of mind in which he approaches a problem and reader, he is being honest, certainly, but his self-revelation may have the effect of persuading the reader to follow the same emotional path. With Arnold and many other writers the two uses of tone are even more inextricably fused. Arnold argues for a temper of mind, rather than for a set of specific doctrines. In his prose, therefore, tone *is* the argument, in large measure: ingratiation and personality become one, for the case stands or falls depending on whether Arnold's feelings and attitudes are attractive to his readers.[31] His use of language is presentational in that a full understanding of his prose depends on a grasp of the emotional pattern which it presents.

Feeling enters discursive prose, then, as expression and as persuasion. In addition there is a third way, I think, which is almost beyond the power of language to describe. A sentence, at its inception, raises questions rather than answering them. The first word or two may limit the field of possible things-to-be-said, but they do not

---

[29] Kenneth Burke, *Permanence and Change* (New York, 1935), p. 71.   [30] See Reuben Arthur Brower, *The Fields of Light* (New York, 1951), Chap. I, for this view of tone.   [31] I am indebted for this notion to John Holloway, *The Victorian Sage* (London, 1953), p. 207.

really transmit information. They may name something, or set an attitude toward something, or indicate a shift in direction from a previous sentence, but they always give rise to questions such as "What about it?" or "What am I to think of in that way?" These demands for completion of a sequence are of course subverbal; they are the vaguest sort of dissatisfaction with suspended thought, with a rational process not properly concluded. As the sentence progresses some of the demands are satisfied, others deferred, others complicated, and meanwhile new ones are created. But with the end of the sentence comes a kind of balance which results from something having been *said*. There may be a new set of indefinite expectations which remain for future sentences to gratify or disappoint, but one circle is completed, one temporary equilibrium gained. The very act of predication is an emotional act, with rhythms of its own. To state something is first to create imbalance, curiosity, where previously there was nothing, and then to bring about a new balance. So prose builds on the emotional force of coming to know, of pinning down part of what has previously been formless and resolving the tensions which exist between the human organism and unstructured experience. Mrs. Langer speaks of the

> feeling that naturally inheres in studious thinking, the growing intensity of a problem as it becomes more and more complex, and at the same time more definite and "thinkable," until the demand for answer is urgent, touched with impatience; the holding back of assent as the explanation is prepared; the cadential feeling of solution, and expansion of consciousness in new knowledge.[32]

To emotion, then, as well as to epistemic choice, the stylistic critic must turn his attention. This part of the study is and always has been particularly enticing, perhaps because the individual character of a writer emerges with special clarity in the patterns of feeling which are habitual with him. The epistemic part of style, moreover—a writer's method of dissecting the universe, as expressed by the infinite number of choices he makes—is likely to seem indistinguishable from what he overtly *says*. Yet this is all the more reason for pursuing stylistic meaning through the maze of surface meaning. That which is not immediately obvious may be just as central to the spirit of the writer, and therefore just as valuable to know, as that which starts up unbidden from the page. And, finally, it should be said that a dichotomy between thought and emotion, though useful, is artificial. A writer's characteristic way of manipulating experience is organically related to his feelings about coming to know; his attitude toward the reader and toward the process of communicating is also part of the whole.

The view of style which I have been outlining clearly takes prose as a serious literary venture. What Leo Spitzer says of the purely imaginative forms is also true of good discursive prose: "the lifeblood of the poetic creation is everywhere the same, whether we tap the organism at 'language' or 'ideas,' at 'plot' or at 'composition.'"[32] This rather mystical theory makes good sense if "lifeblood" is translatable to "modes

---

[32] *Feeling and Form*, p. 302.   [33] *Linguistics and Literary History* (Princeton, 1948), p. 18.

of experience and habits of feeling." Spitzer's dictum means only that a work of prose can be self-consistent just as a good poem is, its fabric all of a piece. Such a view is the direct antithesis of the older one, which saw style as sugar-coating; if my hypothesis is legitimate, style is just as useful a key to total meaning as is any other element. For this reason, and for no other, it is worth studying: to say something about style is to contribute fresh insight into the artistic contours of the work as a whole.

FROM *The Novelist's Medium and the Novelist's Art*

❦ DAVID LODGE ❦

David Lodge's *Language of Fiction: Essays in Criticism and Verbal Analysis of the English Novel* (1966) divides into two parts: a theoretical section, in which the author engages with a number of pronouncements by different critics to establish that the esthetic status of fiction and its language is comparable to that of poetry; and a series of essays on particular novels, in which he treats such stylistic matters as vocabulary in *Mansfield Park*, imagery in *Jane Eyre*, and rhetoric in *Hard Times*.

In the first section, to truncate his argument severely, Lodge demonstrates the uniqueness of a novel's language on practical grounds, in part, by showing it to be as unamenable in its own way to precise translation into a foreign language as poetry (whose greater compression and heightened phonological dimension make accurate translation impossible). In addition, he contends—drawing on the work of the philosopher J. M. Cameron—that the language of a novel (like that of a poem) is unique, non-paraphrasable, on the theoretical grounds that in dealing with literature we have no external criteria that allow us to decide whether a description of actuality is true or false, thus no viable possibility of entertaining an alternative description, but only "these words in this order." Thus Lodge takes the position that literary language and the particulars it renders have a special status: they less refer to an external world than create a reality within the text, less represent one world than realize another.

Lodge goes on to review several sorts of stylistic analysis. The philologically conditioned approach exemplified by Leo Spitzer or Stephen Ullmann, he suggests, is somewhat undermined by the fact that both critics seize on "deviations from normal usage" where "normal usage" often refers to a linguistic context outside the literary work. And he takes issue with the structuralist approach of a critic like Michael Riffaterre because it does not yield a truly scientific way of determining whether and how any specific stylistic device has worked. Finally, he discounts criticism of fiction that deals too exclusively in "character" or "plot," for he holds that characters and plots are realizable only in the language itself of fiction. Following his own precepts, in the essays that make up the second half of his book Lodge regards the given novel in its entirety as the context in which criticism ought to proceed and devotes his attention to the stylistic features which, through their repetition within that context, have struck him as especially significant.

The two selections reprinted here—both from the first half of Lodge's volume—have been chosen because of their relevance to theoretical problems concerning style in fiction. In one he treats the matter of translation, and in the other he makes his case for the unique functioning of literary language.

The Argument from Translation

THAT POETRY IS UNTRANSLATABLE is a basic tenet of modern criticism and appears to follow logically from any critical theory which holds that form and content are inseparable, and which accounts for the literary effects of a given work principally or exclusively in terms of its verbal organization. Like most of the ideas we have been considering, it starts with the Romantics. Shelley, for instance, talks of the "vanity of translation":

> [I]t were as wise to cast a violet into a crucible that you might discover the formal principle of its colour and odour, as seek to transfuse from one language into another

---

The excerpts from "The Novelist's Medium and the Novelist's Art," by David Lodge, are reprinted from his *Language of Fiction* (London and New York, 1966), pp. 18 ... 23, 30–38, by permission of Routledge & Kegan Paul Ltd. and Columbia University Press.

the creations of a poet. The plant must spring again from its seed, or it will bear no flower,—and this is the burthen of the curse of Babel.[1]

Novels, on the other hand, are apparently translatable, in the sense that we all read translated novels with some confidence in our judgment of them and their authors. Hence, it is argued, the identity of a novel cannot be determined by the words of which it is composed—as a poem is so determined—because this identity is not changed when the novel is translated into other, different words.

... Translation from one tongue to another is altogether too complicated and mysterious a process to provide clear-cut conclusions about the novelist's art, but I believe it can be convincingly argued that novels are non-paraphrasable. I describe such an argument below [see page 59]. But I propose to consider further the argument from translation because of its pragmatic plausibility, and because it raises interesting questions about literature and language.

Let me lay my hand on my heart and aver that although I have read many foreign novels in translation with great pleasure and benefit, and have passed judgment on them, I have never felt that I "possessed" any of them in the sense in which I possess the English novels I read and admire. I invite the reader to ask himself if this is not his own experience, and if it is not accountable in the end only in terms of the insecurity felt in the process of reading: the accumulative effect of innumerable, minute uncertainties, awkwardnesses, anomalies, and ambiguities in the language. That this sense of insecurity does not entirely inhibit our critical faculties can be explained. It is virtually impossible for an educated and sensitive reader to read a translated novel without realizing that it *is* translated, even if for some reason he overlooks the title-page and relies on internal evidence alone. Thus the reader makes a "contract" with a translated novel which is different from the one he makes with a novel in his own language. He approaches it with a recognition of cultural differences which obstruct communication; he expects to feel insecure in the verbal world of a translated novel, just as he expects to feel insecure in a foreign country in whose language he is not fluent.

The question of translation bristles with problems, particularly of verification. To test the closeness of any translation to its original, one would have to be not only bilingual but—to coin a rather ugly phrase—bi-cultural, i.e. possessed of the whole complex of emotions, associations, and ideas which intricately relate a nation's language to its life and tradition, but possessed not only of one such complex—as we all are to some extent—but of two. Writers like Conrad or Beckett might qualify for such an undertaking, but most of us must rely on the comparatively clumsy method of comparative analysis, carried out in the recognition of our unequal competence in the two things compared. I propose to do a little exercise of this kind with a view to showing the kinds of changes which may occur in translations of prose fiction. I shall compare a sentence from Proust with its translation by Scott Moncrieff, usually acknowledged to be a fine translator.

[1] Shelley, "A Defence of Poetry," *Peacock's Four Ages of Poetry, Shelley's Defence of Poetry, Browning's Essay on Shelley*, edited by H. F. Brett-Smith (The Percy Reprints No. 3) (Oxford, 1921), p. 29.

Proust and Scott Moncrieff Compared

THE SENTENCE comes from the first section of "Overture" of *Du Côté de Chez Swann*, where the narrator says that his only consolation when, as a child, he went to bed, was when his mother came upstairs to kiss him good night. He continues:

> Mais ce bonsoir durait si peu de temps, elle redescendait si vite, que le moment où je l'entendais monter, puis où passait dans le couloir à double porte le bruit léger de sa robe de jardin en mousseline bleue, à laquelle pendaient de petits cordons de paille tressée, était pour moi un moment douloureux.[2]

Scott Moncrieff translates:

> But this goodnight lasted for so short a time: she went down again so soon that the moment in which I heard her climb the stairs, and then caught the sound of her garden dress of blue muslin, from which hung little tassels of plaited straw, rustling along the double-doored corridor, was for me a moment of the keenest sorrow.[3]

The narrator, here, is describing, or, more precisely, remembering, a particular action of his mother's, and his own emotional response to it. It is a complex response. Though triggered off by the sense of hearing, it is also clearly visual—i.e. the child in bed reconstructs the appearance of his mother from the evidence of his hearing, assisted by his visual memory. The sentence thus exemplifies in microcosm the synaesthesia which informs the whole novel's treatment of memory. Then, although the passage communicates a sense of joy, in the loving description of the mother's person, it asserts that the moment was one of sorrow, because, although the mother's movements presaged the long-desired kiss, they also implied that the kiss would soon be over, and that there would be nothing left to look forward to for the rest of the night. We encounter another central theme of the novel—time: its elusiveness, its inexorable movement forward, careless of the emotional content of this or that moment for any individual.

If this is a valid account of the meaning of the sentence, we will find, I think, that this meaning is vitally connected with the linguistic form of the sentence; and it may be interesting to see how much of this has been carried over in translation. For convenience of reference, Proust's sentence may be broken down into clauses as follows:

1. Mais ce bonsoir durait si peu de temps,
2. elle redescendait si vite,
3. que le moment...
4. où je l'entendais monter,
5. puis où passait dans le couloir à double porte le bruit léger de sa robe de jardin en mousseline bleue,
6. à laquelle pendaient de petits cordons de paille tressée,
7. ... était pour moi un moment douloureux.

[2] Marcel Proust, *Du Côté de Chez Swann*, 42nd impression (Paris, 1919), p. 18.
[3] Marcel Proust, *Swann's Way*, translated by C. K. Scott Moncrieff (Penguin edition, 1957), p. 20.

The most obvious syntactical feature of the sentence is the long-delayed predicate of clause 3, which is separated from its subject by three subordinate clauses (4, 5, and 6) so extended that the word *moment* has to be repeated (not, of course, that this is the only reason for the repetition). This separation and delay expresses the most important tensions and paradoxes of the narrator's emotion. For, when we come at last to the statement that the moment announced several lines before was one of sorrow, it is, notwithstanding the logical explanations provided by clauses 1 and 2, with a faint shock of surprise, because the description of what was happening in that moment suggested love and affection and joy.

This delaying of the predicate is available to the English translator, and, as we see, he has used it. But the effect of this delay is supported and amplified by two inversions in clauses 5 and 6, only the second and less important of which Scott Moncrieff has managed to accommodate. The delay of the predicate *était pour moi un moment douloureux* expresses an irony that works against the narrator, which might be crudely expressed as "all good things come to an end." But the delay of the subjects in clauses 5 and 6 indicates the narrator's resistance to this fact. The verbs *passait* and *pendaient* are followed by nouns which are lengthily and elaborately qualified, suggesting (to me at least) that against the inexorable passing of time the boy is desperately pitting his keen sensuous responsiveness to his mother's person, expressed in the nouns and adjectives. It is as if, by extending and concentrating on the catalogue of concrete details, he can arrest time; but the hopelessness of this effort is indicated by the return to this predicate of clause 3, which will not be held off any longer.

The principles of English prose enable Scott Moncrieff to retain the second inversion—*from which hung*—but not the first: *when passed* would be awkward and jarring.[4] He is obliged to transfer the verb from the mother (or, more exactly, from the sound of her dress) to the narrator, and this involves other changes. He has to specify the sound of the dress as a *rustle*. Proust does not specify, but merely suggests a sound in the sibilants of *passait*, *mousseline* and *tressée*. The transfer of the verb from the sound to the narrator means that the *double-doored corridor* has to be shifted to the end of the subordinate clauses. In Proust's sentence, the order of words and phrases follows the pattern of the narrator's thought, which tends towards finer and finer, more and more anguished concentration on smaller and smaller details of his beloved mother's appearance. The clause which immediately precedes the explicit declaration of sorrow is the description, in affectionate detail, of the little tassels of plaited straw. In Moncrieff, however, this crucial position is occupied by the relatively unimportant double-doored corridor. The translation also produces (to my ear, at least) an unfortunate treble-rhyme: *straw . . . double-doored corridor.*

In the above comparison I have confined myself to what can be studied objectively in language: word-order, tense, clause structure, and the more obviously mimetic use of sound. I have not attempted to penetrate into the mystery of tongues, to consider, for instance, whether *of the keenest sorrow* can convey to an English reader exactly what *douloureux* conveys to a French reader. So far as it goes, the experiment suggests

---

[4] One might also note that English lacks an exact equivalent to the French imperfect tense.

that Scott Moncrieff has succeeded in conveying a good deal of the meaning of the original (in so far as that original meaning is discernible by myself) but that he has also lost a good deal. The loss is felt not on the level of "mere sense" but in the higher categories of Richards's levels of meaning, or in what is sometimes called, in modern linguistics, "delicacy." The degree of loss is not, in my opinion, entirely trivial. And while it is true that not all novelists pose the same kind of problems to a translator as Proust does, it may be that his very virtuosity alerts us to the possibility of aesthetic loss, which we may overlook in the case of writing which is superficially innocent of verbal cunning.[5]

. . . .

Summary of Arguments

I THINK I can best draw together the arguments against considering the novelist as a verbal artist in the sense in which a poet is generally acknowledged to be a verbal artist, by distilling from those considered above and from others which I have not had space to discuss, their essential and most persuasive drift. Let us imagine a kind of "familiar compound ghost" of a critic, putting forward the following view.

"All examples of human discourse can be placed on a scale according to the extent to which each example *draws attention to the way it is manipulating language.* A metaphysical lyric—say, Donne's 'Valediction Forbidding Mourning,' is an example which does so to a very striking extent. Ordinary casual conversation, on the other hand, provides countless examples of discourse which scarcely calls any attention to the way it is manipulating language, for it is concerned to call attention to something specific outside itself—an object, a situation, an emotion. John Robinson, for instance, says to a woman: 'I've got to go away for a while, darling, but don't be upset. I'll soon be back, and I'll be thinking of you all the time.'

Our response to any particular item of discourse, and the kind of comment we feel ready to make on it, are determined by its place on the above-mentioned scale. If asked to comment on 'A Valediction,' we should naturally and properly indicate the way the poet gives interest and particularity to a conventional and generalized idea—parting, with its attendant sadness and consolations—by manipulating language: by selecting, using, and discarding a series of analogies until he settles on one which gathers to itself and reconciles the tensions in the poem, the conduct of this argument-by-analogy being supported by a cunning exploitation of sound and rhythm. Such questions as, 'Does the poem refer to an actual situation? if so, what was the identity of the woman? was Donne sincere?'—these questions have a certain interest, but they are not the first considerations for an educated reader, and their relevance to the poem *qua* poem is doubtful.

Of John Robinson's parting words, however, the reverse is true. If asked to

---

[5] One naturally tends to assume that the changes involved in translation result in a "loss." But there are cases —Baudelaire's translations of Poe, for example—where it seems to have resulted in aesthetic gain.

comment on them (in a context in which such a request would seem natural—i.e. ordinary social intercourse) it would matter very much whether John Robinson was addressing his wife or his mistress, and one would be concerned chiefly with how far his words reflected his real feelings, whether the consolation offered was effective, what light the utterance threw upon the relationship between the two people, and so on. To comment in detail upon the diction and grammar would not be appropriate, or useful.

The novel covers a fairly wide portion of the scale between Donne's poem and John Robinson's utterance, but it leans, on the whole, towards the latter. The novelist creates a fictional likeness of the real world, in which the behaviour and utterances of people arouse the kind of interests, pose the kind of questions, that belong to John Robinson's discourse rather than to John Donne's. The difference between John Robinson's utterance and the utterance of a character in a novel is, of course, that in the real world we comment on such utterances by referring to our empirical knowledge of the context—what we know or suspect or have observed about the people involved. We apply the same kind of knowledge to an utterance in the fictional world, but such knowledge derives from the novelist—it is he who has given us the information we need to satisfy the questions raised by any individual utterance. In recognizing this we are able to make a *literary* judgment of a novel even though the kind of interests aroused by a novel are essentially the same as those aroused by events in life. We assess a novelist according to the success with which he constructs a fictional world in which every action or utterance contributes to our understanding of any other. Since this is a created world we look for a logic, consistency, and design in the whole which eludes us in the real world. In both worlds the same kinds of questions are raised, the same kinds of thought-processes are set in motion, but in the fictional world we have stronger expectations of finding answers and reaching conclusions. In the ordered, selective world of the novelist we gain insights which enrich our understanding of the real world, though such insights can never totally encompass its endless flux. In so far as the activity of the novelist relates to human behaviour, we talk of his *characterization*. In so far as it relates to cause and effect, we talk of his handling of *plot*. Such terms are properly central in formal criticism of the novel because they recognize that the fictional world runs parallel to the experiential world, while being at the same time more ordered and more patterned—in other words, a 'made thing.' Language is the point of departure and the terminus of the criticism of poetry, but only the point of departure of novel-criticism."

I have tried to put this case as persuasively as possible, and there is much in it with which one must agree. It is true that the language of poetry calls attention to itself and thus invites critical attention, whereas the language of prose fiction approximates more to casual speech, and arouses the interests of ordinary life. X's argument is in fact more plausible as an account of the methodology of novel criticism, than as an account of what might be called the epistemology of novel-criticism—i.e. the means by which we come to know what we criticize. I would argue that these means are linguistic in a sense which obliges us to find a method appropriate for dealing with them.

At the end of my discussion of Christopher Caudwell's theories, I suggested that at the heart of the whole debate was a philosophical problem concerning the relationship of literary language to reality. To carry the argument further, I must lean heavily on a contemporary philosopher who is also distinguished by his knowledge and understanding of literature.

J. M. Cameron: These Words in This Order

IN HIS INAUGURAL LECTURE as Professor of Philosophy at Leeds University, entitled "Poetry and Dialectic," J. M. Cameron addressed himself to the question which has most haunted writers and critics since the Romantic period, namely, whether "there are grounds for thinking that truth is applicable to poetic discourse and for putting that value upon it which belongs to those types of discourse in which we make plain to each other and to ourselves the character of human life and of its predicaments."[6] In examining this problem, and in coming to an affirmative conclusion, Professor Cameron makes several points which are highly relevant to the present discussion.

By "poetry" Professor Cameron means all literary discourse, including prose fiction. His argument can sustain this definition because he distinguishes poetic from non-poetic discourse not in terms of the *way* it uses language, but in terms of the *purpose* with which it uses language, that purpose being "the making of fictions." Attempts to define poetry, when "poetry" is used in the wide generic sense, according to the way or ways it uses language nearly always come to grief because there is no linguistic device which is *peculiar* to poetry, in the sense that we could not use it in other types of discourse. This is why linguistic *form* (as distinct from function) should be seen as a continuum, rather than as sharply divided into two kinds.

Still, our instinct is that, since the poet's medium is language, there must be something peculiar about his use of it. This instinct is right, and the definition of poetry as "the making of fictions" will not account for this peculiarity unless it is followed up in a particular way.

The definition of poetry as "the making of fictions" is, as Cameron acknowledges, essentially Aristotle's notion of *mimesis*. What dissatisfies us about Aristotle's and some neo-Aristotelian criticism is that it presents imitation as a process of means to end, in which the verbal means are relegated to an inferior position.[7] Modern, post-Romantic criticism has corrected this tendency by asserting that in poetry what is said is not distinguishable from the way it is said. But it has not been able, or has not

---

[6] Cameron, "Poetry and Dialectic," *The Night Battle* (1962), p. 122.

[7] Wimsatt conveniently illustrates the point in discussing the Chicago school of neo-Aristotelian critics: "Olson and, echoing him recently, the Chicago sympathiser Hoyt Trowbridge say that if a critic begins with the words of a poem, it is just as if he were to say that 'the shape and function of a saw are determined by the steel of which it is made.'" Wimsatt's reply seems unanswerable: "But why wouldn't modern criticism of verbal meaning be more like saying that the goodness of a saw, its capacity to cut, is determined by the steel *fashioned in a certain shape*?" (*The Verbal Icon*, pp. 62–63.)

wished to assert this for poetry in the wide generic sense that would include novels, considered as wholes.

The basis of this assertion was well stated by Coleridge, who seems to have derived it from his excellent schoolmaster, the Rev. James Bowyer:[8]

> whatever lines can be translated into other words of the same language, without diminution of their significance, either in sense, or association, or in any worthy feeling, are so far vicious in their diction.[9]

This is the familiar commonplace of modern criticism, that poetry is distinguished from other kinds of discourse by being non-paraphrasable.... Now, in so far as this argument depends upon practical demonstration, it is most convincing when tested on poems, and particularly lyric poems, where the verbal, syntactical and phonological organization is highly complex, concentrated and "artificial"; and the effect of any small change or omission can be easily appreciated. Few modern critics trouble to prove that poetry is non-paraphrasable, but their justification of every minute part of a good poem on aesthetic grounds implies this. Novels, however, do not, on the whole, invite this kind of analysis, for various reasons: because they are so long, because it is impossible to hold all their words in the mind at once, because their language has the feel of casual speech, and so on. Paraphrase, in the sense of summary, is as indispensable to the novel-critic as close analysis is to the critic of lyric poetry. The natural deduction is that novels are paraphrasable whereas poems are not. But this is a false deduction because close analysis is itself a disguised form of paraphrase, differing from the paraphrase of conventional novel-criticism only in that it tends towards expansion rather than compression. It is the inevitable irony of our position as critics that we are obliged, whatever kind of imaginative work we examine, to paraphrase the unparaphrasable. Whenever we try to express our understanding and appreciation of a literary text, we are obliged to state its meanings in different words; and it is in the *distance* between the original words and our own words, when the latter are brought to their maximum of sensitive and articulate responsiveness, that we feel the uniqueness of the writer's achievement.

To return to Cameron: he cuts through this confusion by providing a *logical* proof of the non-paraphrasability of literary discourse. First, he considers the general question of "how words and expressions and sentences of various logical types get the sense they have," and in particular the traditional notion, very characteristic of eighteenth-century thought, and still vigorous, that "a thought is one thing and the way it is expressed another."[10] He concludes that it is allowable to talk about a sentence and the thought it expresses, because the same thought can be expressed in different words of the same language, or in different languages; but that it does not follow that we can think of "two objects, as it were, the sentence and the thought" because "the notion that there can be thought quite apart from a vehicle of thought

---

[8] Coleridge, *Biographia Literaria*, Chapter I. [9] Coleridge, *Select Poetry and Prose*, edited by Stephen Potter, p. 217. [10] Cameron, *op. cit.*, p. 125.

is a superstition, so far, at least, as human thinking is concerned."[11] He then considers the effects of this superstition on traditional poetics, and how it has been corrected by the Romantics, and by modern critics specializing in close analysis. He then considers the objection that, since this criticism has concerned itself almost exclusively with material that is self-evidently difficult to paraphrase, and since it has been conceded that some discourse can be paraphrased, we cannot be sure that poetry in the wide generic sense is always non-paraphasable.

Cameron takes his stand on the proposition that "some of the entailments that belong to other kinds of discourse are, in poetic discourse, cut."[12] By this he means that

> it is characteristic of a fiction that certain questions cannot appropriately be asked about it. We cannot ask how many children Lady Macbeth had; or what courses Hamlet pursued at the University of Wittenberg; or what kind of caterpillar caused the sickness of the rose in Blake's poem; or whether Mr Jingle's talking, in the year 1827, about the 1830 Revolution, is or is not a case of extrasensory perception.[13]

There is no need to linger over this argument: it is another of the commonplaces of modern criticism. But the logical implications seen in it by Professor Cameron have not, I think, been seen before. Briefly, they are that the distinction we are able to make in ordinary discourse between what is said and the way it is said is a condition of the entailments that are cut in fictional discourse. "When we for example describe the world, how we describe it has much to do with the *force* of our description, very little—provided we make no syntactical blunders—to do with its accuracy." He instances some descriptive uses of language, and concludes:

> what all these instances have in common, and what makes such uses susceptible of paraphrase, is that in each case the adequacy of what is said is governed by some state of affairs, prior to and independent of what is said.... Now, the adequacy of what is said in the form of poetic fiction is not, in any straight-forward sense, governed by any state of affairs prior to and independent of what is said. Fictitious descriptions are neither true nor false in the way real descriptions are true or false and this follows from their being fictions. ... It follows from this that I could not give an *alternative* poetic description, for there could be no criterion (as there would be in the case of a real description) for deciding whether or not the alternative description had succeeded. The poetic description has the form of a description; but it exists only as *this* description, these words in this order. What is said and how it is said are thus not distinguishable in the way they are in other forms of discourse.[14]

This is roughly the half-way stage of Cameron's essay. What he has to say in the latter part is no less interesting. Briefly, his conclusion is that we rightly value poetry because, in its unique combination of universality and rich particularity, it compensates for the inadequacy we find in "concepts drawn from the common stock"[15] to the uniqueness of our own experience as individuals, though without that common stock of concepts

---

[11] *Ibid.*, p. 129.   [12] *Ibid.*, p. 134.   [13] *Ibid.*, p. 133.   [14] *Ibid.*, pp. 136–37.   [15] *Ibid.*, p. 145.

we should not be conscious of experience at all. Thus, I cannot identify in myself a sensation like "pain," or a state of emotion like "being in love," without knowing what those words mean in the public language.

> Nevertheless, because each of us is himself and not another, unique in his history and in his relations to others, a characterization of our individual feelings through concepts drawn from the common stock leaves us with a feeling of injustice; for the feelings are rendered, not in their particularity, but in respect of their likeness to the feelings of others.... The consolation of the poetic representation of human love is that it reveals to us that condition of feeling we share with others—it gives us "the image of man and nature"—but not, or not wholly, as articulated in the common run of concepts, but as articulated in a particular concrete representation that speaks to us and for us in our individual situation, and only *through* this to and for our common humanity. It belongs to the poetic representation that it is wholly individual, these words in this order, and that no paraphrase can be given; so that although we know that this poem that speaks to us and for us speaks also to and for others, it is still as though it speaks to us alone.[16]

Cameron's conclusions do not differ widely from those of other modern literary theorists and aestheticians. What is interesting is the route by which he reaches these conclusions, which enables him to formulate them in a particularly persuasive and precise way. To make one comparison: his description has much in common with Richards's distinction between "emotive" and "referential" language, but it accounts much more satisfactorily for the fact that, on the one hand, emotive language is frequently used in non-poetic discourse, and on the other hand, that the language of a good deal of literature has the appearance of being referential. Similarly, Cameron's vindication of the truth and value of poetic discourse is more satisfying than Richards's psychological theory of literary value as the integration and appeasement of appetencies, because more directly related to the writer's special skills in the medium of language.

It should be emphasized that Cameron's definition of poetic discourse, by reference to the purpose with which it uses language, does not mean that other types of discourse are utterly distinct. Discourse which ostensibly sets out to describe actuality may also use language with a poetic purpose; and this accounts for the fact that many works of an apparently descriptive nature, particularly philosophical treatises, survive the demonstration of their descriptive falsity, and retain a power to affect and interest us, so that we ascribe to them a quasi-literary value. Professor Cameron himself, in another essay, cites Hobbes's *Leviathan* and Pascal's political writings as cases of this kind:

> On particular questions Hobbes and Pascal were right or wrong, what they said was true or false. But the enduring charm of what they said about political man is more to be grasped through the analogy of the poetic whole than through the analogy of Newton's *Principia*. This may go some way to explain what at first sight seems puzzling, and

[16] *Ibid.*, pp. 145–46.

puzzling not only in connection with the thinkers I have named: the co-presence of logical incoherence and a felt power to illuminate political relations.[17]

For my purposes, the most important element in Cameron's essay is his demonstration that all poetic fictions exist only as certain words in a certain order. Clearly, for the purposes of actual criticism, this principle must be modified according to the material under consideration. In the case of drama, for instance, we must allow for the non-verbal and variable elements of theatrical production—movement, spectacle, music, etc. And in discussing orally-transmitted literature we must take into account the constant process of modification and accretion which occurs in any "one" work. But such questions scarcely affect the novel, which of all the literary genres is the one most firmly fixed in the Gutenberg galaxy. It is the characteristic literary product of the printing press. In the eighteenth and nineteenth centuries, of course, novels were often read aloud to an assembled audience—but they were *read*, not recited: the words were fixed on the printed page in the order determined by the novelist. The novelist might subsequently change the words—in which case his revisions were fixed on another printed page, and we have a slightly different novel to deal with. Apart from the possibility of textual corruption having occurred in the process of printing (where the critic must rely upon the assistance of textual scholarship), we may, in citing a reliable text and sticking to it, be confident that we are dealing with an artistic whole.

[17] Cameron, "The Justification of Political Attitudes," *op. cit.*, pp. 82–83.

Style of Distance,
Style of Nearness

❧ THEOPHIL SPOERRI ❧

Theophil Spoerri was long a distinguished professor of Romance literature at the University of Zurich and co-editor with Emil Staiger, professor of German literature at the same university, of *Trivium*, a Swiss quarterly published from 1942 to 1951 which contains so many fine essays on matters of style that it is a crucial document for anyone interested in such criticism. In addition to his many contributions to *Trivium*, Spoerri has written a number of books, including *Renaissance und Barock bei Ariost und Tasso* (1922), a volume—like Fritz Strich's *Deutsche Klassik und Romantik*— deeply influenced by Heinrich Wölfflin's *Principles of Art History; Präludium zur Poesie* (1929), which offers along with its central argument a group of extremely sensitive analyses of poems by Goethe, Eichendorff, and Rilke, among others; and *Die Formwerdung des Menschen* (1938), which develops a theoretical position aimed at integrating the nature and value of literature with the conditions of existence and the capacities of man. These last two volumes, especially, reveal the metaphysical tendencies of Spoerri's criticism—his essentially religious commitment; his conception of the poem realized through its forms as a kind of model for the perennial human task of the individual to realize himself morally; and the Crocean belief that the reader may re-experience the creative process of the artist which has eventuated in the particular work.

The essay reprinted here, published initially in *Trivium* as "Stil der Ferne, Stil der Nähe," shows both Spoerri's proclivity for the sweeping overview and his capacity for delicately detailed analysis. Taking off from Buffon's "Discourse on Style," he posits two archetypal stylistic modes —one of distance, one of nearness—and suggests their relation to the progress of human history, to the development of language, to the very movements of man's consciousness. Maintaining that a writer's texts may enable the critic of style to make "an existential diagnosis of a whole epoch," Spoerri interprets a series of texts by the French Swiss novelist C. F. Ramuz as reflections of the shifting cultural situation in Europe during the first decades of the twentieth century. He uses Proust's description of a kiss in *The Guermantes Way* and several poems by Valéry as extreme examples of the two stylistic modes within the same literary period. Then, in an analysis of Mallarmé's "Sonnet" to Méry Laurent, he movingly traces the interplay between the motifs of distance and nearness within a single poem.

"Le style c'est l'homme": this is the form in which the famous definition of style is usually attributed to Buffon. In his *Discours sur le style*,[1] however, Buffon both said and had in mind something less crude. Toward the end of his speech, he distinguishes between the form and content of a text. Content—"les connaissances, les faits et les découvertes [knowledge, facts, and discoveries]"—is alterable and belongs to the realm of generality. "Ces choses sont hors de l'homme, *le style c'est l'homme même* [These things are external to man, *style is the man himself*]."

What Buffon really meant by such an unchanging and personal style emerges clearly from the speech as a whole—in a word, "le sublime." Only the "sublime" style, says Buffon, measures up to the most lofty, noble topics, and he enumerates these in a very characteristic ranking: "les lois de la Nature, les êtres en général, l'espace, la matière, le mouvement et le temps, l'âme, l'esprit humain, les sentiments, les passions [laws of Nature, beings in general, space, matter, motion and time, the soul, the mind, the sentiments, the passions]." For all other topics, a less elevated style will suffice, though Buffon requires that even such a style be "noble et élevé,

---

[1] *Discours prononcé à l'Académie française par M. de Buffon le jour de sa réception* (August 25, 1753).

"Style of Distance, Style of Nearness," by Theophil Spoerri, here translated by Corinna Babb, originally appeared in *Trivium: Schweizerische Vierteljahresschrift für Literaturwissenschaft und Stilkritik*, II (1944), 25–41. Translated by permission of Atlantis Verlag. Excerpts from the poems of Paul Valéry on pages 73, 74, and 75 are reprinted by permission of Éditions Gallimard. © Éditions Gallimard, all rights reserved.

majestueux et grave." Whatever fails to rise to these two levels of style is contemptuously rejected by Buffon. The sublime style can be attained only by one who surveys nature as an ordered whole from the highest vantage point, and who imitates it from this perspective:

> ... s'il imite la Nature dans sa marche et son travail, s'il s'élève par la contemplation aux vérités les plus sublimes; s'il les réunit, s'il les enchaîne, s'il en forme un tout, un système par la réflexion, il établira sur des fondements inébranlables des monuments immortels.
>
> ... *if he imitates Nature in its development and operation, if he rises through contemplation to the most sublime truths; if he brings these together, interrelates them, and forms them into a whole, a system arrived at by reflection, he will establish, on unshakable foundations, monuments that will last forever.*

One who stands on such a height will feel like the master of the world.

> L'homme n'a connu que tard l'étendue de sa puissance et même il ne la connaît pas encore assez; elle dépend en entier de l'exercice de son intelligence: ainsi plus il observera, plus il cultivera la Nature, plus il aura de moyens pour se la soumettre, et de la facilité pour tirer de son sein des richesses nouvelles, sans diminuer les trésors de son inépuisable fécondité. (*Histoire naturelle: des époques de la Nature*, "Septième ... époque")
>
> *Man has only recently come to recognize the extent of his power, and he still does not know that power sufficiently; it depends entirely on the use of his intelligence: for the more man observes and cultivates Nature, the more he will acquire the means to make her comply and the skill to draw new riches from her breast without depleting the treasures of her inexhaustible fecundity.*

The basic tone which corresponds with such an attitude toward the world is one of majestic calm. "Le vrai bonheur," Buffon wrote to his collaborator Guyton de Morveau in 1762, "est la tranquillité.... on fait mille fois plus de mouvement qu'on n'en devrait faire, et c'est ce mouvement qui trouble et perd tout [True happiness is tranquillity.... one moves a thousand times more than is necessary, and it is this movement which unsettles and ruins everything]."

To the style of elevation and repose, the style of distance, which designates objects —precisely because it views them from afar—with the most general expressions ("les termes les plus généraux"), Buffon juxtaposes, in his *Discours*, a lower style, the style of nearness, which focuses only on the points and angles of things:

> ... l'on ne présente qu'un côté de l'objet ... et ordinairement ce côté qu'on choisit est une pointe, un angle sur lequel on fait jouer l'esprit avec d'autant plus de facilité, qu'on l'éloigne davantage des grandes faces sous lesquelles le bon sens a coutume de considérer les choses.
>
> *... one presents only a part of the object ... and ordinarily the chosen part is a point or angle about which one's mind plays all the more freely as one departs farther from the broad aspects in terms of which common sense is accustomed to consider things.*

The "termes généraux" are replaced by the "traits saillants [striking features]." To the exceptional person of a superior nature ("le petit nombre de ceux qui ont la tête ferme, le goût délicat et le sens exquis [the small number of those who possess a steady mind, delicate judgment and refined sensibility]"), Buffon contrasts the mediocre talent who manipulates the masses with pathetic tones, violent gesticulating, and loud, fast-flowing words. This effect is a purely mechanical one ("purement mécanique"): "*C'est le corps qui parle au corps* [*It is the body which speaks to the body*]."

Could Buffon have been thinking of his contemporary Diderot when he used a phrase so full of aversion? In any case, there is scarcely a greater contrast to the aristocratic and withdrawn Buffon—who, arrayed in lace cuffs, wrote his great history of nature in the turret of Montbard, a castle itself situated among heights—than the noisily plebeian and importunate Diderot, who thrust himself upon people with such impetuous gestures and such a storm of words that they had to flee from this veritable hurricane, stunned as well as black and blue. And there is no better way of characterizing Diderot's literary style than with Buffon's formula: "C'est le corps qui parle au corps." The phrase refers simultaneously to physical nearness (bodily contact) and to its mode of expression (the mimicry of the body).

In reaction against the formal distance of Classicism, of which Buffon was a late representative, an almost pathological yearning for physical nearness developed in the people of the eighteenth century. It revealed itself even among the upper classes in grotesquely repulsive scenes which Diderot gleefully describes in his *Lettres à Sophie Volland*. One can hardly imagine a stranger declaration of love than his letter of October 15, 1759, in which Diderot speaks in dead seriousness of lovers who had themselves buried side by side:

> Peut-être leurs cendres se pressent, se mêlent et s'unissent.... O ma Sophie! il me resterait donc un espoir de vous toucher, de vous sentir, de vous aimer, de vous chercher, de m'unir, de me confondre avec vous quand nous ne serons plus ... si les molécules de votre amant dissous avaient à s'agiter, à s'émouvoir et à rechercher les vôtres éparses dans la nature!
>
> *Perhaps their ashes press upon one another, merge and mingle with one another.... Oh, my Sophie! Thus I would yet have a hope of touching you, of feeling you, of loving you, of seeking and obtaining you, of uniting with you, of becoming one with you when we no longer exist ... if the molecules of your dissolved lover were indeed to stir, to move about, and to seek yours, strewn about in nature!*

Physical nearness finds its stylistic counterpart in the language of the body: in gestures and pantomime. Diderot's style is always most impressive where it is pantomimic. He himself could bestow no higher praise than to say of someone with whom he had conversed, "il est pantomime depuis la tête jusqu'aux pieds [he is pantomime from head to foot]" (Letter to Sophie Volland of October 20, 1760). This is how he describes the conversation of one of his characters, Rameau's nephew:

> Que ne lui vis-je pas faire? Il pleurait, il criait, il soupirait; il regardait, ou attendri, ou tranquille, ou furieux; c'était une femme qui se pâme de douleur; c'était un malheureux livré à tout son désespoir; un temple qui s'élève; des oiseaux qui se taisent au soleil couchant; des eaux ou qui murmurent dans un lieu solitaire et frais ou qui descendent en

torrent du haut des montagnes; un orage, une tempête, la plainte de ceux qui vont périr, mêlée au sifflement des vents, au fracas du tonnerre. C'était la nuit avec ses ténèbres; c'était l'ombre et le silence, car le silence même se peint par des sons.

What did I not see him do? He wept, he cried out, he sighed; he looked about, tenderly moved, or tranquil, or furious; he was a woman fainting with pain; he was a luckless man given over to despair; a temple that rises upward; birds that grow quiet at sunset; brooks that murmur in some cool and lonely place or that gush down in torrents from mountainous heights; a thunderstorm, a tempest, the wail of those about to die mingled with the hissing of the winds, with the crash of thunder. He was night with its darkness; he was the shade and the silence, for even the silence portrays itself through sounds.

After the demonstration comes the theory. The new style so emphatically demanded by Diderot in the following quotation stands in striking contrast to the calm held in such high esteem by Buffon:

Il nous faut des exclamations, des interjections, des suspensions, des interruptions, des affirmations, des négations; nous appelons, nous invoquons, nous crions, nous gémissons, nous pleurons, nous rions franchement. Point d'esprit, point d'épigrammes, point de ces jolies pensées; cela est trop loin de la simple nature.

We must have exclamations, interjections, pauses, interruptions, assertions, negations; we call, we invoke, we shout, we sigh, we shed tears, we laugh loudly. No refined wit, no epigrams, none of these prettily turned thoughts; that is too far from simple nature.

This reaction in the matter of style is closely associated with Rousseau's gospel of a return to nature. But it was the friend of Diderot and of Rousseau, Condillac, who pointed, with prophetic insight, to the common origin of consciousness and language. In his *Essai sur l'origine des connaissances humaines* (1746) and his *Traité des sensations* (1754), he starts with the notion of contact in that he gives the sense of touch priority over all other senses. Out of the sense of touch, which is set in motion by instinct, grows objective knowledge of the world. Bodily motion itself develops into the language of gesture ("langage d'action"). Significant gestures crystallize, through one's living together with other human beings, into generally accepted signs ("signes d'institution"). Through the language of signs, however, man acquires a kind of spiritual sense of touch; the sign enables him to free himself from physical dependence on the world. Yet even in the most abstract sign there remains a trace of the original gesture, of groping or of pointing. Maine de Biran, who so brilliantly continued Condillac's investigations, summed up his own findings in this vivid phrase:

C'est toujours une action, un mouvement, une parole qui... fait revivre le *moi*. Sans cette action exercée sur le corps, l'esprit est comme le géant de la fable, expirant quand il est séparé de la terre.[2]

---

[2] The theory of the birth of mind and language from gesture—as it develops from Condillac via Maine de Biran, Ravaisson, Lachelier, and Lagneau to Bergson—is traced by Gabriel Madinier, *Conscience et mouvement* (Paris, 1938). The latest investigations concerning the intellectual and linguistic growth of children and primitive peoples have in fact confirmed Condillac's views. See Henri Wallon, *De l'acte à la pensée: essai de psychologie comparée* (Paris, 1942); Marcel Jousse, *Études de psychologie linguistique* (Paris, 1925); E. Fenz, *Laut, Wort, Sprache und ihre Deutung* (Vienna, 1940).

It is always some deed, some movement, some phrase which . . . re-animates the I. Unless it thus acts through the body, man's spirit is like the giant of the fable who dies when he is separated from the earth.

In this theory of the "conscience gestuelle," intuitions fundamental to language have become newly alive. That human thought has grown out of the gesture of grasping ["greifen"] is still demonstrable in the abstract concept ["Begriff"] of "comprehension" ["begreifen": literally, "to grope for"; intellectually, "to grasp"] ("erfassen" [literally, "to lay hold of; to comprehend"] = "comprendre" [literally, "to take in; to understand"]). Indeed, man's highest aspiration is expressed in this motion of "grasping," of apprehending—of "reaching toward what lies in front." Paul says,

Nicht daß ich's schon ergriffen habe oder schon vollkommen sei; ich jage ihm aber nach, ob ich's auch ergreifen möchte, nach dem ich von Christo Jesu ergriffen bin.

Not that I have already grasped it or am perfect; but I hunt after it, seeking whether I might also grasp it after I have been in the grasp of Jesus.

Not as though I had already attained, either were already perfect: but I follow after, if that I may apprehend that for which also I am apprehended of Christ Jesus. (Authorized Version)

This reaching for an object, however, already implies the loss of contact. Human thought awakens and lives only at a distance from things and in contradistinction to them. The mind must oppose itself to "objects" ["Gegenstand," the German for "object," means literally "stand against," opposition]; it must be able to imagine— that is, to set before itself ["vorstellen"]—what is to be realized. The greater its "distance" and the more it "abstracts" itself from things, the greater the mastery it can exert over them and the more freedom it has to realize its own possibilities. At the height of this development, man conceives of himself as a "being of distance"; he recognizes that his destiny lies in the direction of freedom, for freedom is identical with the capacity to achieve distance. Man is always in movement precisely because— since he is able to project himself—he is always on the way to himself. Yet all distance aims at becoming nearness. Nearness is what gives meaning to distance. The mind cannot sustain itself in distance alone; at all stages of its development, it depends on contact. Only when it is firmly rooted in the physical can it grow and rise above the physical. And even at its highest point, it will not lose itself in empty space, but find itself through new, creatively transforming contact with the world.

The counterpoint of contact and distance proves to be the basic law of history. All historical development originates in contact, loses itself in distance, and returns again to contact. From the primordial depths of the vegetative-instinctive life, the human mind gradually emerges. Unsure of itself, it gropes through a world in which the corporeal and the spiritual, the material and the immaterial—not yet differentiated from each other—overwhelm it with the horror of the unknown. Out of all this all-too-close contact arise strangely mixed forms of consciousness: magic, which—as a reaction against the threats or temptations of the world—cannot distinguish between spiritual transformation from within and technical mastery from without; mysticism, which—in its timid retreat to an inner world—blurs the boundaries between external and internal; and myth, which seizes on the great archetypes wherein the human spirit has sought, as in a dream, for answers concerning the origin, aim, and end of life, only to consolidate them in a sacral mixture of the grossly sensuous and the imperfectly transcendent.[3] But the mind seeks to free itself more and more from its involvement with things; with increasing strength, it struggles for ever clearer distinctions, ever greater tensions, ever wider perspectives, an ever more inclusive overview. Thus man rises from the "participation mystique" of a magical-mythic existence to technical-intellectual mastery of the world. But how easily does the mind fall victim to its striving for distance and height! It overreaches itself and loses in distance its contact with the natural, organic world. Life becomes inhuman; it hardens into the strictly ordered regularity of temporal sequences and into the divisive barriers of a fully delineated space. The inevitable reaction is a return to the sources of being, a submersion in the fluidity of nature. The human spirit is summoned back from its austere distance to the loving nearness of the sensual. In these pendulum swings of history, it becomes evident that the center of gravity is never on one side or the other, but in the middle, and that a true climax is reached only where distance and nearness interact in tension-filled equilibrium.

This whole development, with all its oscillations, is marvellously displayed in language. At first, language emerges from the dull stirrings of physical, instinctive existence as an utterance of the whole body and of the whole soul. The more primitive a man is and the more uncontrolled his instinctual life, the more he will gesticulate. Along with the increasing distance of the mind from things themselves goes the transformation of bodily mimicry into an increasingly abstract language of signs. The gesture changes into the spoken or written word. Language becomes more and more thin and rigid—until the reaction of the spirit in favor of instinct occurs, and language reincarnates itself, pulsing once more with the blood of life and gaining strength from its contact with the earth.

It is poetry which watches over all changes in language. Not only was poetry the mother tongue of mankind in the beginnings of history, but it remains so throughout the ages. It is the protectress of life and the guardian of equilibrium. Again and again it brings the mind back from rigidity, confusion, and error. Again and again poetry, mediating between body and spirit, between the visible and the meaningful, between space and time, allows the *gesture* to be revitalized in the spoken word. From the vibrant tension between rest and motion, poetry creates *rhythm*. At the precise midpoint between nearness and distance, it projects man and world as *image*. Just as the physician forms an impression—on the basis of behavior, pulse beat, and facial expression—of the condition of a patient, so the stylistic critic can evolve—from the typical

---

[3] These intermediate or mixed forms are to be differentiated from the pure archetypes of the magical, the mystical, and the mythic, which always lie at the very root of life where it burgeons in primal, unspoiled innocence. (For the distinction between archetypal and later magic, see E. Mally, *Erlebnis und Wirklichkeit* [Leipzig, 1935].)

gesture of speech, the rhythmic movement, and the imagery of a poetic work—an existential diagnosis of a whole epoch.

An exceptionally symptomatic case for our time is the work of the French Swiss C. F. Ramuz. After a preparatory period—which coincided with the naturalistic-psychological tendencies prevalent at the turn of the century, yet contained in embryo all the germs of his later development—a new force bursts forth, erupting under the impression of the First World War. The elemental powers—which on ethnic and political levels were to become the fate of Europe in the form of a collective, sacral commitment to blood, soil, and race—appear with terrifying clarity in the world of the poet long before they invaded the everyday world. With the instinct of a seer, this Swiss writer shapes his magical, mythic picture of the world.[4] The heavily flowing style and the massive mimicry seem to arise from the deepest substrata of language. The world is newly created out of gesture:

> Ils doivent d'abord se les [les bras et les jambes] refaire et se refaire eux-mêmes, avant de se servir d'eux-mêmes, puis commencent à s'en servir, s'étant remis debout, tendant le bras, posant le pied sur le plancher; mais ils se disent: " Le plancher est là."
> Ils sont refaits, le plancher est refait; ils vont au mur, le mur est refait.
> <div align="right">(<i>Les Signes parmi nous</i>)</div>
>
> *First of all, they must again make them [their arms and legs] for themselves and make themselves all over before they can make any use of themselves, then begin to make use of themselves, having gotten up, extending an arm, placing a foot on the floor; but they say to themselves: " The floor is there."*
> *They are re-made, the floor is re-made; they walk toward the wall, the wall is re-made.*

Here, things do not merely exist: they act out what they are. They close in on man; they assault him. The fact that they possess a life of their own threatens man. But he stands defenseless, for the spiritual powers that might be of help are still too distant:

> ... il y avait que le ciel allait de son côté,—nous, on est trop petits pour qu'il puisse s'occuper de nous, pour qu'il puisse seulement se douter qu'on est là, quand il regarde du haut de ses montagnes.
>
> *... it was that the sky had its own way,—for us, one is too small for it to concern itself with us, for it even to suspect that one is there when it looks down from the top of its mountains.*

All human life and activity is silenced in this spellbound world.

> Mais il n'y avait ni enfants, ni femmes, ni hommes, ni bruit de voix, ni bruit de scie, ni bruit de faux, ni cris de poules, ni quand on plante un clou, ni quand on rabote une planche; et, portant ses regards autour de lui, Joseph continuait de se faire mal aux yeux à des pierres, à toujours des pierres, à rien que des pierres; et à toujours personne, et à cette absence de tout mouvement et de tout bruit. (*La Grande Peur dans la montagne*)
>
> *But there were neither children, nor women, nor men, nor the sound of a voice, nor the sound of a saw, nor the sound of a scythe, nor the clamor of hens, nor when one drives in a nail, nor when one sands down a board; and, looking around, Joseph continued to get his eyes hurt by stones, always*

---

[4] See E. Brock, "Das Magische im Stil von C. F. Ramuz," *Trivium*, I.

by stones, by nothing but stones; and always by nobody, and by this absence of all movement and of all sound.

In the novels of Ramuz's middle period, the magical power of things increases to the point of catastrophe—as it did in actuality on European soil. The visions of the Swiss poet appear to us like apocalyptic prophecies of what is happening in our own day.[5]

But Ramuz knew, even before his intuitions were realized in history, that a return to the forces of the earth and too close a contact with things can only lead to a dead end. Thus the works of his third creative period, which started in the thirties, became a passionate search for equilibrium between the world of things and the world of the spirit. The transcendent spirit, represented by the sky, keeps its infinite distance from the human world, but only a slight displacement of accent is needed to convert the alienating distance into a living relationship. The mountain landscape of *La Grande Peur dans la montagne* (1926) finds its counterpart in *La Guerre aux papiers* (1942):

> Les vraies révolutions se font là-haut, et elles nous détournent des autres. C'est qu'on est avant tout paysan, par chez nous. On est esclave des saisons; c'est elles qui commandent. C'est le soleil qui nous fait lever. . . . Ce n'est pas nous qui faisons, c'est lui qui fait. . . . On confie, voilà tout, on confie à quelqu'un quelquechose d'où on dépend. On coopère, on collabore. Mais le quelqu'un avec qui on collabore a ses volontés qui ne sont pas toujours les nôtres. . . . Et nous, tout petits, allons sous le ciel avec notre toute petite ombre, tandis qu'il est là-haut, dans sa toutepuissance, s'occupant peu de nous, nous ignorant peut-être.
>
> *The real revolutions are made up there, and they draw us from the others. One is above all a farmer, with us. One is slave to the seasons; it is they that command. It is the sun that makes us get up. . . . It is not we who act, it is the sun that acts. . . . One trusts, that is all; one entrusts someone with something on which one depends. One cooperates, one collaborates. But the someone with whom one collaborates has whims that are not always ours. . . . And we, quite tiny, walk under the sky with a very tiny shadow, while it is up there, very mighty, barely noting us, not recognizing us perhaps.*

Things still make their weight felt, but man is gaining power over them through work.

> Une chose n'est faite que pour être défaite, puis être refaite par nous, puis être défaite à nouveau. On y consent parce qu'il faut bien, mais avec fatigue. . . . Il s'était levé, ce matin-là, comme toujours; il avait été travailler au jardin. Il faut bien se défendre contre les choses, quand même on sait qu'elles sont plus fortes que vous et l'emporteront pour finir.
> (*Adam et Ève*)

---

[5] One could point to numerous other traits in Ramuz's style which characterize the undifferentiated primitiveness of our time. The mingling of elements so typical for the style of nearness—in contrast to the distinguishing of elements peculiar to the style of distance—is shown in Ramuz's preference for the collective *on* [we, one], in his mixing of different tenses within the same sentence, in his shifting between subjective and objective modes of expression. All this may be the expression of a natural, primitive talent which truly lacks the capacity for differentiation or the manifestation of a later, conscious return to the undifferentiated, of a flight to the anonymity of the impersonal *on*. Similarly, the dynamism in Ramuz's style amalgamates newly erupting instincts with the mechanical movement characteristic of a late stage in civilization—a dynamism that also reminds one at moments of the technique of motion pictures.

> *A thing is done only to be undone, then to be re-done by us, then to be undone again. One goes along because one has to, but wearily. . . . He had gotten up this morning as always; he had been working in the garden. One must defend oneself against things anyhow, even if one knows that they are stronger than you and will prevail in the end.*

Man now sets himself at a distance from things. He builds the world anew according to his own measure and by his own power:

> Maintenant, il regarde, il voit. Les objets se mettent pour lui les uns en avant des autres; les objets ont de nouveau entre eux des distances plus ou moins grandes. L'espace s'organise aux alentours de sa personne en hauteur et en profondeur. Le soleil l'aide. Le soleil d'abord voulait l'empêcher, il n'y a pas réussi. L'homme force le soleil à l'aider; si tu ne veux pas, vois-tu, je te force; et ça c'est un caillou, ça c'est un caillou. (*Derborence*)
>
> *Now he looks, he sees. Objects place themselves for him, some in front of others; things again have greater or lesser distances between them. Space organizes itself all around him in height and in depth. The sun is helping. At first the sun wanted to hinder him, it has not succeeded. Man forces the sun to assist him; look here, if you are not willing, I force you; and that over there is a pebble, that is indeed a pebble.*

Ramuz's language is the same. But he has abandoned the heavy monotone of litany, though he retains his fundamental, gently rocking rhythm. In the movement of the sentences, back and forth, is revealed more and more sharply an intellectually controlled parallelism creating equilibrium.

> Mais il n'y a point de vraie solitude pour le cœur, quand il s'est donné. Un trou se fait, l'amour le comble. Il répare à mesure les ruines, et remplit les vides à mesure.
> (*Si le Soleil ne revenait pas*)
>
> *But there is no true solitude for the heart that has given itself away. An emptiness is created, love makes up for it. It repairs the ruins gradually, and it fills the blank spaces by and by.*

And still what is most profound is expressed through gestures, but gesture now creates a relationship among human beings, becoming the unspoken language of love, of submission, of everything inexpressible. This new development is most impressively evident at the end of *Derborence*. How unpretentious and forceful and lucid has language become here! Nothing disturbs the quiet movement of events. Everything is kept at the most basic level. Only the man's gestures of help are thrown into relief and elaborated. And in great, measured parallelisms, the eternal equilibrium between man and woman is revealed.

> C'est un homme et une femme. Ils s'approchent, ils sont ensemble.
> Et c'est elle, et c'est lui, car ils n'en pouvaient plus douter, s'étant mis debout pour mieux voir; et c'est bien elle, et elle aura su faire, elle a su dire, elle le ramène;—tandis qu'ils auraient voulu appeler et n'osaient pas, ils auraient voulu dire quelquechose et se taisent.
> Car on voyait que l'homme aidait la femme aux passages difficiles: là où il y avait une pierre à sauter, il la prenait dans ses bras. Il faisait quelques pas en avant d'elle, comme

pour chercher le bon chemin; l'ayant trouvé, il se tournait vers elle. Il lui tendait la main; elle lui tendait la main.

Et, au fin sommet de la paroi, la tranche du glacier était comme un rayon de miel, toute ruisselante de couleurs, toute étincelante de lumière, toute découlante de vie; mais, derrière ceux qui venaient, la combe entière entrait définitivement dans la nuit et le silence, dans le froid et dans la mort.

It is a man and a woman. They move toward each other, they are together.

And it is she, and it is he, for they could no longer be in doubt, having stood up to see better; and it is certainly she, and she will have known what to do, she has known what to say, she brings him back;—while they would have liked to call out and did not dare, they would have liked to say something and remained quiet.

For one could see that the man helped the woman at the rough places: where there was a rock to pass over, he took her in his arms. He kept a few paces ahead of her, as if to look for the best path; having found it, he turned toward her. He held out his hand to her; she held out her hand to him.

And, at the very top of the mountain, the slender edge of the glacier was like a comb of honey, streaming with colors, glistening with light, flowing with life; but, behind those two who came, the entire valley fell at last into night and silence, into cold and into death.

The counterpoint between distance and nearness becomes particularly tense when operative in two men of the same generation. And all the more exciting in the case of Marcel Proust and Paul Valéry, since they both move at the extreme limit of culture, in contrast to their primitive contemporary Ramuz.

The famous description of the kiss in Marcel Proust (*Le Côté de Guermantes II*) is an extreme example of arrested contact. As the man draws near with infinite slowness, the appearance of the girl changes:

... en laissant mon regard glisser sur le beau globe rose de ses joues, dont les surfaces doucement incurvées venaient mourir aux pieds des premiers plissements de ses beaux cheveux noirs qui couraient en chaînes mouvementées, soulevaient leurs contreforts escarpés et modelaient les ondulations de leurs vallées, je dus me dire: "Enfin... je vais savoir le goût de la rose inconnue que sont les joues d'Albertine?..." ... au fur et à mesure que ma bouche commença à s'approcher des joues que mes regards lui avaient proposé d'embrasser, ceux-ci se déplaçant virent des joues nouvelles; le cou, aperçu de plus près et comme à la loupe, montra, dans ses gros grains, une robustesse qui modifia le caractère de la figure.... dans ce court trajet de mes lèvres vers sa joue, c'est dix Albertines que je vis; cette seule jeune fille étant comme une déesse à plusieurs têtes, celle que j'avais vue en dernier, si je tentais de m'approcher d'elle, faisait place à une autre. Du moins tant que je ne l'avais pas touchée, cette tête, je la voyais, un léger parfum venait d'elle jusqu'à moi. Mais hélas!... tout d'un coup, mes yeux cessèrent de voir, à son tour mon nez, s'écrasant, ne perçut plus aucune odeur, et sans connaître pour cela davantage le goût du rose désiré, j'appris, à ces détestables signes, qu'enfin j'étais en train d'embrasser la joue d'Albertine.

... letting my eyes glide over the beautiful globe, the pink globe of her cheeks, whose gently curved surfaces died away at the foot of the first locks of her beautiful black hair, which flowed in sinuous chains, thrust up steep escarpments, and modeled undulating valleys, I could not help but say: "At last... I am going to know the taste of the unknown rose in the cheeks of Albertine?..."

... gradually, as my mouth began to approach the cheeks that my eyes had proposed to it to kiss, my eyes, changing position, saw different cheeks; the throat, seen from nearby and as if through a magnifying glass, revealed in its coarse texture a robustness that modified the character of the face. ... in this brief passage of my lips toward her cheek, it was ten Albertines that I saw, this single girl being like a goddess with many heads, the one that I saw last, if I tried to draw near it, giving way to another. At least so long as I didn't touch it, that head, I saw it; a faint perfume came to me from it. But alas! ... suddenly my eyes ceased to see; in its turn my nose, crushed, no longer perceived any fragrance; and without coming to know any better the taste of the desired rose, I learned, by these detestable signs, that I was at last in the act of kissing the cheek of Albertine.

The dissolving of the human figure into a many-headed idol—one might also be reminded of a filmstrip, which separates movement into a sequence of stills—parallels the magnified slowing-down of the event. At the moment of contact, movement ceases entirely, and all anticipation is stifled in an emptiness of sensation that resembles death. Indeed, it is as an exercise for dying that Proust quite consciously handles this technique: "It is, after all," he says in *A l'ombre des jeunes filles en fleurs*, "a way like any other to solve the problem of existence: to get close enough to things and people which appeared so beautiful and mysterious to us from afar, only to find that there is neither beauty nor mystery in them—this is one of the many hygienic regimens which help us to pass away life and await death."

The counterpart to Proust's description of the kiss is Paul Valéry's poem "Les Pas." The lover, resting on his bed, hears steps drawing near. The approach of the beloved carries infinite promise for him. And yet he finds the hovering between expectation and fulfillment so blissful a state that he holds back the kiss, shying away from contact:

> Ne hâte pas cet acte tendre,
> Douceur d'être et de n'être pas,
> Car j'ai vécu de vous attendre,
> Et mon cœur n'était que vos pas.
>
> *Do not hasten this tender act,*
> *A delight in being and not being,*
> *For I have lived only in awaiting you,*
> *And my heart was one with your step.*

If with Proust the human figure dissolves in contact, with Valéry it dissolves in distance. This dehumanizing occurs as a visible event in "Cantique des colonnes." After the introductory chords—which, as in the great dialogue *Eupalinos* [by Valéry], celebrate the harmony of music and architecture—the hymn praising the formation of the pillars is heard.

> Si froides et dorées
> Nous fûmes de nos lits
> Par le ciseau tirées,
> Pour devenir ces lys!

> *So cold and golden*
> *We were from our beds*
> *Drawn by the chisel,*
> *To become these lilies!*

They rise up before our eyes, shedding all human form to become pure function.

> Servantes sans genoux,
> Sourires sans figures,
> La belle devant nous
> Se sent les jambes pures.
>
> *Servant girls without knees,*
> *Smiles without faces,*
> *The beautiful girl before us*
> *Feels herself sheer legs.*

Nose, ears, eyes are obliterated ("Le nez sous le bandeau... nos riches oreilles / Sourdes... les yeux / Noirs pour l'éternité [The nose tightly banded... our rich ears / Deaf... our eyes / Blinded for eternity]"). Progressive abstraction is expressed verbally ("Nous allons sans les dieux / A la divinité! [We move without the gods / Toward divinity!]") as well as rhythmically ("Filles des nombres d'or, / Fortes des lois du ciel [Girls of golden numbers, / Strong through heaven's laws]"), and it reaches a climax in the psalm on time, a time that is endlessly stretched out in space:

> Nous marchons dans le temps
> Et nos corps éclatants
> Ont des pas ineffables
> Qui marquent dans les fables...
>
> *We march on in time*
> *And our bodies, bursting into splendor,*
> *Have ineffable footsteps*
> *Which imprint themselves in fables...*

Here a basic tendency of the human spirit becomes visible: to seek out that supreme energy which preserves—beyond the contingency inhering in any empirical, determined form—the very power to form. Or as Socrates says in *Eupalinos* in reference to music and architecture:

> Les arts dont nous parlons doivent... au moyen de nombres et de rapports de nombres, enfanter en nous non point une fable, mais cette puissance cachée qui fait toutes les fables.
>
> *The arts of which we speak must... through numbers and the relations of numbers, give birth in us, not to a fable, but to that hidden power which creates all fables.*

If Proust suffers the loss of distance in nearness and therefore stifles in contact, Valéry suffers the loss of nearness in distance, with the result that organic growth withers in a technical, mathematical world. But just as Proust, in his *Recherche du temps perdu*, returns from the deadly limits of the most extreme spatialization to immerse himself in the eternally non-spatial—that is, in the time of remembering, *Le Temps retrouvé*—so Valéry always turns back from the ultimate limits of abstraction and seeks contact with the flow of life. Thus the strange and abrupt reversals in all Valéry's great poems ("Le Cimetière marin": "Non, non!... Debout!... il faut tenter de vivre! [No, no!... Get up!... one must endeavor to live!]"). The whole of "Narcisse" dramatizes such a reversal, man's return on himself. Narcissus' power to project imaginatively becomes paralyzed as he contemplates his own image, and his spirit succumbs to the attraction of the physical. At the contact of the kiss, the infinitely attractive image mirrored in the water breaks apart:

> Hélas! corps misérable, il est temps de s'unir...
> Penche-toi... Baise-toi. Tremble de tout ton être!
> L'insaisissable amour que tu me vins promettre
> Passe, et dans un frisson, brise Narcisse, et fuit...
>
> *Alas! miserable body, it is time to unite...*
> *Bend down... Kiss yourself. Tremble in your whole being!*
> *The love that you have just promised me, not to be seized,*
> *Is passing, and, in a shiver, breaks Narcissus and flees...*

In the relation of one human being to another, the relationship between distance and nearness is decisive, for only in the mean between contact and distance can the lover find the tact, the "touch," which converts the beloved into a true partner. Neither in Proust nor in Valéry does one discover such a "being with," such mutuality, between lover and beloved. Where love does indeed disentangle itself from a perverse, narcissistic tendency, it overpowers the partner, whom it treats like a helpless object. Émilie Teste's quiet disclosures about the way in which she is loved are terrifying ("Il a une vigueur et une présence effrayante dans les mains. Je me sens dans les prises d'un statuaire, d'un médecin, d'un assassin, sous leurs actions brutales et précises [He has a force and a dreadful presence in his hands. I feel myself in the grip of a sculptor, a doctor, an assassin, submitting to their brutal and precise actions]," [Valéry's] *Lettre de Madame Émilie Teste*).

With Stéphane Mallarmé, the dialectic between nearness and distance rises to an almost inexpressible tension. In contrast to the poems of distance ("Hérodiade"), with their hieratic stiffness, stand the poems of contact ("L'Après-midi d'un faune"), with their warm and relaxed sensuality. Wonderfully pure, however, is the interplay of distance and nearness in the "Sonnet" to Méry Laurent:

> O si chère de loin et proche et blanche, si
> Délicieusement toi, Méry, que je songe
> A quelque baume rare émané par mensonge
> Sur aucun bouquetier de cristal obscurci...
>
> *Oh, so dear from far away, so near, and so white, so*
> *Deliciously you, Méry, that I dream*

> *Of some rare perfume exhaled—unreally—*
> *Above any vase of obscured crystal* . . .

Already in the first sounds of the poem, the theme of distance and nearness is intoned: initially by the intimate yet tenderly respectful "chère," and finally by the "blanche," which alludes simultaneously to a distancing purity and to the alluring charm of a womanly body inviting touch. The "si" at the end of the line reaches over toward the long-drawn-out "Délicieusement toi, Méry"—whereupon her beauty, beyond capturing in its transcendence, is rendered by an image of absence: "you bring to mind a rare perfume emanating—unreally—from an unimaginable vase of pale crystal . . . ." All the negative expressions act to prevent a hardening into the tangible, the material. Thus the dominant movement here is a thrust beyond all firmly defined forms into the "primal distance." But this irrevocable development of love, which pours forth in the fullness of time, cannot tear the lover away from the present and the presence of the beloved. Like a rose in summer, she blooms for him in her radiant smile:

> Le sais-tu, oui! pour moi voici des ans, voici
> Toujours que ton sourire éblouissant prolonge
> La même rose avec son bel été qui plonge
> Dans autrefois et puis dans le futur aussi.
>
> *You know it, yes! for me it has been years, it is*
> *Forever that your blossoming smile prolongs*
> *The same rose with its beautiful summer that plunges*
> *Into bygone times and then into the future also.*

Now even the lover plunges into the depths of time; listening, he attends to the night, and to his own darkness, in order to hear and to understand—wonderful ambiguity of the French "entendre"—the "heart of being." Here the essential meaning of distance is made manifest: to disengage oneself from the ordinary, outward version of the "I" through turning inward to become aware of the nocturnal depth of the self. But such a self cannot exist in isolation: it must turn outward, express itself to the beloved. The listening to the inner self is conjoined with the most intimate address of love by the "Ou," which identifies the two. And the lover's heart is elated by the gently whispered "sœur." In this chaste and tender word, distance and nearness are once more intoned simultaneously. "Sister" refers to the nearest, most tender relationship between the sexes; at the same time, it erects a protective barrier against any nearness which threatens to intermix or to consume.

> Mon cœur qui dans les nuits parfois cherche à s'entendre
> Ou de quel dernier mot t'appeler le plus tendre
> S'exalte en celui rien que chuchoté de sœur . . .
>
> *My heart, which in the nights sometimes seeks to hear and to understand itself,*
> *Or to call you with some last, most tender word,*
> *Exalts itself in nothing but the softly whispered sister* . . .

But the lover does not stop at this point: he does not listen only to the inner self. Or, much better: inasmuch as he is not listening to the outward version of the "I" but to the expressing, the emerging, of the inner self, he opens himself to a coexisting "you." "Only because existence as such is determined through selfhood can an 'I myself' relate to a 'you yourself'" (Martin Heidegger, *Vom Wesen des Grundes*, Husserl-Festschrift [Halle, 1929]). The lover allows himself to be taught by the woman. Out of her womanly fullness and delicacy, she teaches him a way of saying which is also a way of doing: to speak to her most intimately through a kiss on her hair. Thus contact is again established with the elemental since, for the poet, the hair of the beloved is synonymous with the streaming, archetypal force of Eros itself. Yet the restraint of the gesture expresses once more, and definitively, love's union of the endless with the immediate, of the transcendent with the actual.

> N'était, très grand trésor et tête si petite,
> Que tu m'enseignes bien toute une autre douceur
> Tout bas par le baiser seul dans tes cheveux dite.
>
> *Were it not, very great treasure and head so small,*
> *That you teach me a quite different sweetness*
> *By the kiss alone, softly spoken in your hair.*

It is a miracle that such rich life can be engendered by French, a language which sounds so thin and brittle—a miracle which becomes all the more staggering if one thinks of the fatal struggle with his means of expression to which Mallarmé sacrificed his life. In a similarly tense dialectic between life and intellect—but one in which he was supported by the grace of the German language—Friedrich Hölderlin wrote his poems. He was granted the power to perceive the great counterpoint between nearness and distance at its most profound, pre-mythical level and to mold it in divine images. Bacchus is the god of nearness, in whose presence all barriers fall, everything fixed becomes fluid, and all sober rationality dissolves in a rapt yielding to nature. Hercules, on the contrary, is the god of light. "He has introduced the making of distinctions, clear consciousness, laws, language, order, all which tears us from the lap of the mother" (Emil Staiger, "Hölderlin," *Schweizer Monatshefte* [May 1943]).[6] But everything sheerly mythical is transcended by Him whom Hölderlin hesitantly calls "Der Einzige," the "Only One," and who, as the Incarnation of the Word, unites all opposites within himself.

> Wie Fürsten ist Herkules. Gemeingeist Bacchus. Christus aber ist
> Das Ende.
>
> *Like princes is Hercules. Common to all is Bacchus' spirit. Christ, however, is*
> *The ultimate.*

However, what Hölderlin, along with all other poets, unfolds in great images is captured by the philosopher Martin Heidegger in so lucid and concise a formulation

---

[6] Hölderlin's use of myth is further discussed by Emil Staiger in his Introduction to Friedrich Hölderlin's *Werke* (Zurich, 1944), I, 7–29. (Translator's note)

that the "most distant mountains" of the human landscape can yet be encompassed in a *single* look:

> Und so ist der Mensch, als existierende Transzendenz überschwingend in Möglichkeiten, ein *Wesen der Ferne*. Nur durch ursprüngliche Fernen, die er sich in seiner Transzendenz zu allem Seienden bildet, kommt in ihm die wahre Nähe zu den Dingen ins Steigen. Und nur das Hörenkönnen in die Ferne zeitigt dem Dasein als Selbst das Erwachen der Antwort des Mitdaseins, im Mitsein mit dem es die Ichheit drangeben kann, um sich als eigentliches Selbst zu gewinnen. (*Vom Wesen des Grundes*)

> *And thus man, as an existing transcendence overflowing with possibilities, is a being of distance. Only through those primary distances which he forms for himself in his transcendence relative to all that exists, can there arise in him the true nearness to things. And only its capacity to hear what is distant can foster, in the existent self, the awakening of the answer of coexistence; in living with this answer, the self can yield up the "I" in order to achieve its true self.*

On the Continuity of American Poetry

ROY HARVEY PEARCE

Roy Harvey Pearce is most widely known as the author of *The Continuity of American Poetry* (1961), an important book which contains as one of its chapters an expanded version of the essay reprinted below. In both the essay and the book as a whole, Pearce reveals his essential concern with the relationship of poetry to its historical and cultural setting, as well as with the continuing significance of earlier literature for writers of the present and for contemporary culture.

In his role as an "historian of a national imagination," Pearce identifies through his book several characteristic features of American poetry: the persisting need of the poets to justify their activity in the face of a dominantly anti-poetic culture; the modernity of the poetry, which derives in part from the poet's self-conscious use of language and in part from his tendency to make poems which—instead of encouraging the reader to "contemplate" them as finished "creations"—invite him "to participate in the creating" of the poems; and the pervasive self-awareness evidenced in the poetry, which arises from the fact that "the American poet has always felt obliged, for well and for ill, to catch himself in the act of being a poet." Through the exploration of such qualities Pearce charts the whole course of American poetry, discussing the Puritan writers, the attempts at an American epic, the Fireside poets, and such twentieth-century artists as Eliot and Stevens—along with the major nineteenth-century poets treated more briefly in the essay reproduced here.

Many of the characteristics Pearce examines at large in his book are adumbrated in the present essay, where he attempts to establish the fundamental egocentrism in poems by Poe, Emerson, Whitman, and Emily Dickinson. Since he seeks to illuminate "a basic major American style" in their works—the kind of style that he elsewhere describes as "expressive of the life" of the poet's "community" and so never existing "as such in a poem," though it provides the poet with "the terms in which he may work toward his own unique style"—Pearce does not subject the poetic texts cited to the sort of detailed verbal analysis which typifies most of the other selections in this anthology. But he quotes a number of poems in order to discriminate carefully between the varieties of egocentrism manifested by the poets with whom he deals: Poe's display of "imaginative experience for its own sake"; Emerson's efforts to render "an egocentrism which transmutes itself into universality by being fully acknowledged for what it is"; Whitman's attempts to recreate a world "out there," which affect us finally as celebrations of his own creativity; and Emily Dickinson's commitment to "being herself and accommodating her view of the world to that concern."

Toward the end of the essay Pearce constructs a definition of the typical nineteenth-century American poem, going on to indicate how this mode has been reacted against by some twentieth-century poets and renewed in the work of others. While in general Pearce views the basic style that concerns him here as rooted in history and expressive of American culture, he alludes from time to time in his remarks on specific passages to their effect upon the reader and to the fact that such a mode may make special demands on the audience to participate, as it were, in the processes dramatized by the poems.

"On the Continuity of American Poetry," by Roy Harvey Pearce, is reprinted by permission from *The Hudson Review*, Vol. X, No. 4 (Winter 1957–58), 518–39. Copyright © 1958 by The Hudson Review, Inc. Excerpts from the poems of Emily Dickinson on pages 91, 92, and 93 are reprinted by permission of the publishers and the Trustees of Amherst College from Thomas H. Johnson, Editor, *The Poems of Emily Dickinson*, Cambridge, Mass.: The Belknap Press of Harvard University Press. Copyright, 1951, 1955, by The President and Fellows of Harvard College.

ON THE CONTINUITY OF AMERICAN POETRY

To the Memory of William Hildreth (1904-1954)

> "He says No! in thunder; but the Devil himself can not make him say *yes*. For all men who say *yes*, lie; and all men who say *no*, —why they are in the happy condition of judicious unincumbered travellers in Europe; they cross the frontiers into Eternity with nothing but a carpet-bag,—that is to say, the Ego."

How, and to what extent, has our history made our poetry?—or more precisely, made it possible for our poets to make our poetry? This is a question which we have lately again been much concerned to answer. The richest and most exciting answer we have been given, which shifts the basic terms somewhat, declares that myth has made our poetry and that history (social, economic, intellectual, linguistic, etc.) is in this case just a reductionist term for myth. Mythographic criticism would thus save our poetry (as it presumably would save any poetry) at once from pure (i.e., formalist) criticism and pure (i.e., departmentalized) history. This is not a small enterprise, to be sure; and it appears to have been a successful one. But somehow, so it seems to me, another, quite fundamental question has in the process not even been asked: How has our poetry made our history? The question can be put in other ways: What has our poetry's "use" been for us? What possibilities of the creative imagination has it manifested? What kind of understanding of our history has it made possible? What has our poetry been to us and we to it?

The following notes are meant to make a beginning toward answering such a question. They are intended to establish a working hypothesis as to the continuity of American poetry in the nineteenth century and beyond, and to suggest a way whereby we might see it as a whole—indeed, see its very wholeness. Establishing the pattern of continuity will in turn perhaps be a way of seeing what poetry has "done" in America—and so of becoming increasingly self-conscious of one aspect of our national self-consciousness. For surely the history that our poetry has made is the history of ourselves, or our consciousness of ourselves.

IN VOLUME II, Book 1, Chapter 17, of *Democracy in America*, Tocqueville speaks thus of literature in the United States:

> Nothing conceivable is so petty, so insipid, so crowded with paltry interests, in one word so anti-poetic, as the life of a man in the United States. But among the thoughts which it suggests there is always one which is full of poetry, and that is the hidden nerve which gives vigour to the frame.

Then, a page or so later, he says explicitly what that thought is not and what it is:

> Among a democratic people poetry will not be fed with legendary lays or the memorials of old traditions. The poet will not attempt to people the universe with supernatural beings in whom his readers and his own fancy have ceased to believe; nor will he present

virtues and vices in the mask of frigid personification, which are better received under their own features. All these resources fail him; but Man remains, and the poet needs no more.

What Tocqueville observes in this celebrated discussion is crucial to my hypothesis, and so I venture to convert it into two basic terms. (1) *An anti-poetic culture.* This, taking a metalinguistic leap, I would translate into: *An anti-poetic language,* since language makes immediately available the values and forms of culture. I thus take the passage to refer not only to the paucity of possible "subjects" for American poems, but also to the nineteenth-century American attitude toward poetry itself. This attitude too was expressed in the language which his culture gave the poet; it thus necessarily conditioned and qualified his discovery of a "subject." The second of my basic terms has to do with this problem of "subject." (2) *A putatively poetic conception of Man.* Here there is a certainty that in the (as yet perhaps unrealized) idea of Man there necessarily lies the prime source of poetry in America. Nothing else is available; but nothing else is needed.

Put together the two terms come to something like this: Man in America exists in spite of—as well as in terms of—the anti-poetics which the values and forms of his culture seem to have made inevitable. Here we must look for the full implications of Tocqueville's observations. We may note, if we assent to them, that for the poet there was the necessity of getting at and expressing the significance of Man in terms—language, the myriad aspects of culture it embodies, and the anti-poetic attitude it sets—which actively militated against the very existence of poems. The paradox is as total as paradoxes ever can be. And from the point of view of one who puts Tocqueville's observations together, as he doesn't quite, the burden on the poet theoretically was terrific, forcing him willy-nilly to work at his task as though it were that of breaking through the limits of his culture in order to make its very self-induced blindness to poetry a means to poetic insight. Through his own sense of the anti-poetic life of men in his society, he had to discover the poetic Man immanent in that life; he had to make Man not only a possibility but an actuality; as poet, he had virtually to create Man. He had to discover how the very qualities of that anti-poetic life, if they were fully comprehended, would be seen to derive from Man, Man who was poetry. He had to achieve, in the nigh-on-to obsessive word of the nineteenth (and perhaps the twentieth) century, a poetry of the Self. In his work, that self-consciousness which we take to be the universal mode of poetry had as its prime quality a consciousness of the self defined in terms of its ultimate resistance to consciousness of other selves.

The situation gave rise, in the writer who would be absolutely true to his vocation, to a private poetry aspiring to be universal, yet only on its own terms; an egocentric poetry which insisted that in its egocentrism lay its universality; a poetry which in looking deeply into—then often flouting or distorting or playing with—its culture's anti-poetic values, would make them over; a poetry of the self trying, by virtue of its very working as poetry, to universalize itself; a poetry of sudden breakthroughs and brief consolidations, not of planned strategies and magisterial control; a poetry, as we have always claimed it to be, even when we have not been careful to define what we were claiming, "romantic" in its strength and in its weakness.

I SHALL TREAT as poets whose work variously manifests the principles I have sketched above: Poe, Emerson, Whitman, and Emily Dickinson. They are certainly our major nineteenth-century poets. And they are different enough one from another to manifest a creative uniqueness, an artistic greatness, without the existence of which there would be no point in trying to define what they have in common. For, if my analysis seems to take us away from their individuality, it is only so that we can eventually return to it, so as to know it more fully as a living historical possibility which bears immediately upon our existence in our time.

In what follows, I shall try to indicate how that uniqueness is in itself expressive of, among other things, what we can see now to be a necessarily analogous conception of the poet's and the poem's function, and how there is thus to be perceived a basic major American style—by which term I mean to include both the angle of vision and what is envisioned. I shall consider some of our poets' best (and most anthologized) works as a whole, without regard to its chronology. For it seems to me that the goal of a historian of a national imagination (or an aspect of it) must be to comprehend totally and conspectively the uniqueness of a series of styles conceived as variants on a basic style. It might even turn out that the poets owe as much to the basic style as they do to their own individual creative powers. But that is indeed a chicken-and-egg question which I dare only raise, expecting that theoreticians of culture will continue to be critically minded enough some day to help us answer it. My concern here will be to suggest, with the following brief, foreshortened analyses, how the uniquely variant styles of some of our major poets manifest their origins in that basic style which in turn makes for wholeness and continuity among them.

Poe is obviously the poet of dream-work. The very obviousness makes for a kind of overinsistence which to American readers at least must seem to be no less than vulgar. To recall the gross characteristics of Poe's poems: Metrical effects are forced until they become virtually hypnotic, and language is chosen primarily because it carries exotic, unworldly meaning, or can be made to do so. Thus in the opening lines of "The Sleeper":

>   At midnight, in the month of June,
>   I stand beneath the mystic moon.
>   An opiate vapor, dewy, dim,
>   Exhales from out her golden rim,
>   And softly dripping, drop by drop,
>   Upon the quiet mountain top,
>   Steals drowsily and musically
>   Into the universal valley.

Here the effect is of a willed irrelevance to day-to-day reality. But we do sense the willed quality; and we are shocked into attention by it. What annoys us here (and the effect is everywhere in Poe's poems, even those with an ostensibly firmer argument) is that the poem seems to exist simply as an attention-getting device. Indeed, in some of his more ambitious criticism, Poe was in effect willing to settle on this as one of the chief aims of poetry. For what else is his inordinately technical criticism but an insistence that the poet mind his business, which was chiefly one of expressive technique?

Expressive of what? one now asks. And in the poems the answer would seem to be only expressive of itself, as expression. Here we must ask further what it meant for Poe to make poems whose sole strength consists in this extraordinary weakness. And we can view him as what he set out to be—a kind of culture hero of the imagination. His contemporaries would worry much lest life turn out to be an empty dream. And he would show how in dreams there was manifest the naked power of the imagination. It was, in point of fact, imaginative experience which Poe's anti-poetic society could make little use of—imaginative experience for its own sake, in belles lettres. As we have come to know, his society's "official" philosophy, Scottish Common Sense, put such a low valuation on the products of the imagination that they were granted a right to exist only in so far as they served practical, "social" ends. The critics and imaginative writers whom Poe battled were nursed on Blair's *Rhetoric*, or any number of versions and imitations of it. Poe battled them in his criticism, certainly; and in doing so, eclectically used any philosophical help he could find in his wide-ranging and, as it seems to me, quite superficial reading. But his principal weapon was his own genius and his devotion to the creative power, realizable in the supernally beautiful, that he knew to be beyond the ken of Common Sense and orthodox rhetoric.

It is tragic that his poems exist for us for nothing but their overinsistent exhibitions of the imagination indulging itself in demonstrations of its own power. But it is this fact, apparently, that helped French poets, not so sensitive to the vulgarities of that overinsistence as Americans can now be, write poems of a seriousness which Poe could not reach. Moreover, it is the fact of Poe's poetic gift which set the pattern of his fiction—with its concern to explore the delicately harrowing relations between the world of common sense and that of the dream. Because his fiction has pattern, we can say that it is greater than his poetry, which has only force. But we must always remember that the life of the fiction is one which seems to have been released by poetic powers and that these powers are unmistakably and unforgettably in the poems. The poems take Poe's anti-poetic world as a given and strain to expose the mysterious poetic power which he feels informs it. That such a world exists is a prime assumption without which the poems would have little or no meaning for us. They depend for their force upon a dialectic of simple opposition to the world for which they are written. Yet they make little contact with that world. They exist, as it were, to remind us of a possibility, "out of space—out of time," which by definition is never actualizable in a "real," common-sense situation.

The authentic poet is Israfel, whose world is the simple negative of this one. Poe must strive to be Israfel, so to escape the very world in which even Israfel would "not sing so wildly well / A mortal melody." He makes his poems seem always to be striving to be out there, apart from his world—and ours too, so far as it might share his world's assumptions as to the significance of imaginative experience. The poems project disembodied creativity, so to speak—the force of an imagination driven to be true to itself at all costs. (In *Eureka*, we must remember, Poe tried to construct a rationale for such disembodied creativity; the net effect of the work is at the least one of helpless megalomania, at the most one of willful demonism.) The egocentrism of Poe's poems achieves its greatest value for us by being finally, in its very agonizingly self-indulgent lyricism, an unsharable egocentrism. The poet is freed to be true to his sense of his self and his vocation, but only at the cost of cutting himself off from his vulgarly substantial world. What his act, his poetic act, means is considerably more than it is. This perhaps is the inevitable fate of a man who is more of a culture hero than an artist.

In Emerson's poetry too there is a primary egocentrism, but it is intended to be an egocentrism which transmutes itself into universality by being fully acknowledged for what it is. Emerson indeed says goodbye to the proud world; but then he proceeds to take it home with him. Discovering the genuine and authentic Man—I return to Tocqueville's terms—Emerson would exhibit him in the very act of creating his society, his world, so that it cannot be *really* anti-poetic—if it is well enough known, as it would be in poems. As R. W. B. Lewis, reviving an old and valuable notion, has recently pointed out, Emerson (in one of his moods) conceived of the genuine and authentic Man as still another Adam: "Here's for the plain old Adam," Lewis quotes him as writing in his *Journals*, "the simple genuine self against the whole world." The opposition, self against the (anti-poetic) world, is evident everywhere in Emerson, of course; it is especially sharp in the poems, where it becomes a means of transmutation of the world into something freshly seen, fully found, and so a manifestation of the Adamic principle itself.

This principle works on the materials of Emerson's real world (he would have perhaps called it the world of appearance) in two ways: as it focuses on scene or thought; as it treats the natural world (I use "natural" in the conventional, non-Emersonian sense) or the world of ideas. In the first case—in "scenic" poems like "The Humble-Bee," "The Snow Storm," and in parts of "Wood Notes," "Seashore," and "Each and All,"—there is an attempt to achieve directly ("organically" in Emerson's Coleridgean language) that sense of the natural object which will reveal its meaning and thus make it available to the Reason (i.e., intuition). The end of such a poem is not so much to let us know the object as to know by means of it. What we are to come to know, as Emerson stated explicitly again and again in his essays, is that the poet is somehow one with it. But what we do come to know, as such poems work, is something a little different: the poet makes it one with himself. Adam gives his own name to what he sees and so creates (or recreates) his name and his self.

In the second case, that in which Emerson's Adamic principle treats of the world of ideas, we find poems whose subject is explicitly human actions and beliefs. Such actions and beliefs have for Emerson a paradoxical relation to the world in which they occur, being at once of it and apart from it; and in the poems he would resolve this paradox. In poems like "Each and All" and "Wood Notes" the resolution is managed partly by the descriptive-participative technique which I have already described. But in such poems there is need for more than this, since systematic thought, the dialectics of specifically human actions and beliefs, is involved. The means to this further resolution is characteristically a kind of poetic logic, or pseudo-logic.

The poet knows that true insight into his problem is possible only through a transcendental resolving of his paradox, and he works accordingly—presenting both (or all) sides of the paradox and making it appear to resolve itself in a moment of more-than-human insight. For the non-transcendentalist reader, poems which work thus can be said essentially to dramatize the resolution. For Emerson as transcendentalist poet, the poems can be said actually to create the resolution. For the reader, that is to say, there is no final transmutation of the egocentric into the universal, of Man into the world, and *vice-versa*. The egocentrism of Old Adam is there, and we mark it and its limitations as such. Emerson, for us, cannot get over the obstacle presented to his poetic aspiration by language in its very givenness, its referential quality, its component of anti-poetry. He can, however, make us know what it is creatively to struggle against that obstacle and, in struggling, to know himself all the better.

We feel the presence of a kindred obstacle especially in "philosophical" poems like "Hamatreya" and "Brahma." Properly to read these poems, I think, we must assume from the beginning the resolvability of the paradox around which they turn. There is nothing in the detailed life of the men named in "Hamatreya" which makes inevitable either the "Earth-Song" or the poet's acceptance of it. And in "Brahma," the unresolved details of the paradoxes persist unless we assume with the poet that merely by presenting them he presents also the resolution which is immanent in them. The resolution might well be there, but we are made to feel overpoweringly that the poet, this Man, has put it there.

Likewise, we hear the ineluctably autobiographical voice of the poet in poems of the order of "Bacchus." Here the conceiving and creating ego asks for

> Wine of wine,
> Blood of the world,
> Form of forms, and mould of statures,
> That I intoxicated,
> And by the draught assimilated,
> May float at pleasure through all natures;
> The bird-language rightly spell,
> And that which roses say so well.

In the end the poet is intoxicated by nature and so is able, as he reports, truly to conceive of her and all her manifestations. The point is that here, as everywhere in his poems, the kind of meaning Emerson demands of poetry only he as poet can give to it. The ego is lost so that the ego may be saved; the poet is supremely possessed, but by himself. (Characteristically, at moments of insight, he must chant hypnotically, as here in "Bacchus" and in the "Earth-Song" section of "Hamatreya.") What is manifest in the best poems is not a union and identification of ego and nature, even though the poems nominally argue for that; it is rather an interpretation and definition of nature by a creative assertion of the ego. Even if he would, the poet cannot erase the opposition between himself and his world.

One can find this conception of poetry and the poet adumbrated in Emerson's essay "The Poet" if one reads it in the light of the performance of the poems, not of Emerson's transcendentalist hopes and presuppositions. Emerson's poet is "isolated among his contemporaries by his truth and his art...." He is "the man without impediment, who sees and handles that which others dream of, traverses the whole scale of experience, and is representative of man, in virtue of being the largest power to receive and impart." As for the poet's relation to his world: "All the facts of the animal economy, sex, nutriment, gestation, birth, growth, are symbols of the passage of the world into the soul of man...." And as for the American poet and his nominally anti-poetic world: "We have yet had no genius in America, with tyrannous eye, which knew the value of our incomparable materials, and saw, in the barbarism and materialism of the times, another carnival of the same gods whose picture he so much admires in Homer.... Our log-rolling, our stumps and their politics, our fisheries, our Negroes and Indians, our boasts and our repudiations, the wrath of rogues and the pusillanimity of honest men, the northern trade, the southern planting, the western clearing, Oregon and Texas, are yet unsung. Yet America is a poem in our eyes...." To quote from "The Poet" thus is certainly to interpret it by deletion and selection. For the essay above all makes it clear that Emerson felt that the poet, in "receiving and imparting" the symbols of nature, transformed them into a "new and higher fact," a *single* fact, the One, the Over-soul, God. Yet we are justified, I think, in taking this belief of Emerson's as simply his personal means to making and believing in poems, and then in asking what he is able to make his poems do. He may conceive of poetry as vatic; yet his poems do not work vatically. They are too much *his* poems; their effect is one of an act of creation, not of revelation. What we observe is that in his poetry at its most powerful, to quote from "The Poet," again out of context, "The Universe is the externization of the soul." As we read the poems, Man externizes himself into his anti-poetic world, makes it an aspect of his conception of himself, but still remains Man in an anti-poetic world.

In the context of these notes, we can take Whitman to be the supremely realized Emersonian poet, sufficiently free of and insecure in theoretical concerns to let his ego roam and transform the world into an aspect of itself. If there ever was one, his is a true voice of feeling. Both the preface to the 1855 *Leaves of Grass* and "By Blue Ontario's Shore," its poetic counterpart, are essentially expansions of "The Poet." And Whitman's conception of the forms of love whereby one is to achieve identity with the myriad aspects of the cosmos—this conception is a development of the Emersonian conception of the power of the poet as universal man. So much, I take it, is commonplace critical knowledge. What must be pointed out in these notes is the way in which the ego is made not only to assert but to preserve itself in the poems, the way in which the ego's tremendous creative power militates against that fusion of ego and cosmos which seems to have been Whitman's great desire. Emphasizing the desire (sharing it, perhaps), we have too often tended to mistake it for the effect, and the meaning, of the poetry itself.

The ego asserts itself Adamically, by naming. Yet the names are not new names; in Whitman's poems, in the great catalogues, they are taken to have preexisted, as it were, but not yet really to have been known. The items which the poems so lovingly name are put together as they have never been before, so that they seem to be related only by the creative force of the poetic ego operative on them. There is little or no "qualitative progression" in the poems, for the persons and things which are made to inhabit them hardly interact. They are not conceived as modifying and qualifying one another, but are referred back to their creator, who does with them as his sensibility wills. The catalogues are thus an inevitable expressive form for one who would collocate all the world in the "Kosmos" of his self.

This is the poet's great power. And for all his apparent insistence that the collocation is out there, ready to be discovered so that the poet may recreate it, we feel the power to be so much uniquely and egocentrically his that the collocation is likewise his, and his alone. Whereas in what I have called Emerson's scenic poems, the natural world is said to reveal itself to Man (but, in my argument, poetically does not), in Whitman's poems the poet is explicitly and insistently shown making for natural revelation by the very creative act of his poem. Whitman glories almost exclusively in the first-person singular; Emerson trusts it, true enough, but would discover it in the third-person too. (Whitman, we may recall, said of *Leaves of Grass*, that it was the attempt "to put *a Person*; a human being [myself, in the latter half of the Nineteenth Century, in America] freely, fully and truly on record.") Essentially, there is no third-person in Whitman's world. Hence there is no formal control in the poems but that which stems from the self revealing the world to itself. All experience, all thought, all belief, all appearance is referred back to the ego; or rather treated in such a way as to appear to have emanated from the ego:

> And I know that the hand of God is the promise of my own,
> And I know that the spirit of God is the brother of my own,
> And that all the men ever born are also my brothers,
>   and the women my sisters and lovers,
> And that a kelson of the creation is love,
> And limitless are leaves stiff or drooping in the fields,
> And brown ants in the little wells beneath them,
> And mossy scabs of the worm fence, heap'd stones, elder,
>   mullein, and poke-weed.

Here—the passage is from the fifth section of "Song of Myself"—Whitman aspires at once to be objective and to achieve some sort of union with his world; yet his very power of naming, describing, and collocating is such that his reader cannot but be overwhelmingly, even critically, aware of the single ego which creates that world. Whitman's objectivity here is that of an impressionist, hence an aspect of his all-suffusing subjectivity. We are reminded that in poetry at least narcissism can be creative, since it can be a means to discovering and defining creativity.

The great example (there are others almost as great) is "The Sleepers," in which the ego supposedly is shown celebrating its oneness with all other egos. The poem moves, nonetheless, in a direction in which Whitman likely did not consciously intend it to. There emerges a sense of the sheer creativity involved in such a celebration, a sense so strong as to argue against the very oneness which is the poet's intended subject. In the night, in sleep, the poet is able, so he argues, to lose his sense of individuated self and to achieve vital union with all other selves. This is the argument, but only the argument. The poem begins thus:

> I wander all night in my vision,
> Stepping with light feet, swiftly and noiselessly stepping and stopping,
> Bending with open eyes over the shut eyes of sleepers,
> Wandering and confused, lost to myself, ill-assorted, contradictory,
> Pausing, gazing, bending, and stopping.

"My vision" is of course the crucial phrase here. For as the poem develops, the night is made out to be the poet's lover, rendering him utterly passive. In this state he envisions himself as possessing and possessed by all men and all women, good and evil, now so undifferentiated as to be universally beautiful. And he comes to see that it is "the night and sleep [which have] liken'd them and restored them." The night then is finally given its richest definition:

> I too pass from the night,
> I stay a while away O night, but I return to you again and love you.
>
> Why should I be afraid to trust myself to you?
> I am not afraid, I have been well brought forward by you,
> I love the rich running day, but I do not desert her in whom I lay so long,
> I know not how I came of you and I know not where I go with you,
>   but I know I came well and shall go well.
>
> I will stop only a time with the night, and rise betimes,
> I will duly pass the day O my mother, and duly return to you.

It is thus a primal source of creativity, lover and genetrix, to which the poet must return, even as he must leave it for his daily life. Crucially, it is a source within the poet, the deepest aspect of himself as authentic person. Returning to his mother, he returns to himself as dreamer-creator, returns to the act with which the poem begins; for it is he who has "liken'd and restored" all to beauty.

Whatever Whitman's conscious philosophical intention, the form of the poem, its movement from the picture of the envisioning poet, to a series of catalogues and narratives of what he envisions, to the discovery that the act of envisioning makes all beautiful, then finally to the realization of the source of envisioning power—all this demonstrates a poet sufficiently conscious of his own commitment to isolated, egocentric creativity to manifest it even as he tries to transcend it. For us, the poem is the act of envisioning the soul as beautiful. The account of the source of the vision, its meaning and rationale, is part of that act and derives its power from the actor, not from the transcendental, pantheistic world-view toward which he aspires. Whereas in "The Sleepers" Whitman argues for a transcendent One which would *per se* universalize the ego, he expresses the act of the ego striving to universalize itself by recreating the world in its own image. The poet here is the one who elsewhere wrote of the "noiseless patient spider" which "to explore the vacant vast surrounding" has "launched forth filament, filament, filament out of itself...."

Whitman may have looked to a sort of Hegelian Absolute; he may well have felt that he was achieving it—which is to say, losing himself in cosmic process. Yet his poems show that, being compulsively a person, he could not. Sometimes, as in "Out of the Cradle Endlessly Rocking" and "When Lilacs Last in the Dooryard Bloom'd," he establishes his relation to cosmic process by developing in an argument a series of carefully defined, clearly symbolic, but nonetheless ego-centered relationships. More often he celebrates aspects of process itself, but always, committed to the dialectics of the poetic mode which he worked out, as a simple, separate participant.

He is, in the last analysis, the lonely observer who cannot but make the world participate with him:

> I sit and look out upon all the sorrows of the world,
>   and upon all oppression and shame,
> I hear secret convulsive sobs from young men at anguish with themselves,
>   remorseful after deeds done....

As this poem develops, we sense overpoweringly that Whitman is not of what he sees, "all the meanness and agony without end," but rather makes it of himself. The meaning of the poem is concentrated in the verbs and the adjective which make up the last line: "See, hear, and am silent." Involved in Whitman's conception of the poetic act are seeing, hearing, and being silent, as well as sounding the barbaric yawp. The one makes for the possibility of the other, keeps the poet somehow apart from the very anti-poetic world which he would infuse with his love, protects him from the potentially suicidal force of that love, does not let him be anyone but himself, and thus makes for the positive achievement of his kind of poetry.

I think we may even say that, at its points of achievement, this conception of the poetic act saves Whitman from the sort of grandiose mysticism for which he seems so often to have yearned and also from the excesses of the "Personalism" which he as often preached. That he is, in spite of his learning, necessarily cut off from large areas of knowledge and large forms of discipline (subsumable under some such word as "tradition") is obvious enough, a sign of the weakness which is complementary to the strength of his poems. His conception of poetry, as we can make it out by reading his work critically, not only made for his poems; it also protected him from the world to which he perforce addressed them. For it demanded that the anti-poetic world be translatable into self, expressible thus in poetry, or have no claim to reality at all.

We cannot help but see that this is to a degree a mutilating conception of reality. Yet it is at the same time a source of strength, for Whitman perhaps *the* source of strength.

The achievement of Emily Dickinson is the surest, in a way the simplest, of those I treat in these notes. I am not suggesting that her achievement is less than that of the others. On the contrary, I would say the purity and integrity of her best work makes for the fullest and most direct expression of what I have claimed to be the egocentrism of the basic nineteenth-century American style. In Emily Dickinson we do not sense, as we do in Emerson and Whitman, the compulsion to be oneself in spite of the world and yet somehow to be oneself in terms of the world—no compulsion, in short, toward the transcendental dialectic. In Emerson and Whitman, poetic egocentrism, striving so often to be itself expressively and something else dialectically, emerges in powerful fits and starts, almost out of control, as a result of a break in the dialectical tension (between self and world) which the poets' very artistry (taking the form of an overwhelming sense of the claims of self) will not let them maintain. This sort of tension does not exist in Emily Dickinson's poems. Rather, she is simply and starkly concerned with being herself and accommodating her view of the world to that concern. Whatever her picture of herself as a Little Tippler tasting "a liquor never brewed" owes to Emerson's "Bacchus," the poems are essentially different in kind; for she gives no indication of trying to achieve Emerson's intended transcendental sacramentalism and thus of losing herself in her world. Here, as everywhere, she does not try to merge with nature, but rather to conceive of it. The conceiving self is primary; the poems explicitly celebrate the act of conception and no more. This limitation is so fully realized as to be the occasion of celebration:

> Adventure most unto itself
> The Soul condemned to be—
> Attended by a single Hound
> It's own identity.

The poems are thus, in all their restrictiveness, the purest of poems done in the basic nineteenth-century style.

We can take these most famous lines quite literally, I think:

> This is my letter to the World
> That never wrote to Me—
> The simple News that Nature told—
> With tender Majesty....

Emily Dickinson always reported to the world her sense of herself and nature—in short, her sense of the world. It is not a matter of egotism, but rather one of a humble, tragic, pathetic, even humorous realization of limitations. The sense of limitation, realized as sharply as it is, is indeed her greatest spiritual strength and forces her poems into their triumphant egocentrism. This has been often observed in one way or another of her poems anatomizing her own psyche and its adventures. I think, for example, of variations on the theme of the self defining itself as they occur in poems like "I felt a Cleaving in My Mind," "Renunciation—is a piercing Virtue," "Much Madness is divinest Sense," "The Soul selects her own Society," "I died for Beauty...," and "I dreaded that first Robin, so." Moreover there are the poems on religion in which she, as has often been remarked, now takes one stand and now another. In effect, she refuses to settle down to a definite theology even as she appears to assume that there very likely is one. What are God and immortality to me? she asks again and again. Trying to answer her own questions, she finds a new answer each time. That in this case the answers all seem to be variations on an expressive (as opposed to a repressive) Edwardsean Puritanism—this fact is not material to the working of any one of her poems. It is in the nature of the poems to refuse to point to anything but themselves as they are being made.

This self-sufficiency is above all apparent in the sort of poems in which egocentrism would have (and did have, in Emerson and Whitman) its greatest struggle to survive —poems of the natural world. (Poe, in his concern to demonstrate the value of the darkly egocentric origins and supernal life of the imagination, never got as far as poetizing the natural world; this is an aspect of the hyperexpressionism of his poems.) In a poem like the celebrated "A Route of Evanescence," the very objectivity of the natural scene is a product of the poet's control of the language with which she pictures it. The metaphors testify to the poet's controlling presence; and at the end ("The mail from Tunis, probably, / An easy Morning's Ride—"), the commentary gives an interpretative assertion in which we discover that the poet has fully taken over and used what she has seen and created out of her seeing. We are forced to focus our interest on her, as the poem's maker.

Beyond this, if Emily Dickinson directly relates the natural world to her own sense of herself, it is by a kind of allegory, in which self and nature are kept quite separate. I would cite as examples here, among many others, three poems which Yvor Winters (in his essay on Emily Dickinson, in *Maule's Curse*) has analyzed from this point of view: "A Light exists in Spring / Not present in the Year," "As imperceptibly as Grief / The Summer lapsed away,"—and "There's a certain Slant of light, / Winter Afternoons." In these poems the natural images are selected explicitly as they contribute to a definition of a moral experience; they are not, in any sense, there for their own sakes, scenically; the language in which they are cast has no meaning except as it is focused on the moral experience involved; nature is made to be, as it were, the self allegorized. So, in the last stanza of the third poem named:

> When it comes, the Landscape listens—
> Shadows—hold their breath—
> When it goes, 'tis like the Distance
> On the look of Death—

The qualities here imputed to the natural scene are human qualities, but their humanness explicitly derives from the situation of the poet-protagonist—as though the objective reality of nature were irrelevant, whereas the felt quality were everything. We may observe that the transaction in which Nature "told" Emily Dickinson this "simple News" was an involved one, since she told it to Nature first.

The function of these poems, then, is to let us see the poet in the act of making poems, and thus of making herself—or her understanding of herself. A useful analogy perhaps is Melville's Ishmael, impressing upon us that he is writing his novel after the fact, making us assent to his utter freedom to adduce material from whatever quarter he wishes and to write from various points of view and in various forms, just so he may understand what has happened to himself, just so he may create himself, or at least the possibility of himself. The great conglomeration of Emily Dickinson's poetry is indeed a kind of *Moby Dick*. Her poetry has its own kind of proliferation and plenitude, and its own kind of incompleteness; for the very lack of "system" in the poetry, the very openendedness of its conception of the creating self, is such that there is, properly speaking, no end and no beginning—just life being made even as it is being lived through.

Of something like this, I think, Emily Dickinson must have been conscious—although she puts it in her own typically restrictive terms—since, in spite of the overarching of her imaginative grasp toward things, there was for her no Whale, just her own soul in her own world. Thus there is the poem which begins:

> I dwell in Possibility—
> A fairer House than Prose—
> More numerous of Windows—
> Superior—for Doors—

and ends:

> For Occupation—This—
> The spreading wide my narrow Hands
> To gather Paradise—

Moreover, she could conceive precisely of the risks and losses of creating a world entirely unto the self:

> Perception of an object costs
> Precise the Object's loss—
> Perception in itself a Gain
> Replying to it's Price—
> The Object Absolute—is nought—
> Perception sets it fair
> And then upbraids a Perfectness
> That situates so far—

Above all, it is *her* world, framed by variations on the hymn stanza and seemingcasual rhymes, held together by a variety of subtle internal echoings and parallels, modulated (as the Johnson text now lets us see) by an improvised kind of punctuation (mostly dashes)—all of which let us sense a quality of vital annotation, as though the moment had to be put down *now*, the only time it would ever exist for her whose moment it was. She is the Puritan diarist who no longer has to believe that her acutely sensed private experiences are valuable and explicable only as types of something larger than they—something given from above, from outside herself. Which is to say, she is the extreme American Protestant self which, when it comes fully alive in its greatest poems, is in effect able to set its institutional and religious commitments aside and be radically and unflinchingly itself, radically and unflinchingly free. In that freedom there is at once loss, denial, pain, release, certainty, and victory.

In what sense, finally, does Emily Dickinson's poetry come out of the sort of anti-poetic world of which Tocqueville wrote? In the simplest sense: that in its very egocentric limitation (of whose biographical origin we are now certain), it finds its greatest strength and achievement; for herein it gives life to those clichés of the self which an anti-poetic society was perforce bringing into dominance. It battles against and wins out over the mass media of the psyche. Professor Whicher's observation on this matter, in *This Was a Poet*, goes even deeper than he seems to have intended it to: "Her poems were demonstrations that the simplest commonplaces of life in America could be vitalized and made precious to the mind."

What Emily Dickinson never achieved, nor could try to achieve, one guesses, was a philosophical poetry which, in its submission to traditional intellectual and artistic disciplines, would allow the ego to discover its formal relations to other egos and to celebrate not only the relations but their forms—the grand myths so to speak. (That a "philosophy" is deducible from her poems and the record of her life is yet another matter.) But, as I have argued, neither could Whitman or Emerson, who tried at once to hold to their egocentrism and to be philosophical poets; nor, I venture to say, could Poe, who left us *Eureka*, a pseudo-poem in which the work of the creative imagination, its very existence and function rationalized, is transformed into painfully amateurish dialectics. For many reasons, none of which are immediately relevant to the kind of analysis I have undertaken, Emily Dickinson held close to, and thereby most richly developed, the egocentric style which I am suggesting is basic in nineteenth-century poetry. This was her triumph. Reading her along with Poe, Emerson, and Whitman, we can say that this was in part their triumph too, and thus, almost in spite of itself, one of the triumphs of their culture.

HAVING PUT DOWN my hypothesis and annotated it, I now propose a definition of the ideal type of major nineteenth-century American poem. This poem is one which portrays the simple, separating inwardness of Man as that which at once forms and is formed by a vision of the world in which it has its being. Expressively this poem is one which makes us aware of the operation of the creative imagination as an act of self-definition—thus, whether the poet wills it or not, of self-limitation. The poem may nominally argue for many things, may have many subjects, may be descriptive of the world at large; but always it will implicitly argue for one thing—the vital necessity of its own existence and of the ego which creates and informs it. Its essential argument is the life of poetry itself, as this life makes viable a conception of man as radically free to know, be, and make himself. Herein lies perhaps the crucial quality of its so-called romanticism.[1] The historian is able to observe after the fact: What other kind of poem could be written in an anti-poetic society by one whose very vocation (which we must take as a given) committed him to the primacy of the idea of Man? What could he do but try to use the language his culture gave him and convert its implicit anti-poetry to a celebration of the one Man he could fully know, himself? That he often wanted to write a poetry as cosmic as it was personal is beside the point in this analysis of his basic style—the style he willy-nilly shared with others of his vocation. This perhaps was his crucial role in his culture: to preserve and make possible of realization the idea of Man as a simple, separate person, an authentic self.

Certainly in much twentieth-century American poetry, as we have come to assure ourselves, this is still the poet's essential role. It is true, however, that at the end of the first decade of our century, the dominant poetic mode of the nineteenth century, its basic style, seemed to have spent itself. We can, for example, see this happening in the work of E. A. Robinson, in which is portrayed the emptiness of many selves (known not as first-persons, but as third-), surviving as persons, if they do, only by their capacity to live heroically with their illusions. The mode of such poetry, deriving so much stylistically from that of its great precursors, seems to have been unsatisfactory for Robinson; for he moved to a series of dramatic but shapeless, quasi-philosophic poems in which he tried to erect the principle of the self living on illusions to a positive belief in the world which guaranteed something beyond illusions. He could not, however, convert disillusioned inwardness to illusioned outwardness, especially by the fiat of making short negative poems long, positive, and "dramatic." He was equipped as a poet, as had been Poe, Emerson, Whitman, and Emily

---

[1] At this point the reader, like the author, might want at least to raise the proper comparatist question as to the relevance of English and European "romantic" poetry—with *its* conception of the role (or roles) of the self—to the American poetry under discussion. Since the question is not directly relevant to the discussion, the author has come to feel that it should be raised and answered only in a footnote. In the first place: I am concerned to move centripetally, to define the basic style only in such a way as to relate it to some of the basic issues in American culture; I hope thus to make the poetry more available historically, as it were, to the American reader who is of that culture and to the non-American who would understand it. And in the second place: I should hazard the guess that the basic American style may be differentiated from the basic European and English style (or styles) precisely to the degree that it centers on the confused dialectic involved in having oneself and losing it, of being apart from society even as one redefines the integrative force of society in terms of that very apartness. The burden of being oneself seems to be more bearable (or better borne) in the English and European romantic poetry that I know; the anguish, and the triumph of the anguish, seems to be purer; the diversitarianism, more completely achieved; the basic style (or styles), more fully realized. But this is a guess that only the proper comparatist is entitled to make and to evaluate. And I like to think that he had best begin with "nationalistic" considerations like those in my essay. I take refuge, in short, in the wise opening words of Américo Castro's "Presence of the Sultan Saladin in the Romance Literatures," *Diogenes*, No. 8 (Autumn 1954), pp. 13–36: "Cultural phenomena never exist except in connexion with the agents of human life that make them possible and endow them with their authentic value. Culture is not of itself a fertilising rain—nothing human can be 'of itself' an island of abstraction. Literary themes, then, are things that happen in and to someone's historical life. Their value is manifested to its full extent when the theme that interests us is seen as the expression, through an individual, of a particular people, who, in giving life to the literary theme, achieves its self-realisation in terms of a value structure. . . ."

Dickinson before him, primarily to explore necessarily fragmented inwardness, not to construct whole, well-ordered systems.

More important is the reaction against the basic nineteenth-century style (or against its turn-of-the-century failures) in Pound and Eliot. They set about to create a whole new poetic mode, one in which the ego would be defined by sources outside of itself, in which its aim would be not to create and shape itself but to seek the discipline whereby it might achieve the form and wholeness which seemed otherwise unattainable. Nonetheless, as it becomes more and more apparent to us, Pound and Eliot and their tradition are not all of twentieth-century American poetry. I would suggest that the basic style of the nineteenth century has existed in the twentieth as a minor line, which now looks again to become the major line. I refer of course to the line of poets whose work culminates in that of Wallace Stevens. In these poets—some of them are as different from Stevens as Cummings, Williams, Marianne Moore, and Roethke—the American way of poetry is still, to misecho Mr. Trilling's phrase, that of the imposing self. And it is a way still as significant as much for what it cannot successfully deal with (in all, a sense of culture as having something like an autonomous validity), as for what it can (a sense of the self as valid only when autonomous). That, in recently rediscovering this way and the neo-Romanticism it validates, we have not concerned ourselves much with what it cannot deal with—this is our misfortune.

Thinking of our nineteenth-century poetry in relation to that of the twentieth which carries on the basic style, we may note how the twentieth-century subject is now so often the very possibility of poetry itself. I venture to think that this means that Tocqueville's observations about literature in the United States still hold; only, as we all too well know, the terms are now more extreme, the urgencies more desperate, and the poet more and more aware of his crucial, lonely, and imperious role as trustee of our imaginative language. He is, we are in the habit of saying, a "purer" poet. And we tend to suspect and resent his purity and the imperiousness and loneliness that go with it. We wonder what his fierce pursuit of the verbally adequate (which is to say, the beautiful) has to do with us and we with it. We begin to be uneasy about what we so often take to be estheticism for estheticism's sake. At this point, I suggest that we can try to think historically and see that it is not estheticism but the impulse to creativity which is at the heart of this matter. Moreover, we might try to see how he makes this creativity out to be, if not humanity itself, at least the first step toward the achievement of humanity. Granting the situation of our culture, this might have been and still be, for good and for bad, our prime "use" of poetry. In any case, the opening lines of Stevens' "Of Modern Poetry" may well describe for us the ideal type of poems, nineteenth- and twentieth-century poems, conceived in the basic style, definition of which has been the purpose of these notes:

> The poem of the mind in the act of finding
> What will suffice.

My hypothesis leads me to suggest that thus it has always had to be with some of our major poets and with that part of ourselves to which they speak.

The Baroque Style in Prose

❧ MORRIS W. CROLL ❧

Morris Croll's "The Baroque Style in Prose," published originally in 1929, has proved a seminal work in the analysis of late sixteenth-century and of seventeenth-century prose. As Croll indicates in this essay, he had earlier traced the theories and "the triumph of the anti-Ciceronian movement" (in a series of articles treating the history of "Attic prose" and such figures as Muret, Lipsius, Montaigne, and Bacon), but in the selection at hand he sets himself "to describe" and exemplify "the *form* of anti-Ciceronian, or baroque, prose." And he so succeeds that a number of later scholars, pre-eminent among them George Williamson in *The Senecan Amble* (1951) and Jonas Barish in *Ben Jonson and the Language of Prose Comedy* (1960), have been able to take off in one way or another from Croll's insights, revising, developing, and refining them.

Obviously Croll views anti-Ciceronian verbal practices as grounded in theory. And it is worth noting that he persistently describes the baroque style, not as a pane of glass through which the reader may see into the private experience of the writer, but as a vehicle by which the writer dramatizes himself, represents himself for the reader as engaged in a particular activity. The "modernism" of the anti-Ciceronian movement is quite "self-conscious," Croll declares, and the writers with whom he deals "preferred the forms that express [that is, dramatize] the energy and labor of minds seeking the truth"—they deliberately "portray, not a thought, but a mind thinking, or, in Pascal's words, *la peinture de la pensée.*" Although Croll's application of "baroque" to literature no doubt helped to establish a term that has often been used in bewildering ways, the real strength of this essay lies in his careful attempt to differentiate between two versions of the baroque style through a meticulous examination of syntax.

Morris Croll's essays have been collected and edited by J. M. Patrick and R. O. Evans, working with J. M. Wallace and R. J. Schoeck, in the volume *Style, Rhetoric, and Rhythm* (Princeton, N.J., 1966).

Introduction

IN THE LATTER YEARS of the sixteenth century a change declared itself in the purposes and forms of the arts of Western Europe for which it is hard to find a satisfactory name. One would like to describe it, because of some interesting parallels with a later movement, as the first modern manifestation of the Romantic Spirit; and it did, in fact, arise out of a revolt against the classicism of the high Renaissance. But the terms "romantic" and "classical" are both perplexing and unphilosophical; and their use should not be extended. It would be much clearer and more exact to describe the change in question as a radical effort to adapt traditional modes and forms of expression to the uses of a self-conscious modernism; and the style that it produced was actually called in several of the arts—notably in architecture and prose-writing—the "modern" or "new" style. But the term that most conveniently describes it is "baroque." This term, which was at first used only in architecture, has lately been extended to cover the facts that present themselves at the same time in sculpture and in painting; and it may now properly be used to describe, or at least to name, the characteristic modes of expression in all the arts during a certain period—the period, that is, between the high Renaissance and the eighteenth century; a period that begins in the last quarter of the sixteenth century, reaches a culmination at about 1630, and thenceforward gradually modifies its character under new influences.

Expressiveness rather than formal beauty was the pretension of the new movement, as it is of every movement that calls itself modern. It disdained complacency, suavity, copiousness, emptiness, ease, and in avoiding these qualities sometimes obtained

---

"The Baroque Style in Prose," by Morris W. Croll, is reprinted from *Studies in English Philology*, edited by Kemp Malone and Martin Ruud, pp. 427-56. University of Minnesota Press, Minneapolis. © Copyright 1929 by the University of Minnesota, renewed 1957 by Kemp Malone. Translations in brackets and italics are new to the present edition.

effects of contortion or obscurity, which it was not always willing to regard as faults. It preferred the forms that express the energy and labor of minds seeking the truth, not without dust and heat, to the forms that express a contented sense of the enjoyment and possession of it. In a single word, the motions of souls, not their states of rest, had become the themes of art.

The meaning of these antitheses may be easily illustrated in the history of Venetian painting, which passes, in a period not longer than one generation, from the self-contained and relatively symmetrical designs of Titian, through the swirls of Tintoretto, to the contorted and aspiring lines that make the paintings of El Greco so restless and exciting. Poetry moves in the same way at about the same time; and we could metaphorically apply the terms by which we distinguish El Greco from Titian to the contrast between the rhythms of Spenser and the Petrarchans, on one hand, and the rhythms of Donne, on the other, between the style of Ariosto and the style of Tasso. In the sculptures of Bernini (in his portrait busts as well as in his more famous and theatrical compositions) we may again observe how ideas of motion take the place of ideas of rest; and the operation of this principle is constantly to be observed also in the school of architecture associated with the same artist's name. "In the façade of a Baroque church," says Geoffrey Scott, "a movement, which in the midst of a Bramantesque design would be destructive and repugnant, is turned to account and made the basis of a more dramatic, but not less satisfying treatment, the motive of which is not peace, but energy."[1]

And finally the change that takes place in the prose style of the same period—the change, that is, from Ciceronian to anti-Ciceronian forms and ideas—is exactly parallel with those that were occurring in the other arts, and is perhaps more useful to the student of the baroque impulse than any of the others, because it was more self-conscious, more definitely theorized by its leaders, and more clearly described by its friends and foes. In some previous studies I have considered the triumph of the anti-Ciceronian movement at considerable length; but I have been concerned chiefly with the theory of the new style; and my critics have complained, justly, that I have been too difficult, or even abstract. In the present study I hope to correct this defect. Its purpose is to describe the *form* of anti-Ciceronian, or baroque, prose.

There are of course several elements of prose technique: diction, or the choice of words; the choice of figures; the principle of balance or rhythm; the form of the period, or sentence; and in a full description of baroque prose all of these elements would have to be considered. The last-mentioned of them—the form of the period—is, however, the most important and the determinant of the others; and this alone is to be the subject of discussion in the following pages.

The anti-Ciceronian period was sometimes described in the seventeenth century as an "exploded" period; and this metaphor is very apt if it is taken as describing solely its outward appearance, the mere fact of its form. For example, here is a period from Sir Henry Wotton, a typical expression of the political craft of the age:

[1] *The Architecture of Humanism*, p. 225.

Men must beware of running down steep places with weighty bodies; they once in motion, *suo feruntur pondere;* steps are not then voluntary.

The members of this period stand farther apart one from another than they would in a Ciceronian sentence; there are no syntactic connectives between them whatever; and semicolons or colons are necessary to its proper punctuation. In fact, it has the appearance of having been disrupted by an explosion within.

The metaphor would be false, however, if it should be taken as describing the manner in which this form has been arrived at. For it would mean that the writer first shaped a round and complete oratorical period in his mind and then partly undid his work. And this, of course, does not happen. Wotton gave this passage its form, not by demolishing a Ciceronian period, but by omitting several of the steps by which roundness and smoothness of composition might have been attained. He has deliberately avoided the processes of mental revision in order to express his idea when it is nearer the point of its origin in his mind.

We must stop for a moment on the word *deliberately*. The negligence of the anti-Ciceronian masters, their disdain of revision, their dependence upon casual and emergent devices of construction, might sometimes be mistaken for mere indifference to art or contempt of form; and it is, in fact, true that Montaigne and Burton, even Pascal and Browne, are sometimes led by a dislike of formality into too licentious a freedom. Yet even their extravagances are purposive, and express a creed that is at the same time philosophical and artistic. Their purpose was to portray, not a thought, but a mind thinking, or, in Pascal's words, *la peinture de la pensée* [the painting of thought]. They knew that an idea separated from the act of experiencing it is not the idea that was experienced. The ardor of its conception in the mind is a necessary part of its truth; and unless it can be conveyed to another mind in something of the form of its occurrence, either it has changed into some other idea or it has ceased to be an idea, to have any existence whatever except a verbal one. It was the latter fate that happened to it, they believed, in the Ciceronian periods of sixteenth-century Latin rhetoricians. The successive processes of revision to which these periods had been submitted had removed them from reality by just so many steps. For themselves, they preferred to present the truth of experience in a less concocted form, and deliberately chose as the moment of expression that in which the idea first clearly objectifies itself in the mind, in which, therefore, each of its parts still preserves its own peculiar emphasis and an independent vigor of its own—in brief, the moment in which truth is still *imagined*.

The form of a prose period conceived in such a theory of style will differ in every feature from that of the conventional period of an oratorical, or Ciceronian, style; but its most conspicuous difference will appear in the way it connects its members or clauses one with another. In the period quoted above from Wotton the members are syntactically wholly free; there are no ligatures whatever between one and another. But there is another type of anti-Ciceronian period, in which the ordinary marks of logical succession—conjunctions, pronouns, etc.—are usually present, but are of such a kind or are used in such a way as to bind the members together in a characteristically

THE BAROQUE STYLE IN PROSE [101]

loose and casual manner. The difference between the two types thus described may seem somewhat unimportant; and it is true that they run into each other and cannot always be sharply distinguished. The most representative anti-Ciceronians, like Montaigne and Browne, use them both and intermingle them. But at their extremes they are not only distinguishable; they serve to distinguish different types, or schools, of seventeenth-century style. They derive from different models, belong to different traditions, and sometimes define the philosophical affiliations of the authors who prefer them.

They will be considered here separately; the first we will call, by a well-known seventeenth-century name, the *période coupée*, or in an English equivalent, the "curt period" (so also the *stile coupé*, or the "curt style"); the other by the name of the "loose period" (and the "loose style"); though several other appropriate titles suggest themselves in each case.[2]

Stile Coupé

ONE EXAMPLE of the *période coupée* has already been given. Here are others:[3]

Pour moy, qui ne demande qu'à devenir plus sage, non plus sçavant ou éloquent, ces ordonnances logiciennes et aristoteliques ne sont pas à propos; je veulx qu'on commence par le dernier poinct: j'entends assez que c'est que Mort et Volupté; qu'on ne s'amuse pas à les anatomizer.—Montaigne, *Essais*, II, 10, "Des Livres."

For myself, who asks only to become wiser, not more learned or eloquent, these logical and Aristotelian orderings are not to the point; I want us to begin with the conclusion: I know well enough what Death and Pleasure are; let us not amuse ourselves in dissecting them.

'Tis not worth the reading, I yield it, I desire thee not to lose time in perusing so vain a subject, I should peradventure be loth myself to read him or thee so writing; 'tis not *operae pretium*.—Burton, *Anatomy of Melancholy*, "To the Reader."

No armor can defend a fearful heart. It will kill itself within.—Felltham, *Resolves*, "Of Fear and Cowardice."

Mais il faut parier; cela n'est pas volontaire; vous êtes embarqués.—Pascal, *Pensées*, Article II.

But one must wager; that is not voluntary; you have embarked.

L'éloquence continue ennuie.
Les princes et les rois jouent quelquefois. Ils ne sont pas toujours sur leurs trônes; ils

---

[2] For example, the *stile coupé* was sometimes called *stile serré* ("serried style"), and Francis Thompson has used this term in describing a kind of period common in Browne. For synonyms of "loose style" see a succeeding section of this paper [pp. 107-15].

[3] The punctuation in all cases is that of editions which profess to follow in this respect good seventeenth-century editions or manuscripts.

s'y ennuient: la grandeur a besoin d'être quittée pour être sentie.—Pascal, *Pensées*, "Sur l'Éloquence."

Continued eloquence bores.
Princes and kings play sometimes. They are not always on their thrones; they are bored there: greatness needs to be put aside in order to be felt.

The world that I regard is myself; it is the microcosm of my own frame that I cast mine eye on: for the other, I use it but like my globe, and turn it round sometimes for my recreation.—Browne, *Religio Medici*, II, 11.

Il y a des hommes qui attendent à être dévots et religieux que tout le monde se déclare impie et libertin: ce sera alors le parti du vulgaire; ils sauront s'en dégager.—La Bruyère, *Des Esprits Forts*.

There are some men who wait to become devout and religious until everyone declares himself an infidel and freethinker: that will then be the cause of the vulgar; they will know how to disengage themselves from it.

In all of these passages, as in the period quoted from Wotton, there are no two main members that are syntactically connected. But it is apparent also that the characteristic style that they have in common contains several other features besides this.

In the first place, each member is as short as the most alert intelligence would have it. The period consists, as some of its admirers were wont to say, of the nerves and muscles of speech alone; it is as hard-bitten, as free of soft or superfluous flesh, as "one of Caesar's soldiers."[4]

Second, there is a characteristic order, or mode of progression, in a curt period that may be regarded either as a necessary consequence of its omission of connectives or as the causes and explanation of this. We may describe it best by observing that the first member is likely to be a self-contained and complete statement of the whole idea of the period. It is so because writers in this style like to avoid prearrangements and preparations; they begin, as Montaigne puts it, at *le dernier poinct*, the point aimed at. The first member therefore exhausts the mere fact of the idea; logically there is nothing more to say. But it does not exhaust its imaginative truth or the energy of its conception. It is followed, therefore, by other members, each with a new tone or emphasis, each expressing a new apprehension of the truth expressed in the first. We may describe the progress of a curt period, therefore, as a series of imaginative moments occurring in a logical pause or suspension. Or—to be less obscure—we may compare it with successive flashes of a jewel or prism as it is turned about on its axis and takes the light in different ways.

It is true, of course, that in a series of propositions there will always be some logical process; the truth stated will undergo some development or change. For example, in the sentence from Montaigne on page 101, the later members add something to the

---

[4] The phrase comes from a midseventeenth-century work on prose style (*Precetti*, reprinted in Milan, 1822) by Daniello Bartoli, and is there applied to *il dir moderno*.

idea; and in the quotation from Pascal's *Pensées sur l'Éloquence*, on the same page, the thought suddenly enlarges in the final member. Yet the method of advance is not logical; the form does not express it. Each member, in its main intention, is a separate act of imaginative realization.

In the third place, one of the characteristics of the curt style is deliberate asymmetry of the members of a period; and it is this trait that especially betrays the modernistic character of the style. The chief mark of a conventional, or "classical," art, like that of the sixteenth century, is an approximation to evenness in the size and form of the balanced parts of a design; the mark of a modernistic art, like that of the seventeenth, and the nineteenth and twentieth, centuries, is the desire to achieve an effect of balance or rhythm among parts that are obviously not alike—the love of "some strangeness in the proportions."

In a prose style asymmetry may be produced by varying the length of the members within a period. For example, part of the effect of a sentence from Bishop Hall is due to a variation in this respect among members which nevertheless produce the effect of balance or rhythmic design.

> What if they [crosses and adversities] be unpleasant? They are physic; it is enough if they be wholesome.[5]—Hall, *Heaven upon Earth*, XIII.

But the desired effect is more characteristically produced by conspicuous differences of form, either with or without differences of length. For instance, a characteristic method of the seventeenth century was to begin a succession of members with different kinds of subject-words. In the sentence from Wotton (page 100) the first two members have personal subjects, the third the impersonal "steps"; in the following from Pascal the opposite change is made.

> Mais il faut parier; cela n'est pas volontaire; vous êtes embarqués.
> *But one must wager; that is not voluntary; you have embarked.*

In both of these periods, moreover, each of the three members has a distinct and individual turn of phrase, meant to be different from the others. Again, in the period of La Bruyère quoted on page 102 each new member involves a shift of the mind to a new subject. (Observe also the asymmetry of the members in point of length.)

Sometimes, again, asymmetry is produced by a change from literal to metaphoric statement, or by the reverse, or by a change from one metaphor to another, as in the last example quoted from Pascal, where the metaphor of one embarked upon a ship abruptly takes the place of that of a man engaged in a bet. Or there may be a leap from the concrete to the abstract form; and this is an eminently characteristic feature of the *stile coupé* because this style is always tending toward the aphorism,

---

[5] Note how exactly this reproduces a movement characteristic of Seneca: *Quid tua, uter* [Caesar or Pompey] *vincat? Potest melior vincere: non potest non pejor esse qui vicerit* [What is it to you, which of the two (Caesar or Pompey) conquers? It is possible for the better man to win: it is not possible for him who will have conquered not to be the worse].

or *pensée*, as its ideal form. The second passage quoted from Pascal, on pages 101-102, illustrates this in a striking way. It is evident that in the first three members [of the second paragraph]—all concrete, about kings and princes—the author's mind is turning toward a general truth, which emerges complete and abstract in the last member: *la grandeur a besoin d'être quittée pour être sentie*.

The curt style, then, is not characterized only by the trait from which it takes its name, its omission of connectives. It has the four marks that have been described: first, studied brevity of members; second, the hovering, imaginative order; third, asymmetry; and fourth, the omission of the ordinary syntactic ligatures. None of these should, of course, be thought of separately from the others. Each of them is related to the rest and more or less involves them; and when they are all taken together they constitute a definite rhetoric, which was employed during the period from 1575 to 1675 with as clear a knowledge of its tradition and its proper models as the sixteenth-century Ciceronians had of the history of the rhetoric that they preferred.

In brief, it is a Senecan style; and, although the imitation of Seneca never quite shook off the imputation of literary heresy that had been put upon it by the Augustan purism of the preceding age, and certain amusing cautions and reservations were therefore felt to be necessary, yet nearly all of the theorists of the new style succeeded in expressing their devotion to their real master in one way or another. Moreover, they were well aware that the characteristic traits of Seneca's style were not his alone, but had been elaborated before him in the Stoic schools of the Hellenistic period; and all the earlier practitioners of the *stile coupé*, Montaigne (in his first phase), Lipsius, Hall, Charron, etc., write not only as literary Senecans, but rather more as philosophical Stoics.

Senecanism and Stoicism are, then, the primary implications of *stile coupé*. It must be observed, however, that a style once established in general use may cast away the associations in which it originated; and this is what happened in the history of the curt style. Montaigne, for instance, confessed that he had so thoroughly learned Seneca's way of writing that he could not wholly change it even when his ideas and tastes had changed and he had come to prefer other masters. And the same thing is to be observed in many writers of the latter part of the century: St. Évremond, Halifax, and La Bruyère, for instance. Though these writers are all definitely anti-Stoic and anti-Senecan, all of them show that they had learned the curt style too well ever to unlearn it or to avoid its characteristic forms; and there was no great exaggeration in Shaftesbury's complaint, at the very end of the century, that no other movement of style than Seneca's—what he calls the "Senecan amble"—had been heard in prose for a hundred years past.

The curt or serried style depends for its full effect upon the union of the several formal traits that have been described in the preceding section. We have assumed hitherto that these traits are as rigorous and unalterable as if they were prescribed by a rule; and in the examples cited there have been no significant departures from any of them. But of course slight variations are common even in passages that produce the effect of *stile coupé;* and some searching is necessary to discover examples as pure as those that have been cited. This is so evidently true that it would need no illustration except for the fact that certain kinds of period eminently characteristic of seventeenth-century prose arise from a partial violation of the "rules" laid down. Two of these may be briefly described.

a. In a number of writers (Browne, Felltham, and South, for example) we often find a period of two members connected by *and, or,* or *nor,* which evidently has the character of *stile coupé* because the conjunction has no logical *plus* force whatever. It merely connects two efforts of the imagination to realize the same idea; two as-it-were synchronous statements of it. The following from Browne will be recognized as characteristic of him:

> 'Tis true, there is an edge in all firm belief, and with an easy metaphor we may say the sword of faith.—*Religio Medici,* I, 10.

Again:

> Therefore I perceive a man may be twice a child before the days of dotage; and stand in need of Aeson's bath before threescore.—*Ibid.,* I, 42.

Often, too, in a period consisting of a larger number of members the last two are connected by an *and* or the like. But this case can be illustrated in connection with the one that immediately follows.

b. The rule that the successive members of a *période coupée* are of different and often opposed forms, are asymmetrical instead of symmetrical, is sometimes partly violated inasmuch as these members begin with the same word or form of words, for example, with the same pronoun-subject, symmetry, parallelism, and some regularity of rhythm thus introducing themselves into a style that is designed primarily and chiefly to express a dislike of these frivolities. It is to be observed, however, that the members that begin with this suggestion of oratorical pattern usually break it in the words that follow. Except for their beginnings they are as asymmetrical as we expect them to be, and reveal that constant novelty and unexpectedness that is so characteristic of the "baroque" in all the arts.

One illustration is to be found in the style of the "character" writings that enjoyed so great a popularity in the seventeenth century. The frequent recurrence of the same subject-word, usually *he* or *they,* is the mannerism of this style, and is sometimes carried over into other kinds of prose in the latter part of the century, as, for instance, in writings of La Bruyère that are not included within the limits of the character genre,[6] and in passages of Dryden. It is indeed so conspicuous a mannerism that it may serve to conceal what is after all the more significant feature of the "character" style, namely, the constant variation and contrast of form in members that begin in this formulistic manner.

The style of the "character," however, is that of a highly specialized genre; and

---

[6] For instance, in the famous passage "De l'Homme" describing the beastlike life of the peasants of France.

the form of the period with reiterated introductory formula can be shown in its more typical character in other kinds of prose, as, for example, in a passage from Browne describing the Christian Stoicism of his age:

> Let not the twelve but the two tables be thy law: let Pythagoras be thy remembrancer, not thy textuary and final instructor: and learn the vanity of the world rather from Solomon than Phocylydes.[7]—*Christian Morals*, p. xxi.

Browne touches lightly on these repetitions, and uses them not too frequently. Balzac uses them characteristically and significantly. A paragraph from his *Entretiens* (No. XVIII, "De Montaigne et de ses Escrits") may be quoted both in illustration of this fact and for the interest of its subject matter:

> Nous demeurasmes d'accord que l'Autheur qui veut imiter Seneque commence par tout et finit par tout. Son Discours n'est pas un corps entier: c'est un corps en pieces; ce sont des membres couppez; et quoy que les parties soient proches les unes des autres, elles ne laissent pas d'estre separées. Non seulement il n'y a point de nerfs qui les joignent; il n'y a pas mesme de cordes ou d'aiguillettes qui les attachent ensemble: tant cet Autheur est ennemy de toutes sortes de liaisons, soit de la Nature, soit de l'Art: tant il s'esloigne de ces bons exemples que vous imitez si parfaitement.

> *We remain agreed that the author who wishes to imitate Seneca begins anywhere and ends anywhere. His discourse is not a whole body: it is a body in pieces; they are separated members; and even if the parts are near one another, they do not cease to be separate. Not only are there no sinews which join them; there are not even strings or threads which attach them to each other: so much is this author an enemy of all sorts of connections, be they of Nature or of Art: so much does he depart from the good examples which you imitate so perfectly.*

The passage illustrates exactly Balzac's position in the prose development of the seventeenth century. Montaigne is indeed—in spite of his strictures upon him—his master. He aims, like Montaigne, at the philosophic ease and naturalness of the *genus humile;* he has his taste for aphorism, his taste for metaphor; he is full of "points," and loves to make them show; in short, he is "baroque." But by several means, and chiefly by the kinds of repetition illustrated in this passage (*c'est . . . ce sont; il n'y a point . . . il n'y a pas mesme; tant . . . tant*), he succeeds in introducing that effect of art, of form, of rhythm, for which Descartes and so many other of his contemporaries admired him. He combines in short the "wit" of the seventeenth century with at least the appearance of being "a regular writer," which came, in the forties and fifties, to be regarded in France as highly desirable. In his political writings, and especially in *Le Prince*, his iterated opening formula becomes too evident a mannerism, and on page after page one reads periods of the same form: two or three members beginning alike and a final member much longer and more elaborate than the preceding that may or may not begin in the same way. The effect is extremely rhetorical.

---

[7] The period occurs in the midst of a paragraph in which each main member of each period begins with a verb in the imperative mood.

Finally, we have to observe that the typical *période coupée* need not be so short as the examples of it cited at the beginning of the present section. On the contrary, it may continue, without connectives and with all its highly accentuated peculiarities of form, to the length of five or six members. Seneca offered many models for this protracted aphoristic manner, as in the following passage from the *Naturales Quæstiones* (vii, 31):

> There are mysteries that are not unveiled the first day: Eleusis keepeth back something for those who come again to ask her. Nature telleth not all her secrets at once. We think we have been initiated: we are still waiting in her vestibule. Those secret treasures do not lie open promiscuously to every one: they are kept close and reserved in an inner shrine.

Similar in form is this six-member period from Browne's *Religio Medici* (I, 7):

> To see ourselves again we need not look for Plato's year: every man is not only himself; there have been many Diogeneses, and as many Timons, though but few of that name; men are lived over again; the world is now as it was in ages past; there was none then but there hath been some one since that parallels him, and is, as it were, his revived self.[8]

What has been said in a previous section of the characteristic mode of progression in *stile coupé* is strikingly illustrated in such passages as these. Logically they do not move. At the end they are saying exactly what they were at the beginning. Their advance is wholly in the direction of a more vivid imaginative realization: a metaphor revolves, as it were, displaying its different facets; a series of metaphors flash their lights; or a chain of "points" and paradoxes reveals the energy of a single apprehension in the writer's mind. In the latter part of the seventeenth century a number of critics satirize this peculiarity of the Senecan form. Father Bouhours, for instance, observed that with all its pretensions to brevity and significance this style makes less progress in five or six successive statements than a Ciceronian period will often make in one long and comprehensive construction. The criticism is, of course, sound if the only mode of progression is the logical one; but in fact there is a progress of imaginative apprehension, a revolving and upward motion of the mind as it rises in energy, and views the same point from new levels; and this spiral movement is characteristic of baroque prose.

The Loose Style

IN THE PRECEDING PAGES we have been illustrating a kind of period in which the members are in most cases syntactically disjunct, and we have seen that in this style the members are characteristically short. It is necessary now to illustrate the other type of anti-Ciceronian style spoken of at the beginning, in which the members are usually

---

[8] Felltham uses this manner with too much self-consciousness. See, for instance, a passage on the terse style (*Resolves*, I, 20) beginning: "They that speak to Children assume a pretty lisping."

connected by syntactic ligatures, and in which, therefore, both the members and the period as a whole may be, and in fact usually are, as long as in the Ciceronian style, or even longer.

It is more difficult to find an appropriate name for this kind of style than for the other. The "trailing" or "linked" style would describe a relation between the members of the period that is frequent and indeed characteristic, but is perhaps too specific a name. "Libertine" indicates exactly both the form of the style and the philosophical associations that it often implies; but it is wiser to avoid these implications in a purely descriptive treatment. There is but one term that is exact and covers the ground: the term "loose period" or "loose style"; and it is this that we will usually employ. In applying this term, however, the reader must be on his guard against a use of it that slipped into many rhetorical treatises of the nineteenth century. In these works the "loose sentence" was defined as one that has its main clause near the beginning; and an antithetical term, "periodic sentence"—an improper one—was devised to name the opposite arrangement. "Loose period" is used here without reference to this confusing distinction.

In order to show its meaning we must proceed by means of examples; and we will take first a sentence—if, indeed, we can call it a sentence—in which Bacon contrasts the "Magistral" method of writing works of learning with the method of "Probation" appropriate to "induced knowledge," "the latter whereof [he says] seemeth to be *via deserta et interclusa*."

> For as knowledges are now delivered, there is a kind of contract of error between the deliverer and the receiver: for he that delivereth knowledge desireth to deliver it in such form as may be best believed, and not as may be best examined; and he that receiveth knowledge desireth rather present satisfaction than expectant inquiry; and so rather not to doubt than not to err: glory making the author not to lay open his weakness, and sloth making the disciple not to know his strength.—*Advancement of Learning*, Book I.

The passage is fortunate because it states the philosophy in which anti-Ciceronian prose has its origin and motive. But our present business is with its form; and in order to illustrate this we will place beside it another passage from another author.

> Elle [l'Imagination] ne peut rendre sages les fous; mais elle les rend heureux à l'envi de la raison, qui ne peut rendre ses amis que misérables, l'une les couvrant de gloire, l'autre de honte.[9]—Pascal, *Pensées*, "L'Imagination."

> It [the imagination] cannot make wise men of fools; but it makes them happy and competes with reason, which can only render its friends miserable, the one covering them with glory, the other with shame.

There is a striking similarity in the way these two periods proceed. In each case an antithesis is stated in the opening members; then the member in which the second part of the antithesis is stated puts out a dependent member. The symmetrical development

---

[9] There should, rhetorically speaking, be semicolons, not commas, after *raison* and *misérables*.

announced at the beginning is thus interrupted and cannot be resumed. The period must find a way out, a syntactic way of carrying on and completing the idea it carries. In both cases the situation is met in the same way, by a concluding member having the form of an absolute-participle construction, in which the antithetical idea of the whole is sharply, aphoristically resumed.

The two passages, in short, are written as if they were meant to illustrate in style what Bacon calls "the method of induced knowledge"; either they have no predetermined plan or they violate it at will; their progression adapts itself to the movements of a mind discovering truth as it goes, thinking while it writes. At the same time, and for the same reason, they illustrate the character of the style that we call "baroque." See, for instance, how symmetry is first made and then broken, as it is in so many baroque designs in painting and architecture; how there is constant swift adaptation of form to the emergencies that arise in an energetic and unpremeditated forward movement; and observe, further, that these signs of spontaneity and improvisation occur in passages loaded with as heavy a content as rhetoric ever has to carry. That is to say, they combine the effect of great mass with the effect of rapid motion; and there is no better formula than this to describe the ideal of the baroque design in all the arts.

But these generalizations are beyond our present purpose. We are to study the loose period first, as we did the curt period, by observing the character of its syntactic links. In the two sentences quoted there are, with a single exception, but two modes of connection employed. The first is by co-ordinating conjunctions, the conjunctions, that is, that allow the mind to move straight on from the point it has reached. They do not necessarily refer back to any particular point in the preceding member; nor do they commit the following member to a predetermined form. In other words, they are the loose conjunctions, and disjoin the members they join as widely as possible. *And*, *but*, and *for* are the ones employed in the two sentences; and these are of course the necessary and universal ones. Other favorites of the loose style are *whereas*, *nor* (= *and not*), and the correlatives *though* ... *yet*, *as* ... *so*. Second, each of the two periods contains a member with an absolute-participle construction. In the loose style many members have this form, and not only (as in the two periods quoted) at the ends of periods, but elsewhere. Sir Thomas Browne often has them early in a period, as some passages to be cited in another connection will show. This is a phenomenon easily explained. For the absolute construction is the one that commits itself least and lends itself best to the solution of difficulties that arise in the course of a spontaneous and unpremeditated progress. It may state either a cause, or a consequence, or a mere attendant circumstance; it may be concessive or justificatory; it may be a summary of the preceding or a supplement to it; it may express an idea related to the whole of the period in which it occurs, or one related only to the last preceding member.

The co-ordinating conjunctions and the absolute-participle construction indicate, then, the character of the loose period. Like the *stile coupé*, it is meant to portray the natural, or thinking, order; and it expresses even better than the curt period the anti-Ciceronian prejudice against formality of procedure and the rhetoric of the schools.

For the omission of connectives in the *stile coupé* implies, as we have seen, a very definite kind of rhetorical form, which was practiced in direct imitation of classical models, and usually retained the associations that it had won in the Stoic schools of antiquity. The associations of the loose style, on the other hand, are all with the more skeptical phases of seventeenth-century thought—with what was then usually called "Libertinism"; and it appears characteristically in writers who are professed opponents of determined and rigorous philosophic attitudes. It is the style of Bacon and of Montaigne (after he has found himself), of La Mothe le Vayer, and of Sir Thomas Browne. It appears always in the letters of Donne; it appears in Pascal's *Pensées;* and, in the latter part of the century, when Libertinism had positively won the favor of the world away from Stoicism, it enjoyed a self-conscious revival, under the influence of Montaigne, in the writings of St. Évremond, Halifax, and Temple. Indeed, it is evident that although the Senecan *stile coupé* attracted more critical attention throughout the century, its greatest achievements in prose were rather in the loose or Libertine manner. But it must also be said that most of the skeptics of the century had undergone a strong Senecan influence; and the styles of Montaigne, Browne, Pascal, and Halifax, for instance, can only be described as displaying in varying ways a mingling of Stoic and Libertine traits.

Besides the two syntactic forms that have been mentioned—the co-ordinating conjunctions and the absolute construction—there are no others that lend themselves by their nature to the loose style, except the parenthesis, which we need not illustrate here. But it must not be supposed that it tends to exclude other modes of connection. On the contrary, it obtains its characteristic effects from the syntactic forms that are logically more strict and binding, such as the relative pronouns and the subordinating conjunctions, by using them in a way peculiar to itself. That is to say, it uses them as the necessary logical means of advancing the idea, but relaxes at will the tight construction which they seem to impose; so that they have exactly the same effect as the loose connections previously described and must be punctuated in the same way. In other words, the parts that they connect are no more closely knit together than it chooses they shall be; and the reader of the most characteristic seventeenth-century prose soon learns to give a greater independence and autonomy to subordinate members than he would dare to do in reading any other.

The method may be shown by a single long sentence from Sir Thomas Browne:

> I could never perceive any rational consequence from those many texts which prohibit the children of Israel to pollute themselves with the temples of the heathens; we being all Christians, and not divided by such detested impieties *as* might profane our prayers, or the place wherein we make them; *or that* a resolved conscience may not adore her Creator anywhere, *especially* in places devoted to his service; *where,* if their devotions offend him, mine may please him; if theirs profane it, mine may hallow it.[10]— *Religio Medici,* I, 3.

---

[10] Italics are mine.

The period begins with a statement complete in itself, which does not syntactically imply anything to follow it; an absolute participle carries on, in the second member. Thereafter the connectives are chiefly subordinating conjunctions. Observe particularly the use of *as, or that*, and *where*: how slight these ligatures are in view of the length and mass of the members they must carry. They are frail and small hinges for the weights that turn on them; and the period abounds and expands in nonchalant disregard of their tight, frail logic.

This example displays the principle; but of course a single passage can illustrate only a few grammatical forms. Some of those used with a characteristic looseness in English prose of the seventeenth century are: relative clauses beginning with *which*, or with *whereto, wherein*, etc.; participial constructions of the kind scornfully called "dangling" by the grammarians; words in a merely appositional relation with some noun or pronoun preceding, yet constituting a semi-independent member of a period; and of course such subordinating conjunctions as are illustrated above. It is unnecessary to illustrate these various cases.

The connections of a period cannot be considered separately from the order of the connected members; and, in fact, it is the desired order of development that determines the character of the connections rather than the reverse. In the oratorical period the arrangement of the members is "round" or "circular," in the sense that they are all so placed with reference to a central or climactic member that they point forward or back to it and give it its appropriate emphasis. This order is what is meant by the names *periodos, circuitus*, and "*round composition*," by which the oratorical period has been variously called; and it is the chief object of the many revisions to which its form is submitted.

The loose period does not try for this form, but rather seeks to avoid it. Its purpose is to express, as far as may be, the order in which an idea presents itself when it is first experienced. It begins, therefore, without premeditation, stating its idea in the first form that occurs; the second member is determined by the situation in which the mind finds itself after the first has been spoken; and so on throughout the period, each member being an emergency of the situation. The period—in theory, at least—is not made; it becomes. It completes itself and takes on form in the course of the motion of mind which it expresses. Montaigne, in short, exactly described the theory of the loose style when he said: *J'ecris volontiers sans project; le premier trait produit le second* [I write freely and without plan; the first stroke produces the second].

The figure of a circle, therefore, is not a possible description of the form of a loose period; it requires rather the metaphor of a chain, whose links join end to end. The "linked" or "trailing" period is, in fact, as we have observed, an appropriate name for it. But there is a special case for which this term might better be reserved, unless we should choose to invent a more specific one, such as "end-linking," or "terminal linking," to describe it. It is when a member depends, not upon the general idea, or the main word, of the preceding member, but upon its final word or phrase alone. And this is, in fact, a frequent, even a characteristic, kind of linking in certain authors, notably Sir Thomas Browne and his imitators. The sentence last quoted offers two or three illustrations of it: the connective words *as, especially,* and *where* all refer to the immediately preceding words or phrases; and in another period by the same author there is one very conspicuous and characteristic instance.

> As there were many reformers, so likewise many reformations; every country proceeding in a particular way and method, according as their national interest, together with their constitution and clime, inclined them: some angrily and with extremity; others calmly and with mediocrity, not rending, but easily dividing, the community, and leaving an honest possibility of a reconciliation; *which* though peaceable spirits do desire, and may conceive that revolution of time and the mercies of God may effect, yet that judgment that shall consider the present antipathies between the two extremes,—their contrarities in condition, affection, and opinion,—may with the same hopes expect a union in the poles of heaven.—*Religio Medici,* I, 4.

Here the word *which* introduces a new development of the idea, running to as much as five lines of print; yet syntactically it refers only to the last preceding word, *reconciliation*. The whole long passage has been quoted, however, not for this reason alone, but because it illustrates so perfectly all that has been said of the order and connection of the loose period. It begins, characteristically, with a sharply formulated complete statement, implying nothing of what is to follow. Its next move is achieved by means of an absolute-participle construction.[11] This buds off a couple of appositional members; one of these budding again two new members by means of dangling participles. Then a *which* picks up the trail, and at once the sentence becomes involved in the complex, and apparently tight, organization of a *though ... yet* construction. Nevertheless it still moves freely, digressing as it will, extricates itself from the complex form by a kind of *anacoluthon* (in the *yet* clause), broadening its scope, and gathering new confluents, till it ends, like a river, in an opening view.

The period, that is, moves straight onward everywhere from the point it has reached; and its construction shows ideally what we mean by the linked or trailing order. It is Browne's peculiar mastery of this construction that gives his writing constantly the effect of being, not the result of a meditation, but an actual meditation in process. He writes like a philosophical scientist making notes of his observation as it occurs. We see his pen move and stop as he thinks. To write thus, and at the same time to create beauty of cadence in the phrases and rhythm in the design—and so Browne constantly does—is to achieve a triumph in what Montaigne called "the art of being natural"; it is the eloquence, described by Pascal, that mocks at formal eloquence.

The period just quoted serves to introduce a final point concerning the form of the loose period. We have already observed that the second half of this period, beginning with *which*, has a complex suspended syntax apparently like that of the typical oratorical sentence. The anti-Ciceronian writer usually avoids such forms, it is true; most of his sentences are punctuated by colons and semicolons. But, of course, he will often

---

[11] Observe that the period from Browne quoted on p. 110 begins with movements of the same kind.

find himself involved in a suspended construction from which he cannot escape. It remains to show that even in these cases he still proceeds in the anti-Ciceronian manner, and succeeds in following, in spite of the syntactic formalities to which he commits himself, his own emergent and experimental order. Indeed, it is to be observed that the characteristic quality of the loose style may appear more clearly in such difficult forms than in others. For baroque art always displays itself best when it works in heavy masses and resistant materials, and out of the struggle between a fixed pattern and an energetic forward movement often arrives at those strong and expressive disproportions in which it delights.

We shall return to Browne in a moment in illustration of the point, but we shall take up a simpler case first. In a well-known sentence, Pascal, bringing out the force of imagination, draws a picture of a venerable magistrate seated in church, ready to listen to a worthy sermon. *Le voilà prêt à l'ouïr avec un respect exemplaire* [There he is, ready to listen to it with exemplary respect].

> Que le prédicateur vienne à paraître: si la nature lui a donné une voix enrouée et un tour de visage bizarre, que son barbier l'ait mal rasé, si le hasard l'a encore barbouillé de surcroît, quelque grandes vérités qu'il annonce, je parie la perte de la gravité de notre sénateur.
>
> *Suppose the preacher appears: if nature has given him a hoarse voice and a bizarre countenance, let his barber have shaved him badly, if chance has also smeared him with dirt on top of it all, whatever the great truths he announces, I'll wager that our magistrate will lose his great air.*

Unquestionably a faulty sentence by all the school-rules! It begins without foreseeing its end, and has to shift the reader's glance from the preacher to the magistrate in the midst of its progress by whatever means it can. Observe the abruptness of the form of the member *quelque grandes vérités*. Observe the sudden appearance of the first person in the last member. Yet the critic who would condemn its rhetorical form would have also to declare that there is no art in those vivid dramatic narratives that so often appear in the conversation of animated talkers; for this period moves in an order very common in such conversation.[12]

In this passage the free and anti-Ciceronian character of the movement is chiefly due to its dramatic vividness and speed. It follows the order of life. Sometimes, however, we can see plainly that it is the mystical speculation of the seventeenth century that changes the regular form of the period and shapes it to its own ends. Sir Thomas Browne provides many interesting illustrations, as, for instance, in the period quoted in the preceding section, and in the following:

> I would gladly know how Moses, with an actual fire, calcined or burnt the golden calf into powder: for that mystical metal of gold, whose solary and celestial nature I admire,

---

[12] It may be said that Pascal's *Pensées* should not be cited in illustration of prose form because they were written without revision and without thought of publication. But a good deal of characteristic prose of the time was so written; and the effect at which Bacon, Burton, Browne, and many others aimed was of prose written in that way.

exposed unto the violence of fire, grows only hot, and liquefies, but consumeth not; so when the consumable and volatile pieces of our bodies shall be refined into a more impregnable and fixed temper, like gold, though they suffer from the action of flames, they shall never perish, but lie immortal in the arms of fire.—*Religio Medici*, I, 50.

With the first half of this long construction we are not now concerned. In its second half, however, beginning with *so when*, we see one of those complex movements that have led some critics to speak of Browne as—of all things!—a Ciceronian. It is in fact the opposite of that. A Ciceronian period closes in at the end; it reaches its height of expansion and emphasis at the middle or just beyond, and ends composedly. Browne's sentence, on the contrary, opens constantly outward; its motions become more animated and vigorous as it proceeds; and it ends, as his sentences are likely to do, in a vision of vast space or time, losing itself in an *altitudo*, a hint of infinity. As, in a previously quoted period, everything led up to the phrase, "a union in the poles of heaven," so in this everything leads up to the concluding phrase, "but lie immortal in the arms of fire." And as we study the form of the structure we can even observe where this ending revealed itself, or, at least, how it was prepared. The phrase *like gold* is the key to the form of the whole. After a slow expository member, this phrase, so strikingly wrenched from its logical position, breaks the established and expected rhythm, and is a signal of more agitated movement, of an ascending effort of imaginative realization that continues to the end. In a different medium, the period closely parallels the technique of an El Greco composition, where broken and tortuous lines in the body of the design prepare the eye for curves that leap upward beyond the limits of the canvas.

The forms that the loose period may assume are infinite, and it would be merely pedantic to attempt a classification of them. In one of the passages quoted we have seen the dramatic sense of reality triumphing over rhetorical formalism; in another, the form of a mystical exaltation. For the purpose of description—not classification—it will be convenient to observe still a third way in which a loose period may escape from the formal commitments of elaborate syntax. It is illustrated in a passage in Montaigne's essay "Des Livres" (II, 10), praising the simple and uncritical kind of history that he likes so much. In the course of the period he mentions *le bon Froissard* as an example, and proceeds so far (six lines of print) in a description of his method that he cannot get back to his general idea by means of his original syntactic form, or at least cannot do so without very artificial devices. He completes the sentence where it is, but completes his idea in a pair of curt (*coupés*) sentences separated by a colon from the preceding: *C'est la matière de l'histoire nue et informe; chascun en peult faire son proufit autant qu'il a d'entendement* [This is the material of history, bare and unshaped; each one can profit from it according to his own understanding]. This is a method often used by anti-Ciceronians to extricate themselves from the coils of a situation in which they have become involved by following the "natural" order. A better example of it is to be seen in a passage from Pascal's essay on "Imagination," from which another passage has already been cited.

Le plus grand philosophe du monde, sur une planche plus large qu'il ne faut, s'il y a au-dessous un précipice, quoique sa raison le convainque de sa sûreté, son imagination prévaudra. Plusieurs n'en sauraient soutenir la pensée sans pâlir et suer.—*Pensées*, "L'Imagination."

The greatest philosopher in the world, standing on a plank larger than necessary, if there is an abyss beneath, although his reason convince him of his safety, his imagination will prevail. Some could not sustain the thought without growing pale and sweating.

Nothing could better illustrate the "order of nature"; writing, that is, in the exact order in which the matter presents itself. It begins by naming the subject, *le plus grand philosophe*, without foreseeing the syntax by which it is to continue. Then it throws in the elements of the situation, using any syntax that suggests itself at the moment, proceeding with perfect dramatic sequence, but wholly without logical sequence, until at last the sentence has lost touch with its stated subject. Accordingly, this subject is merely left hanging, and a new one, *son imagination*, takes its place. It is a violent, or rather a nonchalant, *anacoluthon*. The sentence has then, after a fashion, completed itself. But there is an uneasy feeling in the mind. After all, *le plus grand philosophe* has done nothing; both form and idea are incomplete. Pascal adds another member (for, whatever the punctuation, the *plusieurs* sentence is a member of the period), which completely meets the situation, though a grammatical purist may well object that the antecedent of *plusieurs* was in the singular number.

Pascal is usually spoken of as a "classical" writer; but the term means nothing as applied to him except that he is a writer of tried artistic soundness. He is, in fact, as modernistic, as bold a breaker of the rules and forms of rhetoric, as his master Montaigne, though he is also a much more careful artist. *La vraie éloquence*, he said, *se moque de l'éloquence*.

Two kinds of style have been analyzed in the preceding pages: the concise, serried, abrupt *stile coupé*, and the informal, meditative, and "natural" loose style. It is necessary to repeat—once more—that in the best writers these two styles do not appear separately in passages of any length, and that in most of them they intermingle in relations far too complex for description. They represent two sides of the seventeenth-century mind: its sententiousness, its penetrating wit, its Stoic intensity, on the one hand, and its dislike of formalism, its roving and self-exploring curiosity, in brief, its skeptical tendency, on the other. And these two habits of mind are generally not separated one from the other; nor are they even always exactly distinguishable. Indeed, as they begin to separate or to be opposed to each other in the second half of the century we are aware of the approach of a new age and a new spirit. The seventeenth century, as we are here considering it, is equally and at once Stoic and Libertine; and the prose that is most characteristic of it expresses these two sides of its mind in easy and natural relations one with the other.

The Punctuation of the Seventeenth-Century Period

The "long sentence" of the anti-Ciceronian age has received a remarkable amount of attention ever since it began to be corrected and go out of use; and there have been two conflicting views concerning it. The older doctrine—not yet quite extinct—was that the long sentences of Montaigne, Bacon, Browne, and Taylor were sentences of the same kind as those of Cicero and his sixteenth-century imitators; only they were badly and crudely made, monstrosities due to some wave of ignorance that submerged the syntactic area of the seventeenth-century mind. Their true character, it was thought, would be shown by substituting commas for their semicolons and colons; for then we should see that they are quaint failures in the attempt to achieve sentence-unity.

The other view is the opposite of this, namely, that we should put periods in the place of many of its semicolons and colons. We should then see that what look like long sentences are really brief and aphoristic ones. The contemporary punctuation of our authors is again to be corrected, but now in a different sense. This is the view urged by Faguet in writing of Montaigne, and by Sir Edmund Gosse concerning the prose of Browne and Taylor.

This later view is useful in correcting some of the errors of the earlier one. But, in fact, one of them is just as false as the other; and both of them illustrate the difficulties experienced by minds trained solely in the logical and grammatical aspects of language in interpreting the forms of style that prevailed before the eighteenth century. In order to understand the punctuation of the seventeenth century we have to consider the relation between the grammatical term *sentence* and the rhetorical term *period*.

The things named by these terms are identical. *Period* names the rhetorical, or oral, aspect of the same thing that is called in grammar a *sentence*; and in theory the same act of composition that produces a perfectly logical grammatical unit would produce at the same time a perfectly rhythmical pattern of sound. But, in fact, no utterance ever fulfills both of these functions perfectly, and either one or the other of them is always foremost in a writer's mind. One or the other is foremost also in every theory of literary education; and the historian may sometimes distinguish literary periods by the relative emphasis they put upon grammatical and rhetorical considerations. In general we may say, though there may be exceptions, that before the eighteenth century rhetoric occupied much more attention than grammar in the minds of teachers and their pupils. It was so, for instance, in the Middle Ages, as is clear from their manuals of study and the curricula of their schools. It was still true in the sixteenth century; and the most striking characteristic of the literary prose of that century, both in Latin and in the vernacular tongues, was its devotion to the conventional and formal patterns of school-rhetoric.

The laws of grammatical form, it is true, were not at all disturbed or strained at this time by the predominance of rhetorical motives. There was no difficulty whatever in saying what these rhetoricians had to say in perfect accordance with logical syntax because they had, in fact, so little to say that only the most elementary syntax was necessary for its purposes. Furthermore, the rhetorical forms they liked were so symmetrical, so obvious, that they almost imposed a regular syntax by their own form.

But a new situation arose when the leaders of seventeenth-century rationalism—Lipsius, Montaigne, Bacon—became the teachers of style. The ambition of these writers was to conduct an experimental investigation of the moral realities of their time, and to achieve a style appropriate to the expression of their discoveries and of the mental effort by which they were conducted. The content of style became, as it were, suddenly greater and more difficult; and the stylistic formalities of the preceding age were unable to bear the burden. An immense rhetorical complexity and license took the place of the simplicity and purism of the sixteenth century; and, since the age had not yet learned to think much about grammatical propriety, the rules of syntax were made to bear the expenses of the new freedom. In the examples of seventeenth-century prose that have been discussed in the preceding pages some of the results are apparent. The syntactic connections of a sentence become loose and casual; great strains are imposed upon tenuous, frail links; parentheses are abused; digression becomes licentious; *anacoluthon* is frequent and passes unnoticed; even the limits of sentences are not clearly marked, and it is sometimes difficult to say where one begins and another ends.

Evidently the process of disintegration could not go on forever. A stylistic reform was inevitable, and it must take the direction of a new formalism or "correctness." The direction that it actually took was determined by the Cartesian philosophy, or at least by the same time-spirit in which the Cartesian philosophy had its origin. The intellect, that is to say, became the arbiter of form, the dictator of artistic practice as of philosophical inquiry. The sources of error, in the view of the Cartesians, are imagination and dependence upon sense-impressions. Its correctives are found in what they call "reason" (which here means "intellect"), and an exact distinction of categories.

To this mode of thought we are to trace almost all the features of modern literary education and criticism, or at least of what we should have called modern a generation ago: the study of the precise meaning of words; the reference to dictionaries as literary authorities; the study of the sentence as a logical unit alone; the careful circumscription of its limits and the gradual reduction of its length; the disappearance of semicolons and colons; the attempt to reduce grammar to an exact science; the idea that forms of speech are always either correct or incorrect; the complete subjection of the laws of motion and expression in style to the laws of logic and standardization—in short, the triumph, during two centuries, of grammatical over rhetorical ideas.

This is not the place to consider what we have gained or lost by this literary philosophy, or whether the precision we have aimed at has compensated us for the powers of expression and the flexibility of motion that we have lost; we have only to say that we must not apply the ideas we have learned from it to the explanation of seventeenth-century style. In brief, we must not measure the customs of the age of semicolons and colons by the customs of the age of commas and periods. The only possible punctuation of seventeenth-century prose is that which it used itself. We might sometimes reveal its grammar more clearly by repunctuating it with commas or periods, but we should certainly destroy its rhetoric.

FROM *The Primary Language of Poetry in the 1540's and 1640's*

❧ JOSEPHINE MILES ☙

In 1948 Josephine Miles began publishing a series of monographs about "the primary language of English poetry" which were later collected in *The Continuity of Poetic Language*. Her studies are based on statistics—which Miss Miles has since qualified somewhat—involving the choice of twenty English poets published in the fourth decade of each century from the sixteenth to the twentieth; the examination of some 1,000 lines by each poet, usually the first 1,000 of the work specified in her tables, unless "two works of the poet in the period seem very different"; and the count of "every adjective, noun, and verb" within the 1,000-line segments. Thus she draws up tables to indicate the given poet's proportioning of adjective, noun, and verb; the degree to which he employs the "majority vocabulary" of the decade; his "individual stresses" in vocabulary; and his preferred poetic forms. On the basis of these tables, she generalizes about the decades in question, though carefully insisting that her statements can be construed only as applying to "the lines under consideration." And she buttresses her claims about the poets' language in the specific decade through also exploring its prose and the critical ideas applied in or to the decade.

To speak merely of statistics does a disservice to Miss Miles, for in her prose she translates them into clear and perceptive accounts of the separate decades. Yet the statistics are essential to *The Continuity of Poetic Language*, since she seeks to describe what might better be termed period styles than individual styles. No poet, she argues, is absolutely free to do what he will with language: it—his very medium—is to some extent "set" for him "as for every one else by social situation in time and place," and "even further set by literary conventions." To be sure, any poet reveals his individuality in his poems through interacting with the language thus "set" for him, but in this book Miss Miles focuses primarily on "the contemporary agreements in the practice of individual poets. In such agreements, not consciously compacted, the poets indicate what they together accept from their language as valuable for their poetry; they show shared choices and stresses in meanings, statement forms, and sound patterns; they present in all its variation the common poetic material of their time." In concentrating on these "agreements," however, Miss Miles does not lose sight of any poet's individuality, as the following selections from "The Primary Language of Poetry in the 1540's and 1640's" will make clear.

To select as radically as I have does less than justice to the substance and development of Miss Miles's argument. But I have chosen portions from her book to at least suggest the way in which she closes with English poetry of the 1640's: first, a composite description of the decade's favored vocabulary and an exemplar of its poetry; second, an account of the proportionings of adjective, verb, and noun, in the course of which two styles begin to emerge within the decade; next, a survey and interpretation of the tables (I have included Table 1 to show the range of data on which her discussion of the 1640's is built, but I have omitted Tables 3a and 3b, which reveal minor agreements and individual differences); then, an elaboration of the distinction between two styles of the decade, the one discursive, as exemplified in Jonson and Donne, the other epithetical and descriptive, as in Dryden and Milton; finally, a brief comparison (much more fully articulated in the original) between the poetry of the 1640's and that of the 1540's.

The excerpts have been chosen, then, to illustrate the analysis of what I have called a period style, but this time in connection with a particular nation's poetry, as opposed to Morris Croll's analysis in the preceding essay of a style adopted by a European intellectual movement. I should add that Josephine Miles has gone on from examining the English poetry of specific decades in *The Continuity of Poetic Language* to charting the developments within whole centuries in her *Eras and Modes in English Poetry* (1957).

THE WORDS appearing most often in the volumes of poetry in the bookstalls of the 1640's were these: 4 adjectives, *fair, good, great, sweet;* 10 nouns, *day, earth, eye, god, heart, heaven, love, man, soul, time;* 11 verbs, *bring, come, find, give, go, know, make, see, take, tell, think.* They took logical shape in complex declarative or exclamatory sentences about relationship, and they took melodic form to the beat of the iambic and the couplet. The poetry sounds like this "Divine Mistris" of Carew, in which are a half-dozen of these words at work:

>In Nature's peeces still I see
>Some errour that might mended bee;
>Something my wish could still remove,
>Alter, or adde; but my faire Love
>Was fram'd by hands farre more divine;
>For she hath every beauteous line:
>Yet I had beene farre happier,
>Had Nature, that made me, made her;
>Then likenes might (that love creates)
>Have made her love what now she hates:
>Yet I confesse I cannot spare
>From her just shape the smallest haire;
>Nor need I beg from all the store
>Of heaven for her one beautie more:
>Shee hath too much divinity for mee:
>You Gods! teach her some more humanitie.

These couplets make a play of reason, an argument for preference, a choice between divinitie and humanitie, by a hyperbole of too perfect beauty, and a plea to perfection for more human kindness. Starting with a beautiful piece of nature, putting it in a human relationship of love and desire, finding its flaw in feeling, in natural relation, the poem makes its "explanation" by extension into a supernatural realm, and thus by an exaggeration beyond the physical, literally metaphysical, requests correction direct from the gods through their own powers over the human rather than the divine. It is a complicated situation, being in love: the realms of the natural, the human, the divine—all are involved in it.

The same involvement shows itself in the major nouns of the decade as a whole. *Day, earth, time* are nature's; *eye, heart, love, man,* human, with divine overtones; and *god, heaven, soul,* divine with human connections. The adjectives suggest the split between the sensory affection of *fair* and *sweet* and the more moral standard of *good* and *great;* and the verbs are equally useful in either sphere of activity, human or divine, *giving, knowing, making, seeing, taking, telling* being especially suited to heavenly intercessions, and *coming, going, thinking* more mortal. In Carew's poem, the human

---

The excerpts from "The Primary Language of Poetry in the 1540's and 1640's," by Josephine Miles, are reprinted from her *The Continuity of Poetic Language* (New York, 1965), pp. 4–6, 12–13, 28–31, 39–40, 65–72, 82–90, 100 . . . 102, by permission of The Regents of the University of California.

fair love which is the center as object, creator, and activity is *seen* by the poet who has been *made* by nature, and who turns to *heaven* and the gods in his overpowering sense of divinity—a sense not qualitatively lofty or sublime, but abstractly reasoned or conceived by the logical extensions of metaphorical trope. So the terms are blended by interchange from realm to realm, the very function of trope, and the love by being part of all realms, by being fair, beautiful, perfect, divine, yet subject to nature and humanity, maintains the center of the argument and the petition, the structure of "In Nature ... but my Love ... Yet I had beene ... Yet I confesse ... You Gods! teach her ... ," which sounds so logically formed within the bounds of human reference, yet which, by its interchange of reference, is spread to the bounds of metaphysics. The couplets which carry the argument are five-accented, end-stopped, with some easy variations in foot and caesura and carry-over; they provide most strongly the sound effect of measure, with little else of assonantal or consonantal interplay; the intricacy, therefore, is left to concept, and the trope does the major job of creation in the piece, the creation of a love both natural and divine.

.   .   .   .

Not only the vocabulary itself, but its proportioning, reveals change within stability and idiosyncrasy within the common cause of poetry. In the 1640's, the poets seem consistently to use about one verb to a line, varying no more than from Milton's 8 to Donne's 12 verbs in 10 lines, with some noteworthy early exceptions. In construction as in content the verb seems least variable. The noun, on the other hand, normally varies from one to two in a line, from Donne's 11 in 10 lines to Waller's 19, and thus may equal or double the verb. The adjective may range at extremes from one-half to one and one-half per line, from Jonson's 6 to Milton's 12 and Fletcher's 14 in 10 lines, and thus displays the widest variety in support of its nouns. A plenitude of nouns seems usually to make for a plenitude of adjectives, so that the two may be considered together as a substantival force, as very strong for example in Waller, Milton, and More, where substantival vocabulary is three times as great as predicative, in contrast to the decade's standard twice as great. Proportioning may well be a defining aspect of style.[1] There is a describable difference between the poet who crowds his lines, themselves relatively inflexible in their usual four- or five-foot length, with the separately meaningful nouns and adjectives of substantiation, and the predicating poet who intercomplicates with connectives. There is a vivid technical difference between the highly predicated, meagerly modified poetry of the 1540's and at least part of the highly modified poetry of the 1640's. The difference may suggest, too, the nature of a difference in two styles which persist through the century, the difference between a Skelton, Wyatt, Jonson, Donne sort of predicative style and a Sackville, Spenser, Quarles, Waller, Milton sort of qualitative style. Both sorts are

[1] Little systematic study has been made, more in German than in English, and more with emphasis on prose than with interest in poetry. David Boder's suggestion for an "Adjective-Verb Quotient" (*Psychological Record*, III: 309–44) is interesting, although its bases of classification are difficult. Vernon Lee's distinguishing, in *The Handling of Words*, p. 74, of two prose styles, the active (a two-to-one proportion of substantival elements) and the qualitative (three-to-one), is surprisingly close to what the poetry presents here.

1640's: Table 1* The Poems in Chronological Order: Their Sound and Structure and Proportion

Date	Poet and work (first 1,000 lines)	Form	Adjective	Noun	Verb
1640	CAREW, THOMAS. *Poems.* Preface by W. C. Hazlitt. Roxburghe Library, 1870.	4'–5' cpl. Addr.	8	15	11
	DONNE, JOHN. *Songs and Sonets. Works* (London, 1640).	4'–5' st. Addr.	7	13	12
	HARVEY, CHRISTOPHER. *The Synagogue. Complete Poems,* ed. Grosart, Fuller Worthies' Library, 1874.	5'–3' st. Addr.	6	12	10
	JONSON, BEN. *Under-wood. The Poems,* ed. B. H. Newdigate (Oxford, Blackwell, 1936).	5'–4' st. Addr.	6	14	12
1641	SANDYS, GEORGE. *Song of Solomon, Jeremiah. Poetical Works,* ed. R. Hooper (London, 1872), Vol. II.	5'–4' cpl. Addr.	8	17	9
1642	DENHAM, JOHN. *Cooper's Hill* (1668 text), etc. *Poetical Works,* ed. T. H. Banks (Yale University Press, 1928).	5' cpl. Descr.	7	15	9
	MORE, HENRY. *Psychozoia Platonica. Complete Poems,* ed. Grosart, Chertsey Worthies' Library, 1878.	5', Sp. st. Narr., addr.	12	18	10
1644	QUARLES, FRANCIS. *Shepheards Oracles. Complete Works,* ed. Grosart, Chertsey Worthies' Library, 1881.	5' cpl. Descr., dial.	10	17	13
1645	MILTON, JOHN. "Christ's Nativity," "L'Allegro," "Il Penseroso," "Lycidas," "Comus." *Minor Poems,* ed. M. Y. Hughes (New York, Doubleday-Doran, 1939).	4'–5' ll. Narr., addr.	12	16	8
	WALLER, EDMUND. *Poems. Poetical Works,* ed. Charles. C. Clarke (Edinburgh, 1862).	5' cpl.	11	19	10

*[Key to abbreviations:
  cpl.   *couplet*   narr.   *narrative*
  addr.   *address*   descr.   *description*
  st.   *stanza*   dial.   *dialogue*
  Sp. st.   *Spenserian stanza*   avg.   *average*]

to be seen in the great Elizabethan years between: Breton, Gascoigne, Googe, Turberville, Daniel continue the Wyatt line toward Jonson and Donne and the majority of the 1640's, but more poets in the decade after Spenser are more fully substantial, in the Miltonic direction. We may therefore see proportioning in parallel as well as in nucleus, and, as most directly important, in the simple impact of the individual poem.

1640's: Table 1 (Continued)

Date	Poet and work (first 1,000 lines)	Form	Adjective	Noun	Verb
	WITHER, GEORGE. *Vox Pacifica*. *Miscellaneous Works*, Publications, Spenser Society, No. 13, 2d coll., 1872.	5' st. Narr., addr.	7	14	11
1646	CRASHAW, RICHARD. *Steps to the Temple. Poems*, ed. A. R. Waller (Cambridge University Press, 1904).	4'–5' st. Descr., addr.	10	18	11
	SHIRLEY, JAMES. *Poems*, ed. Ray L. Armstrong (New York, King's Crown Press, Columbia University, 1941).	4' cpl., st. Narr., addr.	7	14	11
	SUCKLING, JOHN. *Fragmenta Aurea. The Works*, ed. A. Hamilton Thompson (London, 1910).	4' cpl., st. avg. Narr., addr.	6	13	12
	VAUGHAN, HENRY. *Silex Scintillans*, 1650, and *Poems*. *Works*, ed. Grosart, Fuller Worthies' Library, 1871.	2'–5', avg. 4' st. Addr.	7	13	9
1647	CLEVELAND, JOHN. *Poems*, ed. Berdan, 1903.	4'–5' st. Addr.	7	17	10
	COWLEY, ABRAHAM. *The Mistress. Works* (8th ed., London, 1693).	4'–5' st.	7	13	11
1648	HERRICK, ROBERT. *The Hesperides. Complete Poems*, ed. Grosart, 3 vols. (London, 1876).	4'–5' st. Addr., narr.	7	13	11
1649	DRYDEN, JOHN. "Upon the Death of Lord Hastings," in *Lacrymae Musarum*, 1649; and later elegies, in *Poetical Works*, ed. W. D. Christie (New York, Macmillan, 1921).	5' cpl. Addr.	10	16	10
	LOVELACE, RICHARD. *Lucasta. The Poems*, ed. C. H. Wilkinson (Oxford, Clarendon Press, 1925).	4'–5' cpl., st. Addr.	8	13	10

The tables for the 1640's show, in the full detail of a decade, the wide range of agreed experiment, the deep sort of individualism, the clear division into kinds. It was a full-bodied poetic decade which began with the posthumous poems of Carew, Donne, and Jonson, moved to Milton, Waller, Crashaw, and ended with the maturity of Herrick, the youth of Dryden. Its titles are religious, philosophical, pastoral, political, amorous, elegiac. Its forms are more often now stanzaic than coupleted, though the couplet maintains its strength within the stanza. Its vocative address is most common, in the tradition of Wyatt and Surrey, and the older narrative structure is subordinate. Its average proportioning is much like that of the preceding century's, with a slightly increased stress on the adjectival. Carew's 8-15-11 closely represents it.

1640's: Table 2   Proportions in Order of Adjectival Emphasis

Poet	Adjectives	Nouns	Verbs
HARVEY	6	12	10
SUCKLING	6	13	12
JONSON	6	14	12
WITHER	7	14	11
DONNE	7	13	12
VAUGHAN	7	13	9
COWLEY	7	13	11
SHIRLEY	7	14	11
HERRICK	7	13	11
DENHAM	7	15	9
CLEVELAND	7	17	10
LOVELACE	8	13	10
CAREW	8	15	11
SANDYS	8	17	9
DRYDEN	10	16	10
QUARLES	10	17	13
CRASHAW	10	18	11
WALLER	11	19	10
MILTON	12	16	8
MORE	12	18	10

Its range has widened considerably: from the usual 6 or 7 adjectives in 10 lines of Jonson and Donne to the 12 in 10 of Milton and More: in this decade are a half dozen poets who employ one epithet or more per line, making with their many nouns and few verbs a substantival ratio sometimes three times the predicative, and therefore collaborating in a style of effect strongly different from the average in the period and from most but Sackville's in the 1540's. Verbs and nouns have consolidated rather than widened; from Milton's 8 to Quarles' 13 verbs and from Donne's 13 to Waller's 19 nouns is not so wide a gap as that of the 1540's, for both noun and verb have lessened somewhat in extremes, as adjective has expanded. In other words, in the 1640's there is less variety in the proportioning of parts of speech and, indeed, a good deal of close agreement; but at the same time, through the agency of adjectival usage, two stylistic extremes are clarified, the larger, the Donnic, in continuity from the 1540's, the smaller, the Miltonic, in continuity it may be surmised from the intervening decades of Spenser. Table 2, by its arrangement on the adjectival basis, makes clear the two sorts of proportions which amount to styles, with Donne's few nouns, Milton's few verbs, not idiosyncratic but individualistically typical.

Table 3 presents the higher ratio of adjectives in specific form, two more major ones, *fair* and *sweet*, of a sense quality to accompany increase of *day*, *heart*, *love*, and addition of *earth*, *eye*, *heaven*, *soul*, most closely and consistently massed at the Miltonic or adjectival side of the page. Verbs, both old and new, are stronger at the Donnic side, as proportioning also would have led one to expect. In major unanimities, *eye* has been added to *man* while both *find* and *give* have supplemented *make* and *see*.

THE PRIMARY LANGUAGE OF POETRY

The decade is a more receptive, a more admiring, a more closely interworking one, as the many pairs of opposites suggest. Extra-strong uses like Vaughan's *day*, Shirley's and Crashaw's *eye*, Harvey's and Sandys' *God*, Carew's *heart*, the many Miltonic *heavens*, Donne's great *love* outverbalizing all the rest in his characteristic repetition, Jonson's *man*, Dryden's *soul*, and the many *makes*, represent again, as one reads down the list, the consolidations in the 1640's both in agreement and in emphatic repetition. Across the page, on the other hand, the blanks in the interest of Denham, Cleveland, Milton in most of the standard nouns reveal an individualism still strong as Skelton's, a 50 per cent disagreement. And, further, the two sides of the page present two sides of the poetry, one predicative, the other substantive, even in the mass of major words.

. . . .

1640's: Table 3   Majority Vocabulary: In 1,000 Lines 10 Uses by 10 Poets or More

Word	Harvey	Suckling	Wither	Jonson	Donne	Vaughan	Cowley	Shirley	Herrick	Denham	Cleveland	Lovelace	Carew	Sandys	Dryden	Quarles	Crashaw	Waller	Milton	More	Total no. of users
fair		10				10	20	15				15	20	15		15	35	30	10	10	12
good	30	20	10	25	20			10	10	10	10	10			20	25	10	15	10	30	16
great	10	15	15	10			15	15		20			15		10	20	10	20	20	25	14
sweet				10					15		10			15	10		15	10	10	10	10
day		10	15	10	15	30	10	10	10			15	10	15	15	20	15		10		15
earth	10					10	10					10	10	10	10	10	10			10	10
eye		15	10	15	20	10	10	30	10	10	10	20	25	20	10	25	50	20	15	10	19
God	30		25	10		10	15			10		10	15	30	10	10	15	10	10	15	15
heart	10	15	15	10	25		15	25	10			10	30	15	10	20	15	15		10	16
heaven	10				15	15	10				15		10	10	10	45	30	15			11
love		50		30	110		60	35	40	20	20	15		65	25	10	15	40		15	16
man	30	30	20	45	20	10	30	15	20	15	15	10	10	10		10	15	15		25	18
soul	10			15	15	15	15			10		15	15	20	35	10	10			15	13
time	10	15	15		10	10	10					10	10		10	20					10
bring	10	15	20			15	10	10	10	10		10				10	10	10			12
come		20	15	10	15	20	15	20	30	10				15	15	15	20	10	15		15
find	10	15	15	10	30	15	15	10	10	15		10	10	10	10	20	10	10	15		18
give		15	15	10	10	10	20	15	20	10	20	10		20	10	25	20	15	10	10	19
go			10		15	10	10		20		10				10		10		10	10	11
know	10	20	15	25	15	15	20	10	20	15	10	15	20		20	25	10	15	10		18
make	25	25	25	45	30	15	30	35	30	30	20	20	20	15	15	45	45	30	10	25	20
see	25	15	25	25	20	25	25	30	20	10	15	25	15	15	15	15	55	15	10	25	20
take	15	15	10	20	10	10	15			15			10	10	15					10	12
tell		10	10	15	10		10	10	10					10		20		10		10	11
think	10	20	10	15	20	10	15		10	10	10				20	10					21
Total of major words used	16	20	18	19	17	19	22	19	17	15	14	18	16	19	19	23	22	18	15	17	

On a scale representing the decade's range of poetic reference, with Harvey at one end and More at the other, Jonson and Donne rest beside Harvey; Waller and Milton beside More. The minor men mark the limits, the major men are beside them just within the limits. The matter of difference, then, is more than a matter of minor followers of two great traditions, the Elizabethan and the Jacobean, the Spenserian and the Metaphysical, the Neo-Platonic and the Neo-Aristotelian, the Cavalier and the Puritan; and it is less than the matter of these traditions themselves with all their ramifications. Centrally it is a matter of how poets write poetry, and how in any one time, while sharing the interests and manners of that time, poets make choices as wide apart as possible, within the range of choice afforded them by the idiom of the time. So *Under-wood* opposes "Lycidas," the posthumous work, the youthful; so Wither's poems oppose Waller's in 1645; so Vaughan as one kind of metaphysician opposes Crashaw as another in 1646; so the mature Herrick's *Hesperides* of 1648 opposes the immature Dryden's "Hastings" of 1649. So the focus of a unity of time brings clear the variety of type; and so in converse the individual reaches are seen to be bound and confirmed in the common grasp.

Perhaps the poet best to represent the solidest ramifications of the extreme position is Ben Jonson, to whom many younger poets were pleased to call themselves "son," as they modified his position toward the central agreement of their own.[2] Most modern critics think of Jonson, I suppose, as a strong and mild but somewhat dull example of what was most standard in his age. Rather, he was a radical poet, allied with Donne against a large field. He was a poet of the power of predicates and infrequent epithets. He was a poet of both Lord and Lady.

> Heare mee, O God!
> A broken heart,
> Is my best part:
> Use still thy rod,
> That I may prove
> Therein, thy Love....

and,

> Let it not your wonder move,
> Lesse your laughter; that I love.
> Though I now write fiftie yeares,
> I have had, and have my Peeres;
> Poets, though devine are men:
> Some have lov'd as old agen.
> And it is not alwayes face,
> Clothes, or Fortune gives the grace;
> Or the feature, or the youth:

---

[2] Saintsbury would agree, calling Jonson "the greatest single tutor and teacher of the verse of the mid-seventeenth century"—that era which revealed the "almost incomprehensible blowing of the wind of the spirit in a particular direction for a certain space of time." *Minor Poets of the Caroline Period*, I, vii.

> But the Language, and the Truth,
> With the Ardor, and the Passion,
> Gives the Lover weight, and fashion.

Thus he begins a hymn to God the Father, thus he begins "A Celebration of Charis" in *Ten Lyrick Peeces*. Love is again the bond between, and art is again the immortalizing force. Every word in the two passages is essentially familiar to the reader of the poetry of the 1640's. Adjectives are scarce, and there is a verb to almost every line. The structure is rhymed, coupleted, addressed. These are indeed poems of the 1640's, but with restraint.

For Jonson, three of the time's four major adjectives, six of the ten nouns, ten of the eleven verbs, were major. He stressed *good, great, sweet,* but not *fair; day, eye, god, heart, love, man,* but not the abstractions of *heaven, soul,* and *time;* his verbs were active and strong, *know, make, see, tell* used more often apiece than most other poets used them. Among secondary terms, he ignored the sensory in favor of epithets like *poor* and *true*, nouns like *face, life, name, nature, son, world,* verbs like *call, grow, look, love*. He ignored the *bright, dark, rich, soft* of a Crashaw, the *king* of a Wither, the *sun* and *tear* of a Donne or Carew, the *seem* and *shine* of a Cowley. His common, active language was neither one of appearances nor one of speculations, but rather one of event in thought or deed, and so slighted the aesthetics of substance and quality.

Most of the poems in *Under-wood* are stanzaic, the rest tetrameter couplet, or pentameter. The stanzas have not so much the intricate qualities of songs as the neat qualities of couplets. Here is one of the most metrically complex of the brief poems:

> On A Lovers Dust
> Made Sand for an Houre Glasse
>
> Doe but consider this small dust,
>   Here running in the Glasse,
>   By Atomes mov'd;
>   Could you beleeve, that this,
>   The body was
>   Of one that lov'd?
> And in his Mrs. flame, playing like a flye,
>   Turn'd to cinders by her eye?
> Yes; and in death, as life unblest,
>   To have't exprest,
> Even ashes of lovers find no rest.

The variations of accent play around the four-accent base of the first and last lines, which in themselves provide the idea of the poem, and which carry the echo of the major rhyme. The various rhymes set up in the first three lines are extended through the rest, with the exception of the couplet of former life, the *fly-eye* couplet; and the last line finishes with a sort of delayed couplet neatness. Not so elaborate in rhyme and accent interweaving as Cowley for example, Jonson exhibits a sense of patness, and perhaps more ear for inner pattern in the cross reference of consonants in this poem.

Note, too, how it is characteristic of his use of language. Adjectives, except verbal ones, are at a minimum. Dust, glass, atoms, body, flame, fly, cinders, ashes, lovers, the nouns extend the central figure. The central thought, on the other hand, in either first and last line, or the first question, is carried by verbs in the now familiar structure of address: "Doe but consider . . . / Could you beleeve, that this, / The body was / Of one that lov'd?"

Of the two dozen or so first poems of *Under-wood*, two-thirds begin with some form of address: Let . . . , See, . . . , Guess, . . . , Come, let us . . . , Oh, doe not . . . , Consider, . . . , Take pity . . . , If, Sackville, . . . , Wake, friend, . . . , and so on,—and many then proceed through persuasion or illustration to a conclusion or question which keeps involved the subject of address. Only a few contain a simple narrative or listing progression, as "A Nymph's Passion" begins, "I love, and he loves me againe, / Yet dare I not tell who"; and then lists the qualities of her lover throughout five stanzas of telling yet not telling. Full of "eyes so round and bright," Summer sky, and love's Torches, such lines still contain some complexity of argument, and as so complex are more actually characteristic than the more famous "O so white! O so soft! O so sweet is she!" of the fourth Charis lyric.

I should suggest as representative of the true idiosyncrasy of Jonson's style the first lines of "An Epistle to Master John Selden."

> I know to whom I write: Here, I am sure,
> Though I am short, I cannot be obscure:
> Lesse shall I for the Art or dressing care,
> Truth, and the Graces best, when naked are.
> Your Booke, my Selden, I have read, and much
> Was trusted, that you thought my judgement such
> To aske it: though in most of workes it be
> A pennance, where a man may not be free,
> Rather than Office, where it doth or may
> Chance that the Friends affection proves allay
> Unto the Censure. Yours all need doth flie
> Of this so vitious Humanitie.

The sixteen verbs in these twelve lines are a great excess for poetry, but they are the very excess which Jonson, like Wither, Vaughan, and Donne felt to be poetic. The couplets are average enough, the address and argument familiar, the vocabulary of art, truth, grace, office, and friendship, strong and common; the special sound which Jonson gives to the language lies in brevity and persistency of statement. Sentences are to be weighed as sentences.

Fond of paradox like his time, Jonson presents to us, then, his own stylistic paradox. He is at once radical and conventional. He invents no new major or even secondary vocabulary, he shares the verse forms and thought forms of the decade following his death; yet he uses to an extreme that trait of his time which put up to poetry the activity of predication, which made the poem a process in which reader and writer both proposed, demonstrated, argued, disproved, questioned, responded, and so participated. Such a process and emphasis colored sound and syntax, as well as reference, filling the poem with the tone and structure of talk. As adjective and noun present substance, so predicate presents relationship and response. It was this sense of relationship which Jonson drew upon, if not always with skill, yet always with sympathy, to make a significance for his poetic sons, who moderately, and each in his own way, went to do likewise.

John Donne, whom Jonson admired and referred to with refrain-like consistency in his talks with Drummond, shared the poetic speech, yet spoke likewise in his own way. Elsewhere[3] I have tried to describe his way with adjectives and adjective structures, his scanty and conceptual use of them. Now it is possible to see that much of his method he shared with his late contemporaries, and that it was associated also with scant use of nouns and strong use of verbs. Donne, in fact, used fewer nouns than any other of the twenty poets, and more verbs than any but Jonson. He, too, pushed to an extreme the style which he shared. Most of the major terms he agreed on with Wither, Jonson, Vaughan, and then used one of these, *love*, more than a hundred times in a thousand lines, more than twice the amount of anybody else's most enthusiastic repetition. In his own special adjectives, the thousand lines of *bad*, *new*, *old*, *true*, reflect the emphasis of his whole concordance. In his secondary nouns, to the Jonsonian *face*, *name*, *world*, he adds characteristically more concrete emphases, on *death*, *tear*, *sun*, *thing*, and his temporal interest in *year*. In secondary verbs, his noun insistences are repeated in to *die* and to *love*. The traits which seemed so strong in adjective usage, then—the strong repetitive use of a few terms, the vivid appearance of some emphasis upon objects in the outer world, the preoccupation with negatives, and with time,—seem to be repeated through all the textures of his reference, and to singularize him in the midst of his wide stylistic agreements upon man, love, goodness, death, and thought, in stanza and couplet arguments with his love, and with, in his intensive fashion, himself.

"Love's Usury" sets forth many of its author's qualities in these matters.

> For every houre that thou wilt spare mee now,
>   I will allow,
> Usurious God of Love, twenty to thee,
> When with my browne, my gray haires equall bee;
> Till then, Love, let my body raigne, and let
> Mee Travell, sojourne, snatch, plot, have, forget,
> Resume my last yeares relict: think that yet
>   We'had never met.

The couplet rhyme in stanzaic form is familiar, and the structure of address and request. The God of Love is familiar, even under the special epithet put upon him. The browne and gray are characteristically used by Donne as epithets not of sense

---

[3] *Major Adjectives in English Poetry.*

but of concept. The hour and year are part of his preoccupation, the body too, and the relict one of his noted technical references. The rest are verbs in great variety and some familiarity in *let, think, met*, their excess of fourteen in eight lines suggesting Donne's active emphasis. The stanza is a 1640 stanza, earlier written though it was, in vocabulary, sound, and structure of argument; it is especially Donne's in its self-assertion. The next two stanzas develop an excessive paradox with authority. The average petition takes on a kind of bargaining power with Donne's desperate and direct attack.

> Spare mee till then, I'll beare it, though she bee
> One that loves mee.

This is the poetry, the music, the rhyme, the thought, the argument, of pure verbs. Or recall "A Feaver," for an example of Donne's neatness:

> Oh doe not die, for I shall hate
> All women so, when thou art gone,
> That thee I shall not celebrate,
> When I remember, thou wast one. . . .
>
> These burning fits but meteors bee,
> Whose matter in thee is soone spent.
> Thy beauty, and all parts, which are thee,
> Are unchangeable firmament.
>
> Yet t'was of my minde, seising thee,
> Though it in thee cannot persever.
> For I had rather owner bee
> Of thee one houre, than all else ever.

In these verses the address is to the love rather than the god, the phrasing compacter, the rhyming closer, the argument still involved in analogies, but the stress is the same, assertive and predicative. Adjectives, except for the numerals, and *unchangeable*, are minor; nouns provide a selection for illustrative reference; it is the verbs which make the sense, as the whole of the first stanza suggests.

Like Jonson, like his sons, Donne varies the patterns of his many poems, but maintains as close norm the four- or five-beat line rhymed in couplets. He maintains, too, the norm of conversation, in plea, query, imperative, beginning: "I wonder, by my troth, what thou, and I"; "Goe, and catche"; "Now thou hast lov'd me"; "Busie old foole"; "For Godsake hold your tongue"; "Sweetest love"; "'Tis true, 'tis day"; "I'll tell thee now"; "Let me powre forth"; "Marke but this flea"; and so on; and ending in a kind of agreement or resolution in "none can die"; "I may thinke so too"; "thy spheare"; "A patterne of your love"; "ne'r parted bee"; "to marke when, and where the darke eclipses bee"; "and hastes the others death"— these concluding phrases being the last part, often, of a coupleted, a fully completed, ending. Recognizably Donne's as many of these phrases are to us, in content and structural suggestion they could begin or end most poems of the decade, except when some felicity or audacity even in so brief compass marks the extra power of mind and skill of craft. And of that skill of craft Donne, like Cowley and his colleagues, was aware. He shared the self-consciousness which analogized lover and poet, body and book, and which therefore expressed in every double turn of phrase a seriousness of relative vision.

. . . .

In this ceremonial manner [typical of Waller and, to some degree, of Denham], something thoroughgoing and persistent has been added to the poetry of the 1640's. Waller's occasional poems, with their scenic backgrounds, are not characteristic of the number of poets we have been observing; not of Cowley, Carew, Donne, not even of the masque-writing Jonson or the Biblical Sandys. Rather, suggestions of Waller's descriptive pomp may be remembered from poets of the epithetical pole, from More's Spenserians, Crashaw's lengthening decorative line, the pastoral backgrounds to Quarles' dialogues. The poets of epithet and substantive are the poets also of an altered or altering structure, a structure descriptive rather than discursive.

Dryden was the most temperate of these reformers, steering his poetic course down center and only gradually shifting from Donne's "wit" to Waller's "poetry."[4] His first poem, "Upon the Death of Lord Hastings," published together with thirty-two other elegies on the young lord's death, in *Lachrymae Musarum* in 1649—and by this date justifying Dryden's inclusion here, though most of his poems are later[5]—begins in medium fashion with an addressed question rather abstractly assumed, a ceremonious but not a descriptive manner:

> Must noble Hastings immaturely die,
> The honour of his ancient family?
> Beauty and learning thus together meet
> To bring a winding for a wedding sheet?
> Must Virtue prove Death's harbinger? must she,
> With him expiring, feel mortality?

The sharpness of the sad inquiring paradox is its "wit"; the smoothness of even-paced, poised, and balanced line is its "poetry," for Dryden.

Though the sharp and abstract terms of wit maintain the nature of Dryden's writing, they are increasingly modified toward the smooth and descriptive. Epistle or "To . . ." poems are relatively infrequent, and occasion poems have taken their place. Set beside the active personal address of "To the memory of Mr. Oldham,"

> Farewell, too little and too lately known,
> Whom I began to think and call my own,

---

[4] "Doctor Donne, the greatest wit, though not the best poet, of our nation." Dedication to "Eleonora," 1692.

[5] Andrew Marvell, also appearing early in the same volume, uses much the same reference and structure pattern as Dryden's.

the more static frame of "On the Monument of the Marquis of Winchester," which is filled to its limits with far-reaching epithets:

> He who in impious times undaunted stood
> And midst rebellions durst be just and good, ...
> Such souls are rare, but mighty patterns given
> To earth were meant for ornaments to Heaven.

Or the first of "Eleonora":

> As when some great and gracious monarch dies,
> Soft whispers first and mournful murmurs rise
> Among the sad attendants; then the sound
> Soon gathers voice and spreads the news around, ...
> So slowly, by degrees, unwilling Fame
> Did matchless Eleonora's fate proclaim,
> Till public as the loss the news became.

In the latter regular and substantial procedures of numbers rather than in the former colloquialism is to be seen the major framework of Dryden's verse. Wit and master of the abstract though he seems in comparison with Pope, the frame even of his satires is descriptive and ceremonial in Waller's and Milton's manner. So "Absalom and Achitophel":

> In pious times, ere priestcraft did begin,
> Before polygamy was made a sin,
> Where man on many multiplied his kind,
> Ere one to one was cursedly confined,

and "MacFlecknoe":

> All human things are subject to decay
> And, when Fate summons, monarchs must obey

and "Religio Laici":

> Dim as the borrowed beams of moon and stars
> To lonely, weary, wandering travellers
> Is Reason to the soul: ...

and "The Hind and the Panther":

> A milk-white Hind, immortal and unchanged,
> Fed on the lawns and in the forest ranged;
> Without unspotted, innocent within,
> She feared no danger, for she knew no sin.

These stately beginnings employ the standard vocabulary and substance of the 1640's, of goodness and soul, earth and heaven, greatness and fate, fear and mortality, piety and sin, monarch and man, for Dryden was faithful to the major terms, and not highly inventive of his own. But the vocabulary here is given a fuller measure than by most poets of the 1640's: every line marked to its full extent, more substantives, and more epithets for them, a range of generalization and liberality of remark which is limited less by logic of situation or extent of the attender's listening and reasoning powers than by the poise and balance of the even lines themselves. Here is almost the classical "golden" line of Ovid, as Dryden describes it in his *Essay on Translation*: "two substantives and two adjectives, with a verb betwixt them to keep the peace." It is a line which omits, in the spirit of the Dedication to the *Aeneis*, articles, pronouns, "and other barbarities on which our speech is built by the faults of our forefathers." It is a full and framing line. Short poems are fewer; the ends, being farther from the beginnings, are less poetically conditioned by them in close patterns, and provide often a kind of descriptive frame, rather than an end in any directed sense. The famous ode to Mrs. Anne Killigrew, for example, begins with semiscene:

> Thou youngest virgin-daughter of the skies,
> Made in the last promotion of the blest;
> Whose palms, new plucked from Paradise,
> In spreading branches more sublimely rise,
> Rich with immortal green above the rest:

and ends with semiscene, after a wide tracing through the realms of poetry, pastoral, and politics:

> There thou, sweet saint, before the quire shall go,
> As harbinger of Heaven, the way to show,
> The way which thou so well hast learned below.

Not exposition of the central point of death, but amplification of the central quality of goodness, has been achieved. In this manner of narrative sweep and setting, under precise and ingenious variety of metrical control with the regular line, the poetry of qualification expands.

Milton is, as may be surmised, such poetry's major master. He sweeps and expands every part of it: loosens its rhyme, draws out its sentence structure, extends its periods, elaborates its argument, piles up its scenes, increases its epithets, originates its main terms' emphases, and moves farthest from its central agreements as from the agreements of all the poetry in its time. What Crashaw does in exaggerating and intensifying the metaphysical norm, and what More does in earnestly and thoroughly following a borrowed mode as far from the norm as possible, Milton combines, making, with the fervor of the one and the persistence of the other, a massive shift in the decade's tone and content.

His poems published in 1645 have many metrical styles. The "Nativity" plays in complex lyrical fashion upon the short couplet base, as do so many Cavalier love poems. "L'Allegro" and "Il Penseroso" are in standard octosyllabics. But "Lycidas" frees the rhyme and accent pattern, upon a blank verse base, and "Comus" works in blank verse, with interludes. This volume at the middle of the decade mixed much that was familiar with much that was surprising in sound; so too in sense.

Milton used fewer, less than two-thirds, of the major terms than almost any other poet. He was short on the standard epithets of *good, fair, great, sweet;* he stressed almost none of the nouns but *god, heaven, eye;* he used with any enthusiasm only *come,* and *go,* and *see.* Among secondary terms, he shared with Waller a preference for *high;* with Vaughan, Herrick, Lovelace, Sandys, Crashaw, More, a preference for *night;* with Donne, Vaughan, and Carew for *sun;* with many for *hear* and *live;* with Cowley, Shirley, Dryden for *sing.* All these terms share a tone, I think; not one of cerebration, but one of sensory range and vitality. So too his own special repetitions caught not verbs, not actions, but felt nouns like *air* and *light,* and minor epithets like *bright, dark, gentle, solemn, foul, mighty, mortal, loud, sad, soft, fresh, green,* making a steady sensory adjectival texture.

Milton used more adjectives and fewer verbs in these poems of 1645 than any poet of the decade. And he made this shift in poetic emphasis without any great change in poetic line, using about the same proportion of four- and five-accent lengths that Jonson did with reverse emphasis. Milton said no more in the line, but something different. Not "I know to whom I write," but

> Hence loathed Melancholy
> Of Cerberus and blackest midnight born,
> In Stygian Cave forlorn
> 'Mongst horrid shapes, and shrieks, and sights unholy, . . .

The structure follows from this approach. As address here takes the formal and "passionate" shape of invocation, and as paradox here takes the more sensuous shape of simple contrast, so:

> But come thou Goddess fair and free,
> In Heav'n yclep'd Euphrosyne, . . .
>
> And if I give thee honour due,
> Mirth, admit me of thy crew
> To live with her, and live with thee, . . .
>
> To hear the Lark . . .
>
> Straight mine eye hath caught new pleasures
> Whilst the Lantskip round it measures,
> Russet Lawns and Fallows Gray, . . .
>
> Hard by, a Cottage chimney smokes, . . .
>
> Tow'red cities please us then, . . .
>
> These delights if thou canst give,
> Mirth, with thee I mean to live.

The progression is serial, not syllogistic; descriptive, not reasoning; and within each separate stage, a list of items, of color, variety, allusion, provides the illustrative substance.

In many separate poetical aspects, then, and in their interrelation, Milton constructed what was in his time an extreme of style. One may venture to call "Miltonic," at least Miltonic for the 1640's, a verse in which the content and structure require more adjectives than verbs, and in which participial adjectives dominate numerical, and descriptive all others, and in which few conceptual terms are shared, the nouns and verbs like the epithets being scenic and sensory; in which the linear pattern has an extreme length, flow, and fullness, the sharpness of rhyme exchanged for the sonority of internal correspondences, the amount of content as distinguished from connectives greater per line; in which the structure of thought is demonstrative and cumulative, a structure of description.

"Lycidas" may serve as an example of the way these traits function, and may suggest the major contrast to the elegiac technique of Donne or Jonson. Its open sound and motion, and ceremonial stress, and regular qualitative series are all familiar as a kind.

> Yet once more, O ye Laurels, and once more
> Ye Myrtles brown, with Ivy never sere,
> I come to pluck your Berries harsh and crude,
> And with forc'd fingers rude,
> Shatter your leaves before the mellowing year.
> Bitter constraint, and sad occasion dear,
> Compels me to disturb your season due:
> For Lycidas is dead, dead ere his prime,
> Young Lycidas, and hath not left his peer:
> Who would not sing for Lycidas?

The strongest content of these lines consists in the brown, sere, harsh, crude, rude, mellowing, bitter, sad, dear, due, young, dead, dead, rather than in I come, shatter, compels, hath not left, would not sing, which are less frequent and less full of the significance of atmosphere. The sound, like the sense, repeats its theme, in the length of once more . . . once more, the fall from *b*s to *d*s in dead, and dead, the linear and cross-linear alliteration. The structure of the sentence begins by address, as we may expect, but it is the ceremonial address of invocation. From then on, there is little complexity of subordination; the statements work in an accumulating parallel fashion. The steps of the whole poem move thus: Lycidas must not go unwept. Begin, then, to sing as I would be sung. We saw together the rural sights. Now Lycidas will see them no more. Where were ye Nymphs, and where your aid, when he died? What avail the earnest shepherd's labours? Neptune, Camus, report upon Lycidas, and St. Peter regrets the sacrifice of good shepherds for bad. Return, Sicilian Muse, and bid the Vales cast their beauties here for Lycidas, wherever far away his bones are hurled. Weep no more, Shepherds, for Lycidas has mounted high and will be the Genius of the shore. So sang the swain, and rose: Tomorrow to fresh Woods, and Pastures new.

Each of these stages, simple and uncomplicated in its logic, is made elaborate by its scenes and allusions. Each is given scope by pastoral, classical, political, or Biblical reference, and is given substance by the epitheted setting: first the bitter shrubs, then the dewy fields, the face of Orpheus down the swift Hebrus, Amaryllis in the shade, the level brine, the scrannel Pipes of wretched straw, the Bells and Flowrets of a thousand hues, the stormy Hebrides, the Saints above, the Oaks and rills, all listed in their features and associations.

The richness of "Lycidas" resides in these features and associations, the scope and density of their coverage, rather than in the working out of thought in syntax. Once more—Begin—the change—Alas—But now—Next—Last—Return—Weep no more—Thus sang—is the syntax of demonstrative performance, pulling the stops in the tones of music, now loud, now soft, now near, now far. Within its simplest frames comes the full variety of qualitative reference.

Much of this reference is central to the decade: sad occasion, denial vain, gentle Muse, fair peace, flock, fountain, fresh dews of night, bright, Heav'n's descent, glad sound, sacred head, foul contagion, dread voice, flowers, eyes, tears, world, great vision, nuptial song, blest Kingdoms, joy and love, dead, weep, singing, glory. Some is especially Milton's: forc'd fingers rude, wat'ry bier, high Lawns, morn, sultry horn, westering wheel, gadding Vine, shaggy top, hideous roar, gust of rugged wings, Inwrought with figures dim, lean and flashy songs, the Pansy freakt with jet, whelming tide, fable of Bellerus, In solemn troops, and sweet Societies—all these which by accentuation of sound pattern, of sensory quality, of participial suspension, of height, power, decoration, and ceremony, did not abandon the standard content but increased and dowered it.

. . . .

The life of the poet is the life of his poetic medium; it comes to him from the past, speaks to him and through him in the present, survives for him into the future. It is never his life alone; even in the rarest materials of measure, word, and syntax, and more complexly in the whole sentences and sentiments of his time and type of poetry, it is shared. The highest degree of individuality makes choices and uses of major material less than halfway original, commonly agreeing, if not with a contemporaneous majority, at least with a minority kind, or with an earlier or later majority. So Cowley and Shirley were of the majority in their time, and shared with yet differed from Quarles, who agreed with a somewhat fuller emphasis; so Harvey and Wither looked back to earlier uses as Baldwin and Sackville had looked forward. So Donne with his many verbs, negatives, abstractions, repetitions, and Milton with his many epithets, qualities, heights and depths, and Vaughan with his condensed clouds and Crashaw with his expanded tears, and Harvey and More with their deliberate imitations of the extremes of types, and Jonson and Dryden with their radical neutralities, all stressing as they did their particular variations upon theme, yet assumed the presence and the power of the theme as the language of their time and of their poetic heritage enunciated it.

. . . Certain very specific qualities mark the theme the poets of the 1640's spoke:

qualities rising, as we have seen, from the opposition and interplay of the realms of the human and divine. The major vocabulary speaks for just these realms, as in the 1540's it had not; the four-accented couplet measure, its variety in length, stress, rhyme, and their relations, rather than in inner harmonizings, indicates the tight external control of the poetic craftsman over these double worlds; the vocative petition and supplication and argument of structure temper this control with the suggestion of mortal humility under the poetic arrogance, the tenuous position of earthly lover and spiritual sinner and traditional subject of the muse.

The storytelling, third-person narrative, primarily human though often allegorical, of the sixteenth century has turned to prayer, first- and second-personal, playful or solemn but in forms intensely rational, binding, such is the classical power of art and the force of metaphysical belief, the worlds of earth and heaven not naturally bound. Activities of construction and discovery are primary for almost all poets; the nouns of man, his love and his vision, his epithet of goodness, belong to most. The world of secondary stresses is a world of physical parts, of temporal measures, of human values and standards conditioned by the divine. Few external objects are major, and these of the heavenly landscape, air, cloud, sun, fire, or of the pastoral, lamb, sheep, water, flower, rose, in the special contexts of individual choice or tradition. Few sheer feelings are major—love, tears, joy, woe, and the adjectival happy, proud, sad. Neither strongly objective nor strongly subjective, the secondary vocabulary is rather one of concept: of old, high, true, of death, nature, power, sin, of fate, foe, folly, wit, and word; and in this character it matches the primary terms of earth and heaven, God and man, heart and soul.

This is the poetry often called witty, conceited or conceptual, figurative, Cavalier, Puritan, Platonic, Petrarchan, heroic, lyric, baroque, metaphysical. Its major language shows how easily it is all of these. The structure is one of reason, the terms abstract, the minor earthly detail figuring forth the spiritual, the Cavalier making a heaven of earth, the Puritan an earth of heaven, the various secular and religious versions of Platonism preserving the idea in the object, the expanse of imagination magnificent and domesticated, the individual cry strong and controlled, the reaches and juxtapositions daring and elaborate, the physical always and powerfully subordinated to and informed by the metaphysical, God in heart, soul in eye, time in day.

FROM *Language*

❧ FRITZ STRICH ❧

Fritz Strich—professor for many years, first in Munich and later in Bern —has written frequently on German literature, his books ranging from *Die Mythologie in der deutschen Literatur von Klopstock bis Wagner* (1910), through *Goethe und die Weltliteratur* (1946) and *Der Dichter und die Zeit* (1947) to *Kunst und Leben* (1950), and including *Deutsche Klassik und Romantik, oder Vollendung und Unendlichkeit* (1922), the volume in which the selections translated here originally appeared. In *Deutsche Klassik und Romantik*, Strich is deeply influenced—as he handsomely acknowledges—by Heinrich Wölfflin, whose categories for distinguishing between renaissance and baroque style in *Principles of Art History* inform Strich's comparison of the Classical with the Romantic spirit in Germany and his differentiations between their characteristic literary products.

Strich grounds his argument in an essential polarity that he discerns in the human spirit itself, which—aware that the given "I" is necessarily transitory—is impelled to commit itself to an ideal of permanence, reaching out by an act of will to some realm of enduring value. But the ideal of permanence, of eternity, may take either of two forms, "Vollendung" or "Unendlichkeit." "Vollendung"—the conception associated with German Classicism—refers to that which is so complete in itself, so fully realized, that it seems exempt from change and so may endure timelessly through time. "Unendlichkeit"—the conception associated with German Romanticism—also refers to a version of eternity, in that what can never end can never be completed and thus remains in perpetual transformation and development, in endless becoming. The two conceptions eventuate in very different types of art, according to Strich (and here one can see the influence of Wölfflin most plainly): "Vollendung" is linked with the static, with shut forms, with clarity, with a unity achieved through the subordination of many precisely articulated details, whereas "Unendlichkeit" is linked with the dynamic, with open forms, with darkness, with a unity of movement in which imprecisely articulated details blend with one another. No summary of Strich's book can do justice to the host of distinctions that he elaborates—through chapters on man, the object, rhythm and rhyme, the inner form, the tragic and the comic—between German Classicism and Romanticism. Suffice it to say that, in comparing the two, he educes differing attitudes toward history, time, space, nature, love, and death, relating these attitudes to his governing categories of "Vollendung" and "Unendlichkeit" and illustrating the attitudes with references to a variety of literary texts.

The extracts given here come from Strich's chapter on language. The first is a brief, general comparison of Classical and Romantic conceptions of speech, a comparison which Strich goes on to develop in the book itself by contrasting two views about the origin of language, the relation of sound to meaning, the coining of words, imagery, metaphor, and word play. In the second, longer extract, Strich seeks to support his claims with quotations from Goethe, Kleist, Novalis, and Hölderlin, exploring such matters as word coinage, syntax, and the use of parallelism.

THE QUESTION, strange as it may sound, must yet be asked: can the Classical spirit ever realize itself fully in language, or is language—by its very nature as verbal expression—not bound to destroy what Classicism most basically strives for? Winckelmann spoke of the "still grandeur" of all Classical art, and does not stillness here also imply speechlessness in every sense of the word? Goethe wanted to create a still figure in Iphigenie, but is it really possible for such a figure to speak a language, to express its stillness in words? If such questions seem meaningless to the reader, it must be pointed out that Goethe wrestled desperately with them; in fact, they underlie his whole yearning for the plastic arts. He believed that he could never translate his

The excerpts from "Language," by Fritz Strich, here translated by Corinna Babb, are taken from Strich's *Deutsche Klassik und Romantik* (Munich, 1924), pp. 187–88, 204–14. Translated by permission of Francke Verlag.

ultimate vision into language—neither into German, which presented him with special obstacles, nor into any other language—for "das Wort bemüht sich nur umsonst, Gestalten schöpferisch aufzubaun [the word struggles in vain to body forth original figures]." Although Goethe wrested the utmost in the way of representational possibilities from his language, still he was not satisfied. Indeed, he must have felt it his tragic destiny to be born a poet, not a sculptor. For those beings that he envisioned could only be shaped in stone. After all, the ultimate aim of the Classical spirit, which seeks deliverance from time, is to achieve a spatial structure. That is why every Classical poetic style has shown a clear tendency toward sculpture. In the same vein, Schiller complained that language—instead of representing the object entrusted to it—robs it of sensuousness and individuality, transforming it into an intellectual abstraction; thus he contended that language could only describe, could never truly create (to Körner, June 20, 1793). Whenever Schiller wrote about the essence of beauty and art, he was always speaking about sculpture, really, and envisioning the figures of Greek art. Similarly, the esthetic of the Classical Goethe was an esthetic of the plastic arts. There is a fundamental hostility between forms that exist independently of time and language, which unfolds in time.

But now to look at the other side of the question. It was the goal of Romanticism to convert everything—not just words—into language. The very essence of Romanticism is language. But what does it seek to express with all its words and symbols? What is endless; what is unutterable. A true Romantic must also have felt it a tragic destiny to be born a poet. For words were never adequate to serve his ultimate purpose. He, too, had to struggle painfully with language, which proved much too confining a form for the boundless content of the spirit. Whereas Classical art sought its solution in approaching the condition of sculpture, Romantic art strove to become music. For while Classicism believed that its conception of the eternal idea could best be rendered in the language of the plastic arts, Romanticism thought that its experience of the one, infinite spirit could only be expressed in the language of music.

.   .   .   .

It could not normally be the goal of Classicism to free itself from what Romanticism felt to be the domination of language and its illusive character, for these were not the terms in which the Classical spirit experienced language. It did not seek to reach behind language any more than it sought to reach behind the appearances—illusory for the Romantics—of the phenomenal world. If Goethe suffered because of language, he did so only because the verbal representation never seemed quite to coincide with the phenomenon itself. And he felt that the Romantics, whenever they attempted to penetrate behind the veil of words, were guilty of using language artificially. If Goethe uses superlatives in his late style—"allschönest," "allbegabtest," "letzteste" ["the most beautiful of all," "the most gifted of all," "the very ultimate"] —these remain utterly opposed to those of the Romantics. For Goethe endeavors to express through his superlatives the purest essence, the quintessential concept—never violating the just measure of things by dissolving them in limitless feeling. The "all"—so common an element in the verbal combinations of Goethe's late style—no longer refers, as in the style of his youth, to a chaotic unity, an "all-oneness" in which every individual form must ultimately lose its contours; rather, the word refers to a cosmic interrelatedness, a manifold unity ordering its individual parts. The new compounds, which appear in his late style as often as they appeared during his *Sturm und Drang* period, no longer struggle as they did then against the precise articulation and delimitation of objects and words; rather, as in the language of Sophocles, they mass together, in the simultaneity of one plastic vision, what in the consecutiveness of time could never be isolated as such a unity ("Pappelzitterzweig," "Feuerwirbelsturm" [literally, "poplar-trembling-branch," "fire-hurricane"]). To stress the multiplicity inherent in this concept of unity, however, Goethe may in turn keep separate verbal elements that could be combined ("Farb und Bogen," "Thron und Stufe" [literally, "color and arc," "throne and step"]), thus attributing independence, individuality, and equality to the different parts. Thereby he mirrors in language once more a cosmos made up of individual units which simultaneously function as parts yet serve the whole.

Similar principles govern the sentence and its members. But first one must point out how the style of a period may easily come into conflict with that of a genre and how a period style will show itself to be more suited to one genre than to another. It follows from the objectivity of the epic perspective—in which a world seems to present itself to us, its contours and form apparently unmediated through the vision of any artist—that epic language weighs everything on the same scale. It does not subordinate or deal in dependent relations; rather, each part here acts at once as a separate entity and as a link in a chain—all of which makes for the epic's special coherence in which things steadily follow one another in time and stand next to one another in space. However, where things thrust against one another, where there are superiority and subordination, where effects are being generated out of causes, where conditions are being imposed and removed, where nothing is self-contained and everything stands in relation to something else—there we are in the realm of the dramatic style. Lyric style, finally, is typified by neither its perspective nor its aim, but by the interpenetration of form and feeling. It does not place one thing after another or relate one thing to another; instead, everything merges with everything else, all words becoming the tones of a melody whose line cannot be broken up in any way.

In what has just been said, of course, only general tendencies and extreme cases have been described. Yet it is manifest that a Classical style—in spite of Classicism's concern with preserving the distinctions between genres and forms—will remain predisposed toward the even measure of the epic, even when used in dramas or lyrics. The Classical attitude, after all, is related to the epic perspective. Schiller himself observed how, while at work under Goethe's influence on *Wallenstein*, he was overcome by an epic spirit which simplified and evened out the language of this drama. And his translation of *Macbeth*, in which Schiller endeavored to render Shakespeare's highly animated, richly hypotactic language in measured, even speech, was as much a translation from a dramatic into an epic mode as from a baroque to a Classical style.

Obviously, prose is in itself more suited than metered language to expressing relationships. One can see clearly in seventeenth-century literature that the many involuted forms so prevalent in baroque prose are not used to nearly the same extent in the poetry of the time. Even in Goethe's case, there exists a marked difference between his prose epics and his poetic epics. Moreover, in the revisions of his prose, as has often been noted, Goethe reveals a consistent tendency to cut down the number of subordinate clauses, changing them into independent clauses or at least into parts of a main clause in order to transform the subordinate construction into a coordinate one. Here is the original version of a sentence:

Wir vermeiden große Beschwerlichkeiten, gewinnen Zeit und Geld, anstatt daß jener Weg, welchen uns das Publikum vorschlägt und nach dem ich mich ... erkundigt habe, uns so weit abwärts führt und in so schlimme Wege verwickelt, daß ich nicht weiß, ob wir Hoffnung haben können, uns vor der schlimmen Jahrszeit wieder heraus zu finden, und das Ziel unserer Reise, das wir uns vorgesetzt, zu erreichen.

We avoid serious inconvenience, we gain time and money, instead of allowing that other route— which is suggested by the public and about which I ... have inquired—to lead us so far astray and get us involved with such bad roads that I do not know whether we can hope to find our way again before the bad season of the year and reach the goal that we have set for ourselves in our journey.

Goethe's revision is as follows:

Der Umweg bringt uns auch dahin, aber in welche schlimme Wege verwickelt er uns, wie weit führt er uns ab! Können wir Hoffnung haben, uns in der späten Jahrszeit wieder heraus zu finden, und was für Zeit und Geld werden wir indessen zersplittern!

The detour will bring us there also, but what bad roads it will get us involved with, how far it will lead us astray! Can we ever hope to find our way again in the late season of the year? And how much time and money will meanwhile be frittered away!

One has only to set the prose of Goethe beside Kleist's and two different worlds of style open up.

In modern philology there is a controversy over the origin and basic nature of the sentence (Wundt and Paul). Is the sentence, even before it is spoken, a self-contained and determinate image of thought which splits up into verbal units only because it is being converted into language, or is the sentence the vehicle for a thought which acquires existence and clarity only as and while it is being spoken? The truth is that this controversy concerns a question of style which cannot be settled dogmatically. There are sentences of the one kind and of the other, and which category a sentence belongs to is easily seen. In his treatise "Über die allmähliche Verfertigung der Gedanken beim Reden [Of the Gradual Completion of Thought in Speech]," Kleist has given us his answer: nothing exists before the act of speech but a shadowy, dimly suspected conception; nothing is completed; thought and image develop only in the process of speaking, just as truth comes to light only gradually through questioning in a trial; language is such a trial, such a dramatic act; it truly completes thought.

Obviously one would not make such an assertion about the Classical style of Goethe. The clarity of perspective, the balance, the structuring of Goethe's sentences could only result from a conception complete prior to its verbal formulation. The sentence served him as a kind of space to be occupied by an already developed concept. Kleist's language, on the contrary, is the perfect illustration of his theory. One usually refers to the involuted form of his sentences as "Einschachtelung" ["encapsulation": sentences composed of intricately interrelated units, one enclosed within another]. But how false is this metaphor! For Kleist's sentence is precisely not a circumscribed, static space into which other, smaller spaces can be fitted; it has no existence as an idea apart from its articulation. His sentence is one that unfolds in time, one that—as development and creative deed—shapes the world of language into history. The decisive thing here is not, as in the case of Goethe, whether a given sentence member, once begun, comes to completion, thus gaining independence and definition. At each moment, rather, language seizes on what is now, at this very instant, to be said. Until the sentence is finished, everything remains in a state of openness: becoming, growing, forming itself and clarifying itself. It is as if thought has first to be chiseled out of the stone block of language, emerging from shapelessness with each new word as it gradually acquires contour and depth.

Indeed, this form is three-dimensional. Consider these passages by Kleist and by Goethe:

Der Forstmeister fragte, *ob* er nicht glaube, daß die Person, die die Frau Marquise suche, sich finden werde?—"Unzweifelhaft!" versetzte der Graf, *indessen* er mit ganzer Seele über dem Papier lag und den Sinn desselben gierig verschlang. *Darauf, nachdem* er einen Augenblick, *während* er das Blatt zusammenlegte, an das Fenster getreten war, sagte er: "*Nun* ist es gut! Nun weiß ich, was ich zu tun habe!" kehrte sich *sodann* um, und fragte den Forstmeister noch, auf eine verbindliche Art, *ob* man ihn bald wiedersehen werde; empfahl sich ihm, und ging, völlig ausgesöhnt mit seinem Schicksal fort. (Kleist)

The forester asked whether *he did not think that the person whom the Marquise was looking for could be found.*—"*Without a doubt!*" *replied the Count,* while *he was poring over the sheet of paper and avidly devouring its contents.* Thereupon, after *having momentarily stepped to the window* as *he folded the paper, he said,* "*Now all is well! Now I know what I have to do!*" upon which *he turned away, yet still asked the forester in an obliging way* whether *one would soon see him again; he bid him adieu and left, completely reconciled to his fate.*

Dieser stieg nun die Terrassen hinunter, musterte im Vorbeigehen Gewächshäuser und Treibebeete, bis er ans Wasser, dann über einen Steg an den Ort kam, wo sich der Pfad nach den neuen Anlagen in zwei Arme teilte. Den einen, der über den Kirchhof ziemlich gerade nach der Felswand hinging, ließ er liegen, um den andern einzuschlagen, der sich links etwas weiter durch anmutiges Gebüsch sachte hinaufwand; da, wo beide zusammentrafen, setzte er sich für einen Augenblick auf einer wohlangebrachten Bank nieder, betrat sodann den eigentlichen Stieg und sah sich durch allerlei Treppen und Absätze auf dem schmalen, bald mehr, bald weniger steilen Wege endlich zur Mooshütte geleitet.
(Goethe)

He now walked down through the terraces, examined in passing the greenhouses and hotbeds, until he came to the water, then over a footbridge, to the point beyond the newly laid-out grounds where the path forked. He disregarded one path, which led rather directly through the churchyard to the face of the cliff, in order to strike off on the other, which wound, somewhat farther on, gradually upward to the left through graceful shrubs; at the place where the two paths came together again, he sat down for a moment on a welcome bench, then began the real climb and found himself at last conducted to the Mooshütte *over all kinds of steps and ledges along a narrow path, now more and now less steep.*

The form of Goethe's sentence lifts its content out of time. From the standpoint of the beholder, everything appears to move in a single plane, equally distant and equally past, and the decisive factor for the sequence of the story is its steady progression occurring at a fixed distance from the observer. Kleist, however, abandons this sort of standpoint to plunge into the depths of time. He shifts about and rearranges things so that their pure and continuous sequence is transformed into a three-dimensional time. A moment of the past becomes present for him and serves as the standpoint for his narrative. From this perspective, however, some events appear to lie still further in the past, others are contemporaneous, and still others belong to the future. Kleist's sentence creates these dimensions in time. One can verify this: it would be possible to transpose the same content into a strict sequence. But the content would then have lost all its attraction for Kleist through being deprived of movement. Kleist had to place himself in the "midst of time," as Hölderlin once said of himself, and he could not treat it as something passing by out there, at a distance from himself. This is what makes for the special plasticity of his language. Goethe, of course, would have called it the reverse of plastic because for him the sculptured was something freed from time. But Kleist's is a baroque sculpture, as is evident from the ways in which his language structures both time and space. Yet the temporal depths of this language create by all odds the more expressive effects: even where the structure of a sentence by Kleist appears to generate a spatial image of incredible plasticity, it is still in truth precisely the temporal interrelationships shaped by the language that allow for the sculptural effect.

This is by no means the verbal mode of the Romantic period as a whole; rather, it is an isolated occurrence in that period and the expression of Kleist's peculiarly strong-willed personality. It would almost appear that one could not conceive of a greater contrast than that between his language and Novalis'. Yet the two styles do resemble one another in one decisive respect. For Novalis' language shapes its materials in comparable forms of time and history. Only it does so in the spirit of the gothic rather than of the baroque. Kleist's involuted structures and depths have given way, in the language of Novalis, to the arrangement of words in many simply built sentences. A mode that Goethe used for the expression of painfully restrained movement (as at the end of *Werther*) has become the basic form of the narrative in *Ofterdingen*, characterized by its quiet, steady forward-movement. It would be wrong to explain such simplicity as the expression of an old-fashioned, childlike spirituality. This style is much too self-conscious for one not to recognize a deeper purpose in it. There is no doubt that Novalis himself believed he wrote a truly historical style.

LANGUAGE [145]

We know well what he understood by *history*: a free and creative development—exempt from causality—which possesses no coherence other than that which unites the tones of a melody. Since this language presents the narrative in so simple a form, without constructing any relationships apart from the purely melodic advance from one sentence to the next, it develops creatively and freely—just as does time—and is thus the true language of history.

> Heinrich war erhitzt, und nur spät gegen Morgen schlief er ein. In wunderliche Träume flößen die Gedanken seiner Seele zusammen. Ein tiefer blauer Strom schimmerte aus der grünen Ebene herauf. Auf der glatten Fläche schwamm ein Kahn. Mathilde saß und ruderte. Sie war mit Kränzen geschmückt, sang ein einfaches Lied und sah nach ihm mit sanfter Wehmut herüber. Seine Brust war beklommen. Er wußte nicht warum. Der Himmel war heiter, die Flut ruhig. Ihr himmlisches Gesicht spiegelte sich in den Wellen. Auf einmal fing der Kahn an sich umzudrehen. Er rief ihr ängstlich zu. Sie lächelte und legte das Ruder in den Kahn der sich immerwährend drehte. Eine ungeheure Bangigkeit ergriff ihn. Er stürzte sich in den Strom; aber er konnte nicht fort, das Wasser trug ihn. Sie winkte, sie schien ihm etwas sagen zu wollen, der Kahn schöpfte schon Wasser; doch lächelte sie mit einer unsäglichen Innigkeit und sah heiter in den Wirbel hinein. Auf einmal zog es sie hinunter. Eine leise Luft strich über den Strom, der ebenso ruhig und glänzend floß wie vorher. Die entsetzliche Angst raubte ihm das Bewußtsein. Das Herz schlug nicht mehr. Er kam erst zu sich, als er sich auf trockenem Boden fühlte. Er mochte weit geschwommen sein, es war eine fremde Gegend. Er wußte nicht, wie ihm geschehen war. Sein Gemüt war verschwunden. Gedankenlos ging er tiefer ins Land. Entsetzlich matt fühlte er sich. Eine kleine Quelle kam aus einem Hügel, sie tönte wie lauter Glocken. Mit der Hand schöpfte er einige Tropfen und netzte seine dürren Lippen. Wie ein banger Traum lag die schreckliche Begebenheit hinter ihm. Immer weiter und weiter ging er, Blumen und Bäume redeten ihn an. Ihm wurde so wohl und heimatlich zu Sinne. Da hörte er jenes einfache Lied wieder. Er lief den Tönen nach. Auf einmal hielt ihn jemand am Gewande zurück. "Lieber Heinrich," rief eine bekannte Stimme. Er sah sich um, und Mathilde schloß ihn in ihre Arme. "Warum liefst du vor mir, liebes Herz," sagte sie tiefatmend. "Kaum konnte ich dich einholen." Heinrich weinte. Er drückte sie an sich.— "Wo ist der Strom?" rief er mit Tränen. "Siehst du nicht seine blauen Wellen über uns?" Er sah hinauf, und der blaue Strom floß leise über ihrem Haupte. "Wo sind wir, liebe Mathilde?" "Bei unsern Eltern." "Bleiben wir zusammen?" "Ewig," versetzte sie, indem sie ihre Lippen an die seinigen drückte und ihn so umschloß, dass sie nicht wieder von ihm konnte. Sie sagte ihm ein wunderbares geheimes Wort in den Mund, was sein ganzes Wesen durchklang. Er wollte es wiederholen, als sein Großvater rief und er aufwachte. Er hätte sein Leben darum geben mögen, das Wort noch zu wissen.
>
> *Heinrich felt feverish, and only toward morning did he fall asleep. In wonderfully strange dreams the thoughts of his soul flowed together. A deep blue stream shimmered from the green plain below. On its even surface glided a boat. Mathilde sat and rowed. She was decked with garlands, sang a simple song and looked over to him tenderly and pensively. His chest was tight. He did not know why. The sky was serene, the water quiet. Her heavenly face was mirrored in the waves. All at once the boat started turning. He called out anxiously to her. She smiled and laid the oar in the boat, which kept turning all the while. A terrible fear took hold of him. He plunged into the current; but he could not get away, the water held him. She beckoned, she seemed to want to say something to him; the boat was taking in water already, yet she smiled with unutterable tenderness*

and gazed serenely into the whirlpool. All at once she was drawn below. A soft breeze touched the stream, which flowed along as calm and radiant as before. Overwhelming fear robbed him of consciousness. His heart ceased to beat. He came to himself only when he felt himself on dry land. He might have swum a long way; the surroundings were foreign. He did not know what had become of him. His soul had vanished. Absent-mindedly he went farther inland. He felt utterly spent. A small spring welled out from a hill; it sounded like many bells. With his hand he scooped up a few drops and wet his parched lips. Like a haunting dream, the dreadful event lay behind him. On and on he walked; flowers and trees addressed him. He began to feel at ease, as if he were at home. Then he heard the simple song again. He ran after the sound. All at once somebody held him back by the coat. "Dear Heinrich," a familiar voice called. He looked around and Mathilde embraced him. "Why did you run ahead of me, dear heart," she said, breathing heavily. "I could scarcely overtake you." Heinrich wept. He pressed her to him.—"Where is the river?" he called out, with tears in his eyes. "Don't you see its blue waves above us?" He looked up, and the blue stream flowed softly above her head. "Where are we, dear Mathilde?" "With our parents." "Will we remain together?" "Forever," she replied, while she pressed her lips to his and clasped him, never to let him go. She breathed a rare, secret word between his lips, one that reverberated through his whole being. He wanted to say it after her, when his grandfather summoned him and he woke up. He would willingly have given his life still to possess that word.

The language of [Hölderlin's] Hyperion belongs to yet another type of Romanticism. Here the sentence seems open and endless. If Goethe's Classical sentence structure contains the primary and definitive elements of a conception completed before its expression in language, in Hölderlin's sentences a feeling—through the process of becoming language—again evolves in the dimension of time, transforming itself and growing in that it remains ever open to the influx of new life. This feeling cannot "complete itself" even in the manner of Kleist, cannot arrive at a conclusion, not even gradually; it can only increase in intensity and depth. What is endless is also inexhaustible and thus perpetually requires new expression. This is what happens in Hölderlin's sentences, where words continually acquire new tonalities. They persist in transforming themselves and keep piling up, and where language is open to such a process, the possibility for growth is infinite; even when the sentence looks closed, the feeling continues to reach out beyond the finished form.

"Jawohl, mein Alabanda," sagt' ich; "da geh'n wir heiter in den Kampf, da treibt uns himmlisch Feuer zu Taten, wenn unser Geist vom Bilde solcher Naturen verjüngt ist, und da läuft man auch nach einem kleinen Ziele nicht, da sorgt man nicht für dies und das, und künstelt, den Geist nicht achtend, von außen, und trinkt um des Kelches willen den Wein; da ruh'n wir dann erst, Alabanda, wenn des Genius Wonne kein Geheimnis mehr ist, dann erst, wenn die Augen all in Triumphbogen sich wandeln, wo der Menschengeist, der langabwesende, hervorglänzt aus den Irren und Leiden und siegesfroh den väterlichen Äther grüßt.—Ha! an der Fahne allein soll niemand unser künftig Volk erkennen; es muß sich alles verjüngen, es muß von Grund aus anders sein; voll Ernsts die Lust und heiter alle Arbeit! Nichts, auch das Kleinste, das Alltäglichste nicht ohne den Geist und die Götter! Lieb und Haß und jeder Laut von uns muß die gemeinere Welt befremden und auch kein Augenblick darf *einmal* noch uns mahnen an die platte Vergangenheit!"

"Indeed, my Alabanda," I said; "then we'll go into battle serenely; then heavenly fire will drive us to action, once our spirit is rejuvenated through the example of such Natures, and then one will no longer run after petty goals, or busy oneself with all sorts of trifles, or strive for effect without regard for the meaning, or drink wine for the sake of the goblet; then we'll rest only, Alabanda, when the exultation of genius is no longer a secret, only when eyes are all transformed into arches of triumph where the human spirit, long absent, shines forth from the errors and sufferings and hails the heavenly aether victoriously.—Indeed, no one shall, in the future, recognize our people by their flag only; everything must become young again, everything must be changed utterly; full of earnestness the joy, and serene all our labor! Nothing—not even the smallest, the most commonplace—without a spiritual meaning and without the gods! Love and hate and every sound we utter must be set apart from the more vulgar world, and no moment may remind us even once of our platitudinous past!"

It is commonly said that Hyperion's language is Greek in character, and yet one could not designate it more falsely. It stands much nearer to the language of the Orient. For it progresses through parallelism, which Friedrich Schlegel once called the "geflügelte Urform der poetischen Bewegung [winged archetype of poetic movement]." As the soul, according to the belief of the Orient, migrates through the changing shapes of a constantly renewed life, so—in this parallel structure—a word, an image, or a sentence moves through the changing shapes of its expression, always the same, yet never identical with itself. For its permanence consists in transformation. It is a movement not through space but through time, a deepening, a growing in intensity. In company with an inner transformation of this sort, the repetition of form [characteristic of parallelism] expresses precisely the unity and permanence of what is being transformed. It is a perfectly open form which can endure through ever further transformations.

There is only one way in which this form may close itself off internally—namely, if the parallelism becomes an antithesis—and this is, of course, the only form in which parallelism ever entered the language of Classicism. A thought turns into its contrary, one pole becoming its opposite. Here, as before, a unity persists within the elements undergoing transformation. But the transformation itself reaches a conclusion. For the two poles—encompassing as they do opposite extremes—are not susceptible to further transformation. The possibilities are exhausted; the circle is completed. The language of Schiller is informed by a spirit of antithesis, and not only when it is philosophical. Goethe shapes antithetically those verses that are already antithetical in their rhythmic structure: alexandrines and pentameters. Antithesis could serve as the idiom of Classical polarity. When the inner polarity of the whole world became visible to Goethe late in life—a polarity through which each thing achieves its form and being—he made his language so transparent that the antithetical spirit emerges from his words: "dunkelhell," "gelassenkühn," "zartkräftig," "westöstlich," "Wechseldauer" [literally, "dark-light," "relaxed-audacious," "delicate-powerful," "western-eastern," "change-permanence"].

Linguistic Perspectivism
in the Don Quijote

❧ LEO SPITZER ❧

Certainly Leo Spitzer is among the two or three most widely known stylistic critics of the twentieth century. Master of many languages, he has written prolifically on matters involving philology, literary interpretation, and stylistic analysis, and his essays have appeared in journals the world over. Among his important books are *Stilstudien*, 2 vols. (1928), *Romanische Literaturstudien, 1936–1956* (1959), and *Linguistics and Literary History: Essays in Stylistics* (1948). This last volume, probably his best-known work in America, contains an introductory essay in which Spitzer outlines his assumptions about language and his critical method, chapters on texts by Racine, Diderot, and Claudel, and the following essay on Cervantes' *Don Quijote*.

Spitzer's position seems to me to derive, however loosely, from Benedetto Croce. For Croce, intuition is an activity of the spirit, but an activity that necessarily and simultaneously realizes itself in expression. Since the artist's intuition and expression are thus identical, we are presumably enabled—though Croce also insists that expression is definitively characterized by its achieved forms—to recreate the particular poetic process the artist has gone through if we examine his expression sensitively. For Spitzer, the language of a nation reflects its cultural and psychological activity—"*Wortwandel ist Kulturwandel und Seelenwandel*"—an idea which allies him generally with Karl Vossler, who also derives from Croce and who has concerned himself with the interrelations of the French language and French culture in the book *Frankreichs Kultur im Spiegel seiner Sprachentwicklung* (1913). Spitzer, however, concentrates primarily on individual styles, searching out the ways in which they are indicative of the minds of the particular artists: "The individual stylistic deviation from the general norm must represent a historical step taken by the writer, I argued: it must reveal a shift of the soul of the epoch, a shift of which the writer has become conscious and which he would translate into a necessarily new linguistic form; perhaps it would be possible to determine the historical step, psychological as well as linguistic?"

The mode of analysis that Spitzer describes in *Linguistics and Literary History*—an application of the "philological circle"—comprises "first observing details about the superficial appearance of the particular work ... then, grouping these details and seeking to integrate them into a creative principle which may have been present in the soul of the artist ... finally, making the return trip to all the other groups of observations in order to find whether the 'inward form' one has tentatively constructed gives an account of the whole." Thus the critic would arrive at "the common spiritual etymon, the psychological root, of several individual 'traits of style'" in the given writer, completing an analytic process which begins, for Spitzer himself, with an "awareness of having been struck by a detail" that registers as significant. In many of his essays, Spitzer claims to work back through the style only so far as to the artistic self of the writer (Croce, we may remember, distinguishes between an author's "practical" and "poetical personality," suggesting that the latter alone is deducible from a literary text). But on occasion—as in the chapter on Diderot in *Linguistics and Literary History*—Spitzer tries "to penetrate to the soul not only of the author but of the man" himself—an enterprise "legitimate only in the case of a modern author: one who enjoys the freedom permitted by the conception of the 'original genius.'"

In the essay on *Don Quijote* reprinted here, Spitzer explores a number of stylistic details—the varying names attributed to individual characters; the several etymologies presented for particular common or proper nouns; Cervantes' flexible attitude toward "refined word-usage," "dialects and jargons"—to discover their common denominator in the "linguistic perspectivism" of Cervantes. Through this perspectivism Cervantes establishes himself as a kind of God controlling the world of his book: the details of style become the means by which he asserts his creative freedom as an artist. Spitzer goes one step further, however, to declare that Cervantes, despite his exalted position in presiding as artist over the relativistic world of the novel, "never denies God," remaining "subservient to the divine" —though Spitzer bases this claim on the episode of the *Cautivo*, an episode which has been interpreted by others as questioning God and which in any case seems to reveal the same sort of linguistic perspectivism as the rest of *Don Quijote*.

While one may thus find Spitzer's ultimate deduction about Cervantes excessive in the light of the sheerly stylistic evidence at hand, the critic's verbal analysis itself is everywhere illuminating. Indeed, though his method has frequently come under attack—as in Jean Hytier's "La Méthode de M. Leo Spitzer," *The Romanic Review*, XLI (1950), 42-59—Spitzer's writings constitute a major body of stylistic criticism, individual, sensitive, provocative, full of insight.

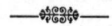

M∪CH, though not too much, has been written about Cervantes' master novel. Yet, we are still far from understanding it in its general plan and in its details as well as we do, for instance, Dante's *Commedia* or Goethe's *Faust*—and we are relatively further from an understanding of the whole than of the details. The main critical works of recent years, which represent gigantic strides forward toward the understanding of the whole, are, in my opinion, Américo Castro's *El pensamiento de Cervantes* (Madrid, 1925), in which the themes of Cervantes' poetry of ideas are stated, and Joaquín Casalduero's article in *Revista de Filología Hispánica*, II, 323, "La composición de 'El Ingenioso Hidalgo Don Quijote de la Mancha,'" in which the artistic architecture of the novel, as based on the themes recognized by Castro, is pointed out. As for the style of the novel, Helmut Hatzfeld, in his book *Don Quijote als Wortkunstwerk* (Leipzig, 1927), has attempted to distinguish different "styles" determined by previous literary traditions (the pastoral or chivalric styles, the style of Boccaccio, etc.)—without, however, achieving what I should call an integration of the historical styles into one Cervantine style in which the personality of the writer would manifest itself. Perhaps it is better not to break up the unity of a work of art into historical units which, in any case, are extraneous to Cervantes and, instead, to proceed according to a method by which one would seek to move from the periphery toward the center of the artistic globe—thus remaining within the work of art. Any one outward feature, when sufficiently followed up to the center, must yield us insight into the artistic whole, whose unity will thus have been respected. The choice of the particular phenomenon, then, would appear to be of secondary importance: any single one must, according to my ideology, give final results.

"Linguistic Perspectivism in the *Don Quijote*," in Leo Spitzer, *Linguistics and Literary History: Essays in Stylistics* (copyright 1948 by Princeton University Press; Princeton Paperback, 1967), pp. 42-85. Reprinted by permission of Princeton University Press. Material in double brackets and italic block translations are new to this edition.

Accordingly, I shall choose certain linguistic phenomena (of, at first glance, slight importance for Cervantes' artistic cosmos) which I shall attempt to reduce to a common denominator, later to bring this into relationship with the "pensamiento," the *Weltanschauung*, of Cervantes.

Any reader of the *Quijote* is struck by the instability of the names of the main characters of the novel: in the first chapter we are told by Cervantes that the protagonist has been called, by the sources of "this so truthful story," alternatively Quixada, Quesada, or Quixana (this last, according to Cervantes, being the best "conjecture"); from this assortment the "ingenioso hidalgo [ingenious gentleman]" chose, before starting his knightly career, the name that he was to bear in the whole book: Quijote. When, at the end, he is cured of the fever of quixotism and repudiates *Amadís de Gaula* and the rest of the novels of chivalry, he recovers his unpretentious prosaic original name (II, 74): "ya no soy don Quijote de la Mancha, sino Alonso Quixano a quien mis buenas costumbres me dieron renombre de Bueno [I am no longer Don Quijote of La Mancha, but Alonso Quixano, whose good habits won me the name of the Good]"; and the final scene of his Christian death and regeneration seems rounded out by a kind of baptism, as this "loco" becomes a "cuerdo [sane man]" (the change of name is thrice mentioned in this final chapter, as if the author wanted to din it into our heads that the old Adam is dead); in his will, "Quixano" calls his niece Antonia by the name Quixana, as if to emphasize that he is now a "bourgeois rangé" to the extent of having a family bearing his own (everyday) name. The first-mentioned name Quixada is also used in recognition of the reasonable side of the protagonist's nature: earlier (I, 5) he was referred to, by an acquaintance who knew him in the days before his madness, as "señor Quixada." Again, just as Quesada, Quixada, or Quixana became a Quijote when he fancied himself a knight, so, when his chivalric dreams seem about to give way to those of pastoral life, he imagines himself to be called "el pastor Quijotiz" (and his companion, Sancho Panza, "el pastor Pancino").[1] In another episode, Dorotea, who plays the role of Princess Micomicona (I, 30), feigns that her presumptive rescuer is called "[si mal no me acuerdo,] don Azote o don Jigote [[if I remember correctly,] Sir Scourge or Sir Mincemeat]." And the Countess Trifaldi jocundly endows him with the superlative for which she seems to have a predilection: "Quijotísimo." As for his epithet "de la Mancha," this is coined (I, 1) after Amadís de Gaula. Later, he will be called by the name, first given him by Sancho, "el caballero de la Triste Figura [the Knight of the Sorrowful Countenance]," still later by "el caballero de los Leones [the Knight of the Lions]" (in II, 27–29, this change is strongly emphasized, and a certain character is rebuked by Sancho for having disregarded the distinction).[2]

---

[1] And in that same pastoral game (II, 67) Sansón Carrasco would become "el pastor Sansonino" or "el pastor Carrascón" (two names!), the barber > "Nicolás Miculoso" (after *Nemoroso*, as Quijote explains), *el Cura* > "el pastor Curiambro" (reminiscence of the giant Caraculiambro?); as for the name of Sancho's wife, however, the squire, who always pays heed to the *convenientia* of words and objects, agrees only to "Teresona" as the pastoral name for his fat Teresa. We see why he cannot agree to "Teresaina": this name, proposed by Sansón Carrasco (II, 73), is so evocative of the ethereal music of the flute (*dulzaina*) that Don Quijote must laugh at "la aplicación del nombre [the application of the name]."

[2] A pendant to Quijote, the believer in an unreal order of virtue, is Cardenio, the lover who cannot face that

It is obviously required by chivalric decorum that whoever enters the sphere of the knight Don Quijote must also change his or her name: Aldonza Lorenza > Dulcinea ("nombre a su parecer músico y peregrino y significativo [a name that seemed to him musical and unusual and significant]"), Tolosa > Doña Tolosa, la Molinera > Doña Molinera (I, 3), and the anonymous nag receives the name of Rocinante ("nombre a su parecer alto, sonoro y significativo [a name that seemed to him lofty, sonorous, and significant]": note the parallel wording appearing in the justifications for the names given to Dulcinea and to the nag); incidentally, the ass from which Sancho is inseparable is not deemed worthy of a change of name that would be indicative of a change of rank. Although Sancho Panza, the peasant squire, undergoes no change of name similar to that of his master,[3] and is resolved always to remain (governor or no governor) plain Sancho without the addition of "don" (II, 4), there is some uncertainty in regard to his name, too, since, in the text of Cide Hamete Benengeli, the Arabian chronicler whose manuscript Cervantes purports to have found at the moment when other sources gave out (I, 9), there is a picture of thick-set Sancho with "la barriga grande, el tallo corto y las zancas largas [a big belly, a short body and long shanks]," bearing the inscription: "Sancho Zancas."

It is, however, in regard to the name of Sancho's wife, that the greatest confusion obtains: Sancho calls her first "Juana Gutiérrez, mi oíslo [my old woman]" (I, 7); a few lines later, he ponders whether a crown would fit "la cabeza de [the head of] Mari Gutiérrez"—which change the more intelligent commentators, seeking to avoid bringing the charge of inconsistency against Cervantes, rightly explain by the fact that *Mari* had come to represent simply a generic and interchangeable name for women. But in II, 5, Sancho's wife calls herself Teresa Cascajo; from then on she is either Teresa Panza or Teresa Sancho, "mujer de [wife of] Sancho Panza"; of the name Teresa itself she says (II, 5): "Teresa me pusieron en el bautismo, nombre

---

injustice which so often obtains in the reality of love. Thus we will not be astonished to find that the onomastic pattern, dear to the romances of chivalry, represented by *caballero de la Triste Figura* is also applied to Cardenio: he is alternatively called (by the shepherds who tell his story) *Roto de la Mala Figura* [the Tattered One of Sorry Countenance], *caballero de la Sierra* [Knight of the Sierra], *caballero del Bosque* [Knight of the Forest]—before he himself is allowed to state his simple, real name: "Mi nombre es Cardenio."

The importance of the *name* for the Middle Ages appears here most clearly; any knight of romance, Amadís or Perceval or Yvain, is presented as undergoing an inner evolution, whose outward manifestations are the different "adventures" which mark his career; and it is by virtue of these adventures that he acquires different names, each of which is revelatory of the particular stage attained; in this way, the evolution is clearly labeled for the reader. Yvain acquires a new dignity, so to speak, when he becomes the "Chevalier au Lion"; "Orlando innamorato" is a different person from "Orlando furioso." Consequently, a mistake in names is no slight mistake: it is a sin against the law of inner evolution which presides over the events of a heroic life. It is significant that Don Quijote speaks (I, 18) of "la ventura aquella de Amadís [de Grecia], *cuando se llamaba el caballero de la Ardiente Espada*, que fué una de las mejores espadas que tuvo caballero en el mundo [that adventure of Amadís [of Greece], *when he was called the Knight of the Burning Sword*, which was one of the finest swords ever owned by any knight in the world]." It is precisely because this extraordinary sword distinguishes objectively one of the exemplary phases of the evolution of the knight that the name under which he appears has a somewhat objective, temporally definable validity.

[3] In II, 2, Sancho reports with pride that, though Don Quijote and his beloved are being celebrated by the historiographer Cide Hamete Berenjena [sic], under their fanciful names ("El ingenioso hidalgo," "Dulcinea del Toboso"), his name has suffered no such treatment: "que me mientan... *con mi mesmo nombre de Sancho Panza* [that they mention me... *by my real name of Sancho Panza*]."

mondo y escueto... [They baptized me Teresa, a plain and simple name...]." Evidently we have to do with a woman named Juana Teresa Gutiérrez, who becomes a Juana Panza or Teresa Panza when called after her husband, or... Cascajo when called after her father. Occasionally, however, according to the mood of the situation, she may be called "Teresaina" (II, 73) or "Teresona [*-ona* is a generally unflattering augmentative ending]" (II, 67: because of her "gordura [stoutness]").[4]

There are other cases, slightly different from those enumerated so far, in which the ignorance and weak memory of Sancho seem to create a "polyonomasia": here we can hardly think in terms of different traditions offered by chroniclers (as in the case of the names of Quijote), or of popular variation (as in that of the names of Sancho's wife): Sancho must multiply names simply because all the forms of names that he retains are only approximations to the real ones; they are variable because he cannot take a firm hold on them; he indulges in what linguists call "popular etymologies," i.e. he alters names according to the associations most convenient to his intellectual horizon. Sometimes he offers several variations, but even when only one alteration is involved, the effect of polyonomasia still remains because of the fact that the real name is also present in the reader's mind. Mambrino (I, 19–21), of whose helmet he speaks, becomes "Malandrino" (a "moro [Moor]"), "Malino" (= the Evil One), or "Martino" (a common first name); Fortinbras > feo [ugly] Blas (I, 15); Cide Hamete Benengeli > "...Berenjena [egg plant]" (II, 2; this Sancho justifies with the remark: "...los moros son amigos de berenjenas [...the Moors are fond of egg plant]"[5]); Señora Rodríguez de Grijalva > Señora González (II, 31); Magalona > "la señora Magellanes o Magalona" (II, 41). A similar alteration of names is practiced by the *ama* [housekeeper] who (I, 7) contends that the books which we know to have fallen prey to the *auto-da-fé* (I, 6) had been ravished by the sorcerer Muñatón: Don Quijote corrects this to "Frestón." "Never mind Frestón or Tritón," answers the *ama*, "provided it is a name ending in *-ton*": word forms that are unalterable for the learned Don Quijote are quite exchangeable in the mind of the uncultured *ama*.

The names of the Countess Trifaldi are in a class by themselves since, in addition to the instability of names conditioned by a masquerade, there are involved the alterations to which Sancho is prone: here there coexist polyonomasias of the first

---

[4] Again, we have evidence of the importance of nomenclature: a change of suffix, in itself, may be equivalent to a change of linguistic perspective.

In another incident (I, 22), from one of the secondary episodes, we are told that, when the guard speaks of his prisoner, Ginés de Pasamonte, as "el famoso Ginés de Pasamonte, que por otro nombre llaman Ginesillo de Parapilla [the famous Ginés de Pasamonte, whom they also call Ginesillo de Parapilla]," the other retorts: "Señor Comisario,... no andemos ahora a deslindar nombres y sobrenombres, Ginés me llamo, y no Ginesillo, y Pasamonte es mi alcurnia, y no Parapilla, como voacé dice... algún día sabrá alguno si me llamo Ginesillo de Parapilla o no.... Yo haré que no me lo llamen [Mr. Deputy,... let's not get into defining names and surnames, Ginés is my name, and not Ginesillo, and Pasamonte is my family name, and not Parapilla, as you are saying... someday someone will know whether my name is Ginesillo Parapilla or not.... I'll make them stop calling me that]." Again, just as in the case of Sancho's rebuke to the one who had altered Quijote's title, Cervantes takes occasion to show the natural indignation aroused by a violation of the "perspective" which the bearer of the name has chosen and under which he has a right to appear.

[5] The same type of justification of a mispronunciation by the invention *ad hoc* of a (secondary) relationship is found in II, 2, when Sancho, in order to explain his version of the Arabic name *Benengeli* (i.e. Berenjena), refers to the Moors' predilection for *berenjenas*.

and second degrees. The Countess is first (II, 36) introduced to us (by her messenger Trifaldín el de la Barba Blanca) as "la condesa Trifaldi, por otro nombre llamada la dueña Dolorida [the Countess Trifaldi, also known as the Doleful Duenna]"; one of the two names is her authentic one, the other her "name within the world of romance" (just as Don Quijote is also the "caballero de la Triste Figura"). When she appears in the pageant (II, 38) of the *carro triunfal* her name "Trifaldi" is given the following explanation: "la cola, o falda, o como llamarla quisieren, era de tres colas [the train, or skirt, or whatever they might wish to call it, had three flounces]"; the "mathematical" (geometrical) figure of her skirt with three flounces (or trains?) is so striking that every spectator must interpret her name as "la condesa de las Tres Faldas." But the scrupulous chronicler Benengeli, who, like Cervantes, seems to care about even the minor details of the fiction-within-the-fiction, is said by Cervantes to have stated that the character was really called "la condesa *Lobuna*" —allegedly because of the presence of wolves in her domain (he adds that, according to onomastic traditions in princely houses she would have been called "la condesa Zorruna" if foxes had been prevalent in her domain)—but that she had dropped this name in favor of the more novel one derived from the form of her skirt. Now, this etymology of the name "Trifaldi," as stated by the chronicler (and as made evident to the eye of the spectators who see the masquerade skirt), had been somewhat anticipated by Sancho's popular etymology in II, 37: "esta condesa Tres Faldas o Tres Colas (que en mi tierra faldas y colas, colas y faldas, todo es uno [where I come from skirts and trains, trains and skirts, it's all the same thing])." Ultimately we are presented with an array of (possible) names for the same character: la condesa Trifaldi, de Tres Faldas, de Tres Colas (the latter name would be due to what the modern linguist in his jargon calls "synonymic derivation"), Lobuna ("Zorruna" again being a "synonymic derivate"[6]), dueña Dolorida—a list as impressive as that of the names of Don Quijote.

Now those commentators who, in general, take the line of emphasizing the satiric intent of Cervantes, will point out that the variety of names attributed to the protagonist by Cervantes is simply an imitation of the pseudo-historical tendencies of the authors of chivalric novels who, in order to show their accurateness as historians,

---

[6] Sancho offers us another example of popular "synonymic derivation": *rata* "rate, installment of payment" has been understood by him as "rat," which, with him, must lead to *gata* "cat." As a matter of fact, the procedure by which developments take place in argot is not basically different from this: *dauphin* "dolphin" > "pimp" in French argot was interpreted as *dos fin* [delicate back] so that a *dos vert* [a green back, an untried back] could follow. The modern linguist would say that Sancho has the makings of an excellent subject for an inquirer such as Gilliéron, who wanted to seize, on the spot, the working of the popular imagination. When faced with the problem of language, Sancho is not lazy and passive, as he is in general (and in this incessant linguistic criticism and linguistic activity, side by side with inactivity in other realms of life, he is typically Spanish): he asks himself why the Spanish battle cry is ¡*Santiago y cierra España*! [Santiago and close Spain!]: "¿Está por ventura España abierta, y de modo que es menester cerrarla, o qué ceremonia es esta? [Is by any chance Spain open, so that it is necessary to close her, or what ceremony is this?]." Erroneously he seeks to interpret, by contemporary patterns, a way of speech obscured by historic development. While he does not know as much historical grammar as does Rodríguez Marín, the modern commentator of the *Don Quijote*, he shows himself to be aware of the basic problem of linguistics: the opaqueness of certain ways of speech.

pretend to have resorted to different sources.[7] In the case of the names of Sancho's wife, some commentators point out, as we have seen, that the polyonomasia is due to the onomastic habits of the period; in the alterations of the name "Mambrino" they usually see a satire on Sancho's ignorance; in the case of the Condesa Trifaldi I have seen no explanation (Rodríguez Marín's edition points out possible "historical" sources for the costume itself of "tres colas o faldas"). But, evidently, there must be a common pattern of thought behind all these cases, which would explain (1) the importance given to a name or change of name, (2) the etymological concern with names, (3) the polyonomasia in itself.

Now it happens that just these three features are well known to the medievalist (less, perhaps, to students of Renaissance literature): they ultimately derive from Biblical studies and from ancient philology: one need only think of Saint Jerome's explanation of Hebrew names or of Isidore's "Etymologies"—and of the etymologizing habits of all great medieval poets. The names in the Bible were treated with seriousness; in the Old Testament the name, or rather the names of God were all-important (Exodus, VI, 2–3: "I am *Iahve*, and I have appeared to Abraham, Isaak and Jacob as *El Schaddai*, under the name of Jahve I was not known to them," cf. ibid., III, 14); the many *nomina sacra* revealed the many aspects through which the divine might make itself felt (cf. *PMLA*, LVI, 13 *seq.*). Nor does the importance of the name decrease with the New Testamentary divinity (Christ is Immanuel). And, in the New Testament, a tendency appears which will have great influence on medieval chivalry: the change of name subsequent to baptism will be imitated by the change of name undergone by the newly dubbed knight. In all these sacred (or, sacramental) names or changes of names, etymology plays a large part, because the true meaning (the etymon) may reveal eternal verities latent in the words—indeed, it was possible for many etymologies to be proposed for the same word, since God may have deposited different meanings in a single term: polyonomasia and polyetymology. Both these techniques are generally applied to a greater degree to proper names than to common nouns—because the former, "untranslatable" as they are by their nature, participate more in the mysterious aspect of human language: they are less motivated. In proper names the medieval mind could see reflected more of the multivalence of the world full of arcana. The Middle Ages were characterized by an admiration as well for the correspondence between word and thing as for the mystery which makes this correspondence unstable.

By all this I do not mean to deny that Cervantes followed the models pointed out to us by the commentators: what I do say is that, in doing so, he was also following certain accepted medieval patterns (which, however, he submitted to a new

---

[7] Accordingly, this variety of names would be on one level with such pseudo-historical interruptions of the narrative as we have seen in I, 2, when Cervantes pretends to hesitate about which particular adventure of his protagonist to narrate first: it seems that there are some *autores* ("authors" or "authorities") who say that the adventure of Puerto Lápice was the first; others contend the same about that of the windmills, while Cervantes, himself, has ascertained, from the annals of La Mancha ... etc.

We shall see later, however, that the pseudo-historical device has implications much more important than the parodying of chronicles.

interpretation: that of his critical intelligence). It is possible, for example, in the case of the name "Trifaldi," to see on the surface a medieval imagination at work: the name is given an interpretation (*Trifaldi* = *tres faldas*) which, from our modern linguistic or historical point of view, is evidently wrong but which would have delighted a medieval mind, ever ready to accept any interpretation offering a clarification of the mystery of words.[8] The ancient and medieval etymologies are indeed rarely those a modern linguist would offer, trained as he is to respect the formational procedures current in human language; the aim of those etymologies was to establish the connection between a given word and other existing words as an homage to God whose wisdom may have ordained these very relationships. The etymological connections that the medieval etymologist sees are direct relationships established between words vaguely associated because of their homonymic ring—not the relationships established by "historical grammar" or those obtained by decomposition of the word into its morphological elements.[9] In other words, we are offered edifying ideal possibilities, not deterministic historical realities; Isidore will connect *sol* and *solus* because of the ideological beauty of this relationship, not *sol* and ἥλιος as the comparative grammarian of today must do.

But, if the equation *Trifaldi* = *tres faldas* represents a "medieval" etymology, Cervantes himself did not take too seriously his own etymologizing: he must have been perfectly well aware of the historically real explanation—that which prompted him to coin the word. *Trifaldi* is evidently a regressive form from *Trifaldín*, which name, in turn, is the farcical Italian *Truffaldino* "nome di personaggio ridicolo e basso di commedia [name of the ridiculous and base character of comedy]" (Tomm.- Bellini); the reference to *truffare* "to cheat" is apposite, in our story, given the farcical episode intended to delude Don Quijote and Sancho. Thus the name of the messenger *Trifaldín* is (historically) not a diminutive of *Trifaldi*, as it might seem, but, on the contrary, was preexistent, in Cervantes' mind, to the name of the mistress. The etymology of "tres faldas" is, historically speaking, entirely out of place. We have to face here the same para-etymological vein in which Rabelais (facetiously imitating medieval practice, while exemplifying the joyous freedom with which the Renaissance writer could play with words) explained the name *Gargantua* by *que grand tu as* [sc. *le gosier*]! [what a huge [sc. throat, voice] you have!] and *Beauce* by [*je trouve*] *beau ce* [sc. *pays*] [[I find] beautiful this [sc. country]]. In this story, the para-etymological play with names serves to underline the deceitfulness of outward

---

[8] It is in the medieval vein that Cervantes, in the Trifaldi episode (II, 40), has the name of the horse *Clavileño el Alígero* explained as follows: "cuyo nombre conviene con el ser de leño y con la clavija que trae en la frente y con la ligereza con que camina [whose name is appropriate because of the fact that he is made of wood and the peg that he has in his forehead and the swiftness with which he moves]": *convenir, convenientia* are the medieval (originally Ciceronian) expressions for "harmony"—as well as "grammatical accord," harmony between word and meaning, etc.

[9] A characteristic trait of the ancient and medieval etymological procedures was to explain by compounds where the modern linguist would assume derivation: Thus Eng. *dismal* was explained by *dies mali* instead of as a derivative from OF *disme* "dîme" (cf. *MLN*, LVII, 602). In the same vein is the decomposition of the derivative *Truff-ald-[ino]* into the two parts *tri* + *fald*-. Compare also Sancho's decomposition (II, 3) of *gramática* into *grama* (the herb) + *tica* (the meaning of the latter word has not yet been elucidated by commentators).

evidence; what for Quijote and Sancho are wondrous events are, in reality, only *burlas* [[tricks]] in a baroque world of histrionics and disingenuity.[10]

The disingenuous procedure of offering such "medieval" etymologies as would occur to his characters (for the simpleton Sancho as well as the learned Arab Benengeli are medieval primitives) is also exemplified in the case of the nag Rocinante, whose name is interpreted by Don Quijote[11] in the style of Isidore: the horse was a "rocín antes"—which may mean either "a nag before" ("previously a nag," "an erstwhile nag") or "a nag before all others": "antes de todos los rocines del mundo." Two explanations are given of one word, as was the general medieval practice[12]—not the *one* historically true significance according to which the name was actually coined: viz. *rocín* + the noble and "literary" participial ending *–ante*. Cervantes was perfectly aware of the correct etymology but he allowed his medieval Don Quijote to offer a more "significant" one. He knew also the explanation of the name *Quijote* (= *quij-* "jaw" + the comic suffix *–ote*, derived from *jigote* [[mincemeat]], etc.), while his protagonist, who adopted this name, thought of it as patterned on *Lanzarote*.[13]

---

[10] The trick intended for the protagonists is revealed in the midst of the pageant, when the majordomo, who plays the Countess, corrects himself: "a este su criado, *digo, a esta su criada* [[for this your manservant, I mean, your lady in waiting]]."

It may be stated that such baroque effects are on the increase in the second part of the *Quijote*, where pageants, *burlas*, and *truffe* flourish (cf. "Las bodas de Camacho y Quiteria [[The wedding of Camacho and Quiteria]]"). In Part I we are shown the aggressive Don Quijote and his grumbling but faithful follower Sancho challenging the outward world—meeting, in their adventures, with a flux of humanity in a series of chance encounters against the fluid background of roadsides and inns. In Part II, however, the couple appear rather as being challenged than as challenging the world—and this world, the world of the big city, the world of the aristocracy, is now more formidable, more firmly constituted. The resistance of the first environment was not sufficient to bring about the necessary cure of the knight: Quijote must be brought to face the criticism of the higher spheres of society, where he is victimized with sophisticated *burlas*. The aristocrats play theater for Don Quijote and Sancho (in a way that may remind us of Shakespeare's Sly—and the "governorship" of Sancho resembles Sly's temporary courtship). And theater, like *sueño* [[dream]], is bound to end with an awakening from illusion. This is a baroque theme.

If Mr. Stephen Gilman (*Revista de Filología Hispánica*, V, 148) is right in claiming for Avellaneda's continuation of the *Quijote* a baroque style, it might be apposite to add that Cervantes himself, whether prompted by his competitor or not (and I personally think, rather not), went the same path of "baroquization" in his own continuation of the story.

[11] Don Quijote himself explains words according to an Isidorian scheme: e.g. when he takes it upon himself to explain *albogues* (II, 67), he begins by describing the "res" designated by the word ("albogues son unas chapas ... [[pastoral flutes are some metal plates ...]]"), and follows this with the etymon: it is originally Arabic, he says, as the prefix *al–* suggests. Don Quijote cannot stop here, however; giving full rein to his associative imagination, he goes on to mention other Arabic words in Spanish likewise characterized by *al–* and ends by including certain loan-words with a termination in *–í*.

[12] The same "twofold pattern" is followed for the etymology of the (legendary, medieval) island of which Sancho is to become the ruler (II, 45): "la ínsula Baratería, o ya porque el lugar se llamaba Baratario o ya por el barato con que se le había dado el gobierno [[Baratería Island, either because the place was called Baratario or because of the low price for which the government was handed over]]"; here, the first etymology is the formal or tautological one which Cervantes slyly proposes (in order to remain faithful to the dichotomy) as an alternative to the second—which is the historically "real" etymology.

[13] My reason for believing that the hidalgo had *Lanzarote* in mind when he changed his name, is found in the episode of I, 2, where Don Quijote adapts the text of the old *romance* to his own situation, substituting his own name for that of the protagonist: "Nunca fuera caballero / De damas tan bien servido / Como fuera don Quijote / Cuando de su aldea vino [[There was never a knight / So well served by ladies / As was

Thus we may conclude that, while, for the medieval world, the procedures of polyonomasia and polyetymologia amounted to a recognition of the working of the divine in the world, Cervantes used the same devices in order to reveal the multivalence which words possess for different human minds: he who has coined the names put into them other meanings than those conceived of by the characters themselves: a *Trifaldín* who is for Cervantes a *truffatore*, a cheater or practical joker, is understood by Don Quijote and Sancho to be the servant of a Countess *Trifaldi* who wears a three-flounce skirt.

Perhaps this procedure is symptomatic of something basic to the texture of our novel; perhaps a linguistic analysis of the names can carry us further toward the center, allowing us to catch a glimpse of the general attitude of the creator of the novel toward his characters. This creator must see that the world, as it is offered to man, is susceptible of many explanations, just as names are susceptible of many etymologies; individuals may be deluded by the perspectives according to which they see the world as well as by the etymological connections which they establish. Consequently, we may assume that the linguistic perspectivism of Cervantes is reflected in his invention of plot and characters; and, just as, by means of polyonomasia and polyetymologia, Cervantes makes the world of words appear different to his different characters, while he himself may have his own, the coiner's, view of these names, similarly he watches the story he narrates from his own private vantage point: the way in which the characters conceive of the situations in which they are involved may be not at all the way in which Cervantes sees them—though this latter way is not always made clear to the reader. In other words, Cervantes' perspectivism, linguistic and otherwise,[14] would allow him qua artist to stand above, and sometimes aloof from, the misconceptions of his characters. Later we will have more to say about what lies behind this attitude of Cervantes; suffice it for us here, where we are given the first opportunity to look into the working of the (linguistic) imagination

---

Don Quijote / When from his village he came]]." The suffix *-ote* (as in *monigote, machacote* [bumpkin, importunate one]]) has a comic ring for the reader but not, evidently, for the coiner of the name.

We have a somewhat similar bivalence in the case of the name *Rocinante*—though here, of course, it is not the suffix but the radical which provides the comic effect. The noble connotation of *-ante*, that participial ending which had dropped out of current use in Old Romance languages, is to be found, with a nuance of high distinction, in such epic names as OF *Baligant, Tervagant*, and in common nouns such as OF *aumirant* (Sp. *almirante* [admiral]]) and Sp. *emperante* (found along with *emperador* in the *Libro de buen amor*). Thus, our learned knight, with his "epic imagination," came naturally by his predilection for such a pattern of nomenclature.

As for the factual etymology of the word *quijote* (< OF *cuissot* [thigh-piece]] "cuissart"), this has been established by Malkiel, *Language*, XXI, 156. Mr. Malkiel, however, confuses historical linguistics with the study of a work of art when he writes: "The etymology of this word naturally aroused the curiosity of Cervantes." In reality, Cervantes has not shown himself interested in the etymology of the common noun *quijote*, but in that of the proper name *Quijote*; and the latter was not, for him, derived from OF *cuissot*, but from *Lanzarote*, and from the group *Quijada, Quijano* (whatever the origin of these may be).

[14] As a nonlinguistic example of such perspectivism, we may point to the passage made famous by Hume: two kinsmen of Sancho, called upon to give their opinion of a hogshead of wine, find it excellent, in the main, except for a peculiar flavor—on which they disagree. The one insists it has a leathery taste, the other, a metallic taste. When they have finally drunk their way to the bottom of the cask, they find a rusty iron key with a leather strap attached.

of the novelist, to have summarily indicated the relationship between his linguistic ambivalences and his general perspectivism.[15]

If, now, we turn back for a moment to Sancho's mispronunciations of names—which, as we have seen, was one of the contributing factors to the polyonomasia of the novel—we will recognize a particular application of Cervantes' linguistic perspectivism at work: to Sancho's uncultured mind, "Mambrino" must appear now as "Malino," now as "Martino," etc. In this, there is no suggestion of smugness on the part of Cervantes, as there might be with modern intellectual writers who would mock the linguistic "abuses" of ignorant characters; Cervantes presents "Malino," "Martino," etc., simply as the "linguistic appearances" of what, for Don Quijote, for example, can evidently be only Mambrino.[16] This lack of auctorial criticism in the face of so much linguistic relativity tends to shake the reader's confidence in established word usage. Of course, we are apt to rely on the correctness of Don Quijote's use of words and names; but who knows whether the knight, who is so often mistaken in his attempts to define reality (as he is precisely in his identification of the helmet

---

[15] It is not astonishing that Dostoievski, that great absolutist who delighted in showing up the relativity in human affairs, should have imitated the polyonomasia of Cervantes: In *Crime and Punishment*, the monomaniac Raskolnikov (whose name, related to *raskolnik* "heretic," suggests his monomania) has a friend named *Razumichin* (related to *razum* "reason"), who is the flexible, optimistic, helpful, and loquacious defender of reason: his flexibility of mind is mirrored in the alterations to which his name is subjected by other characters in the novel: *Vrazumichin* (to *vrazumlyaty* "to explain") and *Rassudkin* (to *rassudok* "judgment").

[16] Sancho, who appears so often as the representative of that Catholic positivism which takes the world, as it is, as God-given, without envisaging the possibility of a more ideal order, expresses his linguistic doubts about the mysterious, significant, and musical names of Quijote's making, just as he usually (though not always) suspects the arcana of the world of enchantment that his master visualizes: (I, 28): "... no eran fantasmas ni hombres encantados, como vuestra merced dice, sino hombres de carne y de hueso *como nosotros*, y todos, según los oí nombrar... tenían sus nombres: que el uno se llamaba Pedro Martínez y el otro Tenorio Hernández, y el Ventero oí que se llamaba Juan Palomeque el Zurdo [... they were not phantoms or enchanted men, as you say, but men of flesh and bone *like us*, and all, from what I heard... had names: one was named Pedro Martínez and the other Tenorio Hernández, and the innkeeper I heard called Juan Palomeque the Left-Handed]." When he hears from Quijote's lips the fantastic names of beings from a world he does not believe to exist, he tries to bring these names down to earth, to adapt them to his homely environment. And in I, 29, when it is explained to him that the princess Micomicona is called so after her estate Micomicón in Guinea, Sancho is happy only when he can find a parallel in the names of the common people he knows, such as Pedro de Alcalá, Juan de Úbeda, Diego de Valladolid, who are named after their birthplaces.

Evidently, the names in the world of Don Quijote must be, in opposition to the homespun names of Sancho's world, the more grandiloquent the less they cover of reality: they are of the grotesque, that is, the comically frightening kind, that distinguishes the names of Pulci's and Rabelais' giants: we find (I, 18) Caraculiambro de Malindranía; el grande emperador Alifarfarón, señor de la grande isla Trapobana; Pentapolín del Arremangado Brazo; Espartafilando del Bosque, duque de Nestria; (I, 30) Pandafilando de la Fosca Vista—which last is transposed by Sancho (in accord with the feeling he has acquired for linguistic correspondences between his master's speech and his own: $f > h$, *-ando* > *-ado*) into *Pandahilado*; similarly, the poetic name *Fili* becomes, with Sancho, *hilo* (I, 23): Sancho's capacity of transposition is the linguistic equivalent of his capacity for adopting the fanciful schemes of Don Quijote. Another aspect of Sancho's positivistic approach is his lack of that symbolic feeling so characteristic of his master. He gauges symbolic actions according to their "positive" or pragmatic value in actual life: when Don Quijote invites him, in order to symbolize the Christian democracy of men, to sit at his table with him and the shepherds, Sancho refuses because of the inconvenience of having to be on his best behavior at the master's table. On the other hand (for Cervantes knows always an "on-the-other-hand"), Sancho's unmystical attitude is capable of producing good results: he is, during his governorship, able to uncover the swindle involving the money concealed in the staff, precisely because he disregards the symbolic value of the staff.

of Mambrino), has hit this time upon the right name, whether this name is not as much of a dream as are the fantastic adventures he envisions (we are reminded of the baroque theme *par excellence* "... que los sueños sueños son ⟦... that dreams are dreams⟧")? Why should, then, "Mambrino" and not "Malino" or "Martino" be the name representing *reality*? The same insistence on "correctness" of word-usage, as applied to the nonexistent, occurs in the scene where Quijote listens to the *ama*'s cock-and-bull story of the theft of the books by "the sorcerer Muñatón," and finds nothing to correct therein but the name: not "Muñatón" but "Frestón": Frestón and Mambrino are names correct in irreality (in books), representing naught in reality. Evidently we are offered in Don Quijote a caricature of the humanist[17] who is versed in books and bookish names, but is unconcerned as to their valid relationship to reality (he has a pendant in the *licenciado*, to whom Don Quijote tells the fantastic story of his descent to the "cueva de Montesinos ⟦Cave of Montesinos⟧," and who is outspokenly qualified by Cervantes as a "humanista").[18]

In these two incidents we have a suggestion of a theme which informs our whole novel: the problem of the reality of literature. I belong with those critics who take seriously Cervantes' statement of purpose: "derribar la máquina mal fundada de los libros de caballería ⟦to demolish the badly founded structure of the chivalric novels⟧"; this statement, which indicts a particular literary genre, is, in fact, a recognition of the potential danger of "the book." And, in its larger sense, the *Quijote* is an indictment of the bookish side of Humanism,[19] a creed in which, seventy years earlier, Rabelais had so firmly believed, and an indictment of the "word-world" in which the Renaissance had delighted without qualms. Whereas the writers of the Renaissance were able to build up their word-worlds out of sheer exuberance, free to "play" linguistically because of their basic confidence in life—with the baroque artist Des-

[17] For us to apply this label to the knight striving to revive a medieval chivalric world, in the midst of his contemporary world of mass armies employing firearms, may seem surprising to the reader. But the humanistic world was a continuation of the medieval world: and what Don Quijote seeks to revive and reenact are humanistic dreams of antiquarians. The humanist tends to revive, by the strength of his imagination, a more beautiful past, regardless of how it may fit into his time; this is the ideal strength and the weakness of any humanist, and Cervantes has described both aspects.

[18] It has not been sufficiently emphasized that Cervantes, as so often happens (e.g. in the case of the diptychs Marcela–Don Quijote, Cardenio–Don Quijote, el Cautivo–el Oidor; or in Don Quijote's speech on "armas y letras"), is proceeding by offering pendant pictures when he opposes to Don Quijote's vision in *la cueva de Montesinos* the speech of the *licenciado* on the humanistic books which he intends to write. Both turn to the past: the one seeks to relive it in the present, the other, to exhume it and transmit it through his books; both attempts, illustrating the same pattern of thought, are equally futile. Don Quijote's account of his visions is welcomed by the *licenciado* as a new "source" for his complication of fanciful lore—while these same visions have been inspired by that same sort of lore.

[19] Cervantes himself must have been vulnerable to the humanistic "book-virus": he tells us that he used to pick up every printed scrap of paper—surely not, like Saint Francis, because some sacred words might be on it, but in order to live through the printed words a vicarious existence, in the fashion of his Don Quijote, i.e. as a "novel-reader."

Cervantes must also, like any humanist, have delighted in the deciphering of old documents: he tells us of the adventure of having Benengeli's Arabic deciphered for his benefit; in the story of the *Cautivo*, the Arabic letter of Lela Zoraida is puzzled out; and, in II, 39, a Syriac text is referred to: "escritas en lengua siríaca unas letras, que habiéndose declarada en la candayesca, y ahora en la castellana, encierran esta sentencia ⟦some letters written in the Syriac tongue, which, having been rendered in Candayan, and then in Castilian, contain this sentence⟧." To be polyglot is to delight in many perspectives.

engaño, disillusionment is allowed to color all things of the world, including books and their words, which possess only the reality of a *sueño*. Words are no longer, as they had been in the Middle Ages, depositories of truths nor, as they had been in the Renaissance, an expansion of life: they are, like the books in which they are contained, sources of hesitation, error, deception—"dreams."

The same linguistic perspectivism is present in Cervantes' treatment of common nouns. For the most part we have to do with the confusion, or the criticism, engendered by the clash of two linguistic standards determined mainly by social status.[20] Here, too, in this continuous give-and-take between cultured and uncultured speakers, there is given a suggestion of linguistic relativism that is willed by Cervantes. The opposition between two different ways of speech takes different forms: it may be Sancho who is interrupted and corrected by Don Quijote: in I, 32 [*hereje o*] *flemático* is corrected to *cismático* [heretic or phlegmatic > disturbed]; in II, 7 *relucido* > *reducido* [brilliant > convinced]; II, 8 *sorbiese* > *asolviese* [might swallow > absolve]; II, 9 *cananeas* > *hacaneas* [Canaanites > nags]; II, 19 *friscal* > *fiscal* ["crickety" > "critical," according to Samuel Putnam's translation].[21] Particularly interesting are the cases in

---

[20] It could be said, of nearly every character in the *Quijote*, that he appears located at his own particular linguistic level, somewhere along a hierarchic ladder. The Duchess, for example, who is quite conscious of her social and linguistic superiority over Sancho, and who takes care to distinguish her speech from his (II, 32: "la flor de las ceremonias, o cirimonias, *como vos decís* [the flower of ceremonies, or cirimonies, *as you say*]"), must be shown her inferiority, at least in matters linguistic, to Don Quijote: when the latter has occasion to speak of "la retórica ciceroniana y *demostina* [the Ciceronian and *Demosthene* rhetoric]," the Duchess asks about the significance of the last word, remarking "que es vocablo que no he oído en todos los días de mi vida [it is a word that I have never heard in all the days of my life]," and is taunted by her husband: "habéis andado deslumbrada en tal pregunta [you have shown your ignorance with such a question]." Thus the same character has a chance to snub and be snubbed linguistically—as well as otherwise.

On the other hand we may ask ourselves: does Cervantes the superhumanist smile here at the reader over the head of the humanistic character Don Quijote? For the adjective *demostino* (an evidently popular haplology for *demostenino* "of Demosthenes") is incorrectly formed. Is Cervantes here revindicating again for himself a position above his protagonist by having Quijote the scholar make elementary mistakes?

Even when the characters lapse into a foreign language, there is a difference according to social classes—the standard "second language" in Cervantes' time being Italian. Don Quijote, being a Spanish humanist, must, of course, know Italian: he expressly states (II, 52) that he knows "somewhat" of Tuscan and can sing some stanzas of Ariosto; he examines a printer as to his knowledge of Italian vocabulary ("does he know that *pignatta* corresponds to Sp. *olla* [pot]?"); and he occasionally inserts Italian forms into his facetious speeches: II, 24: "Notable *espilorchería*, como dice el italiano [Notable *espilorchería* ("avariciousness"), as the Italian would say]"; II, 25: "Dígame vuestra merced, señor adivino: ¿que peje pillamo? [Tell me, Sir Diviner, *what kind of fish will we catch?* (i.e. "how will things turn out?")]." Here we have rather far-fetched idioms by which the humanist Quijote shows how conversant he is with the nuances that are better expressed in Italian than in Spanish.

We also find, in our novel, Italianisms used in the speech of the lower strata of society, where they seem to suggest the language of conviviality: the Ventero says of Maese Pedro (II, 25): "... es hombre galante (como dicen en Italia) y bon compaño [... he is a gallant man (as they say in Italy) and a good companion]"; in the drinking scene between Sancho, his ex-companion Ricote, and the other pseudo-pilgrims, a *lingua franca* version of Italian is used at the height of their merriment (II, 54): "Español y Tudesqui tuto uno: bon compaño [Spanish and German, it's all the same: good companion]"—(Sancho:) "Bon compaño, juradí [Good companion, I swear to God]." Clemencín and Rodríguez Marín are therefore wrong when they object to a *caro patrón mío* in the mouth of Sancho (II, 23); this is not humanistic Italian but the language of plain people indulging in exuberant gaiety.

Thus we have two types of Italianate Spanish, according to social strata.

[21] Compare, for other mispronunciations of Sancho (II, 68): *trogloditas* > *tortolitas*, *bárbaros* > *barberos*, *antropófagos* > *astropajos*, *scitas* > *perritas a quien dicen cita cita*.

which the term used by Sancho and the correction offered by Quijote are in the relationship of etymological doublets (popular and learned developments of the same root): (I, 12): *cris–eclipse* [[dagger–eclipse]], *estil–estéril* [["style"–"sterile"*; these terms are actually used by Pedro, not Sancho]] (how admirably has Cervantes anticipated the discoveries of nineteenth-century linguistics!). Again, it may be a question of Sancho's reaction to the language of the knight which the squire either misunderstands (in I, 8 Quijote's *homicidios* "murders" is transposed by Sancho into the more familiar, semipopular doublet *omecillos* "feuds") or fails to understand (in II, 29 Quijote must explain the meaning of *longincuos* ["por tan longincuos caminos [[over such distant roads]]"], which he "translates" by *apartados* [[distant]]). In general, Don Quijote shows more tolerance for linguistic ignorance (in regard to the *longincuos* just mentioned, he excuses Sancho with the words: "y no es maravilla que no lo entiendes, que no estás tú obligado a saber latín [[and it's no wonder that you don't understand it, since you are not required to know Latin]]") than his uncultured associates (who seem more concerned with things than with words) do for linguistic pedantry: they often blame the knight for his *jerigonza* [[jargon, gibberish]] (I, 11), for his *griego* [[Greek]] (I, 16). And, when Don Quijote reproves Sancho for his use of *abernuncio* instead of *abrenuncio* [[fie]], the squire retorts: "Déjeme vuestra grandeza, que no estoy agora para mirar en sotilezas ni en letras más o menos [[Let me alone, my lord, for I'm not about to think about subtleties or extra or missing letters]]" (similarly, in II, 3, when the *bachiller* Sansón Carrasco corrects *presonajes* to *personajes*, Sancho remarks: "¡Otro reprochador de voquibles tenemos! Pues andense a eso y no acabaremos en toda la vida [[We have another one who criticizes language! Go on at this rate, and we won't finish in a lifetime]]"). Sancho adopts the attitude of a Mathurin Régnier, opposing the "éplucheurs de mots [[nigglers about words]]"! It may happen that the same Sancho, the advocate of naturalness in language, turns purist for the moment[22] for the edification of his wife, and corrects her *revuelto*

---

[22] It was to be expected that when Sancho became governor he would establish a linguistic level of his own, above that of his subjects. And, in fact, he once satirizes the way of speaking of a peasant by ironically carrying further a grammatical mistake of the latter; the scene in question could not be better analyzed than in the words of Morel-Fatio (*Romania*, XVI, 476):

> Lorsque le paysan vient conter son cas au gouverneur de Barataria, il cherche dans sa mémoire le mot juridique qui exprime décemment l'acte qu'il a commis [that is, *yacer* "to lie, sleep with"], et au lieu de "hizo que *yoguiésemos*," imparfait du subjonctif dont il n'avait conservé qu'un vague souvenir, il dit *yogásemos*... comme si l'infinitif était *yogar*. Sancho, qui, depuis qu'il est gouverneur, s'étudie à parler correctement, saisit avec joie l'occasion de souligner une grosse faute grammaticale chez un de ses semblables: "Faites en sorte, mon brave homme, de ne plus *yogar* avec personne," dit-il avec un sourire protecteur et appuyant sur le mot. Il y a là une finesse qu'ont dû sentir la plupart des lecteurs du *Don Quichotte*.

> *When the peasant comes to tell his story to the governor of Barataria, he searches his memory for a legal term that expresses decorously the act he has committed [that is,* yacer *"to lie, sleep with"], and in place of "*hizo que* yoguiésemos," an imperfect subjunctive of which he has retained only a vague memory, he says* yogásemos ... *as if the infinitive were* yogar. *Sancho, who, since he has been governor, makes a point of speaking correctly, joyfully seizes the occasion to underline a gross grammatical error made by one of his fellows: "See to it, my good man, that you do not* yogar *with anyone any more," says he with a patronizing smile, emphasizing the word. In this, there is a finesse that most readers of* the Don Quijote *must have felt.*

Sancho, the perpetrator of so many linguistic sins, is not insensitive to those committed by his subjects; his linguistic personality varies according to his interlocutor.

[revolved] to *resuelto* [resolved] (II, 5); but then he must hear from her lips—oh, relativity of human things!—the same reproach he was wont to administer to his master: "No os pongáis a disputar, marido, conmigo. ¡Yo hablo como Dios es servido, y no me meto en más dibujos! [Don't start to argue with me, husband. I speak as God wishes, and I don't get myself into other descriptions!]" (here, she is referring to the language of God, Who, as Sancho himself had already claimed, is the great "Entendedor [Understander]" of all kinds of speech).[23] Another example of the linguistic intolerance of the common people is the retort of the shepherd who has been corrected for having said *más años que sarna* [more years than mange] instead of... *que Sarra* [... than Sarah (wife of Abraham)]; "Harto vive la sarna [Mange is good enough]," he answers, "y si es, señor, que me habéis de andar zahiriendo [= 'éplucher'] a cada paso los vocablos no acabaremos en un año [and if, sir, you must go on reproaching me for my language at every step, we won't finish in a year]." In this case Don Quijote apologizes, and admits that there is as much sense to the one as to the other expression (in other words, he is brought to recognize the wisdom of "popular etymology"). Indeed, Don Quijote the humanist is made to learn new words, popular graphic expressions unknown to him—such as terms descriptive of *naturalia turpia* which the high-minded knight was wont to eschew in his conversation (I, 48: *hacer aguas* "to urinate"; Sancho is triumphant: "¿Es posible que no entienda vuestra merced hacer aguas mayores o menores? [Is it possible that your Grace doesn't understand what making a major or a minor is?]"), or low argot expressions (I, 22: *gurapas* [galleys], *canario* [literally, "canary"; one who confesses his crime], from the language of galley-slaves). And—the acme of shame for a humanist!—it may even happen that he has to be instructed in Latinisms by Sancho (with whom they appear, of course, in garbled form), as when he fails to understand his squire's remark: "quien infierno tiene *nula es retencia* [Sancho misquotes *nulla est redemptio* ('there is no redemption'), saying something like 'for him whom Hell holds there is no retention']" (I, 25): it is significant that Sancho the Catholic Positivist is more familiar with ecclesiastical Latin terms than is his master, the idealistic humanist. Thus, Don Quijote is shown not only as a teacher but also as a student of language; his word-usage is by no means accepted as an ideal. And the reader is allowed to suppose that, to Cervantes himself, the language of the knight was not

---

[23] This idea, which is a medieval one, is clearly expressed by Sancho when his wife contends that, since the time he became a member of the knight-errantry, she is no longer able to understand him (II, 5): "Basta que me entienda Dios, mujer, que El es el Entendedor de todas cosas [It is enough that God understands me, wife, for He is the Understander of all things]." The same reliance on God appears in II, 7, when Sancho, whose remark, "yo soy tan fócil [I am so focile]" (*fócil* evidently representing a combination of *dócil* + *fácil* [docile + facile]) has not been understood by Quijote, explains: "soy tan así [I am so much that way]"; when this does not help, he exclaims: "Pues si no me puede entender, no sé cómo lo diga; no sé más, y Dios sea conmigo [Well, if you can't understand me, then I don't know how I might say it; I don't know anything more, God help me]." The coinage *fócil*, however nonexistent it may be in common language, covers the reality of Sancho's inner being, which is defined simply as "being as he is," and which he trusts God may recognize. (Don Quijote, himself, must admit [II, 20] that Sancho, in spite of his "rústicos términos," would make a good preacher; and Sancho concurs boastfully, immediately introducing a solecism: "Bien predica quien bien vive, y no sé otras *tologías* [He preaches well who lives well, and I do not know any other thologies ("theologies")].")

above reproach: when, in his solemn challenges or declarations of love, Quijote indulges in archaic phonetics (*f-* instead of *h-*) and morphology (uncontracted verb forms), this is not so different from the *a Dios prazca* of Sancho, or the *voacé* of one of the captives.

It seems to me that Cervantes means to present the problem of the Good Language in all its possibilities, without finally establishing an absolute: on the one hand, Sancho is allowed to state his ideal of linguistic tolerance (II, 19):

> "Pues sabe que no me he criado en la corte ni he estudiado en Salamanca para saber si añado o quito alguna letra a mis vocablos; no hay para qué obligar al sayagués a que hable como el toledano, y toledanos puede haber que no las corten en el aire en esto del hablar polido."
>
> *"Well, you know that I wasn't raised at court, nor have I studied at Salamanca to know whether I add or drop some letter in my words; there's no reason to oblige the man from Sayago to talk like one from Toledo, and there may be some Toledans who aren't so good at this business of polished talk."*

On the other, Don Quijote may assert his ideal of an "illustrated language" (in the sense of Du Bellay): when Sancho fails to understand the Latinism *erutar* (II, 43), Don Quijote remarks:

> "*Erutar*, Sancho, quiere decir 'regoldar,' y éste es uno de los más torpes vocablos que tiene la lengua castellana, aunque es más significativo. La gente curiosa se ha acogido al latín, y al *regoldar* dice *erutar*, y a los *regüeldos, erutaciones*; y cuando algunos no entienden sus términos, importa poco, que el uso los irá introduciendo con el tiempo, que con facilidad se entiendan; y esto es enriquecer la lengua, sobre quien tiene poder el vulgo y el uso."
>
> *"Eruct, Sancho, means 'belch,' which is one of the ugliest words in the Castilian language, though a most expressive one. Fastidious people have resorted to the Latin forms, and for* regoldar *they say* erutar, *and for* regüeldos, erutaciones; *and when some do not understand their terms, it matters little, for in time their use will become general, and they will be easily understood; and this is to enrich the language, over which the people and usage hold power."*

Thus, Don Quijote would create a more refined word-usage—though, at the same time, he realizes that the ultimate decision as to the enrichment of the language rests with the people; and he does not deny the expressivity of the popular expressions. Sancho's principle of linguistic expressivity, which is in line with his advocacy of the natural, of that which is inborn in man, must be seen *together* with Quijote's principle of linguistic refinement—which is a reflection of his consistent advocacy of the ideal: by positing the two points of view, the one problem in question is dialectically developed. It is obvious that in the passage on *erutar* we have a plea for a cultured language—though the ratification by the common people is urged. But this is not the same as saying that Cervantes himself is here pleading for linguistic refinement: rather, I believe, he takes no final stand but is mainly interested in a dialectical play, in bringing out the manifold facets of the problem involved. Sancho has a way of deciding problems trenchantly; Don Quijote is more aware of complexities; Cervantes stands above them both: to him, the two expressions *regoldar* and *erutar* serve to reveal so many perspectives of language.[24]

Within the framework of linguistic perspectivism fits also Cervantes' attitude toward dialects and jargons. Whereas, to Dante, all dialects appeared as inferior (though inferior in different degrees) realizations of a Platonic-Christian ideal pattern of language, as embodied in the *vulgare illustre*, Cervantes saw them as ways of speech which exist as individual realities and which have their justification in themselves. The basic Cervantine conception of perspectivism did not allow for the Platonic or Christian ideal of language: according to the creator of Don Quijote, dialects are simply the different reflections of reality (they are "styles," as the equally tolerant linguist of today would say), among which no one can take precedence over the other. Borgese, in "Il senso della letteratura italiana" (*Quaderni di Domani*, Buenos Aires, 1933), speaks definitively of Dante's conception of the *vulgare illustre*:

> Si veda nel *De vulgari eloquentia* com' egli si costruisca una lingua italiana che abbia carattere di perfezione divina, che sia, diremmo, una lingua celestiale e di angeli, di religione e di ragione; tanto che questa lingua, illustre, antica, cardinale, cortegiana, non si trova per natura in nessun luogo, e il parlare nativo di questo o di quel luogo, il dialetto di questa o quella città, è tanto più o meno nobile quanto più o meno s'avvicina a quell' ideale, così come un colore è più o meno cospicuo, più o meno luminoso, secondo che somigli al bianco o gli contrasti. Il bianco, il puro, il tutto-luce, l'astratto . . . da Dante è considerato . . . come tipo supremo del bello.
>
> *It can be seen in the* De vulgari eloquentia *how he constructs for himself an Italian language which is to have a character of divine perfection, which is, we may say, a celestial language of angels, of religion and of reason; so much so that this language, illustrious, ancient, ecclesiastical, courtly, cannot, because of its nature, be found anywhere; and the native speech of this or that place, the dialect of this or that city, is more or less noble to the degree that it approaches this ideal, just as a color is more or less conspicuous, more or less luminous, insofar as it resembles white or contrasts with it. The white, the pure, the pellucid, the abstract . . . is considered by Dante . . . the supreme type of the beautiful.*

Cervantes, on the contrary, delights in the different shades, in the particular gradations and nuances, in the gamut of colors between white and black, in the transitions between the abstract and the concrete. Hence we may explain the frequent excursions of Cervantes into what today we would call "dialectal geography"—I, 2: "un pescado que en Castilla llaman *abadejo* y en Andalucía *bacalao* y en otras partes *curadillo*, y en otras *truchuela* [a fish which in Castile they call *abadejo* and in Andalusia *bacalao* and in other areas *curadillo*, and in others *truchuela*]" (in fact, a modern Catalonian linguist, Montoliu, has been able to base his study of the synonyms for "mackerel" on this passage); I, 41: "*Tagarinos* llaman en Berbería a los moros de Aragón, y a los de

---

[24] The attitude of Cervantes toward the popular adages is no different from that toward popular words: Sancho is given to piling up such stereotyped word material indiscriminately; Don Quijote, who is himself prone to quote adages, admires Sancho's spontaneity and fluency in this regard, as well as the original and natural wisdom which they reveal—though he advocates more restraint in their use; Cervantes does not commit himself one way or the other.

Granada *mudéjares*, y en el reino de Fez llaman a los mudéjares *elches* ⟦In Barbary they call the Aragonese Moors *tagarinos*, and those from Granada *mudéjares*, and in the kingdom of Fez they call the mudéjares *elches*⟧."[25] In these lexicological variants, Cervantes must have seen not a striving toward the approximation of an ideal, but only the variegated phantasmagoria of human approaches to reality: each variant has its own justification, but all of them alike reflect no more than human "dreams." Don Quijote is allowed to expose the inadequacy of such chance designations, as appear in any one dialect, by punning on the word *truchuela* "mackerel": "Como hay muchas truchuelas, podrán servir de una trucha ⟦Since there are many *truchuelas*, they can be used as one trout⟧," where he interprets (or pretends to interpret) *truchuela* as "little trout." What, ultimately, is offered here is a criticism of the arbitrariness of any fixed expression in human language (*Sprachkritik*): the criticism which underlies the unspoken question, "Why should a mackerel be called a small trout?" Again, when Don Quijote hears the expression *cantor* ⟦one who confesses⟧ used in reference to the galley-slaves, he asks the candid question (I, 22): "¿Por músicos y cantores van también a galeras? ⟦Do musicians and singers go to the galleys too?⟧" Thus the literal interpretation of the expression serves to put into relief the macabre and ironic flavor of its metaphorical use [*cantar* = *cantar en el ansia* "to 'sing' under torture"]. Here we witness the bewilderment of Don Quijote, who tries to hold words to a strict account; we may, perhaps, sense a criticism of Quijote's too-literal approach toward language—but this, in itself, would amount to a criticism of the ambiguity of human speech. Cervantes is satisfied, however, merely to suggest the linguistic problem, without any didactic expansion.

A masterpiece of linguistic perspectivism is offered in the transposition, by Sancho, of the high-flown jargon of love contained in Don Quijote's letter to Dulcinea, of which the squire has remembered the spirit, if not the exact words. Sancho, like most primitive persons, has an excellent acoustic memory, "toma de memoria ⟦takes from memory⟧" and "tiene en su memoria ⟦holds in his memory⟧" (in line with medieval practice, he does not "memorize," cf. my article on *decorar* in *Revista de Filología Hispánica*, VI, 176, 283), but, in attempting to cope with Don Quijote's florid language, he must necessarily "transpose," remembering what he *thinks* Quijote has said. In this way, "soberana y alta señora ⟦supreme and highborn lady⟧" becomes "alta y sobajada señora ⟦high and worn-out lady⟧"—which the barber corrects to "... sobrehumana o soberana ⟦... superhuman or supreme⟧": for this single term of address we are presented with three versions, resulting in a polyonomasia, as in the case of the proper names. Again, "de punto de ausencia y el llagado de las telas del corazón ⟦(stabbed) by the point of absence and wounded in the depths of his heart⟧" > "el llego y falto de sueño y el ferido ⟦the ignorant and sleepless and wounded one⟧" (it is as though Sancho, while indulging in Isidorian

---

[25] In the *entremés* "Los habladores" a character is made to accumulate synonyms in different languages: "Una criada se llama en Valencia *fadrina*, en Italia *masara*, en Francia *gaspirria*, en Alemania *filomiquia*, en la corte *sirvienta*, en Vizcaya *moscorra*, y entre pícaros *daifa* ⟦A maid in Valencia is called *fadrina*, in Italy *masara*, in France *gaspirria*, in Germany *filomiquia*, at the court *sirvienta*, in Biscay *moscorra*, and among rogues *daifa*⟧." Here we have the raw material (*copia verborum*) on which Cervantes will draw in the *Quijote*.

etymologies, is shrewdly diagnosing his master). In such linguistic exchanges we have a parallel to the numerous dialogues between the knight and the squire which, as is well known, are inserted into the novel in order to show the different perspectives under which the same events must appear to two persons of such different backgrounds. This means that, in our novel, things are represented, not for what they are in themselves, but only as things spoken about or thought about; and this involves breaking the narrative presentation into two points of view. There can be no certainty about the "unbroken" reality of the events; the only unquestionable truth on which the reader may depend is the will of the artist who chose to break up a multivalent reality into different perspectives. In other words: perspectivism suggests an Archimedean principle outside of the plot—and the Archimedes must be Cervantes himself.

In Part II of the novel, the nickname "los del rebuzno [those from the braying town]" is loaded with a double-entendre: the Spanish variants of Gothamites draw on the doubtful art of braying for their proud war slogan: their banner bears the verse "no rebuznaron en balde / el uno y otro alcalde [they did not bray in vain / the two justices]" (the "regidores [aldermen]" have been promoted to "alcaldes" in the course of history and—evidently—thanks to the compulsion of rhyme). Here, Don Quijote is entrusted by Cervantes with exploding the vanity of such sectional patriotism: the humanistic knight, in a masterful speech which includes a series of Spanish ethnical nicknames (which take the modern philologian, Rodríguez Marín, over four full pages to explain): "los de la Reloja, los cazoleros, berenjeneros, ballenatos, jaboneros," shows the excessive vanity, originating in the flesh, not in the spirit, in the devil, not in true Catholicism, that is underlying the townspeople's attitude of resenting nicknames—i.e. of investing such trifling expressions of the language with disproportionate symbolic value. The Don Quijote who, on other occasions, is only too apt to introduce symbolism and general principles into everyday life, is here inspired by Cervantes to expose the vanity of misplaced symbolizing and generalization. The epithet "los del rebuzno" is thus made to shine with the double light of a stupidity—that wants to be taken seriously; of a local peculiarity—that aspires to "national" importance. The reader is free to go ahead and extend this criticism to other national slogans. That here Cervantes is endorsing Don Quijote seems beyond doubt since, when the novelist introduces this incident, he, speaking in his own right, attributes the adoption of the communal slogan to the activity of "the devil who never sleeps" and who is forever building "quimeras de no nada [chimeras of nothing]"—we might say: to a baroque devil who delights in deluding man. The chimeric and self-deluding quality of human vanity could hardly be illustrated more effectively than in this story, where the art of braying is first inflated and then deflated before our eyes, appearing as a "special language of human vanity."[26] And we may

---

[26] The raw material from which Cervantes drew the first episode is, according to Rodríguez Marín, a folk-tale (I would say, of the *Schildbürger*-tale variety). But, obviously, the introduction therein of the baroque element is a Cervantine touch. It is also in line with this element that the chimeric expedition of the townspeople, who are bent on conquering the whole countryside, should end in the beating administered to Sancho—a victory which, if they had been familiar with the ancient Greek custom, says Cervantes, they would have celebrated by raising a monument, a "trofeo."

see in Cervantes' twofold treatment of the problem of nicknames another example of his baroque attitude (what is true, what is dream?)—this time, toward language. Is not human language, also, *vanitas vanitatum*, is it not sometimes a "braying" of a sort? Cervantes does not outspokenly say so.

The double point of view into which Cervantes is wont to break up the reality he describes may also appear in connection with one key-word, recurring throughout a given episode, upon which Cervantes casts two different lighting effects. We have a most successful example of this in the two chapters II, 25 and 27, where our interest is focused on the motif "braying like an ass." The connecting link between the two chapters is evidently "vanity": it is vanity that prompts the two *regidores* of the Mancha de Aragón to try to out-bray each other, as they search for the lost animal which they want to decoy and whose answering bray each seems to hear—only to learn, at the end, that the braying he heard was that of the other *regidor* (the ass, meanwhile, having died). It is vanity, again, that induces the townspeople—who, after this adventure, were called "los del rebuzno" by the inhabitants of neighboring villages—to sally forth to do battle with their deriders. And it is also due to vanity, on Sancho's part, that he, while deprecating, along with Don Quijote, the gift of imitating an ass, cannot refrain from showing off his own prowess in this regard before the townspeople—who straightway turn upon him in anger and beat him.

The vanity of "braying" shares with all other vanities the one characteristic that an inconsequential feature is invested with a symbolic value which it cannot, in the light of reason, deserve. Thus a duality (sham value vs. real value) offers itself to the artist for exploitation. In the first chapter, Cervantes has the two *regidores* address each other with doubtful compliments: "de vos a un asno, compadre, no hay alguna diferencia en cuanto toca al rebuznar [between you and an ass, my friend, there is no difference as far as braying is concerned]" or "[you are the] más perito rebuznador del mundo [most skillful brayer in the world]." In the word *rebuznador*, there is a striving after the noble ring of *campeador* [champion], *emperador* [emperor]—which is drowned out by the blatant voice of the unregenerate animal: an ambivalence which exposes the hollow pretense.

There is one case in which Cervantes' perspectivism has crystallized into a bifocal word-formation; in Don Quijote's remark: "eso que a ti te parece bacía de barbero me parece a mí el yelmo de Mambrino, y a otro le parecerá otra cosa [that which seems to you to be a barber's basin seems to me Mambrino's helmet, and to another it will seem to be something else]" (I, 25),[27] there is contained a *Weltanschauung* which Américo Castro has, in a masterly fashion, recognized as a philosophical criticism (typical of the Renaissance) of the senses ("el engaño a los ojos [optical illusion]"); and this vision finds its linguistic expression, highly daring for Cervantes' time, in the coinage *baciyelmo*, with which the tolerant Sancho concludes the debate about the identity of the shining object—as if he were reasoning: "if a thing appears to me as *a*, to you as *b*, it may be, in reality, neither *a* nor *b*, but *a* + *b*" (a similar tolerance is shown by Don Quijote a little later in the same episode, when he remarks, in the

---

[27] The same pattern is evident in other passages: what is the *cueva de Montesinos* for Quijote is a "pit of hell" for Sancho: "'¿Infierno le llamáis?' dijo Don Quijote ['Hell you call it?' said Don Quijote]," II, 22.

argument about the hypothetical nature of the hypothetical Mambrino: "Así que, Sancho, deja ese caballo, o asno, o lo que quisieras que sea [[So, Sancho, leave that horse, or ass, or whatever you would like it to be]]"; Quijote, however, does not go so far as to coin a *caballiasno). Now, it is evident to any linguist that, when shaping *baciyelmo*, Cervantes must have had in mind an existing formation of the same type; and his pattern must have been that which furnished designations of hybrid animals— i.e. of a fantastic deviation from Nature—so that this quality of the fantastic and the grotesque is automatically transferred to the coinage *baciyelmo*; such a form does not guarantee the "actual" existence of any such entity $a + b$. In most cases, Cervantes must obey language, though he questions it: a basin he can only call "bacía," a helmet, only "yelmo"; with the creation of *baciyelmo*, however, he frees himself from linguistic limitations.[28] Here, as elsewhere, I would emphasize, more than Castro (whose task it was to show us the conformity to Renaissance thinking of what Cervantes himself has called his "espíritu lego [[lay spirit]]"), the artistic freedom conquered by Cervantes. In the predicament indicated by (the paradigmatic) "... o lo que quisieras que sea," the artist has asserted his own free will.

Now, from what has been said it would appear that the artist Cervantes uses linguistic perspectivism only in order to assert his own creative freedom; and this linguistic perspectivism, as I have already suggested, is only one facet of the general spirit of relativism which has been recognized by most critics as characteristic of our novel.[29] Such perspectivism, however, had, in the age of Cervantes, to acknowledge

---

[28] Linguistically speaking, *baciyelmo* fits into the group of *dvandva* formations designating hybrids in Spanish: *marimacho* [[masculine woman]], *serpihombre* [[serpent-man]] (Góngora); an object, like an animate being, may present a hybrid aspect, and be represented by the same pattern: *arquibanco* [[bench with drawers]], *catricofre* [[bed lounge]] (and *baciyelmo*). As Miss Hatcher will show, in a forthcoming article, this Renaissance type in Spanish word-formation goes ultimately back to Greek: ἀνδρογύνης-τραγέλαφος, in Latinized form: *masculo-femina, hircocervus*—and *tunico-pallium*. Thus Cervantes has expressed his perspectivistic vision in a word-formational pattern of the Renaissance reserved for hybrids.

[29] Interesting, in connection with Cervantes' linguistic perspectivism, are the many puns that appear in the *Quijote*: (I, 2) Don Quijote calls the innkeeper a *castellano* because the inn appears to him as a *castillo* in which he will be dubbed knight; but the innkeeper thinks that he has been called a "Castilian" "por haberle parecido de los sanos ['the toughs'] de Castilla [[for having seemed to him one of the toughs from Castile]]." I, 3: "No se curó ['did not care'] el harriero destas razones (y fuera mejor que se curase porque fuera curarse ['be cured'] en salud) [[The muleteer did not care about these reasons (and it would have been better if he had, for he might have saved his health)]]." II, 36: [Someone takes money] "no para tomar el mono ['because of having taken the donkey'] sino la mona ['in order to get tipsy'] [[not because of having taken the donkey but in order to get tipsy]]." II, 66: when the lackey says to Sancho, "tu amo debe de ser un loco [[your master must be mad]]," the squire answers: "¿Cómo debe? No debe nada a nadie; que todo lo paga, y más cuando la moneda es locura [[What do you mean? He doesn't owe anything to anyone; he pays everything, and especially when the coin is madness]]."

The pun is a bifocal manner of expression which relaxes and relativizes the firmness with which language usually appears to speaking man.

Sometimes the "word-world," in Renaissance fashion, encroaches on outward reality. The word *donas* in the phrase *ni dones ni donas* is an entirely fantastic formation, without any reality behind it (since the feminine of *don* is *doña* or *dueña*): it is to be explained as an extraction from *don(es)* and susceptible of usage in connection with this word alone—just as *ínsulos* is possible only in the phrase *ni ínsulas ni ínsulos*. Such formations are intended to exclude from consideration all possible varieties of the species denoted by the radical—a tendency to be found in many languages: cf. Turk. *šapka yok mapka yok* "[I have] no cap no nothing" (*mapka* being a nonce-word patterned on *šapka*). But by the very creation of a name for that which exists only at the moment it is denied, the nonexistent entity is endowed with a certain (fantastic) reality.

ultimately a realm of the absolute—which was, in his case, that of Spanish Catholicism. Cervantes, while glorying in his role of the artist who can stay aloof from the "engaños a los ojos," the "sueños" of this world, and create his own, always sees himself as overshadowed by supernal forces: the artist Cervantes never denies God, or His institutions, the King and the State. God, then, cannot be attracted into the artist's linguistic perspectivism; rather is Cervantes' God placed above the perspectives of language; He is said to be, as we have seen, the supreme "Entendedor" of the language He has created—just as Cervantes, from his lower vantage-point, seeks to be. Perhaps we may assume with Cervantes the old Neo-Platonic belief in an artistic Maker who is enthroned above the manifold facets and perspectives of the world.

The story of the *Cautivo* (I, 37 seq.), one of the many tales interpolated into the main plot, exemplifies linguistic perspectivism made subservient to the divine. The maiden betrothed to the ex-captive, who enters the stage dressed and veiled in Moorish fashion and who, without speaking a word, bows to the company in Moorish fashion, gives from the beginning the impression "que . . . devía de ser mora y que no sabía hablar cristiano [[that . . . she must be a Moor and that she didn't know how to speak Christian]]" (note the expression *hablar cristiano* [instead of *hablar castellano*] which, with its identification of "Spanish" and "Christian," anticipates the religious motif basic to the story). Dorotea is the one to ask the all-important question: "¿esta señora es mora o cristiana? [[is this lady a Moor or a Christian?]]"—to which the Cautivo answers that she is a Moor in her costume and in her body, but in her soul, a great Christian, although not yet baptized—but "Dios será servido que presto se bautice [[God willing, she will soon be baptized]]" (again, we may see in this mention of God not only a conventional form but a suggestion of the main problem, which is the working of Divine Grace). The Cautivo, speaking in Arabic, asks his betrothed to lift her veil in order to show forth her enchanting beauty; when asked about her name, he gives it in the Arabic form: *lela Zoraida*. And now the Moorish girl herself speaks for the first time: "No, no Zoraida: María, María"—repeating this statement twice more (the last time half in Arabic, half in Spanish: "Sí, sí, María: Zoraida *macange* ['not at all']"). The change of name which she claims—evidently in anticipation of the change of name which will accompany her baptism—is of deep significance; it is a profession of faith, of conversion. We will learn later that she must become a María because, since her early childhood, she had been taken under the mantle of the Virgin.

After this first appearance of "Zoraida-María," whose two names are nothing but the linguistic reflection of her double nature, the episode is interrupted by Don Quijote's speech on *armas y letras*; thus, after the briefest of introductions, we must lose sight for a while of Zoraida-María, the puzzle of whose twofold name and Januslike personality remains suspended in midair. The interruption is significant: Cervantes, in the episodic short stories, follows for the most part a technique opposed to that of the main plot: in the latter we are always shown first the objective reality of events, so that when they later become distorted after having passed through the alembic of Don Quijote's mind (Sancho, in general, remains more true to the reality he has experienced) we, from the knowledge we have previously gained, are proof against the knight's folly. But, in the short stories, on the contrary, Cervantes' technique is to tantalize us with glimpses into what seems an incredible situation, worthy of Quijote's own imagination (in our own story there suddenly appears before the group of Don Quijote's friends assembled in an inn, an exotic-looking woman, dressed in outlandish gear, with her companion who has to talk for her) and with all the connotations of the unreal; and the author is careful to protract our suspense to the utmost before giving us the solution of the initial puzzle. Thus the interpolations of these episodic short stories, whose reality is at least as fantastic as the most daring dreams of the mad knight, offer another revelation of the perspectivism of Cervantes; we have to do not only with the opposition between prosaic reality and fantastic dreams: reality itself can be both prosaic and fantastic. If, in the main plot, Cervantes has carried out his program of "derribar la máquina mal fundada [demolishing the badly founded structure]" of the fantastic, he has taken care to rebuild this machinery in the by-stories. And our tale of the Captive is an excellent illustration of this rule.

When, after Don Quijote's speech, the Captive tells his story *ab ovo*, explaining how the startling fact of a "Zoraida–María" came to pass, we are allowed a glimpse into the historic reality of that hybrid world of Mohammedans and Christians, which was the equivalent in Cervantes' time of the *fronterizo* milieu of the romances—only, a more complicated variant because of the two different groups representative of the Mohammedan faith then facing the Spaniards: the Turks and the Arabs, the former the more ruthless type, the latter (to which Lela Zoraida and her father belong) the type more amenable to the Christian way of life. Indeed, the Arabs themselves seem to feel more akin to the Christian civilization than to the Turkish (the girl's father calls the Turks *canes* [Lat. "dogs"]; it is ironic that later, after he has been deeply wronged by the Christians, he must call them *perros* [Sp. "dogs"]).

As the Captive tells the story of the tragic events that took place against the background of the warring Turkish Empire, he embellishes his (Spanish-language) narrative with words from Turkish and Arabic, offering a linguistic mosaic that adds to the local color of his story. If we compare the Turkish words with the Arabic, we will note the sharpest of contrasts: the former are of a factual reference, narrowly descriptive, with no transcendental connotations (for the Turks are excluded from the possibility of Enlightenment by Grace): *leventes* [naval infantry], *bagarinos* [rowers], *baño* [bath] (wrongly offered as a Turkish word for "prison"), *pasamaques* [sandals], *zoltanís* [coins], *gilecuelco* [captive's coat]; we find also the pejorative epithet *Uchalí Fartax* "que quiere decir en lengua turquesca el renegado tiñoso, porque lo era [which means in Turkish 'the mean renegade,' because he was one]" (again, the *convenientia* between names and objects!). The Arabic words, on the contrary, are nearly always connected with things religious and, more specifically, with things Christian—so that a kind of transposition (or perspectivism) is achieved: "Lela Marién" instead of "Nuestra Señora la Virgen María [Our Lady the Virgin Mary]"; "Alá" for the Christian God, and also the interjection "quelá" in the same reference; *nizarani* for "Christians"; *la zalá cristianesca* for "the Christian prayer," in which the adjective *cristianesco* (instead of *cristiano*), formed after *morisco*, *turquesco*, has something of the same transposed character, as if the Christian rites were seen from the outside. And, in addition to the linguistic medley offered the reader directly, there is a reference to the polyglot habits among the protagonists of the story. Zoraida, for example, chooses Arabic as the private language in which to talk and write to the Captive, but converses with the Christians (as also does her father) in the *lingua franca*—which language is characterized by the Captive as "lengua que en toda la Berbería, y aun en Constantinopla se habla entre cautivos y moros, que ni es morisca ni castellana ni de otra nación alguna, sino una mezcla de todas las lenguas, con la cual todos nos entendemos [the tongue that in all Barbary, and even in Constantinople, is spoken between captives and Moors, which is neither Moorish nor Castilian nor of any other nation, but a mixture of all languages, with which we all understand each other]," or "la bastarda lengua que ... allí se usa [the bastard tongue which ... is used there]": a characterization, it may be noted, which is not basically different from that offered in our times by Schuchardt ("Mischsprache," "Verkehrßprache."), the student of *lingua franca*, of the Creole languages, etc., and the advocate of an international artificial language. Castilian, Turkish, Arabic, with reminiscences of *lingua franca*: why this Babelic confusion of tongues in our story? It does not suffice to appeal to the historical fact that these languages were actually spoken at the time in the Ottoman Empire, where Cervantes himself had lived as a captive: for, in addition to the foreign phrases that might serve simply for local color, we have to do evidently with an express concern for each individual language as such—to the extent that we are always informed in which language a certain speech, letter, or dialogue was couched. It seems to me that Cervantes would point out that differences of language do not, by principle, hinder the working of Christian Grace—though he evidently grades the languages according to their penetrability by things Christian: Turkish is presented as on a lower level than Arabic—which lends itself so easily to the transposition of Christian concepts.[30] And this linguistic transposition of things Christian into things Moorish reflects only the transposed situation of a Moor who becomes a Christian;

---

[30] In the story of Ana Félix, the Christian daughter of the Morisco Ricote, we see again how closely connected are language and faith: she explains (II, 53): "Tuve una madre cristiana ... mamé la Fé católica con la leche; criéme con buenas costumbres; ni en la lengua ni en ellas jamás, a mi parecer, di señales de ser morisca [I had a Christian mother ... I drank in the Catholic Faith with her milk; I grew up with good habits; neither in my language nor ever in those habits, in my opinion, did I show signs of being Moorish]." The reader should note the expression *mamar la fé con la leche*: the same expression is used in Cervantes (II, 16) of the mother tongue: "todos los poetas antiguos escribieron en la lengua que mamaron con la leche [all the ancient poets wrote in the language that they drank in with their mothers' milk]"; and Castro has pointed out the origin of this metaphor (Bembo, *Della volgar lingua*, 1525: "... nella latina [sc. *lingua*] essi [the Romans] tutti nascevano e quella insieme col latte dalle nutriei loro beeano ... [... they [the Romans] were born to Latin and drank it in with the milk of their sustenance ...]"). Here, we are at the bottom of the concept of *Muttersprache*, *langue maternelle*, *mother tongue*, which ultimately go back to an Augustinian concept: the Christian learns the name of God from his mother ("hoc nomen salvatoris mei ... in ipso adhuc lacte matris tenerum cor meum biberat [this name of my Savior ... my young heart had imbibed all along in the very milk of my mother]"): the "name of God" is the most important and the most intimate linguistic knowledge the mother can impart to her child; thus (and this is in harmony with Christianity, which, in general, tends to present spiritual truths behind a human veil), the concept of "mother tongue" is vitally connected with that of maternal religion (cf. *Monatshefte für deutschen Unterricht*, XXXVI, 120).

the story of the Captive and of Zoraida-María shows Grace working toward the salvation of a disbeliever and toward the sacramental union, by a Christian marriage, of two beings of different races: above the divergence of race and language[31] God understands the Christian longing of Zoraida for the *Alá cristiano*. It was the Virgin Mary, of whom she had learned from a Christian nurse, who inspired her to rescue the Christian soldier and to flee with him to a Christian country in order there to be baptized and married. When Zoraida speaks of Alá, everyone knows that the Christian God is meant—Whose true nature shines through the linguistic disguise. The same symbol is carried out on another plane: when, from her window, Zoraida's white hand is seen, adorned with Moorish jewels (*ajorcas*), waving a Christian cross, the *ajorcas* are naturally overshadowed by the cross.[32] Again, in the case of Zoraida's letters to the prisoners, written in Arabic but adorned with the sign of the Cross, it is clear that these indications of different cultural climates clearly express only one thing: her will to be a Christian. It is not the language, the gesture, the costume, or the body that matter to Him, but the meaning behind all the exterior manifestations: the soul. God, Cervantes is telling us, can recognize behind the "perspective" of a disbeliever, His true faithful follower.

I cannot quite agree with Castro, who seems to see mainly the human side of the episode, when he says (*El pensamiento de Cervantes*, p. 147): "Amor y religión (ésta como envoltura de aquél) llevan a Zoraida tras su cautivo [love and religion (the latter as a development of the former) carry Zoraida after her Captive]," and

[31] In the other Moorish story in our novel, that of the expelled Ricote who, having fled to Germany, comes back in the disguise of a German pilgrim to Spain (II, 54), the exile mixes German (¡*Guelte*! ¡*Guelte*!) into his Spanish—a language which he knows as well as does Sancho, whose "neighborhood shopkeeper" he had been. Cervantes describes Sancho's inability to understand the Germanate jargon of Ricote, whose identity he fails at first to recognize. Later, the pilgrim throws aside his incognito and hails Sancho "en voz alta y muy castellana [in a loud and very Castilian voice]"; "Ricote, sin tropezar nada en su lengua morisca, en la pura castellana le [to Sancho] dijo las siguientes palabras [Ricote, without falling into his Moorish language, in pure Castilian said [to Sancho] the following words]." In the ensuing drinking scene, Sancho, in his mellow tipsiness, finally ends up by speaking the esperanto of *lingua franca*. In this episode we must infer that the difficulties of linguistic understanding are all artificially contrived: here are *Ricote el morisco* and *Sancho el bueno*, who have lived side by side for many years and who are quite able to understand each other perfectly, who have the same habits of living, eating, and drinking—and are separated from each other only by the (arbitrary) fact of the Morisco's exile.

Ricote is as good a Spaniard as is Sancho (perhaps also a more gifted one: this comes out in his ironic question, so natural with emigrants who, returning to their mother country, see themselves in a position inferior to their merits: "¿Faltaban hombres más hábiles para gobernadores que tú eres? [There weren't any men more able than you to be governors?]"), and his daughter is a perfect Christian; nevertheless, as exiles, they have been the victims of an arbitrary death-blow. But, by his exile, Ricote has not only learned to say *guelte* instead of *limosna* [alms]: he has come to know religious tolerance as he saw it practiced in Augsburg, in the heart of Protestantism. No bolder words could have been written, in Counter-Reformation Spain, about religious freedom, than are expressed here by Ricote. Nevertheless, the same Ricote bows submissively before the expulsion of the Moors by the Spanish King and his minister, which has plunged him and his family into despair and misery. Cervantes seems here more interested in the dialectic play of arguments, in the facets and perspectives of the problem, than in giving a decision on the moral issue. To the Spanish subject-matter of the novel, the stories of Moorish emigrants, renegades, and converts add a new perspective, that of Spain seen from the outside—a perspective of "spiritual geography."

[32] The same double light is cast on the *caña*, that angling rod dropped by Zoraida to the captives, which is first only a utensil, an astute device, and then becomes a symbol of the miracle ("*milagro*") of a twofold salvation.

considers the story to be one of "armonía entre seres concordados [[harmony between concordant beings]]." Rather, I should say that religion is the kernel, love the envelopment; we have here a drama of Divine Grace working against all possible handicaps and using the love between Moor and Christian as a means to an end: the conversion of Zoraida (and, incidentally, the return of a renegade [33] to the bosom of the Church); therefore Cervantes has devised his story against the background of the Spanish-Turkish wars, which ended with the victory of the Spaniards at Lepanto and in which, as Titian has represented it, Spain succors Christian faith. I concur absolutely with Castro, however, when he goes on to say that this story of abduction is the most violent and the most tragic of all the episodes in the novel: Zoraida, in her zeal to receive holy baptism and the sacrament of Christian marriage, must cheat her father, must see him subjected by her doings to the violence of the Christians who truss him up and finally leave him marooned on a desert island, where he cries out to his daughter, alternately cursing and beseeching her. Here is a good Arab, meek and truthful to Christians, who is thrown back to the Mohammedan god by the ruthless deed of his Christian daughter. That such sins may be committed for the rescue of a soul can only be explained, Cervantes seems to tell us, by the incalculable will of Providence. Why should these sins be made corollary to the salvation of the particular soul of Zoraida—while the soul of her father becomes thereby utterly lost to salvation? What whimsicality of God! I should say that this scene exhibits not so much the "abismos de lo humano," as Castro has it, but rather "abismos de lo divino." No harmonious earthly marriage could be concluded on the bases of such a terrifying violation of the Fourth Commandment; but God is able to put the laws of morality out of function in order to reach His own goal.

In our story, which is the story of a great deceit, the words referring to "deceit" take on a particularly subtle double-entendre. When, for example, Zoraida, in one of her letters to the Captive, says: "no te fies de ningún moro, porque son todos *marfuzes* [[do not trust any Moor, because they are all treacherous]]" of her Moslem coreligionists, she is using an originally Arabic word for "treacherous" which had come to be borrowed by the Spaniards probably to refer, primarily, to the treachery of the Mohammedans (meaning something like "false as a Moor"); the choice of this word, which sounds rather strange when used by an Arab, must mean that Zoraida is judging the Arabs according to Christian prejudices (it is ironical that, in this story, it is the Arabs who are faithful and kind, and the Christians who are "marfuzes"— although working toward a goal presumably willed by Providence). Again, the

---

[33] In this tale, the "renegade" develops before our eyes and gradually comes to take on stature; he shows his eagerness to help in the escape of the prisoners: after his repentance, when he swears by the cross to change from a "foul" member of the Church to a true member, the Christian fugitives put themselves "en las manos de Dios y en las del renegado [[in the hands of God and in those of the renegade]]" (as though God's hands used those of the renegade for His purposes). Later, it is true, his plan is abandoned for another one ("Dios, que lo ordenaba de otra manera, no dió lugar al buen deseo que nuestro renegado tenía [[God, who had ordained otherwise, did not give occasion for the fine wish that our renegade had]]"), but, nevertheless, he is saved along with the whole party and succeeds in his desire "a reducirse por medio de la santa Inquisición al gremio santísimo de la Iglesia [[to enter through the sacred Inquisition unto the most sacred body of the Church]]."

accusation of cheating is reversed when Zoraida, speaking as a Moor to the Christian Captive, in the presence of her father, remarks: "... vosotros cristianos siempre mentís en cuanto decís, y os hacéis pobres por engañar a los moros [... you Christians always lie in whatever you say, and you demean yourselves by lying to the Moors]"; here, where her judgment is, indeed, factually justified, she is actually speaking disingenuously—in order to further the stratagem planned by the Christians. The discrepancy between words and meaning, between judgment and behavior, has reached such proportions that we can view only with perplexity the "abismo del divino" which makes it possible that such evil means are accepted to further a noble purpose; the story offers us no way out but to try to share Zoraida's belief in the beneficent intervention of Lela Marién, who has prompted the good-wicked enterprise ("plega a Alá, padre mío, que Lela Marién, que ha sido la causa de que yo sea cristiana, ella te consuele en tu tristeza [let it please Allah, my father, that Lela Marién, who has caused me to be a Christian, will console you in your sadness]"). When Zoraida, speaking to her father, states of her deed "que parece tan buena como tú, padre amado, la juzgas por mala [which to me seems as good, beloved father, as to you it seems evil]," we are offered basically the same perspectivistic pattern that we have noted in the case of the *baciyelmo*: it is implied, evidently, that Lela Marién knows of no perspectivism. There can be no doubt that what Cervantes is dealing with here is the tortuous and Jesuitic divinity that he was able to see in his time— whose decisions he accepts, while bringing out all the complications involved. Along with the submission to the divine there is instituted a tragic trial against it, a trial on moral grounds, and, on these grounds, the condemnation is unmitigated; the sacramental force of a father's curse is not entirely counterbalanced by the sacramental force of the Christian rites, the desire for which on Zoraida's part brought about the father's plight. Perhaps no writer, remaining within the boundaries of orthodox religion, has revealed more of the perplexities inherent in the theocratic order (a Nietzsche might have called this story an example of the immorality of God and have advocated the overthrow of such a God—whereas Cervantes quietly stays within the boundaries of the Christian fold). And this acme of submissive daring has been achieved by placing the divine beyond the perspectives which appear to the human eye.

Zoraida herself, for all her religious fervor, innocence, and supernatural beauty, is, at the same time, capable of great wickedness. And again linguistic perspectivism is invoked in order to bring this side of her nature into relief. There is a moment when the band of fugitives pass the promontory called, after the mistress of Roderick, the last of the Gothic Kings, *cabo de la Cava Rumia* "... de la mala mujer cristiana [... of the evil Christian woman]"; they insist, however, that to them it is not the "abrigo de mala mujer, sino puerto seguro de nuestro remedio [coat of the evil woman, but the sure port of our remedy]." Now, when the name of this infamous woman, who sinned for love, is brought before the reader, he cannot fail to think of Zoraida—though, in the comparison with the Arabic prostitute "por quien se perdió España [for whom Spain was lost]," the betrothed of the Captive must appear as a pure woman, who refused to live in a state of sin before her marriage. At the same time, however, Cervantes may wish us to realize how close was Zoraida to the abyss, and to see the ward of the Virgin, for a moment, under the perspective of la Cava.

IF WE LOOK BACK NOW over the development of this essay, we will see that we have been led from a plethora of names, words, languages, from polyonomasia, polyetymologia, and polyglottism, to the linguistic perspectivism of the artist Cervantes who knows that the transparence of language is a fact for God alone. And, at this point, I may be allowed to repeat, as a kind of epitomizing epilogue, the final passages of a lecture on the *Quijote* which I have given at several universities—which, I trust, will serve to round out the linguistic details I have pointed out earlier and to put them into relationship with the whole of the novel: a relationship which, in the course of our linguistic discussion, has already been tentatively indicated. After explaining that the *Quijote* appeals as well to children as to adults because of its combination of imagination and criticism, and that the modern genre of the critical novel, which started with a criticism of books and of a bookish culture (a criticism of the romances of chivalry) and came to be expanded to a new integration of the critical and the imaginative, was the discovery of Cervantes, I continued thus:

It is one of the great miracles of history (which is generally regarded deterministically by professional historians, who present individual phenomena as enclosed within tight compartments), that the greatest deeds sometimes occur at a place and time when the historian would least expect them. It is a historical miracle that, in the Spain of the Counter-Reformation, when the trend was toward the reestablishment of authoritarian discipline, an artist should have arisen who, thirty-two years before Descartes' *Discours de la méthode* (that autobiography of an independent philosophical thought, as Lanson has called it), was to give us a narrative which is simply one exaltation of the independent mind of man—and of a particularly powerful type of man: of the artist. It is not Italy, with its Ariosto and Tasso, not France with its Rabelais and Ronsard, but Spain that gave us a narrative which is a monument to the narrator qua narrator, qua artist. For, let us not be mistaken: the real protagonist of this novel is not Quijote, with his continual misrepresentation of reality, or Sancho with his skeptical half-endorsement of quixotism—and surely not any of the central figures of the illusionistic by-stories: the hero is Cervantes, the artist himself, who combines a critical and illusionistic art according to his free will. From the moment we open the book[34] to the moment we put it

---

[34] In this connection, we should consider the famous opening sentence of the novel: "En un lugar de la Mancha de cuyo nombre no quiero acordarme [[In a place in La Mancha whose name I do not wish to recall]]." All the explanations hitherto offered—the silly autobiographical one (Cervantes had personal reasons for not wanting to remember the name); that based on literary history, proposed by Casalduero (Cervantes opposes his novel to the romances of chivalry, which claimed to know exactly wherefrom their heroes hailed); the folkloristic one of María Rosa Lida (the sentence is in line with the beginning of folk-tales)— fail to take into sufficient consideration the functional value, for the novel, of the attitude of the author expressed therein—which, in my opinion, is the glorification of the freedom of the artist. Even if, for example, Mme. Lida should be right, the transfer of a sentence traditional in folk-tales into this particular novel of Cervantes could give the transferred sentence a new meaning, just as certain folklorisms adopted by Goethe

down, we are given to understand that an almighty overlord is directing us, who leads us where he pleases. The prologue of the whole work shows us Cervantes in the perplexity of an author putting the final touches to his work, and we understand that the "friend" who seemingly came to his aid with a solution was only one voice within the freely fabricating poet. And, on the last page of the book when, after Quijote's Christian death, Cervantes has that Arabian historian Cide Hamete Benengeli lay away his pen, to rest forever, on the top of the cupboard in order to forestall any further spurious continuation (after the manner of Avellaneda) of the novel, we know that the reference to the Arabian pseudo-historian is only a pretext for Cervantes to reclaim for himself the relationship of real father (no longer the "step-father," as in the prologue) to his book. Then the pen delivers itself of a long speech, culminating in the words: "For me alone Don Quijote was born and I for him; his task was to act, mine to write. For we alone are made for each other" ("Para mí solo nació Don Quijote, y yo para él; él supo obrar, y yo escribir; solos los dos somos para en uno"). An imperious *alone* (*solo[s]*)

---

or Heine become more than folklorisms in the lyrical poetry of these poets. By the deliberate assertion of his free will to choose the motifs of his plot, to emphasize or disregard what detail he pleases (and "no quiero" expresses deliberate disregard), Cervantes has founded that genre of "subjective story-telling" which, before him, is found at its incipient state with Boccaccio and which, later, was to inspire Goethe (in the beginning of the *Wahlverwandtschaften*: "Eduard—so nennen wir einen reichen Baron im besten Mannesalter—Eduard hatte... [Edward—thus we name a rich baron in the flower of manhood—Edward had...]"), Laurence Sterne, Fielding, Melville ("Call me Ishmael!").

In an address to the Baltimore Goethe Society, entitled "Laurence Sterne's *Tristram Shandy* and Thomas Mann's *Joseph the Provider*" (later published in *Modern Language Quarterly*, VIII, 101 seq.), Professor Oskar Seidlin pointed out the presence, in both these modern works, of some of the same comic devices (change of names, assumption of fictional sources, introduction of "relativizing dialogues," etc.) which I have been discussing as characteristic of Cervantine perspectivism. Since Thomas Mann himself had stated in 1942 that, during the composition of his *Joseph* he had had two books as his steady companions, *Tristram Shandy* and *Faust*, the stylistic congruences between the German and the English novel are easily explained. On the other hand, the devices of Sterne which reappear with Mann were, in turn, borrowed from Cervantes; and, in this connection, it is relevant to note that, in 1935, Thomas Mann had published his essay on the *Don Quijote*: thus the Cervantine climate may have acted doubly upon him: directly as well as indirectly. And, though the idea expressed in *Joseph the Provider* that the world is "Jehovah's Jest" would not have occurred to Cervantes, who glorified the "artist beneath the dome of God," the great *Entendedor*, the Spanish poet could have subscribed to Mann's idea of "artistic lightness" as man's consolation (*loc. cit.*, New York edition, p. 357): "For lightness, my friend, the artful jest, that is God's very best gift to man, the profoundest knowledge we have of this complex, questionable thing called life. God gave it to humanity so that life's terribly serious face might be forced to wear a smile.... Only in lightness can the spirit of men rise above them [the questions put to us by life]: with a laugh at being faced with the unanswerable, perhaps he can make even God Himself, the great Unanswering, to smile."

It is interesting that Thomas Mann, who, in his *Buddenbrooks*, was still the pure representative of what Walzel has called "objective narration" (in the Spielhagen style), has from the time of his *Magic Mountain* developed consistently in the direction of Cervantine "story-telling" technique; this evolution must be due, not only to the general change in literary trends that has been taking place, but also to Mann's growing consciousness of the triumphant part the artist is called upon to play in modern society.

In this connection I may cite also the opening line of E. M. Forster's novel *Howard's End* (1910): "One may as well begin with Helen's letters to her sister," on which Lionel Trilling, *E. M. Forster* (1943), remarks: "Guiding his stories according to his serious whim... Forster takes full and conscious responsibility for his novels, refusing to share in the increasingly dull assumption of the contemporary novelist, that the writer has nothing to do with the story he tells, and that, *mirabile dictu*, through no intention of his own, the story has chosen to tell itself through him. Like Fielding, he shapes his prose for comment and explanation. He summarizes what he is going to show, introduces new themes when and as it suits him."

which only Cervantes could have said and in which all the Renaissance pride of the poet asserts itself: the poet who was the traditional immortalizer of the great deeds of historical heroes and princes. An Ariosto could have said the same words about the Duke of Ferrara.

The function of eulogizing princes was, as is well known, the basis of the economical situation of the Renaissance artist: he was given sustenance by the prince in return for the immortal glory which he bestowed upon his benefactor (cf. Zilsel, *Die Entstehung des Geniebegriffs*). But Don Quijote is no prince from whom Cervantes could expect to receive a pension, no doer of great deeds in the outer world (his greatness lay only in his warm heart), and not even a being who could be attested in any historical source—however much Cervantes might pretend to such sources. Don Quijote acquired his immortality exclusively at the hands of Cervantes—as the latter well knows and admits. Obviously, Quijote wrought only what Cervantes wrote, and he was born for Cervantes as much as Cervantes was born for him! In the speech of the pen of the pseudo-chronicler we have the most discreet and the most powerful self-glorification of the artist which has ever been written. The artist Cervantes grows by the glory which his characters have attained; and in the novel we see the process by which the figures of Don Quijote and Sancho become living persons, stepping out of the novel, so to speak, to take their places in real life—finally to become immortal historical figures. Thomas Mann, in a recent essay on the *Quijote* (in "Leiden und Grösse der Meister"), has said: "This is quite unique. I know of no other hero of a novel in world literature who would equally, so to speak, live off the glory of his own glorification" ("... ein Romanheld [der] ... von dem Ruhm seines Ruhmes, von seiner Besungenheit lebt"). In the second part of the novel, when the Duke and Duchess ask to see the by now historical figures of Quijote and Panza, the latter says to the Duchess: "I am Don Quijote's squire who is to be found also *in the story* and who is called Sancho Panza—unless they have changed me in the cradle—I mean to say, at the printer's." In such passages, Cervantes willingly destroys the artistic illusion: he, the puppeteer, lets us see the strings of his puppet-show: "see, reader, this is not life, but a stage, a book: art; recognize the life-giving power of the artist as a thing distinct from life!"[35] By multiplying his masks

---

[35] I realize that this is an opinion contrary to that of the writers of the Enlightenment who, in their treatment of the *Don Quijote*, made much of Cervantes' own classicistic pronouncement that art imitates nature. Locke, for example, has written: "Of all the books of fiction, I know none that equals Cervantes's 'History of Don Quijote,' in usefulness [!], pleasantry, and a constant decorum. And indeed no writings can be pleasant, which have not nature at the bottom, and are not drawn after copy." And Sydenham, the English Hippocrates and founder of modern clinical treatment, is reported to have advised young medical students to read the *Don Quijote* instead of books on medicine—because (as Professor Edelstein shows, in *Bulletin of the History of Medicine*, suppl. 3, 1944, p. 54) he evidently thought the Spanish novel offered a deterrent example of a person who views the world in the light of his preconceived ideas instead of that of facts—with which alone Dr. Sydenham was concerned.

Needless to say, my historical interpretation is also at the other pole from the poetic vision of an Unamuno who believes that this story was dictated to Cervantes' pen by the suprapersonal and perennial Spanish character, by the innate Spanish will to immortality by suffering and the "sentimiento trágico de la vida" as embodied in the figures of the quasi-saint Nuestro Señor Don Quijote de la Mancha and of his evangelical squire. In my opinion, it is Cervantes the "artistic dictator," who dictated the story to his pen, and Cer-

(the friend of the prologue, the Arabian historian, sometimes the characters who serve as his mouthpiece), Cervantes seems to strengthen his grip on that whole artistic cosmos. And the strength of the grip is enhanced by the very nature of the protagonists: Quijote is what we would call today a split personality, sometimes rational, sometimes foolish; Sancho, too, at times no less quixotic than his master, is at other times incalculably rational. In this way, the author makes it possible for himself to decide when his characters will act reasonably, when foolishly (no one is more unpredictable than a fool who pretends to wisdom). At the start of his journey with Sancho, Don Quijote promises his squire an island kingdom to be ruled over by him, just as was done in the case of numerous squires in literature. But, acting on his critical judgment (of which he is not devoid), Don Quijote promises to give it to him immediately after their conquest—instead of waiting until the squire has reached old age, as is the custom in the books of chivalry. The quixotic side of Sancho accepts this prospective kingship without questioning its possibility, but his more earthly nature visualizes—and criticizes—the actual scene of the coronation: how would his rustic spouse Juana Gutiérrez look with a crown on her head? Two examples of foolishness, two critical attitudes: none of them is the attitude of the writer, who remains above the two split personalities and the four attitudes.

With the Machiavellian principle "divide and conquer" applied to his characters, the author succeeds in making himself indispensable to the reader: while, in his prologue, Cervantes calls for a critical attitude on our part, he makes us depend all the more on his guidance through the psychological intricacies of the narrative: here, at least, he leaves us no free will. We may even infer that Cervantes rules imperiously over his own self: it was he who felt this self to be split into a critical and an illusionistic part (*desengaño* and *engaño*); but in this baroque Ego he made order, a precarious order, it is true, which was reached only once by Cervantes in all his works—and which was reached in Spain only by Cervantes (for Calderón, Lope, Quevedo, Gracián decided that the world is only illusion and dreams, "que los sueños sueños son"). And indeed only once in world literature has this precarious order come into being: later thinkers and artists did not stop at proclaiming the inanity of the world: they went so far as to doubt the existence of any universal order and to deny a Creator, or at least, when imitating Cervantes' perspectivism (Gide, Proust, Conrad, Joyce, Virginia Woolf, Pirandello),[36] they

---

vantes, no half-Christian like Unamuno, knew how to distinguish the earthly plane from the transcendental. On the former plane he obeyed his own *sovereign reason*. He does, then, not belong to the family of Pascal and Kierkegaard, but to that of Descartes and Goethe.

[36] Pirandello's perspectivism is in this respect different from that of Cervantes: with the latter, it is the *author* who looks for his characters, not the reverse.

I beg also to disagree with those critics who compare Cervantes with El Greco because of the novelist's "modern impressionism." We must be clear about the meaning of the term "impressionism." Cervantes never offers *his own* impressions of outward reality, as does the modern artist of the impressionistic school; he presents simply the impressions which his characters may have had—and, by juxtaposing these different impressions, he implicitly criticizes them all. The program of the modern impressionist, on the other hand, makes impossible the intervention of the critical sense into what he sees. As for the impressionism of El

have failed to sense the unity behind perspectivism—so that, in their hands, the personality of the author is allowed to disintegrate. Cervantes stands at the other pole from that modern dissolution of the personality of the narrator: what grandeur there is in his attempt—made in the last moment before the unified Christian vision of the world was to fall asunder—to restore this vision on the artistic plane, to hold before our eyes a cosmos split into two separate halves: disenchantment and illusion, which, nevertheless, by a miracle, do not fall apart! Modern anarchy checked by a classical will to equipoise (the baroque attitude)! We recognize now that it is not so much that Cervantes' nature is split in two (critic and narrator) because this is required by the nature of Don Quijote, but rather that Don Quijote is a split character because his creator was a critic-poet who felt with almost equal strength the urge of illusionary beauty and of pellucid clarity.

To modern readers the "schizophrenic" Don Quijote might seem to be a typical case of social frustration: a person whose madness is conditioned by the social insignificance into which the caste of the knights had fallen, with the beginnings of modern warfare—just as, in Flaubert's *Un Cœur simple*, we are meant to see as socially conditioned the frustrations of Félicité, the domestic servant, which lead to the aberration of her imagination. I would, however, warn the reader against interpreting Cervantes in terms of Flaubert, since Cervantes himself has done nothing to encourage such a sociological approach. Don Quijote is able to recover his sanity, if only on his death-bed; and his erstwhile madness is but one reflection of that generally human lack of reason—above which the author has chosen to take his stand.[37]

High above this world-wide cosmos of his making, in which hundreds of characters, situations, vistas, themes, plots and subplots are merged, Cervantes' artistic self is enthroned, an all-embracing creative self, Naturelike, Godlike, almighty, all-wise, all-good—and benign: this visibly omnipresent Maker reveals to us the secrets of his creation, he shows us the work of art in the making, and the laws to which it is necessarily subjected. For this artist is Godlike but not deified; far be it from us to conceive of Cervantes as attempting to dethrone God, replacing Him by the artist as a superman. On the contrary, Cervantes always bows before the supernal wisdom of God, as embodied in the teachings of the Catholic Church and the established order of the state and of society. Qua moralist, Cervantes is not

---

Greco, while this involves no criticism of reality as does that of Cervantes (since the ultimate reality he portrays is the divine), it does offer the evanescent reflections of the divine—which may, of course, have prepared the public for the perception of the evanescent in this world, i.e. for modern "impressionistic" perception.

[37] Professor Auerbach, in his book *Mimesis* (Bern, 1946), p. 319, states the lack, in the *Don Quijote* (as in the whole literature of the *siglo de oro*), of any "problematische Erforschung der zeitgenössischen Wirklichkeit," of any "Bewegung in den Tiefen des Lebens," of any search into the social motivations of Don Quijote's madness, and of the life of his age—the underlying idea being that the "real" motivations of life are those of sociology, not of morality, on which Cervantes has based his novel (though, as we have said, he offers us the conflict between different moral standards). The attitude of this critic, which seems to abound in the sense of Carl Becker ("the historian has become the successor of the theologian"), is, in my opinion, contingent on the presupposition that moral values are obsolete in a modern world given to the sociological explanation of history.

at all "perspectivistic."³⁸ Nor can we expect to find in Cervantes any of that romantic revolt of the artist against society. But, on the other hand, the artist Cervantes has extended, by the mere art of his narrative, the Demiurge-like, almost cosmic independence of the artist. His humor, which admits of many strata, perspectives, masks—of relativization and dialectics—bears testimony to his high position above the world. His humor is the freedom of the heights, no fate-bound dionysiac dissolution of the individual into nothingness and night, as with Schopenhauer and Wagner, but a freedom beneath the dome of that religion which affirms the freedom of the will. There is, in the world of his creation, the bracing air with which we may fill our lungs and by which our individual senses and judgment are sharpened; and the crystalline lucidity of an artistic Maker in its manifold reflections and refractions.

³⁸ It should perhaps be pointed out here that "perspectivism" is inherent in Christian thought itself. The pair Don Quijote–Sancho Panza is, after all, a Cervantine replica of the medieval characters Solomon and Marcolf, in whom the wisdom of the sage and that of the common man are contrasted (we may also see in Sancho Panza's *refranes* a later version of the *proverbes au vilain*). Such an exemplary contrast is derived from the evangelic truth that the common man has access to wisdom, as well as the learned man; that the spirit, if not the letter, of the law can be understood by anyone. Here, we have an example of "medieval gradualism," according to which the social or mental level of Christ's followers is ultimately irrelevant. It is for this reason that, in medieval mystery plays, lofty scenes treating the life of Christ may alternate with scurrilous scenes in which shepherds or clowns are allowed to express their "point of view," on the august events in question, in their own unregenerate rustic speech. In this "gradualism," perspectivism is implied; and, to the perspectivism which Cervantes found in the medieval tradition, he added only the artistic aloofness of a Renaissance thinker.

Roland Against Ganelon

❧ ERICH AUERBACH ❦

Erich Auerbach's extraordinary book *Mimesis: The Representation of Reality in Western Literature*—the original German edition of which appeared in 1946 and the English translation in 1953—is founded on Auerbach's meticulous analyses of a series of texts, ranging in time from the *Odyssey* and the Bible to a story by Virginia Woolf, in language through Greek, Latin, French, Italian, Spanish, German, and English, and in genre through epic, history, romance, drama, autobiography, essay, memoir, and the novel. As the subtitle of his book indicates, Auerbach concentrates on the representation of reality in these texts, charting the shifts in both material and its presentation that occur as Western man gradually comes to believe that everyday life with its commonplace details is worth being portrayed seriously, and that the ordinary individual, located in an evolving historical context, may be regarded as problematic or even tragic.

To cite only a few stages that define this development: Auerbach takes as one point of departure the evenly lighted foreground of the Homeric epic, with its fully externalized details; he discovers in Montaigne the first attempt to treat "the random personal life as a whole" and traces the ways in which Montaigne's style recreates for us "a spontaneous apprehension of the unity of his person emerging from the multiplicity of his observations"; he sees Stendahl and Balzac as the originators of modern realism, the former because he situates "the tragically conceived life of a man of low social position"—Julien Sorel—"within the most concrete kind of contemporary history," and the latter because he dramatizes the connection of his characters with their milieux as "a necessary one." Auerbach outlines this development by analyzing specific passages, concerning himself with such traits of style as syntax, diction, and the use of direct discourse. In addition, he repeatedly explores the influence of two related literary matters: the doctrine of the "separation of styles" established in antiquity (which prescribed, for example, that everyday life could be treated only on a comic level), a doctrine that reasserted its power in Classical French tragedy; and the "figural interpretation" that flourished in the Christian Middle Ages, which could work either to minimize or to maximize (as in the case of Dante) the actuality of the given event, since the event was seen as a type of the divine.

From time to time Auerbach associates the verbal features of his texts with some underlying world view, as when he suggests that the mixture of styles in the Bible, its treatment of common people, and its highlighting of fragments of experience which seem "fraught with background" are all expressive of a Christianity whose central belief is in the incarnation of God in man. But he dwells chiefly in *Mimesis* on the modes of representation themselves, differentiating them carefully through precise analyses of comparable texts. In the following selection, a typical one, he establishes the paratactic constructions in the grammar of the *Chanson de Roland*, links them to the sequence of strophes and to the structure of the poem as a whole, and then illuminates their use through references to the *Iliad*, German epics, the Bible, and Latin texts, as well as through a detailed comparison with the Old French *Chanson d'Alexis*. While Auerbach mentions several attitudes reflected in parataxis and also indicates its literary history as a stylistic device, he remains everywhere conscious of style as a thing of purpose which "seeks to arouse ... its auditor" in various ways, as a "representational technique" that "includes the idea of structure which poet and audience apply to the narrated event."

LVIII
Tresvait la noit e apert la clere albe ...   737
Par mi cel host (sonent menut cil graisle).
Li emperere mul fierement chevalchet.
"Seignurs barons," dist li emperere Carles,   740

"Roland Against Ganelon," by Erich Auerbach, is reprinted from his *Mimesis: The Representation of Reality in Western Literature*, translated by Willard R. Trask (copyright 1953 by Princeton University Press; Princeton Paperback, 1968), pp. 96–122. Reprinted by permission of Princeton University Press. Bracketed translations are new to the present edition.

"Veez les porz e les destreiz passages:
Kar me jugez ki ert en la rereguarde."
Guenes respunt: "Rollant, cist miens fillastre:
N'avez baron de si grant vasselage."
Quant l'ot li reis, fierement le reguardet,   745
Si li ad dit: "Vos estes vifs diables.
El cors vos est entree mortel rage.
E ki serat devant mei en l'ansguarde?"
Guenes respunt: "Oger de Denemarche:
N'avez baron ki mielz de lui la facet."   750

LIX
Li quens Rollant, quant il s'oït juger,
Dunc ad parled a lei de chevaler:
"Sire parastre, mult vos dei aveir cher:
La rereguarde avez sur mei jugiet!
N'i perdrat Carles, li reis ki France tient,   755
Men escientre palefreid ne destrer,
Ne mul ne mule que deiet chevalcher,
Ne n'i perdrat ne runcin ne sumer
Que as espees ne seit einz eslegiet."
Guenes respunt: "Veir dites, jol sai bien."   760

LX
Quant ot Rollant qu'il ert en la rereguarde,
Ireement parlat a sun parastre:
"Ahi! culvert, malvais hom de put aire,
Quias le guant me caïst en la place,
Cume fist a tei le bastun devant Carle?"   765

LXI
"Dreiz emperere," dis Rollant le baron,
"Dunez mei l'arc que vos tenez el poign.
Men escientre nel me reproverunt
Que il me chedet cum fist a Guenelun
De sa main destre, quant reçut le bastun."   770
Li empereres en tint sun chef enbrunc,
Si duist sa barbe e detoerst sun gernun,
Ne poet muer que des oilz ne plurt.

LXII
Anpres iço i est Neines venud,
Meillor vassal n'out en la curt de lui,   775
E dist al rei: "Ben l'avez entendut;
Li quens Rollant, il est mult irascut.
La rereguarde est jugee sur lui:
N'avez baron ki jamais la remut.
Dunez li l'arc que vos avez tendut,   780
Si li truvez ki trés bien li aiut!"
Li reis li dunet e Rollant l'a reçut.

LVIII

Night goes and bright dawn appears . . . 737

.   .   .   .   .

Proudly the Emperor rides on horseback.
"Lord Barons," says Emperor Charles, 740
" See those gaps and those narrow passages;
Now decide for me who shall be in the rearguard."
Ganelon answers: " Roland, my stepson:
You have no baron of such great prowess."
When the King hears this, he looks at him fiercely, 745
And thus he spoke to him: " You are a living devil.
Into your body mortal rage has entered.
And who will be before me in the vanguard?"
Ganelon answers: " Ogier the Dane:
You have no baron who would do it better than he." 750

LIX

Count Roland, when he hears himself chosen,
Then spoke as befits a knight:
" Sir stepfather, I must hold you very dear:
The rearguard you have adjudged to me!
Thereby shall Charles, the king who holds France, lose, 755
If I know rightly, neither palfrey nor charger,
Neither mule nor hinny which he is to ride,
Nor shall he lose thereby either hack or sumpter
Which has not first been fought for with sword."
Ganelon answers: " You speak true, I know it well." 760

LX

When Roland hears that he will be in the rearguard,
Angrily he spoke to his stepfather:
"Ah! wretch, bad man of stinking birth,
Did you think the glove would drop from my hand in this place,
As the staff did for you before Charles?" 765

LXI

"Just Emperor," said Roland the baron,
"Give me the bow which you hold in your clenched hand.
If I know rightly, none shall reproach me
That it dropped from my hand as it did for Ganelon,
From his right hand, when he received the staff." 770
The Emperor kept his head bowed,
Stroked his beard and twisted his mustache,
He cannot keep his eyes from weeping.

LXII

After this Naimes came there,
There was no better vassal than he at court, 775
And he said to the King: " Well have you heard it;
Count Roland, he is very angry.

> *The rearguard is allotted to him:*
> *You have no baron who could (would?) change this.*
> *Give him the bow which you have drawn,* 780
> *And find him some to help him very well!"*
> *The King gives it to him, and Roland received it.*

These lines are from the Oxford manuscript of the *Chanson de Roland*. They relate the appointment of Roland to a dangerous post, that of commander of the rearguard of the Frankish army, which is on its way back through the Pyrenees after the campaign in Spain. The choice is made at the suggestion of Roland's stepfather Ganelon. The manner of it corresponds to an earlier episode, the choice of Ganelon for the post of Charles's emissary to Marsilius, King of the Saracens, at the suggestion of Roland (ll. 274 ff.). Both occurrences are rooted in an old enmity between the two barons, who are at odds over matters of money and property and seek to destroy one another (l. 3758). Any emissary to Marsilius, it was known from earlier experiences, was in great danger of losing his life. The events of Ganelon's mission showed that it would have cost him too his life, if he had not proposed to the Saracen King the treacherous bargain which at the same time would satisfy his own hatred and thirst for revenge: he promises the King that he will deliver into his hands the rearguard of the Frankish army, with Roland and his twelve closest friends, the douzepers, whom he represents (rightly) to be the war party at the Frankish court. He has now come back to the Frankish camp with Marsilius' insincere offer of peace and submission. The return of the army to France has begun. And Ganelon, to carry out the plan he has agreed upon with Marsilius, still has to arrange that Roland shall be appointed to the rearguard. This takes place in the lines quoted above.

The occurrence is related in five strophes (laisses). The first contains Ganelon's proposal and Charles's immediate reaction. The second, third, and fourth are concerned with Roland's attitude toward the proposal. The fifth takes up Naimes's intervention and the final appointment of Roland by the Emperor. The first laisse begins with an introduction of three lines, three paratactically juxtaposed principal clauses which describe the early morning departure of the army (the subject immediately preceding was the past night and a dream of the Emperor's). Next comes the scene of the proposal, which is given in the form of a double exchange of speech and rejoinder: demand that a choice be made, reply (with proposal), counterquestion, and counterreply. Both pairs of speeches are fitted into the simplest stereotyped frame (*dist, respunt, dit, respunt*). After the first pair, they are interrupted by line 745, the only one containing a brief temporal hypotaxis. Everything else is in the form of principal clauses, juxtaposed and opposed like blocks, with a paratactic independence still further emphasized by mention of the speaking subject each time (especially striking, 740, *li emperere Carles*, although he is also the subject of the preceding sentence). Let us now examine the individual speeches. Charles's demand contains a causal train of reasoning: since we are to traverse a difficult terrain, choose for me. ... But in keeping with the Emperor's proudly confident demeanor (*mult fierement*), it is presented paratactically in two principal clauses, a demonstrative clause (see the difficult terrain) and an imperative clause. In answer—like a gauntlet flung down—comes Ganelon's proposal, again a parataxis, with three members: first the name, then a reference, filled with triumphant revenge, to the kinship (*cist miens fillastre*, as a reminiscence of the corresponding *mis parastre*, l. 277, and l. 287, *ço set hom ben que jo sui tis parastres* [men know well that I am your stepfather]), and finally the supporting argument with its conventional praise, no doubt uttered in a tone of scornful irony. After this we have the brief dramatic pause with Charles's fierce look. His reply—likewise purely paratactic in form—begins with violent expressions which show that he sees through Ganelon's plan, but also, as is later confirmed by Naimes, that he has in his power no effective means of rejecting the proposal. Perhaps we may interpret his concluding question as a sort of counterattack: I need Roland for the vanguard! If this interpretation is correct, Ganelon at any rate disposes of the counterattack at once, and the identity of structure between his second speech and his first emphasizes the slashing abruptness of his demeanor. His position is apparently very strong, and he is quite certain of victory. In syntax too, this laisse answers blow with blow.

To this keenness and finality of statement there is a certain contrast in the fact that many things in the scene are not particularly clear. We can hardly be expected to assume that the Emperor is bound by the proposal of a single one of his barons. In fact, in similar cases elsewhere (for example, in the previous case of Ganelon's appointment, ll. 278-9 and 321-2; see also l. 243), explicit mention is made of the assent of the entire army. It may be conjectured that in the present instance the same assent is given without its being mentioned, or that the Emperor knows that there can be no doubt that it would be given. But even so, even if our text conceals a portion of the tradition—the fact that Roland has enemies among the Franks, who would be glad to see him given a dangerous assignment and removed from the Emperor's entourage, possibly for fear his influence might reverse the decision to end the war—even so it is puzzling that the Emperor should have failed to make arrangements beforehand for a solution agreeable to him, so that his call for a choice puts him in a position from which he knows no escape. He must after all be aware of what currents of thought prevail among his men, and in addition he has been warned by a dream. This connects with another enigma: how well does he see through Ganelon, how well does he know beforehand what is going to happen? We cannot assume that he is informed of Ganelon's plan in all its details. But if he is not, his reaction to the proposal (*vos estes vifs diables*, etc.) seems exaggerated. The Emperor's entire position is unclear; and despite all the authoritative definiteness which he manifests from time to time, he seems as it were somnambulistically paralyzed. The important and symbolic position—almost that of a Prince of God—in which he appears as the head of all Christendom and as the paragon of knightly perfection, is in strange contrast to his impotence. Although he hesitates, although he even sheds tears, although he foresees the impending disaster to some not clearly definable extent, he cannot prevent it. He is dependent upon his barons, and among them there is none who can change the situation at all (or should we say, who will? That depends on how we interpret line 779). In the same way, later on, at Ganelon's trial, he would be obliged to leave his nephew Roland's death unavenged were it not that, finally, a single knight is prepared to defend his cause. It is possible to find various explanations for all this: for example, the weakness of the central power in the feudal order of society, a weakness which, though it had hardly developed by Charlemagne's time, was certainly prevalent later, at the time when the *Chanson de Roland* originated; then, too, semireligious, semilegendary concepts of the kind found with many royal figures in the courtly romance, concepts which, to the personification of the great Emperor, add an admixture of passive, martyrlike, and somnambulistically paralyzed traits. Furthermore, his relation to Ganelon seems to contain elements of the Christ-Judas pattern.

The poem itself in any case gives no analyses or explanations whatever of the mysterious aspects of this and other events. We have to contribute them ourselves, and they rather detract from our aesthetic appreciation. The poet explains nothing; and yet the things which happen are stated with a paratactic bluntness which says that everything must happen as it does happen, it could not be otherwise, and there is no need for explanatory connectives. This, as the reader knows, refers not only to the events but also to the views and principles which form the basis of the actions of the persons concerned. The knightly will to fight, the concept of honor, the mutual loyalty of brothers in arms, the community of the clan, the Christian dogma, the allocation of right and wrong to Christians and infidels, are probably the most important of these views. They are few in number. They give a narrow picture in which only one stratum of society appears, and even that stratum in a greatly simplified form. They are posited without argument as pure theses: these are the facts. No argument, no explanatory discussion whatever is called for when, for example, the statement is made: *paien unt tort et chrestiens unt dreit* (l. 1015: heathens are wrong and Christians are right), although the life of the infidel knights—except for the names of their gods—seems hardly different from that of the Christians. Often, it is true, they are referred to as depraved and horrible, at times in fantastic and symbolic ways, but they are knights too, and the structure of their society seems to be exactly the same as that of Christian society. The parallel extends to minor details and thus serves to render the narrowness of the representation of life still more striking. The Christianity of the Christians is simply a stipulation. It exhausts itself in the creed and the liturgic formulas that go with it. Furthermore it is, in a very extreme sense, made to serve the knightly will to fight and political expansion. The penance laid upon the Franks when they pray and receive absolution before going into battle is to fight hard; whoever falls in the fight is a martyr and can surely expect a place in Paradise. Conversions by force which involve the killing of those who offer resistance are works with which God is well pleased. This attitude, astonishing as a Christian attitude and non-existent as such in earlier times, is not based, here in the *Chanson de Roland*, on a given historical situation, as it was in Spain, whence it would seem to have stemmed. Nor is any other explanation of it given. That is the way it is—a paratactic situation made up of theses which, extremely narrow as they are, are yet full of contradictions.

Let us go on to the second part of the scene—Roland's reaction. It is the theme of three laisses. In the first two Roland addresses Ganelon, in the third the Emperor. His speeches contain three motifs of various strength and variously crossed: (1) a tremendously assertive and ferocious pride, (2) hatred for Ganelon, and (3), much weaker, devotion to the Emperor and the desire to serve him. (1) and (2) are crossed in such a way that (1) appears first, with great force, but even here is already imbued with (2) and (3). Roland loves danger and seeks it; he cannot be frightened. Furthermore he sets great value upon his prestige. He refuses to grant Ganelon the briefest moment of triumph. And so his first consideration is to point out emphatically, for all to hear, that he, unlike Ganelon in a comparable situation, has not lost his composure. Hence his expression of gratitude to Ganelon, which in view of the enmity between them—well known to all present—can have only an effect of irony and scorn. Hence too the enumeration of the various mounts and beasts of burden not one of which will he abandon without fight—a powerful, demonstrative, and very successful assertion of his pride and courage which even Ganelon is obliged to recognize, although in doing so he may well have his own thoughts in the back of his mind, for it is precisely Roland's intrepid self-confidence on which he relies in his plan to destroy him. But in any case, Ganelon's momentary triumph is spoiled. For, once Roland has made his attitude sufficiently known, he can give the reins to his hatred and contempt, which now assume the form of a scornful triumph on his part: you see, you scoundrel, I do not conduct myself as you did that time; and even when he stands before Charles to receive the bow, his expression of ready obedience, formulated so as to reveal impatience, is once again interspersed with his scornful and triumphant comparison between his behavior and Ganelon's.

The whole scene—Roland's display of self-confidence, followed by his sustained, repetitive, and triumphant outburst of hatred and scorn—is spread out over three laisses, and since the first two are addressed to Ganelon, with very similar opening phrases, distinguished only by the adverbial modifiers—the first time *a lei de chevaler*, the second time *ireement*—since furthermore a superficial and purely rational examination seems to show their contents to be incongruous—the first appearing friendly and the second angry—numerous editors and critics have doubted the authenticity of the text and have cut out one of the two laisses, usually the second. That this cannot be right was pointed out by Bédier in his commentary (Paris, Piazza, 1927, p. 151), and this—as the foregoing analysis may serve to indicate—is my view too. The second laisse presupposes the first. The attitude revealed in the first laisse, which stands in sharp contrast to Ganelon's attitude in that earlier scene, supplies the justification for the triumphant hatred of the second. I should like to corroborate this result by another, a stylistic, consideration. This kind of repeated resumption of the same situation in consecutive laisses, in a manner which at first leaves the reader in doubt as to whether he is confronted with a new scene or a complementary treatment of the first, is very frequent in the *Chanson de Roland* (as well as elsewhere in the *chansons de geste*). There are other instances where such resumptions occasion surprising shifts, as is the case in the passage here under discussion. In laisses 40, 41, and 42, the question which King Marsilius repeats three times in almost identical terms—i.e., when will Charles, who after all is getting on in years, tire of war—is answered by Ganelon in three different ways, of which the first gives not the least inkling of what the others will be. In his first answer Ganelon speaks exclusively in praise of Charles, and it is only in the second and third that he names Roland and his companions as warmongers, thus taking his first step toward treason; in the following laisse, 43, he at last speaks plainly, and Charles is no longer referred to in friendly terms. Even before this, Ganelon's attitude in Marsilius' presence is not to be understood in purely rational terms. He displays such hostility and haughtiness that his purpose seems to be to irritate the King at all costs, and negotiation and treason appear to be out of the question. In other instances (laisses 5 and 6, 79 to 81, 83 to 86, 129 and 130, 133 to 135, 137 to 139, 146 and 147, etc.) there is no real contradiction between the content of one laisse and that of another, but here too one and the same point of departure is frequently used to push ahead in different directions or over different distances. When in laisse 80 Oliver climbs to the top of a hill and from there sees the approaching Saracen army, he summons Roland and talks to him of Ganelon's treason. In laisse 81, which also begins with Oliver's climbing the hill, no mention is made of Roland, but Oliver comes down as quickly as possible to report back to the Franks. In laisses 83 to 85, where Oliver thrice asks Roland to blow his horn and thrice receives the same negative reply, the function of the repetition is to make the scene more intense; as, in the *Chanson de Roland* generally, both the urgent-intense and the manifold-simultaneous are represented by the repetition and addition of many, and frequently of artfully varied, individual occurrences. The series of knights who assume a place in the action, as well as the series of battle scenes, are instances of this procedure. Laisses 129 to 131, where Roland himself proposes to blow his horn (prepared in laisse 128 and extremely artful in the expression of Roland's self-conscious regret), correspond to the earlier scene although the actors have exchanged roles. This time it is Oliver who thrice replies in the negative. His three answers are constructed with considerable psychological finesse. The first, with concealed irony, repeats Roland's own counterarguments but suddenly changes to a spontaneous outburst of sympathy (or admiration) at the sight of Roland's blood-stained arms. The second again begins ironically, and concludes in an outburst of anger. It is not until we reach the third that we have Oliver's reproaches and his grief formulated in an orderly manner. In the three laisses of the horn signal—133 to 135, presumably involving a threefold blowing of the horn—the effect which the horn produces upon the Franks is developed differently each time. Taken together, to be sure, the three effects represent a development too, that is, from surprise and confusion to a complete realization of the state of affairs (which Ganelon endeavors to prevent), but this development is not evenly progressive but spastic, now gaining, now losing ground, like generation or birth.

Varied repetition of the same theme is a technique stemming from medieval Latin poetics, which in turn draws it from antique rhetoric. This fact has recently been pointed out once again by Faral and E. R. Curtius. But neither the form nor the stylistic effect of the "regressions" in the *Chanson de Roland* can thus be explained or even described. It would seem that the series of similar events and the resumption of previous statements are phenomena related in character to the parataxis of sentence structure. Whether one comprehensive representation is replaced by a reiterative enumeration of individual scenes similar in form and progress; whether one intense action is replaced by a repetition of the same action, beginning at the same starting point time and again; or whether finally, instead of a process of complex and periodic development, we have repeated returns to the starting point, each one proceeding to elaborate a different element or motif: in all cases rationally organized condensations are avoided in favor of a halting, spasmodic, juxtapositive, and pro- and retrogressive method in which causal, modal, and even temporal relations are obscured. (In the very first laisse of the poem, the last line, *nes poet guarder que mals ne l'i ateignet* [he cannot prevent evil from overtaking him], looks very far into the future.) Time and again there is a new start; every resumption is complete in itself and independent; the next is simply juxtaposed to it, and the relation between the two is often left hanging. This too is a type of epic retardation in Goethe's and Schiller's sense (cf. [Auerbach, *Mimesis*], pp. 4 ff.), but it is not managed through interpolations and episodes but through progression and retrogression within the principal action itself. This procedure is very markedly epic; it is even recitationally epic, for a listener arriving in the course of the recitation receives a coherent impression. At the same time it is a technique of subdividing the course of events into numerous rigid little divisions, mutually delimited by the use of stereotyped phrases.

Roland's three speeches are not as brief as the Emperor's and Ganelon's in the first laisse, but they too have no periodic flow. The long sentence of laisse 59 is merely an enumeration with repeated breaks. In all three laisses the subordinate clauses are of the simplest type; they are independent to a very high degree. Anything like flow of discourse does not arise. The rhythm of the *Chanson de Roland* is never flowing, as is that of the antique epic. Every line marks a new start, every stanza represents a new approach. This impression, already produced by the prevailing parataxis, is increased by the generally clumsy and ungrammatical handling of connections whenever a rare attempt is made to use somewhat more complex hypotaxes. Another factor is the assonant strophic pattern, which gives every line the appearance of an independent unit while the entire strophe appears to be a bundle of independent parts, as though sticks or spears of equal length and with similar points were bundled together. Consider for example Ganelon's speech in support of accepting Marsilius' offer of peace (ll. 220 ff.), which contains a long sentence:

> Quant ço vos mandet li reis Marsiliun 222
> Qu'il devendrat jointes ses mains tis hum
> E tute Espaigne tendrat par vostre dun,
> Puis recevrat la lei que nus tenum, 225
> Ki ço vos lodet que cest plait degetuns,
> Ne li chalt, sire, de quel mort nus muriuns.
>
> *If this is the message King Marsilius sends,* 222
> *That he will become—his hands folded—your vassal,*
> *And will hold all of Spain in fief to you,*
> *Then will take the faith which we hold,* 225
> *He who recommends to you that we reject this proposal,*
> *To him it does not matter, Sire, what kind of death we die.*

The principal clause (*ne li chalt...*) comes at the end. But the beginning of the period does not consider what the pattern of the main clause is going to be and consequently —after the content of Marsilius' message has been stated—a shift in construction proves necessary. The *quant*-clause with its subordinate statements of the content (*que... e... puis...*)—which itself loses sight of its structure before it is half finished (*puis recevrat...* already begins breaking away from the anchorage in *que*)—remains an anacoluthon, and the emphatically anticipated *ki*-clause starts a new pattern. But in addition to this type of sentence structure, which is hypotactic in external appearance but in reality quite paratactic, there is also the subdivision in meaning according to the individual lines, the sharp incisions marked by the assonance in *u*, and the somewhat less emphatic but clearly noticeable caesuras in the middle of the line, which in all cases indicate units of meaning as well. No indeed—periodicity and flow of discourse are not among the characteristics of this style. It is admirably homogeneous, for the attitudes of the personages are so strongly molded and limited by the narrow range of the established order in which they move, that their thoughts, feelings, and passions can find room in such lines. The copious and connected argumentation of which Homer's heroes are so fond is wholly outside of their ken; and by the same token they are without any free-flowing, dynamic, and impulsive movement in expression. The words which the Emperor Charles utters when he hears the call of the horn (ll. 1768-9),

> Ce dist li reis: "Jo oi le corn Rollant.
> Unc nel sunast se ne fust cumbatant."
>
> *This said the King: "I hear Roland's horn.*
> *Never would he sound it if he were not fighting."*

have often been compared with the corresponding lines in Vigny's poem "Le Cor,"

> Malheur! C'est mon neveu! malheur! car si Roland
> Appelle à son secours, ce doit être en mourant,
>
> [*Disaster! It's my nephew! disaster! because if Roland*
> *Calls for help, he must be dying,*]

which is extremely informative in the present connection. But it is not necessary to adduce a romantic parallel; the same purpose can be served by classical and later European texts from periods preceding Romanticism. Consider Roland's death prayer (ll. 2384 ff.) or the formally quite similar prayer uttered by the Emperor before the battle against Baligant (ll. 3100 ff.). These follow liturgical models and consequently display a comparatively prolonged sweep in their syntax. Roland's prayer reads:

> Veire Paterne, ki unkes ne mentis,   2384
> Seint Lazaron de mort resurrexis
> E Daniel des leons guaresis,
> Guaris de mei l'anme de tuz perilz
> Pur les pecchez que en ma vie fis!

ROLAND AGAINST GANELON

> True Father, who never lied, 2384
> Who resurrected Saint Lazarus from the dead
> And saved Daniel from the lions,
> Save my soul from all dangers
> On account of the sins which I committed in my life!

and the Emperor's:

> Veire Paterne, hoi cest jor me defend, 3100
> Ki guaresis Jonas tut veirement
> De la baleine ki en sun cors l'aveit,
> E esparignas le rei de Niniven
> E Daniel del merveillus turment
> Enz en la fosse des leons o fut enz, 3105
> Les .III. enfanz tut en un fou ardant!
> La tue amurs me seit hoi en present!
> Par ta mercit, se te plaist, me cunsent
> Que mun nevold poisse venger Rollant!

> True Father, help me now on this day, 3100
> Thou who didst Jonas truly save
> From the whale which had him in its belly,
> And spared the King of Nineveh,
> And Daniel from the terrible torture
> In the lions' den wherein he was, 3105
> And the three men from the burning oven:
> Let Thy love be with me today.
> Through Thy mercy, if it please Thee, grant me
> That I may avenge my nephew Roland.

In this rigidly stereotyped use of the figures of redemption (figures which, as the literature of mysticism shows, can be employed in a very differently dynamic fashion), as well as in the almost static and reiterative manner of the apostrophizing supplication, there is, to be sure, a strong element of emotion, but there is also the narrow definitiveness of a spatially limited and perfectly unambiguous view of God, the universe, and fate. If we confront this with any prayer from the *Iliad*—I choose at random 305 ff.,

> πότνι' Ἀθηναίη ἐρυσίπτολι, δῖα θεάων,
> ἆξον δὴ ἔγχος Διομήδεος ἠδὲ καὶ αὐτὸν,
> πρηνέα δὸς πεσέειν Σκαιῶν προπάροιθε πυλάων

> Mighty Athena, protectress of the city, sublime goddess,
> Turn Diomedes' lance and make him
> Fall headlong before the Skaean gates!

with a violent upsurge in the movement of imploration (ἠδὲ καὶ αὐτὸν πρηνέα δὸς πεσέειν)—we discover how much greater possibilities for freely flowing, urgent, and imploring movements are to be found in Homer, and that his world, though certainly limited, yet has a much less rigid structure. The significant feature here is obviously not the run-on lines (which are frequent in antique versification) but the broad sweep of the richly nuanced sentence movement. This can equally well be displayed in rhymed verse without enjambment, whether the lines are short or long. And it appears quite early in Old French, as early as the twelfth century, in the octosyllabic rhymes of courtly romance or in shorter rhymed tales. If one compares the octosyllabic line of an old heroic epic, the fragment of *Gormund et Isembard*, which sounds like a series of detached and sharply marked bugle calls (*criant l'enseigne al rei baron, / la Loovis, le fiz Charlun* [crying the motto of the brave king, that of Louis, son of Charles]), with the fluent, sometimes verbose, sometimes lyrical octosyllabic line of the courtly romance, one will quickly grasp the difference between rigid and fluent-connective syntax. And very soon indeed widely sweeping rhetorical movement appears in the courtly style. The following lines are from the *Folie Tristan* (after Bartsch, *Chrestomathie de l'ancien Français*, 12ᵉ éd., pièce 24):

> en ki me purreie fier,   31
> quant Ysolt ne me deingne amer,
> quant Ysolt a si vil me tient
> k'ore de mei ne li suvient?
>
> *In whom can I have confidence,*   31
> *If Ysolt deigns not to love me,*
> *If Ysolt considers me so despicable*
> *That she does not now remember me?*

This is an urgent movement of grief in the form of a rhetorical question with two similarly constructed subordinate clauses of which the second is broader in scope, while the whole passage displays ascending rhythm. In pattern, it is reminiscent of, though much simpler than, the famous lines in Racine's *Bérénice* (4, 5):

> Dans un mois, dans un an, comment souffrirons-nous,
> Seigneur, que tant de mers me séparent de vous:
> Que le jour recommence et que le jour finisse,
> Sans que jamais Titus puisse voir Bérénice,
> Sans que, de tout le jour, je puisse voir Titus?
>
> [*In a month, in a year, how shall we endure it,*
> *My Lord, that so many oceans separate me from you:*
> *That the day will begin and the day end*
> *Without Titus' ever being able to see Bérénice,*
> *Without, in all the day, my being able to see Titus?*]

Let us briefly complete the analysis of our text. At the end of laisse 61 the Emperor still hesitates to hand the bow to Roland, who stands before him, and thus definitely to give him the order. He bows his head, he strokes his beard, he weeps. The intervention of Naimes, which concludes the scene, is again entirely paratactic in structure.

The modal connections implied in his remarks are not grammatically expressed. Otherwise the passage would have to read: "You have heard how angry Roland is because his name has been suggested for the rearguard. But since there is no baron who could (or: would?) fill his place, give him the bow, but at least make certain that his support is strong enough." The beautiful concluding line is also paratactic.

In the classical languages paratactic constructions belong to the low style; they are oral rather than written, comic and realistic rather than elevated. But here parataxis belongs to the elevated style. This is a new form of the elevated style, not dependent on periodic structure and rhetorical figures but on the power of juxtaposed and independent verbal blocks. An elevated style operating with paratactic elements is not, in itself, something new in Europe. The style of the Bible has this characteristic (cf. our first chapter). Here we may recall the discussion concerning the sublime character of the sentence *dixitque Deus: fiat lux, et facta est lux* (Genesis 1:3) which Boileau and Huet carried on in the seventeenth century in connection with the essay *On the Sublime* attributed to Longinus. The sublime in this sentence from Genesis is not contained in a magnificent display of rolling periods nor in the splendor of abundant figures of speech but in the impressive brevity which is in such contrast to the immense content and which for that very reason has a note of obscurity which fills the listener with a shuddering awe. It is precisely the absence of causal connectives, the naked statement of what happens—the statement which replaces deduction and comprehension by an amazed beholding that does not even seek to comprehend—which gives the sentence its grandeur. But the case of the *chanson de geste* is completely different. The subject here is not the awesome riddle of creation and the Creator, not the creature man's relationship to one and the other. The subject of the *Chanson de Roland* is narrow, and for the men who figure in it nothing of fundamental significance is problematic. All the categories of this life and the next are unambiguous, immutable, fixed in rigid formulations. To be sure, rational comprehension has no direct access to them, but that is an observation which we ourselves make; the poem and its contemporary audience felt no such concern. They live safely and confidently in the rigid and narrow established order within which the duties of life, their distribution according to estates (cf. the division of labor between knights and monks, ll. 1877 ff.), the character of supernatural forces, and mankind's relationship thereto are regulated in the simplest way. Within this frame there are abundant and delicate emotions; there is also a certain motley variegation in external phenomena; but the frame is so restricted and rigid that properly problematic situations, let alone tragedy, can hardly arise. There are no conflicts which deserve to be called tragic.

The early Germanic epic texts which have come down to us also exhibit paratactic construction; here too the warrior ethics of a nobility dominates, with its strict definitions of honor, justice, and ordeal by battle. And yet the final impression is quite different. The verbal blocks are more loosely juxtaposed, the space about the occurrences and the heaven above them are incomparably wider, destiny is more enigmatic, and the structure of society is not so rigidly established. The mere fact that the most famous Germanic epics, from the *Hildebrandslied* to the *Nibelungenlied*, derive their historical setting from the wild and spacious epoch of the tribal migrations rather than from the solidly established structure of the age of feudalism, gives them greater breadth and freedom. The Germanic themes of the age of the migrations did not reach Gallo-Roman territory, or at least they could not strike root here. And Christianity has almost no significance at all for the Germanic heroic epic. Free and immediate forces, still unsubdued by settled forms, are stronger in it, and the human roots—so at least it seems to me—go deeper. We cannot say of the Germanic poems of the heroic epic cycle, as we said of the *Chanson de Roland*, that the problematic and tragic element is lacking in them. Hildebrand is more directly human and tragic than Roland, and how much more deeply motivated are the conflicts in the *Nibelungenlied* than the hatred between Roland and Ganelon!

Yet we do encounter the same restricted and definitely established cosmos when we take up an early Romance religious text. We have several of these which precede the *Chanson de Roland* chronologically. The most important is the *Chanson d'Alexis*, a saint's legend, which crystallized in the eleventh century in an Old French form still extant in several manuscripts. According to the legend, Alexis was the late-born only son of a noble Roman family. He was carefully educated, entered the Emperor's service, and in accordance with his father's wishes was to marry a virgin of equal rank. He obeyed, but on the bridal night he left his wife without having touched her and lived for seventeen years as a poor beggar in a strange land (Edessa in northeastern Syria, the modern Turkish Urfa), that he might serve only God. Leaving his refuge to escape being revered as a saint, he was driven back to Rome by a storm. There he passed another seventeen years, still unrecognized and living as a despised beggar under the steps of his father's house, unmoved by the sorrow of his parents and his wife, whose laments he often heard without revealing his identity. Not until after his death was he finally and miraculously recognized and thenceforth revered as a saint. The attitudes reflected in this text are different entirely from those of the *Chanson de Roland*. But it exhibits the same paratactic and rigid style, the same narrowness, indisputability, and fixity of all categories. Everything is settled, white or black, good or bad, and never requires further search or justification. Temptation is there, to be sure, but there is no realm of problem. On the one hand there is serving God, forsaking the world and seeking eternal bliss—on the other, natural life in the world, which leads to "great sorrow." There are no other levels of consciousness, and external reality—the many additional phenomena which have their place in the universe and which ought somehow to constitute the frame for the occurrences of the narrative—is submitted to such reduction that nothing survives but an insubstantial background for the life of the saint. About him are grouped, accompanying his activities with appropriate pantomime, his father, mother, and bride. A few other characters required by the action appear, but they are even more shadowy. Everything else is completely schematized, both sociologically and geographically speaking. This is the more surprising since the scene seems to embrace the extent and variety of the entire Roman Empire. Nothing remains of West and East but churches, voices from on high, praying multitudes—nothing but the ever identical environment of the life of a saint; even as in the *Chanson de Roland*, the same social structure—that of feudalism—and the same ethos is dominant throughout, among both pagans and Christians. But here this is much more pronounced. The world has become very small and narrow; and in it everything revolves rigidly and immutably about a single question, which has been answered in advance and which it is man's duty to answer rightly. He knows what road he must follow, or better, there is but one road open to him, there is no other. He knows too that he will reach a fork in the road, and that then he must turn right although the tempter will try to entice him to turn left. Everything else has vanished, the whole sweeping infinity of the outer and inner worlds, with its innumerable possibilities, configurations, and strata.

This, without doubt, is not Germanic; nor is it, I believe, Christian; at least it is not the necessary and original version of Christianity. For Christianity, the product of a variety of premises, and coming to grips with a variety of realities, has proved itself—before and after this period—incomparably more elastic, more rich, and more complexly stratified. This narrowness can hardly be original at all; it contains too many and too various inherited elements for that; it is not narrowness, it is a narrowing process. It is the process of rigidification and reduction which late antiquity underwent and which has figured in other earlier chapters. To be sure, a significant part is played in it by the simplified, reduced form which Christianity assumed in its clash with exhausted or barbaric peoples.

In the Old French *Chanson d'Alexis* the scene of the bridal night, which is one of the high points of the poem, reads as follows (stanzas 11 to 15, text after Bartsch, *Chrestomathie*, 12ᵉ éd.):

11
Quant li jorz passet ed il fut anoitiet,
ço dist li pedre: "filz, quer t'en va colchier,
avuec ta spouse, al comant Deu del ciel."
ne volst li enfes son pedre corrocier,
vait en la chambre o sa gentil moillier.

12
Com vit le lit, esguardat la pulcele,
donc li remembret de son seignour celeste
que plus ad chier que tote rien terrestre;
"e! Deus," dist il, "si forz pechiez m'apresset!
s'or ne m'en fui, molt criem que ne t'en perde."

13
Quant en la chambre furent tuit soul remes,
danz Alexis la prist ad apeler:
la mortel vide li prist molt a blasmer,
de la celeste li mostrat veritet;
mais lui ert tart qued il s'en fust tornez.

14
"Oz mei, pulcele, celui tien ad espous
Qui nos redemst de son sanc precious.

en icest siecle nen at parfite amour:
la vide est fraile, n'i at durable onour;
ceste ledece revert a grant tristour."

15
Quant sa raison li at tote mostrede,
donc li comandet les renges de sa spede,
ed un anel dont il l'out esposede.
donc en ist fors de la chambre son pedre;
en mie nuit s'en fuit de la contrede.

11
When the day was passed and night had come,
Thus spake his father: "Son, now go to bed,
With your spouse, as the God of Heaven commands."
The son did not want to anger his father;
He goes into the chamber with his gentle wife.

12
When he saw the bed, he looked at the maiden,
Then he remembers his Heavenly Lord
Whom he holds more dear than any earthly thing:
"Ah, God!" said he, "how strongly sin presses upon me!
If I flee not now, much I fear that I shall thereby lose Thee."

13
When they were left all alone in the chamber,
Master Alexis began to speak to her:
Mortal life he began to chide to her,
Of heavenly life he showed her the truth;
But much he wished that he were gone from there.

14
" Hear me, maiden, take Him for spouse
Who redeemed us with his precious blood.
In this world there is no perfect love:
Life is frail, there is no lasting honor in it;
this joy becomes great sorrow."

15
When he had set forth all his mind to her,
He gives her the thong of his sword
And a ring with which he had married her.
Then he went out of the chamber in his father's house;
In the middle of the night he fled from the country.

However different the tenor of the two poems may be, the stylistic resemblance to the *Chanson de Roland* is very striking. In both, the paratactic principle goes far beyond mere technique of sentence structure. In both we have the same repeated returning to fresh starts, the same spasmodic progression and retrogression, the same independence of the individual occurrences and their constituent parts. Stanza 13 recapitulates the situation at the beginning of stanza 12, but carries the action further and in a different direction. Stanza 14 repeats, concretely and in direct discourse, the statement made in stanza 13 (of which, however, the last line had already gone further). Instead of the construction, "When they were alone in the room, he remembered . . . , and said 'Listen . . .'", we have the following arrangement: 1. "When he was in the room, he remembered . . ." 2. "When they were in the room, he said that . . ." (indirect discourse) 3. "Listen, (he said) . . . ." Each of the stanzas presents a complete and autonomous scene. The impression of a unified, progressive event whose advance binds together the various elements is much weaker than the impression of a juxtaposition of three very similar but separate scenes. One may generalize on the basis of this impression: the *Chanson d'Alexis* is a string of autonomous, loosely interrelated events, a series of mutually quite independent scenes from the life of a saint, each of which contains an expressive yet simple gesture. The father ordering Alexis to join his bride in the chamber; Alexis at the bedside, speaking to his bride; Alexis at Edessa distributing his worldly goods to the poor; Alexis the beggar; the servants sent out after him but failing to recognize him and giving him an alms; the mother's lament; the conversation between mother and bride; and so forth. It is a cycle of scenes. Each one of these occurrences contains one decisive gesture with only a loose temporal or causal connection with those that follow or precede. Many of them (the mother's lament, for example) are subdivided into several similar and individually independent pictures. Every picture has as it were a frame of its own. Each stands by itself in the sense that nothing new or unexpected happens in it and that it contains no propulsive force which demands the next. And the intervals are empty. But it is with no dark and profound emptiness, in which much befalls and much is prepared, in which we hold our breath in trembling expectation, the emptiness sometimes conjured up in the style of the Bible, with its intervals which make us ponder. Instead, it is a colorless duration without relief or substance, sometimes only a moment, sometimes seventeen years, sometimes wholly indefinable.

    The course of events is thus resolved into a series of pictures; it is, as it were, parceled out. The *Chanson de Roland* taken as a whole is more compressed; the coherence is clearer; the individual picture sometimes displays more movement. But the representational technique (and this means more than mere technical procedure, it includes the idea of structure which poet and audience apply to the narrated event) is still exactly the same: it strings independent pictures together like beads. The intervals in the *Chanson de Roland* are not always so very empty and flat; landscape sometimes intrudes; we see or hear armies riding through valleys and mountain passes—yet the occurrences are still strung together in such a fashion that, time and again, completely independent and self-contained scenes result. The number of the characters who maintain the action is very small in the *Chanson de Roland* too; all the others—although they are far more varied than in the Alexis—seem mere types. Those participating in the action of the individual scenes are fixed to the spot; it is but rarely that a newcomer joins their number; and when that occurs (Naimes or Turpin acting as mediators), there is a sharp break. The variously altering relationship between a large number of persons, with the consequent involvements and element of adventure so characteristic of epic elsewhere, is here completely lacking. So much the stronger is the element of impressive gestures, both in the Alexis and the Roland. The urge to establish connections and pursue developments is feeble. Even within an individual scene, the development, if any, is halting and laborious. But the gestures of the scenic moment are simply and plastically impressive in the highest degree.

This impressiveness of gestures and attitudes is obviously the purpose of the technique under consideration when it divides the course of events into a mosaic of parceled pictures. The scenic moment with its gestures is given such power that it assumes the stature of a moral model. The various phases of the story of the hero or the traitor or the saint are concretized in gestures to such an extent that the pictured scenes, in the impression they produce, closely approach the character of symbols or figures, even in cases where it is not possible to trace any symbolic or figural signification. But very often such a signification can be traced: in the *Chanson de Roland* it is present in the person of Charlemagne, in the description of many characteristics of the pagan knights, and of course in the prayers. As for the *Chanson d'Alexis*, E. R. Curtius' excellent interpretation (*Zeitschrift für romanische Philologie*, 56, 113 ff., especially pp. 122 and 124) conclusively supports the idea of a figural fulfillment in the beyond. This figural tradition played no small part in discrediting the horizontal, historical connections between events and in encouraging rigidification of all categories. Thus the prayers cited above exhibit the figures of redemption completely rigidified. The parceling of the events of the Old Testament, which are interpreted figurally in isolation from their historic context, has become a formula. The figures—as on the sarcophagi of late antiquity—are placed side by side paratactically. They no longer have any reality, they only have signification. With respect to the events of this world, a similar tendency prevails: to remove them from their horizontal context, to isolate the individual fragments, to force them into a fixed frame, and, within it, to make them impressive gesturally, so that they appear as exemplary, as models, as significant, and to leave all "the rest" in abeyance. It is easy to see that such a procedure permits but a small, extremely narrow portion of reality to assume visual plasticity, that portion which the crystallized idioms of the established categories are able to convey. But small as it may be, it does assume visual plasticity, and this shows that the high point of the process of rigidification has been passed. It is precisely in the isolated pictures that the germs of a revival are to be found.

The Latin text which may be assumed to have been the source for the French *Chanson d'Alexis* (it will be found in the *Acta Sanctorum* of July 17; it is here cited after Förster-Koschwitz, *Altfranzösisches Übungsbuch*, sixth edition, 1921, pp. 299 ff.) is perhaps not much older than the French version, for the legend, which originated in Syria, can be traced in the West only at a comparatively late date. But it exhibits the form of the saint's legend of late antiquity much more purely. Its treatment of the bridal night deviates from the Old French version in a highly characteristic fashion:

> Vespere autem facto dixit Euphemianus filio suo; "Intra, fili, in cubiculum et visita sponsam tuam." Ut autem intravit, coepit nobilissimus juvenis et in Christo sapien-

tissimus instruere sponsam suam et plura ei sacramenta disserere, deinde tradidit ei annulum suum aureum et rendam, id est caput baltei, quo cingebatur, involuta in prandeo et purpureo sudario, dixitque ei: "Suscipe haec et conserva, usque dum Domino placuerit, et Dominus sit inter nos." Post haec accepit de substantia sua et discessit ad mare. . . .

When it was evening, Euphemianus said to his son: "Go into the bedroom, son, and visit your wife." But when he entered, the noble youth began most sagely to teach his wife of Christ and to explain to her many holy things, then he gave her his golden ring and the thong of his sword wrapped in a purple cloth of silk and spoke to her: "Take these and keep them as long as it pleases the Lord, and the Lord be between us." After that he took some of his wealth and went down to the sea. . . .

It will have been noticed that the Latin text is likewise almost wholly paratactic. But it does not exploit the possibilities of parataxis; it has not come to know them. It has leveled and flattened the whole scene to complete uniformity. The narration proceeds without any ups and downs, without change of tone, "monotonously": so that not only the frame but even the picture within it remains motionless, is rigid and without dynamism. The inner struggle which the temptation brings about in Alexis' soul and for which the Old French version has the simplest and most beautiful expression, is not even mentioned. There seems to be no temptation at all. And the great movement of Alexis' words in direct discourse to his bride (*Oz mei, pulcele* . . .) —one of the strongest movements of the entire Old French poem, in which Alexis rises to his full stature and which is the first outbreaking of his real nature—is evidently something the French poet created out of the pale Latin words of his source. The flight too first becomes dramatic in the French text. The Latin version is much smoother and more uniformly progressive; but the human movement is weak, is barely alluded to, as if the story had to do with a ghost and not a living being. The same impression continues as one reads on. A really human formulation can be found only in the vernacular version. New in it (and we mention only the most important points) are the mother's lament in the deserted room and, later, the saint's inner struggle when the storm drives him back to Rome. Here Alexis hesitates before taking upon himself the most difficult trial of all, which is to live as an unknown beggar in his father's house, where day after day he sees his nearest relatives mourning for him. He wishes that the cup might pass from him; yet he accepts it. The Latin text knows no hesitation and no inner struggle, here as in the scene of the bridal night. Alexis goes to his father's house because he does not want the burden to fall on anyone else.

It was vernacular poetry—our comparison of these two texts seems to show—which first imparted relief to the individual pictures, so that their characters took on life and human fullness. This life, to be sure, is restricted by the rigidity and narrowness of the categories, which persist unalterably, and it fails all too easily for lack of progressive movement; but it is precisely through the resistance offered by the frame of rigid categories that it acquires impressiveness and force. It was the vernacular poets who first saw man as a living being and found the form in which parataxis possesses poetic power. Instead of a thin, monotonous trickle of juxtapositions, we now have the laisse form, with its abrupt advances and regressions and its abundance of energetic new beginnings, which is a new elevated style. If the life which this stylistic procedure can seize upon is narrowly restricted and without diversity, it is nevertheless a full life, a life of human emotion, a powerful life, a great relief after the pale, intangible style of the late antique legend. The vernacular poets also knew how to exploit direct discourse in terms of tone and gesture. We have already referred to Alexis' address to his bride and to his mother's lament. In addition we may mention the words in which, after his return to Rome, the saint asks his father for food and shelter. In the French version they have a concrete and direct appeal to which the Latin text could not possibly attain. The French passage reads:

> Eufemiiens, bels sire, riches om,
> quer me herberge por Deu en ta maison;
> soz ton degret me fai un grabaton
> empor ton fil dont tu as tel dolour;
> toz sui enfers, sim pais por soue amour. . . .
>
> *Euphemianus, noble lord, wealthy man,*
> *May it please thee to give me shelter in thy house for the sake of God.*
> *Under thy stairs arrange a sickbed for me,*
> *For thy son's sake through whom thou hast such great sorrow.*
> *I am very ill; so feed me for the sake of thy love to him. . . .*

and the Latin parallel:

> Serve Dei, respice in me et fac mecum misericordiam, quia pauper sum et peregrinus, et jube me suscipi in domo tua, ut pascar de micis mensae tuae et Deus benedicat annos tuos et ei quem habes in peregre misereatur.
>
> *Servant of God, look at me and be charitable to me, for I am poor and a stranger; and give orders that I be received in thy house, so that I may feed upon the crumbs from thy table, and may God bless thy years and have mercy on him whom you have wandering far from home.*

We observed earlier that it would be a mistake simply to make Christianity responsible for the rigidity and narrowness which appear in the late antique legend and from which the vernacular texts are able to emancipate themselves only gradually. In our earlier chapters we attempted to show that the first effect of the Judaeo-Christian manner of dealing with the events in the world of reality led to anything but rigidity and narrowness. The hiddenness of God and finally his *parousia*, his incarnation in the common form of an ordinary life, these concepts—we tried to show—brought about a dynamic movement in the basic conception of life, a swing of the pendulum in the realms of morals and sociology, which went far beyond the classic-antique norm for the imitation of real life and living growth. Even the Church Fathers, Augustine in particular, have not by any means come down to us as schematized figures pursuing a rigidly preordained course, and Augustine's friend, Alypius, whose inner upheaval at the gladiatorial games we discussed in an earlier passage, comes fully alive as he struggles, is defeated, and finally recovers. Rigid, narrow, and unproblematic schematization is originally completely alien to the Christian concept of reality. It is true, to be sure, that the rigidifying process is furthered to a considerable degree by the figural interpretation of real events, which, as Christianity became established and spread, grew increasingly influential and which, in its treatment of actual events, dissolved their content of reality, leaving them only their content of meaning. As dogma was established, as the Church's task became more and more a matter of organization, its problem that of winning over peoples completely unprepared and unacquainted with Christian principles, figural interpretation must inevitably become a simple and rigid scheme. But the problem of the process of rigidification as a whole goes deeper; it is linked to the decline of the culture of antiquity. It is not Christianity which brought about the process of rigidification, but rather Christianity was drawn into it. With the collapse of the Western Roman Empire and the principle of order which it embodied—a principle which had itself been long characterized by certain senile traits of calcification—the inner coherence of the *orbis terrarum* disintegrated too, and a new world could only be rebuilt from its parceled fragments. During the process, the politically and psychologically crude ethos of the newly emerging peoples everywhere clashed with the surviving institutions of Rome, the vestiges of antique culture, which retained a tremendous prestige despite decline and rigidification. It was a clash of the very young and the age-old, and at first the very young was paralyzed, until it had managed to come to terms with the vestiges of tradition, until it had filled them with its own life and brought them to a new florescence. The process of rigidification was naturally least pronounced in countries where the culture of late antiquity had never played a dominant role, that is, in the countries at the center of the Germanic world; it was considerably more pronounced in the Romance countries, where a real clash occurred, and perhaps it is no accident that France—where the Germanic influence was stronger than in any other Romance country—was the first to begin emancipating itself from that influence.

It appears to me that the first elevated style of the European Middle Ages arose at the moment when the single event is filled with life. That is why this style is so rich in individual scenes of great effectiveness, scenes in which only a very few characters confront one another, in which the gestures and speeches of a brief occurrence come out in sharp relief. The characters, facing one another at close quarters, without much room for movement, nevertheless stand there as individuals clearly set off from one another. What is said of them never degenerates into mere talk; it always remains a solemn statement in which every address, every phrase, and indeed every word, has a value of its own, separate and emphatic, with no trace of softness and no relaxed flow. Confronting the reality of life, this style is neither able nor willing to deal with its breadths or depths. It is limited in time, place, and social milieu. It simplifies the events of the past by stylizing and idealizing them. The feeling it seeks to arouse in its auditor is admiration and amazement for a distant world, whose instincts and ideals, though they certainly remain his own, yet evolve in such uncompromising purity and freedom, in comparison with the friction and resistance of real life, as his practical existence could not possibly attain. Human movements and great, towering exemplary figures appear with striking effect; his own life is not there at all. To be sure, in the very tone of the *Chanson de Roland* there is a great deal of contemporaneity. It does not begin with an announcement which removes the events to a distant past ("Long ago it came to pass . . . Of olden days I will sing . . .") but with a strongly immediate note, as though Charles, our great Emperor, were almost still a living man. The naive transfer of events three centuries past into the ethos of feudal society of the early crusading period, the exploitation of the subject matter in the interest of ecclesiatic and feudal propaganda, give the poem a quality of living presentness. Something like a nascent national consciousness is even perceptible in it. When we read—to choose a simple illustration—the line in which Roland tries to organize the imminent attack of the Frankish knights (1165):

> Seignurs barons, suef, le pas tenant!
>
> [*Lords Barons, gently, keeping step!*]

we hear the echo of a common scene of contemporary feudal cavalry maneuvers. But these are isolated instances. Class limitation, idealization, simplification, and the shimmering veil of legend prevail.

The style of the French heroic epic is an elevated style in which the structural concept of reality is still extremely rigid and which succeeds in representing only a narrow portion of objective life circumscribed by distance in time, simplification of perspective, and class limitations. I shall be saying nothing new, but merely reformulating what I have said many times, if I add that in this style the separation of the realm of the heroic and sublime from that of the practical and everyday is a matter of course. Strata other than that at the top of the feudal system simply do not appear. The economic bases of society are not even mentioned. This is carried much further than in the heroic epic of the early Germanic and Middle High German periods and is also in striking contrast to the heroic epic of Spain, which begins to appear but little later. Yet the *chanson de geste*, and the *Chanson de Roland* in particular, was popular. It is true that these poems deal exclusively with the exploits of the upper stratum of feudal society, but there is no doubt that they address the common people as well. The explanation may be that despite the marked material and juridic differences between the various strata of the lay population they were as yet essentially on the same intellectual level; that, indeed, the ideals men cherished were still uniform, or at least that secular ideals other than those of knighthood and heroism were not ready to be put into practice and into words. That the *chanson de geste* was a force and an influence on all levels of society is shown by the fact that about the end of the eleventh century the clergy—whose attitude toward vernacular lay literature had not theretofore been benevolent—began to exploit the heroic epic for their own purpose. The fact that these themes survived for centuries, that they were recast in ever new versions and quickly sank to the level of country-fair entertainment, proves their enduring popularity among the lower classes. For audiences of the eleventh, twelfth, and thirteenth centuries the heroic epic was history; in it the historical tradition of earlier ages was alive. No other tradition existed, at least none accessible to those audiences. It is only about the year 1200 that the first vernacular chronicles are composed, but they do not relate the past, they are eye-witness accounts of contemporary events, and even so they are strongly influenced by the epic style. And indeed, the heroic epic *is* history, at least insofar as it recalls actual historical conditions—however much it may distort and simplify them—and insofar as its characters always perform a historico-political function. This historico-political element is abandoned by the courtly novel, which consequently has a completely new relationship to the objective world of reality.

Diction

❧ W. K. WIMSATT, JR. ❧

In his introduction to *The Prose Style of Samuel Johnson*—a book which was first published in 1941 and which has already established itself as a classic treatment of an author's characteristic means of expression—W. K. Wimsatt, Jr., develops a theory of "style as meaning." The primary nature of words is to convey meaning, he contends, even when they are used as an "esthetic medium" (that is, in a context where aspects of sound or rhythmic arrangement may also be significant), which is to say that words and style cannot be discussed in isolation from "a meaning" or regarded as providing alternative ways of saying exactly the same thing: "If a word is to be placed here or there in a sentence in order to be effective, to have due weight, this ought to be thought of not as a juggling of words round a meaning to give the meaning emphatic expression, but as a choice of a more emphatic rather than a less emphatic meaning, or, strictly, the choice of the meaning needed, for meaning exists through emphasis; a change of emphasis is a change of meaning."

Thus Wimsatt conceives of words and the rhetorical pattern into which they may be deployed as essentially "expressive" of meaning. And since he defines *style* itself as "the last and most detailed elaboration of meaning," he concentrates in his book on examining "those rhetorical topics which have special relevance to the Johnsonian style," which Johnson typically calls on to make his meaning: chiefly parallelism, antithesis, and abstract diction, but also "'inversion' and its special form 'chiasmus.'" Wimsatt's recurrent use of *expressive* and his insistence on *meaning* indicate that he views language itself as ultimately transitive, as affecting an audience. Yet the weight of his particular analyses falls on the ways in which Johnson's words render meaning within the text rather than on the responses they elicit from the reader.

One symptom of Wimsatt's primary concern for the text itself—to come at the matter for a moment from the other side—is his distinction in the chapter reproduced here between the possible sources of Johnson's vocabulary and the stylistic evaluation of it: "The opportunities which a man has to learn this or that kind of vocabulary are certainly a part of his literary history and an important part, but they do not affect the description of his style as expression." Within the chapter, Wimsatt treats the generality of Johnson's diction, its abstraction, and Johnson's use of "words which have a scientific or philosophic flavor" (the latter is a topic that Wimsatt has developed in a separate book, *Philosophic Words* [1948]). Not the least of the chapter's merits is Wimsatt's careful laying of the groundwork for his analysis of Johnson's diction through distinguishing between three sets of terms often loosely employed in describing words: *particular* and *general*, *concrete* and *abstract*, *sensory* and *non-sensory*.

IN HIS PARALLELISM we have seen Johnson more interested in the alignment of reasoning, the relation of premises to conclusions, than in the individuality of the premises themselves. In his antitheses we have seen him intent on showing the respect in which he does mean something by telling the respect in which he does not mean it. Both these are ways of attaining generalization, of referring to their relevant classifications the concrete or specific objects employed as the texture, really only illustrative, of thoughtful discourse. They are ways of insisting on the formal over the material. And in yet another important way Johnson did the same—in his peculiar choice of words, the distinctively Johnsonian vocabulary.

The critics have not differed much over what words are Johnsonian. "Words of Latin and Greek origin," says Schmidt, "... technical terms of philosophy, medicine and law," and he gives a long list of nouns ending in "ion."[1] "Pompous and long," says Matthew Arnold.[2] "In a learned language," says Macaulay, "... in a language

---

[1] [Heinrich] Schmidt [*Der Prosastil Samuel Johnson's* (Marburg, 1905),] pp. 4–8.
[2] *The Six Chief Lives from Johnson's "Lives of the Poets"* (London, 1878), p. xix.

"Diction," by W. K. Wimsatt, Jr., is reprinted from *The Prose Style of Samuel Johnson* (New Haven, Conn., and London, 1963), pp. 50–62, by permission of Yale University Press. Copyright © 1941 by Yale University Press.

in which nobody ever quarrels, or drives bargains, or makes love, in a language in which nobody ever thinks. ... It is well known that he made less use than any other eminent writer of those strong plain words, Anglo-Saxon or Norman-French, of which the roots lie in the inmost depths of our language; and that he felt a vicious partiality for terms which long after our own speech had been fixed, were borrowed from the Greek and Latin...."[3] "None but 'tall, opaque words' taken from the 'first row of the rubric,'" says Hazlitt—"words with the greatest number of syllables, or Latin phrases with merely English terminations."[4]

Scarcely a criticism of Johnson's style has been written without the mention of "long" words or "Latin" words. And the early, more vituperative criticisms abound in epithets like "polysyllabic," "pedantic," "hard," "obscure," "bombastic," "cumbrous."[5] "The teeth-breaking diction of Johnson" was Walpole's expression.[6] "This may be a bookseller's project at bottom," said Archibald Campbell; "he might write his *Ramblers* to make a dictionary necessary, and afterwards compile his dictionary to explain his *Ramblers*."[7]

But we must approach the matter somewhat more thoughtfully. In the first place, if an expressive tendency sometimes leads an author to violate idiom, his violations may be exhibited as curiosities, and in proportion to their frequency the author may be more or less censured—for idiom, currency, is one of the conditions of effectiveness in the arbitrary medium of language. Yet these violations, understood however perfectly as violations, are no account of the expressive tendency that produced them. Professor Taylor has well said: "The whole tale is never told when one merely turns his pages—as one easily may—and unearths such a list of musty curiosities as the following: *proemial, momentaneous, interstitial, supplantation, supervenient, annuitant, obtunds, pravity, divaricate, amendations, propagate, procerity,* and *operose*."[8] And the perhaps even more exaggerated examples with which O. F. Christie amuses himself are amusing only, not seriously instructive.[9]

Nor is it a stylistic evaluation of Johnson's words to consider where he learned them. The opportunities which a man has to learn this or that kind of vocabulary are certainly a part of his literary history and an important part, but they do not affect the

---

[3] T. B. Macaulay, "Essay on Johnson," in *Macaulay's and Carlyle's Essays on Samuel Johnson*, edited by William Strunk, Jr. (New York, 1895), pp. 60–62.

[4] [*The Complete Works of William Hazlitt*, edited by P. P.] Howe [(London, 1930–34),] VIII, 243, *Table Talk*, 1822, Essay XXIV, "On Familiar Style." Cf. *Howe* IV, 371.

[5] Some selections may be conveniently consulted in W. Vaughan Reynolds' "Reception of Johnson's Prose Style," *Review of English Studies*, XI (1935), 145–62.

[6] Horace Walpole, *Letters*, edited by Mrs. Paget Toynbee (Oxford, 1904), IX, 173, 3 April 1775.

[7] *Lexiphanes*, second edition (London, 1767), pp. 108–09.

[8] [Warner] Taylor ["The Prose Style of Samuel Johnson," *University of Wisconsin Studies in Language and Literature*, No. 2, *Studies by Members of the Department of English* (Madison, 1918),] p. 25.

[9] [O. F.] Christie [*Johnson the Essayist* (London, 1924),] pp. 27–28. From Johnson's works: speculatist, adscititious, abscinded, officinal, indiscerptible, papilionaceous, colorifick, frigorifick, fugacity, alexipharmick, equiponderant, reposited, orbity, catharticks, argumental, equilibrations, concatenations, oraculous, subducted, intenerate, oppugner, divaricate, irremeable. From Boswell's *Life:* formular, conglobulate, anfractuosities, labefactation, peregrinity, depeditation. Christie studies Johnson's treatment of these words in the *Dictionary*.

description of his style as expression. The question whether Johnson's vocabulary is traceable to his work on the *Dictionary* is irrelevant here. And so is the question whether it is traceable to his classical education. It is not to the purpose to call his words Latin. Their derivation may have a historical connection with their type of meaning, but for the analysis of meaning this is an accident. If Johnson had been a Roman, he would probably have used Greek words. As a matter of fact it is possible that he uses almost as many Greek as Latin words.[10] Again, it is but little more to the purpose to appeal to Johnson's *Plan of a Dictionary* and his *Preface to the Dictionary* and deduce from these his theory of propriety in English. If we consider Johnson's objection to "Gallick structure and phrase," his belief that the cultivation of the learned languages had helped to perfect and fix our language,[11] we may understand some of the limitations of his vocabulary but hardly his way of using it. A lexicographical principle is not a stylistic, not an expressive one.

If we would philosophize on Johnson's use of words, we must go again to his meaning, we must describe his words as tending to have certain kinds of meaning. At once then we see the inadequacy of simple lists of words or statistics of the occurrence of certain kinds of words defined merely by qualities that may be observed in them when isolated. What is needed is the context. For the "same" type of word becomes a different type in a different use. An impressive list of nouns in "ion," for example, such as Schmidt presents, may warrant the presumption that some way of using these has been of extraordinary frequency. But what the way is we may miss, because words in "ion" have been used by different writers in different ways.

IN TALKING OF Johnson's words there are in general three pairs of opposed notions that must be mentioned and usually have been, either more or less explicitly: the particular and the general, the concrete and the abstract, the sensory and the non-sensory. At the risk of being obvious I enter into a short discussion of the meaning and interrelation of these terms.

Generality in writing is more a matter of whole meaning than of diction, or at any rate it is hardly to be measured in terms of the latter. General terms, as opposed to particular terms, embrace almost the whole language. Only proper nouns, personal pronouns, and demonstrative adjectives and pronouns are in themselves particular.[12] And all particulars in thoughtful writing have an illustrative value, that is to say, a class value. Particularity is often a mere form, as when Addison introduces Eugenius in *Spectator* No. 177, or when Johnson devotes the whole of *Idler* No. 71 to Dick Shifter. All class terms are general, and those that are less general ought to be called

---

[10] Professor Chandler reports of the first thousand words of our passage from the *Life of Pope* that the percentage of classical words is 55.8, but that of Latin words only 26.3 ([Zilpha E.] Chandler [*An Analysis of the Stylistic Technique of Addison, Johnson, Hazlitt, and Pater,* University of Iowa Humanistic Studies, Vol. IV, No. 3 (Iowa City, 1928),] p. 42).

[11] Cf. *Christie* pp. 26–27. Cf. [Wimsatt, *The Prose Style of Samuel Johnson,*] p. 104.

[12] Of course any word may be particular, or "singular," in use. "That tree" is a singular term. So is "the second oak tree on the left of the road past the white wooden gates."

more specific rather than more particular. Any given class word is more general or more specific according to the generic idea with relevance to which it is used. If I mention horses in a field in an enumeration of farm animals, I have been fairly specific. If I mention only horses in describing a racing farm, I have been general. For this, to be equally specific, I should know the breeds of horses, distinguish the mares, the stallions and the geldings, the fillies and the colts. And this is only to consider genera and species according to one order. There is also the matter of intersection of species. An apple in an orchard is not an apple in a lunch basket. Any term when put in different contexts assumes by implication relations to different generic scales. Further, an adjective or an abstract noun will have a more or less specific value according to the concrete noun with which it is associated. "Green woods" are less specific than "green hat," for the woods are expected to be green.

The act of generalization is a step toward that other which is called abstraction. In order to form the class concept "animals" it is necessary to see a number of dissimilar objects under an aspect which they have in common; nevertheless the concept is still of the actual objects. It is the act of attending to this concept itself which is better called abstraction. The aspect, adjectival when considered as embodied in the object, is invested with substantiality of its own; and we have "animality."[13] As a usual thing the more general the idea by the first process, the more likely the mind is to find a use in the abstraction. "Animality" is a more common abstraction than "horsiness" or "equinity," and the latter more common than "colthood" or "coltiness." The more specific the class notion becomes, the more difficult it is to conceive it abstractly or at least to find an abstract word for it. And so abstraction depends on generalization, and an author's tendency to abstraction is likely to be in proportion to his tendency to generalization.

The foregoing may have suggested the standing of the terms "sensory" and "non-sensory" in our inquiry. They are as relative as "particular" and "general." Even an onomatopoeic word has some arbitrary, generalized value, or it is not a word. And even an abstract word referring to a mental state, like "thoughtfulness," is abstracted from experiences which are partly sensory and must faintly suggest them. For thinking is done through the imagination, and the imagination draws its material from the senses. An abstract word like "greenness" has much more sensory value than a concrete word like "man." All that can be said in general is that particular or more specific words tend to be more sensory than general or abstract ones. There are more physical qualities connoted in the word "colt" than in "equine." And it may be added that verbs of thought, even the more specific ones, like "speculate," "ponder," "muse," those which are dead metaphors, have little sensory content, while adjectives denoting qualities perceptible to the senses, "green," "harsh," "fragrant," have the greatest, though even this is diluted by frequent metaphorical use, as when one speaks of "harsh manners." A writer's proportion of sensory values will correspond to his use of the specific. And as no single class word can be called

---

[13] Cf. Abraham Wolf, *Textbook of Logic* (London, 1930), pp. 118–19; Désiré Cardinal Mercier, *Cours de Philosophie*, Vol. I, *Logique* (Louvain, 1902), p. 102; Richard Whately, *Logic*, in *Encyclopaedia Metropolitana*, First Division (London, 1851), Introduction, pp. 25–26.

DICTION [211]

absolutely specific or absolutely general, so no word can be called absolutely sensory or absolutely non-sensory. The terms are contraries rather than contradictories.

IT IS rather as a character of general meaning than as a detail of meaning,[14] as style, that one must be content to consider Johnson's tendency to generalization. It is possible to produce a list of words from Hazlitt like the following:

> brilliance, buckles, lake, lamp, library, lustre, mariner, masquerade-dress, bosom, brow, dew-drops, garden, glass, spring, sun, pale, paste, cottage, glittering, smooth, soft, stamped, stripped, trembles, laugh, wandered, winged.[15]

And to make a list from Johnson to set beside them:

> objects, present, schemes, felicity, commodious, serious, ridiculed, wantoning, blessings, transmit, futurity, progressive, horizon, allurements, fear, fatigue, contemplation, harvest, maxims, caution, propriety, usefulness, levity, distinction, vehemence, inquietude, fruition.[16]

We may call Hazlitt's words sensory and specific, Johnson's non-sensory and general.[17] Yet it is only in a vague and collective sense that this is so, and only because we know the contexts too that we accept these lists as representative of any quality of meaning. Though many of Johnson's words in the above list could not by any use have much sensory value, it is only the use of a word that ever gives it any. It may be instructive to compile the following list from the same *Rambler*:

> raillery, gay, wantoning, shine, glide, flowery, gradual, horizon, flights, steps, eyes, ground, harvest, blights, inundations, sweep, reaping, riot, slipped, magnifying, crown, island, squire, mirth, plants, sun, gardens, physick, catharticks, lenitives, dispel, cloud, luminaries, library, caressed, huddled, fluctuating, immersed.[18]

Not even at first glance so promising as Hazlitt's bright array. Yet who without the context could guess the dryly non-sensory, intellectual use of these words, the semi-metaphorical "track so smooth and so flowery," "flights of the human mind," "horizon of his prospects," or "steps to a certain point," or the flat illustrative value of "an

---

[14] Under this head, however, one might place Johnson's fondness for relative clauses of characteristic (i.e., classification), especially those with a completely indefinite antecedent—"he that," "that which," "what," etc. I note, for example, five of these in our passage from the *Life of Pope* and no fewer than nine in *Rambler* No. 2.
[15] Professor Chandler's list chosen from the passage of the lecture "On Dryden and Pope" (*Chandler* p. 62).
[16] From *Rambler* No. 2, [Samuel Johnson] *Works* [edited by John Hawkins (London, 1787),] V, 7–10.
[17] Professor Chandler reports that in the first thousand words of the passage from the *Life of Pope* there are only three sensory adjectives out of sixty-nine, and out of 105 verbs only seven "denoting action" (*Chandler* pp. 43–44).
[18] *Works* V, 7–13.

island to bestow on his worthy squire"? And if we limit the inquiry to the matter of specific or general, it is even more hopeless to define or count. Anyone looking for general words would have to admit that in our first list from *Rambler* No. 2 "schemes" and "fear" are rather general. Yet which is more general? And where is the line to be drawn? On which side of these words? Or between the two?

On the other hand, Johnson's bent for generality cannot be denied. It is part of his moral purpose. It is derived from the very subjects of his essays and suggested in their titles. It is apparent as a character of his general meaning on almost any page.[19] And if he is interested in generality, in the classes to which things belong, the aspects which unify groups of objects, he becomes at moments even more interested in these aspects as things in themselves, as metaphysical realities. Allowing the physical objects to be pressed out of sight,[20] he erects the metaphysicalities or abstractions into the substantives of his discourse. And in order to accommodate these substantives he resorts at times to certain extraordinary distortions of prose.

Some examples may be seen in the following paragraphs from *Rambler* No. 2:

> This quality of looking forward into futurity seems the unavoidable condition of a being, whose motions are gradual, and whose life is progressive: as his powers are limited, he must use means for the attainment of his ends, and intend first what he performs last; as by continual advances from his first stage of existence, he is perpetually varying the horizon of his prospects, he must always discover new motives of action, new excitements of fear, and allurements of desire.[21]

Johnson has gone far out of his way to bring in the two very general abstractions "quality" and "condition," where the concrete form would be simply: "To look forward into the future seems unavoidable for a being whose motions are gradual." Then "attainment" is an abstraction, and instead of "for the attainment of his ends,"

---

[19] Only Johnson's extraordinary contentment with generality could prompt some of the criticisms that have been made of his writing. Northcote said that the character of Zachariah Mudge in the *London Chronicle*, 2 May 1769, "was like one of Kneller's portraits,—it would do for anybody" ([James Boswell] *Life [of Johnson*, edited by George B. Hill and L. F. Powell (Oxford, 1934),] IV, 77, n. 1). Boswell's friend Dempster wrote "that a great part of what was in his 'Journey to the Western Islands of Scotland,' had been in his mind before he left London" (*Life* III, 301). Hawkins says of the same work, "His web was spun, not from objects that presented themselves to his view, but from his own pre-existent ideas" (*Works* I, 482). John Nichols told Boswell that the *Debates in Parliament* "were frequently written from very slender materials, and often from none at all,—the mere coinage of his own imagination" (*Life* IV, 408. Cf. *Life* I, 506-07, Appendix A). Miss Talbot complained to Mrs. Carter of the *Rambler*, "Why then does he not write now and then on the living manners of the times?—The stage,—the follies and fashions" (*Series of Letters between Mrs. Elizabeth Carter and Miss Catherine Talbot*, edited by Montagu Pennington (London, 1809), I, 371).

Cf. [Wimsatt, *The Prose Style of Samuel Johnson*,] pp. 93-94, for evidence of Johnson's consciousness and justification of his use of generality.

[20] Professor Chandler reports that in the first thousand words of the passage from the *Life of Pope* the percentage of concrete words is only 19.7, while in the same number of words from Addison it is 38.3 and from Hazlitt, 32.3 (*Chandler* p. 43). She reports also that "Johnson uses comparatively few nouns,—fewer *in proportion to his vocabulary* than any of our other writers," 37.8 per cent to Hazlitt's 44.6 and Addison's 41.8 (p. 42). The italics are mine. He might use the same nouns a good many times each. It is also possible that her definition of abstraction includes generalization.

[21] *Works* V, 9, *Rambler* No. 2.

the verbal form "to attain his ends" would be preferred by many writers.[22] But the closing phrases of this paragraph show Johnson in his most abnormal employment of the abstract noun in place of another part of speech—the linking of noun to noun, or piling of noun upon noun, by the preposition "of." In "attainment of his ends" the verbal notion is so strong that this objective genitive construction is hardly noticed as containing two nouns. The meaning of such genitive constructions can, however, vary widely, according to the nature of the nouns and their relation to each other. We may have, for example, the subjective genitive, "fear of men" (for death); the objective, "fear of death" (by men); the qualitative, "house of stone"; and so on, through many shades of meaning perhaps uncatalogued by grammarians.[23] What Johnson specializes in is a form of the *appositional* genitive in which one noun is abstract, or both. "He must always discover new motives of action, new excitements of fear, and allurements of desire." The last two members of this triplet are a development of the first and taken together are parallel to it. The relations of the three pairs of words connected by "of" are different. "*Motives* of action" are *motives for* action —namely, "fear" and "desire," which, though parallel to "motives," occupy the position of second noun in the last two phrases. The element of action disappears at the end of the phrase, and in its place, but at the beginning, appear the two words "excitements" and "allurements," abstract, in appositional relation to "fear" and "desire." The notion "fear" (itself perhaps abstract) has the quality of exciting pulled out of it and formed into a second abstraction; so "allurements" is pulled out of "desire"; and the pairs of abstractions float in unstable expansion, each ready to collapse into one. The use of verbs would have made the expressions more concrete: "new fears to excite him and desires to allure him," and perhaps would have created a more apparent shade of tautology (multiplication irrelevant to the context).

In the first paragraph of the same *Rambler* occurs the expression:

> ridiculed, with all the pleasantry of wit, and exaggerated with all the amplifications of rhetoric.[24]

But "wit" is not an agent who displays "pleasantry"; both are qualities of mind or talk displayed by some agent, or better two aspects of the same mental actions or

---

[22] Robert R. Aurner says of Addison's prose, "The unusually large number of gerunds or verbal nouns adds to the natural liveliness and resiliency of his writing, and makes it seem active, kinetic, and verbal as with Dryden's, rather than heavy, potential, and substantive as with Johnson's" ("The History of Certain Aspects of the Structure of the English Sentence," *Philological Quarterly*, II (1923), 200).

The relation of abstraction to the parts of speech is roughly this: Abstract words are nouns, though of course not all nouns are abstract. Adjectives refer to qualities conceived as *in things*; when the things are concrete, so are the adjectives. Finite verbs are adjectives predicated. The gerund and infinitive are hence abstract substantives. "Green" is to "greenness" as the participle (adjective) "running" is to "to run." Nevertheless, we tend to conceive physical actions as separable from their agents and hence concrete. We go to see a race (a running), but not to see a greenness. A more persuasive abstract suggestion is obtained from those verbs, mostly of mental action, which admit a noun form on the same root. With the words "thought" or "attention" we lose most of the idea of action for that of quality.

[23] For a more elaborate treatment, see John H. Scott and Zilpha E. Chandler, *Phrasal Patterns in English Prose* (New York, 1932), pp. 125-35.

[24] *Works* V, 8.

talk. To say "the pleasantries of wit" is to make one grow out of the other, like a hump on the hump of the camel. A more ordinary form would be "pleasantry and wit," a typical Johnsonian doublet for emphasis, but less abstract, for here the two terms are parallel, each capable of an abstract or a concrete interpretation. Much the same may be said for "amplifications of rhetoric." If rhetoric is personified into a rhetorical speaker, the construction may be interpreted as a subjective genitive, with "amplifications" referring to the amplified things said by this speaker. But one is more likely to conceive "rhetoric" as a way of speaking or writing and "amplifications" as another, if a more specific, aspect of the same way.[25]

Along with these abstractions may be noted the passive voice and the absence of concrete nouns denoting agents. The abstractions assume the responsibility of the agent and are usually in an oblique case. "It has been marked with every epithet of contempt."[26] Or the verb itself becomes an abstraction, the agent disappears, and what would be the object is connected with the abstraction of a verb by some other verb. "Which escape vulgar observation,"[27] instead of "which people do not commonly observe." Or the abstraction not only assumes the responsibility of the agent but fills his shoes as subject of the action. "That vehemence of desire which presses through right and wrong to its gratification, or that anxious inquietude which is justly chargeable with distrust of heaven."[28] An abstraction of an abstraction pressing through right and wrong to another abstraction. In the *Life of Watts*, we have "Mr. Pinhorne ... to whom the gratitude of his scholar afterwards inscribed a Latin ode."[29] In *The False Alarm*, "Lampoon itself would disdain to speak ill."[30] Or in any part of the sentence, as subject, as object of verb, as object of preposition, may appear abstractions that are but the faintest shade removed from personification.[31]

---

[25] Schmidt groups these constructions under "Fülle des Ausdrucks," along with word pairs. "Sinnverwandte Substantive subordiniert" he calls them and gives a list, in which the following are good examples of synonymy (nearness of relevant meaning, emphasis rather than range): "the coldness of neglect" (*Works* VI, 307, *Rambler* No. 119); "the infirmities of decrepitude" (*Works* V, 379, *Rambler* No. 59); "the gloom of sorrow" (*Works* V, 334, *Rambler* No. 52). He gives a shorter list where the noun is modified not by an abstraction but by an equivalent adjective (*Schmidt* pp. 9–12). *Rambler* No. 30, from which he selects "lazy idleness" (*Works* V, 198), was written by Catherine Talbot ([William P.] Courtney [*A Bibliography of Samuel Johnson* (Oxford, 1915),] p. 25).

[26] *Works* V, 8, *Rambler* No. 2.

[27] *Ibid.*, p. 8. Once before, in a conspicuous place, Johnson used the abstract "observation" less fortunately:

    Let observation with extensive view,
    Survey mankind, from China to Peru.

"Let observation with extensive observation observe mankind extensively." (For the origin and development of this paraphrase see *Life* I, 193, n. 3, 537, Appendix G.)

[28] *Works* V, 10, *Rambler* No. 2. [29] *Works* IV, 179. [30] *Works* X, 5.

[31] As early as 1787 the Reverend Robert Burrowes published his "Essay on the Stile of Doctor Samuel Johnson," which in some respects is as penetrating as anything since written [*Transactions of the Royal Irish Academy*, Vol. I (Dublin, 1787), "Polite Literature," pp. 27–56]. "The instrument, the motive, or the quality therefore," he writes, "which ordinary writers would have in the oblique case, usually takes the lead in Johnson's sentences; while the person, which in connected writing is often expressed by some weak pronoun, is either intirely omitted, or thrown into a less conspicuous part. Thus, 'fruition left them nothing to ask, and innocence left them nothing to fear,'—'trifles written by idleness and published by vanity,'—'wealth may, by hiring flattery, or laying diligence asleep, confirm error or harden stupidity' ... and we are teized

The danger of constant abstraction, besides its leading to occasional violation of idiom, is, like the danger of other types of meaning we have considered, that of irrelevant meaning. A series of metaphysical substantives engrafted into a discourse, standing out like shadows from every concrete substantive or rising like ghosts in the level road of verbs and adjectives, is a series of meanings that may point in many wrong directions. Abstraction is the conjuring into substantiality of qualities which in the physical world have not this dignity. Many qualities, quite relevantly named, are nevertheless, like the paint on a bench, better for lying flat. Enough has been said by many a writer[32] on the virtue of concrete nouns and active verbs—how they touch directly what is meant, cut swiftly to the heart of matters. Although in every context some abstractions may be relevantly named, it does not follow that abstraction is a safe prescription for any of the things sometimes vaguely associated with good writing, for dignity or sublimity, force or authority.

BUT THE TWO TRAITS of generalization and abstraction lead Johnson to a third which I consider to be preeminently the Johnsonian trait of vocabulary—the use of general or abstract words which have a scientific or philosophic flavor. "Philosophick" he called them himself.[33] There are certain words for denoting objects which may not denote these any more generically than other words denoting the same objects, but which suggest that the objects are to be thought of as a class, rather than as individuals; they emphasize by their tone the aspect under which the class is conceived and have little or no connotation of complete appearance or the physical accidentals which clothe individuals of the class. These terms speak as having been coined by men who knew more accurately than common men the precise aspect, or complex of aspects, that constitute the class, who named classes only after studying them and with the advantages of vast preliminary erudition, men who understood the nature of things. These, in short, are scientific terms, what Schmidt recognizes as the "technical terms of philosophy, medicine and law,"[34] careful terms, and because careful, weighty, carrying authority. Such, for example, is the word "equine." As a noun it refers to no other object than a horse, but it suggests that the writer knows what a horse is; as an adjective it means "horselike," yet it is one word, established, whereas there is that of the makeshift, unready, unauthoritative, about "horselike." The difference is most apparent in terms which actually belong to science. But it appears all through the language. It is the difference between "domicile" and "home," between

---

with the repeated mention of 'ear of greatness,'—'the bosom of suspicion,'—and 'the eye of wealth, of hope, and of beauty'" (p. 45). Burrowes devotes three pages to abstractions of various kinds, closely paralleling much that I have said above. He collects some examples that I should not venture to exhibit as typical: "places of little frequentation," "circumstances of no elegant recital," "with emulation of price," "the library which is of late erection," "too much temerity of conclusion" (pp. 46–7).

The two parts of Burrowes' essay were reprinted anonymously and as original, verbatim, in the Port Folio (Series V), Vol. XI (Philadelphia, 1821), pp. 300–09; Vol. XII (1821), pp. 32–42.

[32] See for example the trenchant lecture "On Jargon" by Sir Arthur Quiller-Couch, *On the Art of Writing* (Cambridge, England, 1916), pp. 96–103.

[33] [Wimsatt, *The Prose Style of Samuel Johnson*,] p. 109.

[34] *Ante* p. 207.

"cursive" and "running," between "incise" and "cut," even, by extension of the implication, between "frequently" and "often."

It happens that almost all of these terms, if not all of them, are Latin and Greek. This is the accident of their derivation, that the learned tongues were levied upon for the terminology of philosophy and then for that of the growing physical sciences, "natural philosophy," and that the learned tongues were Latin and Greek.[35] So Latin and Greek derivation becomes implicitly learned and authoritative; the character is more or less extended to all words of direct Latin or Greek derivation, whether strictly scientific or not, down to adverbs of such common occurrence as "frequently" and "subsequently." In these the character is of course very faint but can become noticeable by multiplication.

It happens too that Latin and Greek learned derivatives are long.[36] And to length of words I am ready to grant some expressive value—that of emphasis. The scientific authority, the deliberation and certainty, is backed up by a thump on the table. The big word is big enough to enforce its big meaning,[37] to increase the strength of the less emphatic parts of the sentence, to clinch the already more emphatic parts. If Johnson would use a doublet of nearly synonymous words mainly for emphasis, why not one big one, or a doublet of big ones?

In considering philosophic words we have of course the same problem of context as with the specific and sensory. We must proceed, not by statistics, but by examining the function of such words as may securely be called Johnsonian. When Johnson said of *The Rehearsal*, "It has not wit enough to keep it sweet," then in correction of himself, "It has not vitality enough to preserve it from putrefaction,"[38] he composed in the second version what I believe everyone will admit to be a highly characteristic Johnsonian expression. Moreover, it cannot be disputed that its character depends largely on the diction. Yet one bent on listing Johnsonian words could hardly stop in manageable limits if words like "vitality," "preserve," "putrefaction," were to be included. "Such was the intense vitality of the Béarnese prince." Surely the word "vitality" itself has its innocence. And see what Carlyle could do with the plural. "He was full of bright speech and argument; radiant with arrowy vitalities." "Putrefaction" is less exonerable; its use shines through it more, and perhaps did even more

---

[35] Cf. Otto Jespersen, *Growth and Structure of the English Language* (New York, 1923), pp. 115–16.

[36] Professor Taylor counts the number of syllables per word of sections of Johnson's prose and finds the average high, 1.55 in exposition, 1.53 in biographical narrative. "Wordsworth's *We Are Seven* averages 1.18 syllables per word; a section from James's *Psychology* that I have in mind, 2.07. Between the two styles lies the ocean. I have come to the conclusion through analyzing many passages that *normal* exposition—by which limitation I mean to exclude simple personal prose on the one hand and technical prose on the other—will fall between 1.45 and 1.50 syllables per word, and that normal descriptive or narrative prose will find its limits between 1.30 and 1.40" (*Taylor* pp. 27, 30). He finds that Macaulay has about the same word length as Johnson, and De Quincey a somewhat greater. (But of course they may not use long words in the same way as Johnson. "Philosophick" words are long words, but long words, not necessarily "philosophick" words.) Johnson's word length remains about the same throughout his career (*Taylor* pp. 29–30). Cf. [Wimsatt, *The Prose Style of Samuel Johnson*,] p. 87.

[37] Cf. Herbert Spencer, "The Philosophy of Style," in Lane Cooper's *Theories of Style* (New York, 1907), pp. 276–77.

[38] *Life* IV, 320.

in Johnson's day. Yet Marryat in 1833 was certainly not being Johnsonian when he wrote: "The body is never allowed to remain many hours unburied in the tropical climates, where putrefaction is so rapid." And even in 1756 Gray wrote to Wharton: "I maintain that one sick rich patient has more of pestilence and putrefaction about him than a whole ward of sick poor."[39] And for the word "preserve," who would care to list its humble uses? It is when "vitality" is the alternative to "wit," or to what would be of its own generic level, "life," that its philosophic character is seen. And "putrefaction" loses its philosophic character when applied in a matter-of-fact, gruesome way to a corpse, or disgustingly to a sick man, but shows this character in full when used in the abstract realm of literary criticism. "Preserve" in this context shows perfectly how a common word (not directly Latin in derivation, but French) becomes philosophic when it displaces a still more common word. The Old English "cēpan" might father a sturdy enough plain English word, but never a philosophic one.

As a further illustration I offer the following sentence from *Rambler* No. 2:

> In agriculture, one of the most simple and necessary employments, no man turns up the ground but because he thinks of the harvest, that harvest which blights may intercept, which inundations may sweep away, or which death or calamity may hinder him from reaping.[40]

"Agriculture" is the "philosophic" term for "farming"; "intercept," for "cut off"; "inundations," for "floods." The terms "harvest," "blights," "sweep away" are non-philosophic or plain, of the same rank as the alternatives just suggested. In this sentence there would perhaps be small loss of meaning were all of the six terms plain.

The danger is once more that of irrelevant meaning. If it is remembered that a "philosophic" word has a kind of meaning, a connotation, which its plain equivalent lacks, it will be easily understood that to use "philosophic" diction constantly is to give to writing an irrelevant overtone, to emphasize or attempt to emphasize every word in a monotonous uproar. It is to Johnson's "philosophic" diction that Hazlitt refers when he says: "He always translated his ideas into the highest and most imposing form of expression,"[41] and when he says again, "The fault of Dr. Johnson's style is, that it reduces all things to the same artificial and unmeaning level."[42]

---

[39] *New English Dictionary*, "vitality," 3, 4; "putrefaction," 1, 1.b.   [40] *Works* V, 9.   [41] Howe IV, 371, "On Manner," in the *Examiner*, 27 August 1815.
[42] Howe VI, 101–02, *Lectures on the English Comic Writers*, 1819, Lecture V, "On the Periodical Essayists."

K. Čapek's Prose as Lyrical Melody and as Dialogue

JAN MUKAŘOVSKÝ

Jan Mukařovský was a member of the Prague Linguistic Circle that flourished in the late 1920's, a group which was influenced by the Russian Formalists' work of the early 1920's and went on to develop a structuralist approach to literature. Like the Russian Formalists, the Prague School reacted against more traditional methods of scholarship which seemed to pay insufficient attention to literary texts themselves, and it insisted on the esthetic status of literature through differentiating between ordinary discourse, which aims primarily at expeditious communication, and artistic discourse, which tends to make language itself the object of our notice, to "foreground" its qualities. The critical approach of the group is illustrated in *A Prague School Reader on Esthetics, Literary Structure, and Style* (1964), a collection of essays by various members which Paul Garvin has done a signal service in translating from the Czech.

To elaborate slightly upon the premises of the group and to provide a background for the particular essay on Karel Čapek reprinted here, I quote several passages from more theoretical essays by Mukařovský (also as translated by Garvin in the *Prague School Reader*). "Poetic language," Mukařovský claims, "is thus not a brand of the standard [language]," but "this is not to deny the close connection between the two, which consists in the fact that, for poetry, the standard language is the background against which is reflected the esthetically intentional distortion of the linguistic components of the work, in other words, the intentional violation of the norm of the standard." "In poetic language foregrounding achieves maximum intensity to the extent of pushing communication into the background as the objective of expression and of being used for its own sake; it is not used in the services of communication, but in order to place in the foreground the act of expression, the act of speech itself." Although foregrounding distinctively characterizes much of the language in a literary work, the esthetic whole includes other elements as well and becomes a structure integrated through a variety of interrelationships: "What does specifically characterize poetic language in an esthetic sense is something else [something other than the mere number of foregrounded components]: the work of poetry forms a complex, yet unified, esthetic structure into which enter as constituents all of its components, foregrounded or not, as well as their interrelationships. This makes the work of poetry different from any communicative response, where at all times only the foregrounded elements are esthetically relevant. The predominance of the esthetic function in poetic language, by contrast with communicative speech, thus consists in the esthetic relevance of the utterance as a whole."

In the following essay, Mukařovský explores "intonation"—which is linguistically foregrounded in various ways—in the works of Čapek to suggest that *"a soft undulation without abrupt boundary markers"* is a dominant characteristic of Čapek's verbal manner. Mukařovský builds his case on Čapek's unusual use of the semicolon and dash, his employment of intonational units to create patterns of repetition or contrast, his management of dialogue, and the ultimate invasion of his narrative prose by dialogue. Although the critic mentions several possible sources for Čapek's concern with intonation, including the author's "subjective awareness of language" and his reading of certain lyric poets, Mukařovský's analysis focuses on the texts themselves, and the overriding question to which he addresses himself is how intonation operates as a "formative device" within them.

"K. Čapek's Prose as Lyrical Melody and as Dialogue," by Jan Mukařovský, is reprinted by permission from *A Prague School Reader on Esthetics, Literary Structure, and Style*, edited and translated by Paul L. Garvin. Georgetown University Press, 1964, pp. 133–49. Garvin identifies the original essay as appearing in *Slovo a slovesnost*, V (1939), 1–12.

[first paragraph omitted]

THE TITLE of our study seems to indicate a limitation of the material; it is therefore necessary to mention that in taking our departure from the *phonetic* aspects of Čapek's prose this does not mean, considering the close interrelatedness of *all* the components of any verbal response, that the phonetic aspects are the final goal of our analysis; and finally, though giving our primary attention to Čapek's *prose*, we will be unable, in view of the close interrelatedness of all of Čapek's poetic creation, to avoid his lyrical, and especially his dramatical, works. His epic prose is of course the very core of Čapek's work, as is clear from the fact that it is the carrier of the poet's personal development. Its thematic, and especially stylistic, modifiability from the first works to the last is greater than that of his drama: his style changes almost from book to book, whereas in the drama, at least from *R. U. R.* to *Matka* [The Mother], his dialogue technique remains about the same. The developmental changeability of Čapek's prose thus is extremely great: even a casual comparison of his first book, *Krakonošova zahrada* [Krakonoš's Garden], with his next to last, *První parta* [The First Rescue Party], shows clearly that almost everything has changed: the style, the subject matter, the attitude to reality—in the former, a brittle prose lyric, in the latter a style leaning on conversational speech; in the former, cavaliers, rich roués, beautiful women, in the latter miners dirty with coal dust; in the former, an underestimation of everyday reality and a turning away from it, in the latter, an attentive penetration into its recesses. In spite of all this, even these extreme milestones are connected by something other than the mere name of the author: it is the identity of a certain basic structural principle. And thus two basic questions arise in connection with Čapek's work: 1. What is this basic principle uniting Čapek's works in spite of their developmental differentiation? 2. What caused this developmental differentiation? We shall attempt to answer both of these questions by an analysis of the phonetic aspects, not because we think that this is the only place where Čapek's poetic personality manifests itself, but because it is the most accessible starting point for an analysis.

The most distinctive, and also the most permanent, mark of the phonetic side of Čapek's prose is its melodiousness, in other words, the *dominant status of intonation*; beginning with the first book and ending with the last, Čapek's prose is carried along and organized by intonation not only in terms of its phonetic aspect but, as will be shown subsequently, in regard to its meaning aspect as well; this is equally true of Čapek's dramatic dialogue.

It seems that intonation was for Čapek's subjective awareness of language the most important organizing factor of the verbal response, that component of language for the nuances of which he had the finest perceptive capacity. In the short story *Elegie* [Elegy] in the collection *Boží muka* [The Passion of Our Lord] he describes the orator's subjective impression of his own speech as follows: "At times he would listen to his own voice; it seemed to him to be thick and run together, heavy in its cadences and unnatural in its accents; and he would listen to it bitterly and with dislike." In *Historie dirigenta Kaliny* [The Story of Kalina, the Conductor], one of his *Povídky z druhé kapsy* [Stories from My Other Pocket], Čapek tells the story of a musician who uses the intonation of an unknown language to guess at the content of the verbal response: "Listen, that wasn't love talk, a musician would know that; lovers' speech has an entirely different cadence and does not sound so closed in, love talk is a deep cello, but this was a high bass, played in a kind of presto rubato, in a single position, as if this man had been repeating the same thing over and over again. It almost frightened me." Although both of these quotes are from short stories and are the statements, or thoughts, of fictitious personages, they have documentary value as far as the author's own perceptive capacity and his attitude to the sound of language are concerned.

The fact that intonation was the dominant feature of Čapek's verbal responses is, however, attested for us above all by the author's own texts in their graphic aspect: Čapek's treatment of punctuation very often departs from established conventions; we sometimes find subordinate clauses without the preceding comma [mandatory in Czech orthography], in those places where the intonational pause due to the comma might break up the continuity of the intonational line in an undesirable location; at other times again, we find commas where the convention does not require them, and where they serve, in the given case, to characterize the intonational line; we can also observe Čapek's liking for a punctuation mark that is otherwise quite rare, namely the semicolon, the probable reason being that the semicolon, although it serves to end a sentence as well as a period, does not separate it intonationally as radically from the following sentence.

Even more characteristic than his use of semicolons is the manner in which Čapek uses the dash, especially at the end of sentence units. Čapek very frequently uses a dash where the spelling convention requires a period; for evidence, we can look into any of his books; for instance, the short story *Otcové* [The Fathers] (from *Trapné povídky* [Embarrassing Stories]): "The small little casket moves higher and pulls the black crowd after itself; a small little casket, a small little death in white clothes and with a broken candle; here is where she used to walk hand in hand with her father—"; "The silence extends tortuously, heavily, oppressively—"; "The young priest is beginning to swing the censer; the chains give a light rattle, the smoke is rising and trembling—." In all of these examples, of course, the reason for the dash appears to be a certain semantic indefiniteness of the conclusion of the sentence; the dash serves to indicate the impulse of emotion or thought, not expressed in words, which follows the sentence. There are, however, also cases in which the dash expresses, when the sentence meaning is properly self-contained, a sudden change in the direction of thought from one sentence to the next: "He already had a certain plan and a detailed guess; but now all of this is sort of falling apart by itself—A new alternative for action is rapidly taking shape"; "The more usual something is, the more easily it can happen. Some facts usually appear together, not because of some necessary causality, but sort of accidentally, out of sheer habit and unwittingly—In one word, it does not depend on us" (*Boží muka* [The Passion of Our Lord], *Lída* [a girl's name]). Elsewhere, finally, the dash is used for purely intonational reasons, to let the sentence terminate without a steep cadence: "Power can only decide about things; in this is its force and obviousness—The only self-evident judgement is a command" (*Boží muka*, *Hora* [The Mountain]). The dash is in general used frequently by Čapek; it occurs frequently in the middle of his sentences, for the most varied stylistic purposes, but always with an intonational function: "And Jevíšek felt pain, enthusiasm, horror—love and hurt, pleasure, tears and a passionate courage" (*Boží muka*, *Hora*); "He sat down and talked —not one word to touch the fact that something had happened, that he had been looking for her, that there was something to explain" (*Trapné povídky* [Embarrassing Stories], *Helena* [Helen]). Even more frequent than in narration or exposition is Čapek's use of the dash in his dialogues, both in his novels and short stories, and in his dramas. It serves to indicate a pause in the conversation, a hesitation in excited or shy speech (Galén [Dr. Galen] in *Bílá nemoc* [The White Sickness]), the search for a suitable or considerate expression, a sudden silence, a sudden turn of the mind, failure to answer or a mere change in the direction of thought, a hesitation of the voice, an informal conversational tone.

Let us give some examples from the drama *Matka* [The Mother]: "I don't know; but I wouldn't want to try it a second time—wow! A ghastly feeling!" "But Ma, haven't I explained this to you so many times—I didn't want you to worry"; "I was like a father to these other children—so wise and responsible—And then all of a sudden, bang, off you go to the equator to die there of yellow fever"; "You could have been at home and treated people—or help bring children into the world—." Very frequent in the dramatic dialogue is the use of the dash in cases where a sentence begun by one person is continued by another. Such a shift in the sentence may be motivated in the most varied ways; sometimes it becomes a complex and sophisticated game. Thus in the preface to the drama *R. U. R.*

> HELEN: I have come—
> DOMIN: —to take a look at our factory production of people. Like all our visitors. Please, go right ahead.
> HELEN: I thought it was forbidden—
> DOMIN: —to enter the factory, but of course. Except that everybody comes here with somebody's recommendation, Miss Glory.
> HELEN: And you show everybody around?
> DOMIN: Only certain things. The manufacture of artificial human beings, miss, is a factory secret.
> HELEN: If only you knew how—
> DOMIN: —immensely interested you are in this. Old Europe talks of nothing else.
> HELEN: Why don't you let me finish?
> DOMIN: Forgive me, please. Were you going to say something else?
> HELEN: I just wanted to ask—
> DOMIN: —whether just this once I couldn't show you around the factory, after all. But of course, Miss Glory.
> HELEN: How did you know that that's what I was going to ask?
> DOMIN: They all ask the same.

The cutting into an unfinished sentence is here motivated by the very common nature of the questions; at the same time, it also serves to give a hint of Domin's superiority, his somewhat charlatanlike eloquence, etc. Completely different is the semantic function of the cutting in in the following dialogue from the second act of *R. U. R.*

> FABRY: You did well, Miss Helen. The robots can't reproduce. The robots will die out. Twenty years from now—
> HALLEMEIER: —not one of the scoundrels will be left.
> DR. GALL: But humanity will remain. Twenty years from now the world will be man's, even if it's only a few savages on a small island—
> FABRY: —it'll be a beginning. And as long as there is a beginning somewhere, it'll be all right. In a thousand years, they'll catch up with us and then they'll get ahead of us—
> DOMIN: —and they'll achieve in reality what we have only been stammering about in our minds.

The sentence is here taken over by the other person not in order "to cut him off," but in order to divide the lyrical part, in the manner of a litany, among persons of different pitch ranges and colors of the voice. The dash grapheme [grafický znak] here appears as the carrier of pure intonation, without special semantic or characterizing function.

We have discussed in some detail one of the punctuation marks used by Čapek, the dash, in order to show how intonation is the dominant phonetic feature of Čapek's prose, but also to show the nature of this intonation. The very circumstance that Čapek has a special preference for the semicolon and the dash, punctuation marks which, by comparison with the period, moderate the intonational cadence when placed at the end of a complex intonational unit, is evidence of the fact that *Čapek's intonation tends towards a soft undulation without abrupt boundary markers*. The examples of cutting in on unfinished speech in dialogue showed that this tendency also reflects itself in the semantic structure as a desire to remove, or at least soften up, the sharp boundaries between the statements of the various persons: a dialogue so structured tends to function, both phonetically and semantically, as a single uninterrupted phonetic and semantic band, as changing as multicolored bunting. We shall speak later of the consequences of this for the structure of Čapek's dramatic text; here we only wish to point to the weakening of the boundary marks as a significant feature of Čapek's intonation. This quality would be confirmed by a more detailed analysis for which there is no space here; we will content ourselves with some indications only. We must first be reminded of another circumstance which comes to the fore particularly conspicuously in the prose of Čapek's last period beginning with the trilogy *Hordubal—Povětroň* [The Meteorite]—*Obyčejný život* [An Ordinary Life], namely the frequent omission in the transition from the poet's text to direct speech of the colon and quotation marks, for instance: "The other day, however, Standa ran over to town and straight to the bookstore. Do you by any chance have a textbook in Swedish? No, they didn't have it; and so Standa was at a loss as to what he could do for Mr. Hansen" (*První parta* [The First Rescue Party], II); "Some woman standing next to (Standa) is shaking the grate and yelling, let me in there, let me in there, I got a husband in there!" (ibid.). This circumstance likewise attests the weakened borders between intonational segments. Another kind of proof can be found by tentatively rearranging the word order in sentences that lend themselves to it, that is, in sentences where the rearrangement would not lead to a distortion of the normal word order. Thus, in the first act of the drama *Matka* [The Mother] we find the sentence: "Nu, pravda, ale má-li někdo pět dětí, nemusí proto ještě být špatným vojákem, miláčku [Well, that's true, but just because somebody has five children, that doesn't make him a bad soldier]." If we changed the word order to read: "Nu, pravda, ale má-li někdo pět dětí, proto ještě nemusí být špatným vojákem," the word order of the passage would be no less normal, but a sharp intonational break would be introduced at the border of the two clauses, because after the word dětí [children] carrying the final cadence of the first clause would follow the words proto ještě [therefore yet; corresponding to "just because" in the free translation above] which are less strongly stressed than nemusí [need not; corresponds to part of "doesn't make him" in the free translation], and thus the intonational distinctiveness of the preceding cadence would be reinforced. The sentence "Byl by ses vrátil ke mně a k dětem... a odešel z armády [You would have come back to me and the children... and left the army]," though interrupted by a series of dots (that is, a pause in the pronunciation), yet has not lost its intonational continuity. Were we to repeat in it, however, the auxiliary verb byl bys [you would have] with the second participle as well, to read "Byl by ses vrátil ke mně a k dětem... a byl bys odešel z armády," the meaning would not be changed, but the second clause would be intonationally much more independent from the first than is the case in Čapek's own version.

The intonation of Čapek's prose and dialogue is thus flowing. This characteristic alone does not yet, however, make it into the formative artistic device which it undoubtedly is for Čapek: the uninterrupted undulation of Čapek's intonation in and of itself could simply be an individual characteristic of his style, based on the predominance of the melodic properties of the voice over the dynamic (since dynamic intensity as manifested by strong stresses keeps breaking up the intonational line). How then does Čapek's intonation become a formative device?

It may not be out of place here to mention the genesis of Čapek's prose. In the preface to *Krakonošova zahrada* [Krakonoš's Garden], Karel and Josef Čapek reveal the literary influences to which they were subject in their beginnings. And amazingly enough, among the Czech authors whom they mention as their models, there isn't one prose writer; the three names given by them are all of them lyrical poets: [Karel] Hlaváček [1874-1898, a decadent poet], [S. K.] Neumann [1875-, a socialist poet], and [Viktor] Dyk [1877-1931, a nationalist poet]. Let us further remember that the young Čapek during the [First World] War translated modern French poetry, and that these translations by a prose writer have become, by the lyric poet's own admission, the source of [Vítězslav] Nezval's [1920-, a modern poet] melodious verse (see the preface to the second edition of *Francouzská poesie* [French Poetry], Prague, 1936); Čapek here discovered the new melody of Czech verse based on the utilization of normal word order. And let us finally not forget that the first dramatic work by the brothers Čapek is written in verse and, in addition to the dramatic portions, also contains a beautiful lyrical passage... based on intonational parallelism:

[one paragraph of verse omitted]

If we summarize all of the facts mentioned, the genesis of Čapek's epic and dramatic intonation is clear: both have their origin in lyric poetry. Where K. Čapek, as was shown above, influenced the development of Czech lyrical poetry, and exerted his influence precisely in his capacity as prose writer, by depriving lyric poetry of the petrified tradition of word-order inversions driven to extremes by the school of [Jaroslav] Vrchlický [1853-1912, leading member of the Lumír Group], among epic writers he was, on the contrary, a disciple of lyric poetry. The artistic utilization of intonation in his writings therefore has to be looked for in that direction.

It is well known that the artistic utilization of intonation in lyric poetry is done mainly in two ways: by the method of repetition, and by the method of contrast; we find both in Čapek's epic prose, as well as in his dramatic dialogue.

Repetition consists in the recurrent use of a certain intonational unit, for instance of a question or exclamation:

> My God, is Lída really just the nth case among many? And not something unique and beautiful? And not a wonder of life? And *if I'm right*, what good, what good indeed, are her "unknown motives," her suffering, her striving for decision? (*Boží muka, Lída*)

> Will I never get rid of this? Why can't I get Lída's misfortune out of my head? Why am I so concerned with fate, anyhow? How did this mania come upon me? (ibid.)

> You beautiful? Why beautiful? Is hair beautiful when it only oppresses you? Are eyes beautiful when you close them? Are lips beautiful, when you only bite down on them until it hurts? What is beauty, what's the point in being beautiful? (*R. U. R.*, act III)

> I'm sorry for science! Sorry for technology! for Domin! for myself! for all of us! It is our fault, ours! For the sake of our grandeur, for someone's profits, for progress, for I don't know what splendid things, we have killed humanity! Why don't you just burst with grandeur! Not even Genghis Khan has built himself such a tremendous mausoleum of human bones! (*R. U. R.*, act II)

We may also deal with the repetition of an intonational motif carried and strengthened by the recurrence of a word, grammatical form (for instance, the imperative), particle (for instance, the negation):

> If one stood up there above the quarries, one would see the entire village as if in the palm of one's hand; one would see the child running home, sobbing and crying; one would see the tiny figure of a man rush out and speed across the village with the excited haste of an ant. (*Boží muka, Hora*)

> Dear God, enlighten Domin and all those who have lost their way; destroy their work and help people to return to their worry and work; keep the human race from perdition; don't allow them to be harmed in soul and body; rid us from the robots and protect Miss Helen, amen. (*R. U. R.*, act I)

> Oh Helen, Robot Helen, never will your body come to life, never will you be a lover, never a mother; these perfect hands will never play with a newborn babe, never will you see your beauty in the beauty of your child— (*R. U. R.*, act I)

An intonational scheme once created may, however, in the consciousness (or rather, subconscious) of the poet become fixed as a permanent formula which may occur in mutually very distant places of his work; such a formula becomes a permanent part of the poet's inventory of formative devices. Thus, we find in the short story *Hora* (*Boží muka*), at the beginning of one of the chapters, the sentence "Sadder than the night is the break of dawn." It contains an inverted word order: the sentence starts with the predicative complement. Since this is the beginning of a new section of the text, there is no reason for the inversion by virtue of the preceding context, and the sentence construction therefore functions as an intonational unit called forth simply by the artistic intent, as a melodious motif, as it were. And we find that same melodious motif, again at the beginning, but this time at the beginning of the story as a whole, in *Historie beze slov* [Story Without Words] (*Boží muka*): "Deep are the woods at night, like a bottomless sea..."

Similarly, the entire intonational unit cited once before, namely:

> If one stood up there above the quarries, one would see the entire village as if in the palm of one's hand; one would see the child running home, sobbing and crying; one would see the tiny figure of a man rush out and speed across the village with the excited haste of an ant   (*Boží muka*, *Hora*),

recurs in the further context of the story, in a place at a distance from the first, without any connection with the first passage, once again in this form:

> Jevíšek turned his skyblue, myopic gaze at his guests; he saw Pilbauer motionless and engrossed in thought, his eyes lowered as if he were remembering something; he saw Slavík consuming himself with the grief of reproach and self-torture; he saw the commissioner, bending worn out and tired with the sadness and weakness of a sick child.
> (ibid.)

In both of these cases, the repetition of the word "saw" ("would see") introduced a certain recurrent intonational schema; the dual occurrence of this unit is, however, not in any way connected, the second passage is in no way designed to remind the reader of the first.

We deal with something else in the following case, taken again from the story *Hora*. We find the following passage there:

> "There are that many of you?" said the voice with supreme bitterness. "What a shame! What'll I do now? God, oh God, what'll I do?"
> Jevíšek stiffened with painful embarrassment.
> "Jesus Christ," the voice lamented, "what'll I do now? They've surrounded the mountain... Christ Jesus!"
> A bright whiteness filled Jevíšek's heart. "Sir," he began tremulously.
> "What'll I do now," the voice shook in the fog. "I'm lost! Lost! Lost! Oh God, how is it possible!"
> "I'll help you, Sir," exclaimed Jevíšek hastily.

"You want to betray me," moaned the voice. "Our Father who art in heaven, hallowed be thy name, thy kingdom come, thy will be done ... thy will be done ... Let me escape! Please God, let me escape!"

The words of the trapped criminal here alternate with mentions of Jevíšek or with his replies. The part of the criminal is in this carried by a constantly repeated intonational motif with two peaks: "There are that many of you?"—"What'll I do?"—"Jesus Christ!"—"What'll I do now?"—"They've surrounded the mountain"—"Christ Jesus!"—"What'll I do now?"—"Let me escape!"—"Let me escape!" As can be seen, the intonational motif is carried by various groupings, some of which recur more than once, especially the groupings "What'll I do (now)?" and "Let me escape!" Well, these very word groups recur in the story in *another* place as well, shortly after the cited passage, so that their first occurrence is still fresh in the memory of the reader. But they are no longer spoken by the criminal, they are now thoughts in the "inner" monologue of the tired police commissioner, who imagines himself a little schoolboy in class before a severe teacher: "Christ, Lord, where can I hide? What'll I do? Let me escape! Oh God, let me escape!" We are here dealing with a direct allusion to the preceding scene, an allusion, the purpose of which is compositional: the intonational motif is here utilized over a larger section of text as part of the compositional blueprint. It is something along the lines of a Wagnerian leitmotiv, expressing the analogy of the new situation to the previous one. At this point, we could enter into a discussion of repetition in general, not only of intonations but of words, and especially of subject matter, as a permanent and unusually frequent compositional device in Čapek's prose and drama; let us be content with a single example as an indication. We will again find it in the short story *Hora* which we have just dealt with: both at the beginning and at the end of this short story there occurs the motif of a corpse crushed by a fall and lying with the face to the ground; in the first case, it is the body of the murder victim lying under a rocky ledge near the village, in the second case the body of the murderer below a rock somewhere in the woods; the action of the story took place between these two situations: the murderer was discovered and punished himself; the repeated motif by its recurrence serves to underline even more the change in the situation that occurred during the narration.

We have discussed the repetition of intonational motifs as a formative device in Čapek's style; now we turn to the second, opposite, device, namely the *contrast* arising from the direct, and intentional, confrontation of various sharply different intonational schemas. Let us give an example:

It seemed to him highly poetic that Lída had run away: he was in a kind of ecstasy; he was pleased beyond measure and not even aware of the fact that he was alone and quiet for the whole night. (*Boží muka, Lída*)

At the borders of the main clauses of this short text there is a gradual alternation of colon, semicolon, the conjunction "and" [in the original, the equivalent of "not even aware" is literally "he was not even aware," i.e., a coordinate main clause];

to each of these transitions there corresponds in the pronunciation a different intonational cadence; this variety, placing the various types of cadences into mutual contrast, is here artistically intentional. Similarly, in the next example we find several intonational units in contrast with each other:

> Nothing in this picture is hidden any more: The large body with its face in the bloody mud, the crazy spread of the limbs as if it wanted to jump up again—jump up now, after all this, and wipe the dirt off the forehead! Oh, what a sight! two hands there regretfully sticking from the hideous crushed matter, full of mud, oh God, and yet so human, those hands! Nothing in this picture— (*Boží muka*, Hora)

First the falling intonation up to the colon, repeated once more in the passage before the following comma; then an intonational gradation beginning with the conjunction "as if" up to the second "jump up"; then a monotonous intonation divided into several segments, enclosed by the dual repetition of the word "hands," which is first given as an introductory intonational peak, then as a concluding cadence; finally, a repetition of the initial words of the paragraph, but without the verb—intonationally, the effect of an incomplete sentence intonation.

The artistic intent is in both cases clearly directed towards heaping the most varied intonational units into the shortest span of text. It may of course also occur that the grouping of different intonations is repeated several times, which gives rise to a regular pattern, something like an intonational stanza; this device is used particularly in Čapek's dramatic dialogue and monologue. Thus for instance:

> HELEN: I've been afraid of the robots.
> DOMIN: Why?
> HELEN: They might come to hate us, or something.
> ALQUIST: They do. (*R. U. R.*, act II)

Here an intonational unit comes about independently of the persons uttering the various replies, a unit tying all of the replies together: a longer intonational segment twice alternates with a shorter one. An example from a dramatic monologue:

> Christ Lord God, take care of my boy. Mary, Mother of charity, have mercy on me and protect my children. Christ Jesus, give my boy back to me. Mary, Mother of God, pray for my children. Christ on the cross, have mercy on my children.
> (*Matka* [The Mother], act II)

Here, there is a regular alternation of the intonation of the vocative with that of the exclamatory sentence; the alternation of these two intonation patterns produces, by deliberate artistic intent, the impression of a litany, the traces of which we can find in Čapek quite frequently, the litany being the classical model of an intonational blueprint based on contrast.

As a last example of the artistic utilization of intonation by Čapek, let us mention the use of the "language of the birds," that is, the intonational schemas of bird song superimposed upon words, in the play *Loupežník* [The Robber]:

1ST BIRD: No toto, no toto, jejej! To je, to je, to je, co?
2ND BIRD: Čilý kluk, čilý, čilý, vid'? Čilý jako mník, vid'? vid'? vid'?
3RD BIRD: Kluku, kluku, kluku!
1ST BIRD: Co to? Co to? Mimi, chodí ti po bytu, po bytu cizí pán!
3RD BIRD: Kuku! Kuku!
MIMI: Co tam dělá?
2ND BIRD: Vidí byt, byt, byt!
4TH BIRD: Pátrá, pátrá.
MIMI: Ach, ptáčkové, co mám s ním dělat?
2ND BIRD: Nic, nic, nic. Líbí se ti, vid'?
4TH BIRD: Párek.
1ST BIRD: Neradím. Toho ne, toho ne, i toto. Ani za nic.
MIMI: Fiu fiu fiuí—
1ST BIRD: Tu já, tu, tu, tu? Vidíš? Vidíš?
2ND BIRD: Díky, díky, díky!
4TH BIRD: —brý ráno!
MIMI: Vrána. Špatné znamení. Co to znamená?
3RD BIRD: Muka, muka, muka . . . muka, muka, muka, muka . . .
MIMI: Už dost!

1ST BIRD: *Now then, now then, well, well! That is, that is, that is, what?*
2ND BIRD: *A nimble boy, nimble, nimble, isn't he? Like a jackrabbit, isn't he? isn't he? isn't he?*
3RD BIRD: *Boy, boy, boy!*
1ST BIRD: *What's this? What's this? Mimi, a strange gentleman is walking around in your apartment, in your apartment!*
3RD BIRD: *Coocoo! Coocoo!*
MIMI: *What is he doing there?*
2ND BIRD: *He's seeing the apartment, the apartment, the apartment!*
4TH BIRD: *He's searching, he's searching.*
MIMI: *Gosh, birds, what shall I do with him?*
2ND BIRD: *Nothing, nothing, nothing. You like him, don't you?*
4TH BIRD: *A couple.*
1ST BIRD: *I don't advise it. Not that, not that, not that either. Not for anything.*
MIMI (*lifts her head and whistles to the birds*): *Whee, whee, wheeoo—*
1ST BIRD: *Here me, here, here, here? Do you see? Do you see?*
2ND BIRD: *Thanks, thanks, thanks!*
4TH BIRD: *'morning!*
MIMI: *A crow. A bad sign. What does it mean?*
3RD BIRD (*retreating*): *Torture, torture, torture . . . torture, torture, torture . . .*
MIMI: *Enough now!*

This example shows us a whole series of different intonations and timbres: the human voice, the whistling of the birds transposed into words [by creating onomatopoeic sequences from ordinary Czech morphemes], human whistling, the [onomatopoeic] cawing of the crow, all these form a harmony which is at the very border of dramatic dialogue and lyric poetry.

The analysis which we have undertaken has served to verify the intonational foundation of Čapek's style, a foundation which, as we shall see more closely henceforth, continues unchanged from Čapek's beginnings as a writer to the end of his career. Nevertheless, even a cursory glance at Čapek's prose shows that beginning with *Továrna na absolutno* [The Absolute at Large] and *Krakatit*, but especially with *Povídky z jedné kapsy* [Stories from One of My Pockets] and *Povídky z druhé kapsy* [Stories from My Other Pocket], there penetrates into Čapek's prose another element which from one book to the next gradually changes its shape, until it finally restructures it into the very special form of Čapek's last books. It is usually attributed to the influence of conversational speech—the question is, however, what is to be understood by the term. A certain lexical and phraseological, perhaps also syntactic, coloring? That too, of course; but the real sense of the process undergone by Čapek's prose style is not shown clearly until his last work: it is the ever increasing penetration of dialogue into his prose. There is no doubt that Čapek by his fundamental activity and talent was an epic writer; just as the lyrical poetry which he cultivated concomitantly with his epic beginnings, however, had its permanent influence on his prose, so the dialogue which the mature Čapek as a dramatist mastered supremely was the leavening in the development of his prose style. Before we attempt to define this influence more closely, however, let us for a moment turn our attention to the dialogue of Čapek's dramas itself.

In treating the intonation in Čapek's style, we have not avoided his dramatic language, because the discovery of the dominance of intonation is equally valid for the dialogue prose of his dramas as for the monologue of his prose writings. At this point, we would merely like to give additional emphasis to the importance of intonation in Čapek's dialogue. Let us start with an anecdotal memory told by the poet himself; it concerns the rehearsals before the first performance of *Loupežník* [The Robber]. The concluding lines of the play read as follows:

CORPORAL: And what was it that made you want to kill this robber?
FANKA: I really don't know. Perhaps it's because I'm not young any more and I started feeling sorry for my lost youth.

Fanka's line, however, did not appeal to the actress playing the part, Mrs. Hübner; she could not, as Čapek tells it, achieve a final cadence which would, as it were, put a period after the whole play. And poet and actress together tried something else; the final result was to insert into Fanka's last lines a question by the corporal consisting of the pronominal phrase "for what." The corrected version reads:

FANKA: I really don't know. Perhaps it's because I'm not young any more and I started feeling sorry—
CORPORAL: For what?
FANKA: For my lost youth.

And the final cadence was found. The corporal's question allowed Fanka to make the key words independent, to close off the play with them as if with a clamp; there was actually no need to change the wording, it was enough to change the intonation. We are here unwittingly reminded of the drama *Matka* where the ending of the play again depends simply on the imperative intonation of the last word: "Go!" The anecdote which we cited is typical of Čapek, the dramatist, not only for its own sake, but also because in conversation he would give it as an example of the phonetic aspect of the language of the drama; it is clear what component of language concerned him most. To what extent the dramatic dialogue was an intonational unit to him is also attested by the subject matter of an article which he promised to write for *Slovo a slovesnost* and which he no longer could get around to do: he had in mind a kind of comparison between the drama and the opera, he thought that the dramatist's text already was geared towards the different pitch ranges of the various voices; this, in his opinion, to a large extent serves to determine the distribution of the characters in the blueprint of the play, and the place of each in the dialogue. If this was his view of the dramatic dialogue, it is understandable how he was able to construct so brilliantly scenes of mass dialogue with many participants, such as for instance the first and second act of *R. U. R.*, the scenes of horror before and during the revolt of the robots, in which all the people living in the Rossum factory participated.

It is said about Čapek's dialogue, and the author himself says it, that it is "natural." "Naturalness," however, is a multivalued[1] quality. There is no question but that the naturalistically intended dialogue in *Maryše* by the brothers Mrštík [Alois, 1861–1925; Vilém, 1863–1912] also has its own, and very expressive, "naturalness." Nevertheless, how different isn't it from Čapek's dialogue! If we look at the dialogue in *Maryše* more carefully, the reason for this difference becomes apparent, since the dialogue of this play is not built upon intonation, like Čapek's, but on the effects of the color of the voice, its timbre. Let us, for instance, consider this passage:

> LÍZAL (poisonously): Well—and you wouldn't want six, would you? (Starts laughing) Maryša and four thousand. (He laughs) You're not stupid!... (Becomes serious) if it were a woman that has to be covered with gold before anyone wants her!... But Maryša? [original in Haná dialect, translator]

The great number of stage directions is conspicuous, seemingly referring to the actor's gestures and expressions, but in reality relating to the rapid shifting of vocal timbre required by the dramatist of the actor: "poisonous" speech, speech mixed with laughter, serious speech, rapidly alternate with each other, just as in Čapek there sometimes is an alternation of different kinds of intonation (for examples, see above).

The most characteristic feature of the "naturalness" of Čapek's dialogue is the easy-going transition from reply to reply, from question to answer, from objection to its elimination. The juncture [šev] at which the consecutive utterances of the various persons meet is indeed the most sensitive spot in Čapek's dialogue. We have given

---

[1] Cf. *Almanach Kmene*, Spring 1934, pp. 25 ff.

evidence above of the frequency with which Čapek toys with the cutting in of one person into the unfinished sentence of another. For this sort of thing, of course, the abrupt transitions from one timbre to another such as we find in the Mrštík brothers would impair, rather than increase, the fluency. Čapek's dialogue requires an actor who does not attempt to set off the characters too much: an actor who exaggerates his part emotionally or otherwise, who exaggerates the self of the person whose part he plays, makes it difficult for his fellow actors to take their cues smoothly and breaks up the intonational unity of the dialogue. Čapek's dialogue wants to flow with musical smoothness; broken into pieces, it becomes lifeless. The "naturalness" of Čapek's style is thus not merely the result of a fine ear for the intonational nuances of everyday conversation, but also of a very deliberate artistic effort and of technical adroitness. The same can be said about Čapek's prose which was influenced by the epic dialogue.

What gives Čapek's epic prose its dialogue character? In the beginning, as we have said, it is indicated by simply approaching epic style to conversational speech, the speech of everyday contact which we are most often used to hearing in the form of conversation, as is shown by the term chosen to denote it. At first, only the actual conversations of the characters are close to conversational speech (*Továrna na absolutno* [The Absolute at Large]); later, the style of conversational speech is used to tell the plot itself, put into the mouth of one of the characters as an oral report addressed to the other characters (*Povídky z druhé kapsy* [Stories from My Other Pocket]). In Čapek's travel descriptions we find a conversation of the poet with the reader; the reader here is a silent partner in the conversation, who is constantly being told that his opinion of the matter is important; to him are addressed the minute humorous distortions of reality, on his emotional participation are calculated the lyrical passages; here we can really begin to speak of an interpenetration of prose with dialogue. The most advanced crystallization of this type of prose based on dialogue does not, however, occur until some of Čapek's novels of the latest period, especially *Hordubal* and *Poslední parta* [The Last Rescue Party]. In *Hordubal*, a good part of the plot is presented as the subvocal inner monologue of the participating character, as his imagined conversation with himself, or at times with others; in *První parta* then, the entire narration with all that it contains, be it the narrative passages or the dialogues or thoughts of the characters, is projected into the author's inner monologue. In each word we perceive the author, not as an objective narrator, but as one conversing with himself, using his own voice or the voices of the characters of his novel. There actually is here an uninterrupted dialogue, speech constantly addressed to someone, a conversation in which the poet and the reader are the partners as much as the characters and things told about. He has here put into artistic practice the idea which he has presented in *Povětroň* [The Meteorite]:

> Isn't it strange, though: who knows how sure it is that this life (of the hero of the novel) was just imagination; and just looking at it now, I would say that it was *my own* life. It's me. It's me, the sea and the man, that kiss breathed from the dark shadow of a mouth belongs to me; that man sat under the lighthouse at Hoe because I sat under the lighthouse

at Hoe, and if he lived on Barbados or Barbuda, well, thank God, praise the Lord, I finally got there, too. All this is me; I'm not thinking up anything, I'm just expressing what I am and what I have within me. And if I wrote about Hecuba, or a Babylonian hussy, it would be me; I would be the old woman wailing and rending the wrinkled bags of her breasts, I would be the woman crushed by the lust in the hairy hands of the Assyrian man with the oily beard. Yes, both man, woman and child.

That's why Čapek in this last period of his development perceives human personality as a multitude: "Each of us is we, each is a crowd stretching beyond the range of sight" (*Obyčejný život* [An Ordinary Life], XXXIV). If "each of us is we," then of course all of the inner life of man is a constant inner dialogue moving from partner to partner until it winds up fixed within the range of a single self. These are thus the epistemological foundations of the definitive dialoguization of Čapek's prose; what, then, are the linguistic consequences of this attitude? Let the evidence speak for itself:

What a deal, good God, what a deal; five years of science high school and then finished; your aunt who has been giving you your miserable keep goes off and dies, and now go ahead, boy, and support yourself. You can take your descriptive geometry now, boy, and your logarithms, and whatnot, and keep them; who cares if you were all done in from fear and hard studying and your teachers still weren't satisfied; a poor boy such as yourself, Půlpán, should appreciate the education he's getting, they'd say, and try to get somewhere in life — — — Just go ahead and try, and then your aunt off and dies and that's it for trying descriptive geometry. They shouldn't let poor boys study. Here you sit now with your geometry and your French irregular verbs and can peel the calluses off your hands.

This is the introductory passage of *První parta*: clearly direct speech uttered by some person as yet unknown to us and addressed to himself; the second person who at times is addressed directly (*your* aunt ... goes off and dies; here *you* sit now) is the speaker himself. Was this speech ever uttered aloud, however? Of course not; it is not even cited in quotation marks, since it is a part of the narration itself, part of the exposition of the novel in which we are made familiar with the past biography of the hero. Who then is making this speech? It's actually the author himself, or rather, the character speaking for the author. And we go one step further: we hear the teacher speak to the sloppy student (a poor boy such as yourself, Půlpán . . .); who is speaking these words now? The hero of the novel, to himself. And he does it again for the author who wants to inform us of the way the hero's studies went. There is thus no lack of complexity; in the case of the teacher's words we are dealing, figuratively speaking, with direct speech of the third degree: the teacher—the hero—the author. We find something similar in the beginning of Chapter II of the novel *Hordubal*:

Who is it, who goes there on the other side of the valley? He sees him, a gentleman in boots, perhaps a mechanic or somebody, carrying a little black suitcase and walking up the hill—if he weren't so far off, I'd put my hands to my mouth and holler at him: Bless the Lord, Sir, what time is it? Two in the afternoon, little cowherd; if I weren't so far off, I'd call over to you and ask you whose cows you're herding, and you might show me: that one with the bald spot, that speckled one, that one with the star on her forehead, that red one, that young heifer, they all belong to Hordubal's pasture.

What we find here is a conversation between two persons, but one without quotation marks to set off one utterance from another: the one who speaks here is really but a single person, Hordubal, who is walking along the slope and at the same time also looking at himself with the eyes of the little cowherd tending his cows on the opposite slope. He is merely guessing at what the cowherd might be saying, and he himself, with his subvocal dialogue with himself, is but a product of the consciousness of the author who is here *narrating* Hordubal's return from America to his native village.

This is how Čapek's prose finally changed when it absorbed the dialogue into itself. This is not to say, however, that this new increase in richness and complication in any way masked its original intonational character. On the contrary, it increased the possibilities of the alternation of different intonational units. For confirmation, it is enough to inspect the last example: interrogative, declarative, exclamatory intonations are rapidly alternating in many variations.

Is a conclusion necessary? It is perhaps enough to say that if Czech postwar prose constitutes an effort towards the definitive creation of the Czech prose sentence which is to be both phonetically harmonious and have semantic reach (cf. J. Durych, "O slohu latinském a o slohu českém [Latin Style and Czech Style]," *Slovo a slovesnost*, I [1935], 112 ff.), then Čapek's stylistic creativeness is an important factor in this effort. The mixing of lyric and dramatic style and the infusion of the mixture into epic prose has created, in addition to permanent poetic values, also an important developmental step towards the definitive mastery of thought by language. At the end of this path broken by Čapek and his poetic contemporaries there should loom, if further developments are favorable, the definitive shape of the Czech sentence not only in artistic writing, but in scientific and philosophic as well; for a perfect, both flexible and firm, scientific style has never yet been created without poetic predecessors and models.

King Lear: *The Quality of Nothing*

❦ SIGURD BURCKHARDT ❦

After studying both English and German literature, Sigurd Burckhardt began during the 1950's to publish a series of essays—most often on Shakespeare, but also on such writers as Goethe and Sterne—which are marked by an intense and serious concern with the language of the texts in question. Burckhardt commits himself absolutely to taking the artist at his word, and the result is a mode of analysis that is idiosyncratic, sometimes provoking, and always illuminating. His death in 1966 brought an abrupt end to his work, but his writings on Shakespeare have been collected and published by the Princeton University Press in *Shakespearean Meanings* (1968).

The premises that underlie Burckhardt's analysis of *King Lear* in the following essay are more fully spelled out in another essay reprinted in *Shakespearean Meanings*, "The Poet as Fool and Priest." The poet's medium of language, Burckhardt there argues, is unlike other artistic media in that it is, for the most part, a given: insofar as the words which a poet might employ already possess meanings, he has less than absolute "creative sovereignty" over them; and insofar as words are referential, pointing to things beyond themselves, they are peculiarly substanceless. Through such devices as rhyme, meter, pun, and metaphor, which call attention to words as substances, the poet seeks to endow his medium with a degree of corporeality (an idea that may remind us of the Prague School's insistence on the foregrounding of language in a literary text) at the same time that he seeks to free his words to some extent from their ordinary ranges of significance (their "common denominators" of meaning, inevitable since language is a "social instrument"), all to the end that the poem will embody the particular insight of the poet.

In his essay on *King Lear*, Burckhardt conceives of words as deeds, as dramatic acts, and he charts the course of the tragedy and the development of the king by differentiating between two views of language realized in the play. For Gloster, "words are merely a medium," and reality consists in "matter of fact," in something to be seen, a conception which Burckhardt relates to Gloster's desire to see the letter forged by Edmund, to Gloster's blinding, and to his imagined fall over the sheerly verbal cliff created by Edgar. Lear, on the other hand, conceives of words as creative, immediate, fraught with reality, taking for granted "the sovereign's power to make good his words." Shorn of that power, he yet "chooses immediacy" on the heath in "going out to confront reality nakedly," even at the cost of madness, that "utter nakedness of mind" in which "discourse of reason" gives way to "free association." When he recovers, he adopts a new language, one "intimate," utterly "natural," characterized by "the absence of all style," as if to evade the very nature of language which prevents one from uttering experience directly. Thus the play shows Lear penetrating, beyond the limits of language, to the limits of being. And Shakespeare—though he points, through Lear's experience, to the fact that "the essence . . . of direct confrontation—namely its directness—remains incommunicable; every word violates and distorts it"—nevertheless commits himself, as a poet who must work with language, to dramatizing that fact.

IN HIS FINE PREFACE to *King Lear*, Granville-Barker settles the old critical problem of the implausibility of the two opening scenes with refreshing simplicity: "Shakespeare asks us to allow him the fact of [Gloster's] deception, even as we have allowed him Lear's partition of the kingdom. It is his starting point, the dramatist's 'Let's pretend,' which is as essential to the beginning of a play as a 'Let it be granted' to a proposition of Euclid." This is sound sense and should put an end to all tortured

---

"*King Lear*: The Quality of Nothing," by Sigurd Burckhardt, is reprinted from *The Minnesota Review*, II (1961), 33–50, by permission of The Minnesota Review.

KING LEAR: THE QUALITY OF NOTHING

reasoning about the play's opening, at least where it springs from the question: "How could Shakespeare have done it?" But it must not put an end to the very legitimate, in fact necessary question: "*What* are we expected to pretend?" The more willing we are to grant the poet his premises, the more necessary it is to know exactly what we are granting; else the demonstration will make no sense.

The first two scenes have usually been read as a concentrated exposition of two characters, one rash and despotic, the other weak and gullible, who because of these flaws fall into error. But the scenes are more than that: they are *events*—events which determine the future action. Undoubtedly Lear is rash and Gloster gullible; but since through such different failings they commit exactly the same fault—the banishing of the true and loving child and the preferment of the false one—we are compelled to ask what it is that accounts for the difference in the subsequent fates of the two men—the blindness of one and the madness of the other, for example. If such reasoning sounds forbiddingly rigid in a literary interpretation, I submit that Shakespeare, in this tragedy and in no other, constructed parallel plots of considerable rigor, and that we must assume that he meant something by this structure. He cannot have meant the plots to be merely parallel, one reinforcing the other; for then the subplot would become a mere redundancy, and if ever an action needed no reinforcement of its impact, it is Lear's. There is every reason to think that the apparent similarity of the two plots is like that of controlled experiments, and that the meaning of both lies in the one element which accounts for the difference.

Shakespeare commonly satisfies the positivistic axiom that we can get answers only if we ask the right questions. He certainly does in *Lear*. At the very outset he points up both the sameness and the difference of the two plots by the thematic use of "nothing." This is the word which both Lear and Gloster stumble over; with it, or their response to it, their falls begin—first Lear's:

>   What can you say to draw
>   A third more opulent than your sisters? Speak.
>   Nothing, my lord.
>   Nothing!
>   Nothing.
>   Nothing will come of nothing. Speak again.

And then Gloster's:

> What paper were you reading?
> Nothing, my lord.
> No? What needed, then, that terrible dispatch of it into your pocket? The quality of nothing hath not such need to hide itself. Let's see. Come, if it be nothing, I shall not need spectacles.

The point of this insistent echo cannot be simply the similarity of the two men. It must be subtler and more precise, and it must lie in the quality of "nothing."

HAD SHAKESPEARE only meant to present us, in the first scene, with a wrathful and imperious old man, he could have found a more plausible way to do so. But what he seized upon in the fairy-tale motif and makes the substance of his "Let it be granted" is a particular *speech* situation. The king lays down conditions of discourse under which his daughters' words will have an automatic validity; he acts on the premise that what they say will be true by virtue of their saying it. He will not test their professions of love against the matter of fact of their previous behavior, will not treat the words as signs that are true or false to the degree that they correspond to an extraverbal reality. Rather, he treats them as substances, as entities, which carry their own truth within them; they create for him his daughters' loves, as they are to create—a kind of physical precipitate of this verbal creation—their realms. "Which of you shall we say doth love us most," Lear asks and therewith engages to settle this question as though it were a poetry contest. It is false to ascribe to him here a despot's greed for praise or fawning submission; he makes a fearful mistake, but the mistake is the regal one of taking people *at their word* in the most radical and literal sense. He refuses to submit to the demeaning necessity ordinary men are under: the necessity of suspiciously grubbing for facts by which to judge words. Suspicion, the "looking beneath" words for what, as often as not, they hide rather than reveal, would seem to him a diminution of his royal dignity. He *cannot* be lied to by his daughters, because, in transferring his sovereignty to them, he also endows them with its noblest attribute and prerogative: to speak creatively, substantially, with automatic truth.

The error is a noble one, but it compels both Lear and those who wish him well to a disastrous rigor. It is idle to speculate about Cordelia's pride, her share of responsibility for the consequences of her unbending "plainness." As her asides make clear, she has no choice; the covenant under which she must speak has its own logic. Where there can be no lie, there can be no truth; and since the essential function of speech is to transmit truth, for Cordelia no speech is possible. Her "nothing" is the simple statement of this fact, and her following attempt to return discourse to the sphere where it can be true (or false) is condemned from the start to futility.

For Lear is already committed. He has not yet sworn, as when he later answers Burgundy: "Nothing. I have sworn; I am firm." But he might as well have; with his "Nothing will come of nothing" he has stated the very formula of his belief. He has no choice either—none, that is, except to give up his conception of himself, his royalty and truth. If words are substantial and creative, then his answer to Cordelia is the only possible one. And by the same token he is compelled to banish Kent. What prompts him is not the vanity of the tyrant who cannot bear criticism, or of the king who cannot bear discourtesy; he does not deign even to notice Kent's desperate ill manners, and he enters into no argument about the substance of Kent's charges. Kent's guilt is that he has sought

> To come between our sentence and our power,
> Which nor our nature nor our place can bear.

Lear here tries to banish the inherent "between-ness" of all discourse; with Kent he means to rid himself of the degrading intrusion of "mere" fact into the gapless identity of "sentence" and "power," of sovereign speech and the power of that speech to create what it states.

Thus the king's wrath and rashness receive the precise definition of a verbal *act*. He has rashly committed himself to a particular conception of himself and his office, his nature and place, has in fact identified the two; and he wrathfully resists all attempts to question this conception as questioning his identity. This he sees in, let us say, *immediacy*, in the possibility of getting at truth directly, without any circuitous "between." I shall try to show how this "verbal" reading of the first scene makes explicable, not simply Lear's fall (that can be explained in other ways as well), but the specific kind and direction and even depth of his fall. For the remarkable thing about *King Lear* is that in it the tragic error is "made good" as a word is made good: not by contrition and amendment but by an unyielding perseverance in it, a determination to live by it and its bitter consequences until it has yielded its core of truth.

But first Gloster's analogous stumbling demands attention. Had he responded to Edmund's "Nothing, my lord" as Lear did to Cordelia's—had he taken Edmund at his word—the letter scheme would have come to nothing. But for Gloster speech is the opposite of substantial; he sees in it "mere words," insubstantial signs which, as likely as not, have been made to point in the wrong direction. He is familiar with "the dark and vicious place" of illicit union and has learned the subject's craft of "looking beneath" for the matter of fact. He will not be taken in by words but will trust only to what he can see with his own eyes; there is an ignoble greediness for "the real thing" in his thrice repeated "Let's see" (antiphone to Lear's threefold and royal "Speak!"). And because to him words are merely a medium, he falls victim to a *mediacy* far more abject than Goneril's and Regan's lies; in his eagerness for the matter of fact he gets hold of a forged letter, an indirection squared. (Edmund shrewdly calculates on his father's affinity for the indirect: he tells him that the letter was thrown in at the casement, not delivered in person—"there's the cunning of it." To a mind like Gloster's, this increases the probability of the tale.) Determined as he is to distrust the direct word, he is at the mercy of report, of hearsay, of signs. With this scene, the letter becomes the emblem of the illicit and dangerously mediate—so clearly so that the sight of Lear reading a letter would strike us as somehow incongruous; for a letter is speech reduced to signs, discourse become manifestly indirect. Gloster's belief in signs and portents, ridiculed by Edmund, is further evidence of this affinity; not that it is necessarily wrong, but that it is slavish, implies an abdication of the creative will and a wish to get at the truth by an "outguessing" which Lear would never stoop to.

Gloster, like Lear, will attain his measure of truth—not by abandoning his error, but by being delivered over to it more absolutely than he and we had imagined possible. The problem of immediacy and mediacy, of confrontation and report, of being and meaning is a true paradox, and the truth of paradoxes does not lie in the golden mean between the extremes; it lies in a man's readiness to penetrate through illusion and despair to his particular extreme and at the pole to find himself.

SHAKESPEARE WOULD BE no poet if he gave equal dignity to the two errors; the poet is bound to err on Lear's side, that of thinking speech creatively substantial and truth direct. Every poet, I should guess, is an ironist; knowing, more intimately than the rest of us, the deceptiveness of words, he is condemned to being circuitous, to trying to get the better of his untrustworthy medium by strategems and indirections. But precisely for this reason the true poet is an ironist *in spite of himself*; what he longs for is creative immediacy. From Iago to Melville's Confidence Man and Mann's Felix Krull, poets have portrayed themselves as tricksters and sought the release of truth in this self-exposure. But that is the round-about way, the way of irony.

The difference between Lear and Gloster is to be measured by what one is granted and the other denied: the dignity of direct confrontation. In the end Lear sees Cordelia face to face, and we see both; all Gloster's sufferings never earn him this fulfillment. He can never, literally, *see* Edgar; even in the recognition he is dependent on report, and what is more, this event is withheld from us, buried in Edgar's story. His final release must reach him, and us, mediately.

For this reason it is a mistake to think of Gloster as being, by the loss of his eyes, given "true sight." To be sure, he now becomes aware of things he had been blind to; but we will do well to mind our metaphors in speaking of that awareness. (The trouble with treating *King Lear* under the categories of appearance and reality is not that doing so is false, but that it translates the play's realities too directly into the realm of metaphysics and so loses sight of the metaphorical substance. Both protagonists are deceived by appearance and discover reality; but as their ways of being deceived are not the same, neither are their sufferings and discoveries.) Always a led man, he is now led in the literal sense; always in the dark, he is now enclosed with darkness and made to *feel* the mediacy of report. He is guided to the truth, not by learning to see with an "inner vision" or "the mind's eye," but by a palpable thickening of the wall between him and reality. "I see it feelingly," he tells Lear, or:

> I stumbled when I saw. Full oft 'tis seen,
> Our means secure us, and our mere defects
> Prove our commodities.

("Commodities" is to be understood in this play as related to "accommodate" and "unaccommodated" and thus having the secondary meaning of "clothes.") Similarly, Edgar tells the dying Edmund: "The dark and vicious place where thee he got / Cost him his eyes," thereby likening that place to the darkness into which Gloster is thrust. There is truth in discovering how densely we are enclosed in darkness; that, fittingly, is Gloster's truth.

Seen this way, his painful progress comes to its proper goal at what he thinks the edge of Dover Cliffs. Here we see him, who had swept aside "nothing" as an insubstantial nothing, totally delivered over to the creative power of the word. Edgar's cliff—a poetic lie creating a purely verbal reality—for Gloster assumes the substantiality of fact, because he no longer has any matter of fact to judge it by. Edgar acts from motives and for ends altogether opposite to Edmund's; but for all that he *does* the same thing: he lies. Though the motives will direct our moral judgment, the fact must determine our interpretation. And the fact is that Gloster is saved from despair and suicide by the very deed that plunged him into them; the difference is that now, he being blind, the lie can be "grosser."

There is another difference: Gloster suffers Edgar's lie, while he invited Edmund's. His assertions of superior insight were as mistaken as his desperate attempt to pit his will against the gods'; *his* truth and wisdom lie in obedience, the virtue of the natural subject. He is compelled by blindness to do what, had he done it when he saw, would have saved him from error: take men at their word. In a sense, therefore, his finding his own truth brings him around to Lear's position; that is the way of paradoxes. But the quality of reaching that point remains radically different; his plus is the product of minuses. There is immediacy in Edgar's summoning up of the cliff; but as we the spectators know, it is arrived at by squaring mediacy: blindness times lying equals "truth." When the extremes of a paradox meet, a great deal depends on the direction from which the meeting point is approached.

If the metaphor for Gloster's blindness is covering, that for Lear's madness is stripping. Edgar as Tom o' Bedlam is the touchstone. To Gloster his nakedness is an offense:

> If, for my sake,
> Thou wilt o'ertake us hence a mile or twain
> I' th' way toward Dover, do it for ancient love;
> And bring some covering for this naked soul,
> Which I'll entreat to lead me.

And his madness is a deficiency of reason, the remaining glimmer of which Gloster looks for: "He has some reason, else he could not beg." Lear, on the other hand, sees in the naked madman the true pattern of man stripped and essential, and so he eagerly sets about becoming like him:

> Ha! here's three on 's are sophisticated! Thou art the thing itself; unaccommodated man is no more but such a poor, bare, forked animal as thou art. Off, off, you lendings! come, unbutton here.

(The cadence of "Off, you lendings" will shortly recur in "Out, vile jelly!") Lear resists the efforts of Kent and Gloster to separate him from this "philosopher" and guide him to the covering of a house; madness and nakedness have come to mean truth to him.

How has he come to this? The Fool's jest tells us:

> This is nothing, Fool.
> Then 'tis like the breath of an unfeed lawyer; you gave me nothing for it. Can you make no use of nothing, nuncle?
> Why, no boy; nothing can be made out of nothing.

But the Fool can make use of it:

> Thou wast a pretty fellow when thou hadst no need to care for her frowning; now thou art an O without a figure. I am better than thou art now; I am a Fool, thou art nothing.

Lear discovers that his faith in directness was mistaken because it ultimately did rest on an intervening matter of fact: the sovereign's power to make good his words. The power gone, so is the immediacy; power was the integer before the zero. The formula "Nothing will come of nothing" is now looked at from the other side. In the first scene it had meant for Lear that the sovereign has, and can endow others with, creative power: Say something, and that something will be. Now the axiom has become the formula of impotence, and so the Fool explicates it. The king, who scorned to construe the meaning of words by indirect evidence, is now under the humiliating necessity of interpreting by signs, by "frowns" and "cold looks," of looking for reasons why his orders are disobeyed and his messengers slighted. In the play's most pitiful scene—the bargaining with Goneril and Regan over the number of retainers—he tries to cling to the illusion, to hold on to the shreds of royalty that will cover the nakedness of the zero he has become; and even as we tremble lest he might fail in this attempt, we tremble lest he might succeed. But he fails, is not left even the shreds. The choice is forced upon him between submitting to the subject's lot, learning the arts of indirection in order to have a roof over his head, and going out to confront reality nakedly, with nothing to interpose between himself and the turmoil of unstructured nature. When he discovers that there *is* a gap between sentence and power, he chooses immediacy, nakedness, the truly royal essence of what his still impure image of himself had been. That is why the "foolish, fond old man" of the end is more regal than the king was.

It is common to take Lear's compassionate concern for the Fool and his prayer for the "poor, naked wretches" as evidence of his conversion from a blind pride to an understanding of man's common humanity and of the superficiality of rank and power. And so, of course, they are. But they do *not* constitute a turning point in his fall; they only mark a stage. He is now stripped of the title and additions of a king and so learns what it is to be poor and wretched. But he is not naked yet, nor mad. For a moment it seems as though he might find a halt in his prayer, by identifying himself with the common man, finding consolation and support in a kind of Christian pity and humility; but at that moment Edgar's voice first emerges from the hovel and reads the precise and as yet incomplete measure of Lear's descent:

> Fathom and half, fathom and half!

And Lear's passion for the real and naked immediately instructs him that there are depths yet to be plumbed—those of madness—and a cover yet to be stripped: discourse of reason.

BLINDNESS, since Homer, Tiresias and Oedipus, has behind it a long tradition as a noble affliction; it is the mark of the seer and poet, of the superior being who has penetrated behind the veils of appearance that enclose ordinary men. Madness is quite another thing. To be sure, the tradition of divine frenzy, of seizure by a higher power, is also an old one; man has long paid the tribute of awe to this kind of madness. But Lear's madness, as Shakespeare portrays it, is of a different sort. It does not issue in dark oracles or hint at mysteries; it is very much of this earth. Edgar's feigned madness appears (as it *is*) literary next to it; he trades in the standard goods of seizure and possession: "The foul fiend haunts poor Tom in the voice of a nightingale," or: "Frateretto calls me; and tells me Nero is an angler in the lake of darkness." (Later, with the fallen Gloster, he will continue to deal in devils and divinities.) Lear's madness is the real thing, and it would seem that, once he has talked with his "learned Theban," he has intuitively penetrated Edgar's disguise, sensed that his madness is not of his own, royal kind—an utter nakedness of mind—but a "garment":

> You, sir, I entertain you for one of my hundred: only I do not like the fashion of your garments. You will say they are Persian, but let them be changed.

He does not gibber oracularly about foul fiends nor chill our spines with the stock properties of witchcraft; when he sees himself beset, it is not by Obidicut, Hobbididence, Mahu and Modo, but by dogs:

> The little dogs and all,
> Tray, Blanch, and Sweetheart, see, they bark at me.

To convince us that this very ordinary madness is the truly regal affliction was a formidable task—the more so because it is counterposed to what Shakespeare makes us accept, against all tradition, as the servile suffering of blindness. It seems almost perverse for him so to have stacked the cards against himself; my guess is that only the necessity of truth could have brought him to undertake the attempt.

For the truth is that what we call reality comes to us prefabricated, cut to orderly measure and built into orderly structure by language; poets, at least Shakespeare, did not have to wait for Whorf to discover this truth for them. Discourse of reason, though it may be employed to correct the falsities of this structuring, cannot but remain their victim; every coherent sentence written against the tyranny of words is ultimately a rattling of chains. That is why truth, which cannot reside outside discourse, cannot reside in it either. It is enacted in a confrontation of the real which is either silent and incommunicable or, if it is uttered, madness.

Lear's raving is, as Edgar says, "matter and impertinency mixed, / Reason in madness." It is natural for the commentator to cling to the reason, to talk about the lines exposing the relativity of justice and the deceptiveness of appearance, and to pass over the "impertinencies." But this is an evasion, not only of the scene's terror but of its truth. Shakespeare makes this point clearly. Directly before the entrance of Cordelia's men, Lear "preaches" to Gloster:

> Thou must be patient; we came crying hither;
> Thou know'st, the first time that we smell the air,

> We wawl and cry. I will preach to thee, mark...
> When we are born, we cry that we are come
> To this great stage of fools.—This' a good block.
> It were a delicate strategem to shoe
> A troop of horse with felt. I'll put 't in proof;
> And when I have stol'n upon these son-in-laws,
> Then kill, kill, kill, kill, kill, kill!

The burden of the "preachment" is the same as Edgar's later words about our going hence and coming hither—which means that we should stop quoting them as though they were the distillate of Shakespeare's tragic wisdom. They may be noble to Gloster's ears (and Gloster is most of us most of the time), but Lear knows them for what they are: eloquent commonplaces from the Stoic's repertory. That is why he breaks off in the middle, weary with the formulable precepts of faith or even disillusionment, and turns his mind, or rather perception, back to realities far grimmer, because without any order. Of Gloster's "block," or hat, he sees not the form or social function to which it has been pressed, but the raw material; and this he presses to the purpose of total destruction. (Here again is the garment metaphor, associated with Gloster, stripped by Lear. For the equation garment equals ordered speech, which I have inferred, there is also direct textual warrant:

> GLOSTER: Methinks thy voice is altered and thou speak'st
>   In better phrase and matter than thou didst.
> EDGAR: You're much deceived. In nothing am I changed
>   But in my garments.
> GLOSTER: Methinks you're better spoken.)

This naked directness and substantiality of perception, this apprehension of the "raw material" which makes all wisdom sound brittle, is one mark of Lear's madness. It applies also to words, which for him assume a phonetic corporeality that strips them of meaning and would, if it were consciously done, be called punning: "Peace, peace; this piece of toasted cheese will do 't." The same directness leads Lear's mind along the path of free association, in which ideas and images are not functionally ordered in a reasoned chain but assume a body and life of their own:

> Ha! Goneril with a white beard! They flattered me like a dog and told me I had the white hairs in my beard ere the black ones were there.

The second mark, or theme, of his madness is his royalty; it stands at the beginning, middle and end of this scene:

> No, they cannot touch me for coining; I am the King himself.

> Aye, every inch a king!

> I will be jovial. Come, come; I am a king,
> My masters, know you that?

And Cordelia's Gentleman answers for all of us:

> You are a royal one, and we obey you.

Had Lear held on to his discovery of human fellowship, we would have welcomed and pitied him (as we are always ready to do when we see someone brought down to our level); his tragedy would have been one in the medieval sense: a fall from greatness. We might have been awed, but our awe would have been paid to the eternal powers that make the wheel of fortune turn, not to Lear himself. Edgar states, in rhymes a deal too neat, the force of such tragedies:

> When we our betters see bearing our woes,
> We scarcely think our miseries our foes.
> Who alone suffers, suffers most i' th' mind,
> Leaving free things and happy shows behind.
> But then the mind much sufferance doth o'erskip,
> When grief has mates, and bearing fellowship.

But Lear is meant, or rather wills, not to o'erskip any sufferance by finding grief-mates; he is the king and has no fellows.

He defines his kingship for us: he cannot be touched for coining. As every coin the king issues is necessarily a true coin, so every word he sovereignly speaks is a true word and every judgment a just judgment. The king can do no wrong—that is what sets him apart from men and forces him, once he understands it, to his fearful directness and confrontation. It is he who justifies:

> None does offend, none, I say, none; I'll able 'em.

But who, then, will "able" *him*? Before he saw Edgar, Lear thought he knew. Though powerless, he could call on the "great gods" to send their "dreadful summoners" and bring criminals before the bar of their "higher" justice. At that point he could still speak of himself as more sinned against than sinning, as having a just claim. Then he knew who was guilty and who was not, because then, for a brief moment, he thought he could find refuge in fellowship and the subject's consoling sense of being *under* the law; he could abdicate and become plaintiff before the court of divine law. Now he knows better. First he summons a court of his own, with the Fool and the Madman as justices, to try his daughters. And finally he summons all mankind, judge and felon, beggar and beadle, into the searing light of his discovery that there is nothing and no one to able him, no "natural law" or "right reason" to mediate between him and chaos. He is the *source* of justice and truth and so can receive none.

It is this knowledge that is his madness—not in the sense that he is mad to think so, but rather that no one who penetrates to this point can stay sane. Here words like truth and justice, the comforting constructs under which sane men seek shelter, cease to have meaning. This is the harvest of Lear's proud faith in the substantiality of his words; Nothing now *has* come of nothing, the word as entity has created its meaning and drawn the universe into the chaos of universal negation. The "name" has become absolute: Lear, utterly divested of all that gives "meaning" to the name of king, is now king "in name only" and so, paradoxically, king absolute and quintessential.

This is "the worst," as Edgar has negatively but precisely defined it:

> The worst is not
> So long as we can say, "This is the worst."

The stress is on the "say." That simplest of sentences implies, in its four ordered words, a whole ordered universe and hierarchy of values. It presupposes a meaningful order. Lear no longer can say it; he has rejected meaning as "mean" in both senses: demeaning and mediate. If in the preceding paragraphs I have been obscure and groping, the obscurity should not cast doubt on my interpretation. For all interpretation is "report," and at this point the interpreter (and the reader) can only say, with Edgar:

> I would not take this from report. It is;
> And my heart breaks at it.

It is—it no longer means. Report and interpretation try to make sense, to clothe the nakedness of being in the decent and orderly garments of rational discourse. They either falsify *Lear* at this point or break at it. It is—the worst.

WHEN LEAR AWAKENS from madness and sleep, he no longer is king; all the respectful solicitude of Cordelia and her servants will not persuade him to it. He has earned his release from the frightful office and will not be distracted from the truth he has won—and for which there is no name but Cordelia. His new state is discontinuous with what he was before: he has had "fresh garments" put on him, but "all the skill I have remembers not these garments"; he does not know where he "did lodge last night," but sees himself surrounded by spirits and souls in bliss. In short, he is transfigured.

With his fresh garments he has put on a new language—and yet what he speaks is nothing new and dark. It is, rather, wholly private, has the intimate directness of people who believe they stand outside all social orders and need not rely on the mediation of custom and authority to give meaning to what they say. It is as natural as the song of the birds:

> We two alone will sing like birds i' th' cage.
> When thou dost ask me blessing, I'll kneel down
> And ask of thee forgiveness. So we'll live,
> And pray, and sing, and tell old tales, and laugh
> At gilded butterflies, and hear poor rogues
> Talk of court news; and we'll talk with them too.

> Who loses and who wins; who's in, who's out;
> And take upon 's the mystery of things
> As if we were God's spies.

As natural and as intimate and as remote. Injustice and justice no longer concern him; he does not want to see Goneril and Regan. Cordelia's eight little, unstructured words suffice him: "(And so) I am, I am" and "No cause, no cause." The first four lifted him from the depths of nothingness, and the last released him from the chain of cause and effect, the iron and ironic consequences of his unchallengeable, "Nothing will come of nothing."

It seems as though irony has been vanquished; in the two scenes in which Lear and Cordelia appear before being led to prison, Shakespeare and Lear almost persuade us, against our better judgment, that the plots and armies swirling around them do not matter, that a realm has been won, even if it is only a bird's cage, where the immediate is possible. But it isn't only the soldiers and Edmund who warn us that this idyll cannot last; it is something in Cordelia's way of speaking:

> We are not the first
> Who with best meaning have incurred the worst.
> For thee, oppressed king, I am cast down;
> Myself could else outfrown false Fortune's frown.

There is the rhyme, so oddly formal at this point and from this woman; there are the antitheses of reasoned discourse, the coining of epigrammatic wisdom of general currency, the play on words. This might be Edgar speaking to Gloster; it ought not to be Cordelia speaking to the new Lear. If we have understood the play rightly, we will be frightened by these lines more than by Edmund's preceding soliloquy. Lear *is* frightened, as his frantic "No, no, no, no!" shows.

What is he warding off? Ultimately, of course, the loss of his daughter, but more immediately the knowledge that she still belongs to that other realm, still is a queen, cannot extricate herself from the world of war and strategem. Goneril and Regan are still what she so pointedly calls them: her sisters and Lear's daughters. The almost unspeakable simplicity of directness, purchased by unspeakable suffering, cannot be the last word, or if it is, must literally be the *last* word. For speech remains tied to the social order—and with it truth.

Since almost anything the interpreter can say about the end of *King Lear* is a trivialization, I will risk one that may seem ludicrous: Shakespeare had to write the end because he had to return to living and writing. If the finding of Cordelia had meant the finding, at whatever cost, of a new "style"—the conquest of irony, the beginning of the direct mode—the conclusion could have been triumphant; we might have been dismissed with the lines about the mystery of things. But the end of *Lear* does not yield a new style; it is the absence of all style. Style is the summary term for the way the poet uses "devices"; it is, therefore, the tribute exacted by the "mystery of things." The essence of the experience of direct confrontation—namely its directness

—remains incommunicable; every word violates and distorts it. It is the pain of this insight, I think, which Shakespeare embodies in the play's last scene.

When Lear, mad, encounters Gloster and Edgar near Dover, his second sentence —following the one about coining—is: "Nature's above art in that respect." The meaning of "nature" in the play is, as Empson has shown, vastly complex, but at this point it is reasonably clear. "Art," for Lear, is all that he has stripped away; he is now the natural king, and his coinages are natural. From this point on, in what concerns Lear directly, art is abandoned, Nature speaks. In Shakespeare—in fact in poetic drama—I know of no "naturalism" to equal the end of this play.

Since I have made so much of immediacy, I may seem to be caught here in a discrepancy. We are made to *see*, with cruel directness, the blinding of Gloster; we are not made to see the killing of Cordelia. But here, too, Shakespeare is rigorously exact. In Gloster's sphere, physical fact is primary; hence the blinding is presented as physical fact, to which the words are a feeble accompaniment. But in Lear's sphere words are primary, so that a physical directness, which with Cordelia's murder would silence all, would be false. *Words* must carry the whole burden, as Lear carries his daughter; to manage things otherwise would have been, for Shakespeare, an evasion of his task and—odd as this may sound—of his pain. Far from sparing himself and us a last, insupportable horror, he makes us bear all of it—in words. For the poet there is, or may be, a release in the abdication from speech: Shakespeare does not allow himself that release. He must speak, or—if speech refuses its office— "howl."

Lear's "Howl, howl, howl, howl!" as he enters with Cordelia's body should have been enough to keep any English poet from entitling a poem "Howl." To howl is a privilege so bitterly earned that only experiences like Lear's can ever justify it in poetry. There is a quality in the last scene which anywhere else we should have to call indecent—an insensibility to all but that one dead body which, except here, would be subhuman:

> Where is your servant Caius?
> He's a good fellow, I can tell you that;
> He'll strike and quickly too. He's dead and rotten.

That is Lear's acknowledgement of Kent's loyalty, of no more account now than the treacheries of Goneril and Regan:

> Your elder daughters have fordone themselves
> And desperately are dead.
>   Aye, so I think.

Lear is not mad, though now we might wish he were. He is totally cut off from everything and everyone, wholly given over to his forlorn hope of a faint breath. It is not even Cordelia as a person that all his senses are fixed on, but only her lips, her breath, her speech:

> Cordelia, Cordelia, stay a little! Ha!
> What is 't thou say'st? Her voice was ever soft,
> Gentle and low; an excellent thing in woman.

And his final words are the cry of the man who cares for nothing more except the hope that truth has breath and voice and that from it issue visible realities:

> Do you see this? Look on her, look, her lips,
> Look there, look there!

He ends, it might seem, where Gloster, with his "Let's see," began. But he dies believing that he has seen living breath, not letters—words, not signs.

Besides this absorption, all else is what Albany calls Edmund's death: "but a trifle." We are, all of us, dismissed. At best we are, with Edgar, among those who must "speak what we feel, not what we ought to say." There can be honesty in speaking what we feel, but what we ought to say is the naked truth, and it cannot be said. Make "nothing" into a substance, and you get Nothing; take it for a mere sign, and you have "nothing." Be king or subject—nothing will be the sum of your earnings. But the uncompromising logic—the logic of life and language, not of syllogisms—with which we work out or more likely let ourselves be led to this sum is, perhaps, something. Since we are dismissed into the stewardship of Edgar, we may be forgiven for covering the shame of silence with saying: "Ripeness is *all*."

The Poet at War with His Language: Remarks on the Newer French Lyric

❦ ELISABETH BROCK-SULZER ❦

Elisabeth Brock-Sulzer, who teaches in Zurich, has written and lectured on a wide range of topics in drama and French literature. A pupil of Theophil Spoerri, the eminent professor of Romance literature at the University of Zurich for some years, Mrs. Brock-Sulzer's first book was *Natur und Mensch im Werke Honoré de Balzacs* (1930), a study of Balzac's descriptive passages and imagery; more recently, she has published *Theater* (1954), a selection of her dramatic criticism, and a study of Dürrenmatt, on whose work she is an authority. During the lifetime of the Swiss quarterly *Trivium* (1942–1951), which devoted so many of its pages to stylistic analyses, Mrs. Brock-Sulzer contributed a series of articles on such writers as Molière and Rimbaud, as well as the essay translated here, which originally appeared under the title "Der Dichter im Kampf mit seiner Sprache."

Mrs. Brock-Sulzer's overriding thesis is that the creative literary artist is almost inevitably at war with his language as it is given him, struggling against and through its forms to win from them his unique expression; and the result of the war—when waged by someone so gifted as Mallarmé —may well be the renewal of the language itself, in the sense that the artist's innovations may point the way to further linguistic developments. In the first segment of her essay, which reveals her mastery of a strain of traditional European literary scholarship, Mrs. Brock-Sulzer establishes the characteristics of the French language itself as it developed from Latin and as it is differentiated from German; she cites such attributes as the relatively strict word order of the French language, its orientation toward the audience's need to understand rather than toward the expressive requirements of the speaker, and its firm observance of the boundaries between classes of words. In the body of the essay, however, she treats two schools of symbolist poetry—one exemplified by Verlaine, the other by Mallarmé—first distinguishing between their poetic ideals and attitudes toward language and then revealing, through the most delicate and meticulous analysis, the reaction of each poet against certain qualities and norms in French, how he remakes the language into an instrument embodying his particular vision. In the case of Mallarmé, especially, Mrs. Brock-Sulzer shows exactly what it means for a poet to struggle with the limitations of his language as she discusses his handling of negation, his dissolution of verbal categories, his interweaving of long and short words, and his revitalization of unimportant words (which normally serve merely as grammatical signs) through placing them so that they bear full poetic weight in his lines. In short, the essay precisely and brilliantly demonstrates how language becomes monumentalized in Mallarmé's symbolist poems.

Although Mrs. Brock-Sulzer is primarily concerned with the artist's creativity as he contends with language, a number of her analyses deal with the ways in which certain aspects of style work dramatically on the audience, as in her commentary on Verlaine's "Pareil à la / Feuille morte," or on Mallarmé's rhyme of "ce l'est" with "–celet," or on the play between caesura and line length in the first verse of "L'Après-midi d'un faune."

If we take a comprehensive look at French literature, we notice how broken in its line of development French lyric poetry has been. The century of Classicism was a fundamentally *un*lyrical epoch, and the Enlightenment continued at least *this* Classical trait; thus it became possible for one of the most delightful creations of

---

"The Poet at War with His Language: Remarks on the Newer French Lyric," by Elisabeth Brock-Sulzer, here translated by Corinna Babb, originally appeared in *Trivium: Schweizerische Vierteljahresschrift für Literaturwissenschaft und Stilkritik*, V (1947), 233–62. Translated by permission of Atlantis Verlag.

French literary art—the lyric poetry of the Renaissance—to be abused or ignored through two whole centuries, until Romanticism opened readers' eyes to it once more. However, the thoroughly *episodic* character of French Romanticism itself is again symptomatic of a characteristically French tendency to shy away from the so-called freedom of the lyric in pursuit of entirely different forms of thought and art. Still, at the very time when a Zola was endeavoring to domesticate the novel in sociology, there quietly emerged a new form of lyric poetry, Symbolism, of which it can truly be said that it brought Romanticism to its full maturity, even if it was later bound to outgrow Romanticism. Although Paul Valéry could speak of France's "lyrical fits,"[1] the remark is certainly no longer applicable now to the poetry of the last 120 years. But of course one cannot simply dismiss a remark made by one of France's greatest lyrical poets. Nor can one quite overlook the fact that in the realization of its Romantic movement—and here one means Romantic in its most general sense—France shows an interrupted development similar to that of Germany in its realization of Classicism. For it would seem quite generally true that Romanticism, in its broadest sense, has more in common with lyric poetry than does Classicism.

But how can one explain this apparent hostility to the lyric in French literary art? After all, we should not forget that it was precisely the French troubadours who forged the lyrical instrument for all Europe. And we should be equally mindful that the French lyric preserved itself during the Renaissance, that breach felt throughout Western culture, and that the French troubadours and trouvères were followed in loose succession by a Villon (who expressed simultaneously the late medieval spirit and the new freedom), by a school of Lyons, by a Pléiade, even if these diverse poets of the late- or post-medieval period were taking a position opposed to the art of the troubadours. In short, the French language can hardly be described as totally unlyrical if one considers its history as a *whole*. However, if one now looks at the nineteenth and twentieth centuries so far as we have been able to experience them, there emerges the spectacle of a war—that might almost be called heroic—which the native French lyric poet is waging against his language.

Only a naive reader would believe that the poet at war with his language is an exception. For in the whole of world literature only a few literary works *of any length* exist which have not been born out of such conflict. The seeds of a poetic composition may always come as a gift, but their growth into a larger poetic work can scarcely occur in the absence of the poet's struggle with his linguistic heritage. Naturally, there are differences of degree. We with a Germanic background, and thus a language which seems especially created for lyrical expression, may be inclined to dismiss the poet's struggle with his medium, language, as something negligible, if in fact we do not regard it as working against the greatness of a poet. We are all too ready to view the innocent, folk-song quality of a poetic work as the alpha and omega of poetic art. Indeed, the greatest, most visionary German lyrical poet, Hölderlin, has described such poetry as "des Lieds kindlich Geschwätz und der Mühn, Süße Vergessenheit

---

[1] "Questions de poésie" in *Variété III*. Especially relevant here are Valéry's studies of Mallarmé in *Variété II* and *Variété III*, to which this essay is much indebted.

bei gegenwärtigem Geiste [the childlike babbling of song and the sweet obliviousness to troubles, coexisting with utter awareness]." And in confirmation of this view, there are of course many German poems which exemplify, incontestably and delightfully, the wonderful success of the poet's first effort, achieved without struggling. These tend to make us forget that, measured against the *whole* of literature, they are the rare exceptions to the rule. Nevertheless—a lyrical quality is more "easily" achieved in German than in French, just as, on the other hand, precision in prose is more "easily" won from French than from German.

We have already seen that this was not always the case. Even though in the sixteenth century Du Bellay found it necessary to *illustrate* the French language—to give it literally more "lustre"—he still was not in any way waging a war against what was later felt to be the essentially prosaic character of French, but only against a language which—like the one encountered by Luther in Germany—did not yet appear capable of competing with Latin in treating anything more than common, everyday events and things. Indications that prose was later to dominate the character of the French language were still too little evident and the possibilities of reacting against this domination too easy for it to be felt as a threat. Only when Malherbes, and the linguistic theoreticians and writers of the seventeenth century who followed, shaped a French *an sich* through concentrating all the powers in their language—somewhat as Richelieu did with the State—only then did there develop a language so exemplary in its codification as to make a fundamentally conflicting critical position a possibility. It was this language of the mature seventeenth century which was later heralded as the "clearest language of Europe": one which, through authors like Voltaire and Anatole France, came to figure in the sensibility of the cultivated European as a kind of Esperanto for the expression of Reason in all its grace and agility.

But precisely how did French manifest itself as the clearest of languages? First of all, in its strict word order, which is mentioned again and again: subject, predicate, object. Named first is not that which is closest to one's feeling, but that which is logically in the foreground. Dominant is a consideration for the reader, who must be oriented as soon as possible, and not a consideration for the expressive requirements of the speaker. Also to be mentioned here is the predominantly analytical character of French prose. And this clarity manifests itself further in the firm, honest, and open way in which particles—the hinges of language—are used. One could cite, for example, the double possibilities in German and in English usage—"Du sagst, daß du kommst" and "Du sagst, du kommest" (just as in English ["You say that you will come" and "You say you will come"])—and contrast these with the single possibility in French— "Tu dis que tu viendras"—where the particle clearly separates the main clause from the subordinate clause. A further reason for the clarity of French is the clear separation of word classes. What accuracy in the rendering of thought is made possible by the fact that the adjective and adverb are differentiated in form (whereas in German they often coincide in form)! What sensitivity to the uniqueness of word classes is manifest in the resistance of the French language to the conversion of verbs and adjectives into substantives—as opposed to German, in which every infinitive can harden into a substantive, and the substantive itself becomes devalued as a designator of things by such indiscriminate transpositions! How faithfully the French language adheres to the gradations of value which exist among the different word classes, always putting words of a subservient class in subordinate positions and appropriately elevating those of a dominant class—a linguistic procedure which can of course be best observed in verse! Never in traditional poetry would the rhyme or the accent be allowed to fall on a logically subordinate word which does not carry a special value of its own. Finally, even the relative poverty of the French vocabulary is, by the genius of the great French prose writers, quite surprisingly shaped into the very tool of clarity. Few elements can indeed become many if the possibilities for combining them are fully exploited; here again interest focuses automatically on the connectives: those forms which do not render things, or material reality, but the process of thought, the rationale of language as it unfolds.

In short, the lucidity of the French language is indisputable where clarification is the criterion, the virtue of speech in question. However, all the advantages mentioned so far are essentially virtues for French *prose*. Poetry appears poorly accoutered if it must rely on them. And poets might well claim that all these conditions so favorable to prose are not necessarily indigenous to French itself. For if we look at the development of the French language, we find that these very traits which make for the clarity of its prose originated, at least in part, as mere expedients to compensate, as much as possible, through substitute constructions for the disappearing Latin inflections. The rigid sentence structure of French today must have first become law when the difference between subjective and objective [nominative and accusative] case disappeared and when there was no other way of bringing order out of chaos than through such strict methods of separation. And what is true for the chief manifestation of this clarity—word order—is also true for other typically Classical traits: the wonderful capacity for manipulating relatively few basic elements; the peculiar articulation of an intermediate realm, halfway between pure abstraction and pure concretion—these things are to be explained as the result less of deliberate intent than of a necessary linguistic development from Latin, a development which was a particularly difficult and interrupted one for the French language. Only later did a Classical linguistic intent—for which the Renaissance poets had in part prepared the way—draw the conclusion from this development and transform with marvellous consistency what had merely happened into something deliberately willed. Here the writers obeyed as well as mastered the destiny of their language. In the seventeenth century, this linguistic will is still informed by a spontaneous creative will. The insistence on concord—which is shown, for instance, in the introduction of personal pronouns in cases where the verb form alone would clearly indicate the person—is not evidence of dull repetitiveness, but strong testimony to the Classicists' strict belief in the principles of symmetry and equilibrium. Even in its most prosaic form, the linguistic instrument was still subject to the deliberate artistic act. True, language was about to solidify, but it still had not and thus was not yet a dead weight on creative expression. If at this time a Bossuet could believe that French might be arrested and codified in its newly gained perfection, and could see in this the most noble task for the Académie, he could do so only because this perfection had just been achieved and thus still allowed glimpses of the road along which language had progressed.[2] At a later date, however, when Rivarol glorified the clarity of French to the rest of Europe,[3] this clarity was already taken for granted, routine, a sign above all of a language for communication which could no longer fully satisfy the demands of self-expression. And what the poets wanted to express at this time was no longer belief in reason but in the absolute power of feeling, no longer exchanges between people in conversation but the monologue bursting from the I. Revolution—even the linguistic one—could not be suppressed. At the time of Romanticism, Sainte-Beuve, the greatest critic of the epoch, could even say: "Le moule de style en usage depuis Balzac jusqu'à Jean-Jacques a sauté en éclats, aussi bien que le moule du vers [The mold of style in use from Balzac to Jean-Jacques has burst in pieces, as has the mold of verse]." Indeed, the rather ominous phrase was coined by Sainte-Beuve that the great Classicists were "un accident immortel," an immortal accident—perhaps a disaster.[4]

But did the Classical linguistic forms themselves truly break down during this Romantic period? If we look at the language of the French Romantic poets from the point of view of our present linguistic situation, or from the perspective of German or English Romanticism, we find it still very much bound to forms stamped by Classicism. Often the originality appears simply in a certain relaxation of contours, so that we might well agree with Rivarol's definition that poetry simply lets the reins of language trail behind.[5] What is radically new, indeed revolutionary, in French Romanticism is its stock of emotions and concepts. But this newness has still not been fully incarnated: Romanticism remains, from an artistic point of view, fragmentary. We can follow this development clearly in the poems of Baudelaire. Even he, who seems always unwilling to waste words, can be seen making one attempt after another through several lines before he seizes on the unalterably right expression for a thoroughly new and original world view. Precisely the most unforgettable verses of this poet are often preceded by stretches of merely rhymed prose, revealing their real poetic density only at the end of the stanza. One thinks, for instance, of the verses in "Recueillement":

> Pendant que des mortels la multitude vile,
> Sous le fouet du plaisir, ce bourreau sans merci,
> Va cueillir des remords dans la fête servile,
> Ma Douleur, donne-moi la main; viens par ici
>
> Loin d'eux....
>
> *While the base multitude of mortals*
> *Under the whip of pleasure, this pitiless torturer,*
> *Go plucking remorse in the slavish feast,*
> *My Sorrow, give me your hand; come this way*
>
> *Far from them....*

---

[2] *Discours de réception à l'Académie française*, 1671. [3] "De l'universalité de la langue française," *Discours à l'Académie de Berlin*, 1784. [4] "Conclusion," *Tableau historique et critique de la poésie française au 16ᵉ siècle*.
[5] "De l'universalité de la langue française."

But the *real* breaking apart of Classical French occurred only in Symbolism and in those subsequent movements which, from the vantage point of the present day, now seem allied with Symbolism.

WHAT VERBAL INNOVATIONS do occur in the lyrics of this late Romanticism? Even if they all share *one* common characteristic, the search for a pure *word magic*, we must distinguish two contradictory tendencies: the one, a search for the *song*; the other, a search for the *fugue*. For one, language is too structured; for the other, it is not structured enough. The former strives for complete freedom: freedom from strict verse patterns, freedom from logical control, freedom from traditional grammar, all in the interests of an entirely unrestricted use of language, a use which approximates a truly vital, not a rational, prose. The latter strives for the utmost concentration, compression of line and stanza, the most precise poetic vision, the strictest sorting of the linguistic materials—indeed, one often has the impression that poets of this second group would like to establish a new grammar which would be far more stringently binding than the old one because it would have to regulate the most condensed form of language, the poem. The first is the way of Verlaine and his many different disciples; the other, the way of Mallarmé, who, though he had no real disciples, still revolutionized the poetry of all modern Europe by his refusal to compromise in his art (just as Rimbaud did by his refusal to compromise in his life). In what follows, an attempt will be made to sketch only the chief characteristics of these two fundamental types of Symbolist poetry.

Let us look first at the advocates of the freer kind of verse. There is an *ars poetica* for the Symbolists, Verlaine's "Art poétique." For, its playfulness and polemics aside, it still furnishes us with certain guiding principles of the chosen method:

> De la musique encore et toujours!
> Que ton vers soit la chose envolée
> Qu'on sent qui fuit d'une âme en allée
> Vers d'autres cieux à d'autres amours.
> (*Jadis et Naguère*)

> *Let there be music again and forever!*
> *May your verse be the winged thing*
> *That one senses which escapes from a soul in passing*
> *Toward other skies to other loves.*

From the standpoint of the Classical ideal, the syntactical structure of this stanza sounds barbarous. How naive, in contrast to Classical practice, is the double genitive construction which Flaubert would have avoided at any cost! "Qu'on sent qui fuit...." Restlessly, one sentence thrusts another out of itself—image of impatient flight. And how maladroit the choice of words: "la chose envolée," "une âme en allée..."! Why "la chose envolée"? Why this "en allée" which seems suspended between movement and immobility? Because all at once exact expression provokes the deepest distrust. Precision means finality; the thought or feeling, once it is fully expressed in the word, appears exhausted, drained of vitality. Life seems conquered by the word. That is exactly what Flaubert *wanted*, as did the great Classicists before him. But Verlaine does not. The quoted stanza is designedly faulty in structure: it has everywhere cracks and crevices through which life and dreams—neither of them ever to be caught fast—can escape. Thus,

> Il faut aussi que tu n'ailles point
> Choisir tes mots sans quelque méprise:
> Rien de plus cher que la chanson grise
> Où l'Indécis au Précis se joint.
>
> *Also, you must never*
> *Choose your words without some mistake:*
> *Nothing more precious than the gray song*
> *Where the Indefinite and the Precise join.*

The choice of words by a poet should be deliberately beside the mark. Not the full, congruent expression, but the slightly oblique one ought to be chosen, so that the union of definiteness and indefiniteness may yield a song that is less than fully resolved. In the discrepancy between the word and its referent lives the truly creative process, both for the creating poet and for the re-creating reader: only in that divergence can life remain in flux. Or, as Mallarmé has said (and here the two so different poets meet):

Nommer un objet, c'est supprimer les trois quarts de la jouissance du poème qui est faite du bonheur de le deviner peu à peu: le suggérer, voilà le rêve. C'est le parfait usage de ce mystère qui constitue le symbole.[6]

To name an object is to suppress three-quarters of the enjoyment of the poem, which consists in the happiness of guessing it little by little: to suggest it—that is the dream. It is the perfect handling of this mystery that constitutes the symbol.

This is the reason why Verlaine never wants the color, only the shade, and why he rejects wit, word plays, and laughter as "impure." This is why he wants no eloquence, why he uses rhyme in a very limited way (at least he claims so here), and why he seeks only that "chose envolée," that verse of the beautiful adventure, "et tout le reste est littérature [and all the rest is mere literature]."

The poem is characteristic of a certain tendency in Symbolism—toward total emancipation from the rational. Every form ordinarily associated with reason—rhetoric, wit, plays on words—is taboo. But we must look more closely. For when Verlaine says,

> Car nous voulons la Nuance encor,
> Pas la Couleur, rien que la nuance!

---

[6] Jules Huret, *Enquête sur l'évolution littéraire*.

> Oh! la nuance seule fiance
> Le rêve au rêve et la flûte au cor!
>
> *For again we want the Nuance,*
> *Not the Color, nothing but the nuance!*
> *Oh! the nuance alone weds*
> *The dream to the dream and the flute to the horn!*

we still discover a purely musical kind of eloquence which is not without a certain triteness and, in its obviousness, hardly jibes with a poet who has just finished holding forth against rhyme. True, the wit that depends on reason is avoided; in its place, however, we have a kind of musical pun ["nuance"—"fiance"] which seems equally alien to the true nature of poetry. Of course, Verlaine was no Boileau of Symbolism. Theorizing was not his forte. And his *ars poetica* is really only intended as a sort of frolic. But if we look at Verlaine's best poems rather than at his theory, we find in them a real approximation of speech to music. The sound of a given word is not an accessory to meaning, but meaning itself:

> Les sanglots longs / Des violons / De l'automne . . .
>
> Il pleure dans mon cœur / Comme il pleut sur la ville. . . .
>
> *The long sobs / Of the violins / Of autumn . . .*
>
> *It rains in my heart / As it rains on the town. . . .*

Or one might mention the poem "Soleils couchants,"[7] in which a four-syllable expression ["soleils couchant(s)"] appears four times within sixteen five-syllable verses: in two rhythmically parallel pairs, but with the syntax always shifting. And yet it is no accident that this superb word music pales in comparison with the quintessentially simple

> Le ciel est, par dessus le toit, / Si bleu, si calme.
>
> *The sky, above the roof, is / So blue, so calm.*

<table>
<tr><td colspan="2" align="center">Soleils couchants</td></tr>
<tr><td>Une aube affaiblie</td><td>*A feeble dawn*</td></tr>
<tr><td>Verse par les champs</td><td>*Pours over the fields*</td></tr>
<tr><td>La mélancholie</td><td>*The melancholy*</td></tr>
<tr><td>Des soleils couchants.</td><td>*Of setting suns.*</td></tr>
<tr><td>La mélancholie</td><td>*The melancholy*</td></tr>
<tr><td>Berce de doux chants</td><td>*Rocks with sweet songs*</td></tr>
<tr><td>Mon cœur qui s'oublie</td><td>*My heart that forgets itself*</td></tr>
<tr><td>Aux soleils couchants.</td><td>*In setting suns.*</td></tr>
<tr><td>Et d'étranges rêves,</td><td>*And strange dreams,*</td></tr>
<tr><td>Comme des soleils</td><td>*Like suns*</td></tr>
<tr><td>Couchant sur les grèves,</td><td>*Setting on the beaches,*</td></tr>
<tr><td>Fantômes vermeils,</td><td>*Rose phantoms,*</td></tr>
<tr><td>Défilent sans trêves,</td><td>*Pass by without pause,*</td></tr>
<tr><td>Défilent, pareils</td><td>*Pass by, like*</td></tr>
<tr><td>A des grands soleils</td><td>*Great suns*</td></tr>
<tr><td>Couchant sur les grèves.</td><td>*Setting on the beaches.*</td></tr>
</table>

(*Poèmes saturniens*)

Here word music no longer usurps one's attention. In fact, one realizes how soon musical language exhausts itself if it follows only musical and not linguistic rules. The failure of the Dadaists could have been predicted from the example of Verlaine. After all, the sound of language can remain creative only when counterpoised with its *meaning*, and one betrays the very essence of poetry if one limits it to sound alone.

Less apparent, yet more important, is a phenomenon like the following:

> Et je m'en vais
> Au vent mauvais
>   Qui m'emporte
> Deçà, delà,
> Pareil à la
>   Feuille morte.
>   ("Chanson d'automne," from *Poèmes saturniens*)
>
> And I walk away
> Into the strong wind
>   Which carries me off
> Now here, now there,
> Like a
>   Dead leaf.

"Pareil à la / Feuille morte" is split into two lines, this division conflicting absolutely with the ordinary unity of the phrase and the traditional rule concerning the juxtaposition of article ["la"] and substantive ["Feuille"]. Are we to see in this disrespect for the natural law a willful dissolution of the verse, an approach to prose, in which case the phrase should read, "Pareil / à la feuille / morte"? Or rather, in keeping with poetry's character, should we observe precisely the unity of each line—"Pareil à la / Feuille morte"—a reading clearly suggested by the rhyme itself? If we read the lines thus, we suddenly become aware of something quite odd. The article is paralleled with the rhyme-word, "delà" (a demonstrative adverb), and thus takes on something of its demonstrative character. The article ceases to be merely a grammatical sign. Nevertheless, it remains irrevocably that at the very moment when the apparently inseparable bond between article and substantive is loosened [through their placement in separate lines], thus producing an incomparably rich graphic effect—the leaf is separated verbally as well as logically from the branch, becoming both internally and externally a dead, wilted leaf.

Such an expressive achievement makes it clear that the freedom which the poet takes—in breaking up the set patterns into which French had hardened—is by no means *negative*. Innovations in language, in order to be more than mere reactions to oppressive forces, must contain within themselves *new* expressive possibilities. Thus one might say that every innovative lyric which is only liberating itself and not developing *toward* something is poetry of an inferior sort. Verlaine still used this freedom primarily to render that flow of experience which can never be wholly captured—the dream. But with many of his disciples—for example, the *vers librists*—freedom often ends up in formlessness and misses the point of art entirely.

Another phenomenon which must at least be mentioned here is Verlaine's use of the vernacular. After all, along with the revolt by the poets against the traditional grammarians and against the fanatics of the Enlightenment, there was a powerful, even if often inarticulate, revolt by the people. And where poets and common people combine to bring about linguistic changes, one is probably at the very heart of language. That the "pauvre" Lélian [Verlaine] heeded the voice of the people is to be expected; but the fact that the esoteric Mallarmé also did shows how basic this revolution was—one which has still not ceased in the French language. In the case of Verlaine, one might cite as an example his preference for repetition and for simple parataxis, which have, as we know, been used so triumphantly in the modern lyric (though with quite a different purpose); one might also cite his simplified use of the negative form, a device also found in intellectual poets like Mallarmé and Valéry; and one could mention his preference for simple pronouns in neuter form—perhaps "sans qui" instead of "sans lequel" [roughly, "without which" instead of "without that which"]. One might further call attention to the particular usage of "chose" ["thing"] which, in Verlaine, Rimbaud, and Mallarmé, took on such important and diverse functions.[8] Here only one instance can be followed up in detail: unquestionably a basic deficiency of French is that, with respect to interrogative pronouns, it possesses only one composite form—"qu'est-ce qui" [literally, "what is it that"]—for the neuter nominative (besides the elliptical "quoi" ["what"]), while it has at its disposal two forms—"qui" ["who"] and "qui est-ce qui" ["who is it that"]—for the personal pronoun. The cōndensed, tersely formulated "qui passe" has no counterpart in an equally terse "quoi passe." In "Dans l'interminable ennui de la plaine,"[9] Verlaine—like others before him—risks the formulation "Quoi donc vous arrive?" ["What is happening to you?"], where the elliptical and thoroughly conventional "Quoi donc?" [literally, "What then?"—the idiomatic equivalent of "What?"] is indeed brought into conjunction with a verb. The poet goes even further in "Charleroi."[10] From "Quoi donc se sent?" ["What is felt?"] he proceeds to "On sent donc quoi?" ["One feels then what?"], only to risk a further leap to "Quoi bruissait / Comme des sistres?" ["What was rattling / Like sistra?"]; and it is certainly no accident that, immediately preceding the uncannily terse "Quoi bruissait," he has placed the competing form "Qu'est-ce que c'est?" [the standard equivalent of "What is it?"], which takes up a whole line. In this context, both forms give the interrogative a new poetic life. In "Qu'est-ce que c'est" the thin hissing sound, incidental to the worn-out grammatical formula, develops into a suggestive onomatopoeia:

> Parfums sinistres!
> Qu'est-ce que c'est?

---

[8] In this connection one might consider the verses by Verlaine quoted on p. 267 of this essay, or call to mind Rimbaud's "Les Effarés," where the material world of baker and bread—so densely textured in contrast with the dreams engendered by the hunger of the starving and dispossessed—becomes almost immaterial and meaningless for the starving through its reduction in their dreams to a "chose," a mere featureless thing.

[9] *Romances sans paroles.*   [10] *Ibid.*

> Quoi bruissait
> Comme des sistres?
>
> *Sinister perfumes!*
> *What is it?*
> *What was rattling*
> *Like sistra?*

In the third line, Verlaine rejects the standard formula that has just been revitalized in favor of the more block-like, elemental "Quoi bruissait."

NOWHERE, however, can one see more penetratingly into a poet's workings with words, and thus into the very web of language, than in the case of Mallarmé. When he defined Symbolist technique as the foreshadowing of a poem and then continued, "C'est le parfait usage de ce mystère qui constitue le symbole," he summed up his entire artistic credo. To *seize* and *shape* the mystery in its *perfection*; the technique of the *arcane* with a constant view to perfection; *craftsmanship* within the realm of *magic*. It has been said that Mallarmé was a poet of few ideas. He was, in the sense that the troubadours were: to render a fundamental human tendency definitively in words seemed to him to require almost the expenditure of one's life. And since he could never be satisfied until he reached perfection according to his own definition, his poetic output was bound to remain very small.

What differentiates him profoundly from Verlaine is that Mallarmé takes liberties with normal discursive French only in order to commit himself all the more deeply to the language itself. His art of suggestiveness is the very opposite of vagueness. In his essay "Crise de vers," he speaks of the flight of song into the realm of unburdened joy, "joie allégée." "Cette visée—je la dis Transposition—Structure, une autre [This aim—I call it Transposition—Structure, a different one]."[11] So, despite a fundamentally Romantic disposition and an intense awareness of the individual's utter isolation, he turns into a Classicist through his unrelenting commitment to art. Transformation, translation into music, but also architecture, "structure"—these are what he requires of his art. No one ever struggled more unremittingly for the inner unity of the poetic line, not even the greatest Roman poets. It is no accident that these are the ones who come to mind when we think of Mallarmé. Roman verse, which excludes all purely connective elements; which deliberately cultivates a poetic language in contrast to the prosaic; which through its rhythm momentarily alienates words from their customary sound in common speech, only to let them fall back again, after this estrangement from themselves, into their usual sound as into something newly won; Roman verse, in which the words often accumulate a special charge after many pages; in which, especially in the case of Vergil, a particular tone is preserved and seeks to realize its possibilities again and again in the linguistic materials—all these are qualities germane to Mallarmé's art. Yet he writes in French—a language constantly muted by its silent "e" and nasal sounds; a language which requires a great deal of space

---

[11] *Divagations*, Paris, Bibliothèque Charpentier, 1897, p. 246.

simply for the mortar that cements the verbal units; a language, furthermore, which has reached a far higher degree of abstraction than did Latin.

How, then, could Mallarmé proceed? Generally, the normal logic of sentence structure is intentionally sacrificed for the sake of compression, of the unique and immutable shape of the poem. Inversion occurs on a scale perhaps never equaled in French. There are examples everywhere, and they are familiar to every reader of Mallarmé. Here it will suffice to give one extreme case, where a relative clause is placed in front of the word to which it refers:

> Mais chez qui du rêve se dore
> Tristement dort une mandore....
> ("Une dentelle s'abolit")
>
> *But a mandola in which dream is gilding itself*
> *Sleeps sadly....*

The relative clause beginning with "chez qui" (= "chez laquelle") depends on the "mandore" at the end of the subsequent line. Such procedures, above all others, make the deciphering of a text by Mallarmé one of the most difficult of philological tasks. What is in German a natural, spontaneous habit must here be exacted forcibly from French, a language which appears to resist such constructions to the utmost. Why does Mallarmé do it? In the first place, surely, to recreate the exact process of vision and to give the verse musical unity. But also to uproot the reader, as it were, from everyday language, to block his analytical tendencies, to fasten his attention initially on the reverberations emanating from the single word—in order to inhibit, one might be tempted to say, any kind of linear progression of thought. Thus one finds, surprisingly enough, that this poet is just as concerned with the reader as are the writers of rational French prose, who attend so closely to the psychology of their audience. But attention to the reader means something else in the realm of poetry than in that of prose: to start with, one must prepare the reader, attune him to poetry and block the expectations he brings from prose.

Furthermore, the very materials of the words are being tested, and they must prove indispensable. It may be no accident that Mallarmé so willingly replaces the bare article with weightier pronouns like "quelque," "tel," "quelconque," "aucun" ["some," "such," "whatever," "any"]—if indeed he does not suppress it altogether. The omission of the comparative particle "comme" ["as, like"] is frequent in Symbolist poetry, a preference which stems less from a desire for concentration than from an endeavor to let the things compared move toward each other in some new realm where the two dissolve into one or vie with each other as if they were two worlds of equal rank. The negative form, which falls into two parts ["ne ... pas," "ne ... plus," "ne ... point," and so on]—surely a weakness of French, and one which the people would certainly have abandoned long ago had it not been for the inhibiting influence of the grammarians—is reduced to a minimum, with the emphasis falling sometimes, in a scholarly, archaic fashion, on the "ne," and sometimes, in the fashion of the people, on the musically richer second element. Among negative forms,

THE POET AT WAR WITH HIS LANGUAGE [263]

Mallarmé prefers "rien," "aucun," and "nul" ["nothing," "none," "no, not any"] because of their fuller, more solid sound.

It has been rightly said that the quintessence of Mallarmé's art and being can easily be deduced from his use of negation, his verbal expression of "absence." But might one not go even further and remark how significant it is—and in line with the intrinsic character of language—that Mallarmé fixes precisely on the point where language itself becomes irresolute and does not appear to know what to do? Philological research has revealed how much interest lies in those areas where the pathological traits of language become noticeable and how creative such seats of disease can become. "Nur eine Sprache, die den Krebs hat, neigt zu Neubildungen [Only a language which has cancer is ready for new formations],"[12] says Karl Kraus, and Gilliéron might well have agreed. Mallarmé fixes on such a seat of disease and reveals in it the possibility for new vitality; he rejuvenates language through the revival of earlier linguistic conditions as often as through the creation of entirely new ones.

Indeed, Mallarmé will tolerate no words unless they are fully actualized. He places each one literally on the scales, that is, in the most sensitive position of the line. There is not one which could not serve as a rhyme-word or be placed before the caesura, if the need should arise—a fact which is not to be interpreted as a devaluation of the rhyme, but rather as a test by fire of the word itself. If he writes,

> O si chère de loin et proche et blanche, si
> Délicieusement toi, Méry, que je songe...
>
> *Oh, so dear from far away, so near, and so white, so*
> *Deliciously you, Méry, that I dream...*

the purely preparatory "si" [at the end of the first line] acquires as a rhyme the weight to balance the long adverb that follows, "Délicieusement" (which itself takes up a full half-line), and this acquired weight affects retroactively the "si" at the beginning of the first line. But, since the "Délicieusement" occupies metrically the first half of the alexandrine, one still cannot move ahead to the "toi" without a slight pause; here, too, an equilibrium with "toi" must first be attained. The flowing expression "si délicieusement toi" is divided by two caesuras in such a way that the three words, while they ascend logically to a climax, become isolated from one another and have to prove themselves separately. Or consider the stanza

> Le sceptre des rivages roses
> Stagnants sur les soirs d'or, ce l'est,
> Ce blanc vol fermé que tu poses
> Contre le feu d'un bracelet.
> ("Autre éventail de Mlle Mallarmé")
>
> *The scepter of rose-colored shores*
> *Stagnant on golden evenings, this is it,*

---

[12] *Sprüche und Widersprüche*, 1924, p. 187.

> *That white flight, folded, which you place*
> *Against the fire of a bracelet.*

From a logical point of view, the stanza is carried by the main clause, "ce l'est," which in its casual sound so unostentatiously supports the comparison of the two worlds, much as the axis of a scale supports the two pans which themselves claim all our attention. On the one side, shores lazily stretched out in a golden twilight with white birds; on the other side, the closed white fan beside the fiery diamonds of a bracelet. Now the main clause, "ce l'est," reappears in its *entirety* as a rhyme with the bare ending of "bracelet" ["–celet"—"ce l'est"] and gives the diminutive form of that word a wholly new weight. The main clause, on the other hand, appears even more as a mere point of suspension through being paralleled with the bare suffix of the diminutive: thus it becomes the precise representation of a bodiless midpoint.

It is well known that Mallarmé, in his ruthless suppression of connectives as forms lacking in substance, went so far as to reduce verbs to mere infinitives; that he showed a preference for participial constructions modeled on Latin; and that he preferred the *passé simple* to the imperfect tense simply because it possesses a much terser sound. To quote just one particularly daring example from "Hérodiade":

> ... Par quel attrait
> Menée et quel matin oublié des prophètes
> Verse, sur les lointains mourants, ses tristes fêtes,
> Le sais-je? ...

> ... *By what charm*
> *Drawn and what morning forgotten by the prophets*
> *Pours its sad festivities over dying distances,*
> *Do I know it?* ...

One might interpret "Par quel attrait / Menée" as a mere contraction of "Par quel attrait suis-je menée [By what charm am I drawn]," or perhaps more correctly as in fact an interrogative attribute that goes with the "je" at the end, despite its deceptive formal parallel with "quel matin oublié."

Less obvious than this device of compression, the difficulty of which strikes every reader, is another procedure of Mallarmé's, one which has proved especially important for the later poetic development of French. Mallarmé likes to accumulate whole colonies of words of a lesser order of concreteness:

> Avec comme pour langage...
>   ("Éventail de Mme Mallarmé")

> Haute à ne la pas toucher....
>   ("Petit Air I")

> *With as for language...*

> *Too high to touch....*

THE POET AT WAR WITH HIS LANGUAGE [265]

He separates prepositions from their substantives and places them next to similarly inferior verbal categories; adverbs he sets side by side with other expressions which anticipate or merely bind. The linguistic mortar is lifted out of language, as it were, and its own substance is put to the test. Mallarmé has created magnificently block-like lines which in their simplicity are reminiscent of Latin:

> Nuit, désespoir et pierrerie
>
> Calme bloc ici-bas chu d'un désastre obscur
>
> Magnifique, total et solitaire, tel
>
> Solitude, récif, étoile
>
> De ce blanc flamboiement l'immuable accalmie
>
> Rien, cette écume, vierge vers.
>
> *Night, despair, and polished stone*
>
> *Firm block, down here, fallen from a mysterious disaster*
>
> *Magnificent, total, and solitary, such*
>
> *Solitude, reef, star*
>
> *The never-changing lull of this white flare*
>
> *Nothing, this foam, virgin verse.*

More important, perhaps, from the point of view of linguistic innovation is the fact that Mallarmé endeavored to create self-contained poetic units precisely out of those elements which until his time had played an incidental and secondary role in French: to transform elements which had earlier been purely functional into the stuff of poetry, to crystallize them as moments in which the strange fusion of concepts still hangs in suspension and so attains a magical freedom. Such verbal deeds reveal a fundamental awareness that in matters of language there is no turning back but only a pushing forward, and that what might be called the thinning out of the French language—a development that seems so hostile to the quintessence of poetry—must *in itself* become the vehicle for new poetic creation. The further significance of this struggle, however, is that through Mallarmé's rooting of those elements in poetry—even if they are no longer used with the same daring by poets after him—the elements have been instilled with new life, and they cannot readily be detached again from their very base in language—no matter how weakly they may be employed.

This peculiar suspension of words—as if they were momentarily savoring their freedom before settling down into concepts—is also effected by Mallarmé's dissolving of the boundaries between verbal categories. In the line "Le vierge, le vivace et le bel aujourd'hui [The fresh, the vivacious, the beautiful today]," it becomes clear only with the third adjective ["bel"] that it has been a question of adjectives all along;

words [such as "vierge" or "vivace," which at first sight may be read as nouns or adjectives] are allowed initially to reverberate for a while in their most fundamental meaning. We are familiar with this pre-positioning of the adjective from German, where it is the rule and can hardly be avoided unless the adjective is placed after the noun and the article repeated, a process which intensifies the adjective.[13] French, however, recognizes a distinction between the subjectively applied adjective placed before the noun and the objectively applied adjective placed after the noun. With the Symbolists, the use of the subjective adjective placed before the noun has gained such supremacy that examples are superfluous. And it is only the natural, almost inevitable consequence of a technique which allows transposition that those words which normally precede the noun in colloquial speech are now suddenly tested through being placed in isolation after the words to which they relate. Or let us consider that fluctuation—deliberately sought by Mallarmé—of the concept between adjectival and adverbial colorings, whose clear distinction had been the very ground for praising French clarity. Mallarmé entitled one sequence of his poems *Chansons bas* [Soft Songs], an abbreviation of *Airs chantés à voix basse* [Airs Sung in a Soft Voice]. By virtue of its isolation, the adverb [bas] is fundamentally enriched, while the substantive power of "chanson" is weakened: indeed, classifying these words in grammatical categories is almost absurd. Or let us look again at the line

> O si chère de loin et proche et blanche, si ....
> *Oh, so dear from far away, so near, and so white, so ....*

The "de loin" is adverbial, yet bound by antithesis to the adjective "proche," with the result that the words contaminate each other, as it were. The adverb, especially since outnumbered by the adjectives "proche" and "blanche" (which are themselves strengthened through consonance), becomes suddenly adjectival in color. Generally, Mallarmé appears to have a special preference for the adverb. Other modern poets, even prose writers, have tried to replace it whenever possible by the non-derivative and so more directly effective adjective. Mallarmé, however, who does not, more or less hypocritically, pretend to avoid all that is intellectual when he writes poetry, again and again places the adverb—which answers so well to the Symbolist demand for the "nuance"—at decisive places in his lines; he glorifies the adverb and validates it poetically.

---

[13] One might recall the frequent use of this verbal possibility by Hölderlin, or consider the following four-line poem by Goethe:

> Alles geben die Götter, die unendlichen   *All things do the gods, the infinite ones, give*
> Ihren Lieblingen ganz;   *To their favorites, entirely;*
> Alle Freuden, die unendlichen,   *All joys, the infinite ones,*
> Alle Schmerzen, die unendlichen ganz.   *All sorrows, the infinite ones, entirely.*

Here the adjective is placed behind the substantive. Does it thereby become objective [and more factual, as does the French adjective in this position]? Yes and no. For the accompanying article converts the adjective into a substantive again. And what about the final "ganz": who would dare to categorize it grammatically? These lines are wonderfully exemplary of the highest form of objectivity which can be reached in German poetry: each one of the words is restored to its primal root form.

THE POET AT WAR WITH HIS LANGUAGE

One more fundamental quality of French which has been subjected to the strictest examination by Mallarmé is the brevity of its words. If French were not built out of such firmly welded groups of words, its overabundance of monosyllabic words might well give it a "hopping" rhythm. A poet who, like Mallarmé, focuses so strongly on the word itself was bound to become more sharply aware of this quality than, say, a Lamartine, who composed in what might be called *torrents* of words (the expression is not used pejoratively here). It appears that Mallarmé has quite consciously juxtaposed long and short words to play them against one another. Of course, one can see other poets exploiting this contrast. La Fontaine, for instance, handled it masterfully, and, to stay within the context of our present discussion, we may refer to a section from Verlaine's "A la promenade":

> Et les amants lutinent les amantes,
>
> De qui la main imperceptible sait
> Parfois donner un soufflet, qu'on échange
> Contre un baiser sur l'extrême phalange
> Du petit doigt, et comme la chose est
>
> Immensément excessive et farouche,
> On est puni par un regard très sec , ...
> *(Fêtes galantes)*
>
> *And the lovers torment their ladies,*
>
> *Whose tiny hand can*
> *Occasionally give a slap, which one exchanges*
> *For a kiss on the extreme phalanx*
> *Of the little finger, and since the affair is*
>
> *Immensely intemperate and fierce,*
> *One is punished by a very dry look . . . .*

Here quite obviously an ironic effect is sought through the contention between short and long, whereas this technique in the hands of Mallarme is no longer so much tied to the representation of objects as it is assimilated in his word alchemy. The first line of

> Magnifique, total et solitaire, tel
> Tremble de s'exhaler . . .
> ("Toast funèbre")
>
> *Magnificent, total, and solitary, such*
> *Trembles to express itself . . .*

comes to life formally in the counterpoint of short and long; and what is extraordinary here, and typical of Mallarmé, is the way in which the pallid "tel"—a word so loved by Mallarmé and again established in its full dignity here—seems to develop before our very ears. All the sounds in "tel" are rehearsed in the preceding words: the "t" three times, the last before an open "ε," as in "tel"; the "l" twice; and the open "ε" in closest proximity to "tel." In this way the concluding "tel" is a summary even in sound of what has gone before; and since it has been thus derived, abstracted, from more full-bodied words, the original abstractness of "tel" has been overcome, the word has become poetically fruitful, so that in its achieved fullness it hovers over the end of the line, to be echoed in the subsequent alliteration:

> ... tel
> Tremble de s'exhaler ....

Other examples would be

> Indomptablement a dû
> ("Petit Air II")
> *Inexorably was bound to*

where consonance of sounds provides a harmonious countermovement to the deliberate imbalance arising from the juxtaposition of long and short words. Or, similarly,

> Victorieusement fui le suicide beau
> *Victoriously fled the handsome suicide*

or

> O si chère de loin et proche et blanche, si
> Délicieusement toi, Méry, que je songe ....

In "Petit Air I," the contrast between long and short words becomes the real theme:

> Quelconque une solitude
> Sans le cygne ni le quai
> Mire sa désuétude
> Au regard que j'abdiquai
>
> Ici de la gloriole
> Haute à ne la pas toucher
> Dont maint ciel se bariole
> Avec les ors de coucher
>
> Mais langoureusement longe
> Comme de blanc linge ôté
> Tel fugace oiseau si plonge
> Exultatrice à côté
>
> Dans l'onde toi devenue
> Ta jubilation nue.
>
> *Just some solitude*
> *Without the swan or the quay*

> *Reflects its disuse*
> *In the look that I have withdrawn*
>
> *Here from vainglory*
> *Too high to touch*
> *By which many a sky gaudily decks itself*
> *With the golds of sunset*
>
> *But langorously coasts*
> *Like white linen discarded*
> *Such a fugitive bird: so plunges*
> *Exulting alongside*
>
> *Into the billow become you*
> *Your naked jubilation.*

"Quelconque une solitude"—broadly drawn out solitude, a phrase where the indefinite article "une" must lose, through "quelconque" [that is, "whatsoever"], all capacity to single out (if one does not want to assign "une" the root sense of "solitary," "alone")—is contrasted with "Sans le cygne ni le quai," where only short words are used to paint this "solitude" (typical here is the definite article ["le"], which is intended not to generalize but to circumscribe and define, becoming almost a demonstrative). The long rhyme-word in "Mire sa désuétude," on the other hand, recreates the atmosphere of the first line. Or, later, "Ici de la gloriole / Haute à ne la pas toucher," in which the unusual word order of "à ne la pas toucher"—with its accumulation of slighter words in the middle of the line—thrusts apart the "haute" and "toucher" to the ends of the line, where their distance from each other renders the unbridgeable gulf between the concepts. Or the third stanza, which appears so top-heavy as to plunge forward, an impression created as much through the tension between very long and very short words as through the paradoxical "plonge / Exultatrice." The last stanza remains true to this pervasive formal leitmotif: "Ta jubilation nue" renders it with unexcelled clarity.

However, what Mallarmé has attempted to do here with the smallest still-meaningful unit of language, the word, he attempts also with the smallest rhythmic unit of the poem, the line. After all, word and line were completely analogous for him, as he suggests in "Crise de vers": "Le vers qui de plusieurs vocables refait un mot total, neuf, étranger à la langue [The line which, out of several small words, fashions one complete word, new, a stranger to the language]."[14] The alternation of long and short words might correspond, in the realm of pure verse, to the technique in which the poet alternates extremely compressed and abbreviated lines with extremely long, relaxed, and flowing ones. In "L'Après-midi d'un faune" we encounter a line concerning which tastes may differ,

> Mais, bast! arcane tel élut pour confident
> *But hush! such mystery chose for confidant*

---

[14] *Divagations*, p. 251.

whose sharp contours are played against

> Le jonc vaste et jumeau dont sous l'azur on joue.
> *The reed, large and double, on which one plays beneath the blue.*

Each of these lines heightens the effect of the other: the sharp contours of the one set off the suppleness and the many connectives of the other, while the more flexible second line serves as a foil to the hard outlines, the absence of particles, in the first.

Here we encounter a phenomenon which, far more than others, testifies to the greatness of Mallarmé: his awareness of the basic unity of the single line. This unity fascinates the reader, often long before he has completely understood the sense of a poem, and it provokes him to solve the riddle underlying such artistry. Characteristic, for example, is Mallarmé's use of repetition, which appears in Verlaine's poetry strictly for the sake of its entertaining or lulling effect. Not so with Mallarmé: here repetition is severely architectural. In

> La tienne si toujours le délice! la tienne
> Oui seule...
> ("Victorieusement fui")
>
> *Yours so always the delight! yours*
> *Yes alone...*

the line is framed by the repeated "la tienne," an effect underlined by the intensifying "Oui." In

> Qui cherche, parcourant le solitaire bond
> Tantôt extérieur de notre vagabond—
> Verlaine? Il est caché parmi l'herbe, Verlaine...
> ("Tombeau")
>
> *Who seeks, in following the solitary bound*
> *Just a while ago external to our vagabond—*
> *Verlaine? He is hidden amidst the grass, Verlaine...*

the repetition [of "Verlaine"] is anticipated by the assonance in "herbe," and the last line, as a leap from the "Verlaine" at the beginning to the "Verlaine" at the end, reflects the leap in the rhyme of the preceding lines from "bond" to "vagabond"—incidentally, a very convincing popular etymology.

Other verses gain their unity from what might be called linking through sound:

> ...Des ondes
> Se bercent et, là-bas, sais-tu pas un pays....
> ("Hérodiade")
>
> *...Waves*
> *Rock each other gently and, down there, don't you know a land....*

The "bercent" connects with "bas," the latter with "pas," and this in turn with "pays," while each half-line begins with "s." Or let us look at the famous line

>Aboli bibelot d'inanité sonore . . . .
>("Ses purs ongles")
>*Abolished bibelot of resounding inanity . . . .*

The theme is given in the first half-line, whose content is then evaluated—in fact, devaluated—by a word which seems happily formed to do just that, "inanité," and then the whole is raised to a more poetic level through "sonore," a word in which the important sounds of the theme ["Aboli bibelot"] ring out, just as the less important sounds are repeated in "inanité."

Given Mallarmé's sensitivity to the unity of the line, he could never use enjambement to weaken that unity. After all, if the end of a line does not coincide with a natural breathing space and yet the poet requires us to stop, the result is a painful tension which impresses itself much more strongly on the reader's feeling than would a sheerly logical pause. An examination of Mallarmé's enjambement reveals his artistry in the clearest light. A few examples will suffice here. From "L'Après-midi d'un faune,"

>Et soufflant dans ses peaux lumineuses, avide
>D'ivresse . . .
>*And breathing into their luminous skins, greedy*
>*With drunkenness . . .*

where the enjambement is a virtual representation of greediness. Similarly, in the following lines from "Hérodiade," the love for life with all its accumulated tension finds its musical counterpart in

>J'aime l'horreur d'être vierge et je veux
>Vivre . . . .
>*I love the horror of being a virgin and I want*
>*To live . . . .*

A particularly artful irregularity shapes the beginning of "L'Après-midi d'un faune":

>Ces nymphes, je les veux perpétuer.
>   Si clair,
>Leur incarnat léger, qu'il voltige dans l'air
>Assoupi de sommeils touffus.
>
>*These nymphs, I want to perpetuate them.*
>   *So bright,*
>*Their light pink, that it floats in the air*
>*Drowsy with tufts of sleep.*

The first line is a false alexandrine insofar as "Si clair," as the typography indicates, belongs formally to what follows. But internally, "Ces nymphes, je les veux perpétuer" is not fragmentary. The blank space after "perpétuer" is completely filled out with the vibrations of the word's meaning, and the shortened half of the line thus preserves, as if carved in stone, a promise of perpetuity. On the other hand, the "Si clair" emerges from an impressionistically woven background like an arabesque, a fragment, and retains this quality in the structure of the sentence as a whole. Especially striking, however, is the unique caesura in the first line:

> Ces nymphes, je les veux / perpétuer.

"Ces nymphes, je les veux" is *one* theme of the poem, the faun's desire for sensual life; "je les veux perpétuer," the transformation of the living into lasting song, is the *other* theme. Thus the caesura is used to anticipate very clearly the two developments that emerge in the poem.[15]

So much for the analysis of particular examples, which in the present context can do no more than stimulate the reader to make further observations himself; now let us try to describe what promises truly to endure in Mallarmé's verbal art. If he has been chided for writing a kind of Super-German in French,[16] the reproach may often be justified in the case of his prose (which there are good grounds for considering a blind alley), but not of his poetry. In essential matters, his linguistic revolution does not run counter to the fundamental character of French; on the contrary, it brings that character boldly into the foreground. He does not have the audacity of certain modern poets, who believe that French poetry can be infused with new blood simply by an unlimited increase in its vocabulary. His art is of the Classical kind in that it attempts "de faire quelque chose de rien [to make something of nothing]," seeks to make maximum use of the wonderful capacity of French to combine diverse elements and thus to thrive on the juggling about of relatively few. His art is similarly Classical in that it does not disavow the strongly rational, abstract character of the French language, but rather uses it poetically. To be sure, he always loves rare words and will even coin them if an emergency arises, yet he uses them sparingly. And he also loves to let the abstract and the concrete flow into each other. Examples can be found at every point, which is of course not accidental but profoundly expressive of Mallarmé's art. He has said of the word, "Je dis: une fleur! et, hors de l'oubli où ma voix relègue aucun contour ... musicalement se lève, idée même et suave, l'absente de tous bouquets! [I say, 'a flower!' and beyond the oblivion to which my voice relegates any firm meaning... there arises musically the idea [of a flower], convincing and sweet, the one which is absent from all bouquets!]."[17] The word "flower"—music,

---

[15] While Albert Thibaudet stresses mainly the impressionistic freshness of this line (*La Poésie de Stéphane Mallarmé*, Éditions de la Nouvelle Revue Française [Paris, 1926], pp. 51 ff.), Ferdinand Lion points out that this ambiguous rhythm mirrors the two tendencies evident in painting during Mallarmé's time. "Ces nymphes, je les veux" would correspond with the attitude of the Impressionists; "je les veux perpétuer," on the other hand, with the reaction of Cézanne.

[16] Thibaudet, *op. cit.*, p. 326.   [17] *Divagations*, p. 251.

idea, and a reality at the farthest remove from the familiar world—here we are in that realm where Mallarmé composes his poems, where words are not the signs of some external reality but make up a transcendent world, one in which the words are abstract, detached, withdrawn from things, yet, as words, become things: namely, sounding, sensuous ideas. It is clear that a fragmented language like French—grafted as it is on a Celtic and Germanic nature—must have proved an especially appropriate vehicle for someone with Mallarmé's perspective and linguistic consciousness. If Classical writers have converted the limitations of a rigid word order into the virtue of clarity, so Mallarmé has transformed the especially abstract character of French into a virtue, creating from it an absolute poetry in which words take on substance. Indeed, one can go even further: precisely *because* French had become a language so dissociated from the poetic, it was destined to root itself newly in the poetic. For only if its basis in Nature seems lost will the spirit set out to find Nature again. Only when language lets the poet starve will he search out its most hidden nourishment at the risk of, indeed for the sake of, his life. Thus it is no accident that Mallarmé has influenced poets far beyond his own country to reconsider the essence of the poetic. Yet the greatest service he performed was for his own language, and this in two ways.

Not only did he give France his poems but he formed a school in the only way that one should—not to train blind imitators, but to teach human beings to discover their individual selves. Indeed, Mallarmé's art cannot be imitated at all, for it would become counterfeit if it were not informed by his particular intensity. And if another poet *did* possess a comparable intensity, then he would necessarily find his own style, one different from Mallarmé's. His closest follower is probably Paul Valéry, mathematician and philosopher, who drew on those traits of Symbolism which are the most unambiguously Classical. Indirectly, almost all contemporary French lyric poets are indebted to Mallarmé, even those who appear to differ from him profoundly. For if they have been able to write a more spontaneous, more natural poetry, it is in part because he opened the way for them. Even when the modern poet seeks a very simple, almost prosaic tone, he does it far less in imitation of Verlaine's song than on account of that spontaneity restored to language by Mallarmé, a spontaneity which has, nonetheless, been validated by the intellect. This must be emphasized: it is necessary again and again for men to push forward to the extreme limits of the possible—whether in action, thought, or artistic creation—in order thus to engender a golden mean which can serve as a basis for new creation. Our own time shows this with utter clarity in all the arts. There is a type of artist who sacrifices himself to open the way for his spiritual descendants. Mallarmé would have been untrue to his daimon, the spirit of relentless introspection, if he had not fully recognized the dangers of his chosen path. His letter to François Coppée is a relevant document in this connection:

> Pour moi voici deux ans que j'ai commis le péché de voir le Rêve dans sa nudité idéale, tandis que je devais amonceler entre lui et moi un mystère de musique et d'oubli. Et maintenant arrivé à la vision horrible d'une œuvre pure, j'ai presque perdu la raison et le sens des paroles les plus familières.

As for me, I have for two years committed the sin of gazing at the Dream in its ideal nakedness, while I ought to have gathered a mystery of music and oblivion between it and me. And now, having arrived at the terrifying vision of a pure work, I have almost lost reason and the sense of the most familiar words.

These words of the poet ought to warn us against belittling Mallarmé's artistic intent. He spoke the words about a body of work that remained small, work that grew out of unimaginable conflict and lay constantly under the threat of the poet's becoming unproductive. And we, whether we approve his art or not, are his beneficiaries. We live at a time when the French language is again capable of becoming poetry, and when poetry does not conflict with the spirit of the language but only with the routine use of the language. Perhaps Mallarmé's poetry will always remain of interest to only a few, as is usually the case with the greatest lyrics. But its power to unlock language reaches out into the future, and above all it may provide the student of grammar with essential and unique insights into the basic character of French and of language itself. That Mallarmé's poetry remains so hermetic is understandable. For the lyric is the most individual, most personal of all literary forms. French, however, is in its ordinary form a language wonderfully suited to communication. Thus the somewhat asocial lyric stands out more strongly in French than it does in German, for instance, where the verbal medium is in general asocial [oriented toward expression rather than communication]. The "Odi profanum vulgus et arceo [I hate the profane crowd and shy away]" applies with full force to Mallarmé, as it applied, after all, to the "trobar clus [hermetic poet]" of the troubadours. (But are we so sure that the German language is not similarly a matter for only a few initiates, at least in its most purely structured *prose* sentences?)

However this may be, it is of great importance, precisely for a person whose native language is German, to study the linguistic endeavors of a poet like Mallarmé. For we are all too easily taken in by the appearance of naturalness and simplicity. And we believe all too readily that artistic enjoyment is purest when it is most easily come by. There is no more rare, no more difficult miracle than simplicity, and nothing in our language has been more often merely simulated. Rarely, however, will the miracle of simplicity be experienced in a more unsettling manner than in certain verses by Mallarmé, which—after all his toil of condensation, compression, and suppression—yield up to us a "song . . . of obliviousness to troubles, coexisting with utter awareness."

*The First Paragraph
of* The Ambassadors:
An Explication

❧ IAN WATT ☙

Ian Watt's *The Rise of the Novel: Studies in Defoe, Richardson and Fielding* (1957)—which so deftly blends critical analysis and social history with an awareness of the novel's development as a genre—is unquestionably one of the most important books on fiction to appear within recent years. And the frequent reprinting, since its first publication in 1960, of the following essay on James suggests that it is of comparable quality. Although Watt's subtitle characterizes his essay as an "explication," his analysis of the first paragraph in *The Ambassadors* is rooted in a discriminating examination of James's style.

Indeed, after differentiating at the start of his article between the traditions of *explication de texte*, "Practical Criticism" as fostered by I. A. Richards, and *Stilforschung*, Watt declares that he himself aims at a mode of explication which "will lead one from the words on the page to matters as low as syntax and as high as ... the total literary structure"—levels of analysis, he suggests, on which explication as it is ordinarily practiced does not proceed. The essay reveals how handsomely he succeeds in his aim. Watt relates such verbal features of the paragraph as the "preference for non-transitive verbs," the "many abstract nouns," and the frequent use of "that" to James's desire to present the operations of Strether's mind from the broader perspective of a narrator who may help us to focus on them, to James's interest in portraying a reality fraught with a "multiplicity of relations," and thus to his concern with developing a "narrative point of view" that is at once "both intensely individual and yet ultimately social."

On the basis of his stylistic analysis, Watt goes on to show how the first paragraph specifically articulates the themes of *The Ambassadors* and how it typifies James's general methods as a novelist. Especially enlightening is Watt's insistence on the mixture of humor and compassion with which James represents Strether's situation—a mixture rendered in the very arrangement of the sentences within the paragraph and in the running "counterpoint of intelligence and bewilderment." Throughout the essay Watt remains intensely conscious of the ways in which James's style works on the reader, whether in commenting on the author's placing of Strether as a character for us—"One reason for the special demand James's fictional prose makes on our attention is surely that there are always at least three levels of development—all of them subjective: the characters' awareness of events; the narrator's seeing of them; and our own trailing perception of the relation between these two"—or in describing the rhetoric which energizes the final sentence in James's paragraph, the suspended structure that dramatizes the "echoing doom started by the connotation of 'apprehension'" and the climactic positioning of "throughout," which endows the word with a "mockingly fateful emphasis" for the audience.

WHEN I WAS ASKED if I would do a piece of explication at this conference, I was deep in Henry James, and beginning *The Ambassadors*: so the passage chose itself; but just what was explication, and how did one do it to prose? I take it that whereas explanation, from *explanare*, suggests a mere making plain by spreading out, explication, from *explicare*, implies a progressive unfolding of a series of literary implications, and thus partakes of our modern preference for multiplicity in method

---

"The First Paragraph of *The Ambassadors*: An Explication," by Ian Watt, is reprinted by permission from *Essays in Criticism*, X (1960), 250–74. The author's note appended to the essay on its first appearance reads: "A paper given at the Ninth Annual Conference of Non-Professorial University Teachers of English, at Oxford on April 5th, 1959. I am grateful for the many criticisms and suggestions made in the course of the subsequent discussion; in preparing the paper for publication I have taken as much account of them as was possible, short of drastic expansion or alteration. I also acknowledge my debt to Dorothea Krook, Frederick C. Crews, and Henry Nash Smith."

and meaning: explanation assumes an ultimate simplicity, explication assumes complexity.

Historically, the most systematic tradition of explication is presumably that which developed out of medieval textual exegesis and became the chief method of literary instruction in French secondary and higher education in the late nineteenth century. *Explication de texte* in France reflects the rationalism of nineteenth-century Positivist scholarship. At its worst the routine application of the method resembles a sort of bayonet drill in which the exposed body of literature is riddled with etymologies and dates before being despatched in a harrowingly insensitive *résumé*. At its best, however, *explication de texte* can be solidly illuminating, and it then serves to remind us that a piece of literature is not necessarily violated if we give systematic attention to such matters as its author, its historical setting, and the formal properties of its language.

Practical Criticism, on the other hand, as it was developed at Cambridge by I. A. Richards, continues the tradition of the British Empiricists. Inductive rather than deductive, it makes a point of excluding linguistic and historical considerations, so as to derive—in appearance at least—all the literary values of a work empirically from the words on the page. In the last thirty years the emphasis of Practical Criticism on the autonomy of the text has revolutionised the approach to literary studies, and has proved itself a technique of supreme value for teaching and examining students; I myself certainly believe that its use should be expanded rather than curtailed. Yet, at least in the form in which I picked it up as a student and have later attempted to pass it on as a teacher, both its pedagogical effects and its basic methodological assumptions seem to me to be open to serious question. For many reasons. Its air of objectivity confers a spurious authority on a process that is often only a rationalisation of an unexamined judgment, and that must always be to some extent subjective; its exclusion of historical factors seems to authorise a more general anti-historicism; and—though this objection is perhaps less generally accepted—it contains an inherent critical bias in the assumption that the part is a complete enough reflection of the literary whole to be profitably appreciated and discussed in isolation from its context. How far this is true, or how far it can be made to appear so by a well-primed practitioner, is a matter of opinion; but it is surely demonstrable that Practical Criticism tends to find the most merit in the kind of writing which has virtues that are in some way separable from their larger context; it favours kinds of writing that are richly concrete in themselves, stylistically brilliant, or composed in relatively small units. It is therefore better suited to verse than to prose; and better suited to certain kinds of either than to others where different and less concentrated merits are appropriate, as in the novel.

As for its pedagogical effects—and here again I have mainly my own past experience in mind—Practical Criticism surely tends to sensitise us towards objects only within a certain range of magnitude: below that threshold it becomes subjective and impressionist, paying very little attention to the humble facts of the grammar and syntax of the words on the page; while, at the other extreme, it often ignores the larger meaning, and the literary and historical contexts of that meaning.

As a practical matter these restrictions may all be necessary for the pupil and salutary for the teacher; and I mention them mainly to justify my present attempt to develop the empirical and inductive methods of Practical Criticism in such a way as to deal with those elements in a literary text whose vibrations are so high or so low that we Ricardian dogs have not yet been trained to bark at them.

It is mainly in these penumbral areas, of course, that the French *explication de texte* habitually operates; but its analyses of grammar and of the literary and historical background are usually a disconnected series of discrete demonstrations which stop short of the unifying critical synthesis that one hopes for. Until fairly recently the same could have been said, and perhaps with greater emphasis, about the German tradition of literary scholarship, with its almost entirely independent pursuit of philology and philosophy. More recent trends in *Stilforschung* however—of which Wolfgang Clemen's *The Development of Shakespeare's Imagery* (Bonn, 1936), was an early example—come closer to, and indeed partly reflect, the more empirical Anglo-American models of literary criticism; while, even more promising perhaps for the study of prose, though seemingly quite independent of the influence of Practical Criticism, is the development, mainly from Romance philology, of what has come to be called "stylistics."

For my purposes, however, it remains not so much a method as a small group of isolated, though spectacular, individual triumphs. I yield to no one in my admiration for Leo Spitzer's *Linguistics and Literary History* (Baltimore, 1948), or for the continual excitement and illumination offered in Erich Auerbach's *Mimesis* (1946: trans. Willard Trask, Princeton, N.J., 1953); their achievements, however, strike me mainly as tributes to the historical imagination and philosophical understanding of the German mind at its best; I find their brilliant commentaries on words or phrases or passages essentially subjective; and if I am tempted to emulate the *bravura* with which they take off from the word on the page to leap into the farthest empyreans of *Kulturgeschichte*, I soon discover that the Cambridge east winds have condemned me to less giddy modes of critical transport.

Yet what other models are there to help one to analyse a paragraph of Jamesian prose? Some of the historical studies of prose style could, conceivably, be applied; but I am fearful of ending up with the proposition that James was a Ciceronian—with Senecan elements, of course, like everyone else. As for the new linguistics, the promises as regards literary analysis seem greater than the present rewards: the most practical consequence of my exposure to Charles Fries's *The Structure of English: An Introduction to the Construction of English Sentences* (New York, 1952), for example, was to deprive me of the innocent pleasure that comes from imagining you know the names of things. Structural linguistics in general is mainly (and rightly) concerned with problems of definition and description at a considerably more basic level of linguistic usage than the analysis of the literary effect of Henry James's grammatical particularities seems to require.

Perhaps the most promising signs of the gaps being filled have come from what are—in that particular area—amateurs: from Francis Berry's *Poets' Grammar* (London, 1958), or Donald Davie's *Articulate Energy* (London, 1955). But they don't help much with prose, of course, and they aren't basically concerned with grammatical structure in the ordinary sense; although Davie's notion that the principle of continuity in poetry is, after all, primarily grammatical and rational, at least lessens the separation between the stylistic domains of poetry and prose, and suggests some ways of studying how syntax channels expressive force.

Virtually helpless,[1] then, I must face the James passage alone as far as any fully developed and acceptable technique for explicating prose is concerned; but there seem to be good reasons why Practical Criticism should be supplemented by some of the approaches of French and German scholarship, and by whatever else will lead one from the words on the page to matters as low as syntax and as high as ideas, or the total literary structure.

> Strether's first question, when he reached the hotel, was about his friend; yet on his learning that Waymarsh was apparently not to arrive till evening he was not wholly disconcerted. A telegram from him bespeaking a room "only if not noisy," reply paid, was produced for the inquirer at the office, so that the understanding they should meet at Chester rather than at Liverpool remained to that extent sound. The same secret principle, however, that had prompted Strether not absolutely to desire Waymarsh's presence at the dock, that had led him thus to postpone for a few hours his enjoyment of it, now operated to make him feel he could still wait without disappointment. They would dine together at the worst, and, with all respect to dear old Waymarsh—if not even, for that matter, to himself—there was little fear that in the sequel they shouldn't see enough of each other. The principle I have just mentioned as operating had been, with the most newly disembarked of the two men, wholly instinctive—the fruit of a sharp sense that, delightful as it would be to find himself looking, after so much separation, into his comrade's face, his business would be a trifle bungled should he simply arrange for this countenance to present itself to the nearing steamer as the first "note" of Europe. Mixed with everything was the apprehension, already, on Strether's part, that it would, at best, throughout, prove the note of Europe in quite a sufficient degree.[2]

---

[1] This was before the appearance of the English Institute's symposium *Style in Prose Fiction* (New York, 1959), which offers, besides two general surveys and a valuable bibliography of the field, stylistic studies of six novelists, including one by Charles R. Crow, of "The Style of Henry James: *The Wings of the Dove*."

[2] Henry James, *The Ambassadors* (Revised Collected Edition, Macmillan, London, 1923). Since there are a few variants that have a bearing on the argument, it seems desirable to give a collation of the main editions; P is the periodical publication (*The North American Review*, CLXXVI, 1903); 1A the first American edition (Harper and Brothers, New York, 1903); 1E the first English edition (Methuen and Co., London, 1903); NY the "New York Edition," New York and London, 1907–1909 (the London Macmillan edition used the sheets of the American edition); CR the "Collected Revised Edition," London and New York, 1921–1931 (which uses the text of the New York Edition). It should perhaps be explained that the most widely used editions in England and America make misleading claims about their text: the "Everyman" edition

It seems a fairly ordinary sort of prose, but for its faint air of elaborate portent; and on second reading its general quality reminds one of what Strether is later to observe —approvingly—in Maria Gostrey: an effect of "expensive, subdued suitability." There's certainly nothing particularly striking in the diction or syntax; none of the immediate drama or rich description that we often get at the beginning of novels; and certainly none of the sensuous concreteness that, until recently, was regarded as a chief criterion of good prose in our long post-imagistic phase: if anything, the passage is conspicuously un-sensuous and un-concrete, a little dull perhaps, and certainly not easy reading.

The difficulty isn't one of particularly long or complicated sentences: actually they're of fairly usual length: I make it an average of 41 words; a little, but not very much, longer than James's average of 35 (in Book 2, ch. 2 of *The Ambassadors*, according to R. W. Short's count, in his very useful article "The Sentence Structure of Henry James," *American Literature*, XVIII [March 1946], 71–88).[3] The main cause of difficulty seems rather to come from what may be called the delayed specification of referents: "Strether" and "the hotel" and "his friend" are mentioned before we are told who or where they are. But this difficulty is so intimately connected with James's general narrative technique that it may be better to begin with purely verbal idiosyncrasies, which are more easily isolated. The most distinctive ones in the passage seem to be these: a preference for non-transitive verbs; many abstract nouns; much use of "that"; a certain amount of elegant variation to avoid piling up personal pronouns and adjectives such as "he," "his" and "him"; and the presence of a great many negatives and near-negatives.

By the preference for non-transitive verbs I mean three related habits: a great reliance on copulatives—"Strether's first question ... *was* about his friend"; "*was* apparently not to arrive": a frequent use of the passive voice—"*was* not wholly *disconcerted*"; "a telegram ... *was produced*"; "his business *would be* a trifle *bungled*": and the employment of many intransitive verbs—"the understanding ... remained ... sound"; "the ... principle ... operated to." My count of all the verbs in the indicative would give a total of 14 passive, copulative or intransitive uses as opposed to only 6 transitive ones: and there are in addition frequent infinitive, participial, or gerundial uses of transitive verbs, in all of which the active nature of the subject-

---

claims to use the text "of the revised Collected Edition," but actually follows the first English edition in the last variant; while the "Anchor" edition, claiming to be "a faithful copy of the text of the Methuen first edition," actually follows the first American edition, including the famous misplaced chapters.

l. 5.   *reply paid* NY, CR; *with the answer paid* P, 1A, 1E.
l. 5.   *inquirer* P, 1A, 1E, CR; *enquirer* NY.
l. 6.   *understanding they* NY, CR; *understanding that they* P, 1A, 1E.
l. 12. *feel he* NY, CR; *feel that he* P, 1A, 1E.
l. 15. *shouldn't* CR; *should n't* NY; *should not* P, 1A, 1E.
ll. 17–18. *newly disembarked* all eds. except P: *newly-disembarked*.
l. 22. *arrange for this countenance to present* NY, CR; *arrange that this countenance should present* P, 1A, 1E.
l. 23. "*note*" *of Europe* CR; "*note*," *for him, of Europe* P, 1A, 1E; "*note*," *of Europe* NY.
l. 25. *that it would* P, 1A, NY, CR; *that he would* 1E.

[3] I am also indebted to the same author's "Henry James's World of Images," *PMLA*, LXVIII (December 1953), 943–60.

verb-and-object sequence is considerably abated—"on his learning"; "bespeaking a room"; "not absolutely to desire"; "led him thus to postpone."

This relative infrequency of transitive verbal usages in the passage is associated with the even more pronounced tendency towards using abstract nouns as subjects of main or subordinate clauses: "question"; "understanding"; "the same secret principle"; "the principle"; "his business." If one takes only the main clauses, there are four such abstract nouns as subjects, while only three main clauses have concrete and particular subjects ("he," or "they").[4]

I detail these features only to establish that in this passage, at least, there is a clear quantitative basis for the common enough view that James's late prose style is characteristically abstract; more explicitly, that the main grammatical subjects are very often nouns for mental ideas, "question," "principle," etc.; and that the verbs—because they are mainly used either non-transitively, or in infinitive, participial and gerundial forms—tend to express states of being rather than particular finite actions affecting objects.

The main use of abstractions is to deal at the same time with many objects or events rather than single and particular ones: and we use verbs that denote states of being rather than actions for exactly the same reason—their much more general applicability. But in this passage, of course, James isn't in the ordinary sense making abstract or general statements; it's narrative, not expository prose; what need exploring, therefore, are the particular literary imperatives which impose on his style so many of the verbal and syntactical qualities of abstract and general discourse; of expository rather than narrative prose.

Consider the first sentence. The obvious narrative way of making things particular and concrete would presumably be "When Strether reached the hotel, he first asked 'Has Mr. Waymarsh arrived yet?'" Why does James say it the way he does? One effect is surely that, instead of a sheer stated event, we get a very special view of it; the mere fact that actuality has been digested into reported speech—the question "was about his friend"—involves a narrator to do the job, to interpret the action, and also a presumed audience that he does it for: and by implication, the heat of the action itself must have cooled off somewhat for the translation and analysis of the events into this form of statement to have had time to occur. Lastly, making the subject of the sentence "question" rather than "he," has the effect of subordinating the particular actor, and therefore the particular act, to a much more general perspective: mental rather than physical, and subjective rather than objective; "question" is a word which involves analysis of a physical event into terms of meaning and intention: it involves, in fact, both Strether's mind and the narrator's. The narrator's, because he interprets Strether's act: if James had sought the most concrete method of taking us into Strether's mind—"'Has Mr. Waymarsh come yet?' I at once asked"—he would have obviated the need for the implied external categoriser of Strether's action. But James disliked

---

[4] Sentences one and four are compound or multiple, but in my count I haven't included the second clause in the latter—"there was little fear": though if we can talk of the clause having a subject it's an abstract one—"fear."

the "mere platitude of statement" involved in first-person narrative; partly, presumably, because it would merge Strether's consciousness into the narrative, and not isolate it for the reader's inspection. For such isolation, a more expository method is needed: no confusion of subject and object, as in first-person narration, but a narrator forcing the reader to pay attention to James's primary objective—Strether's mental and subjective state.

The "multidimensional" quality of the narrative, with its continual implication of a community of three minds—Strether's, James's, and the reader's—isn't signalled very obviously until the fourth sentence—"The principle I have just mentioned as operating..."; but it's already been established tacitly in every detail of diction and structure, and it remains pervasive. One reason for the special demand James's fictional prose makes on our attention is surely that there are always at least three levels of development—all of them subjective: the characters' awareness of events; the narrator's seeing of them; and our own trailing perception of the relation between these two.

The primary location of the narrative in a mental rather than a physical continuum gives the narrative a great freedom from the restrictions of particular time and place. Materially, we are, of course, in Chester, at the hotel—characteristically "the hotel" because a fully particularised specification—"The Pied Bull Inn" say—would be an irrelevant brute fact which would distract attention from the mental train of thought we are invited to partake in. But actually we don't have any pressing sense of time and place: we feel ourselves to be spectators, rather specifically, of Strether's thought processes, which easily and imperceptibly range forwards and backwards both in time and space. Sentence three, for example, begins in the past, at the Liverpool dock; sentence four looks forward to the reunion later that day, and to its many sequels: such transitions of time and place are much easier to effect when the main subjects of the sentences are abstract: a "principle" exists independently of its context.

The multiplicity of relations—between narrator and object, and between the ideas in Strether's mind—held in even suspension throughout the narrative, is presumably the main explanation for the number of "thats" in the passage, as well as of the several examples of elegant variation. There are 9 "thats"—only two of them demonstrative and the rest relative pronouns (or conjunctions or particles if you prefer those terms); actually there were no less than three more of them in the first edition, which James removed from the somewhat more colloquial and informal New York edition; while there are several other "thats" implied—in "the principle [that] I have just mentioned," for instance. The number of "thats" follows from two habits already noted in the passage. "That," rather than "which" or "who," characteristically introduces relative clauses dealing not with persons but with objects, including abstract ideas; and it is also used to introduce reported actual or implied speech ("on his learning that Waymarsh"—not "Mr. Waymarsh isn't here"), or what may be called reported thought ("a sharp sense that ... his business would be a trifle bungled...").

Reported rather than direct speech also creates a pressure towards elegant variation: the use, for example, in sentence one of "his friend," where in direct speech it would be "Mr. Waymarsh" (and the reply—"*He* hasn't come yet"). In the second sentence —"a telegram... was produced for the inquirer"—"inquirer" is needed because "him" has already been used for Waymarsh just above; of course, "the inquirer" is logical enough after the subject of the first sentence has been an abstract noun— "question"; and the epithet also gives James an opportunity for underlining the ironic distance and detachment with which we are invited to view his dedicated "inquirer," Strether. Later, when Strether is "the most newly disembarked of the two men," we see how both elegant variation and the grammatical subordination of physical events are related to the general Jamesian tendency to present characters and actions on a plane of abstract categorisation; the mere statement, "Mr. Waymarsh had already been in England for [so many] months," would itself go far to destroy the primarily mental continuum in which the paragraph as a whole exists.

The last general stylistic feature of the passage to be listed above was the use of negative forms. There are 6 "noes" or "nots" in the first four sentences; four implied negatives—"postpone," "without disappointment," "at the worst," "there was little fear"; and two qualifications that modify positiveness of affirmation— "not wholly," and "to that extent." This abundance of negatives has no doubt several functions: it enacts Strether's tendency to hesitation and qualification; it puts the reader into the right judicial frame of mind; and it has the further effect of subordinating concrete events to their mental reflection; "Waymarsh was... not to arrive," for example, is not a concrete statement of a physical event: it is subjective— because it implies an expectation in Strether's mind (which was not fulfilled); and it has an abstract quality—because while Waymarsh's arriving would be particular and physical, his *not* arriving is an idea, a non-action. More generally, James's great use of negatives or near-negatives may also, perhaps, be regarded as part of his subjective and abstractive tendency: there are no negatives in nature but only in the human consciousness.

THE MOST OBVIOUS grammatical features of what Richard Chase has called Henry James's "infinitely syntactical language" (*The American Novel and Its Tradition*, New York, 1957), can, then, be shown to reflect the essential imperatives of his narrative point of view; and they could therefore lead into a discussion of the philosophical qualities of his mind, as they are discussed, for example, by Dorothea Krook in her notable article "The Method of the Later Works of Henry James" (*London Magazine*, I [1954], 55-70); our passage surely exemplifies James's power "to generalise to the furthest limit the particulars of experience," and with it the characteristic way in which both his "perceptions of the world itself and his perceptions of the logic of his perceptions of the world... happen simultaneously, are the parts of a single comprehensive experience." Another aspect of the connection between James's metaphysic and his method as a novelist has inspired a stimulating stylistic study—Carlo Izzo's "Henry James, Scrittore Sintattico" (*Studi Americani*, II [1956], 127-42). The connection between thought and style finds its historical perspective in John Henry Raleigh's illuminating study "Henry James: The Poetics of Empiricism"

(*PMLA*, LXVI [1951], 107–23), which establishes connections between Lockean epistemology and James's extreme, almost anarchic, individualism; while this epistemological preoccupation, which is central to Quentin Anderson's view of how James worked out his father's cosmology in fictional terms (*The American Henry James*, New Brunswick, 1957), also leads towards another large general question, the concern with "point of view," which became a crucial problem in the history and criticism of fiction under the influence of the sceptical relativism of the late nineteenth century.

In James's case, the problem is fairly complicated. He may be classed as an "Impressionist," concerned, that is, to show not so much the events themselves, but the impressions which they make on the characters. But James's continual need to generalise and place and order, combined with his absolute demand for a point of view that would be plastic enough to allow him freedom for the formal "architectonics" of the novelist's craft, eventually involved him in a very idiosyncratic kind of multiple Impressionism: idiosyncratic because the dual presence of Strether's consciousness and of that of the narrator, who translates what he sees there into more general terms, makes the narrative point of view both intensely individual and yet ultimately social.

Another possible direction of investigation would be to show that the abstractness and indirection of James's style are essentially the result of this characteristic multiplicity of his vision. There is, for example, the story reported by Edith Wharton that after his first stroke James told Lady Prothero that "in the very act of falling ... he heard in the room a voice which was distinctly, it seemed, not his own, saying: 'So here it is at last, the distinguished thing.'" James, apparently, could not but see even his own most fateful personal experience, except as evoked by some other observer's voice in terms of the long historical and literary tradition of death. Carlo Izzo regards this tendency as typical of the Alexandrian style, where there is a marked disparity between the rich inheritance of the means of literary expression, and the meaner creative world which it is used to express; but the defence of the Jamesian habit of mind must surely be that what the human vision shares with that of animals is presumably the perception of concrete images, not the power to conceive universals: such was Aristotle's notion of man's distinguishing capacity. The universals in the present context are presumably the awareness that behind every petty individual circumstance there ramifies an endless network of general moral, social and historical relations. Henry James's style can therefore be seen as a supremely civilised effort to relate every event and every moment of life to the full complexity of its circumambient conditions.

Obviously James's multiple awareness can go too far; and in the later novels it often poses the special problem that we do not quite know whether the awareness implied in a given passage is the narrator's or that of his character. Most simply, a pronoun referring to the subject of a preceding clause is always liable to give trouble if one hasn't been very much aware of what the grammatical subject of that preceding clause was; in the last sentence of the paragraph, for example, "the apprehension, already, on Strether's part, that it would, at best, ... prove the note of Europe," "it" refers to Waymarsh's countenance: but this isn't at first obvious; which is no doubt why, in his revision of the periodical version for the English edition, James replaced "it" by "he"—simpler, grammatically, but losing some of the ironic visual precision of the original. More seriously, because the narrator's consciousness and Strether's are both present, we often don't know whose mental operations and evaluative judgments are involved in particular cases. We pass, for instance, from the objective analysis of sentence three, where the analytic terminology of "the same secret principle" must be the responsibility of the narrator, to what must be a verbatim quotation of Strether's mind in sentence four: "with all respect to dear old Waymarsh" is obviously Strether's licensed familiarity.

But although the various difficulties of tense, voice, and reference require a vigilance of attention in the reader which some have found too much to give, they are not in themselves very considerable: and what perhaps is much more in need of attention is how the difficulties arising from the multiplicity of points of view don't by any means prevent James from ordering all the elements of his narrative style into an amazingly precise means of expression: and it is this positive, and in the present case, as it seems to me, triumphant, mastery of the difficulties which I want next to consider.

Our passage is not, I think, James either at his most memorable or at his most idiosyncratic: *The Ambassadors* is written with considerable sobriety and has, for example, little of the vivid and direct style of the early part of *The Wings of the Dove*, or of the happy symbolic complexities of *The Golden Bowl*. Still, the passage is fairly typical of the later James; and I think it can be proved that all or at least nearly all the idiosyncrasies of diction or syntax in the present passage are fully justified by the particular emphases they create.

The most flagrant eccentricity of diction is presumably that where James writes "the most newly disembarked of the two men" (lines 17–18). "Most" may very well be a mere slip; and it must certainly seem indefensible to anyone who takes it as an absolute rule that the comparative must always be used when only two items are involved.[5] But a defence is at least possible. "Most newly disembarked" means something rather different from "more newly disembarked." James, it may be surmised, did not want to compare the recency of the two men's arrival, but to inform us that Strether's arrival was "very" or as we might say, "most" recent; the use of the superlative also had the advantage of suggesting the long and fateful tradition of transatlantic disembarkations in general.

The reasons for the other main syntactical idiosyncrasies in the passage are much clearer. In the first part of the opening sentence, for example, the separation of subject —"question"—from verb—"was"—by the longish temporal clause "when he reached the hotel," is no doubt a dislocation of normal sentence structure; but, of course, "Strether" must be the first word of the novel: while, even more important, the delayed placing of the temporal clause, forces a pause after "question" and thus gives it a very significant resonance. Similarly with the last sentence; it has several peculiarities, of which the placing of "throughout" seems the most obvious. The sentence has three parts: the first and last are comparatively straightforward, but the

[5] Though consider *Rasselas*, Ch. XXVIII: "Both conditions may be bad, but they cannot both be worst."

middle is a massed block of portentous qualifications: "Mixed with everything was the apprehension, — already, on Strether's part, that it would, at best, throughout, — prove the note of Europe in quite a sufficient degree." The echoing doom started by the connotation of "apprehension" reverberates through "already," ("much more to come later") "on Strether's part" ("even he knows") and "at best" ("the worst has been envisaged, too"); but it is the final collapse of the terse rhythm of the parenthesis that isolates the rather awkwardly placed "throughout," and this enables James to sound the fine full fatal note; there is no limit to the poignant eloquence of "throughout." It was this effect, of course, which dictated the preceding inversion which places "apprehension" not at the start of the sentence, but in the middle where, largely freed from its syntactical nexus, it may be directly exposed to its salvos of qualification.

The mockingly fateful emphasis on "throughout" tells us, if nothing had before, that James's tone is in the last analysis ironic, comic, or better, as I shall try to suggest, humorous. The general reasons for this have already been suggested. To use Maynard Mack's distinction (in his Preface to *Joseph Andrews*, Rinehart Editions, New York, 1948), "the comic artist subordinates the presentation of life as experience, where the relationship between ourselves and the characters experiencing it is a primary one, to the presentation of life as a spectacle, where the primary relation is between himself and us as onlookers." In the James passage, the primacy of the relation between the narrator and the reader has already been noted, as has its connection with the abstraction of the diction, which brings home the distance between the narrator and Strether. Of course, the application of abstract diction to particular persons always tends towards irony,[6] because it imposes a dual way of looking at them: few of us can survive being presented as general representatives of humanity.

The paragraph, of course, is based on one of the classic contradictions in psychological comedy—Strether's reluctance to admit to himself that he has very mixed feelings about his friend: and James develops this with the narrative equivalent of *commedia dell' arte* technique: virtuoso feats of ironic balance, comic exaggeration, and deceptive hesitation conduct us on a complicated progress towards the foreordained illumination.

In structure, to begin with, the six sentences form three groups of two: each pair of them gives one aspect of Strether's delay; and they are arranged in an ascending order of complication so that the fifth sentence—72 words—is almost twice as long as any other, and is succeeded by the final sentence, the punch line, which is noticeably the shortest—26 words. The development of the ideas is as controlled as the sentence structure. Strether is obviously a man with an enormous sense of responsibility about personal relationships; so his first question is about his friend. That loyal *empressement*, however, is immediately checked by the balanced twin negatives that follow: "on his learning that Waymarsh *was*... *not* to arrive till evening he *was not* wholly disconcerted": one of the diagnostic elements of irony, surely, is hyperbole qualified

---

[6] As I have argued in "The Ironic Tradition in Augustan Prose from Swift to Johnson," *Restoration and Augustan Prose* (Los Angeles, 1957).

with mock-scrupulousness, such as we get in "not wholly disconcerted." Why there are limits to Lambert Strether's consternation is to transpire in the next sentence; Waymarsh's telegram bespeaking a room "only if not noisy" is a laconic suggestion of that inarticulate worthy's habitually gloomy expectations—from his past experiences of the indignities of European hotel noise we adumbrate the notion that the cost of their friendly *rencontre* may be his sleeping in the street. In the second part of the sentence we have another similar, though more muted, hint: "the understanding they should meet at Chester rather than at Liverpool remained to that extent sound"; "to that extent," no doubt, but to *any other*?—echo seems to answer "No."

In the second group of sentences we are getting into Strether's mind, and we have been prepared to relish the irony of its ambivalences. The negatived hyperbole of "not absolutely to desire," turns out to mean "postpone"; and, of course, a voluntarily postponed "enjoyment" itself denotes a very modified rapture, although Strether's own consciousness of the problem is apparently no further advanced than that "he could still wait without disappointment." Comically loyal to what he would like to feel, therefore, we have him putting in the consoling reflection that "they would dine together at the worst"; and the ambiguity of "at the worst" is followed by the equally dubious thought: "there was little fear that in the sequel they shouldn't see enough of each other." That they should, in fact, see too much of each other; but social decorum and Strether's own loyalties demand that the outrage of the open statement be veiled in the obscurity of formal negation.

By the time we arrive at the climactic pair of sentences, we have been told enough for more ambitious effects to be possible. The twice-mentioned "secret principle," it appears, is actually "wholly instinctive" (line 18); but in other ways Strether is almost ludicrously self-conscious. The qualified hyperbole of "his business would be a trifle bungled," underlined as it is by the alliteration, prepares us for a half-realised image which amusingly defines Strether's sense of his role: he sees himself, it appears, as the stage-manager of an enterprise in which his solemn obligations as an implicated friend are counterbalanced by his equally ceremonious sense that due decorums must also be attended to when he comes face to face with another friend of long ago—no less a person than Europe. It is, of course, silly of him, as James makes him acknowledge in the characteristic italicising of "the . . . 'note' of Europe";[7] but still, he does have a comically ponderous sense of protocol which leads him to feel that "his business would be a trifle bungled should he simply arrange for this countenance to present itself to the nearing steamer as the first 'note' of Europe." The steamer, one imagines, would not have turned hard astern at the proximity of Waymarsh's sacred rage; but Strether's fitness for ambassadorial functions is defined by his thinking in terms of "arranging" for a certain countenance at the docks to give just the right symbolic greeting.

Strether's notion of what Europe demands also shows us the force of his aesthetic sense. But in the last sentence the metaphor, though it remains equally self-conscious, changes its mode of operation from the dramatic, aesthetic, and diplomatic, to some-

---

[7] See George Knox, "James's Rhetoric of Quotes," *College English*, XVII (1956), 293–97.

thing more scientific: for, although ten years ago I should not have failed to point out, and my readers would not, I suppose, have failed to applaud, the ambiguity of "prove," it now seems to me that we must choose between its two possible meanings. James may be using "prove" to mean that Waymarsh's face will "turn out to be" the "note of Europe" for Strether. But "prove" in this sense is intransitive, and "to be" would have to be supplied; it therefore seems more likely that James is using "prove" in the older sense of "to test": Waymarsh is indeed suited to the role of being the sourly acid test of the siren songs of Europe "in quite a sufficient degree," as Strether puts it with solemn but arch understatement.

The basic developmental structure of the passage, then, is one of progressive and yet artfully delayed clarification; and this pattern is also typical of James's general novelistic method. The reasons for this are suggested in the Preface to *The Princess Casamassima*, where James deals with the problem of maintaining a balance between the intelligence a character must have to be interesting, and the bewilderment which is nevertheless an essential condition of the novel's having surprise, development, and tension: "It seems probable that if we were never bewildered there would never be a story to tell about us."

In the first paragraph of *The Ambassadors* James apprises us both of his hero's supreme qualities and of his associated limitations. Strether's delicate critical intelligence is often blinkered by a highly vulnerable mixture of moral generosity towards others combined with an obsessive sense of personal inadequacy; we see the tension in relation to Waymarsh, as later we are to see it in relation to all his other friends; and we understand, long before Strether, how deeply it bewilders him; most poignantly about the true nature of Chad, Madame de Vionnet—and himself.

This counterpoint of intelligence and bewilderment is, of course, another reason for the split narrative point of view we've already noted: we and the narrator are inside Strether's mind, and yet we are also outside it, knowing more about Strether than he knows about himself. This is the classic posture of irony. Yet I think that to insist too exclusively on the ironic function of James's narrative point of view would be mistaken.

Irony has lately been enshrined as the supreme deity in the critical pantheon: but, I wonder, is there really anything so wonderful about being distant and objective? Who wants to see life only or mainly in intellectual terms? In art as in life we no doubt can have need of intellectual distance as well as of emotional commitment; but the uninvolvement of the artist surely doesn't go very far without the total involvement of the person; or, at least, without a deeper human involvement than irony customarily establishes. One could, I suppose, call the aesthetically perfect balance between distance and involvement, open or positive irony: but I'm not sure that humour isn't a better word, especially when the final balance is tipped in favour of involvement, of ultimate commitment to the characters; and I hope that our next critical movement will be the New Gelastics.

At all events, although the first paragraph alone doesn't allow the point to be established fully here, it seems to me that James's attitude to Strether is better described as humorous than ironical; we must learn like Maria Gostrey, to see him "at last all comically, all tragically." James's later novels in general are most intellectual; but they are also, surely, his most compassionate: and in this particular paragraph Strether's dilemma is developed in such a way that we feel for him even more than we smile at him. This balance of intention, I think, probably explains why James keeps his irony so quiet in tone: we must be aware of Strether's "secret" ambivalence towards Waymarsh, but not to the point that his unawareness of it would verge on fatuity; and our controlling sympathy for the causes of Strether's ambivalence turns what might have been irony into something closer to what Constance Rourke characterises as James's typical "low-keyed humor of defeat" (*American Humor*, 1931).

That James's final attitude is humorous rather than ironic is further suggested by the likeness of the basic structural technique of the paragraph to that of the funny story—the incremental involvement in an endemic human perplexity which can only be resolved by laughter's final acceptance of contradiction and absurdity. We don't, in the end, see Strether's probing hesitations mainly as an ironic indication by James of mankind's general muddlement; we find it, increasingly, a touching example of how, despite all their inevitable incongruities and shortcomings, human ties remain only, but still, human.

Here it is perhaps James's very slowness and deliberation throughout the narrative which gives us our best supporting evidence: greater love hath no man than hearing his friend out patiently.

THE FUNCTION of an introductory paragraph in a novel is presumably to introduce: and this paragraph surely has the distinction of being a supremely complex and inclusive introduction to a novel. It introduces the hero, of course, and one of his companions; also the time; the place; something of what's gone before. But James has carefully avoided giving us the usual retrospective beginning, that pile of details which he scornfully termed a "mere seated mass of information." All the details are scrupulously presented as reflections from the novel's essential centre—the narrator's patterning of the ideas going forwards and backwards in Strether's mind. Of course, this initially makes the novel more difficult, because what we probably think of as primary—event and its setting—is subordinated to what James thinks is—the mental drama of the hero's consciousness, which, of course, is not told but shown: scenically dramatised. At the same time, by selecting thoughts and events which are representative of the book as a whole, and narrating them with an abstractness which suggests their larger import, James introduces the most general themes of the novel.

James, we saw, carefully arranged to make "Strether's first question," the first three words; and, of course, throughout the novel, Strether is to go on asking questions—and getting increasingly dusty answers. This, it may be added, is stressed by the apparent aposiopesis: for a "first" question when no second is mentioned, is surely an intimation that more are—in a way unknown to us or to Strether—yet to come. The later dislocations of normal word-order already noted above emphasise other major themes; the "secret principle" in Strether's mind, and the antithesis Waymarsh-Europe, for instance.

The extent to which these processes were conscious on James's part cannot, of course, be resolved; but it is significant that the meeting with Maria Gostrey was interposed before the meeting with Waymarsh, which James had originally planned as his beginning in the long (20,000-word) scenario of the plot which he prepared for *Harper's*. The unexpected meeting had many advantages; not least that James could repeat the first paragraph's pattern of delayed clarification in the structure of the first chapter as a whole. On Strether's mind we get a momentously clear judgment at the end of the second paragraph: "there was detachment in his zeal, and curiosity in his indifference"; but then the meeting with Maria Gostrey, and its gay opportunities for a much fuller presentation of Strether's mind, intervene before Waymarsh himself finally appears at the end of the chapter; only then is the joke behind Strether's uneasy hesitations in the first paragraph brought to its hilariously blunt climax: "It was already upon him even at that distance—Mr. Waymarsh was for *his* part joyless."

One way of evaluating James's achievement in this paragraph, I suppose, would be to compare the opening of James's other novels, and with those of previous writers: but it would take too long to do more than sketch the possibilities of this approach. James's early openings certainly have some of the banality of the "mere seated mass of information": in *Roderick Hudson* (1876), for example: "Rowland Mallet had made his arrangements to sail for Europe on the 5th of September, and having in the interval a fortnight to spare, he determined to spend it with his cousin Cecilia, the widow of a nephew of his father...." Later, James showed a much more comprehensive notion of what the introductory paragraph should attempt: even in the relatively simple and concrete opening of *The Wings of the Dove* (1902): "She waited, Kate Croy, for her father to come in, but he kept her unconscionably, and there were moments at which she showed herself, in the glass over the mantle, a face positively pale with irritation that had brought her to the point of going away without sight of him...." "She waited, Kate Croy"—an odd parenthetic apposition artfully contrived to prefigure her role throughout the novel—to wait.

One could, I suppose, find this sort of symbolic prefiguring in the work of earlier novelists; but never, I imagine, in association with all the other levels of introductory function that James manages to combine in a single paragraph. Jane Austen has her famous thematic irony in the opening of *Pride and Prejudice* (1813): "It is a truth universally acknowledged, that a single man in possession of a good fortune must be in want of a wife"; but pride and prejudice must come later. Dickens can hurl us overpoweringly into *Bleak House* (1852–1853), into its time and place and general theme; but characters and opening action have to wait:

> London... Michaelmas Term lately over, and the Lord Chancellor sitting in Lincoln's Inn Hall. Implacable November weather. As much mud in the streets, as if the waters had but newly retired from the face of the earth, and it would not be wonderful to meet a Megalosaurus, forty feet long or so, waddling like an elephantine lizard up Holborn-Hill. Smoke lowering down from chimney-pots....

In Dickens, characteristically, we get a loud note that sets the tone, rather than a polyphonic series of chords that contain all the later melodic developments, as in James. And either the Dickens method, or the "mere seated mass of information," seem to be commonest kinds of opening in nineteenth-century novels. For openings that suggest something of James's ambitious attempt to achieve a prologue that is a synchronic introduction of all the main aspects of the narrative, I think that Conrad is his closest rival. But Conrad, whether in expository or dramatic vein, tends to an arresting initial vigour that has dangers which James's more muted tones avoid. In *An Outcast of the Islands* (1896), for example:

> When he stepped off the straight and narrow path of his peculiar honesty, it was with an inward assertion of unflinching resolve to fall back again into the monotonous but safe stride of virtue as soon as his little excursion into the wayside quagmires had produced the desired effect. It was going to be a short episode—a sentence in brackets, so to speak, in the flowing tale of his life....

Conrad's sardonic force has enormous immediate impact; but it surely gives too much away: the character, Willems, has been dissected so vigorously that it takes great effort for Conrad—and the reader—to revivify him later. The danger lurks even in the masterly combination of physical notation and symbolic evaluation at the beginning of *Lord Jim* (1900): "He was an inch, perhaps two, under six feet...": the heroic proportion is for ever missed, by an inch, perhaps two; which is perhaps too much, to begin with.

It is not for me to assess how far I have succeeded in carrying out the general intentions with which I began, or how far similar methods of analysis would be applicable to other kinds of prose. As regards the explication of the passage itself, the main argument must by now be sufficiently clear, although a full demonstration would require a much wider sampling both of other novels and of other passages in *The Ambassadors*.[8] The most obvious and demonstrable features of James's prose style, its vocabulary and syntax, are direct reflections of his attitude to life and his conception of the novel; and these features, like the relation of the paragraph to the rest of the novel, and to other novels, make clear that the notorious idiosyncrasies of Jamesian prose are directly related to the imperatives which led him to develop a narrative texture as richly complicated and as highly organised as that of poetry.

No wonder James scorned translation and rejoiced, as he so engagingly confessed to his French translator, Auguste Monod, that his later works were "locked fast in the golden cage of the *intraduisible*." Translation could hardly do justice to a paragraph in which so many levels of meaning and implication are kept in continuous operation; in which the usual introductory exposition of time, place, character, and previous action, are rendered through an immediate immersion in the processes of the hero's

---

[8] A similar analysis of eight other paragraphs selected at fifty-page intervals revealed that, as would be expected, there is much variation: the tendency to use non-transitive verbs, and abstract nouns as subjects, for instance, seems to be strong throughout the novel, though especially so in analytic rather than narrative passages; but the frequent use of "that" and of negative forms of statement does not recur significantly.

mind as he's involved in perplexities which are characteristic of the novel as a whole and which are articulated in a mode of comic development which is essentially that, not only of the following chapter, but of the total structure. To have done all that is to have gone far towards demonstrating the contention which James announced at the end of the Preface to *The Ambassadors*, that "the Novel remains still, under the right persuasion, the most independent, most elastic, most prodigious of literary forms"; and the variety and complexity of the functions carried out in the book's quite short first paragraph also suggest that, contrary to some notions, the demonstration is, as James claimed, made with "a splendid particular economy."

Matthew Arnold

❧ JOHN HOLLOWAY ❧

In *The Victorian Sage*, first published in 1953, John Holloway examines how six nineteenth-century English writers—Carlyle, Disraeli, George Eliot, Newman, Arnold, and Hardy—mediate in various ways through their works the impression of a sage. This type of sage, as Holloway defines him, is endowed with a view of life "partly philosophical and partly moral" which equips him to deal with ultimate questions, and his distinctive activity consists in recreating this "somehow esoteric insight" for his reader. Characteristically, the job of the sage is to convey his wisdom through opening the eyes of the reader, stimulating him to a new awareness, for the reality in question is less an utterly "new" one than "old things" as viewed from a new perspective. According to Holloway's summary in his introduction: "... the sage has a special problem in expounding or in proving what he wants to say. He does not and probably cannot rely on logical and formal argument alone or even much at all. His main task is to quicken his reader's perceptiveness; and he does this by making a far wider appeal than the exclusively rational appeal. He draws upon resources cognate, at least, with those of the artist in words. He gives expression to his outlook imaginatively. What he has to say is not a matter just of 'content' or narrow paraphrasable meaning, but is transfused by the whole texture of his writing as it constitutes an experience for the reader."

Thus when he comes to take up the various "sages" in the body of his book, Holloway analyzes such matters as their uses of figurative language or cryptic utterances, their ways of defining key words, of manipulating tone, or of converting exposition itself into a mode of proof. In the chapter reprinted here, Holloway shows how Arnold assumes a dramatic presence through the very texture of his prose—through tone, special forms of argument, procedures of definition, characterization of his opponents, and irony—and thus conveys his message to the reader. Throughout this chapter, as elsewhere in *The Victorian Sage*, it is clear that Holloway conceives of style as functioning dramatically; indeed, this book is the most sustained example I know of stylistic criticism that focuses on the ways in which language affects an audience.

Arnold's Doctrine and Temper

"ONE at last has a chance of *getting* at the English public. Such a public as it is, and such a work as one wants to do with it! ... Partly nature, partly time and study have also by this time taught me thoroughly the precious truth that everything turns upon one's exercising the power of *persuasion*, of charm; that without this all fury, energy, reasoning power, acquirement are thrown away."[1] These few words lay bare the very core of Arnold's "criticism of life," because there was one thing that he never allowed himself to forget. This was that to be successful, the moralist must do what success requires, and that success in this field requires, above all things, patience and self-control. "Where shall we find language innocent enough, how shall we make the spotless purity of our intentions evident enough, to enable us to say ... that the British Constitution itself" is "a colossal machine for the manufacture of Philistines? ... how is Mr. Carlyle to say it and not be misunderstood, after his furious raid into this field with his *Latter-Day Pamphlets*?"[2] By the fullness and

---

[1] Letter to Arnold's mother, 29th October 1863 (*Works*, xiii. 266). References in this Chapter are given to the volume and page of the De Luxe Edition of Arnold's *Works* (15 vols.), Macmillan, London, 1903; and when one book or essay is quoted from several times in succession, its title is indicated only in the first of the corresponding footnotes. The following abbreviations are used:

    CA   *Culture and Anarchy* (1869)
    DA   *Discourses in America* (1885)
    EC.i   *Essays in Criticism*, Series I (1865)
    FE   *A French Eton* (1864)
    FG   *Friendship's Garland* (1871)
    LD   *Literature and Dogma* (1873)
    ME   *Mixed Essays* (1879)
    ST.P   *St. Paul and Protestantism* (1870)

[2] *The Function of Criticism*: EC.i. (iii. 28–9).

"Matthew Arnold," by John Holloway, is reprinted from his *The Victorian Sage: Studies in Argument* Hamden, Conn., and London, 1962), pp. 202–43, by arrangement with Archon Books.

care and circumspection with which he moulds and adjusts his work to the persuasive task, Arnold sets an entirely new standard—goes further here even than Newman. Yet his work does not tempt us to acquiesce in his outlook ignorant of what we are doing; it is persuasive through being a memorable specimen of what that outlook produces, a specimen powerful in illuminating his position and helping his readers to see its attraction and strength. It is what distinguishes art in literature that Arnold directs to the necessities of persuasion: he aims to transform the reader's outlook, and he makes a call upon every part of his nature.

Arnold's polemics were less irresponsible than those of Carlyle, because his effort to persuade was much more sustained and planned; and his task was a more elusive one than Newman's, because he had no rigid doctrines to argue for, only attitudes. His work inculcates not a set of ultimate beliefs—a "Life-Philosophy"—but simply certain habits and a certain temper of mind. He limits his ambitions; he advocates not so much any definite view, as the mental prerequisites of forming views. "The old recipe, to think a little more and bustle a little less";[3] "... between all these there is indeed much necessity for methods of insight and moderation";[4] "the free spontaneous play of consciousness with which culture tries to float our stock habits of thinking and acting ... to *float* them, to prevent their being stiff and stark pieces of petrifaction any longer ... our main business at the present moment is not so much to work away at certain crude reforms ... as to create ... a frame of mind out of which the schemes of really fruitful reforms may with time grow."[5] It is the frame of mind that is crucial; to what conclusions it will lead, once adopted, is for Arnold a secondary matter. Much of his work is negative: he wants to deprecate what is crude and exaggerated, to leave questions open where they have been precipitately closed. He seldom rejects an opposing view outright; all he does is to regret its undue haste or narrowness, or see in it an excess of something by no means intrinsically bad. "There is a catchword which, I know, will be used against me ... cries and catchwords ... are very apt to receive an application, or to be used with an absoluteness, which does not belong to them ... and ... narrow our spirit and ... hurt our practice."[6] In this sentence Arnold condemns his opponents' frame of mind, and suggests a better, all in one.

If he ever advances a more positive doctrine, it is usually of a kind by now familiar: the vital but essentially simple truths that seem to be the sage's peculiar province. What he says of his defence of a classical education is, "I put this forward on the strength of some facts not at all recondite, very far from it; facts capable of being stated in the simplest possible fashion"—the facts are simply those of "the constitution of human nature."[7] Like other moralists, he regards his important function as that merely of bringing familiar knowledge alive. "The larger the scale on which the violation of reason's law is practised ... the greater must be the confusion and final trouble. Surely no laudations of free-trade ... can tell us anything ... which it more concerns us to know than that! and not only to know, but to have the knowledge

---

[3] *My Countrymen* (vi. 388).   [4] Letter to Arnold's mother, 9th November 1870 (xiv. 241).   [5] CA. (vi.212-13).   [6] FE. (xii. 49).   [7] DA. (iv. 330).

present.... But we all know it already! some one will say, it is the simplest law of prudence. But how little reality must there be in our knowledge."[8]

Clearly then, Arnold rigorously circumscribes his work. It suggests an approach; or it is deliberately negative and inconclusive, or where positive its statements are deliberately commonplace and familiar. These restrictions greatly affect that element of Arnold's work which comes nearest to the speculative or metaphysical; for although he disclaims all ability for subtle philosophizing, yet, like Carlyle, like Newman, he too has a philosophy of history, a bedrock *credo*. He too writes of "the natural current there is in human affairs, and ... its continual working";[9] and the fault of his opponents, like theirs, is that "they cannot see the way the world is going, and the future does not belong to them."[10] Further than this, he goes on occasionally to make success a test or sign of rightness: "sure loss and defeat at last... ought to govern ...action,"[11] he writes, or even "that providential order which forbids the final supremacy of imperfect things."[12] But this line of thought is not prominent in his work; and moreover, its development is entirely different in Arnold and in, say, Carlyle.

That difference becomes immediately plain if we complete the last quotation but one: "sure loss and defeat at last, *from coming into conflict with truth and nature*"; or take such a remark as "this contravention of the natural order has produced, as such contravention always must produce, a certain confusion and false movement, of which we are beginning to feel, in almost every direction, the inconvenience."[13] The contrast is inescapable. All the apocalyptic quality of Carlyle's historical determinism is gone; the trend of events is governed not by some everready and apocalyptic Hand, but by a gentle Platonic harmony between virtue, reason, and reality. The course of history is not grand, simple and mysterious, but neat and orderly, now one thing and now another, according to time and place. There are epochs of "expansion" and of "concentration."[14] Hellenism, the urgent need in Arnold's own time, would have been in the Dark Ages "unsound at that particular moment of man's development... premature."[15] Different virtues and different measures require to be insisted on in different countries.[16] France may lack political freedom, England may rely on it to excess; England's chief need is greater amenity, France's greater purity, America's, a more elevated seriousness. Each may benefit by addition even of what is harmful elsewhere. One can now see the place in Arnold's work of how he grossly simplifies in writing of national characteristics. It helps him to modify optimistic determinism, as a philosophy of history, so that it seems reasonable and unmysterious, multiple in its aspects—as indeed every unmysterious thing is—yet simple to grasp, having no surprises for the calm, enlightened, unprejudiced observer.

Arnold has a doctrine of man which is the counterpart of this doctrine of history. It too contains nothing paradoxical or mysterious or not readily acceptable. Man, like the world itself and its history, is a complex of different elements which are

---

[8] CA. (vi. 208–9). [9] vi. 37. [10] *My Countrymen* (vi. 376). [11] ME. (x. 127–8). [12] FE. (xii. 76). [13] CA. (vi. 139–40). [14] See *e.g.* CA. (vi. 59–62) and *The Function of Criticism* (iii. 14–15). [15] CA. (vi. 130). [16] See "A Courteous Explanation" (vi. 398) and *Numbers* (iv. 283), *passim*.

readily brought together into a simple and natural unity. These are the "facts not at all recondite, very far from it," touched upon above. "We set ourselves to enumerate the powers which go to the building of human life, and say that they are the power of conduct, the power of intellect and knowledge, the power of beauty, and the power of social life and manners ... this scheme, though drawn in rough and plain lines enough ... does yet give a fairly true representation. ... Human nature is built up by these powers; we have the need for them all ... the several powers ... are not isolated, but there is ... a perpetual tendency to relate them one to another in divers ways."[17] Humanity is a "composite thing," its elements so "intertwined" that one can temporarily do duty for another; but ultimately there must be "mutual understanding and balance," there must be genuine and organic integration, if the "true and smooth order of humanity's development" is not to be arrested.[18] The "natural rational life"—the juxtaposition, virtual equivalence of the adjectives, has significance —is one with "body, intelligence, and soul all taken care of."[19] These may be commonplaces; but for the present enquiry that is their interest.

This is so, because such a view offers, as it were, a minimum target to the critic; its quality of platitude enables Arnold largely to escape the burden of proof—or rather, to use an apter word, the business of justifying or arguing for a metaphysics, which constrains the other authors we have examined to a style of rhetoric, eloquence, exaltation or mystery. And such a style would inevitably have clashed with Arnold's central concern—to advocate a gentle critical reasonableness of mind. With such essentially simple and commonplace premisses, he could avoid a kind of writing which it would certainly have been hard to unite with the temper of mind he admired. Thus in Arnold there are little or no rhetorical fireworks. Metaphor and imagery are (except very occasionally for certain quite new uses) absent to a degree nothing short of extraordinary by comparison with Newman or Carlyle or George Eliot; and although definitions of words, in a sense at least, are not uncommon, they occur for purposes much more restricted than elsewhere, and are such that the element of prestidigitation—which would have been the alien element—is almost entirely lacking from them. Yet at the same time, Arnold's premisses are important for their substance: they offer a real justification for his method of compromise—that is, of seeing more than one side to any problem, and stressing or adding just what the given case requires, even though intrinsically this may be subordinate. But they do not dictate anything in the details of his approach. Others could start with the same premisses and probably reach any detailed conclusions they liked. What significance they had for Arnold is determined in the whole texture of his writing. If he offers anything of wisdom or sanity or mental poise, it is to be found in the whole experience of reading him, in a sense of what intellectual urbanity is that transpires rather from his handling of problems than from his answers to them. He mediates not a view of the world, but a habit of mind. Let us see how this is done.

To a degree quite unusual among polemical writers, Arnold's persuasive energy goes to build up, little by little, an intimate and a favourable impression of his own

[17] DA. (iv. 331).   [18] CA. (vi. 143–4).   [19] *My Countrymen* (vi. 374).

personality as an author, and an unfavourable impression, equally clear if less intimate and more generalized, of the personalities of his opponents. Over and over again one finds the discussion taking shape between these two poles; and this is natural, because Arnold's chief purpose is to recommend one temper of mind, and condemn another, and such things are more readily sensed through contact than understood through description. No author, of course, can give a favourable impression of his own temper of mind, except obliquely and discreetly. When Arnold writes of himself at length, it is usually in a depreciatory vein; but he causes us to glimpse his personality through various devices, and of these, as with Newman, perhaps the most conspicuous is tone. Indeed he adopts a tone not unlike Newman's, save that it is usually less grave and calm, more whimsical and apologetic. Newman, after all, thought he had a powerful silent ally as Arnold did not.

Thus in the first few lines of the Preface to *Essays in Criticism*, Series I, we find "indeed, it is not in my nature—some of my critics would rather say, not in my power—to dispute on behalf of any opinion, even my own, very obstinately. To try and approach truth on one side after another, not to strive or cry, nor to persist in pressing forward, on any one side, with violence and self-will—it is only thus, it seems to me, that mortals may hope to gain any vision" of truth.[20] Here the opinion is mediated to us through becoming acquainted with the author; and the second sentence, though not the first, reveals how close is the link with Newman.[21] "No, we are all seekers still!" Arnold writes later in the same Preface.[22] This tone is frequent elsewhere: "in differing from them, however, I wish to proceed with the utmost caution and diffidence . . . the tone of tentative enquiry . . . is the tone I would wish to take and not to depart from";[23] "at present I neither praise it nor blame it; I simply count it as one of the votes";[24] "I have no pet scheme to press, no crochet to gratify, no fanatical zeal. . . . All I say is. . . .";[25] "the line I am going to follow is . . . so extremely simple, that perhaps it may be followed without failure even by one who for a more ambitious line of discussion would be quite incompetent";[26] "even though to a certain extent I am disposed to agree with Mr. Frederic Harrison . . . I am not sure that I do not think. . . . Therefore I propose now to try and enquire, in the simple unsystematic way which best suits both my taste and my powers. . . ."[27] Such phrases as these, running throughout the fabric of his work, create an image for us of the intelligent, modest, urbane Arnold who *is* what he advocates.

But he controls more than his own tone—he foists a contrasting tone on his opponents. He puts imaginary speeches into their mouths. "I criticized Bishop Colenso's speculative confusion. Immediately there was a cry raised: 'What is this? here is a liberal attacking a liberal. Do you not belong to the movement? Are you not a friend of truth? . . . Why make these invidious differences? both books are excellent, admirable, liberal; Bishop Colenso's perhaps the most so, because it is the boldest. . . . Be silent therefore; or rather speak, speak as loud as you can! and go into ecstasies.'" And, as if the contrast were not by now sharp enough, he concludes

---

[20] iii, p. v. [21] See [Holloway, *The Victorian Sage*], p. 161. [22] iii, p. xi. [23] DA. (iv. 330). [24] ME. (x. 55). [25] FE. (xii. 44). [26] DA. (iv. 321–2). [27] CA. (vi. 4).

tersely "but criticism cannot follow this coarse and indiscriminate method."[28] It is the tone of the expression that shows the coarseness of the method; and similarly it is the tone of his opponents he points to and condemns in such remarks as "Surely, if they knew this, those friends of progress, who have confidently pronounced the remains of the ancient world to be so much lumber ... might be inclined to reconsider their sentence."[29] But the inclination to reconsider, or even much to consider, is rather what they lack. It will be necessary to return to this point in examining the very distinctive contribution made to our impression of Arnold and of his opponents by irony.

Forms of Argument

ARNOLD IS ALSO like Newman, and unlike Carlyle (and George Eliot in her discursive works), in developing our sense of his temper of mind, and of the kind of thinking he is doing, through the distinctive forms of his argument. Newman and Arnold both employ the *argumentum ad hominem*. In Newman this form is common, it is constantly employed on points of detail, and the effect of its frequency is to amplify our sense of the great integrated system of reality, as the author conceives it. Arnold uses the argument much less often, and then in respect only of some fundamental issue. "I speak to an audience with a high standard of civilization. If I say that certain things ... do not come up to a high standard ... I need not prove how and why they do not; you will feel instinctively ... I need not prove that a high standard of civilization is desirable; you will instinctively feel that it is."[30] *God and the Bible* is "meant for those who, won by the modern spirit to habits of intellectual seriousness, cannot receive what sets those habits at naught."[31] In *Literature and Dogma*,[32] he writes approvingly of how Newman relies on this form of argument. But in his own case its oblique contribution is less to give the impression of system and precision than of circumspection in argument and modesty on the part of the author.

Again, like Newman, Arnold enlists the negative evidence. Scientists are likely to have an incomplete understanding of human nature not through their limitations, but actually through their special talents and interests.[33] Frederic Harrison may be right in arguing that men of culture are just the class who cannot be trusted with power in modern society; but this confirms, not his own attack on men of culture, but Arnold's on the society that cannot use them.[34] As for the Nonconformists, "the very example [America] that they bring forward to help their case makes against them";[35] their knowledge of the Bible, which they make their infallible stay, is a typical specimen of knowledge and ignorance muddled together;[36] and when they rely on a "fetish or mechanical maxim" to bring about an improvement in the state of affairs, they only succeed in adding slightly to the "confusion and hostility."[37] The administration of Athens under Eubulus, which at the time it would have seemed "very impertinent"

---

[28] *The Function of Criticism* (iii. 32). [29] ME. (x. 37). [30] ME. (x. 58). [31] viii, p. xxxiv. [32] vii. 318.
[33] DA. (iv. 336–7). [34] CA. (vi. 3). [35] vi, p. xxx. [36] vi. 153–4. [37] vi. 172–3.

to condemn, was exactly what led to the collapse of the city.[38] Burke, bitterest enemy of the French Revolution, can yet at the very end of his work return upon himself to explain how a great change in human affairs might under certain circumstances be proper and inevitable.[39] The general tendency of these arguments is not to suggest any grand system, but a polite irony in things that sooner or later makes cocksure people look silly.[40]

The appendage to *Friendship's Garland* called "A Courteous Explanation" is especially interesting here. First, it is an argument that finds support for Arnold's case where one would least expect it. "Horace," siding with the complacent English journals, has attacked him for depreciating the value of free speech in England; Arnold quietly observes that at all events this new opponent readily follows his own lead in criticizing compatriots. "How 'Horace' does give it to his poor countrymen...! So did Monsieur de Tocqueville, so does Monsieur Renan. I lay up the example for my own edification, and I commend it to the editor of the *Morning Star* for his."[41] Second, Arnold discredits his opponent, in the same unruffled style, by a *tu quoque* argument. "This brings me to the one little point of difference (for there is just one) between 'Horace' and me."[42] "Horace" has accused him of giving no thought to the needs of foreign countries. But does he give any thought to it himself? —far from it: he wants the English to be told not what they, but what the French need to hear. "'Horace' and his friends are evidently Orleanists, and I have always observed that Orleanists are rather sly."[43] When Arnold has finished, "Horace" looks less sly than silly—or at least, one more opponent of the abrupt, unreflecting, unsubtle kind that Arnold seems so often to be dealing with.

Perhaps the two forms of argument most distinctive of Arnold are *distinguo* arguments which keep the reader sensitized to his unrelaxing circumspection, and concessive arguments which emphasize his modesty. "'Let us distinguish,' replied the envious foreigners" (who here are speaking for Arnold himself) "let us distinguish. We named three powers... which go to spread... rational humane life.... Your middle class, we agreed, has the first.... But this only brings us a certain way...."[44] Or again, "It is not State-action in itself which the middle and lower classes of a nation ought to deprecate; it is State-action exercised by a hostile class."[45] "Just as France owes her fearful troubles to other things and her civilizedness to equality, so we owe our immunity from fearful troubles to other things, and our uncivilizedness to inequality."[46] In *A French Eton*[47] he distinguishes the quite contrasting needs of schools providing for the different classes of society: those for the aristocracy need "the notion of a sort of republican fellowship, the practice of a plain life in common,

---

[38] DA. (iv. 288–9). [39] *The Function of Criticism* (iii. 16).

[40] The example of Burke is different. (*a*) In this respect he is an *example* of the temper of mind Arnold wishes to recommend. (*b*) Arnold recommends his *own* temper of mind by taking a virtual opponent as a praiseworthy example. (*c*) Burke's concession shows all the same how Arnold's opponents are (if intelligent enough) constrained by the nature of events to introduce exceptions and thereby accept Arnold's view. Burke is the opponent who is wise, and retreats; Frederic Harrison and the Nonconformists blunder obstinately on.

[41] FG. (vi. 397).   [42] vi. 398.   [43] *Ibid.*   [44] FG. (vi. 376–7).   [45] ME. (x. 34).   [46] ME. (x. 83).   [47] FE. (xii. 40).

the habit of self-help"; while those for the middle classes need training in "largeness of soul and personal dignity," and those for the lower, in "feeling, gentleness, humanity."[48] The same form of argument underlies a passage quoted earlier, Arnold's version of the attacks on him for his attack on Bishop Colenso:[49] the method of his opponents is coarse and indiscriminate just because they think that all "differences" are "invidious." "The practical man is not apt for fine distinctions, and yet in these distinctions truth and the highest culture greatly find their account."[50] Arnold finds his account in them, because they not only lead him to the conclusions he desires, but give his thought and writing a distinctive temper in the process.

Concession in argument necessarily does little to advance the proof for one's own case; and for Arnold (believing as he did that there were many propositions true in the abstract but not needing stress in his own times) it must necessarily have had little value, save obliquely in mitigating the tone of his work, or helping to create an impression of his personality. Its comparative frequency is thus a clear sign how these oblique functions are important. "We ought to have no difficulty in conceding to Mr. Sidgwick that...fire and strength...has its high value as well as culture";[51] "Hellenism...has its dangers, as has been fully granted";[52] "there are many things to be said on behalf of this exclusive attention of ours to liberty."[53] Sometimes the concession is "placed," as it were, by a subsequent *distinguo* argument: "the final aim of both Hellenism and Hebraism...is no doubt the same: man's perfection or salvation...still, they pursue this aim by very different courses...so long as we do not forget that both...are profound and admirable...we can hardly insist too strongly on the divergence of line and of operation by which they proceed."[54] Sometimes, too, Arnold does something explicit to relate the concession he makes to his tone, and to our conception of himself: "it is impossible that all these remonstrances and reproofs should not affect me, and I shall try my very best...to profit by the objections I have heard and read."[55] One might say here that the substantial significance of the concession is virtually nil—Arnold gives no hint of what it is he is disposed to agree with—but just for that reason, perhaps, the oblique contribution is at its most direct and powerful. There is, of course, in that last remark, a hint also of something quite other than penitent humility.

The reader must have noticed that through the forms of his arguments Arnold does something to develop our notion of his opponents, as well as of himself. The abiding consciousness of those with whom he disagrees—it is something quite distinctive in Arnold's work—finds remarkable expression in *Friendship's Garland*. This is very largely a work discrediting the opinions of others; and in the main it proceeds by methods of irony, which will be examined below. One cannot help noticing that Arnold offers almost no objections of substance to the practical measures he most clearly condemns. But three times—coloured and half-concealed, certainly, by his satirical flashes—an argument does appear. This is how he takes up the case made out for the Deceased Wife's Sisters Bill: "Let us pursue his fine regenerating idea...let

---

[48] *I.e.* distinctions which would not confirm class distinctions, but mitigate them.   [49] See above, p. 298.
[50] *The Function of Criticism* (iii. 28).   [51] CA. (vi. 146).   [52] vi. 155.   [53] vi. 54.   [54] vi. 121–5.   [55] vi. 45–6.

us deal with this question as a whole... this is not enough... for my part, my resolve is formed... as a sop to those toothless old Cerberuses, the bishops... we will accord the continuance of the prohibition which forbids a man to marry his grandmother. But in other directions there shall be freedom."[56] Then he attacks the "gospel of liberty" in the same way. "... have we ever given liberty... a full trial? The Lord Chancellor has, indeed, provided for Mr. Beales... *but why is Mr. Bradlaugh not yet a Dean*? These, Sir, are the omissions, these the failures to carry into full effect our own great principles which drive earnest Liberals to despair!"[57] Finally he turns, with this same weapon, to the nostrum of publicity: it is true that the government and the courts have recently refused to have sordid divorce and other cases heard *in camera*. "All this was as it should be; so far, so good. But was the publicity thus secured for these cases perfectly full and entire? Were there some places which the details did not reach? There were few, but there were some... I say, make the price of the *London Gazette* a halfpenny; change its name to the *London Gazette and Divorce Intelligencer*;... distribute it *gratis* to mechanics' institutes, workmen's halls, seminaries for the young... and then you will be giving the principle of publicity a full trial."[58] All these arguments take the form of the *reductio ad absurdum*; and above all, what they contribute to is our sense of the personality and the intellectual temper of those with whom Arnold disagrees. Caricature of the arguments is done in a style that indicates the true nature of the authors: it is Arnold's opponents, ultimately, who are being reduced to the absurd.

The Value Frame

ARNOLD'S PREOCCUPATION, as we have seen, is with what states of mind and what attitudes are desirable in human society, and more particularly with what is the desirable temper of mind in which to conduct an enquiry. Apart from a rationalist historical determinism, which plays a minor role in his thought, he had no metaphysics which might form apparent premises for the moral principles he wished to assert. But because a certain temper of mind—the characteristic urbanity and amenity of Arnold—is so pervasively recommended to the reader by the whole texture of his writing, he had a quite distinctive means for both making and justifying value-judgements in other fields. He could praise and justify praise, or condemn and justify condemnation, by suggesting that the topic or the belief under discussion would appeal, or fail to appeal, to the frame of mind which appears throughout his work as the fundamental good.

This distinctive method is to preface or envelop the main assertion in clauses which invite the reader to view it with favour or disfavour, and suggest grounds for the attitude he is to adopt. These *value frames*, as they might be called, serve several

---

[56] FG. (vi. 307–9). The quotation abridges to the point of destruction a very entertaining piece of satire, though Arnold was sailing too near the wind to give his climax its real point.
[57] vi. 336. Mr. Bradlaugh was the well-known atheist and champion of birth-control.   [58] vi. 337–8.

different purposes in Arnold's work, and are sometimes very elaborate. Although by their nature they do not obtrude on the casual reader's notice, yet their influence on the texture of argument is great. It should perhaps be said that when they are quoted, one feels at first that the mere trimmings of a sentence have been given and its substantial part omitted: but this impression rapidly fades. Consider an example first: "The aspirations of culture, which is the study of perfection, are not satisfied unless [what men say when they may say what they like, is worth saying]."[59] Here the two elements, first praise, second the grounds for praise, are fairly clear: first, a condition such as the assertion describes would satisfy one whose concern was for *perfection*, and this is as much as to call it *good*; second, it would satisfy the *cultured, aspiring* and *studious*, and these qualities—which *Culture and Anarchy* from beginning to end has endeared to us—are here the grounds of goodness. Compare "the flexibility which sweetness and light give, and which is one of the rewards of culture pursued in good faith, enables a man to see that. . . ."[60] Here one senses that the praise itself lies in "rewards," the grounds of praise in "flexibility," "sweetness," "light," "culture" and "good faith": these are the qualities of mind to which the assertion recommends itself.

Another interesting example of this device is, "Surely, now, it is no inconsiderable boon which culture confers on us if in embarrassed times like the present it enables us to [look at the ins and outs of things in this way] without hatred and without partiality and with a disposition to see the good in everybody all round"[61]—here not only can both praise and grounds of praise be located easily, but two further features appear: the first few words, and the reference to embarrassed times like the present, distinguish the author's tone and hint his personality; and the whole sentence not only puts Arnold's key word "culture" to use, but also enriches its meaning, so that it can be employed more compendiously elsewhere. Sometimes it proves vitally important to control the exact significance of these key-words: thus "essential in Hellenism is [the impulse to the development of the whole man, to connecting and harmonizing all parts of him, perfecting him]"[62] recommends a certain impulse, gives grounds for the recommendation through the word "Hellenism," whose import is already fairly well determined, and thirdly, amplifies this import itself. And this constant amplification of the import, or rather, constantly bringing it afresh to the reader's notice, allows Arnold to take liberties. He does so with "Hellenism" on the very next page: "that [. . .],—this it is abhorrent to the nature of Hellenism to concede" —the reader can keep in mind, though, that Hellenism even *abhors* with amenity.

It is easy to see how much these value frames do, not only to recommend assertions and offer grounds for them, but also to elucidate and recommend the temper of mind to which they seem true, and above all to show that their strength lies in their appeal to such a temper. "Do not let us fail to see clearly that [. . .]";[63] "when [our religious organizations . . . land us in no better result than this], it is high time to examine

---

[59] CA. (vi. 15). In the following quotations the assertion itself, by contrast with the value frame for it, is put in square brackets or indicated by them.
[60] vi. 28.   [61] vi. 64.   [62] vi. 154.   [63] vi. 25.

carefully their idea of perfection";[64] "[this] is so evident, that no one in Great Britain with clear and calm political judgement, or with fine perception, or with high cultivation, or with large knowledge of the world, doubts it."[65] On the other hand, there are negative instances that show equally clearly how some false proposition is born of the mental temper which Arnold condemns: "Well, then, what an unsound habit of mind it must be which makes us [talk of... as ...]."[66] In either case it is clear that in cultivating this sense of a right "habit of mind" throughout his argument, Arnold equipped himself with a precise and powerful instrument for giving effect to judgements of value.

Some of these examples influence us less because they describe than because they exemplify the right habit of mind; that is to say, they affect the reader less through their meaning than through their tone. "Surely culture is useful in reminding us that [...]"[67] illustrates this tendency. But the significant point, for a comprehensive appreciation of Arnold, is how directly and openly this control of tone develops our sense of the author himself. "Keeping this in view, I have in my own mind often indulged myself with the fancy of [...]";[68] "to me few things are more pathetic than to see [...]";[69] "the philosophers and the prophets, whom I at any rate am disposed to believe ... will tell us that [...]"[70]—above all, "now does anyone, if he simply and naturally reads his consciousness, discover that [...]? For my part, the deeper I go into my own consciousness, and the more simply I abandon myself to it, the more it seems to tell me that [...]"[71]—Arnold is using forms of words that recommend his assertion and that develop our sense of himself, all in one. And because the value frame serves this purpose, it is naturally adapted to serve the complementary purpose: it also, often enough, adds to our impression of his opponents.

These three functions may be performed together through simple antithesis. One example quoted above was incomplete: Arnold wrote, "So when Mr. Carlyle, a man of genius to whom we have all at one time or another been indebted for refreshment and stimulus, says [...] surely culture is useful in reminding us that [...]." Here, words like "refreshment" and "stimulus," and the blunt "says," give a tone to Carlyle's assertion, and the whole phrase controls our impression of Carlyle himself; but Arnold's "culture" is *useful* in *reminding* (it does not simply say); and Arnold hopes to do something more significant than refresh and stimulate. This is very similar to "Mr. Roebuck is never weary of reiterating ... 'May not every man in England say what he likes?'—Mr. Roebuck perpetually asks; and that, he thinks, is quite sufficient.... But the aspirations of culture ... are not satisfied unless, [...] culture indefatigably tries ... to draw ever nearer to a sense of [...]."[72] The contrast is clear; Mr. Roebuck is too satisfied too easily. In the sentence "When Protestantism ... *gives the law* to criticism *too magisterially*, criticism *may* and *must remind* it that [its pretensions, in this respect, are illusive and do it harm],"[73] Arnold's opponents are in the end described explicitly, by the words here printed in brackets; but they, and their critic, and the quality of their respective assertions, are already distinguished

---

[64] vi. 27. [65] ME. (x. 122). [66] CA. (vi. 16). [67] vi. 59. [68] vi. 84. [69] vi. 22. [70] DA. (iv. 314).
[71] CA. (vi. 181). [72] vi. 15. [73] *The Function of Criticism* (iii. 38); my italics.

plainly by the value frame, as the italics make plain. The complex manner in which "its pretensions... do *it* harm" illustrates what was said above about forms of argument should not, by the way, be overlooked.

Arnold is able to endow even the simplest negative with significant and contrasting tone: for example, "And, therefore, when Mr. White asks the same sort of question about America that he has asked about England, and wants to know whether [...] we answer in the same way as we did before, that [as much is not done]."[74] Here there is a subtly suggestive difference in the sameness—White's pestering is monotonous and stupid, Arnold is urbane and patient. Almost exactly this construction comes again: "And if statesmen, either with their tongue in their cheek or with a fine impulsiveness, tell people that [...], there is the more need to tell them the contrary."[75] Sometimes the denial is fuller: "When Mr. Gladstone invites us to call [...] we must surely answer that all this mystical eloquence is not in the least necessary to explain so simple a matter."[76] And while foisting one tone on his opponents, Arnold can provide himself with quite another merely by changing the mood of his verb: "Who, that is not manacled and hoodwinked by his Hebraism, can believe that [...]";[77] "When Mr. Sidgwick says so broadly, that [...] is he not carried away by a turn for broad generalization? does he not forget [...]?"[78]—the question-form itself is all that conveys Arnold's presence, but it is enough.

This quite distinctive device bears both inwards, as it were, and outwards: it suggests an attitude (and grounds for it too) that the reader should take up towards the assertion that it introduces; and through modulations of tone, it can do much to expand and sustain our notion of the writer's personality, and of that of his adversaries. In doing so it is one of the more important techniques creating that bipolarity between himself and them which runs like an axis through Arnold's work.

Definitions

IT TRANSPIRED above that the value frame might not only put one of Arnold's key-words, like "culture," to use, but that it could also control its meaning; and this is to say that the value frame may be inverted in function (or have, as is more likely, two simultaneous functions), and serve as a kind of defining formula. Since definitions proved to be so important a persuasive device in Carlyle, George Eliot and Newman, it is high time to trace the contribution they make in Arnold. But we find that it is surprisingly small. This is not so, of course, in the works of Biblical exegesis— *Literature and Dogma, St. Paul amd Protestantism* or *God and the Bible.* Here Arnold's central purpose is to reinterpret some of the essential concepts of Christianity: he is, in consequence, quite explicit in giving fresh meanings to the key-terms of Scripture, and his argument is full of expressions like "and the sense which this will give us for their words is at least solid,"[79] "a plain solid experimental sense,"[80] "what they

---

[74] CA. (vi, p. xxix).   [75] vi, p. xliii.   [76] ME. (x. 90).   [77] CA. (vi. 193).   [78] vi. 147.   [79] LD. (vii. 58).
[80] vii. 62.

really do at bottom mean by God is...."[81] He even, at one stage, thinks of using re-defining arguments based on the etymologies of words, and mentions how this method is extremely common in Ruskin's social criticism—but in the end he decides not to use "fanciful helps."[82] These books, however, are not really of the type that concerns our enquiry. They do not seek to convince a reader that the world-view they express is true, so much as to convince him that it is the real world-view of the Old and New Testaments. Arnold's theology is not what Carlyle would have called "Life-Philosophy"; it is a sustained *argumentum ad hominem*, addressed to those already sure that the Bible is true if rightly interpreted. When we turn to Arnold's independent work, we find that re-defining arguments virtually disappear; and at first sight this seems a very strange thing.

They are to be found, doubtless, from time to time—it would be inconceivably odd if Arnold were never to define a term anywhere. But by comparison they are certainly few in number, and what is more important, they lack the characteristic quality of such arguments, because they are trite. The typical re-definition seems to transform the import of a word, giving it a more pointed, provocative, pregnant, influential meaning by seeming to draw on some insight of unusual keenness. By contrast, Arnold's definitions are often textbook definitions; they are dull; they are diaphanous. It is not merely that they cannot facilitate interesting inferences; they preclude them, and this is their job.

Three examples will be sufficient: Arnold's accounts of the *State*, of *Civilization* and of *Human Nature*. If he wishes to be tendentious anywhere, surely it will pay to be tendentious here. But all we find is (1) "*The State*—but what is the State? cry many. ... The full force of the term, *the State* ... no one will master without going a little deeply...." So far all is like Carlyle; not, however, for long. "... but it is possible to give in very plain language an account of it sufficient for all practical purposes. The State is properly just what Burke called it—*the nation in its collective and corporate character*. The State is the representative acting-power of the nation...."[83] (2) "What do we mean by *civilized*?... we will try to answer. Civilization is the humanization of man in society. To be humanized is to comply with the true law of our human nature ... says Lucan 'to keep our measure, and to hold fast our end, and to follow Nature'... to make progress towards this, our true and full humanity. And to be civilized is to make progress towards this in civil society."[84] Nothing could seem less pointed than this. (3) "When we talk of ... full humanity, we think of an advance, not along one line only, but several. ... The power of intellect and science, the power of beauty, the power of social life and manners ... the power of conduct is another great element."[85] This may be true and useful, but it is not new.

The reason for this apparent lack of enterprise is clear. Unlike Carlyle and the rest, Arnold has no wish to draw controversial or unexpected conclusions from his definitions. On the contrary, it was partisanship or legerdemain of this kind that he was

---

[81] vii. 327.   [82] ST.P. (ix. 42).   [83] ME. (x. 40).   [84] x. 61.

[85] x. 62–3. These same four powers are listed in almost identical words in *Literature and Science* (DA., iv. 330–31) as "the powers which go to the building up of human life," or "the constitution of human nature."

resisting. He defines the State, only to rebut the view that States cannot be active except harmfully (far from this, the State is good or bad as we make it, he argues—it all depends upon the details); he defines civilization to rebut a paradoxical conclusion about France by Erskine May; in *Literature and Science* he gives the same account of human nature in its various aspects, so as to rebut the narrow and exclusive pretensions of the scientist. Arnold is using a pattern of argument contrary to the third pattern we distinguished in Newman's work: he is arguing that his opponents use words in unduly narrow and tendentious senses, and demanding that we adopt unsuggestive, everyday senses instead. In short, these passages are true definitions, not re-definitions; the re-definition is a persuasive technique which it is their purpose to reject and discredit.[86]

To be sure, the more usual type of tendentious re-definition is not unknown in Arnold's work—or at least one supposes oneself to have located it from time to time —but here the position is still stranger, for Arnold appears to use the technique for only one word, or rather one pair of synonyms. These synonyms are "culture," and "criticism." It has not been clearly recognized, perhaps, that he distinguishes these two by nothing substantial; but this is surely true. Culture, in its simpler sense, is grounded on "a desire after the things of the mind simply for their own sakes and for the pleasure of seeing them as they are";[87] criticism's rule "may be summed up in one word—disinterestedness,"[88] and it works against obstacles in that "the mass of mankind will never have any ardent zeal for seeing things as they are."[89] True, "there is of culture another view..." where, though not itself active, it is a ground of action—"... it is *a study of perfection*";[90] but there is another view of criticism too, and this time "it obeys an instinct prompting it to try to know the *best* that is known and thought in the world."[91] Most remarkable of all, perhaps, is the fact that Arnold controls the value-implications of both words by giving a particular sense to the single word "curiosity." Each time he shows that this word "in the terms of which may lie a real ambiguity"[92] has, as well as its usual bad sense, a less usual but more important good sense: and then writes, in one place, "this is the true ground to assign for the genuine scientific passion, however manifested, and for culture, viewed simply as a fruit of this passion";[93] and in the other, "criticism, real criticism, is essentially the exercise of this quality." When one remembers that, after all, each of these words is being used as what Arnold would have called "not a term of science, but... a term of common speech, of poetry and eloquence, *thrown out* at a vast object of consciousness not fully covered by it,"[94] their substantial identity is apparent, and that it has not been more emphasized is remarkable.

There is no need to reproduce the argument whereby, especially in *Culture and Anarchy*, Arnold develops this concept—by whichever of the two words we think of it; like the other Victorian prophets, he has been paraphrased often enough. But

---

[86] Arnold occasionally uses re-definitions of the normal type—for example, "What is freedom but machinery? What is population but machinery?..." (CA., vi. 14). But for the most part (though scarcely here in respect of freedom) they are trivial or incidental.
[87] CA. (vi. 6).   [88] *The Function of Criticism* (iii. 20).   [89] iii. 27.   [90] CA. (vi. 7).   [91] *Op. cit.* (iii. 18).
[92] CA. (vi. 5).   [93] vi. 7.   [94] LD. (vii. 191).

the form of this development is significant. Earlier, we mentioned how Newman had a pattern of argument which gradually unfolded the full sense of a word;[95] but his method and Arnold's are entirely different. Newman first *used* his word in an apparently non-controversial way, then strove to show that in allowing him to use it like this the reader had conceded more than he knew. But Arnold is explicit that his definitions are *analyses* of concepts. He announces[96] that he will proceed to enquire "what culture really is"; and further, he does not confine attention to what we must call its alleged essence, and say that this is really something that usually goes by another name (and the essence of this by a third, and so on through a whole series of "charged" expressions, which in Carlyle is frequent). Arnold's method simply takes the reader through subordinate notions that comprise the meaning of his key-term. He analyses, he does not re-interpret; and only when the analysis is complete does he claim that the key-term stands for something good—recapitulating the analysis to show why, and emphasizing that this *is* why. For example, "If culture, then, is a study of perfection, and of harmonious perfection, general perfection, and perfection which consists in becoming something rather than having something . . . it is clear that culture . . . has a very important function to fulfil for mankind";[97] " . . . well, then, how salutary a friend is culture . . . culture begets a satisfaction which is of the highest possible value. . . ."[98] We can see how the tone becomes gradually firmer, as a positive value is set more and more confidently on what "culture" refers to. But Arnold makes it plain that the word carries this favourable tone explicitly because of the sense he gives it—and even admits openly that one may not necessarily be in error to give it another sense. "I must remark . . . that whoever calls anything else culture, may, indeed, call it so if he likes, but then he talks of something quite different."[99] And there is just such a *caveat* in the essay which defines criticism: "But stop, someone will say . . . this criticism of yours is not what we have in our minds when we speak of criticism . . . I am sorry for it . . . I am bound by my own definition of criticism: *a disinterested endeavour to . . .*"[100]—and so on.

Arnold's way of manipulating senses is thus different in kind from that of Newman or Carlyle. His discussions do not suggest, as theirs did, that investigating senses is a kind of discovery. He is really finding a single convenient *name* for a complex of features plainly listed. And this precedes argument in Arnold, whereas the typical re-definition either *is* the crucial stage of an argument, or comes just after it, and shows that what seemed innocent was in fact crucial. Arnold is at no pains to conceal how the definition he adopts is in a sense arbitrary: for him it is an arbitrary but convenient first move. We have seen how the real argument, when it begins, may also control the sense of a key-word like "culture"—sometimes, for example, through its use in a value frame. Yet this control does less to give the word a new sense, than simply to keep the established sense clearly before the reader. It emphasizes, indeed, that Arnold defines "culture" first and then uses it with a constant meaning. Re-definition proper depends on ambiguities.

---

[95] See [Holloway, *The Victorian Sage*], p. 196.   [96] CA. (vi. 4).   [97] CA. (vi. 12–13).   [98] vi. 16, 17.
[99] vi. 67.   [100] *The Function of Criticism* (iii. 41–2).

Articulating the Argument: Arnold and His Opponents

THE DESIRE to have distinctive names for whatever he is discussing is a feature of much of Arnold's work. In Chapter IV of *Culture and Anarchy*, writing of the "energy driving at practice" and the "intelligence driving at those ideas which are ... the basis of right practice," he says "to give these forces names ... we may call them ... Hebraism and Hellenism."[101] Elsewhere we find "these favourite doctrines of theirs I call ... a peculiarly British form of Atheism ... a peculiarly British form of Quietism";[102] or "I may call them the ways of Jacobinism."[103] How Arnold introduces the terms "sweetness and light," or "Barbarians, Philistines, Populace,"[104] is perhaps too well known to need further remark. The effect of some of these is clear enough—they are what may simply be called *hangdog* names. But Arnold gives a reason for using the last three which indicates how they can contribute to the general texture of his prose. "The same desire for clearness," he writes, "... prompts me also to improve my nomenclature ... a little, with a view to making it thereby more manageable."[105] This is important. To be clear and manageable are not new concepts in Arnold's work. They were the distinctive qualities of his tone, because he made this represent his temper of mind. By providing convenient names for his main topics, he not only influences our attitude through the nuance of those names, but articulates his argument with nodal points that soon become familiar, and easy to trace again. The kind of argument that is his at his most typical, an argument that moves gently forward with a smooth, unruffled urbanity, owes not a little to the familiarity of these coinages, as they so constantly reappear. They do not affect the logic of his discussion, but they transform its quality.

The same principle of style also operates more widely. Sometimes he organizes the whole movement of his thought round a single concept denoted by a single constantly recurring word: an example is the essay *Numbers*, through all the earlier part of which runs the idea of a tiny *élite* which is gradually to leaven the whole of society, and for which Arnold borrows the word "remnant." Much more frequently, a whole essay or a whole book is permeated by certain phrases for ideas which have an abiding place of trust in his mind. "Choose equality," "sweetness and light," "our best self," "spontaneity of consciousness," "a free play of the mind," "a full and harmonious development," "perfection at all points," "the best that is known and thought in the world"—these phrases return constantly, and contribute not only through their meaning, but also by their recurrence. They bring the argument nearer to that easy limpidity which its author wishes to recommend. By being careful to repeat himself verbally, Arnold brings into a bright light the essential simplicity of his thought. He orders his argument with familiar landmarks. By this means he can hope to attune the reader to his message, just as the rich verbal confusion of Carlyle attunes a reader to an outlook which is quite different.

And the key-phrases work to Arnold's advantage not only by their recurrence, but also by their origin. The first three in the list above are all borrowed—from

---

[101] CA. (vi. 121). [102] vi. 109-10. [103] vi. 36. [104] vi. 20, 79 ff. [105] vi. 82.

Menander, Swift and Plato respectively. That they are borrowed in this way may add to the weight they carry, or it may not. But quoting authorities is so common in Arnold that it adds something quite distinctive to our impression of him as we read. Through it we see his modesty, his circumspection, and, oddly enough, his independence—not of mind, but of prejudice or strong emotion such as might provoke personal, precipitate, passionate comment. His use of authorities is a contrast to that of Carlyle. Carlyle overwhelmingly gives the impression of willingness to form and express opinions; his "quotations" are incidental and subordinate. The reader recognizes them as a game, an expression of the author's exuberance, his intellectual self-confidence and high spirits. Arnold really quotes, he does not invent authorities; and time and again his quotation is introduced at the crucial stage, and his authority constitutes the rock of his argument.

Consider some examples. The discourse *Literature and Science* begins by drawing entirely from Plato, and the fact that Arnold by no means expects his audience to defer to Plato's authority only emphasizes the very aspect of using an authority that we are discussing. Later, however, at a really crucial point in the argument, Arnold reverts to Plato. He has been arguing that men have in their nature four "powers" or tendencies, intellectual, moral, aesthetic and social; and that just as they have a need to relate the points of their knowledge into a system, so they have a need to relate these four powers into a system. How is he to suggest that this need is worthy to be given free play? At this point Arnold withdraws from his argument, and makes a quite fresh start to introduce the authority of Diotima in the *Symposium*. All desire, says Diotima, is at bottom desire for the good; "and therefore this fundamental desire it is, I suppose ... which acts in us when we feel the impulse for relating our knowledge to our sense for conduct and our sense for beauty. At any rate, with men in general the instinct exists ... and ... it will be admitted, is innocent, and human nature is preserved by our following the lead of its innocent instincts."[106] In the address on *Equality*[107] Arnold goes even further. He begins by asserting that in the Burial Service is to be found the maxim "evil communications corrupt good manners"; but this is quite irrelevant and is never referred to again. Its only significance is to have been quoted from Menander; from whom another maxim (not already quoted anywhere) is "choose equality and flee greed."[108] With that the argument can begin; but as it proceeds, George Sand, Turgot, Voltaire, Burke, M. de Lavelaye, Hamerton, Bossuet, the Book of Proverbs, Pepys and Charles Sumner come one after another, if not to confirm an opinion, at least to provide one which can be discussed and examined. At every turn Arnold seems to avoid taking the initiative, or forcing on the reader something which is merely his own. He even makes his method explicit on one issue: "now the interesting point for us is ... to know how far other European communities, left in the same situation with us ... have dealt with these inequalities."[109] All the time he is building up our sense of an author who thinks others' opinions more important than his own.

Perhaps it is also worth mentioning, as examples of some special importance, the

---

[106] DA. (iv. 333).   [107] ME. (x. 46).   [108] x. 47.   [109] ME. (x. 52).

first paragraphs of the discourse *Numbers*, deriving as they do from one of Johnson's sayings; and the authority of Burke appealed to at a crucial stage in the essay on *The Function of Criticism*;[110] and the works of Biblical exegesis, which constitute one sustained appeal to authority. But the method is so common with Arnold that it cannot be overlooked. Nor can we overlook its significance, if only because Arnold at one point states it: "I am grown so cowed by all the rebuke my original speculations have drawn upon me that I find myself more and more filling the part of a mere listener."[111] Arnold quotes the views of others, rather than express his own, because this modifies our sense of his argument and our view of him. This is not simply to say that he conciliates the reader by refusing to disagree with him, or instruct him directly. Had Carlyle attempted to conciliate in this way he would have had to be at special pains to prevent its being a quite false note, thoroughly discordant with his argument. Once again, our concern is not with a superficial trick of persuasion, but with some modulation of style which is a genuine aid because, through developing our sense of the writer's personality, it genuinely mediates his point of view. That Arnold sometimes uses this method to excess is undeniable; the problem is to sense its point, where it is used aptly.

Quotation, however, is something which Arnold is fonder of inflicting on his opponents than on his models. *My Countrymen*, for example, opens with a grand review of those who have disagreed with him: the *Saturday Review*, Mr. Bazley (M.P. for Manchester), Mr. Miall, the *Daily Telegraph*, the *Daily News*, Mr. Lowe, John Bright, the *Morning Star*, they are all there, marshalled against Arnold, by himself. *Culture and Anarchy* begins similarly—with Bright, the *Daily Telegraph*, and Frederic Harrison; so does *The Function of Criticism*. In *Equality*, Arnold begins with his opponents—Disraeli, Erskine May, Gladstone, Froude, Lowe, Sir William Molesworth—the moment he has done with Menander. The modest, fair, urbane Arnold shows in what seems like an attempt to do justice to the other side. But Arnold uses his opponents further. He quotes from them, and uses these quotations over and over again; wanting his readers to notice less their meaning (which is often uncertain) than their general tenor and their tone. He thus equips himself with a set of—let us say catch-phrases rather than key-phrases—that crystallize the views he is resisting in the same simple and recurrent form as his most favoured expressions crystallize his own views. Both the false and the true are presented with the same urbane simplicity; and while we see Arnold's personality behind his selection and presentation of these phrases, and behind their calm and genial reiteration, we see his opponents in the catch-phrases themselves, a little more clearly and a little more disastrously each time. His own account of these phrases was "profligate expenditure of claptrap."[112]

Certainly, he collected some gems. Frederic Harrison was unfortunate enough to "seek vainly in Mr. A. a system of philosophy with principles coherent, interdependent, subordinate, and derivative."[113] Arnold never really let him forget it subsequently. Harrison it was too who told the working class that "theirs are the brightest powers of sympathy and the readiest powers of action."[114] Under Arnold's

---

[110] See above, p. 300. [111] FG. (vi. 391). [112] vi. 258. [113] vi. 299. [114] CA. (vi. 101).

reiteration, the readiness takes on a fresh colour, the brightness gets a little rubbed. Arnold also lets us savour Frederic Harrison's account of the middle classes, "their earnest good sense which penetrates through sophisms, ignores commonplaces, and gives to conventional illusions their true value";[115] and John Bright's "thoughtfulness and intelligence of the people of the great towns";[116] and *The Times'* comment on East End children. "Now their brief spring is over. There is no one to blame for this; it is the result of Nature's simplest laws!";[117] and Robert Buchanan's account in the same context of "that divine philoprogenitiveness.... He would *swarm* the earth with beings...."[118] and his "line of poetry":

'Tis the old story of the fig-leaf time.

The newspaper account of why a certain Mr. Smith committed suicide, that he "laboured under the apprehension that he would come to poverty, and that he was eternally lost,"[119] does service too; so does Roebuck's "I look around me and ask what is the state of England? Is not every man able to say what he likes? I ask you whether the world over, or in past history, there is anything like it? Nothing. I pray that our unrivalled happiness may last"[120]—which is a recurrent theme in *The Function of Criticism*, and reappears in *Culture and Anarchy*.[121] "The Dissidence of Dissent and the Protestantism of the Protestant religion," which began life as a motto on the *Nonconformist*, is resurrected in both *Culture and Anarchy* and the *Discourses in America*.[122] *The Times'* instruction to the British Government to speak out "with promptitude and energy" enlivens *Friendship's Garland*,[123] where Lowe's fatuous "the destiny of England is in the great heart of England" also rears its empty head.[124] The desire of the Bishops of Winchester and Gloucester to "do something for the honour of the Eternal Godhead" is saluted every so often throughout *Literature and Dogma*;[125] and choicest of all perhaps, the "great sexual insurrection of our Anglo-Teutonic race,"[126] product of a disciple of Hepworth Dixon, is one of Arnold's most treasured literary possessions.

Now clearly, to introduce or reiterate so many phrases of this kind does not in itself render the texture of Arnold's argument simpler and more urbane: their straightforward effect is to make it more variegated and less urbane, and it will be necessary to see how he so "places" them in their context that this direct tendency is overruled, and the tone of the quotation is prevented from interfering with the tone of the main text. But what these quotations simplify for us is our conception of Arnold's opponents and their shortcomings. Time and again, always in the same way, they epitomize for us the defect of temper which is what above all Arnold is condemning. In one simple, natural perception, we see what this defect is; and every time they are repeated, the flaw they reveal shows a little more clearly.

The defective temper of mind which Arnold makes plain in what his opponents say, is also plain in what they do. He has no need of rhetoric or eloquence or complex

---

[115] CA. (vi. 101). [116] vi. p. xxiv. [117] vi. 201. [118] vi. 202-3. [119] vi. 157. [120] iii. 23-5. [121] vi. 110. [122] vi. 23, and DA. (iv. 375). [123] FG. (vi. 322). [124] vi. 321, 371. [125] *E.g.* vii. 4, 6-7, 33, 162, 183, 237, 239, 273, 288, 304, 364. [126] CA. (vi. 190 and 191); FG. (vi. 306 and 307).

argumentation: the simple facts are silently eloquent by themselves. For this purpose, inventions are as good as realities. *Friendship's Garland* is almost a series of fictitious anecdotes of invented revealing incidents—the Philistine Bottles giving Arnold's hero Arminius a jingoistic number of *Punch* in the train, or sitting in all the Deceased Wife's Sisters Bill glory of his suburban residence; the Honourable Charles Clifford addressing the crowd from the footboard of his hansom; Dr. Russell of *The Times* vainly striving to get astride his warhorse; Cole's Truss Manufactory in Trafalgar Square—"the finest site in Europe";[127] Lord Elcho's hat—"to my mind the mere cock of his lordship's hat is one of the most aristocratic things we have."[128] The technique reappears in *The Function of Criticism*: trying to indicate the fault of temper in a whole series of writings, Arnold again takes a single striking case. "Their fault is...one which they have in common with the British College of Health in the New Road...with the lion and the statue of the Goddess Hygeia...the grand name without the grand thing."[129]

"The grand name without the grand thing"—Arnold is not unaware that, if he selects his opponents astutely, their names alone will be enough to expose their defects; and the method is ingenious, for although it says little explicitly, it makes one unable even to think of Arnold's victim without automatically seeing him in an unfavourable light. Beside the British College of Health we have "Cole's Truss Manufactory,"[130] and the "*British Banner*":[131] Arnold adds "I am not quite sure it was the *British Banner*, but it was some newspaper of the same stamp," which seems to show that he knew how the name, if only he could bring it in, would argue for him. It is not, however, only the sham pomposity of names that he enlists in his argument. "Has anyone reflected," he writes, "what a touch of grossness in our race...is shown by the natural growth amongst us of such hideous names—Higginbottom, Stiggins, Bugg!"[132] In *Friendship's Garland* Arnold hints at the ludicrous, and also at the ugly, in his opponents, by invented names like "Viscount Lumpington," "the Reverend Esau Hittall," and "Bottles Esquire."[133] Elsewhere, for the same purpose, he selects from the material available. The result is Mr. Bazley, Mr. Blewitt, Mr. Bradlaugh, Mr. Blowitz (perhaps Arnold saw something banausic in the initial B), Miss Cobbes and Mr. Murphy. There are other names, too, which might be added to this list; and if any doubt remains whether the method genuinely colours Arnold's argument, a passage in *Culture and Anarchy* shows him somersaulting an opponent's argument of an exactly opposite kind: "'Well, but,' says Mr. Hepworth Dixon, 'a theory which has been accepted by men like Judge Edmonds, Dr. Hare, Elder Frederick and Professor Bush!'... Such are, in brief, the bases of what Newman Weeks, Sarah Horton, Deborah Butler, and the associated brethren, proclaimed in Rolt's Hall as the New Covenant!" Evidently, Arnold hints, "Mr. Hepworth Dixon" is taken in by *not* the grand name without the grand thing. He goes on, "If he was summing up an account of the doctrine of Plato, or of St. Paul...Mr. Hepworth Dixon could not be more earnestly reverential." And now Arnold replies with his

---

[127] vi. 249. [128] vi. 262. [129] *The Function of Criticism* (iii. 36). [130] *Loc. cit.* [131] CA. (vi. 96). [132] *The Function of Criticism* (iii. 26). [133] FG. (vi. 286).

own selection of names: "But the question is, Have personages like Judge Edmonds, and Newman Weeks, and Elderess Polly and Elderess Antoinette, and the rest of Mr. Hepworth Dixon's heroes and heroines, anything of the weight and significance ... that Plato and St. Paul have?"[134] Here the first parade of names is enough to reveal the intellectual defects of Arnold's opponent, and the second is enough to conclude the discussion.

Arnold's comment on the ugliness of English names occurs in a passage when he is more serious, and is using a judiciously chosen example in another way, less to epitomize an outlook, than to reveal what it omits. It is of particular interest, not only because Arnold is using quotation, authority, the value frame, and example in a single integrated argument, but also because the contrast between the tone of the text itself and that of the inserted passages is particularly vivid. First, he quotes Sir Charles Adderley, "the old Anglo-Saxon race ... the best breed in the world," and Mr. Roebuck, "the world over or in past history, is there anything like it? Nothing." Against this comes a simple quotation from Goethe, framed or "placed" by the phrase "clearly this is a better line of reflection"—we see at once how the counter-move is directed against a certain mental temper, and recommends its opposite. Then Arnold returns to his opponents. They would not contradict Goethe, it is simply that they "lose sight" of what he saw: they are carried away by controversy, they "go a little beyond the point and say stoutly—"; so long as they are countered in the same spirit, "so long will the strain swell louder and louder." Instead of this, Arnold proposes another spirit, which he sees in simply giving, without comment, one example, one simple fact. "Let criticism ... *in the most candid spirit* ... confront with our dithyramb *this* ..." (my italics):

> A shocking child murder has just been committed at Nottingham. A girl named Wragg left the workhouse there on Saturday morning with her young illegitimate child. The child was soon afterwards found dead on Mapperly Hills, having been strangled. Wragg is in custody.

"Nothing but that," he goes on, "but in juxtaposition with the absolute eulogies ... how eloquent, how suggestive are those few lines ... there is profit for the spirit in such contrasts. ... Mr. Roebuck will have a poor opinion of an adversary who replies to his defiant songs of triumph only by murmuring under his breath, *Wragg is in custody*; but in no other way will these songs of triumph be induced gradually to moderate themselves, to get rid of what in them is excessive and offensive, and to fall into a softer and truer key."[135]

Irony

IN THAT PASSAGE the sustained contrast between two tempers of mind, one which Arnold seeks to recommend or maintain, and one which he detects in his opponents, is so clear that the problem of how he maintains this duality is now inescapable; and

---

[134] CA. (vi. 97–9).   [135] *The Function of Criticism* (iii. 25–7).

his chief method, beyond question, is irony. It is widely agreed that by irony an author can seem to the casual or uninformed reader to say one thing, but really say something quite different, clear only to the reader who is initiated or more attentive. But why should such a roundabout method of communication ever be employed? Usually it is hard enough, one would suppose, to convey one's meaning straightforwardly—why, not content with one difficulty, does an author invent another? Sometimes, perhaps, because irony can be like a sophisticated intellectual game, which writer and reader alike may enjoy for its own sake. But there may be a more substantial reason. Irony is a powerful and genuine instrument of persuasion. The meaning of a statement—especially one praising or blaming what is being spoken of, or doing anything of a similar kind—usually determines a characteristic tone in which it is reasonable to write or utter that statement. Outright condemnation of essentials tends to sound indignant, partial condemnation of details to sound mildly disapproving, plain description to sound detached, praise to sound admiring. These are no more than tendencies, but they are tendencies strong enough to be inconvenient to writers who, for example, particularly desire not to sound indignant or benignant; and irony is a means whereby a writer may say something in a tone that normally would be inappropriate to it. How easily that will influence the impression he gives the reader of himself, need not be laboured.

Quintilian says that to write ironically is to praise by blaming, or to blame by praising; of which two the last, of course, is the commoner. This is a method which Arnold uses fairly often. But, more than Quintilian's formula suggests, Arnold adapts the nuance of his blame, and of his praise too, so that it serves the general impression he wishes to give. The blame behind his seeming-innocent praise is relatively constant in kind; the praise itself is such that the uncomprehending complacence with which one fancies his opponents would receive it is enough to condemn them; there is no random hitting, because Arnold's irony is adapted so as to be exactly right for the general tenor of his work. Mr. Gladstone is

> that attractive and ever-victorious rhetorician[136]

who

> concludes in his copious and eloquent way.[137]

Other examples of this lethal innocence are

> the ingenious and inexhaustible Mr. Blowitz, of our great London *Times*[138]
>
> a hundred vigorous and influential writers[139]
>
> the newspapers... who have that trenchant authoritative style[140]
>
> this brisk and flourishing movement[141]

[136] DA. (iv. 280).   [137] ME. (x. 49).   [138] DA. (iv. 311).   [139] FG. (vi. 368–9).   [140] vi. 353.   [141] DA. (iv. 321).

> our great orator, Mr. Bright . . . never weary of telling us[142]
>
> my nostrums of State Schools for those much too wise to want them, and of an Academy for people who have an inimitable style already[143]
>
> before I called Dixon's style lithe and sinewy[144]
>
> Mr. Lowe's powerful and much admired speech against Reform.[145]

There is no mistaking the trend of these passages. At first glance, they constitute just that genial, deferential praise which we might expect the urbane Arnold genuinely to give to his more forceful colleagues; but when the second meaning comes home, they are seen to diagnose just the smug, busy over-confidence that Arnold has made his inveterate enemy.

In this way Arnold makes his irony show both what he is like, and what his opponents are like. Images can do this as well as descriptions. In *A Courteous Explanation* he finds occasion to write: "[Horace] and his friends have lost their tails, and want to get them back."[146] The tail here is a symbol of political liberty. But it is not long before Arnold is utilizing its ironic possibilities:

> I think our "true political Liberty" a beautiful bushy object . . . it struck me there was a danger of our trading too extensively upon our tails, and, in fact, running to tail altogether. . . . Our highest class, besides having of course true political liberty,—that regulation tail that every Briton of us is blessed with,—is altogether so beautiful and splendid (and above all, as Mr. Carlyle says, polite) that for my part I hardly presume to enquire what it has or has not in the way of heads.[147]

Clearly, this beautiful bushy tail is—may one say it?—a two-edged weapon. There is a very similar passage at the end of *Friendship's Garland*, in the letter alleged to have been written by "A Young Lion" from Paris; the hand is the hand of a lithe disciple of Hepworth Dixon, but of course the voice is the voice of Arnold:

> While Sala was speaking, a group had formed before the hotel near us, and our attention was drawn to its central figure. Dr. Russell, of the *Times*, was preparing to mount his war-horse. You know the sort of thing,—he has described it himself over and over again. Bismarck at his horse's head, the Crown Prince holding his stirrup, and the old King of Prussia hoisting Russell into the saddle. When he was there, the distinguished public servant waved his hand in acknowledgement, and rode slowly down the street, accompanied by the *gamins* of Versailles, who even in their present dejection could not forbear a few involuntary cries of "Quel homme!"[148]

—by now the exact nuance of the blame behind the praise is beginning to be apparent, the warhorse has become a hobbyhorse, and Arnold, once more, is depicting in his opponents the perennial source of his dislike.

The ambivalency between praise and blame that makes this passage ironical depends very much upon Arnold's giving it to an alleged author doing duty for the real author

---

[142] iv. 285.   [143] FG. (vi. 353–4).   [144] vi. 306.   [145] vi. 369.   [146] vi. 400.   [147] vi. 400–401.   [148] vi. 345.

whom we sense in the background. It is one of his favourite devices to invent figures to speak his opinions for him. In part its contribution is like that suggested above for quotations and authorities; but in part too it sustains that divorce of tone and statement which is the office of irony. Thus, in *My Countrymen*, it is "certain foreigners" who deliver the attack on English life—and a most forceful and outspoken attack it is. But Arnold appears only as their interlocutor in defence of England—an anxious, embarrassed, excessively reasonable defender perhaps (as Arnold was likely to be for any cause) but a defender all the same.

> I used often to think what a short and ready way one of our hardhitting English newspapers would take with these scorners ... but being myself a mere seeker after truth, with nothing trenchant or authoritative about me, I could do no more than look shocked and begin to ask questions. "What!" I said, "you hold the England of today cheap...?" ... Though I could not bear without a shudder this insult to the earnest good sense which, as the *Morning Star* says, may be fairly set down as the general characteristic of England and Englishmen everywhere.... I begged my acquaintances to explain a little more fully....
> "... and intelligence [they said]... your middle class has absolutely none." I was aghast. I thought of this great class, every morning and evening extolled for its clear manly intelligence by a hundred vigorous and influential writers....[149]

But he has just been sent a copy of a speech by Mr. Lowe, telling how the English middle class has been performing unrivalled exploits:

> I took it out of my pocket. "Now," said I to my envious, carping foreigners, "just listen to me ... Mr. Lowe shall answer you...." What I had urged, or rather what I had borrowed from Mr. Lowe, seemed to me exceedingly forcible, and I looked anxiously for its effect on my hearers. They did not appear so much disconcerted as I had hoped.[150]

In *Friendship's Garland* Arnold uses the same device to escape the awkward tone implied by what he wants to say. Here it is the mythical Prussian, Arminius von Thunder-den-Tronkh, who delivers Arnold's attack direct. And Arnold, speaking in his own person, writes:

> In confidence I will own to you that he makes himself intensely disagreeable. He has the harsh, arrogant Prussian way of turning up his nose at things and laying down the law about them; and though, as a lover of intellect, I admire him, and, as a seeker of truth, I value his frankness, yet, as an Englishman, and a member of what the *Daily Telegraph* calls "the Imperial race," I feel so uncomfortable under it, that I want, through your kindness, to call to my aid the great British public, which never loses heart and has always a bold front and a rough word ready for its assailants.[151]

Arminius himself is a likeable figure, with his pink face and blue eyes, his shaggy blond hair, his ancient blue pilot-coat, and pipe belching interminable smoke. But

[149] FG. (vi. 363–9).   [150] vi. 369–71.   [151] vi. 243–4.

although his personality may be likeable, it is very different from Arnold's, and he can do what would be disastrous for Arnold himself. Arminius and his creator go down to Reigate by rail, and in the carriage is, as Arnold calls him, "one of our representative industrial men (something in the bottle way)." When the manufacturer begins to talk politics, Arnold tries to soothe the conversation with "a few sentences taken from Mr. Gladstone's advice to the Roumanians." But—"The dolt! The dunderhead! His ignorance of the situation, his ignorance of Germany, his ignorance of what makes nations great, his ignorance of what makes life worth living, his ignorance of everything except bottles—those infernal bottles!"—that is Arminius's comment.[152] On another occasion, Arnold "runs" to appease him with a "powerful letter" by Mr. Goldwin Smith, published in the *Daily News*, and "pronouncing in favour of the Prussian alliance... 'At last I have got what will please you,'" cries he. But Arminius only gives a sardonic smile, and puts it all down ungraciously to the Prussian needle-gun.[153] "Your precious *Telegraph*,"[154] he says bluntly; and of *The Times*, "that astonishing paper."[155] Arnold contrasts Arminius and himself directly: "'You make me look rather a fool, Arminius,' I began, 'by what you primed me with....' 'I dare say you looked a fool,' says my Prussian boor, 'but what did I tell you?'"[156] Even Arminius himself is made to emphasize just the contrast Arnold wishes us to see. "I have a regard for this Mr. Matthew Arnold, but I have taken his measure.... Again and again I have seen him anxiously ruminating over what his adversary has happened to say against his ideas; and when I tell him (if the idea were mine) that his adversary is a *dummkopf*, and that he must stand up to him firm and square, he begins to smile, and tells me that what is probably passing through his adversary's mind is so and so."[157]

This example introduces one of Arnold's most characteristic manoeuvres. Having introduced imaginary characters to speak for him, he recommends himself to the reader by interruptions that deny their excesses. Here he adds to Arminius's comment the footnote, "A very ill-natured and exaggerated description of my (I hope) not unamiable candour." In the Dedicatory Letter to *Friendship's Garland* he reports Arminius *verbatim* at length and then appears in his own person to retract: "I doubt whether this is sound, Leo, and, at any rate, the D.T. [*Daily Telegraph*] should have been more respectfully mentioned."[158] Arminius asserts dogmatically that Mr. Lowe is descended from Voltaire's insufferable optimist Pangloss: Arnold says that he believes there is no more than "a kinship in the spirit"—Arminius, he fears, was suffering from a fixed idea.[159] Later, Arminius records an unbelievable interview with Lowe. Arnold observes gravely that since everything he makes Lowe say actually appeared in Lowe's printed speeches, there is reason to fear that the interview was only imaginary.[160] When Arminius tirades against the style of the *Daily Telegraph*, Arnold writes, "though I do certainly think its prose a little full-bodied, yet I cannot bear to hear Arminius apply such a term to it as 'incorrigibly lewd'; and I always remonstrate with him. 'No, Arminius,' I always say, 'I hope not *incorrigibly*.'"[161]

[152] vi. 245. [153] vi. 246. [154] vi. 235. [155] vi. 275. [156] vi. 274. [157] vi. 252–3. [158] FG. (vi. 237).
[159] vi. 260. [160] vi. 272 n. [161] vi. 284.

And Arnold has a delightful footnote to "Young Lion's" account of Dr. Russell mounting on horseback, in which he confesses sadly to not having found, in Russell's correspondence, quite the confirmatory descriptions that "Leo" spoke of. "Repeatedly I have seemed to be on the trace of what my friend meant, but the particular description he alludes to I have never been lucky enough to light upon."[162] Sometimes the retraction by Arnold is implicit in one word, as when, pretending to report Arminius's own words about his inventor, he writes "the newspapers which you are stupid [sic] enough to quote with admiration."[163]

The general effect of this device, however, might possibly be misunderstood. Only a child would see Arnold in these disclaimers alone. To a reader acquainted with the methods of irony the first rough impression of his personality, coming perhaps from these by themselves, is immediately corrected by a sense that he is author of the whole tissue of assertion dramatized in character and disclaimer with an edge to it. The undercurrent of meaning establishes that he is fully in earnest, has something he thinks it important to say. But concern for his message has not carried him away, and we see him still able to select exactly the most telling mode in which to express it; we are made to feel that there is no self-importance in a man who can so depreciate himself, even in play. Arnold develops both that first rough impression of himself, and the more complete impression, by explicit means: "for posterity's sake, I keep out of harm's way as much as I can.... I sit shivering in my garret, listening nervously to the voices of indignant Philistines asking the way to Grub Street.... I write with a bit of coal on the lining of my hat."[164] Here the reference to posterity reminds the reader that it is all a game, though one, perhaps, that serves a serious end. So it is when in *Culture and Anarchy*, he, after some havering, offers himself as an example of the Aristotelian extreme of *defect* in possessing the virtues of his own class. "Perhaps there might be a want of urbanity in singling out this or that personage as the representative of defect ... but with oneself one may always, without impropriety, deal quite freely; and, indeed, this sort of plain dealing with oneself has in it, as all the moralists tell us, something very wholesome. So I will venture to humbly offer myself as an illustration of defect in those forces and qualities which make our middle class what it is."[165] He has done nothing, he confesses, to help uproot the evils of church-rates, for example. He quite lacks the "perfect self-satisfaction" current among the Philistines. "But these confessions," he concludes, "though salutary, are bitter and unpleasant." Here again the effect is two-fold: first, simply, of Arnold offering himself humbly as an example of defect; and second, less simply, of Arnold being sufficiently at ease and in command of himself (despite the unmistakable note of seriousness) to play a nice, an elaborate game of self-apology that is also in a way self-praise. But these impressions converge to make a single effect: that if Arnold ever had, like Dr. Russell, a warhorse, it had the same history as the Cheshire cat, and there is nothing left of it but the grin.

---

[162] vi. 347 n.   [163] vi. 235.   [164] vi. 395–6.
[165] CA. (vi. 80–81). Cf. vi. 90, "I again take myself as a sort of *corpus vile* to serve for illustration in a matter where serving for illustration may not by everyone be thought agreeable."

This double sense in the reader of Arnold first as simply a man in the situation he describes, and second as a writer forming that situation, arises also when he contrasts himself and his opponents. The *Saturday Review*, he says,[166] maintains that we have "found our philosophy"; but when obliged to travel almost daily on a branch line close to the scene of a railway murder, Arnold found his fellow-travellers so demoralized by fear that to begin with he thought they disproved this. "Myself a transcendentalist" (the *Saturday Review* has accused him of it) "I escaped the infection; and day after day, I used to ply my fellow-travellers with ... consolations ... 'suppose the worst to happen,' I said, addressing a portly jeweller from Cheapside; 'suppose even yourself to be the victim; *il n'y a pas d'homme necessaire*' .... All was of no avail. Nothing could moderate ... their passionate, absorbing, almost bloodthirsty clinging to life ... but the *Saturday Review* suggests a touching explanation ... the ardent longing of a faithful Benthamite ... to see his religion in the full and final blaze of its triumph." Here our impression is in part of Arnold living through the experience, and in part of him as its gleeful inventor; and of his opponents, partly in their fictitious guise of Arnold's jeweller, partly in their real form, the *Saturday Review* that can write as it does in a world of branch lines, railway murders, and fat poltroons. Nor is it impossible for Arnold to modify his effect by giving us a sense of himself as writer, even when he is most serious. The passage from *The Times*, quoted above,[167] about conditions in the East End, is fitted by Arnold into a personal experience. "This firm philosophy," he writes, "I seek to call to mind when I am in the East of London ... and indeed, to fortify myself against the depressing sights ... I have transcribed from the *Times* one strain ... full of the finest economical doctrine, and always carry it about with me...."[168] Then he continues by quoting Buchanan on the Divine Philoprogenitiveness, observes that this must be a *penchant* he shares with "the poorer class of Irish" and continues "and these beautiful words, too, I carry about with me in the East of London, and often read them there." Buchanan's "fine line" of poetry, too, "naturally connects itself, when one is in the East of London, with God's desire to *swarm* the earth with beings." There is no mistaking the bitterness, but our sense of Arnold himself is largely a sense of the control and the grim humour that give to that bitterness this expression.

These more elaborate examples, then, confirm the view that Arnold uses irony to widen his range of assertion, while still remaining within the range of tone that his outlook demands. It is one further method whereby he conveys a certain temper of mind by example rather than description, and it emphasizes once more that this temper is essentially what his work strives to express. This explains, too, why he is so prominent himself in his writings, why his personality is progressively revealed in a favourable light that the hostile reader, revolting from Arnold's whole attempt to persuade, labels complacency. Nothing will rigorously prove this label mistaken; but we tend less, perhaps, to call Arnold's method complacent, once we have equipped ourselves with a proper knowledge of its detail, and its function.

[166] EC.i. (iii, pp. ix–x).   [167] See p. 312.   [168] CA. (vi. 201).

FROM *Observations on the Style of Ernest Hemingway*

HARRY LEVIN

A distinguished critic and scholar, Harry Levin has done as much as anyone in America to foster the study of comparative literature through his teaching and the example of his writing. His many published volumes —which include *The Gates of Horn: A Study of Five French Realists* (1963) and *The Power of Blackness: Hawthorne, Poe, Melville* (1958), books on Joyce, Marlowe, and Shakespeare, and two collections of essays, *Contexts of Criticism* (1957) and *Refractions* (1966)—testify to the range of his interests and to his erudition. As a critic, Levin has always been particularly attentive to the relationships of literature to society and of past to present, while as a comparatist he has sought to view "all literature as one organic process, a continuous and cumulative whole." These intellectual commitments inform the discussion of Hemingway reprinted here; in addition, the essay reveals the concern with style that has characterized much of Levin's criticism.

In the course of this essay, Levin notes certain similarities between Hemingway's work and that of Fielding, Cervantes, and Joyce; he allies Hemingway with earlier American writers; and he places Hemingway in the period of the 1920's with its reaction against the "disparity between rhetoric and experience" that "became so evident during the First World War...." But for the most part, Levin explores the ways in which

Hemingway's conviction that knowledge is equivalent to experience affects his style, giving rise to a verbal mode whose "effectiveness lies in virtually persuading us that it is not writing at all." The critic examines Hemingway's stripped-down vocabulary, his handling of verbs, and his reliance on nouns (the words that "come closest to things"), showing how the author creates a syntax which "approximates the actual flow of experience," which renders an essentially linear sequence of images in a manner often analogous to "cinematographic presentation." Levin's commentary on the style itself leans in the main, it seems to me, toward describing the effect of Hemingway's verbal modes on the reader, their capacity to engender in the audience a sense of being involved in unmediated experience. But toward the close of the essay, Levin considers the relationship of the style to the man—to the public image of himself that Hemingway created as well as to the personal attitudes and qualities manifested in his writings.

In an introductory note added to this article on its reprinting in his *Contexts of Criticism*, Levin remarks that "these observations began as a book review"—of *Ernest Hemingway: The Man and His Work*, edited by John K. M. McCaffery—"and continued as *explication de texte*." I have reluctantly omitted the first section of the essay, which concludes with the question to which the critic addresses himself in the remaining sections, all of which are reprinted here: "Ought we not then, first and last, to be discussing the characteristics of his prose, when we talk about a man who—as Archibald MacLeish has written—'whittled a style for his time'?"

M*r*. Hemingway, in his turn, would hardly be himself—which he is, of course, quite as consciously as any writer could be—if he did not take a dim view of criticism. This is understandable and, as he would say, right: since criticism, ever seeking perspective, moves in the very opposite direction from his object, which has been immediacy. His ardent quest for experience has involved him in a lifelong campaign against everything that tends to get in its way, including those more or less labored efforts to interpret and communicate it which may be regarded—if not disregarded—as academic. Those of us who live in the shelter of the academy will not be put off by his disregard; for most of us have more occasion than he to be

The excerpt from "Observations on the Style of Ernest Hemingway," by Harry Levin, is reprinted from *Contexts of Criticism* (Cambridge, Mass., 1958), pp. 144–67, by permission of the author.

repelled by the encrustations of pedantry; and many of us are predisposed to sympathize with him, as well as with ourselves, when he tells us what is lacking in critics and scholars. That he continues to do so is a mark of attention which ought not to go unappreciated. Thus currently, in introducing a brilliant young Italian novelist to American readers, he departs from his subject to drive home a critical contrast:

> The Italy that [Elio Vittorini] learned and the America that the American boys learned [writes Ernest Hemingway, making a skillful transition] has little to do with the Academic Italy or America that periodically attacks all writing like a dust storm and is always, until everything shall be completely dry, dispersed by rain.

Since Hemingway is sparing in his use of metaphors, the one he introduces here is significant. "Dryasdust" has long been the layman's stock epithet for the results of scholarly inquiry; while drought, as evoked by T. S. Eliot, has become a basic symbol of modern anxiety. The country that seems to interest Hemingway most, Spain, is in some respects a literal wasteland; and his account of it—memorably his sound track for the Joris Ivens film, *The Spanish Earth*—emphasizes its dryness. Water, the contrasting element, for Hemingway as for his fellow men, symbolizes the purification and renewal of life. Rain beats out a cadence which runs through his work: through *A Farewell to Arms*, for example, where it lays the dust raised by soldiers' boots at the outset, accompanies the retreat from Caporetto, and stays with the hero when the heroine dies—even providing the very last word at the end. It is rain which, in a frequently quoted paragraph, shows up the unreality of "the words sacred, glorious, and sacrifice and the expression in vain." In the present instance, having reduced the contemporary situation to a handful of dust, as it were, Hemingway comes back to that sense of reality which he is willing to share with Vittorini. In the course of a single sentence, utilizing a digressive Ciceronian device, *paralipsis*, he has not only rounded up such writers as he considers academic; he has not only accused them of sterility, by means of that slippery logical shortcut which we professors term an enthymeme; but, like the veteran strategist he is, he has also managed to imply that they are the attackers and that he is fighting a strictly defensive action.

The conflict advances into the next paragraph, which opens on the high note that closed the previous one and then drops down again anticlimactically:

> Rain to an academician is probably, after the first fall has cleared the air, H_2O with, of course, traces of other things.

Even the ultimate source of nature's vitality is no more than a jejune scientific formula to us, if I may illustrate Hemingway's point by paraphrasing his sentence. Whereas —and for a moment it seems as if the theme of fertility would be sounded soon again—but no, the emphasis waxes increasingly negative:

> To a good writer, needing something to bring the dry country alive so that it will not be a desert where only such cactus as New York literary reviews grow dry and sad, inexistent

without the watering of their benefactors, feeding on the dried manure of schism and the dusty taste of disputed dialectics, their only flowering a desiccated criticism as alive as stuffed birds, and their steady mulch the dehydrated cuds of fellow critics; ...

There is more to come, but we had better pause and ruminate upon this particular mouthful. Though we may or may not accept Hemingway's opinion, we must admit that he makes us taste his distaste. Characteristically, he does not countercriticize or state the issue in intellectual terms. Instead he proceeds from agriculture to the dairy, through an atmosphere calculated to make New Yorkers uncomfortable, elaborating his earthy metaphor into a barnyard allegory which culminates in a scatological gesture. The gibe about benefactors is a curious one, since it appears to take commercial success as a literary criterion, and at the same time to identify financial support with spiritual nourishment. The hopeful adjective "alive," repeated in this deadening context, is ironically illustrated by a musty ornithological specimen: so much for criticism! Such a phrase as "disputed dialectics," which is unduly alliterative, slightly tautological, and—like "cactus"—ambiguously singular or plural, touches a sphere where the author seems ill at ease. He seems more sure of his ground when, after this muttered parenthesis, he returns to his starting point, turns the prepositional object into a subject, and sets out again toward his predicate, toward an affirmation of mellow fruitfulness:

... such a writer finds rain to be made of knowledge, experience, wine, bread, oil, salt, vinegar, bed, early mornings, nights, days, the sea, men, women, dogs, beloved motor cars, bicycles, hills and valleys, the appearance and disappearance of trains on straight and curved tracks, love, honor and disobey, music, chamber music and chamber pots, negative and positive Wassermanns, the arrival and non-arrival of expected munitions and/or reinforcements, replacements or your brother.

These are the "other things" missed by the academician and discerned by the "good writer"—whether he be Vittorini or Hemingway. It is by no means a casual inventory; each successive item, artfully chosen, has its meaningful place in the author's scheme of things. Knowledge is equated with experience, rendered concrete by the staple fare of existence, and wet down by essential liquids redolent of the Mediterranean; bed, with its double range of elementary associations, initiates a temporal cycle which revolves toward the timeless sea. Men, women, and dogs follow each other in unrelieved sequence; but the term of endearment, "beloved," is reserved for motor cars; while wavering alternatives suggest the movement of other vehicles over the land. Then come the great abstractions, love and honor, which are undercut by a cynical negation of the marriage ceremony, "disobey." Since chamber music sounds highbrow, it must be balanced against the downright vulgarity of chamber pots. The pangs of sex are scientifically neutralized by the reference to Wassermann tests, and the agonies of war are deliberately stated in the cool and/or colorless jargon of military dispatches. The final choice, "replacements or your brother," possibly echoes a twist of continental slang (*et ton frère!*); but, more than that, it suddenly replaces a strategic loss with a personal bereavement.

The sentence, though extended, is not periodic: instead of suspending its burden, it falls back on *anacoluthon*, the rhetoric of the gradual breakdown and the fresh start. Hence, the first half is an uncharacteristic and unsuccessful endeavor to complete an elaborate grammatical structure which soon gets out of control. The second half thereupon brings the subject as quickly and simply as possible to its object, which opens up at once into the familiar Hemingway catalogue, where effects can be gained *seriatim* by order rather than by construction. After the chain of words has reached its climactic phrase, "your brother," it is rounded out by another transitional sentence:

> All these are a part of rain to a good writer along with your hated or beloved mother, may she rest in peace or in pieces, porcupine quills, cock grouse drumming on a basswood log, the smell of sweet-grass and fresh smoked leather and Sicily.

This time love dares to appear in its primary human connection, but only in ambivalence with hatred, and the hazards of sentimentality are hysterically avoided by a trite pun. And though the final images resolve the paragraph by coming back to the Sicilian locale of Vittorini's novel, they savor more of the northern woods of Hemingway's Upper Peninsula. Meanwhile the digression has served its purpose for him and for ourselves; it has given us nothing less than his definition of knowledge—not book-knowledge, of course, but the real thing. Thus Robert Jordan decides to write a book about his adventures in Spain: "But only about the things he knew, truly, and about what he knew." Such a book is Hemingway's novel about him, *For Whom the Bell Tolls*; and what he knew, there put into words, is already one remove away from experience. And when Hemingway writes about Vittorini's novel, unaccustomed though he is to operating on the plane of criticism, he is two removes away from the objects he mentions in his analysis—or should I call it a hydroanalysis? Critics—and I have in mind Wyndham Lewis—have called his writing "the prose of reality." It seems to come closer to life than other prose, possibly too close for Mr. Lewis, yet for better or worse it happens to be literature. Its effectiveness lies in virtually persuading us that it is not writing at all. But though it may feel like walks in the rain or punches in the jaw, to be literal, it consists of words on the page. It is full of half-concealed art and self-revealing artifice. Since Hemingway is endlessly willing to explicate such artful and artificial pursuits as bullfighting and military tactics, he ought not to flinch under technical scrutiny.

Hemingway's hatred for the profession of letters stems quite obviously from a lover's quarrel. When Richard Gordon is reviled by his dissatisfied wife in *To Have and Have Not*, her most embittered epithet is "you writer." Yet Hemingway's writing abounds in salutes to various fellow writers, from the waitress' anecdote about Henry James in *The Torrents of Spring* to Colonel Cantwell's spiritual affinity with D'Annunzio. And from Nick Adams, who takes Meredith and Chesterton along on fishing trips, to Hemingway himself, who arranges to be interviewed on American literature in *Green Hills of Africa*, his heroes do not shy away from critical discussion. His titles, so often quoted from books by earlier writers, have been so apt that they have all but established a convention. He shows an almost academic fondness, as well as a remarkable flair, for epigraphs: the Colonel dies with a quotation on his lips. Like all of us, Hemingway has been influenced by T. S. Eliot's taste for Elizabethan drama and metaphysical poetry. Thus Hemingway's title, "In Another Country," is borrowed from a passage he elsewhere cites, which he might have found in Marlowe's *Jew of Malta* or possibly in Eliot's "Portrait of a Lady." *A Farewell to Arms*, which echoes Lovelace's title, quotes in passing from Marvell's "To His Coy Mistress," echoed more recently by Robert Penn Warren, which is parodied in *Death in the Afternoon*. Hemingway is no exception to the rule that makes parody the starting point for realistic fiction. Just as Fielding took off from Richardson, so Hemingway takes off from Sherwood Anderson—indeed his first novel, *The Torrents of Spring*, which parodies Anderson's *Dark Laughter*, is explicit in its acknowledgments to *Joseph Andrews*. It has passages, however, which read today like a pastiche of the later Hemingway:

> Yogi was worried. There was something on his mind. It was spring, there was no doubt of that now, and he did not want a woman. He had worried about it a lot lately. There was no question about it. He did not want a woman. He couldn't explain it to himself. He had gone to the Public Library and asked for a book the night before. He looked at the librarian. He did not want her. Somehow she meant nothing to him.

A recoil from bookishness, after a preliminary immersion in it, provided Fielding's master, Cervantes, with the original impetus for the novel. In "A Banal Story" Hemingway provides us with his own variation on the theme of *Don Quixote*, where a writer sits reading about romance in a magazine advertisement, while in far-off Madrid a bullfighter dies and is buried. The ironic contrast—romantic preconception exploded by contact with harsh reality—is basic with Hemingway, as it has been with all novelists who have written effectively about war. The realism of his generation reacted, not only against Wilsonian idealism, but against Wilsonian rhetoric. Hence the famous paragraph from the Caporetto episode describing Frederic Henry's embarrassment before such abstract words as "glory" and "honor," which seem to him obscene beside the concrete names of places and numbers of roads. For a Spaniard, Hemingway notes in *Death in the Afternoon*, the abstraction may still have concreteness: honor may be "as real a thing as water, wine, or olive oil." It is not so for us: "All our words from loose using have lost their edge." And "The Gambler, the Nun, and the Radio" brings forward a clinching example: "Liberty, what we believed in, now the name of a Macfadden publication." That same story trails off in a litany which reduces a Marxist slogan to meaninglessness: "the opium of the people" is everything and nothing. Even more desolating, in "A Clean, Well-Lighted Place," is the reduction of the Lord's prayer to nothingness: "Our nada who art in nada..." Since words have become inflated and devalued, Hemingway is willing to recognize no values save those which can be immediately felt and directly pointed out. It is his verbal skepticism which leads toward what some critics have called his moral nihilism. Anything serious had better be said with a smile, stranger.

The classic echo, "irony and pity," jingles through *The Sun Also Rises* like a singing commercial.

There is something in common between this attitude and the familiar British habit of understatement. "No pleasure in anything if you mouth it too much," says Wilson, the guide in "The Short, Happy Life of Francis Macomber." Yet Jake, the narrator of *The Sun Also Rises*, protests—in the name of American garrulity—that the English use fewer words than the Eskimos. Spanish, the language of Hemingway's preference, is at once emotive and highly formal. His Spanish, to judge from *Death in the Afternoon*, is just as ungrammatical as his English. In "The Undefeated" his Spanish bullfighters are made to speak the slang of American prizefighters. Americanisms and Hispanisms, archaic and polyglot elements are so intermingled in *For Whom the Bell Tolls* that it calls to mind what Ben Jonson said of *The Faerie Queene*: "Spenser writ no language." Hemingway offers a succinct example by translating "*Eras mucho caballo*" as "Thou wert plenty of horse." It is somewhat paradoxical that a writer, having severely cut down his English vocabulary, should augment it by continual importation from other languages, including the Swahili. But this is a facet of the larger paradox that a writer so essentially American should set the bulk of his work against foreign backgrounds. His characters, expatriates for the most part, wander through the ruins of Babel, smattering many tongues and speaking a demotic version of their own. Obscenity presents another linguistic problem, for which Hemingway is not responsible; but his coy ways of circumventing the taboos of censorship are more of a distraction than the conventional blanks. When he does permit himself an expression not usually considered printable, in *Death in the Afternoon*, the context is significant. His interlocutor, the Old Lady, requests a definition and he politely responds: "Madam, we apply the term now to describe unsoundness in abstract conversation or, indeed, any overmetaphysical tendency in speech."

For language, as for literature, his feeling is strongly ambivalent. Perhaps it could be summed up by Pascal's maxim: "True eloquence makes fun of eloquence." Like the notorious General Cambronne, Hemingway feels that one short spontaneous vulgarism is more honest than all those grandiloquent slogans which rhetoricians dream up long after the battle. The disparity between rhetoric and experience, which became so evident during the First World War, prompted the 'twenties to repudiate the genteel stylistic tradition and to accept the American vernacular as our norm of literary discourse. "Literary" is a contradiction in terms, for the resultant style is basically oral; and when the semiliterate speaker takes pen in hand, as Hemingway demonstrates in "One Reader Writes"—as H. L. Mencken demonstrated in "A Short View of Gamalielese"—the result is even more artificial than if it had been written by a writer. A page is always flat, and we need perspective to make it convey the illusion of life in the round. Yet the very fact that words mean so much less to us than the things they represent in our lives is a stimulus to our imaginations. In "Fathers and Sons" young Nick Adams reads that Caruso has been arrested for "mashing," and asks his father the meaning of that expression.

"It is one of the most heinous of crimes," his father answered. Nick's imagination pictured the great tenor doing something strange, bizarre, and heinous with a potato masher to a beautiful lady who looked like the pictures of Anna Held on the inside of cigar boxes. He resolved, with considerable horror, that when he was old enough he would try mashing at least once.

The tone of this passage is not altogether typical of Hemingway. Rather, as the point of view detaches itself affectionately and ironically from the youth, it approximates the early Joyce. This may help to explain why it suggests a more optimistic approach to language than the presumption that, since phrases can be snares and delusions, their scope should be limited to straight denotation. The powers of connotation, the possibilities of oblique suggestion and semantic association, are actually grasped by Hemingway as well as any writer of our time. Thus he can retrospectively endow a cheap and faded term like "mashing" with all the promise and poetry of awakening manhood. When Nick grows up, foreign terms will hold out the same allure to him; like Frederic Henry, he will seek the actuality that resides behind the names of places; and Robert Jordan will first be attracted to Spain as a professional philologist. But none of them will find an equivalence between the word and the thing; and Hemingway, at the end of *Death in the Afternoon*, laments that no book is big enough to do final justice to its living subject. "There was so much to write," the dying writer realizes in "The Snows of Kilimanjaro," and his last thoughts are moving and memorable recollections of some of the many things that will now go unwritten. Walt Whitman stated this challenge and this dilemma, for all good writers, when he spoke of expressing the inexpressible.

THE INEVITABLE COMPROMISE, for Hemingway, is best expressed by his account of Romero's bullfighting style: "the holding of his purity of line through the maximum of exposure." The maximum of exposure—this throws much light upon the restlessness of Hemingway's career, but here we are primarily concerned with the holding of his purity of line. It had to be the simplest and most flexible of lines in order to accommodate itself to his desperate pursuit of material. His purgation of language has aptly been compared, by Robert Penn Warren, to the revival of diction that Wordsworth accomplished with *Lyrical Ballads*. Indeed the question that Coleridge afterward raised might once again be asked: why should the speech of some men be more real than that of others? Today that question restates itself in ideological terms: whether respect for the common man necessitates the adoption of a commonplace standard. Everyone who writes faces the same old problems, and the original writers—like Wordsworth or Hemingway—are those who develop new ways of meeting them. The case of Wordsworth would show us, if that of Hemingway did not, that those who break down conventions tend to substitute conventions of their own. Hemingway's prose is not without precedents; it is interesting to recall that his maiden effort, published by *The Double Dealer* in 1922, parodied the King James Bible. He has his forerunners in American fiction, from Cooper to Jack London, whose conspicuous lack was a style as dynamic as their subject-matter. The ring-tailed roarers of the frontier, such as Davy Crockett, were Colonel Cantwell's brothers under the skin; but as contrasted with the latter's tragic conception of himself, they were mock-heroic and serio-comic figures, who recommend themselves to the reader's condescension. Mark Twain has been the most genuine influence, and Hemingway has acknowledged this by declaring —with sweeping generosity—that *Huckleberry Finn* is the source of all modern American literature.

But Mark Twain was conducting a monologue, a virtual *tour de force* of impersonation, and he ordinarily kept a certain distance between his narrative role and his characters. And among Hemingway's elder contemporaries, Ring Lardner was a kind of ventriloquist, who made devastating use of the vernacular to satirize the vulgarity and stupidity of his dummies. It remained for Hemingway—along with Anderson—to identify himself wholly with the lives he wrote about, not so much entering into them as allowing them to take possession of him, and accepting—along with their sensibilities and perceptions—the limitations of their point of view and the limits of their range of expression. We need make no word-count to be sure that his literary vocabulary, with foreign and technical exceptions, consists of relatively few and short words. The corollary, of course, is that every word sees a good deal of hard use. Furthermore, his syntax is informal to the point of fluidity, simplifying as far as possible the already simple system of English inflections. Thus "who" is normally substituted for "whom," presumably to avoid schoolmarmish correctness; and "that," doing duty for "which," seems somehow less prophetic of complexity. Personal pronouns frequently get involved in what is stigmatized, by teachers of freshman composition, as faulty reference; there are sentences in which it is hard to tell the hunter from his quarry or the bullfighter from the bull. "When his father died he was only a kid and his manager buried him perpetually." So begins, rather confusingly, "The Mother of a Queen." Sometimes it seems as if Hemingway were taking pains to be ungrammatical, as do many educated people out of a twisted sense of *noblesse oblige*. Yet when he comes closest to pronouncing a moral, the last words of Harry Morgan—the analphabetic hero of *To Have and Have Not*—seem to be half-consciously fumbling toward some grammatical resolution: "A man ... ain't got no hasn't got any can't really isn't any way out . . . ."

The effectiveness of Hemingway's method depends very largely upon his keen ear for speech. His conversations are vivid, often dramatic, although he comes to depend too heavily upon them and to scant the other obligations of the novelist. Many of his wisecracks are quotable out of context, but as Gertrude Stein warned him: "Remarks are not literature." He can get his story told, and still be as conversational as he pleases, by telling it in the first person. "Brother, that was some storm," says the narrator, and the reader hears the very tone of his voice. In one of Hemingway's critical digressions, he declares that he has always sought "the real thing, the sequence of motion and fact which [*sic*] made the emotion . . . ." This seems to imply the clear-cut mechanism of verbal stimulus and psychological response that Eliot formulates in his theory of the objective correlative. In practice, however, Hemingway is no more of a behaviorist than Eliot, and the sharp distinction between motion and emotion is soon blurred. Consider his restricted choice of adjectives, and the heavy load of subjective implication carried by such uncertain monosyllables as "fine" and "nice." From examples on nearly every page, we are struck by one which helps to set the scene for *A Farewell to Arms*: "The town was very nice and our house was very fine." Such descriptions—if we may consider them descriptions—are obviously not designed for pictorial effect. When the Colonel is tempted to call some fishing-boats picturesque, he corrects himself: "The hell with picturesque. They are just damned beautiful." Where "picturesque" might sound arty and hence artificial, "beautiful"—with "damned" to take off the curse—is permissible because Hemingway has packed it with his own emotional charge. He even uses it in *For Whom the Bell Tolls* to express his esthetic appreciation of gunfire. Like "fine" and "nice," or "good" and "lovely," it does not describe; it evaluates. It is not a stimulus but a projected response, a projection of the narrator's euphoria in a given situation. Hemingway, in effect, is saying to the reader: *Having wonderful time. Wish you were here.*

In short, he is communicating excitement; and if this communication is received, it establishes a uniquely personal relationship; but when it goes astray, the diction goes flat and vague. Hemingway manages to sustain his reputation for concreteness by an exploring eye for the incidental detail. The one typescript of his that I have seen, his carbon copy of "The Killers" now in the Harvard College Library, would indicate that the arc-light and the tipped-back derby hat were later observations than the rest. Precision at times becomes so arithmetical that, in "The Light of the World," it lines up his characters like a drill-sergeant: "Down at the station there were five whores waiting for the train to come in, and six white men and four Indians." Numbers enlarge the irony that concludes the opening chapter of *A Farewell to Arms* when, after a far from epic invocation, a casual introduction to the landscape, and a dusty record of troops falling back through the autumn, rain brings the cholera which kills "only seven thousand." A trick of multiplication, which Hemingway may have picked up from Gertrude Stein, is to generalize the specific episode: "They always picked the finest places to have the quarrels." When he offers this general view of a restaurant—"It was full of smoke and drinking and singing"—he is an impressionist if not an abstractionist. Thence to expressionism is an easy step: "... the room whirled." It happens that, under pressure from his first American publishers, the author was compelled to modify the phrasing of "Mr. and Mrs. Elliott." In the original version, subsequently restored, the title characters "try to have a baby." In the modified version they "think of having a baby." It could be argued that, in characterizing this rather tepid couple, the later verb is more expressive and no more euphemistic than the earlier one; that "think," at any rate, is not less precise or effectual than "try." But, whereas the sense of effort came naturally, the cerebration was an afterthought.

If we regard the adjective as a luxury, decorative more often than functional, we can well understand why Hemingway doesn't cultivate it. But, assuming that the sentence derives its energy from the verb, we are in for a shock if we expect his verbs to be numerous or varied or emphatic. His usage supports C. K. Ogden's argument that verb-forms are disappearing from English grammar. Without much self-deprivation, Hemingway could get along on the so-called "operators" of

Basic English, the sixteen monosyllabic verbs that stem from movements of the body. The substantive verb *to be* is predominant, characteristically introduced by an expletive. Thus the first story of *In Our Time* begins, and the last one ends, with the story-teller's gambit: "there was," "there were." In the first two pages of *A Farewell to Arms* nearly every other sentence is of this type, and the third page employs the awkward construction "there being." There is—I find the habit contagious—a tendency to immobilize verbs by transposing them into gerunds. Instead of writing *they fought* or *we did not feel*, Hemingway writes "there was fighting" and "there was not the feeling of a storm coming." The subject does little more than point impersonally at its predicate: an object, a situation, an emotion. Yet the idiom, like the French *il y a*, is ambiguous; inversion can turn the gesture of pointing into a physical act; and the indefinite adverb can indicate, if not specify, a definite place. Contrast, with the opening of *A Farewell to Arms*, that of "In Another Country": "In the fall the war was always there, but we did not go to it any more." The negative is even more striking, when Frederic Henry has registered the sensations of his wound, and dares to look at it for the first time, and notes: "My knee wasn't there." The adverb is *there* rather than *here*, the verb is *was* rather than *is*, because we—the readers—are separated from the event in space and time. But the narrator has lived through it, like the Ancient Mariner, and now he chooses his words to grip and transfix us. *Lo!* he says. *Look! I was there.*

GRANTED, then, that Hemingway's diction is thin; that, in the technical sense, his syntax is weak; and that he would rather be caught dead than seeking the *mot juste* or the balanced phrase. Granted that his adjectives are not colorful and his verbs not particularly energetic. Granted that he commits as many literary offenses as Mark Twain brought to book with Fenimore Cooper. What is behind his indubitable punch, the unexampled dynamics of Hemingway's style? How does he manage, as he does, to animate this characteristic sentence from "After the Storm"?

> I said "Who killed him?" and he said "I don't know who killed him but he's dead all right," and it was dark and there was water standing in the street and no lights and windows broke and boats all up in the town and trees blown down and everything all blown and I got a skiff and went out and found my boat where I had her inside of Mango Key and she was all right only she was full of water.

Here is a good example of Hemingway's "sequence of motion and fact." It starts from dialogue and leads into first-person action; but the central description is a single clause, where the expletive takes the place of the observer and his observations are registered one by one. Hence, for the reader, it lives up to Robert Jordan's intention: "You ... feel that all that happened to you." Hemingway puts his emphasis on nouns because, among parts of speech, they come closest to things. Stringing them along by means of conjunctions, he approximates the actual flow of experience. For him, as for Marion Tweedy Bloom, the key word is *and*, with its renewable promise of continuity, occasionally varied by *then* and *so*. The rhetorical scheme is *polysyndeton* — a large name for the childishly simple habit of linking sentences together. The subject, when it is not taken for granted, merely puts us in touch with the predicate: the series of objects that Hemingway wants to point out. Even a preposition can turn this trick as "with" does in this account of El Sordo waiting to see the whites of his enemy's eyes:

> Come on, Comrade Voyager... Keep on coming with your eyes forward... Look. With a red face and blond hair and blue eyes. With no cap on and his moustache is yellow. With blue eyes. With pale blue eyes. With pale blue eyes with something wrong with them. With pale blue eyes that don't focus. Close enough. Too close. Yes, Comrade Voyager. Take it, Comrade Voyager.

Prose gets as near as it can to physical conflict here. The figure enlarges as it advances, the quickening impression grows clear and sharp and almost unbearable, whereupon it is blackened out by El Sordo's rifle. Each clipped sentence, each prepositional phrase, is like a new frame in a strip of film; indeed the whole passage, like so many others, might have been filmed by the camera and projected on the screen. The course of Harry Morgan's launch speeding through the Gulf Stream, or of Frederic Henry's fantasy ascending the elevator with Catherine Barkley, is given this cinematographic presentation. *Green Hills of Africa* voices the long-range ambition of obtaining a fourth and fifth dimension in prose. Yet if the subordinate clause and the complex sentence are the usual ways for writers to obtain a third dimension, Hemingway keeps his writing on a linear plane. He holds the purity of his line by moving in one direction, ignoring sidetracks and avoiding structural complications. By presenting a succession of images, each of which has its brief moment when it commands the reader's undivided attention, he achieves his special vividness and fluidity. For what he lacks in structure he makes up in sequence, carefully ordering visual impressions as he sets them down and ironically juxtaposing the various items on his lists and inventories. "A Way You'll Never Be" opens with a close-up showing the debris on a battlefield, variously specifying munitions, medicaments, and leftovers from a field kitchen, then closing in on the scattered papers with this striking montage-effect: "... group postcards showing the machine-gun unit standing in ranked and ruddy cheerfulness as in a football picture for a college annual; now they were humped and swollen in the grass...." It is not surprising that Hemingway's verse, published by *Poetry* in 1923, is recognizably imagistic in character—and perhaps his later heroics are foreshadowed by the subject of one of those poems, Theodore Roosevelt.

In her observant book, *L'Age du roman américain*, Claude-Edmonde Magny stresses Hemingway's "exaltation of the instant." We can note how this emphasis is reflected in his timing, which—after his placing has bridged the distance from *there* to *here*—strives to close the gap between *then* and *now*. Where Baudelaire's clock said "remember" in many languages, Robert Jordan's memory says: "Now, *ahora, maintenant, heute*." When death interrupts a dream, in "The Snows of Kilimanjaro," the ultimate reality is heralded by a rising insistence upon the word "now." It is not for nothing that Hemingway is the younger contemporary of Proust and Joyce. Though his time is neither *le temps perdu* nor the past nostalgically recaptured, he spends it gathering roses while he can, to the ever accelerating rhythm of headlines and telegrams and loud-speakers. The act, no sooner done than said, becomes simultaneous with the word, no sooner said than felt. Hemingway goes so far, in "Fathers and Sons," as to render a sexual embrace by an onomatopoetic sequence of adverbs. But unlike Damon Runyon and Dickens, he seldom narrates in the present tense, except in such sporting events as "Fifty Grand." Rather, his timeliness expresses itself in continuous forms of the verb and in his fondness for all kinds of participial constructions. These, compounded and multiplied, create an ambiance of overwhelming activity, and the epithets shift from El Sordo's harassed feelings to the impact of the reiterated bullets, as Hemingway recounts "the last lung-aching, leg-dead, mouth-dry, bullet-spatting, bullet-cracking, bullet-singing run up the final slope of the hill." More often the meaning takes the opposite turn, and moves from the external plane into the range of a character's senses, proceeding serially from the visual to the tactile, as it does when the "Wine of Wyoming" is sampled: "It was very light and clear and good and still tasted of the grapes."

When Nick Adams goes fishing, the temperature is very tangibly indicated: "It was getting hot, the sun hot on the back of his neck." The remark about the weather is thereby extended in two directions, toward the distant source of the heat and toward its immediate perception. Again in "Big Two-Hearted River," Nick's fatigue is measured by the weight of his pack: ". . . it was heavy. It was much too heavy." As in the movies, the illusion of movement is produced by repeating the same shot with further modification every time. Whenever a new clause takes more than one step ahead, a subsequent clause repeats it in order to catch up. Repetition, as in "Up in Michigan," brings the advancing narrative back to an initial point of reference. "Liz liked Jim very much. She liked it the way he walked over from the shop and often went to the kitchen door to watch him start down the road. She liked it about his moustache. She liked it about how white his teeth were when he smiled." The opaque verb "like," made increasingly transparent, is utilized five more times in this paragraph; and the fumbling preposition "about" may be an acknowledgment of Hemingway's early debt to Gertrude Stein. The situation is located somewhere between a subjective Liz and an objective Jim. The theme of love is always a test of Hemingway's objectivity. When Frederic kisses Catherine, her responses are not less moving because they are presented through his reflexes; but it is her sentimental conversation which leaves him free to ask himself: "What the hell?" At first glance, in a behavioristic formula which elsewhere recurs, Colonel Cantwell seems so hard-boiled that motions are his only emotions: "He saw that his hand was trembling." But his vision is blurred by conventionally romantic tenderness when he contemplates a heroine whose profile "could break your . . . or anyone else's heart." Hemingway's heroines, when they aren't bitches, are fantasies—or rather, the masculine reader is invited to supply his own, as with the weather in Mark Twain's *American Claimant*. They are pin-up girls.

If beauty lies in the eye of the beholder, Hemingway's purpose is to make his readers beholders. This is easily done when the narration is conducted in the first person; we can sit down and drink, with Jake Barnes, and watch Paris walk by. The interpolated chapters of *In Our Time*, most of them reminiscences from the army, employ the collective *we*; but, except for "My Old Man," the stories themselves are told in the third person. Sometimes, to strengthen the sense of identification, they make direct appeal to the second person; the protagonist of "Soldier's Home" is "you" as well as "he"—and, more generally, "a fellow." With the exception of Jake's confessions, that is to say *The Sun Also Rises*, all of Hemingway's novels are written in the *style indirect libre*—indirect discourse which more or less closely follows the consciousness of a central character. An increasing tendency for the author to intrude, commenting in his own person, is one of the weaknesses of *Across the River*. He derives his strength from a power to visualize episodes through the eyes of those most directly involved; for a page, in "The Short, Happy Life of Francis Macomber," the hunt is actually seen from the beast's point of view. Hemingway's use of interior monologue is effective when sensations from the outer world are entering the stream of a character's consciousness, as they do with such a rush at El Sordo's last stand. But introspection is not Hemingway's genre, and the night-thoughts of *To Have and Have Not* are among his least successful episodes. His best are events, which are never far to seek; things are constantly happening in his world; his leg-man, Nick Adams, happens to be the eye-witness of "The Killers." The state of mind that Hemingway communicates to us is the thrill that Nick got from skiing in "Cross Country Snow," which "plucked Nick's mind out and left him only the wonderful, flying, dropping sensation in his body."

If psychological theories could be proved by works of fiction, Hemingway would lend his authority to the long contested formula of William James, which equates emotion with bodily sensation. Most other serious writers, however, would bear witness to deeper ranges of sensibility and more complex processes of motivation than those he sees fit to describe. Some of them have accused Hemingway of aggressive anti-intellectualism: I am thinking particularly of Aldous Huxley. But Huxley's own work is so pure an example of all that Hemingway has recoiled from, so intellectual in the airiest sense, and so unsupported by felt experience, that the argument has played into Hemingway's hands. We have seen enough of the latter to know that he doesn't really hate books—himself having written a dozen, several of which are, and will remain, the best of their kind. As for his refusal to behave like a man of letters, he reminds us of Hotspur, who professes to be a laconic philistine and turns out— with no little grandiloquence—to be the most poetic character in Shakespeare's play. Furthermore, it is not Hemingway, but the slogan-mongers of our epoch, who have debased the language; he has been attempting to restore some decent degree of correspondence between words and things; and the task of verification is a heavy one, which throws the individual back on his personal resources of awareness. That he has succeeded within limits, and with considerable strain, is less important than that he has succeeded, that a few more aspects of life have been captured for literature. Meanwhile the word continues to dematerialize, and has to be made flesh all over again;

the first-hand perception, once it gets written down, becomes the second-hand notation; and the writer, who attains his individuality by repudiating literary affectation, ends by finding that he has struck a new pose and founded another school.

It is understandable why no critique of Hemingway, including this one, can speak for long of the style without speaking of the man. Improving on Buffon, Mark Schorer recently wrote: "[Hemingway's] style is not only his subject, it is his view of life." It could also be called his way of life, his *Lebensstil*. It has led him to live his books, to brave the maximum of exposure, to tour the world in an endless search for wars and their moral equivalents. It has cast him in the special role of our agent, our plenipotentiary, our roving correspondent on whom we depend for news from the fighting fronts of modern consciousness. Here he is, the man who was there. His writing seems so intent upon the actual, so impersonal in its surfaces, that it momentarily prompts us to overlook the personality behind them. That would be a serious mistake; for the point of view, though brilliantly intense, is narrowly focused and obliquely angled. We must ask: who is this guide to whom we have entrusted ourselves on intimate terms in dangerous places? Where are his limitations? What are his values? We may well discover that they differ from our assumptions, when he shows us a photograph of a bullfighter close to a bull, and comments: "If there is no blood on his belly afterwards you ought to get your money back." We may be ungrateful to question such curiosity, when we are indebted to it for many enlargements of our vicarious knowledge; and it may well spring from the callowness of the tourist rather than the morbidity of the *voyeur*, from the American zest of the fan who pays his money to reckon the carnage. When Spain's great poet, García Lorca, celebrated the very same theme, averting his gaze from the spilling of the blood, his refrain was "¡Que no quiero verla!" ("I do not want to see it!").

Yet Hemingway wants to see everything—or possibly he wants to be in a position to tell us that he has seen everything. While the boy Nick, his seeing eye, eagerly watches a Caesarian childbirth in "Indian Camp," the far from impassive husband turns away; and it is later discovered that he has killed himself. "He couldn't stand things..." so runs the diagnosis of Nick's father, the doctor. This, for Nick, is an initiation to suffering and death; but with the sunrise, shortly afterward, youth and well-being reassert themselves; and the end of the story reaffirms the generalization that Hazlitt once drew: "No young man ever thinks he shall die." It is easy enough for such a young man to stand things, for he is not yet painfully involved in them; he is not a sufferer but a wide-eyed onlooker, to whom the word "mashing" holds out mysterious enticements. Hemingway's projection of this attitude has given his best work perennial youthfulness; it has also armed his critics with the accusation that, like his Robert Cohen, he is "a case of arrested development." If this be so, his plight is generalized by the Englishman Wilson, who observes that "Americans stay little boys... all their lives." And the object of Wilson's observation, Francis Macomber, would furnish a classic case-history for Adler, if not for Freud—the masculine sense of inferiority which seeks to overcome itself by acts of prowess, both sanguinary and sexual. Despite these two sources of excitement, the story is a plaintive modulation of two rather dissonant themes: *None but the brave deserves the fair* and *The female of the species is more deadly than the male.* After Francis Macomber has demonstrated his manhood, the next step is death. The world that remains most alive to Hemingway is that stretch between puberty and maturity which is strictly governed by the ephebic code: a world of mixed apprehension and bravado before the rite of passage, the baptism of fire, the introduction to sex.

Afterward comes the boasting, along with such surviving ideals as Hemingway subsumes in the word *cojones*—the English equivalent sounds more skeptical. But for Jake Barnes, all passion spent in the First World War, or for Colonel Cantwell, tired and disgruntled by the Second, the aftermath can only be elegiac. The weather-beaten hero of *Across the River*, which appears in 1950, is fifty years old and uneasily conscious of that fact; whereas "the childish, drunken heroics" of *The Sun Also Rises* took place just about twenty-five years ago. From his spectacular arrival in the 'twenties, Hemingway's course has paralleled that of our century; and now, at its midpoint, he balks like the rest of us before the responsibilities of middle age. When, if ever, does the *enfant du siècle*, that *enfant terrible*, grow up? (Not necessarily when he grows a beard and calls himself "Mr. Papa.") Frederic Henry plunges into the Po much as Huck Finn dived into the Mississippi, but emerges to remind us even more pointedly of Fabrice del Dongo in Stendhal's *Chartreuse de Parme*, and of our great contemporary shift from transatlantic innocence to old-world experience. Certain intimations of later years are present in Hemingway's earlier stories, typically Ad Francis, the slap-happy ex-champ in "The Battler." Even in "Fifty Grand," his most contrived tale, the beat-up prizefighter suffers more than he acts and wins by losing—a situation which has its corollary in the title of Hemingway's third collection, *Winner Take Nothing*. The ultimate article of his credo, which he shares with Malraux and Sartre, is the good fight for the lost cause. And the ultimate protagonist is Jesus in "Today Is Friday," whose crucifixion is treated like an athletic feat, and whose capacity for taking punishment rouses a fellow-feeling in the Roman soldiers. The stoic or masochistic determination to take it brings us back from Hemingway to his medium, which—although it eschews the passive voice—is essentially a receiving instrument, especially sensitized for recording a series of violent shocks.

The paradox of toughness and sensitivity is resolved, and the qualities and defects of his writing are reconciled, if we merely remember that he was—and still is—a poet. That he is not a novelist by vocation, if it were not revealed by his books, could be inferred from his well-known retort to F. Scott Fitzgerald. For Fitzgerald the rich were different—not quantitatively, because they had more money, but qualitatively, because he had a novelistic interest in manners and morals. Again, when we read André Gide's reports from the Congo, we realize what *Green Hills of Africa* lacks in the way of social or psychological insight. As W. M. Frohock has perceived, Hemingway is less concerned with human relations than with his own relationship to the universe—a concern which might have spontaneously flowered into poetry. His talents come out most fully in the texture of his work, whereas the structure tends to be episodic and uncontrived to the point of formlessness. *For Whom the Bell Tolls*, the only one of his six novels that has been carefully constructed, is in some respects an over-expanded short story. Editors rejected his earliest stories on the grounds that they were nothing but sketches and anecdotes, thereby paying incidental tribute to his sense of reality. Fragments of truth, after all, are the best that a writer can offer; and, as Hemingway has said, "... Any part you make will represent the whole if it's made truly." In periods as confusing as the present, when broader and maturer representations are likely to falsify, we are fortunate if we can find authenticity in the lyric cry, the adolescent mood, the tangible feeling, the trigger response. If we think of Hemingway's temperamental kinship with E. E. Cummings, and of Cummings' "Buffalo Bill" or "Olaf glad and big," it is easy to think of Hemingway as a poet. After the attractions and distractions of timeliness have been outdated, together with categorical distinctions between the rich and the poor, perhaps he will be remembered for a poetic vision which renews our interrupted contact with the timeless elements of man's existence: bread, wine, bed, music, and just a few more of the concrete universals. When El Sordo raises his glance from the battlefield, he looks up at the identical patch of the blue sky that Henry Fleming saw in *The Red Badge of Courage* and that looked down on Prince Andrey in *War and Peace*.

Fiction and the "Analogical Matrix"

❧ MARK SCHORER ❧

In both "Technique as Discovery" and "Fiction and the 'Analogical Matrix,'" surely Mark Schorer's most frequently reprinted essays, he argues for the identity of form and content in novels and contends that the verbal texture of fiction deserves the same sort of precise analysis that is normally reserved for poetry. In the second of these essays, the one reprinted here, he pursues his claim through examining several kinds of metaphors in three nineteenth-century English novels: metaphors that lie "buried" in Jane Austen's *Persuasion*, "generally epithetical" metaphors in Emily Brontë's *Wuthering Heights*, and metaphors that "tend always to be, or to become, explicit symbols of psychological or moral conditions" in George Eliot's *Middlemarch*.

Imagery itself, of course, has been treated by a number of critics who, making a variety of assumptions about how words function, study it for many different purposes: some are interested in simply classifying the figures rhetorically; some, like Caroline Spurgeon, in deducing the man behind the work from the imagery he uses; others, in tracing patterns of imagery, motifs, within the given work; and still others, notably Rosamund Tuve, in locating imagery within a rhetorical tradition that presumably defines the author's intention and thus determines how his figures should affect the audience. I have chosen Schorer's essay, though some may disagree with his reading of the novels in question, because it indicates several possibilities for exploring imagery. In the case of Jane Austen's novel, for instance, he dwells on the areas from which the metaphors are drawn, dead though many of the figures are, whereas with George Eliot he discusses the "conceptual portent" of her metaphors as they contribute to the dramatic structure of *Middlemarch*.

More fundamentally, with regard to theoretical questions of stylistic analysis, Schorer maintains in the generalized conclusion to his essay that metaphorical language not only reveals the author by showing "what conceptions the imagination behind that work is able to entertain, how fully and how happily," and serves in the work itself as a "basis of structure," but also functions expressively for the reader through defining and evaluating the novel's theme.

If the novel, as R. P. Blackmur recently proposed, is now to enjoy the kind of attention from criticism that for the past twenty years has been the privilege of poetry, criticism must begin with the simplest assertion: fiction is a literary art. It must begin with the base of language, with the word, with figurative structures, with rhetoric as skeleton and style as body of meaning. A beginning as simple as this must overcome reading habits of long standing; for the novel, written in prose, bears an apparently closer resemblance to discursive forms than it does to poetry, thus easily opening itself to first questions about philosophy or politics, and, traditionally a middle-class vehicle with a reflective social function, it bears an apparently more immediate relation to life than it does to art, thus easily opening itself to first questions about conduct. Yet a novel, like a poem, is not life, it is an image of life; and the critical problem is first of all to analyze the structure of the image. Thus criticism must approach the vast and endlessly ornamented house of fiction with a willingness to do a little at a time and none of it finally, in order to suggest experiences of meaning and of feeling that may be involved in novels, and responsibilities for their style which novelists themselves may forget.

To choose, more or less at random and without premeditated end, one novel by each of only three novelists, and to examine in each only one element in the language, the dominant metaphorical quality—this, positively, is to work piecemeal, and merely to suggest. I emphasize not *metaphor* but *quality*, intending not only the explicit but

"Fiction and the 'Analogical Matrix,'" by Mark Schorer, is reprinted with the permission of Farrar, Straus & Giroux, Inc., and Chatto & Windus from *The World We Imagine* by Mark Schorer, pp. 24–45. Copyright © 1948, 1949, 1968 by Mark Schorer.

the buried and the dead metaphors, and some related traits of diction generally, that whole habit of value association suggested in Scott Buchanan's phrase, the "analogical matrix." The novels are *Persuasion, Wuthering Heights,* and *Middlemarch.*

Persuasion IS A NOVEL of courtship and marriage with a patina of sentimental scruple and moral punctilio and a stylistic base derived from commerce and property, the counting house and the inherited estate. The first is the expression of the characters, the second is the perception of the author. And whether we should decide that a persistent reliance on commerce and property for concepts of value is the habit of Jane Austen's mind, the very grain of her imagination, or that it is a special novelistic intention, is for the moment irrelevant. It is probable that the essence of her comedy resides, in either case, in the discrepancy between social sentiment and social fact, and the social fact is to be discovered not so much in the professions of her characters as in the texture of her style.

We are told at once that the mother of the three Elliot girls felt in dying that in them she left "an awful *legacy* . . . an awful *charge* rather"; that Sir Walter Elliot is devoted to his eldest daughter, Elizabeth (who opens "every ball *of credit*" and is waiting to be "properly *solicited* by baronet-blood"), but feels that his two younger daughters, Mary and Anne, are "of very inferior *value*"—indeed, "Anne's word had no *weight.*" Anne is befriended by Lady Russell, who "had a *value* for rank and consequence," and even though it was Lady Russell no less than Sir Walter who discouraged Anne's marriage, seven years before, to the propertyless Captain Wentworth, Anne "*rated* Lady Russell's influence highly." "Consequence," we are told, "has its *tax,*" and for seven years Anne has been paying it. The problem of the novel is to relieve her of the necessity of paying it and at the same time to increase her value.

We are in a world of substance, a peculiarly material world. Here, indeed, changes are usually named "*material* alterings"—for example, in "style of living" and "degree of consequence." Perhaps the word is used most tellingly in the phrases "a face not materially *disfigured*" and "a material difference in the *discredit* of it"; for *figure* and *credit* suggest the two large areas of metaphorical interest—arithmetic and business.

Time is *divided,* troubles *multiply,* weeks are *calculated,* and even a woman's prettiness is *reckoned.* Thus, one's independence is *purchased*; one is *rendered* happy or unhappy; one is on *terms,* friendly or unfriendly, with others. Young Mr. Elliot has "nothing to *gain* by being on *terms* with Sir Walter," but Lady Russell is convinced that he hopes "to *gain* Anne" even though Anne cannot "know herself to be so *highly rated.*" We are asked to "take all the charms and perfections of Edward's wife upon *credit,*" and "to judge of the general *credit due.*" Captain Wentworth thought that he had *earned* "every blessing." "I have *valued* myself on honourable toils and just *rewards.*" So Mary is in the habit of *claiming* Anne's energies, and Anne does not feel herself "*entitled* to reward." Young ladies have a "*stock* of accomplishments." "Here were *funds* of enjoyment!" Anne does not wish "for the possibility of *exchange.*" Experience is thought of as *venture, reversal, prospect, fortune,* and *allowance.* Anne "*ventured* to recommend a larger *allowance* of prose in" Captain Benwick's "daily study." The death of a wife leaves a man with "*prospects* . . . blighted," and Anne contemplates "the *prospect* of *spending*" two months at Uppercross. In this metaphorical context, even the landscape takes on a special shimmer: "all the *precious* rooms and furniture, groves, and *prospects*." An "arrangement" is *prudent* or *imprudent*, and feelings must be *arranged* as prudently as accounts: no one's "feelings could *interest* her, till she had a little better *arranged* her own." One *pays* addresses, of course, but one is also *repaid* for the "trouble of exertion." "It had *cost* her something to encounter Lady Russell's surprise." A town has *worth*, a song is not *worth* staying for, and Anne "had the full *worth* of" tenderness in "Captain Wentworth's affection." Captain Wentworth's account of Captain Benwick ("whom he had always *valued highly*") "*stamped him* well in the esteem of every listener." "Ten minutes were enough to *certify* that" Mr. Elliot was a sensible man. Stamped, certified; and at last Anne's character is "*fixed* on his mind as perfection itself," which is to say that, like a currency, it has been stabilized.

Moral qualities are persistently put in economic figures: Mary "had no *resources* for solitude" and she had *inherited* "a considerable *share* of the Elliot self-importance." Love, likewise: if Elizabeth is hoping to be *solicited* by baronet-blood, Anne has had to reject the "declarations and proposals" of an improvident sailor. "Alliance" is a peculiarly appropriate word for such prudential arrangements as these, and at the end of the novel, when "the engagement" is "*renewed*," one sees bonded documents. Anne need no longer suffer those fits of dejection in which she contemplates others' "*prosperous* love," for hers at last has prospered, too.

In this context certain colorless words, words of the lightest intention, take on a special weight. The words *account* and *interest* are used hundreds of times in their homeliest sense, yet when we begin to observe that every narration is an *account*, and at least once "an *account* . . . of the *negotiation*," we are reminded that they have more special meanings. When Anne's blighted romance is called "this little history of sorrowful *interest*," we hardly forget that a lack of money was the blight. Is "a man of principle" by any chance a man of substance?

The significance of this metaphorical substructure is clearest, perhaps, not when Jane Austen substitutes material for moral or sentimental values, but when she juxtaposes them. "He had . . . been nothing better than a thick-headed, *unfeeling, unprofitable* Dick Musgrove, who had never done anything to entitle himself to more than the abbreviation of his name, living or dead." More simply, these three from a single paragraph: "a *fund* of good *sense*," "*leisure* to *bestow*," "something that is *entertaining* and *profitable*." "I must endeavour," says Captain Wentworth, in another such juxtaposition near the end of the novel, "I must endeavour to subdue my *mind* to my *fortune*."

Persuasion is a novel in which sensibility—and I am not now raising the question whether it is the sensibility of the author or of her characters or of her characters except for her heroes—a novel in which sensibility is subdued to property.

The novel explicitly asks, what is "the value of an Anne Elliot" and where is the man who will "understand" it? Anne herself feels that her value has sunk:

> A few months hence, and the room now so deserted, occupied by her silent, pensive

self, might be filled again with all that was happy and gay, all that was *glowing and bright* in *prosperous love*, all that was most unlike Anne Elliot!

... Anne felt her spirits not likely to be benefited by an increasing acquaintance among his brother-officers. "These would have been all my friends," was her thought; and she had to struggle against a great tendency to lowness.

"A great *tendency to lowness.*" The phrase clarifies her situation, for Anne's is finally the problem of a stock that has a debased value, and when she thinks of doing good in such a further phrase as "good of a lower standard," we can hardly escape the recognition that this is a novel about marriage as a market, and about the female as marketable, and that the novel makes the observation that to sentimental scruple and moral fastidiousness, as they are revealed to us in the drama, much property is not necessary but *some* is essential—and this is shown us primarily in the style. The basis of the comedy lies in the difference between the two orders of value which the metaphors, like the characters, are all the while busily equating. At the end, in the last sentence, a prosperous sailor's wife, Anne has been relieved of "the tax of consequence," but now "she must *pay the tax* of quick alarm for belonging to that profession which is, if possible, more distinguished in its domestic virtues than in its national importance."

THE STYLE of Jane Austen is so entirely without flamboyance or gesture, the cited illustrations are so commonplace, so perfectly within the order of English idiom, that, unless we remind ourselves that our own habits of speech are even more intimately involved in the life of cash than Jane Austen's, no case at all may appear. Yet the inevitability of individual imaginative habit, the impressive fact that every mind selects its creative gamut from the whole range of possible language, and in thus selecting determines its insights and their scope, in short, its character and the character of its creations, is at once apparent when we open some other novel. Emily Brontë is very different from Jane Austen, yet both were unmarried provincial women, living in the same half of the same century, speaking the same language, both daughters of clergymen, and one might reasonably expect to encounter, even in *Wuthering Heights*, some of those perfectly normal rhetorical figures with which *Persuasion* abounds. There are, I think, none of the same kind. Emily Brontë does not "divide the time" but, on the first page, "the desolation"; "time," when she mentions it, "stagnates," and "prudence" is "diabolical." If there are any figures of the same kind, they are so few, and in their own metaphorical context, function so differently, that the total quality owes nothing to them. Where Wentworth speaks of the "crown" of "all my other success," Lockwood speaks of the "copestone on my rage and humiliation." Both *crown* and *copestone on* mean climax, but "crown" is drawn from rank and money, "copestone" from earth and building. If Nelly Dean's phrase, "the crown of all my wishes," suggests a kingdom at all, it is a heavenly kingdom, quite different from "all my other success." The difference signifies. *Wuthering Heights* has its own sphere of significant experience, and its metaphors, like its epithets and verbs, tell us different things. They tell us, too, of a special problem.

Wuthering Heights, as I understand it, means to be a work of edification: Emily Brontë begins by wishing to instruct her narrator, the dandy, Lockwood, in the nature of a grand passion; she ends by instructing herself in the vanity of human wishes. She means to dramatize with something like approval—the phrase that follows is from *Middlemarch*—"the sense of a stupendous self and an insignificant world." What her metaphors signify is the impermanence of self and the permanence of something larger.

To exalt the power of human feeling, Emily Brontë roots her analogies in the fierce life of animals and in the relentless life of the elements—fire, wind, water. "Wuthering," we are told, is "a significant provincial adjective, descriptive of the atmospheric tumult to which its station is exposed in stormy weather," and, immediately after, that "one may guess the power of the north wind blowing over the edge, by the excessive slant of a few stunted firs at the end of the house; and by a range of gaunt thorns all stretching their limbs one way, as if craving alms of the sun." The application of this landscape to the characters is made explicit in the second half of the novel, when Heathcliff says, "Now, my bonny lad, you are *mine*! And we'll see if one tree won't grow as crooked as another, with the same wind to twist it!" This analogy provides at least half of the metaphorical base of the novel.

Human conditions are like the activities of the landscape, where rains *flood*, blasts *wail*, and the snow and wind *whirl wildly* and *blow* out lights. A serving woman *heaves* "like a sea after a high wind"; a preacher "*poured* forth his zeal in a *shower*"; Mrs. Dean *rushes* to welcome Lockwood, "exclaiming *tumultuously*"; spirits are "at high-water mark"; Linton's soul is as different from Heathcliff's "as a moonbeam from lightning, or frost from fire"; abuse is *lavished* in a *torrent*, or *pours forth* in a *deluge*; illnesses are "*weathered* . . . through"; "sensations" are felt in a *gush*; "your veins are *full* of *ice water*; but mine are *boiling*"; hair *flies*, bodies *toss* or *tremble* like reeds, tears *stream* or *rain down* among ashes; discord and distress arise in a *tumult*; Catherine Linton "was *struck* during a *tempest* of passion with a kind of fit" and "*flew off* in the *height* of it."

Faces, too, are like landscapes: "a *cloud* of meditation" hangs over Nelly Dean's "*ruddy* countenance"; Catherine had "a suddenly *clouded* brow; her humor was a mere *vane* for constantly varying caprices"; "the surface of" the boy Heathcliff's "face and hands was dismally *beclouded*" with dirt; later, his face "*brightened* for a moment; then it was *overcast* afresh." "His forehead . . . *shaded* over with a heavy *cloud*"; and "the *clouded* windows of hell," his eyes, "*flashed*." Hareton, likewise, grows "black as a *thundercloud*"; or *darkens* with a frown. The older Catherine experienced whole "*seasons* of gloom," and the younger Catherine's "heart was *clouded* . . . in double *darkness*." Her "face was just like the *landscape—shadows* and *sunshine* flitting over it in rapid succession; but the *shadows* rested longer, and the *sunshine* was more transient." Sometimes "her eyes are *radiant* with *cloudless* pleasure," and at the end, Hareton shakes off "the *clouds* of ignorance and degradation," and his "*brightening* mind *brightened* his features."

Quite as important as the imagery of wind and cloud and water is the imagery of fire. In every interior, the fire on the hearth is the center of pictorial interest, and the characters sit "*burning* their eyes out before the fire." Eyes *burn* with anguish but do not *melt*; they always *flash* and *sparkle*. Fury *kindles*, temper *kindles*, a "*spark* of spirit" *kindles*. Catherine has a *fiery* disposition, but so do objects and states: words *brand*, shame is *burning*, merriment *expires* quickly, fevers *consume* life; hot coffee and basins *smoke*, they do not steam; and Isabella shrieks "as if witches were running *red-hot* needles into her." Sometimes fire is identified with other elements, as when a servant urges "*flakes* of *flame* up the chimney," or when Isabella complains that the fire causes the wound on her neck, first stopped by the icy cold, to stream and smart.

Metaphors of earth—earth takes more solid and durable forms than the other elements—are interestingly few. Twice Heathcliff is likened to "an arid wilderness of *furze* and *whinstone*"; there is a reference to his "*flinty* gratification"; and once he speaks scornfully of "the *soil* of" Linton's "shallow cares." Earth and vegetation sometimes result in a happy juxtaposition of the vast or the violent and the little or the homely, as when Heathcliff says of Linton that "he might as well plant *an oak in a flowerpot*," or when he threatens to "crush his ribs in like *a rotten hazelnut*," which is like his saying that Catherine's passion could be as readily encompassed by Linton as "the *sea* could be ... contained in that *horse-trough*."

Most of the animals are wild. Hareton's "whiskers encroached *bearishly* over his cheeks," and Heathcliff denies the paternity of "that bear." Hareton had been "cast out like an unfledged *dunnock*," and Heathcliff is a "fierce, pitiless, *wolfish* man." He is also "a *bird* of bad omen" and "an evil *beast*" prowling between a "stray *sheep* ... and the fold, waiting his time to spring and destroy." He has a "*ferocious* gaze" and a *savage* utterance; he *growls* and *howls* "like a beast," and is many times named "a brute," "a beast," "a brute beast." He struggles like a *bear*, he has *sharp cannibal teeth* which *gleam* "through the dark," and "*basilisk* eyes ... *quenched* by sleeplessness." He *gnashes* his teeth and *foams* like a *mad dog*. He is "like a *bull*" to Linton's "*lamb*," and only at the very end, the exhausted end, "he breathed as fast as a *cat*."

For the domestic and the gentler animals are generally used for purposes of harsh satire or vilification. Edgar, "the soft thing," "possessed the power to depart, as much as a *cat* possesses the power to leave a *mouse* half killed, or a *bird* half eaten." He is "not a *lamb*" but "a suckling *leveret*," and his sister is a "pitiful, slavish, mean-minded *brach*," she is among those *worms*, who, "the more they writhe, the more" Heathcliff yearns "to crush out their entrails." Hindley dies in a stupor, "snorting like a *horse*"; "flaying and scalping" would not have roused him, and when the doctor arrives, "the *beast* has changed to *carrion*." Hareton is "an infernal *calf*," and young Linton is a "puling *chicken*" and a "*whelp*." Like a dying dog, he "slowly *trailed* himself off, and lay down," or, like a cold one, he "*shrank* closer to the fire." He "had *shrunk* into a corner of the settle, as quiet as a *mouse*"; he is called "a little perishing *monkey*"; and he "achieved his exit exactly as a *spaniel* might." He is also "an abject *reptile*" and "a *cockatrice*." Hareton, who is capable on occasion of gathering "*venom* with reflection," is once called a "*magpie*," and once said to be "obstinate as a *mule*"—one of the few kindly animal references in the novel. To be sure, Isabella describes herself as though she were a deer: "I *bounded*, *leaped* and *flew* down the steep road; then ... *shot* direct across the moor, *rolling* over banks, and *wading* through marshes." And

Catherine, on the whole, is not abused. She is a "cunning little *fox*" and she runs "like a *mouse*," but chiefly she is "soft and mild as a *dove*."

Emily Brontë's metaphors color all her diction. As her epithets are charged with passion—"jealous guardianship," "vexatious phlegm," "importunate branch"—so her verbs are verbs of violent movement and conflict, both contributing to a rhetorical texture where everything is at a pitch from which it can only subside. The verbs *demand* exhaustion, just as the metaphors *demand* rest. And there is an antithetical chorus in this rhetoric, a contrapuntal warning, which, usually but not only in the voice of Nelly Dean, says, "Hush! Hush!" all through the novel, at the beginning of paragraph after paragraph. At the end, everything *is* hushed. And the moths *fluttering* over Heathcliff's grave and "the soft wind *breathing* through the grass" that grows on it have at last more power than he, for all his passion. These soft and fragile things paradoxically endure.

The passions of animals, if we may speak of them as passions, have meaning in that they are presumably necessary to survival; Heathcliff's passion destroys others, himself, and at last, itself. The tumult of the elements alternates with periods of peace, and the seasons are not only autumn and winter. The *fact* of alternation enables nature to endure. The singleness of Heathcliff's tempestuous and wintry emotional life dooms it. Thus there is a curious and ironic contrast between the condition and the destiny of Heathcliff, and the full facts of those areas of metaphor. When, at the end of the novel, Nelly remarks that "the same moon shone through the window; and the same autumn landscape lay outside" as eighteen years before, she is speaking with metaphorical accuracy; but Heathcliff is *not* the same. He has not indeed come into a "sober, disenchanted maturity"—that will be the privilege of Hareton and the second Cathy; but he has completely changed in the fashion that Joseph described much earlier—"so as by fire." ". . . there is a strange change approaching: I'm in its shadow at present," he declares when he has found that nothing is worth the feeling of it. At last, after all the windy tumult and the tempests, he says, "I have to remind myself to *breathe.* . . ."

If his life, exhausted at the end, has not been, as he once said of it, "a moral teething," and the novel, therefore, no tragedy, the story of his life has been a moral teething for the author. Lockwood is instructed in the nature of a grand passion, but he and Emily Brontë together are instructed in its final fruits: even roaring fires end in a bed of ashes. Her metaphors instruct her, and her verbs. That besides these rhetorical means (which in their functioning make tolerable the almost impossibly inflated style), she should have found structural means as well which give her whole narrative the remote quality of a twice-told tale, the property of an old wife (and so make its melodrama endurable), should reinforce the point. At the end, the voice that drones on is the perdurable voice of the country, Nelly Dean's. No more than Heathcliff did Emily Brontë quite intend that homespun finality. Like the older Catherine, Emily Brontë could have said of her book, "I've dreamed in my life dreams that have stayed with me ever after, and changed my ideas: they've gone through and through me, like wine through water, and altered the color of my mind." Her rhetoric altered the form of her intention. It is her education; it shapes her insight.

Middlemarch IS A NOVEL written on a much grander scale than either of these others, with many points of narrative interest, a much more complex structural pattern, and an important difference in its metaphorical language. Jane Austen's metaphors are generally of the "buried" kind, submerged, woven deep in the ordinary, idiomatic fabric of the language; Emily Brontë's are generally epithetical. George Eliot's tend always to be, or to become, explicit symbols of psychological or moral conditions, and they actually function in such a way as to give symbolical value to much action, as Dorothea's pleasure in planning buildings ("a kind of work which she delighted in") and Casaubon's desire to construct a "Key to all Mythologies." Their significance lies, then, not so much in the choice of area (as, "commerce," or "natural elements" and "animals") as in the choice of function, and one tests them not by their field, their content, but by their conceptual portent. I should like to suggest a set of metaphorical qualities in *Middlemarch* which actually represents a series apparent in the thinking that underlies the dramatic structure. First of all, there are metaphors of unification; then, of antithesis; next, there are metaphors which conceive things as progressive, and then, metaphors of shaping and making, of structure and creative purpose; finally, there are metaphors of what I should call a "muted" apocalypse.

George Eliot's metaphors of unification pivot on her most characteristic verbs—these are of conciliation and reconciliation, of unification, of course, and of inclusion, of mingling, of associating, of merging and mixing, of embracing and comprehending, of connecting, allying, binding together and making room for. The elements to be brought together are as various as the universe—they may be merely "mingled pleasures" or "associated facts which . . . show a mysterious electricity if you touched them," or the relation of urban and rural areas, which "made fresh threads of connection"; again, they may be attitudes—"criticism" and "awe" *mixing*, or qualities *uniting*, as, presumably, "the glories of doctor and saint" in dreary Casaubon, or men themselves making more *energetic alliances* "with impartial nature"; or they may be those yearnings of one individual for another which find completion in love, the institution of marriage, and the literal embrace; or, most important, they may be "lofty conceptions" which embrace multitudinousness—for example, the daily life of Tipton parish and Dorothea Brooke's own "rule of conduct." If only we knew more and felt more, these metaphors insist; for there *is*, we are told, "a knowledge which . . . traces out the suppressed transitions which unite all contrasts." This is religious yearning, and it finds occasional pseudo-religious fulfillment, as after Lydgate's successful cogitations on morphology: he finds himself "in that agreeable after-glow of excitement when thought lapses from examination of a specific object into a suffusive sense of its connections with all the rest of our existence," and one can "float with the repose of unexhausted strength."

The metaphors of unification imply the metaphors of antithesis; the first represent yearnings, the second a recognition of fact. Thus we have metaphors of reality vs. appearance, as : "the large vistas and wide fresh air which she had dreamed of finding in her husband's mind were replaced by anterooms and winding passages which seemed to lead no-whither"; or of chaos vs. order (humorously dramatized by Mr.

Brooke's "documents," which need arranging but get mixed up in pigeon-holes), as Mary Garth's "red fire," which "seemed like a solemn existence calmly independent of the petty passions, the imbecile desires, the straining after worthless uncertainties, which were daily moving her contempt"; or of shapelessness vs. shape, as "a kind Providence furnishes the limpest personality with a little gum or starch in the form of tradition." There are other kinds, of outer vs. inner, for example: "so much subtler is a human mind than the outside tissues which make a sort of blazonry or clock-face for it." It is this, the outer-inner antithesis, which underscores one of George Eliot's favorite words—"inward" or "inwardly," a usage which is frequently annoying because it is tautological, applied to states which can *only* be inward under the circumstances of the fiction, but, for that reason, all the more symptomatic. There are metaphorical antitheses of fact to wish, imbalance to balance, restlessness to repose, and many other opposites. Most important, and perhaps most frequent, are the figures which oppose freedom to various forms of restraint—burdens, ties, bonds, and so on: "he replies by calling himself Pegasus, and every form of prescribed work 'harness,'" to which the answer is, "I shall let him be *tried* by the *test* of freedom." Another example of the restraint-freedom opposition illustrates the way that reported action, when conjoined with these metaphors, pushes both on to explicit symbolism: near the end, Dorothea observes on the road outside her window "a man with a bundle on his back and a woman carrying her baby," and, still nearer the end, when Lydgate has "accepted his narrowed lot," that is, the values of his child-bride, he thinks, "He had chosen this fragile creature, and had taken the burden of her life upon his arms. He must walk as he could, carrying that burden pitifully."

Everyone and everything in this novel is moving on a "way." Life is a *progress*, and it is variously and inevitably described as road, stream, channel, avenue, way, journey, voyage, ride (either on horse or by carriage), vista, chain, line, course, path, and process. To these terms one should add the terms of *growth*, usually biological growth, which carry much the same value. There must be at least a thousand and possibly there are more metaphorical variations on the general idea of life as progress, and this progress is illimitable. At the end of the novel we are told, in words somewhat suggestive of a more orthodox religious spirit than George Eliot, that "every limit is a beginning as well as an ending."

Everything strains forward. Consciousness is a stream. "In Dorothea's mind there was a current into which all thought and feeling were apt sooner or later to flow—the reaching forward of the whole consciousness toward the fullest truth, the least partial good." "Character, too," we are told, "is a process," and it is a process which we recognize by achievement—"the niceties of inward balance, by which man swims and makes his point or else is carried headlong." Like Leopold Bloom, George Eliot's characters think of their existence as "the stream of life in which the stream of life we trace," but with a difference: the personal life finally flows into the "gulf of death," but the general stream flows on, through vistas of endlessly unfolding good, and that good consists of individual achievements of "the fullest truth, the least partial good," of Lydgate's individually *made points*. This is a progressive, in no sense a cyclical view of human history.

These metaphors of progress, like the restraint-freedom antithesis, involve George Eliot in her many complementary metaphors of hindrance to progress. The individual purpose is sometimes confused by "a social life which seemed nothing but a labyrinth of petty courses, a walled-in maze"; sometimes by the inadequacy of the purpose itself, as Casaubon, who "was lost among small closets and winding stairs"; experience and circumstance over and over become "yokes," which slow the progress, for there are those always "who carry a weight of trials"; one may *toil* "under the fetters of a promise" or move, like Lydgate, more haltingly than one had hoped under the *burden* of a responsibility.

These hindrances are, generally speaking, social, not moral. One submits to them in the interests of the whole procession, and when one does not submit—as Dorothea, refusing to devote herself to Casaubon's scholarship after his death—it is because one has discovered that they are not in the interests of the whole procession. The particular interests of the procession are indicated by the extended metaphors drawn from nearly every known field of physical and medical science. It is by the "serene light of science" that we glimpse "a presentiment of endless processes filling the vast spaces planked out of" our "sight by that wordy ignorance which," in the past, we "had supposed to be knowledge." It is by the same light that we are able to recognize our social obligations, according to the Religion of Humanity.

Thus, quite smoothly, we come to that fourth group of prevailing metaphors, those having to do with purpose. They are of shaping, of forming, of making, of framing; they pivot on notions of pattern or rule, measure or structure. They are all words used in metaphors which, explicitly or by implication, reveal the individual directing his destiny by conscious, creative purpose toward the end of absolute human order. Opposed to them are the many metaphors of derogation of the unorganized, notably the human mind, which, at worst, like Mr. Brooke's, availing nothing perceptible in the body politic, is a *mass*.

At the end of this grand vista are the metaphors of what I have called the "muted" apocalypse. The frequency with which George Eliot uses the words *up, high,* and *higher* in metaphorical contexts is equalled only, perhaps, by her use of the word *light,* until one feels a special significance in "giving *up*" and in all the faces that *beam,* all the ideas that *flash* across the mind, and all the things that are all the time being "taken" in *that light* or *this light.* Fire plays a perhaps predictably important metaphorical role, and, together with light, or alternating with it, usually accompanies or is implied by those frequent metaphors in which things are *gloriously* transformed, transfused, or transfigured. Treating this complex of figures as I do, as a kind of apocalyptic drama which of course does not exist in the novel as such, but surely does in the imagination of George Eliot, we are, now, at the moment before climax, all those metaphors involving ideas of veneration and adoration, or worshipful awe; these, in my factitious series, are immediately followed by the climax itself, which is contained in endless use of the word "revelation" and figurative developments from it. Perception, in this novel, is indeed thought of as revelation, and minds and souls are always "opening" to the influx. Things are many times "manifested" or "made manifest," as if life were a perpetual epiphany. If perception is not a "revelation," it is a "divination," and for the ordinary verb, "to recognize," George Eliot usually prefers to use "to divine." It is here that we come upon her unquestionably favorite word, and the center of her most persistent metaphors. For the word "sight" or "feeling" she almost always substitutes the more portentous word "vision." Visions are of every possible kind, from *dim* to *bright* to *blinding*, from *testing* to *guiding*. The observation of any simple physical detail may be a vision; every insight is of course a vision, usually an *inward* vision.

The experience now subsides. If perception is revelation, then it is, secondarily, nourishment, and the recurrence of metaphors in which perception is conceived as spiritual food and drink, and of all the metaphors of *fullness, filling,* and *fulfillment,* is perhaps predictable. It is likewise energizing, in various figurative ways, and in moments of climactic understanding, significantly, a charge of electricity flows through the human organism.

Illumination, revelation, fulfillment. One step remains in this pattern of a classic religious experience; that is expectation. Metaphors of expectation are everywhere; I will represent them in their most frequent form, a phrase so rubbed by usage that it hardly seems metaphorical at all. It is "to look forward," and it appears on nearly every page of *Middlemarch*, a commonplace there too, yet more than that: it is the clue to the whole system of metaphor I have sketched out; it is the clue to a novel, the clue to a mind.

I have separated into a series a metaphorical habit which of course always appears in conflux, and it is only because these metaphors do constantly associate themselves in the novel, that one may justifiably hit upon them as representing George Eliot's selectivity. One of many such elaborate confluences is as follows:

> ... Mr. Casaubon's talk about his great book was *full* of *new vistas*; and this sense of *revelation*, this *surprise of a nearer introduction* to Stoics and Alexandrians, as people who had ideas not totally unlike her own, kept in abeyance for the time her usual eagerness for a *binding theory* which could bring her own life and doctrine into *strict connection* with that amazing past, and give the remotest *sources* of knowledge some *bearing* on her actions. ... she was *looking forward* to *higher initiation* in ideas, as she was *looking forward* to marriage, and *blending* her *dim* conceptions of both.... All her eagerness for acquirement lay within that *full current of sympathetic* motive in which her ideas and impulses were habitually *swept along*. She did not want to deck herself with knowledge—to wear it loose from the *nerves and blood that fed her action*; and if she had written a book she must have done it as St. Theresa did, under the *command of an authority that constrained her conscience*. But something she yearned for by which her *life might be filled* with action at once rational and ardent: and since the time was gone by *for guiding visions* and spiritual directors, since prayer *heightened* yearning, but not instruction, *what lamp* was there but knowledge?

Here are nearly all of them: metaphors of unification, of antithesis (restraint-freedom), of progress, of the apocalypse: height, light, revelation, vision, nourishment, and, of course, the forward look. The passage is not in the least exceptional. In my analytical sketch of such persistent confluences, I separated the elements into a series to demonstrate how completely, step by step, they embody a pseudo-religious philosophy, how absolutely expressive is metaphor, even in fiction, and how systematic it can become. This is a novel of religious yearning without religious object. The unification it desires is the unification of human knowledge in the service of social ends; the antitheses that trouble it (and I observe in this otherwise classic series no antitheses either of Permanence and Change, or of Sin and Grace) are the antitheses between man as he is and man as he could be in this world; the hindrances to life as progress are man's social not his moral flaws; the purposive dedication of individuals will overcome those flaws; we see the fulfillment of all truly intellectual passions, for the greater glory of Man.

Our first observation on the function of metaphor in this novel should, then, be of its *absolutely* expressive character. The second is perhaps less evident, and we may call it the interpretive function of metaphor, the extent to which metaphor comments on subject. The subject of this novel may be Middlemarch, a community, but, as even the title metaphorically suggests, the theme is the nature of progress in what is probably meant to be the typical British community in the nineteenth century. (Observe, too, these names: Brooke, a running course, and Lydgate, his progress blocked by his wife, twice-blocked by his name.) Or we can select subjects within the subject, as the clerical subject interpreted by the pseudo-religious theme; the true "religious" dedication of a Dorothea Brooke, and the characters around her falling into various "religious" postures: Casaubon as the false prophet, Bulstrode as the parody-prophet, Lydgate as the nearly true prophet—a "scientific Phoenix," he is called—somehow deflected from his prophecy, and Ladislaw as the true prophet. Indeed, given the metaphorical texture, one cannot escape the nearly systematic Christ analogy which George Eliot weaves around Ladislaw, omitting from her figure only the supremely important element of Christ's sacrifice, and the reason for which He made it. This is to be expected in a novel which is about progress without guilt. Here, even the heroic characters cannot be said to have inner struggles, for all their "inward visions." Here there is much illumination and nearly no self-doubt; much science, and never a sin. One recognizes from the metaphorical structure that this novel represents a decay of the full religious experience into that part of it which aspires alone: Christian optimism divorced from the basic human tragedy.

The metaphorical complex provides a third, and a more interesting function: a structural function. *Middlemarch* is concerned with nearly every important activity in community life—political, clerical, agricultural, industrial, professional, domestic, of course, even scholarly. It involves many different characters and groups of characters. The relations between some of these characters and even between some of these groups are often extremely tenuous, often merely accidental. The dramatic structure in short, is not very taut, yet one feels, on finishing the book, that this is a superbly constructed work, that, indeed, as foolish Mr. Brooke observes, "We're all one family, you know—it's all one cupboard." What makes it so is thematic rather than dramatic unity.

The measure of Middlemarch is Dorothea's *sublimity*, the interpretive height from which she judges. From her sublimity, everything shades off, all the way down to garrulous Mrs. Cadwallader and villainous Mr. Bulstrode. The metaphors of unification which George Eliot enjoyed to use, those images of intermingling and embracing, are important in a double sense: they express Dorothea's ethical sentiments, and, actually, they and the others bind the material together. They tell us *how to take* each Middlemarcher, *in what light*. They do this chiefly through the creation of symbolic echoes of the major situations in the minor ones, echoes often ironic, sometimes parodies.

Thus, in the imagery of vision, Dorothea's remark, made so early as in Chapter III, has a special ring: "I am rather shortsighted." In the imagery of human progress, Mr. Garth's question about Bulstrode, the pious fraud—"whether he shall settle somewhere else, as a lasting thing"—has such symbolic value. Mr. Garth's own attitude toward agriculture is a thematic parody of the exaltation of Dorothea, Lydgate, and Ladislaw: "the peculiar tone of fervid veneration, of religious regard in which he wrapped it, as a consecrated symbol is wrapped in its gold-fringed linen." In the imagery of structure, a special meaning seems to attach to the word "dwell," when it refers to characters experiencing some state of mind. Lydgate's morphological research is another such symbolic extension of the metaphors of structure. Dorothea's avenue of limes outside her window, leading toward the sunset, becomes, finally, a representation in the landscape of the idea of progress. The political newspapers, notably unenlightened, are called *The Pioneer* and *The Trumpet*, and these are surely parodies, one of the progress metaphors, the other of the apocalyptic. Even that humble rural tavern, the *Weights and Scales*, reminds us of more exalted concern, in this novel, with justice and with metaphors of balance. And so that wretched farm called Freeman's End, which has nearly destroyed its tenant and his family, is an eloquent little drama of the freedom-restraint metaphors.

"We all of us," says George Eliot, "grave or light, get our thoughts entangled in metaphors, and act fatally on the strength of them." If the writing of a novel is a deed, as Conrad liked to think, she spoke truer than she knew.

FOUR TENTATIVE PROPOSALS seem relevant:

1. Metaphorical language gives any style its special quality, and one may even suggest—only a little humorously—that this quality derives in part from the content of the metaphors, that quantity shapes quality. Certainly the particular "dryness" of Jane Austen's style is generated in part by the content of her images of the counting house, and certainly the inflatedness of Emily Brontë's is generated in large part by the prominence of wind and of atmospheric tumult in her metaphors. I cannot, unfortunately, suggest that George Eliot's pleasure in "light" has any notable effect on the quality of her style, but we can say that the content of her conceptions as her metaphors express it predicts a style serious always, solemn probably, and heavy perhaps.

2. Metaphorical language expresses, defines, and evaluates theme, and thereby demonstrates the limits and the special poise within those limits of a given imagination. We have seen three novels in which metaphors in effect answered questions that the novels themselves neglected to ask.

3. Metaphorical language, because it constantly strains toward symbolism, can be in novels as in poems the basis of structure, and it can even be counterposed to dramatic structure. We have observed the structural function in *Middlemarch*. In *Wuthering Heights* we may observe the more complicated contrapuntal function of metaphor in structure. Gerard Manley Hopkins, writing of Greek tragedy, spoke of "two strains of thought running together and like counterpointed," the paraphrasable "overthought," and the "underthought"

> conveyed chiefly in the choice of metaphors etc. used, and often only half realized by the poet himself, not necessarily having any connection with the subject in hand but usually having a connection and suggested by some circumstance of the scene or of the story.

The metaphors of *Wuthering Heights* comprise such an "underthought," for although they are equated in the work, the work itself yet somehow develops a stronger and stronger contrast between the obligations of the human and the non-human creation.

4. Finally, metaphorical language reveals to us the character of any imaginative work in that, more tellingly perhaps than any other elements, it shows us what conceptions the imagination behind that work is able to entertain, how fully and how happily. I mean to say that style *is* conception, and that, for this reason, rhetoric must be considered as existing within—importantly within, and, sometimes, fatally within—what we call poetic. It is really style, and style primarily, that first conceives, then expresses, and finally tests these themes, these subjects, even these "kinds"—Jane Austen's manners, Emily Brontë's passions, George Eliot's morals. "Symbolization," said Susanne Langer (and I could not comfortably close these observations without mentioning her excellent name), "Symbolization is both an end and an instrument." "The right word," said George Eliot, "is always a power, and communicates its definiteness to our action." And "The Eye," said William Blake, "sees more than the heart knows."

Literature as Sentences

❀ RICHARD M. OHMANN ❀

In addition to his theoretical speculations on style, which include the "Prolegomena to the Analysis of Prose Style" reprinted on pages 36–49 of this volume, Richard Ohmann has done a good deal of specific verbal analysis, bringing to bear his knowledge of contemporary developments in linguistics. In his book *Shaw: The Style and the Man* (1962), for instance, he takes off from a claim by Roman Jakobson—that verbal discourse is grounded in two different activities, combination and selection—to develop the idea that Shaw is essentially a "similarity-seeker" rather than a "continuity-seeker" through examining that writer's "modes of order" and "uses of discontinuity." Although Ohmann indicates a number of correlations between Shaw's stylistic traits and the quality of his mind, he also discusses Shaw's "posture of opposition" and rhetoric, thus in part treating his language as dramatic, as acting on an audience in various ways.

In "Literature as Sentences," Ohmann uses "the framework of generative grammar and scraps of its terminology" to analyze three passages from literary texts, in each case differentiating between the "surface structure" of the passage and its "deep structure." Periodically in the essay, he relates his analyses to some of the theoretical points made earlier in the "Prolegomena to the Analysis of Prose Style." For example, he notes that the distinction between content and form is mirrored in the distinction between deep structure (content) and surface structure (form), the latter comprising a way of saying something and so entering the domain of style. Similarly, the concept of choice—the sort of "epistemic choice" described in the "Prolegomena"—reappears here when Ohmann explores Dylan Thomas' deviations from normal syntax (deviation from the norm being, of course, another recurrent motif in stylistic criticism).

One of the strengths of "Literature as Sentences," I think, is Ohmann's ability to illuminate the literary implications of the linguistic structures that he discovers. In analyzing a sentence from "The Secret Sharer," he not only establishes its rhetorical effect but relates its "rhetorical movement" to the theme of the story and then to "the build" of the "literary work" as a whole; in addition, he points out the "extraordinary 'density'" of the sentence, along with "a chaining effect" typical of Conrad's syntax. Although Ohmann's theoretical position tends to commit him to conceiving of style primarily in relation to the writer, his analyses show that he is acutely aware of the particular effects which a given style has upon the reader.

CRITICS PERMIT THEMSELVES, for this or that purpose, to identify literature with great books, with imaginative writing, with expressiveness in writing, with the non-referential and non-pragmatic, with beauty in language, with order, with myth, with structured and formed discourse—the list of definitions is nearly endless—with verbal play, with uses of language that stress the medium itself, with the expression of an age, with dogma, with the *cri de cœur*, with neurosis. Now of course literature is itself and not another thing, to paraphrase Bishop Butler; yet analogies and classifications have merit. For a short space let us think of literature as sentences.

To do so will not tax the imagination, because the work of literature indubitably *is* composed of sentences, most of them well ordered, many of them deviant (no pejorative meant), some of them incomplete. But since much the same holds for dust-jacket copy, the Congressional Record, and transcripts of board meetings, the small effort required to think of literature as sentences may be repaid by a correspondingly small insight into literature as such. Although I do not believe this to be

"Literature as Sentences," by Richard M. Ohmann, is reprinted from *College English*, XXVII (1966), 261–67, with the permission of the National Council of Teachers of English and Richard Ohmann. The stanzas from "A Winter's Tale," by Dylan Thomas, on page 359 are from Dylan Thomas, *The Collected Poems*. Copyright 1946 by New Directions Publishing Corporation. Reprinted by permission of New Directions Publishing Corporation, J. M. Dent & Sons Ltd., and the Trustees for the Copyrights of the late Dylan Thomas.

so, for the moment I shall hold the question in abeyance, and stay mainly within the territory held in common by all forms of discourse. In other words, I am not asking what is special about the sentences *of literature*, but what is special about *sentences* that they should interest the student of literature. Although I employ the framework of generative grammar and scraps of its terminology,[1] what I have to say should not ring in the traditionally educated grammatical ear with outlandish discord.

First, then, the sentence is the primary unit of understanding. Linguists have so trenchantly discredited the old definition—"a sentence is a complete thought"—that the truth therein has fallen into neglect. To be sure, we delimit the class of sentences by formal criteria, but each of the structures that qualifies will express a semantic unity not characteristic of greater or lesser structures. The meanings borne by morphemes, phrases, and clauses hook together to express a meaning that can stand more or less by itself. This point, far from denying the structuralist's definition of a sentence as a single free utterance, or *form*, seems the inevitable corollary of such definitions: forms carry meanings, and it is natural that an independent form should carry an independent meaning. Or, to come at the thing another way, consider that one task of a grammar is to supply structural descriptions, and that the sentence is the unit so described. A structural description specifies the way each part of a sentence is tied to each other part, and the semantic rules of a grammar use the structural description as starting point in interpreting the whole. A reader or hearer does something analogous when he resolves the structures and meanings of sentences, and thereby understands them. Still another way to approach the primacy of the sentence is to notice that the initial symbol for all derivations in a generative grammar is "S" for sentence: the sentence is the domain of grammatical structure—rather like the equation in algebra—and hence the domain of meaning.

These remarks, which will seem truisms to some and heresy to others, cannot be elaborated here. Instead, I want to register an obvious comment on their relevance to literary theory and literary criticism. Criticism, whatever else it does, must interpret works of literature. Theory concerns itself in part with the question, "what things legitimately bear on critical interpretation?" But beyond a doubt, interpretation begins with sentences. Whatever complex apprehension the critic develops of the whole work, that understanding arrives mundanely, sentence by sentence. For this reason, and because the form of a sentence dictates a rudimentary mode of understanding, sentences have a good deal to do with the subliminal meaning (and form) of a literary work. They prepare and direct the reader's attention in particular ways.

My second point about sentences should dispel some of the abstractness of the first. Most sentences directly and obliquely put more linguistic apparatus into operation than is readily apparent, and call on more of the reader's linguistic competence. Typically, a surface structure overlays a deep structure which it may resemble but little, and which determines the "content" of the sentence. For concreteness, take this rather ordinary example, an independent clause from Joyce's "Araby": "Gazing

---

[1] I draw especially on Noam Chomsky, *Aspects of the Theory of Syntax* (Cambridge, Mass., 1965), and Jerrold J. Katz and Paul Postal, *An Integrated Theory of Linguistic Descriptions* (Cambridge, Mass., 1964).

up into the darkness I saw myself as a creature driven and derided by vanity." The surface structure may be represented as follows, using the convention of labeled brackets:[2] $^S[^{Adv}[V + Part\ ^{PP}[P\ ^{NP}[D + N]]]\ ^{Nuc}[N\ ^{VP}[V + N\ ^{PP}[P\ ^{NP}[D + N\ ^{Adj}[V + and + V\ ^{PP}[P + N]]]]]]]]$. The nucleus has a transitive verb with a direct object. In the deep structure, by contrast, the matrix sentence is of the form $^S[NP\ ^{VP}[V + Complement + NP]]$: "I + saw + as a creature + me." It has embedded in it one sentence with an intransitive verb and an adverb of location—"I gazed up into the darkness"—and two additional sentences with transitive verbs and direct objects—"Vanity drove the creature," and "Vanity derided the creature." Since "darkness" and "vanity" are derived nouns, the embedded sentences must in turn contain embeddings, of, say "(Something) is dark" and "(Someone) is vain." Thus the word "vanity," object of a preposition in the surface structure, is subject of two verbs in the deep, and its root is a predicate adjective. The word "creature," object of a preposition in the surface structure, also has a triple function in the deep structure: verbal complement, direct object of "drive," and direct object of "deride." Several transformations (including the passive) deform the six basic sentences, and several others relate them to each other. The complexity goes much farther, but this is enough to suggest that a number of grammatical processes are required to generate the initial sentence and that its structure is moderately involved. Moreover, a reader will not understand the sentence unless he grasps the relations marked in the deep structure. As it draws on a variety of syntactic resources, the sentence also activates a variety of semantic processes and modes of comprehension, yet in brief compass and in a surface *form* that radically permutes *content*.

I choose these terms willfully: that there are interesting grounds here for a form-content division seems to me quite certain. Joyce might have written, "I gazed up into the darkness. I saw myself as a creature. The creature was driven by vanity. The creature was derided by vanity." Or, "Vanity drove and derided the creature I saw myself as, gazer up, gazer into the darkness." Content remains roughly the same, for the basic sentences are unchanged. But the style is different. And each revision structures and screens the content differently. The original sentence acquires part of its meaning and part of its unique character by resonating against those unwritten alternatives. It is at the level of sentences, I would argue, that the distinction between form and content comes clear, and that the intuition of style has its formal equivalent.[3]

Sentences play on structure in still another way, more shadowy, but of considerable interest for criticism. It is a commonplace that not every noun can serve as object of every verb, that a given noun can be modified only by adjectives of certain classes, and so on. For instance, a well-defined group of verbs, including "exasperate," "delight," "please," and "astound," require animate objects; another group, in-

---

[2] Each set of brackets encloses the constituent indicated by its superscript label. The notation is equivalent to a tree diagram. Symbols: S = Sentence, Adv = Adverbial, V = Verb, Part = Particle, PP = Prepositional Phrase, P = Preposition, NP = Noun Phrase, D = Determiner, N = Noun, Nuc = Nucleus, VP = Verb Phrase, Adj = Adjectival.

[3] I have argued the point at length in "Generative Grammars and the Concept of Literary Style," *Word*, 20 (December 1964), 423–39.

LITERATURE AS SENTENCES [357]

cluding "exert," "behave," and "pride," need reflexive objects. Such interdependencies abound in a grammar, which must account for them by subcategorizing nouns, adjectives, and the other major classes.[4] The importance of categorical restrictions is clearest in sentences that disregard them—deviant sentences. It happens that the example from Joyce is slightly deviant in this way: in one of the underlying sentences —"Vanity derided the creature"—a verb that requires a human subject in fact has as its subject the abstract noun "vanity." The dislocation forces the reader to use a supplementary method of interpretation: here, presumably he aligns "vanity" (the word) with the class of human nouns and sees vanity (the thing) as a distinct, active power in the narrator's psyche. Such deviance is so common in metaphor and elsewhere that one scarcely notices it, yet it helps to specify the way things happen in the writer's special world, and the modes of thought appropriate to that world.

I have meant to suggest that sentences normally comprise intricacies of form and meaning whose effects are not the less substantial for their subtlety. From this point, what sorts of critical description follow? Perhaps I can direct attention toward a few tentative answers, out of the many that warrant study, and come finally to a word on critical theory. Two samples must carry the discussion; one is the final sentence of "The Secret Sharer":

> Walking to the taffrail, I was in time to make out, on the very edge of a darkness thrown by a towering black mass like the very gateway of Erebus—yes, I was in time to catch an evanescent glimpse of my white hat left behind to mark the spot where the secret sharer of my cabin and of my thoughts, as though he were my second self, had lowered himself into the water to take his punishment: a free man, a proud swimmer striking out for a new destiny.

I hope others will agree that the sentence justly represents its author: that it portrays a mind energetically stretching to subdue a dazzling experience *outside* the self, in a way that has innumerable counterparts elsewhere in Conrad. How does scrutiny of the deep structure support this intuition? First, notice a matter of emphasis, of rhetoric. The matrix sentence, which lends a surface form to the whole, is "#S# I was in time #S#" (repeated twice). The embedded sentences that complete it are "I walked to the taffrail," "I made out + NP," and "I caught + NP." The point of departure, then, is the narrator himself: where he was, what he did, what he saw. But a glance at the deep structure will explain why one feels a quite different emphasis in the sentence as a whole: seven of the embedded sentences have "sharer" as grammatical subjects; in another three the subject is a noun linked to "sharer" by the copula; in two "sharer" is direct object; and in two more "share" is the verb. Thus thirteen sentences go to the semantic development of "sharer," as follows:

1. The secret sharer had lowered the secret sharer into the water.
2. The secret sharer took his punishment.
3. The secret sharer swam.

[4] Chomsky discusses ways of doing this in *Aspects of the Theory of Syntax*, Chapter 2.

4. The secret sharer was a swimmer.
5. The swimmer was proud.
6. The swimmer struck out for a new destiny.
7. The secret sharer was a man.
8. The man was free.
9. The secret sharer was my second self.
10. The secret sharer had (it).
11. (Someone) punished the secret sharer.
12. (Someone) shared my cabin.
13. (Someone) shared my thoughts.

In a fundamental way, the sentence is mainly *about* Leggatt, although the surface structure indicates otherwise.

Yet the surface structure does not simply throw a false scent, and the way the sentence comes to focus on the secret sharer is also instructive. It begins with the narrator, as we have seen, and "I" is the subject of five basic sentences early on. Then "hat" takes over as the syntactic focus, receiving development in seven base sentences. Finally, the sentence arrives at "sharer." This progression in the deep structure rather precisely mirrors both the rhetorical movement of the sentence from the narrator to Leggatt via the hat that links them, and the thematic effect of the sentence, which is to transfer Leggatt's experience to the narrator via the narrator's vicarious and actual participation in it. Here I shall leave this abbreviated rhetorical analysis, with a cautionary word: I do not mean to suggest that only an examination of deep structure reveals Conrad's skillful emphasis—on the contrary, such an examination supports and in a sense explains what any careful reader of the story notices.

A second critical point adjoins the first. The morpheme "share" appears once in the sentence, but it performs at least twelve separate functions, as the deep structure shows. "I," "hat," and "mass" also play complex roles. Thus at certain points the sentence has extraordinary "density," as I shall call it. Since a reader must register these multiple functions in order to understand the sentence, it is reasonable to suppose that the very process of understanding concentrates his attention on centers of density. Syntactic density, I am suggesting, exercises an important influence on literary comprehension.

Third, by tuning in on deep structures, the critic may often apprehend more fully the build of a literary work. I have already mentioned how the syntax of Conrad's final sentence develops his theme. Consider two related points. First, "The Secret Sharer" is an initiation story in which the hero, through moral and mental effort, locates himself vis à vis society and the natural world, and thus passes into full manhood. The syntax of the last sentence schematizes the relationships he has achieved, in identifying with Leggatt's heroic defection, and in fixing on a point of reference—the hat—that connects him to the darker powers of nature. Second, the syntax and meaning of the last sentence bring to completion the pattern initiated by the syntax and meaning of the first few sentences, which present human beings and natural objects in thought-bewildering disarray. I can do no more than mention these structural connections here, but I am convinced that they supplement and help explain an ordinary critical reading of the story.

Another kind of critical point concerns habits of meaning revealed by sentence structure. One example must suffice. We have already marked how the sentence shifts its focus from "I" to "hat" to "sharer." A similar process goes on in the first part of the sentence: "I" is the initial subject, with "hat" as object. "Hat" is subject of another base sentence that ends with "edge," the object of a preposition in a locative phrase. "Edge" in turn becomes object of a sentence that has "darkness" as subject. "Darkness" is object in one with "mass" as subject, and in much the same way the emphasis passes to "gateway" and "Erebus." The syntax executes a chaining effect here which cuts across various kinds of construction. Chaining is far from the only type of syntactic expansion, but it is one Conrad favors. I would suggest this hypothesis: that syntactically and in other ways Conrad draws heavily on operations that link one thing with another associatively. This may be untrue, or if true it may be unrevealing; certainly it needs clearer expression. But I think it comes close to something that we all notice in Conrad, and in any case the general critical point exemplified here deserves exploration: that each writer tends to exploit deep linguistic resources in characteristic ways—that his style, in other words, rests on syntactic options within sentences (see footnote 3)—and that these syntactic preferences correlate with habits of meaning that tell us something about his mode of conceiving experience.

My other sample passage is the first sentence of Dylan Thomas' "A Winter's Tale":

>   It is a winter's tale
> That the snow blind twilight ferries over the lakes
> And floating fields from the farm in the cup of the vales,
> Gliding windless through the hand folded flakes,
> The pale breath of cattle at the stealthy sail,
>
>   And the stars falling cold,
> And the smell of hay in the snow, and the far owl
> Warning among the folds, and the frozen hold
> Flocked with the sheep white smoke of the farm house cowl
> In the river wended vales where the tale was told.

Some of the language here raises a large and familiar critical question, that of unorthodox grammar in modern poetry, which has traditionally received a somewhat facile answer. We say that loss of confidence in order and reason leads to dislocation of syntax, as if errant grammar were an appeal to the irrational. A cursory examination of deep structure in verse like Thomas', or even in wildly deviant verse like some of Cummings', will show the matter to be more complex than that.

How can deviance be most penetratingly analyzed? Normally, I think, in terms of the base sentences that lie beneath ungrammatical constructions. Surface structure alone does not show "the river wended vales" (line 10) to be deviant, since we have many well-formed constructions of the same word-class sequence: "machine made toys," "sun dried earth," and so on. The particular deviance of "the river wended vales" becomes apparent when we try to refer it to an appropriate underlying structure. A natural one to consider is "the river wends the vales" (cf. "the sun dries the earth"), but of course this makes "wend" a transitive verb, which it is not, except in the idiomatic "wend its way." So does another possibility, "NP + wends the vales with rivers" (cf. "NP + makes the toys by machine"). This reading adds still other kinds of deviance, in that the Noun Phrase will have to be animate, and in that rivers are too cumbersome to be used instrumentally in the way implied. Let us assume that the reader rejects the more flagrant deviance in favor of the less, and we are back to "the river wends the vales." Suppose now that "the vales" is not after all a direct object, but a locative construction, as in "the wolf prowls the forest"; this preserves the intransitivity of "wend," and thereby avoids a serious form of deviance. But notice that there is *no* transformation in English that converts "the wolf prowls the forest" into "the wolf prowled forest," and so this path is blocked as well. Assume, finally, that given a choice between shifting a word like "wend" from one subclass to another and adding a tranformational rule to the grammar, a reader will choose the former course; hence he selects the first interpretation mentioned: "the river wends the vales."

If so, how does he understand the anomalous transitive use of "wend"? Perhaps by assimilating the verb to a certain class that may be either transitive or intransitive: "paint," "rub," and the like. Then he will take "wend" to mean something like "make a mark on the surface of, by traversing"; in fact, this is roughly how I read Thomas' phrase. But I may be wrong, and in any case my goal is not to solve the riddle. Rather, I have been leading up to the point that every syntactically deviant construction has more than one possible interpretation, and that readers resolve the conflict by a process that involves deep and intricately motivated decisions and thus puts to work considerable linguistic knowledge, syntactic as well as semantic.[5] The decisions nearly always go on implicitly, but aside from that I see no reason to think that deviance of this sort is an appeal to, or an expression of, irrationality.

Moreover, when a poet deviates from normal syntax he is not doing what comes most habitually, but is making a special sort of choice. And since there are innumerable kinds of deviance, we should expect that the ones elected by a poem or poet spring from particular semantic impulses, particular ways of looking at experience. For instance, I think such a tendency displays itself in Thomas' lines. The construction just noted conceives the passing of rivers through vales as an agent acting upon an object. Likewise, "flocked" in line 9 becomes a transitive verb, and the spatial connection Thomas refers to—flocks in a hold—is reshaped into an action—flocking—performed by an unnamed agent upon the hold. There are many other examples in

---

[5] See Jerrold J. Katz, "Semi-sentences," in Jerry A. Fodor and Jerrold J. Katz, editors, *The Structure of Language* (1964), pp. 400–16. The same volume includes two other relevant papers, Chomsky, "Degrees of Grammaticalness," pp. 384–89, and Paul Ziff, "On Understanding 'Understanding Utterances,'" pp. 390–99. Samuel R. Levin has briefly discussed ungrammatical poetry within a similar framework in *Linguistic Structures in Poetry* (The Hague, 1962), Chapters 2 and 3.

the poem of deviance that projects unaccustomed activity and process upon nature. Next, notice that beneath line 2 is the sentence "the twilight is blind," in which an inanimate noun takes an animate adjective, and that in line 5 "sail" takes the animate adjective "stealthy." This type of deviance also runs throughout the poem: Thomas sees nature as personal. Again, "twilight" is subject of "ferries," and should thus be a concrete noun, as should the object, "tale." Here and elsewhere in the poem the division between substance and abstraction tends to disappear. Again and again syntactic deviance breaks down categorical boundaries and converts juxtaposition into action, inanimate into human, abstract into physical, static into active. Now, much of Thomas' poetry displays the world as process, as interacting forces and repeating cycles, in which human beings and human thought are indifferently caught up.[6] I suggest that Thomas' syntactical irregularities often serve this vision of things. To say so, of course, is only to extend the natural critical premise that a good poet sets linguistic forms to work for him in the cause of artistic and thematic form. And if he strays from grammatical patterns he does not thereby leave language or reason behind: if anything, he draws the more deeply on linguistic structure and on the processes of human understanding that are implicit in our use of well-formed sentences.

Most of what I have said falls short of adequate precision, and much of the detail rests on conjecture about English grammar, which at this point is by no means fully understood. But I hope that in loosely stringing together several hypotheses about the fundamental role of the sentence I have indicated some areas where a rich exchange between linguistics and critical theory might eventually take place. To wit, the elusive intuition we have of *form* and *content* may turn out to be anchored in a distinction between the surface structures and the deep structures of sentences. If so, syntactic theory will also feed into the theory of *style*. Still more evidently, the proper *analysis* of styles waits on a satisfactory analysis of sentences. Matters of *rhetoric*, such as emphasis and order, also promise to come clearer as we better understand internal relations in sentences. More generally, we may be able to enlarge and deepen our concept of literary *structure* as we are increasingly able to make it subsume linguistic structure—including especially the structure of deviant sentences. And most important, since critical understanding follows and builds on understanding of sentences, generative grammar should eventually be a reliable assistant in the effort of seeing just how a given literary work sifts through a reader's mind, what cognitive and emotional processes it sets in motion, and what organization of experience it encourages. In so far as critical theory concerns itself with meaning, it cannot afford to bypass the complex and elegant structures that lie at the inception of all verbal meaning.

[6] Ralph Maud's fine study, *Entrances to Dylan Thomas' Poetry* (Pittsburgh, 1963), describes the phenomenon well in a chapter called "Process Poems."

Describing Poetic Structures: Two Approaches to Baudelaire's "Les Chats"

MICHAEL RIFFATERRE

As "Describing Poetic Structures: Two Approaches to Baudelaire's 'Les Chats'" makes clear, Michael Riffaterre is a student of style versed both in structuralism and in linguistics. Perhaps the most useful way of introducing the essay is to outline the theoretical position developed by Riffaterre in two other articles—"Criteria for Style Analysis," *Word*, XV (April 1959), 154–74, and "Stylistic Context," *Word*, XVI (August 1960), 207–18—for that position informs the essay reprinted here.

Riffaterre is generally concerned to differentiate between the "stylistic facts" operative in a work of literature and its "linguistic facts," suggesting that "style stresses" whereas "language expresses." More ordinary kinds of discourse, he argues, are likely to be oriented merely toward communication of the message itself and to show a high incidence of predictable verbal forms. In a work "written" with "literary intent," however, the artist seeks to convey not only his message but also his own attitude toward it; thus he chooses the verbal forms of his text with special care, employing a number of unpredictable elements precisely to secure and control the attention of his reader. (This may call to mind the Prague School's conviction that a work with esthetic intent is characterized by the foregrounding of some part of its language, the occurrence of verbal forms which call attention to themselves.) The "stylistic facts" of a work reside in all those linguistic elements which appear as unpredictable in their local contexts (a contention which in effect redefines the idea of deviation from the norm that turns up so frequently in stylistic criticism). To isolate objectively the whole range of unpredictable elements, according to Riffaterre, the analyst should gather the responses of as many readers as he can—however various their literary training—for those responses will identify the "stylistic facts" which the analyst must take into account before proceeding to interpretation.

Many of these ideas are visible in the following essay on Baudelaire's "Les Chats," in which Riffaterre first makes a critique of one structuralist interpretation, that offered by Roman Jakobson and Claude Lévi-Strauss, then treats the poem in accordance with his own method of identifying stylistic data and interpreting them. He attacks Jakobson and Lévi-Strauss essentially on the ground that some of the structures on which they build their reading are merely linguistic facts of the text—that they are not determinant stylistic facts because, existing below the threshold of the reader's perception as he encounters them in context, they cannot strike him as unpredictable and thus significant. Toward the end of the essay, after examining the poem himself, Riffaterre takes issue with Jakobson and Lévi-Strauss's attempt to buttress their interpretation by citing details from other writings by Baudelaire: in Riffaterre's opinion, the critics violate the rule which should govern comparative structural analysis—that comparisons may not properly be made between the mere data appearing in different structures, but only between the structures themselves.

In a variety of ways, then, the following essay serves to illustrate a structuralist approach to a literary work, with Riffaterre claiming to take even more precise account of the verbal forms operative in Baudelaire's text than do Jakobson and Lévi-Strauss. It is also worth emphasizing that, in his theory as well as in his practical analysis, Riffaterre concerns himself explicitly with the effects which language has upon an audience.

POETRY IS LANGUAGE, but it produces effects that language in everyday speech does not consistently produce; a reasonable assumption is that the linguistic analysis of a poem should turn up specific features, and that there is a causal relationship

---

"Describing Poetic Structures: Two Approaches to Baudelaire's 'Les Chats,'" by Michael Riffaterre, is from *Structuralism*, edited with an introduction by Jacques Ehrmann, pp. 188–230. Copyright © 1966 by Yale French Studies. Reprinted by permission of Doubleday & Company, Inc. Translations in brackets and italics are new to the present edition.

between the presence of these features in the text and our empirical feeling that we have before us a poem. The act of communication—the sending of a message from speaker to addressee—is conditioned by the need it fills: the verbal structure of the message depends upon which factor of communication is focused on. In everyday language, used for practical purposes, the focus is usually upon the situational context, the mental or physical reality referred to; sometimes the focus is upon the code used in transmitting the message, that is, upon language itself, if there seems to be some block in the addressee's understanding; and so forth. In the case of verbal art, the focus is upon the message as an end in itself, not just as a means, upon its form as a permanent, unchangeable monument, forever independent of external conditions. The naked eye attributes this enduring, attention-getting quality to a higher unity and more intricate texture: the poem follows more rules (e.g. meter, lexical restrictions, etc.) and displays more conspicuous interrelationships between its constitutive elements than do casual utterances.

For these features Roman Jakobson has proposed a general formula. Selection and combination are the two basic ordering principles of speech. Selection is based upon equivalence (metaphoric relationship), either similarity or dissimilarity; the speaker designates his topic (subject) by choosing one among various available synonyms and then says what he has to say about it (predicate) by another selection from another set of interchangeable words (paradigm). The combining of these words, that is, their contiguity, produces a sentence. Jakobson defines a poetic structure as one characterized by the projection of the principle of equivalence from the axis of selection to the axis of combination.[1] For instance, words are combined into rhythmic, alliterative, and rhymic sequences because of their equivalence in sound, and this inevitably establishes semantic equations between these words; their respective meanings are consequently perceived as related by similarity (hence a metaphor or simile) or dissimilarity (hence an antithesis).

Which is to say that the recurrence of equivalent forms, *parallelism*, is the basic relationship underlying poetry. Of course, since language is a system made up of several levels superimposed one on top of the other (phonetic, phonological, syntactical, semantic, etc.), parallelism manifests itself on any level: so then, a poem is a verbal sequence wherein the same relations between constituents are repeated at various levels and the same story is told in several ways at the same time and at several times in the same way. This can be usefully restated in structural terms once we have called to mind basic definitions: a structure is a system made up of several elements, none of which can undergo a change without effecting changes in all the other elements; thus the system is what mathematicians call an invariant; transformations within it produce a group of models of the same type (that is, mechanically interconvertible shapes), or variants. The invariant, of course, is an abstraction arrived at by defining what remains intact in the face of these conversions; therefore we are able to observe a structure only in the shape of one or another variant. We are now ready to agree with Claude Lévi-Strauss that a poem is a structure containing within

---

[1] "Linguistics and Poetics," *Style in Language*, edited by T. A. Sebeok (New York: 1960), especially pp. 358 ss.

itself its variants ordered on the vertical axis of the different linguistic levels. It is thus possible to describe the poem in isolation, so that we do not need to explain its singularity by dragging in hard-to-define concepts like non-grammaticalness or departure from the norm. Comparison of variants, prerequisite to analysis, is accomplished by simply scanning the text at its various linguistic levels one after the other.

Such is the approach tried out by Jakobson and Lévi-Strauss on "Les Chats," a sonnet of Baudelaire's, and with extraordinary thoroughness.[2] They modestly declare that they are interested only in describing what the poem is made of. Nevertheless they do draw conclusions as to the meaning of the poem and try to relate it to the esthetics and even the psyche of the poet, purlieu of literary scholars. This raises a question: how are we to pass from description to judgment—that is, from a study of the text to a study of its effect upon the reader? The sonnet is a good occasion for such discussion, for critics generally downgrade the poem (*Fleurs du Mal*, LXVI), a product of Baudelaire's early period (1847), and find it less Baudelairean than most of the others. But the poet did not feel that way about it: he thought it good enough to publish in the feuilleton of a friend, in hopes of drumming up some interest; then he selected it for a preview of his abortive *Limbes* (1851); finally, he thought it worth keeping in the edition of the *Fleurs* that he was able to prepare himself. If structuralism can help determine who is right here, we shall have tested its practical workability in matters of literary criticism.

Far more important, however, is the question as to whether unmodified structural linguistics is relevant at all to the analysis of poetry. The authors' method is based on the assumption that any structural system they are able to define in the poem is necessarily a poetic structure. Can we not suppose, on the contrary, that the poem may contain certain structures that play no part in its function and effect as a literary work of art, and that there may be no way for structural linguistics to distinguish between these unmarked structures and those that are literarily active? Conversely, there may well be strictly poetic structures that cannot be recognized as such by an analysis not geared to the specificity of poetic language.

Les Chats

Les amoureux fervents et les savants austères	1
Aiment également, dans leur mûre saison,	2
Les chats puissants et doux, orgueil de la maison,	3
Qui comme eux sont frileux et comme eux sédentaires.	4
Amis de la science et de la volupté,	5
Ils cherchent le silence et l'horreur des ténèbres ;	6
L'Érèbe les eût pris pour ses coursiers funèbres,	7
S'ils pouvaient au servage incliner leur fierté.	8
Ils prennent en songeant les nobles attitudes	9
Des grands sphinx allongés au fond des solitudes,	10
Qui semblent s'endormir dans un rêve sans fin ;	11

---

[2] Jakobson, Roman and Lévi-Strauss, Claude, "*Les Chats* de Charles Baudelaire," *L'Homme*, 2 (1962), 5–21.

Leurs reins féconds sont pleins d'étincelles magiques,   12
Et des parcelles d'or, ainsi qu'un sable fin,   13
Étoilent vaguement leurs prunelles mystiques.   14

Cats*

Fervent lovers and austere scholars   1
Alike love, in their ripe years,   2
The potent and soft cats, pride of the house,   3
Who like them are shivering and like them, sedentary.   4

Friends of learning and voluptuousness,   5
They seek out silence and the horror of the dark;   6
Erebus would have taken them as his somber coursers,   7
If they could bend their pride to servitude.   8

They assume, while musing, the noble attitudes   9
Of the great sphinxes stretched out in the deepest solitudes,   10
Who seem to slumber in an endless dream;   11

Their fertile loins are full of magic sparks,   12
And particles of gold, like a fine sand,   13
Light up vaguely their mystic eyes.   14

Jakobson and Lévi-Strauss submit the text to scannings of its meter, sound texture, grammar, and meaning; they are thus able to collect several sets of the equivalent signs that actualize the sonnet's structure. Let me describe briefly the systems thus obtained, with a sampling of the variants comparatively studied in order to establish these systems. My aim here is only to show how the authors' analysis is carried through. The most significant of their arguments omitted here will be taken up in my discussion of the validity of their approach.

Jakobson and Lévi-Strauss recognize the following complementary or intersecting structures:

1. a *tripartite division* into: *quatrain I*, which represents the cats as passive creatures, observed by outsiders, lovers and scholars; *quatrain II*, where the cats are active but, again, seen as such from the outside, by the powers of darkness; the latter, also seen from outside, are active: they have designs on the cats and are frustrated by the independence of the little beasts; *sestet*, which gives us an inside view of the cat life-style: their attitude may be passive, but they assume that attitude actively. Thus is the active-passive opposition reconciled, or perhaps nullified, and the circle of the sonnet closes.

This tripartite structure is defined by two equivalent models: one grammatical, formed by three complex "sentences" delimited by periods, and further defined by an arithmetic progression in the number of their independent clauses and personal verbal forms (as distinct from forms in the infinitive or participle); one metric (the

---

* [Baudelaire's poem is so meticulously analyzed in the course of the essay that it has seemed best to provide a rather literal translation here. Francis Scarfe has published especially sensitive prose translations of selected poems in his *Baudelaire* (Baltimore: 1961). Translator's note.]

DESCRIBING POETIC STRUCTURES [367]

rhyme systems unify the tercets into a sestet while separating it from the quatrains). These two models are further bound together by the relationship between rhyme and categories: every feminine rhyme coincides with a plural ending, every masculine one with a singular.

2. a *bipartite division* that opposes the octet and the sestet. In the *octet* the cats are seen from an outside observer's point of view and are imprisoned within time and space (²*saison* and ³*maison*, which rhyme and meaning make equivalent). In the *sestet* both viewpoint and space-time limits drop away: the desert bursts the house wide open; the eternity of ¹¹*dans un rêve sans fin* annuls ²*dans leur mûre saison* (in this case the equivalence is an antinomy and is formally established by the parallelism of the *dans* constructions, the only two in the poem). This overall opposition combines with two secondary ones: *quatrain I tercet I* (³*maison*: ¹⁰*solitudes*::²*saison*:¹¹*sans fin*) and *quatrain II tercet II* (cats in darkness vs. cats radiating light).

To take only one of these secondary oppositions: in *quatrain II tercet II*, on the one hand, ¹²*Leurs reins féconds sont pleins* is synonymous with ⁵*Amis . . . de la volupté* (p. 16), and one of the subjects in the quatrain and three subjects in the tercet all alike designate inanimate things; on the other hand, the antinomy of darkness and light is backed up by corresponding sets of equatable items: ⁷*Érèbe* and ⁶*ténèbres* echo each other in meaning and in sound, as do ¹²*étinCELLES*, ¹³*parCELLES d'or*, and ¹⁴*prun-ELLES*.

3. a *chiasma-like division* linking quatrain I and tercet II, where the cats function as objects (³*chats*, ¹²,¹⁴*leurs*), and, on the other hand, quatrain II and tercet I, where they are subjects. The *quatrain I–tercet II* coupling, to which I shall limit this summary, contains the following formal equivalences: both stanzas have more adjectives than the internal strophes; the first and last verbs are both modified by rhyming adverbs (²*Aiment également*, ¹⁴*Étoilent vaguement*); these are the only two stanzas made up of sentences with two subjects for one verb and one object, each subject and object being modified by one adjective; etc. A semantic relationship underlies these formal features: in *quatrain I* a metonymic relationship between the animals and their worshippers (i.e. cats and people live in the same house) generates a metaphoric similarity (⁴*comme eux* twice repeated); the same thing in *tercet II*, where a synecdochic (*pars pro toto*) description of the cats, using different parts of their body, permits their metaphoric identification with the cosmos, or so say the two analysts.

These three systems fit one inside the other and together make of the sonnet a "closed" structure, but they coexist with a *fourth system* that makes the poem an open-ended structure which develops dynamically from the first line to the last: two equal *sestets* (ll. 1–6 and 9–14), separated by a *distich*. Of the four structures, this last is the one most at variance with the stanza and rhyme architecture that defines the sonnet as a genre: the aberrant distich presents features that do not occur anywhere else, against a background of features that occur only elsewhere in the poem, some of them related to those of the distich by antonymy (every single subject-verb group is plural except for ⁷*L'Érèbe les eût pris*; against the rule followed throughout the rest of the poem, ⁷*funèbres*–⁸*fierté* alliterate; etc.). Now Jakobson and Lévi-Strauss regard this distich as a transition: the pseudo-sestet describes objectively a factual situation of the real world; two opposite human categories, sensual and intellectual, are reconciled through their identification with the animal endowed with the diametric traits of both types of men; these traits in turn explain the cats' love for silence and darkness—a predilection that exposes them to temptation. Erebus threatens to confine them to their animal nature by taming them; we are relieved to see him fail. This episode, translated in terms of parallelism, should be seen not just as another antonymy but as "l'unique équivalence rejetée [the unique identification rejected]" (p. 14).

Nevertheless, this rejection has its positive effect: an equivalence with the sphinx can substitute for it. The sphinx, with a human head on an animal body, transposes into myth the identification between real cats and people. Also, the monsters' motionless daydreaming and the cats' sedentariness (likewise characteristic of the human types they symbolize) are synonymous; and the way the cats ape the sphinxes is a new equivalence stated simultaneously at the grammatical level, in the narrative (it is [9]*en songeant* that they look like the [10]*sphinx allongés*), at the morphological level (*allongés* and *songeant* are the only participles in the text), and at the sound level (the two verbs are related by paronomasia). The second *sestet* is devoted to the deepening mystery of this *miracle des chats* (p. 15). Tercet I still sustains the ambiguity: it is difficult to decide whether cats and sphinxes are linked merely to magnify the image of the cats stylistically, or whether we have here the description of actual similarity, the racial bond between the household sphinx and the desert cat. In tercet II, however, substitution of parts of his body for the whole cat dissolves the beast into particles of matter, and the final identification associates these particles with desert sands and transmutes them into stars: the fusion of cats and cosmos has been accomplished. This apotheosis to infinity does not exclude a circular structure from the text. The authors believe there is a parallelism between tercet II and line 1, the myth being seen as a variant on a universal scale of the "constricting" union, inward-turning, when the lover folds his love into his arms, and of the expansive union, outward-turning, when the scholar takes the universe in his embrace; similarly, cats either interiorize the universe, or else they spread themselves out beyond the bounds of time and space (p. 20).

From all the foregoing, we can at least draw the conclusion that these mutually combinatory and complementary structures interplay in a way unique. The poem is like a microcosm, with its own system of references and analogies. We have an absolutely convincing demonstration of the extraordinary concatenation of correspondences that holds together the parts of speech.

The Irrelevance of Grammar

BUT THERE IS no telling which of these systems of correspondences contribute to the poetry of the text. And there is much to be said about the systems that do not.

The divisions proposed explain a good deal of the tension between symmetrical and asymmetrical rhymes and the grammar arrangements upon which the composition of the sonnet rests. The first division is beyond criticism; the second is well substantiated, since it hinges on an articulation (the octet-sestet boundary) which corresponds to a change so sharp that it prompted postulation of the fourth division. Divisions three and four, especially the last, make use of constituents that cannot possibly be perceived by the reader; these constituents must therefore remain alien to the poetic structure, which is supposed to emphasize the form of the message, to make it more "visible," more compelling.

Equivalences established on the basis of purely syntactic similarities would seem particularly dubious—for instance, the parallelism pointed to between the relative clauses of lines 4 and 11: this last allegedly draws the "contour of an imaginary quatrain, a make-believe homologue of the first quatrain" (p. 13). At most, this might be conceivable if the clauses appeared against an empty or uniform context; not in an actual sonnet, whose continual variation of verbal shapes makes a marked contrast necessary in order to impose perception. Even there, the parallelism from one line to another can be superseded by a stronger relation within one of the two lines involved. This happens in the case of the equation urged by Jakobson and Lévi-Strauss between [4]*Qui comme eux sont frileux* and [12]*Leurs reins féconds sont pleins*, on account of their syntactic parallelism and their internal rhymes. In context the difference outweighs the similarities: an internal rhyme like [5]*science*–[6]*silence* is obvious, and so is *eux–frileux*, because identical stresses "confirm" them; but a natural reading of line 12 will have to take into account the tight unity of *Leurs reins féconds*, which demands a pause after *féconds*, the normal caesura disappearing almost because *pleins* cannot be severed from *d'étincelles*; *pleins* is enclitic, which practically cancels out the rhyme. Suppose we read without regard for meaning or grammar: the rhyme resuscitates, but any response to the rhyme in line 4 still appears purely theoretical, for *comme eux sont frileux* is homologous only to *comme eux sédentaires* and is not free to connect elsewhere. For the significant rhyme system, the one that organizes the rhythm and "illustrates" the meaning, is the homophony under equal stress of *comme eux* repeated twice. The *frileux* rhyme is a secondary modulation: it "makes believe" that the line ends at the caesura,[3] thus getting the rhythm off to a fresh start and making the "unexpected" repetition all the more striking; the fact that it rhymes with *comme eux* lays emphasis upon *sédentaires* by contrast—a second *comme eux* led the reader's subconscious sense of balance to expect a second rhyme, and the expectation is beautifully frustrated. We did find a parallelism anyway, but the remoter one has lost the contest, and this suffices to make homologue-collecting an unreliable tool. Extensive similarities at one level are no proof of correspondence: a parallelism is seen between quatrain I and tercet II, based upon the equivalence of two subjects ([1]*Les amoureux fervents, les savants austères* / [13]*des parcelles d'or, un sable fin*), one verb with rhyming adverb ([2]*Aiment également* / [14]*Étoilent vaguement*), one adjective-noun object ([3]*Les chats puissants et doux* / [14]*leurs prunelles mystiques*), in identical sequence (p. 9). But, in any verse structure, I do not see how two variants can be equivalent if the positions of their components are not homologous: meter lends significance to the

---

[3] This structural role of the break is well documented: Malherbe condemned internal rhymes precisely because they had such effects.

space occupied by the sentence. The relation of object to verb in line 14 is not the same as in quatrain I, since the quatrain keeps them apart with parentheses and enjambement, whereas the tercet unites them. Hence inevitably a difference in emphasis and a shift in respective positions within the line. Furthermore, the equation of the subjects is all askew: the components are alike, and we could link *amoureux fervents* vertically with *parcelles d'or* or diagonally with *sable fin*; but the systems they enter are not comparable, for *sable fin* does not stand in the same relation to *parcelles d'or* as *savants* does to *amoureux*. These last two are opposite equals, and their contiguity expresses their polarity; but the contiguity of *parcelles* and *sable* simply repeats twice the same meaning, *ainsi que* indicating a metaphorical relation. *Ainsi que* and *et* may have the same virtual function in language and be classified alike: but not here, where they are neither synonymous nor antonymous. The parallelism suggested by grammar remains virtual because it has no homologue in the meter or in the semantic system.

No segmentation can be pertinent that yields, indifferently, units which *are* part of the poetic structure, and neutral ones that are not. The weak point of the method is indeed the categories used. There is a revealing instance where Jakobson and Lévi-Strauss take literally the technical meaning of *feminine* as used in metrics and grammar and endow the formal feminine categories with esthetic and even ethical values. They are trying to prove a sexual ambiguity in the poem, the motif of the androgyne, and they find some evidence in the "paradoxical choice of feminine substantives as masculine rhymes" (p. 21). True, the gender of French nouns does orient the associations they trigger: this kind of effect is conceivable with words that signify concrete objects or even abstract concepts, as long as they can be humanized or personified—for example, [5]*volupté*, which is more female than *plaisir* would be. It hardly holds, however, in the case of purely technical terminology, where *masculine* means merely "ending on a fully pronounced syllable" and *feminine* merely "ending on an unstressed syllable" (especially where one need not even be aware of these conventions in order to perceive an alternance). By stretching this to the limit, we may discover cases where the feminine rhyme does evoke some such associations because it coincides with the specific feminine gender ending; it is altogether unlikely with masculine rhymes, which do not offer any similar concurrence. Only technicians would think of it (they have thought of it); metalinguistic rationalization of this sort betrays how easily the wariest of analysts slips into a belief in the intrinsic explanatory worth of purely descriptive terms.

The two critics obviously assume that the definition of categories used to collect data is also valid to explain their function in the poetic structure—that linguistic oppositions, for example, automatically entail stylistic differences. The role of liquid phonemes in the sonnet's sound texture, for example, is declared to be significant: quatrain II is certainly characterized by noticeable variations, since this is a stanza where the phonetic dominance shifts from nasal vowels (only 3) to liquid consonants (24); extreme variations cannot fail of their effect. There is, however, a linguistic opposition between /l/ and /r/, particularly marked in French, and this is frequently exploited in poetry in a manner consistent with the phonetic nature of the opposing features. A slight regression of /r/ before /l/ in the tercets is interpreted as "eloquently accompanying the passage from the empirical feline to his mythic transfigurations" (p. 12). But no one is likely to believe that there is any significance in a difference as imperceptible as that between fourteen /l/ and eleven /r/, especially when tercet II, with /l/ enjoying a majority of two, begins with an /r/ cluster (*Leurs reins*) which will surely catch the eye and ear sooner than an inequality attenuated by distribution along the lines. If we look only for sharp changes, then the drop in the number of liquids from quatrain II to tercet I affects both contenders equally, /l/ ending on top by one point; the one smashing victory of /l/ over /r/—three to nothing—occurs in line 5 *before* the transfiguration; in quatrain II, which is also the only place where brutal variations can be found, the liquids go hand in hand for the whole stanza, rejoicing at the peak of their power. Since liquids as a group do appear significant, the authors assume that every essential linguistic feature of the group must also be significant. The fact is, however, that it does not work out that way: the liquids are significant only as a group; their oppositions, *within* the group, though they are actualized and play their part in the linguistic structure, are not actualized in the style.

Conversely, the analytical categories applied can pull together under one label phenomena which are in fact totally different from one another in the poetic structure. A case in point is the plural. Jakobson and Lévi-Strauss rightly note its high frequency and its concurrence with important elements. Because a single grammatical category is applicable to every line of the poem, they see it as a key to the understanding of the sonnet; they quote a pronouncement of the poet that seems to give symbolic meaning to the plural: *Multitude, solitude: termes égaux et convertibles par le poète actif et fécond* [Multitude, solitude: terms equivalent and convertible by the active and imaginative poet]. Better still, the authors see this mutual "convertibility" symbolized in [10]*solitudes*, where "solitude" as the word itself and "multitude" as the morpheme *–s* enjoy togetherness. This argument recalls their confusion of femaleness and feminine gender; they seem to assume that there is always a basic relationship between actual plurality (and what it symbolizes in Baudelaire's eyes) and plural morphemes. Needless to say, there are many exceptions to that general rule—and what is more, one of them occurs right here: [6]*ténèbres* is a conventional, meaningless plural; let us skip it, and also its rhyme companion [7]*funèbres*. We should probably discount all descriptive plurals, since they are dictated by nature and not the poet's choice: *mystiques* would drop out, cats having two *prunelles*, and also *reins*. We can keep *chats* and their human counterparts: collective singulars being available for groups, the plural may well have meaning. But *solitudes*, the pretext for this philosophical foray, will have to go: it is no paradox at a[11]., just a hyperbole, a cliché where *solitudes* means "desert"—an emphatic plural stemming from the Latin. Baudelaire's quotation may apply elsewhere, certainly not here, and no interpretation of the sonnet can be drawn from it. The authors' mistake is understandable. In their search for a plural structure, they needed a unifying factor. The text yielded no sign that the data could be related, yet their common label demanded that they be so related. Faced with this dilemma, the authors must have gladly seized upon the coincidence between *solitudes* and Baudelaire's aphorism: the poet's mental obsession provided just the invariant required.

Had all plural forms not been brought under the one label, there would have been no compulsion to find, at all costs, an equivalence value for every plural form.

But among these data lumped together because of their morphological similarity, there is a group of plurals set apart from the others because of their distribution: that is the plural feminine rhymes. These do form a stylistic structure, because their –*s* endings make the rhyme "richer" for the eye by increasing the number of its repeated components. In [1,4]*austères–sédentaires*, for instance, the *s* reinforces the visual similarity and offsets the spelling vagaries that spoil the transcription of /ɛ/. The way in which the –*s* is related to and functions in the rhyme system has nothing to do with its simultaneous function in the singular-plural opposition, where it carries a meaning: in the rhyme it works only as an eye-catcher. The interrelations of the –*s* rhymes within the conventional rhyme system are what gives them significance. Poetic convention demands, first, that the rhymes of the sonnet should form an invariable pattern alternating feminine and masculine rhymes; second, that this invariant alternation be combined with sound variants within each alternating series. The visual and aural implementation of the variant is constantly reinforced and constantly compels attention, thus strongly individualizing each stanza; this depends entirely upon the poet's creative fancy. The implementation of the invariant, on the contrary, is normally limited to the compulsory masculine-feminine alternation. By adding –*s* to the –*e*, Baudelaire personalizes, so to speak, what was an automatism, reemphasizes the opposition for the eye. A second constant element in the system of the sonnet as a whole gives more weight to the unifying factor in the rhymes, which more effectively countervails the centrifugal tendencies of each stanza to form an independent unit. Every line affected by this addition is thereby made to look longer, and the fact that such a line ends the sonnet contributes to its unity by emphasizing the final item and therefore the reader's consciousness of a terminal accord; since the word thus underlined happens to be *mystiques*, the combination of meaning and visual emphasis, accompanying it like an upbeat, make the end of the poem a point of departure for reverie and wonder. Jakobson and Lévi-Strauss point out that the feminine rhyme is orally actualized, despite the total disappearance of the unstressed end syllable in modern pronunciation, by the presence of a postvocalic sounded consonant in the rhyming syllable, and they remark, indeed, that this coincides with plural morphemes (pp. 7, 11); but they see the plural as a parallel to the postvocalic consonant, that is, reinforcing each rhyme pair, separately, since that consonant varies and therefore structures only the stanza in which it occurs (/r, br, d, k/). In fact, the invariable –*s* creates a frame that tightens the whole sonnet. This structure would not be overlooked if the term chosen did not also cover forms that are grammatically identical but stylistically foreign to these –*s* rhymes; [1]*amoureux*, [3]*doux*, [10]*sphinx* would not further obscure the operation of the –*s* ending; grammatical equivalence would not be equated with stylistic equivalence.

What I have just said should not be construed as a rejection of the principle of equivalence: similarity in dissimilarity, dissimilarity in similarity, are apparent at all levels. But it seems evident that its pertinence cannot be shown by using grammatical terminology, or any preconceived, aprioristic frame. R. Jakobson chose grammar units to make this exegesis and many others because grammar is the natural geometry of language which superimposes abstract, relational systems upon the concrete, lexical material: hence grammar furnishes the analyst with ready-made structural units. All parts of speech, in fact, may function in parallelism and contrasts; the importance of pronouns, long neglected by style analysts—pronouns are, precisely, typical relational units—comes out clearly in the first division of the poem. Jakobson seems to think that any reiteration and contrast of a grammatical concept makes it a poetic device, that the interrelationship of meter, morphological classes, and syntactic construction actualizes the structure and creates the poetic effect.[4] There is no doubt that a linguistic actualization does take place, but the question remains: are the linguistic and poetic actualizations coextensive?

The sonnet is rebuilt by the two critics into a "superpoem," inaccessible to the normal reader, and yet the structures described do not explain what establishes contact between poetry and reader. No grammatical analysis of a poem can give us more than the grammar of the poem.

The Poem as Response

THE LITERARY SCHOLAR, especially of the humanist stripe, has always assumed that grammar failed because it was incomplete, that the narrow, rigorous methods of the *esprit de géométrie* could never catch the subtle, indefinable *je ne sais quoi* that poetry is supposed to be made of. In fact the opposite is true: the linguist sees all the data, and that is precisely the reason he was prone, especially in pre-structuralist times, to define a poetic utterance as abnormal, as language plus something else. The whole idea of structure, of course, is that within the body of the text all parts are bound together and that stylistically neutral components and active ones are interrelated in the same way as the marked and unmarked poles of any opposition. Our only solution is to observe and rearrange the data from a different angle. A proper consideration of the nature of the poetic phenomenon will give us the vantage point required.

First of all, the poetic phenomenon, being linguistic, is not simply the message, the poem, but the whole act of communication. This is a very special act, however, for the speaker—the poet—is not present; any attempt to bring him back only produces interference, because what we know of him we know from history, it is knowledge external to the message, or else we have found it out by rationalizing and distorting the message. The message and the addressee—the reader—are indeed the only factors involved in this communication whose presence is necessary. As for the other factors—language (code), non-verbal context, means of keeping open the channel—the appropriate language of reference is selected from the message, the context is reconstituted from the message, contact is assured by the control the message has over the reader's attention, and depends upon the degree of that control. These special

[4] R. Jakobson, "Poetry of Grammar and Grammar of Poetry" (in Russian), *Poetics, Poetyka* (Warsaw: 1961), pp. 398 ss, especially 403, 408–9.

duties, and the esthetic emphasis characteristic of poetry demand that the message possess features corresponding to those functions. The characteristic common to such devices must be that they are designed to draw responses from the reader—despite any wanderings of his attention, despite the evolution of the code, despite the changes in esthetic fashion.

The pertinent segmentation of the poem must therefore be based on these responses: they pinpoint in the verbal sequence the location of the devices that trigger them. Since literary criticism aims at informing and improving such responses, we seem to have a vicious circle. It is only apparent, however, for what is blurred in a response is its content, the subjective interpretation of that response, which depends on elements exterior to the act of communication. The response itself testifies objectively to the actuality of a contact. Thus two precautions absolutely must be taken: 1) empty the response of its content; I can then use all forms of reaction to the text—idiosyncrasy-oriented responses (positive or negative according to the reader's culture, era, esthetics, personality) and goal-oriented responses (those of the reader with non-literary intent, who may be using the poem as a historical document, for purposes of linguistic analysis, etc.: such a reader will rationalize his responses to fit into his sphere of interest and its technical terminology); 2) multiply the response, to guard against physical interference with contact, such as the reader's fatigue or the evolving of the language since the time the poem was encoded.

This tool of analysis, this "superreader," in no way distorts the special act of communication under study: it simply explores that act more thoroughly by performing it over and over again. It has the enormous advantage of following exactly the normal reading process, of perceiving the poem as its linguistic shape dictates, along the sentence, starting at the beginning (whereas many critics use the end to comment on the start, and so destroy suspense; or else they use diagrams that modify the balance of the text's natural emphasis system—the chiasma-like division in the Jakobson and Lévi-Strauss analysis, or what they call diagonal or vertical correspondences); it has the advantage of screening pertinent structures and only pertinent structures. My "superreader" for "Les Chats" is composed of: to a limited extent, Baudelaire (correction of line 8, placing the sonnet in the ensemble of the collection); Gautier (his long paraphrase of the sonnet, in his preface to the third edition of the *Fleurs*), and Laforgue (some echoes in *Sanglot de la Terre*, "La Première Nuit"); the translations of W. Fowlie, F. L. Freedman, and F. Duke; as many critics as I could find, the more useful being those whose reason for picking out a line had nothing to do with the sonnet; Jakobson and Lévi-Strauss for those points in the text where they deviate from their method (when they are being faithful, their analysis scans everything with even hand and is therefore misleading); Larousse's *Dictionnaire du XIXème siècle* for the entries which quote the sonnet; philological or textbook footnotes; informants such as students of mine and other souls whom fate has thrown my way.

Each point of the text that holds up the superreader is tentatively considered a component of the poetic structure. Experience indicates that such units are always pointed out by a number of informants who usually give divergent rationalizations. These units consist of lexical elements of the sentence interrelated by their contrasting characteristics. They also appear to be linked to one another by relations of opposition. The contrasts they create is what forces them upon the reader's attention; these contrasts result from their unpredictability within the context. This unpredictability is made possible by the fact that at every point in a sentence, the grammatical restrictions limiting the choice of the next word permit a certain degree of predictability. Predictability increases as the number of levels involved and the number of restrictions increase, which happens with any kind of recurrence, like parallelism in general and meter in particular—and where predictability increases, so does the effect of an unpredicted element.

Units of this kind and the systems they constitute form the basis of the following analysis.

Analysis

TITLE

The definite article [les] and the plural lead us to expect a precise and concrete description: against such a backdrop, the spiritualization of the cats will be more arresting. Structurally the title focuses our expectations upon the first recurrence of *chats* in the text, which helps to unify the poem: every pronoun henceforth refers back unequivocally to that word, the only noun thus singled out.

QUATRAIN I

Coming as it does right after the terse title, the contrasting first line gives an even greater sense of plenitude. Twice the slot left empty next to *chats* is filled up with an adjective; this fullness of the nominal group is emphasized by the parallel word order—a symmetry reinforced on another level by the stresses and by the fact that phrases and hemistichs are coterminal. Of course the internal rhyme *fervents–savants* contributes to unification of the line: the similarity between the rhyme fellows (underlined, perhaps, by the contrast of their grammatical dissimilarity) makes up for the caesura and culminates the intonational curve. The enjambement stresses *Aiment*, of course, at grammar level because the reader will compensate for the metric and rhythmic stop by an increased awareness of the grammatical relationship between verb and subjects. But at prosody level it also stresses the end of the line, where the meaning seems to be suspended for a fleeting moment. Thus the line as a whole looks almost like a subtitle, an anticipatory comment on the deep relatedness of *chats*, *amoureux*, and *savants* (this impression will be confirmed every time we come across a pair of nominal phrases; for nowhere in the text is the model Noun-Adjective so symmetrically actualized).

Now this serves to stress the link between the two phrases bound by *et*, as would an equation. Yet scholars and lovers are diametrical opposites, as far apart as Venus Urania and carnal Aphrodite. Here is an archetypal representation of mankind: imagination links lovers and scholars as two kinds of men who can be defined by their opposition. The scholar stricken in his scholarness, despoiled of his wisdom, the ruined scholar, is the scholar in love; the contradiction is as absurd or moving as that of another stereotype, the amorous greybeard. From Aristotle on all fours, bridled, saddled, and mounted by his courtesan, to Professor Delteil besotted by the conflict between love and lexicography in the *Contes d'été* (1852) of Champfleury, Baudelaire's bosom companion, lover and scholar dwell incompatible within the same individual. It is not by chance that Balzac regards chastity as one of the fundamental traits of the man of science; and it is not by chance that in his erotic "Lesbos" Baudelaire resorts to an antithesis between the lascivious spectacle provided by the reprobates, and Plato's *œil austère* [stern eye] indignantly upon it.

Now this opposition is part of a whole psychological structure, the archetypal representation of mankind divided into various classes of men. Yet the opposition is still further strengthened by the fact that its two poles are hyperbolic statements. *Amoureux* and *fervents* are like synonyms repeating each other, since love and fervor are often associated, and *ferveur* is a frequent metonymy for *amour*; *fervent* makes explicit an already obvious quality and implication of the noun and thereby stresses the noun; *fervent* works as would an *épithète de nature* in classical style, the adjective invariably linked to a given noun. *Austère* (or its synonyms) plays the same role in modifying *savant*: it conveys the mood of the meditative scholar as he is conceived in the popular imagination: Hugo's *Mages* [Wise Men] are *les sévères artistes... Les savants, les inventeurs tristes, les puiseurs d'ombre* [stern artists... scholars, sad discoverers, laborers of darkness] (*Contemplations* 3.30.383, 391–4). Thus *fervent* is to *amoureux* and *austères* to *savants* what "noble" is to "lord" or "unsolved" is to "mystery." Scholars and lovers are the standard exemplars of each genus, which means that their relation to each other is also exemplary, and their polarity more widely distanced. Add to this the fact that *fervent* is etymologically related to fire (in "Le Léthé," the lover's fervor fans the fiery pain of unrequited love); *austère* can be associated with cold (e.g. the "austere coldness" of the monastery, in "Le Mauvais Moine").

This context makes for the striking contrast of *Aiment également... Les chats puissants et doux*; this oneness of feeling, this consensus so unexpected, contrasts the two mutually opposing subjects, an effect increased by *également*. The impact of *également* is further stressed on the semantic level because it superimposes a synonymity upon the antonymy of the first line; it is stressed at the same time by the disjunction, since the verb demands an object which is not yet forthcoming; and the disjunction actualizes the caesura—so that in oral reading the meter will give strong support.

The importance of the adverb has another effect: it is a first hint that lovers and scholars have much in common and that the very qualities that mark their separateness also join them. A possible analogy can now be perceived—the analogy that permits Baudelaire to declare that Beauty's lovers *Consumeront leurs jours en d'austères études* [Will use up their days in austere studies]... ("La Beauté"), the analogy that makes passion a common metaphor for the pursuit of knowledge. As we read along, the importance of *également* grows, since its meaning is confirmed by two more resumptions of the theme that there is a profound similarity between cats, lovers, and scholars—but from the viewpoint of the cats (lines 4 and 5): scholars and lovers love cats, cats love science and love.

A similar flashback effect (the word being reinforced by repeating the title) helps to contrast ³*Les chats* with what precedes; the contrast consists in the distance separating the subjects from the object on the plane of reality: this choice among possibilities offered by the connotations of *chat* is oriented, on the verbal plane, by the disjunction as a suspensive or delaying device, and by the disjunction as meaning, since it leads the reader to expect a mature attachment to a commensurate object, not a mere fondness, almost childish, for pets.

Whatever the orientation, the emphasis is undergirded by ³*puissants et doux*. The dual adjectival group itself is set off by the contrast with its homologues, the adjectives in the first line (their positions are identical, their meanings equally positive, but the ratio one to two), and by the inner contrast that makes *doux* an odd combination with *puissants*. This last contrast is so strong that it has become a cliché—about which more will be said later. The expressiveness of the opposition created by *orgueil* is brought out by its contiguity to the pair of adjectives, whose meaning it reinforces. This powerful combination coincides with the descending curve of the sentence: it seems to have run its course, after stating unequivocally that the most widely differing people imaginable will agree at least in their love for cats. The *puissants–doux* opposition now symbolizes the cat's ambivalence, which explains why two antithetical types of men can both love the cat with equal love: each type in its own way has the same combination of power and serenity; the cat mirrors them in the animal world—here, no doubt, one of the correspondences between mankind and the rest of Nature.

The implicit similitude (implicit because it is our own deduction, we have reasoned it from the love of cats) is now made explicit in line 4: the repetition of *comme eux*, with *eux* encompassing both lovers and scholars, knocks out any interpretation that might try to assign the adjectives separately to the two groups (Jakobson and Lévi-Strauss (p. 15) see a paronomasia—to my mind very far-fetched—linking *fervent* and *frileux*: lovers and scholars are equally shivery *and* sedentary); hence the inescapable conclusion that they are identical, since they not only love equally, but equally resemble the cats, their *tertium comparationis*. The initial apparent opposition discloses a deeper identity. Line 4 is a departure from the context: I have shown earlier how strong is the unity of the line and how it brings out the adjectives, especially *sédentaires*; this line is structured so differently from the first three that the coincidence between this contrast and the pattern at the end of the stanza results in a veritable rhythmic clausula. The parallel relative clauses constitute an addition to the *aiment* clause: the momentum of the sound sequence, carried in one breath to the caesura in line 3 and then continued despite the pause, is now all spent; the intonational curve thus also helps make the first stanza a natural unit, not just a conventional one fused in a sestet, as Jakobson and Lévi-Strauss would have it.

At this point, however, the importance of *frileux* and *sédentaires* gives by flashback a new orientation to our sense of the quatrain. The repeated identification *comme eux* ... *comme eux* clinches the demonstration of identity between cats and their human counterparts. In this culminating phrase we might have expected adjectives in keeping with those that preceded, all laudatory; we might even have expected a climaxing allusion to certain glorious qualities common to both parties. Instead we get the mediocrity of *frileux* and *sédentaires*—a comic letdown; all the more galling because these are every bit as true as the preceding adjectives, though they ruin the image that has been built up. *Frileux* is fussy and oldmaidish; Baudelaire used it effectively in a parodic self-portrait, the satirical "Spleen I": *d'un fantôme frileux* [of a shivering ghost]. *Sédentaire* conjures up the image of the constipated stay-at-home, epitome of the unwholesome bourgeois. The reader takes in this surprise but has in mind the whole quatrain, so that *orgueil de la maison* still sounds complimentary, with perhaps a touch of parody in the *maison*, which narrowly limits the sphere of the fame, the scope of the glory: even thus does La Fontaine's fox cut his blandishments to the measure of the crow when he crowns him *phénix de ces bois* [phoenix of this forest]— but keeps the eyrie of the immortal bird in the neighborhood. Similarly, *mûre saison*, a conventional poetic substitute for *l'âge mûr*, may now be felt as a bit too elegiac, whereas without the twist in line 4 it would simply be the expected ornamental phrase needed to beautify everyday reality. Scholars, in the context and on the level of *amoureux*, are in danger of losing their dignity: their austere mien no longer impresses us, now that we see them as chilly homebodies. *Amoureux* [the amorous] is not, like *amants* [lovers], confined to serious or tragic contexts: the shock wave from line 4 destroys the synonymity with *amants* and actualizes the depreciatory or condescending connotations: nineteenth-century dictionaries rank *amoureux* below *amants*; *amoureux*, not *amants*, is the core of many mocking phrases like *amoureux transi* [bashful lover]; and Baudelaire uses it elsewhere only to deride lovers (in the burlesque "La Lune offensée" their silly irresponsibility *sur leurs grabats prospères* [on their prosperous sickbeds]; in "Hymne à la Beauté," where the irony is all his, as a comparison with the source makes clear, their ungainly bed gymnastics: *L'amoureux pantelant incliné sur sa belle* [The quivering lover stretched over his beloved]; whereas his *amants* are never equivocal, always poetic).

QUATRAIN II

The formal singularity of line 5 clearly marks the beginning of a new stanza, just as the character of line 4, more than its mere final position, makes it the ending of the first quatrain. The element of unexpectedness is provided by the apposition, which gives *Amis* a commanding post, while *science* and *volupté* are each in turn spotlighted by the contrast with the comparatively empty *de la* (whose repetition performs the same unifying, characterizing function, for line 5, as did *comme eux* for line 4). Whereas [3]*orgueil*, also an apposition, followed explicit mention of its referent, *Les chats*, here the apposition precedes its referent, [6]*Ils*. Hence a momentary suspension while the reader's mind hesitates over whether to interpret *Amis* as cats or as their admirers or as all of them together. Shortlived it may be, but the ambiguity is enough to emphasize the line, and when line 6 brings the solution, line 5 is sensed as homologous to lines 1–3 and in contrast to them, reversing them, so to say (this becomes more apparent if we rewrite 1–3: **la volupté et la science sont amies des chats*). The contrast between line

5 and the context of 1 is confirmed by the homologous relations of the two other elements in the spotlight: *amoureux–savants, science–volupté*.

The equivalence twice verified from people to cat to people, indicates plainly that their metonymic relationship is so close as to make them interchangeable: it becomes metaphoric, the cats symbolize something common to love and science.

The focus upon *Amis de la science et de la volupté* isolates it—and this isolation is intensified by its typographical concentration, which makes it quite visibly the shortest line of the sonnet. It is so isolated, in fact, that we are made aware of the cliché: the phrase is like *les amis des lettres* [friends of learning] for "intelligentsia," or *les amis de la vérité* [friends of truth], generally for "the opposition" (it seems that Cicero coined it), or *ami de la bouteille* [friend of the bottle], "drunkard." With the added salt of personification, it has become the poetic stereotype for any habitual contiguity or affinity, the relation between "things that seem to have a sympathy for one another," as the dictionary of the Academy puts it in the 1835 edition, citing *Le vin est ami du cœur* [Wine is the friend of the heart], *Il y a des odeurs qui sont amies du cerveau* [There are odors which are friends of the brain], etc. Baudelaire follows suit with *le soir charmant, ami du criminel* [the charming evening, friend of the criminal] ("Le Crépuscule du soir").

It is in the whole second quatrain, that irony is amplified. Jakobson and Lévi-Strauss are blinded by irrelevant parallelisms and do not see this. Other critics reject it because the poet's infatuation with cats makes irony less than likely. Informants, not so well versed in literary biography, *always perceive it*. Martin Turnell is the rare critic who does catch it, but he explains it away as we do an irony in real life: for him it is an "ironical" situation for scholars and lovers, who are supposed to hunt their prey, to be instead engaged in sedentary occupation (significantly, Turnell sees no irony in *frileux*, since it fits in with his exaggerated translation of *mûre saison* as "elderly"); again, for him the second quatrain is in "mock heroic style" because of the discrepancy between the cats' ludicrous ordinariness and high-sounding verse (*Baudelaire: A Study of His Poetry*, pp. 262, 241). His argument is not to the point: a lover of cats would find no discrepancy—Gautier, for one, does not. Irony in literature must be a verbal structure, lest it vary with different readers' opinions as to what is exaggerated or "not really meant." The text must contain some signal that what is being said is not intended to be taken seriously, or that there is some double meaning. The first such structure is the contrast between a pattern of laudative adjectives and the *comparatively* unfavorable connotations of *frileux* and *sédentaires* (without the praise pattern, *frileux* at least looks "serious" or even poetic: Lebrun-Pindare speaks of *la frileuse hirondelle* [the fluttering swallow]). With this first structure as its context, a second structure is now built up in reverse: against the connotative pattern of line 4, the elevated tone of line 5, which would be appropriate to glorify the Medici, actually creates a *verbal* discrepancy which is inescapable, no matter what the reader's personal views on cats may be.

Informants unanimously ignore [6]*Ils cherchent le silence*. Undoubtedly *cherchent* is the poetic or high-tone substitute for *rechercher* [to search out] or *aimer* [to love], but this is no more than the normal transformation of prose into verse: the device marks genre, as do verse and stanza, setting the context apart from everyday contexts. It is expected and not surprising. [6]*Horreur des ténèbres*, on the contrary, draws the attention of every reader: this, of course, is because it contrasts with the first hemistich—a leap from factual-poetic to affective-poetic, and a semantic contrast between a desire and its undesirable object, as in Racine's *chercher la malédiction* [to seek the curse]; it is also because its inner structure, independent of context, brings out the powerful meaning of the group's components, thanks to an analytical subordination that separates *horreur* from its cause, thereby emphasizing twice over the concept of darkness. Moreover, *horreur des ténèbres* is a cliché: a reader of the 1850s would remember it from Racine or Delille as well. The cliché is objectionable only from the esthetic viewpoint that makes novelty the sole criterion of beauty. It may well be hackneyed, but its stereotyped form keeps it from wearing out: the inclusion of this particular cliché as an example in the *Larousse du XIXème siècle* must testify to its continued effectiveness.[5] Now if your reader is uncultivated, the cliché will strike him because of its intrinsic expressiveness; if he is well read, he will recognize it as a literary allusion, at any rate a literary form. Hence a deepening of darkness: here is no mere absence of light but an asylum for the secret life, a privileged abode for meditation, a sanctuary.

The distich (if we follow the division made by Jakobson and Lévi-Strauss) is the apex of both irony and emphasis on darkness. The attention-forcing features are, first, *L'Érèbe*, because it is a mythological allusion, because of its form (the only word in /rɛb/, aside from one name for ornithologists alone), and because it is a personification. Then *coursiers funèbres*, because it completes the mythological picture of a divine charioteer: but what may be conventional in the image is compensated for by [7]*funèbres*, which is effective both because of its meaning and because it repeats its homologue [6]*ténèbres*, first as a stereotyped rhyme and then as a moral transposition of the concept of darkness. And then [8]*servage* and [8]*fierté*, because these are concretized abstractions, as in line 5, and because the line contains a word order inversion within a clause (*au servage*, stressed in its aberrant position by the caesura). Naturally, the discrepancy we felt between [5]*Amis de la science*... and the preceding line is now even wider: Baudelaire invokes Erebus, son of Chaos, potent brother and husband of Night herself, father of Styx and of the Parcae and of Sleep—and states that tomcats like it in the dark. This is like La Fontaine calling a gardener a priest of Flora and Pomona; clearly this climaxes the second irony structure. But it also gives most effective expression to the essential theme: *Érèbe* is the most evocative word of three connected by their sounds (*Érèbe, ténèbres, funèbres*); it summarizes them phonetically. Semantically too, since Erebus means "darkness." (Nodier goes so far as to use it as a common noun in that sense.) We may now say that the concept of darkness has been expressed, in turn, by the appropriate noun, literal but picked from the top of the ladder of expressivity, whose bottom rung might be *obscurité*; and by a metonymy (*horreur*), a metaphor (*funèbres*), a proper noun that is both metonymic as a person and metaphoric as the symbolic value of that person. Thus a paradigm of four synonyms

---

[5] *Horreur* attracts *ténèbres* so powerfully that it once caused Hugo to write *horreur ténébreuse*, without any connection with what he meant (*Dieu, L'Océan d'en haut*, v. 2465).

has been transposed on to the axis of combination. These several variables (let us add the phonetic one that links three key words) represent the invariant "darkness." This, in turn, is part of a system that embraces the cats and science and love: since cats symbolize something common to love and science, this symbol tells us that love and science thrive in darkness.

So that the last two lines of the quatrain are not a separate unit: their many formal differences simply flow from the complexity of a hyperbolic image, and are needed to cap the demonstration. The dramatic temptation imagined by Jakobson and Lévi-Strauss is quite exaggerated. All we have, of course, is a statement that cats and darkness are closely associated, and then the mock hypothesis; in common parlance, I fancy it might go something like this: "They sure love the dark. Gee!—they could be the black horses of Hell, except that, etc. . . ."

Upon this note end the two quatrains and the irony—the reason being that irony has fulfilled its purpose. Intertwined with "serious" statements, irony lends them support. This is not an irony of content, that destroys; it is an irony of style, a way of saying things with tongue in cheek that attracts attention to what is being said. Irony as style is commonly used in the nineteenth century, in monographs or books of vulgarization as a way of establishing contact with the reader. I find it in Toussenel's *L'Esprit des Bêtes* (1848), the first volume of his *Zoologie passionnelle*, inspired by Fourier (we know that Baudelaire read at least the second volume), where the cat is described as the "lover of Night," or in a paper published by the same Toussenel in *L'École normale*, where he celebrates the cat as the chemist, physicist, physician, etc. of the animal kingdom—in short, a friend of science. Irony and theme are the same in E. T. A. Hoffman's *Chat Murr*.

Where Baudelaire utilizes the techniques of conventional poetry, as here, to embellish a lowly subject, his irony warns the reader, at the same time, that this is just a game, indeed, a mere convention, whose limitations he well knows. The praise of cats enables them to embody human qualities and makes their night something more than a time for backfence yowling. This "poetization" of the metaphoric vehicle allows for an ironic contrast, which in turn permits yet higher praise; and this finally prepares the way for a magnification of the cats into sphinxes through the comparison with mythical horses. Irony, by making such grandeur more acceptable to the sceptic and by underscoring it, further aids a shift in emphasis from superficial similarities (*frileux*) to an esoteric sympathy. It is now clear that the polarity of lovers and scholars defined the extreme examples of the class of men who seek the silence and the dark: these are necessary to the success of their respective strivings, so like each other—toward a life fully lived through *volupté*, toward a universe fully explored through science.

FIRST TERCET

The domestic cat's mythologization becomes more specific and to the point. First of all, it is a new sublimation of the cat, this one based upon traditional association, perhaps because cats had their niche in the Pantheon of Egypt and surely because cats are enigmatic. This image is conveyed less by the hardly noticeable [10]*grands* than by the cliché [9]*nobles attitudes* (the fact that the *Larousse du XIXème siècle* quotes the line under *attitude* is sufficient proof of its effectiveness). It is vague, since *attitude* offers us nothing to *see* and is hardly more than a prop on which to hang some adjective like "noble," "great," "grave" that may be needed to give a description its moral meaning. On the one hand, *attitudes* reduces the plastic or visual evocation to a pose—especially for Baudelaire's contemporaries, who still regarded it as a painter's word—but a meaningful pose; for instance, in "Incompatibilité," *attitude* describes the attentive posture of mountains listening to some mysterious message; in "La Beauté" the word lends a monumental majesty to Beauty, who *trône dans l'azur comme un sphinx incompris* [reigns in the sky like an unfathomable sphinx]; it is motionlessness wherever that symbolizes contemplation. On the other hand, *attitudes* also functions as a screen that filters the complex reality of the cat, eliminates his daintiness, his nimble gait, anything that smacks of *volupté*; what is retained is the immobility, and the watchful gaze from under sleepy lids: in short, whatever makes the cat a domestic sphinx. In turn, the image of the original Sphinx is altered: there is no hint here of the details—breasts, claws, etc.—found in the sphinxes of Empire architecture and furniture, in Gautier's "Sphinx" or in the mean catwoman in Gustave Moreau's *Œdipe*—these are all too tangible. [10]*Allongés* is not exact enough to eliminate vagueness, nor is it incompatible with nobility, as is the pose of another of Gautier's sphinxes, *accroupi dans les sables brûlants* [crouched in the scorching sands] ("Le Lion du cirque"). The sphinx is like the "stone ghost," the statue that commands passers-by to think upon the things *qui ne sont pas de la terre* [which are not of the world] (*Salon de 1859*, IX, édition Pléiade, p. 1086).

Thus [9]*nobles attitudes*, stereotype though it is, sums up a meaning in Baudelaire's own symbolic code—"meditation upon things metaphysical"—which is stated again in common language: *songeant, rêve sans fin*—an elevation to eternity.

Sphinx adds to the mimesis of "contemplation" its archetypal esoterism. A context of ordinary words sets in relief the foreignness of *sphinx*; the name alone suffices to evoke, like Flaubert's sphinx, contemplativeness: *mon regard, que rien ne peut dévier, demeure tendu à travers les choses sur un horizon inaccessible* [my gaze, which nothing can turn aside, remains directed past objects at an inaccessible horizon] (*La Tentation de Saint Antoine*, VII, edited by R. Dumesnil, p. 199).

[10]*Solitudes* keeps the reader from substituting the Oedipean sphinx for this brooder: reinforced by *au fond* and again by the plural, it makes clear that desert has been chosen not for the sake of its connotations of barrenness but for what it means to man as a privileged place of meditation: the poet makes a revealing joke about the working of his imagination being founded upon *la Thébaïde que mon cerveau s'est faite* [the desert which my brain has created] (*Salon de 1859*, VII, p. 1071). The interpretation given by Jakobson and Lévi-Strauss is based on the semantic field of "desert": "the fear of cold, which brings chilly cats and hot lovers close to one another . . . finds a suitable climate in the solitude (as austere as the scholars themselves) of the desert (as hot as the lovers) that surrounds the sphinxes" (p. 15). The procedure is obvious: in accordance with the principle of equivalence, *solitudes* is transformed into *désert* as defined by the dictionary; equivalences are then deduced: from "desert" as a limitless expanse, they

DESCRIBING POETIC STRUCTURES [383]

draw the opposition *maison–solitudes*; from "desert" as opposed to "oasis," the equation with *austères*; from "desert" as "burning sands," the opposition to *frileux* and the equation with *fervents*. Unfortunately, this system is not actualized in the poem and therefore cannot be applied. And that for the simple reason that the text says not *désert* but *solitudes*; which is in reality synonymous with *silence* and *ténèbres*, since, like them, it makes contemplation possible (the three are interchangeable: in "Le Gouffre" they describe the universe contemplated by the poet). It may be argued that *sphinx* identifies *solitudes* with white-hot Egypt: but the sonnet does not actualize in words any such image. Even where a poem does contain a precise geographical description of a desert, this is not enough to impose upon the reader associations not verbally actualized as well. In "Spleen II," for instance, the desert is a geographical reality: it is named, and there are allusions to the pyramids and to the Sphinx. Yet the associative system organized around *désert* in the language is supplanted by the symbolic function of the word in the text (that wasteland is boredom), and only where reality is relevant to that symbol do "natural" associations operate (e.g. the pyramid symbolizes dead memories); but the physical climate of the desert yields in the face of meteorological similes whose sole justification is that they express "spleen": *les lourds flocons des neigeuses années* [the heavy flakes of snowy years], and the symbolic mist that shrouds the sphinx *Assoupi dans le fond d'un Saharah brumeux* [Sunk in the depths of a misty Sahara]. "Contemplative life, ataraxy"—the inscape of *solitudes* has no need to conjure up, and in fact excludes, an arid African landscape.[6]

SECOND TERCET

The two tercets are more than conventionally separated by the difference in clause construction between lines 11 and 12: the abundance of nasals, twice as many as in any other line coinciding with their position, emphasizes their role as stanza boundaries (12, with a sequence of /ɛ/, contrasts with the /ã/ pattern of 11).

So long as the cats' "spiritualization" had not been achieved, no physical detail was given that might drag them back down to reality (except in line 4, and this, paradoxically, was just a way of elevating them by comparison). Now that they are a symbol, the poet refers to their physical realities. But each realistic detail is but a springboard to unreality, for an adjective transposes it and makes it a signpost toward surreality. Every one of these adjectives could apply to the Sphinx: thus the creature constitutes a transition from mythic to mystic, and because it stands for esoterism, it is the key to the code the adjectives set up.

"Reality" is imposed upon the reader by [12]*Leurs reins féconds*: the group is striking at every level. The harsh juncture (/r + r/) signalizes it as a beginning and sharpens the rupture with the first tercet. Since that pattern was simplification, abstraction, its rupture must be concrete detail: hence a shift from pronouns that only allude to real subjects (*Ils, Qui*) to descriptive nouns that invite sensory perception. The

---

[6] Cf. Wm. Y. Tindall, *The Literary Symbol* (1955), pp. 130–3. The whole tercet is quite frequently quoted in its entirety, and by critics of all feathers; this effectiveness is probably attributable to the archetypes as much as to the form.

context indicates that *reins* is a metonymy for "back"; but *féconds* suggests that it is a metaphor, "loins," for sexual potency. Then the ambiguity contaminates *étincelles*. On the one hand, *étincelles* describes the sparks (from this viewpoint, *magiques* is hyperbolic); on the other hand, it symbolizes vital parts (*magiques* then being the literal expression of the mystery of life-giving). *Pleins* belongs to colloquial style (compare *terre ... pleine d'escargots* [earth ... full of snails] in "Le Mort joyeux," *ventre plein d'exhalaisons* [belly full of vapors] in "Une Charogne," etc.), and therein it contrasts with the conventional style of *reins féconds*. But at the metaphoric level, it makes *reins* still more concrete. In either case it provides an animal ground that brightens the contrast of *étincelles*, a word we associate with the archetypes of fire and light. These archetypes exerted more power over the imagination in an era when electricity was still untamed and Mesmer still far from forgotten, as attested by the frequency of metaphors based upon galvanism. [12]*Magiques*, however, is the ingredient that keeps the archetype alive forever in the text, even for the rationalistic reader: it exteriorizes a response that the reader made wise by science now represses in his subconscious, the immemorial surprise at a fire that does not burn (poetic themes like the salamander and the lightning bug obviously took their origin from some such feeling). Perhaps this tips the scales in favor of an interpretation of *reins* as a sexual image, since fire and semen, sparks and life, are often metaphorically associated.[7] Most important, the group *étincelles magiques* declares the existence of a second level of reality beneath appearances. Even if there were no archetypes behind it, the group would still suggest them: *étincelles* and *magiques* do not simply add their poetic potentialities to say something like "the sparks have a magical effect"; in a context now dominated by *sphinx* and previously by *ténèbres* and *science*, *magiques* must be interpreted as a substitute for an actual esoteric reference; the sparks are fire but also meaning. The symbolism of the text has moved from darkness and dream to light in darkness.

The last two lines owe their effectiveness to their structure as a suspense narrative (the enjambement, and the severance of the verb *Étoilent* from its subject). The description stresses a physical beauty whose significance is withheld until the reader discovers, at the same time, that all this is about the eyes of the cat, and that those eyes are supernatural.

At the outset, a vision of gold is summoned up, at once to exploit its archetypal symbolism and to transform it into a symbol of light. [13]*Parcelles d'or* is the agent of this alchemy: significantly, *Larousse du XIXème siècle* quotes this whole tercet under *parcelles*. In a "gold" context, *parcelles* actualizes the highly poetic antithesis of infinite value in infinitesimal room. In other words, a hyperbolic rendering of the cats' yellow-flecked eyes: this stylistic sublimation of the color is carried on by the second hemistich, where even the conjunction has been touched by Midas: *ainsi que* is to *comme* [like] what *or* is to *jaune* [yellow]. *Sable*, semantically related to *parcelles* by metonymy, is now its metaphoric substitute, as if all the sand in the placer had turned to gold dust. *Fin* in a "sand" context lays emphasis upon what makes sand more pleasing to the eye and to the naked foot, but in the parallel structure of the line, *fin* is also in a

---

[7] Line 12 exemplifies Bachelard's Novalis complex (*Psychoanalyse du feu*, pp. 47 ss, 87 ss).

"gold" context and its suggestiveness is therefore oriented by the jeweler's technical phrase *or fin*. Furthermore, *parcelles d'or* irresistibly calls forth the compound *paillettes d'or* [grains of gold] frequently used in descriptions of eyes—*deux yeux de chats, phosphorescents, pailletés d'or* [a pair of cat's eyes, phosphorescent, ingrained with gold].[8] Their semantic equivalence and their quasi-homophony make *parcelles d'or* expressive as a modification of the more common compound—the same stylistic mechanism as in the renewal of a cliché, the adaptation of a quotation, or the distortion of a word. Coming immediately after *étincelles*, *parcelles* works as a variation on the motif of sparkling light—a golden fire. At the peak of the rhythmic build-up of two lines unified by one sentence [14]*Étoilent* all alone would have grandeur. The verb itself, with archetype for a root, and normally in the past participle, is as conventional as "starspangled" in English. But its use in any other mode explodes the stereotype, renews the rapport with the semantic field of *étoile*, and stresses the image of light in darkness; for instance, this line of Hugo: *Nul regard n'étoilait la noirceur de leurs yeux* [No look lighted up the blackness of their eyes] (*Les Quatre Vents de l'esprit*, 4.3.3). Not much is needed for such a verb to take on a suggestiveness of the unknown. This is precisely the effect attained by *vaguement*: the adverb seems to annul exactly what differentiates *étoiler* from other verbs of light—its scintillation. Literally taken, the group would be meaningless, but *vaguement* is more like a blanket negation of reality: it gives it the appearance of the unreal. The adverb functions as a device to orient the reader toward a mystical interpretation. Without *vaguement*, a smile *Entrevu vaguement au bord des autres cieux* [Glimpsed vaguely at the edge of other skies] is only the dream of an exotic idyll with some "Malabaraise." The adverb transmutes it into a yearning for eternity ("Lesbos"). As a matter of fact, this function of *vaguement* dovetails so perfectly with the esoteric connotations of *étoiler* that their grouping became a feature of Hugo's metaphysical or fantastic style: in a picture of dawn, for instance—*l'âpre obscurité... s'étoilait au loin de vagues auréoles* [the bitter darkness... lighted up in the distance with vague radiance]—they give the reader warning that this light in darkness is not of the day but of God, a sign to the *voyant* [seer].[9]

In the tercet the group exercises a final dominion over the reader's imagination by gathering up the sparks in the eyes, where they must have significance, and transposing that significance on to an esoteric level. Thus we escape any temptation to downgrade *mystiques* to "mysterious." The full sense of the adjective was borrowed by Baudelaire from theology, "allegorical of a spiritual truth"—which explains why the nouns it modifies must be concrete: e.g. *le grenier mystique* [the mystic granary] ("La Mort des Pauvres"), that is, Death, the Barn where the poor will find stored for their afterlife the rewards that misery harvests for them. Without such a contrast, *mystiques* would be tautological. The contrast here is provided by the precise *prunelles*. This conventional metonymy ceases to be a mere ornament: it emphasizes the gaze, symbol of a

---

[8] Zola, *Nana*, I (edited by Mitterand, 2, p. 1120). Tears cannot dampen their fire: *Votre prunelle, où brille une humide paillette* [The pupil of your eye, where a moist speck of gold glitters], writes Gautier (*Poésies diverses 1833-1838*, "A deux beaux yeux").

[9] *Dieu*, "L'Esprit humain," v. 235. In *Contemplations*, "A celle qui est restée en France," 352-4, the group appears significantly in a passage that seems to list the key words of the Hugolian contemplation.

questing mind. Both Gautier's and Laforgue's reaction testify to the effect of these two words together: they both tried to emulate it. The rhythmic structure of the tercet shows clearly that the poem is ending. Their meaning and the space occupied by the last two lines develop line 12, and this relation is underscored by [13]*Et*. The *ets* of the quatrains bound together phrases of equal length and comparable value, all of them parts of a clause (1, 3, 5, 6) or of a sentence (4): [13]*Et* standing out against a pattern of six lines without similar coordination, links two sentences, the second twice as long as the first. The tercet seems to fan out in a final image: *Et* launches the ascending portion of the sentence, the first one in the sonnet that takes a whole last line to descend uninterrupted. Such an ample intonational curve provides the poem with a rhythm unequivocally terminal, and yet its resounding amplitude echoes the meaning of *mystiques*.

The poem as a whole obviously should be read as both a *blason*, an encomiastic description, a *laus cattorum*, and as a symbolic poem—the cats are at once cats and the hieroglyph of something else. The concluding word, *mystiques*, which is in effect a metalinguistic comment on the image of the cat, implies two meanings and invites us to a new examination of his image in that light. When the reading is over, a global, summative apprehension of the text through rereading and remembering is certainly part of the literary act of communication. Then, the total of all data and knowledge of the ending surges back to modify what we perceived at the beginning (such an effect was observable in the irony of the quatrains). Several different images can be seen as the variants of a single semantic structure—as symbols.

The fact that attentive critics are not aware of any symbolism and see in "Les Chats" a pre-Parnassian work whose "precise" imagery reflects an esthetics of the picturesque[10] may be laid to the title ("poème animalier") and to the absence of the kind of obvious explanatory statement found in most allegorical poems ("Les Hiboux [Owls]," with a similar title, *are* explained as allegory); perhaps, as well, to the necessity for finding in Baudelaire examples that support the favored idea of his development: something Parnassian was needed.

In each instance where the cats are equivalent to something else (men, mythological figures, and a surreal or supernatural image of themselves), they resemble not the appearance of these equivalents but what the latter stand for. The relationship between cats as pets and men as their masters is but an image of the cats' love for science itself and *volupté*. This link between Science and Pleasure is the symbol of the *raison d'être* that Faust and Don Juan have in common—an unending search of the absolute. (Baudelaire is unequivocal: his "Femmes damnées [Doomed women]" are *chercheuses d'infini* [seekers after the infinite]; poetry, art are *la soif insatiable de tout ce qui est au delà* [the insatiable thirst for all that lies beyond] (*Nouvelles histoires extraordinaires*, Conard, pp. xx–xxi).) Now there are two roads to the absolute: there is the quest for the Grail, *le voyage*; and there is the quest within, that is, meditation. *Mûre saison, doux, maison, frileux, sédentaires* repeat insistently that adventure is forsaken: the cats' meditativeness represents the chosen way.

That such is their meaning is confirmed by their relationship to Erebus, an image of

---

[10] M. A. Ruff, *L'Esprit du mal et l'esthétique baudelairienne* (1955), pp. 245, 304; R. B. Chérix, *Commentaire des Fleurs du Mal* (1949), p. 247.

DESCRIBING POETIC STRUCTURES

their love for silence and the dark; and their relationship to the Sphinx, an image of immobile mystic contemplation.

The sonnet structure can thus be described as a sequence of synonymous images, all of them variations on the symbolism of the cat as representative of the contemplative life. The Sphinx simile duplicates the equivalence by making the cat a symbol of this symbol of mystic contemplation. The last stanza reduplicates this by making him a symbol also of the *object* of contemplation: he merges in himself the gaze of the contemplator and the light in darkness that reveals just enough of the hidden treasure to encourage the *chercheur d'absolu* [seeker after the absolute]—a combination of enticement and denial common to many symbols of esoterism (cf. the frequent image of light behind a veil). Thus, beneath this repetitive continuity lies an antithesis that opposes the natural cat, symbol of contemplation, to the supernatural cat, symbol of the contemplated, of the occult truth.

The foregoing interpretation, it seems to me, covers every aspect of the text without contradiction. The antithesis just outlined has the advantage over the exegesis of Jakobson and Lévi-Strauss that it explains the transfiguration of the cats. The poem gives not a "reason" in the world why we should see this transfiguration as a "cosmic" one. The range of their metamorphosis is not that wide: at most, they become like Cheshire-cats with only their phosphorescence left. And this, we can explain if we take them to symbolize the contemplative mind and to represent its poles in turn, being first the eye as gaze and then the eye as mirror. A description of the familiar feline postures suffices to make them acceptable as symbols of the contemplators; but if we are to be made to see the cat as a being related to the supernatural, a parti-pris is required to inform his physical features with a significance; the transfiguration is then the consequence of a stylistic shift of the description from an animal vocabulary with limited connotations (*frileux, sédentaires,* etc.) to a metaphysical one (*magiques, mystiques*) with a boundless power of suggestion.

Comparative Structuralism

ANY LINGERING DOUBT as to the symbolism of the sonnet will vanish once we find other texts, unquestionably symbolic, which are variants of the structure our sonnet actualizes.

Jakobson and Lévi-Strauss conduct such a comparative study in an effort to relate "Les Chats" to the other *Flowers* and to the poet's psychology. Here again their procedure raises the question of pertinence to the literary phenomenon at hand. In my opinion comparative structuralism as they practice it requires a radical readjustment. Their entire commentary emphasized the cats' identification with the cosmos. Another interpretation, a sexual one, was limited to their affinity with *amoureux*. Now, as a sort of afterthought, sexuality takes the spotlight: we are told that in Baudelaire's mind the image of the cat is the image of a woman and that our sonnet has a female-male ambiguity. Hence the bold conclusion: the cat's image symbolizes the poet. The sublimation of the cat symbolizes love cleansed of feminine impurity and knowledge freed of its coldness. The poet is thus ready for a mystic communion with the universe. Now I am not sure I have this quite straight,[11] but I am sure that a chasm has opened up between an almost pedestrian process of analysis and these philosophical fireworks.

These assertions are put forward as proof: 1) the use of feminine words for masculine rhymes suggests androgyny: in my discussion of metalanguage I tried to show that this could not be; 2) the words ³*puissants et doux* amount to a description of cats as women: the sole evidence for this is a line of Brizeux where women are celebrated as *êtres* [beings] *puissants et doux*. Which is not convincing because, as I said before, this is a cliché (a stereotype structure linking *doux* and any adjective incompatible with "sweetness" or "softness"). The cliché corresponds, I believe, to the archetype of the hero strong enough to be kind, from Homer's Hector to Rimbaud's Héraklès whose brow is *terrible et doux* ("Soleil et Chair"). The cliché is in no way used for amazons only. The only time I found it with female connotations, it described not womanhood, but motherhood,[12] which does not apply to *these* cats. 3) Androgyny is again implied by certain ambiguities in the description of the cats; and the cats in "Les Chats," being the same as those in the two poems entitled "Le Chat," must therefore represent Woman. These last two contentions can be best answered by the comparative method.

The principle of comparative structural analysis is quite simple: given several sets of data, no comparison may be drawn between empirical data pertinent to those sets, but solely between the systems within which they occur. Just because they do have common components, one system cannot be used to explain another: they must be isomorphic.

If we now compare texts, we find no correspondences enabling us to see "Les Chats" as equivalent to a "female" structure. There are, to be sure, homologies between the descriptive structures here and those in "Le Chat" (*Fleurs*, LI): the animal is, at the same time, *fort* et *doux*; his domain is a house too (*C'est l'esprit familier du lieu* [He is the familiar spirit of the place]), although the house is located in the poet's inner universe (*Dans ma cervelle* [In my brain]); the creature's gaze has a sphinx-like fixity, and his nature is mystic (*chat mystérieux, chat séraphique, chat étrange* [mysterious cat, seraphic cat, strange cat]); finally, the relationship between the cat and the poet is much the same as that between our cats and their composite counterpart in "Les Chats." The magic motif is here, but treated differently: stroked, the fur emits a magic fragrance instead of sparks. One feature prominent here is not mentioned in our sonnet, the meow—but this is actually another device to suggest the supernatural (the mewing is compared to poetry, to a philter, and so forth), and a variant of the darkness motif (*sa voix, qui perle . . . Dans mon fonds le plus ténébreux* [his voice, which

---

[11] p. 21, "De la constellation initiale du poème, formée par les amoureux et les savants, les chats permettent par leur médiation d'éliminer la femme, laissant face à face—sinon même confondus—le 'poète des Chats,' libéré de l'amour . . . , et l'univers, délivré de l'austérité du savant [Starting with the poem's initial constellation, as it is shaped by the lovers and the scholars, the cats allow, in their role as mediators, the sheerly feminine element to be eliminated, leaving face to face—if not indeed identified with each other—the 'poet of Cats,' liberated from love . . . , and the universe, delivered from the austerity of the scholar]."

[12] A. France, *L'Anneau d'améthyste*, III (p. 126). Abbé Guitrel calls his affection for a young man "maternelle, pour mieux exprimer ce qu'elle contient à la fois de force et de douceur [maternal, the better to express the force and sweetness which it contains simultaneously]."

DESCRIBING POETIC STRUCTURES

forms pearls... in my darkest depths]). I trust I have made the parallelism as convincing as our exegetes could wish. Now for my retort: there is nothing in Le Chat that imposes upon the reader the image of a woman. The descriptive details claimed for femininity apply as aptly to felinity; all the passages that might be alluding to love can be taken just as satisfactorily as mystical (in fact, some of these ambiguities have verbal or content homologues in "La Beauté" and "Hymne à la Beauté"). I am well aware that critics nearly always assume this cat is a girl—one line is even read as pandering to the reader's prurience. Yet all such conclusions lean upon biographical data which is by no means certainly applicable here. And even if the poet *was* inspired by some love affair, the point is that such content is *concealed* by the form or else translated to a distinctly spiritual level; *volupté* is not described in terms of Woman but is interiorized in a reverie about a symbolic cat.

As for "Le Chat" (*Fleurs*, XXXIV), it does conjure up a woman, though only by simile, and it should be noted that the description of the cat in itself does not bring to mind a woman so long as the comparison is not made formal and explicit (*Je vois ma femme en esprit* [I see my wife in my mind's eye]). But then the structure is entirely different from that of *Les Chats* except for the eyes and the sparks; and these are here given unrelated functions: the sparks are purely descriptive, without spiritual connotation; the eyes do not invite entry into their secret world, they are instead turned outwards, directed against the observer. So are the claws and even the *dangereux parfum*.

Lastly, in a prose poem that Jakobson and Lévi-Strauss do not mention, "L'Horloge," Baudelaire compares a mistress with a cat; he seeks eternity in her eyes. Thus cat and woman are identified, and there is some of the spiritual atmosphere of "Les Chats." But form and emphasis are completely different: in fact, the structure of our sonnet seems to be pointedly avoided. Spiritual connotations are dissociated from the "natural" cat-woman likeness: an ironic comment by the poet dismisses them as the far-fetched metaphor of a madrigal in the Góngora (or Samuel Cramer) vein; the mystic élan is negated, as it were, by the "realistic," prosaic style of the traveler telling tales of Chinese superstition. It is the woman who resembles the cat, rather than the other way around, and even that link is broken as soon as it is formed. As space and eternity are visioned in the woman's eyes, they vanish from the cat's lightless eyeballs (*le blanc des yeux* [the whites of the eyes]); as felinity invades the woman (*la belle Féline, la si bien nommée* [the beautiful Féline, so well named]), it deserts the cat (*un fort gros chat* [a very fat cat]).

Of course Baudelaire is perfectly capable of perceiving the cat in the woman, the woman in the cat. He occasionally uses the one as a metaphor of the other. But not always. Whatever the role of the cat in his private erotic imagery, it was not such as to make him write *chat* instinctively when he meant *femme*: whenever he does, we have seen that he feels obliged to provide the reader with an explanation. If *chat* means something besides the little beast, its dual value entails a selection among the descriptive features of the cat's image, the only traits retained being those common to both the animal and what he represents. This selection, in any given instance, must be our reference for interpreting that instance.

Once we have got rid of our false rapprochements, nothing in "Les Chats" calls up Woman. I am not ready to agree that [12]*reins féconds* is ambiguous: like *aine*, it is a euphemism reserved to the male procreative power, whereas *ventre* or *sein* would be used for female fertility. *Chats* and *sphinx* may be androgynous for lexicographers: but in context the masculine gender of *chats* is repeatedly underlined by *ils* and *eux*, by *coursiers* and *amis*. The mythological sphinx was indeed half or one-third female, but French, significantly, shifted from *la* to *le sphinx* during the eighteenth century; Romantic travelers to the Orient and writers of esoteric bent virtually abandoned the Greek female-bosomed monster in favor of the *grand sphinx* of the Pyramids. *Volupté* is not one way or the other (note, however, that the *chat voluptueux* of "La Géante" is definitely a tomcat), but a context containing *savants, science, silence, horreur des ténèbres*, and *funèbres* rather flatly excludes any female presence. The analysts' misreading is due, I believe, to the choice of data exterior to the poems. Since *chats* is the key word, and since Baudelaire's love for cats is well attested, it was logical for our authors to assume that this is a case of obsession, which triggers the word's recurrence. This causal relationship does not, however, extend to any structure: there is no evidence that a stylistic structure corresponds to the psychological one. All that can be said with certainty is that a psychological structure may well "activate" or "sensitize" a word, and that this word will then come easy to the poet, will play a role in a number of structures that have nothing to do with its source within his mind. *Solitudes* and *chats* demonstrate that the semantic structure, the virtual system of representations centered around a word, does not remain present behind every actualization of that word.

Comparative structuralism, if consistently adhered to, should at least rid literary criticism of one great plague: the proclivity to assume that a key word or verbal obsession must always have the same meaning for the author once the obsession has set in. Semantic permanence *is* to be observed among the variants of one structure; but a verbal obsession may serve several structures. Let us give the name *code* to the lexical components that actualize a variant of a structure. We can say that in "Les Chats" three symbolic structures (semantic, but in actual texts only, not in language) representing mystery and two modes of contemplation have been implemented with a *cat-code* (*sphinx* is only a specialization of *chat*, a sub-code). If the structures determined from the data of the sonnet are correct, there should be other codes actualizing them.

The contemplative-life structure subcoded in *sphinx* can be readily verified: I find it in "La Chambre double," where *Les meubles ont des formes allongées, prostrées, alanguies. Les meubles ont l'air de rêver; on les dirait doués d'une vie somnambulique* [The pieces of furniture have forms which are elongated, stretched out, langourous. The pieces of furniture look as if they were dreaming; one could say they are endowed with a trancelike life]. The relational elements are the same: *allongés rêve*, wakefulness under the appearance of sleep; the bed is occupied, but hardly by a woman—like the cats, the "queen of dreams" has been virtually reduced to eyes, instrument of contemplation. Her eyes have the same ambiguity as the eyes of cats: they watch, they demand to be watched; they too are like stars, and these *étoiles noires* [black stars], in a symbolic synthesis, explicitly achieve the simultaneity of darkness and light; and so does everything else in the room: *ici, tout a la suffisante clarté et la délicieuse obscurité de l'harmonie* [here, everything has the self-contained clarity and the delightful obscurity of harmony]. To cast out any possible doubt, the "translation" is given: this room looks like a dream (it *is* a dream), its true nature is *véritablement spirituelle* [truly spiritual]. The code is made up of the stock of images evoked by "bedroom," but the fundamental theme is still the same beatitude represented by the cats, the sphinxes, and their human counterparts: contemplation abolishes time and plunges you into blissful eternity.

Another variant of the structure provides a regular commentary on the second tercet: in "Les Yeux de Berthe," there are dark eyes the description of which is synonymous with our sonnet:

> ... arcanes adorés,
> Vous ressemblez beaucoup à ces grottes *magiques*
> Où, derrière l'amas des ombres léthargiques,
> *Scintillent vaguement* des trésors ignorés!

> ... beloved mysteries,
> You much resemble those magic grottoes
> Where, behind the mass of lethargic shadows,
> Glint vaguely unknown treasures!

Arcanes and *trésors ignorés* develop [14]*mystiques*: these eyes are like the eyes of the Queen of Sheba in Flaubert's *Tentation—de grands yeux noirs, plus sombres que les cavernes mystiques* [big black eyes, darker than the mystic caves][13]—at the very moment she proclaims that she is no woman but a universe, a "succession of mysteries." The motif of treasure shining in the dark is repeated in the mystic antithesis of night as a font of light:

> ... des yeux obscurs, profonds et vastes,
> Comme toi, Nuit immense, éclairés comme toi!

> ... dark eyes, profound and wide,
> Like you, boundless Night, lit up like you!

and then the translation is given:

> Leurs feux sont ces pensers d'Amour, mêlés de Foi,
> Qui pétillent au fond, voluptueux ou chastes.

> Their fires are these thoughts of Love, mingled with Faith,
> Which sparkle in their depths, sensuous or chaste.

Thus is the symbolism of the eyes demonstrated: they are certainly not the eyes of

---

[13] Chapter II, edited by Dumesnil, p. 42. The passage was published in *L'Artiste* of December 21, 1856, and reviewed by Baudelaire one year later.

Baudelaire's mulatto paramour as most critics choose to think. The poet gazes into these eyes and for him they are like intercessors in his contemplation.

This act of intercession by eyes, we find again in "Le Chat" (*Fleurs*, LI), whose genuinely symbolic character I have hinted at before; at the end of the poem the eyes move to where the Church Fathers and the mystics after them set the *oculi animae*. When the poet looks within himself, he finds the eyes interiorized, looking at him from out of the depths of his soul. These eyes of the spirit mirroring the eyes of the body are a definite allusion to the language of esoterism, wherein reciprocity is a metaphor for secret "correspondences." Baudelaire himself refers to this in the prose version of "L'Invitation au Voyage": he invites an allegorical flower to *se mirer, pour parler comme les mystiques, dans sa propre correspondance* [to mirror itself—to speak with the mystics—in its own correlative]. Finally, the parallelism between *Amour* and *amoureux*, and between *Foi* and *savants* demonstrates the metaphysical nature of their symbolism.

Our comparisons supply us with a tool for evaluating the components of Baudelaire's imagery and their role: "eyes," for instance, are not part of a code; they appear invariably and are therefore essential to a structure symbolic of infinity—whose invariant is a relation *fascinating light + darkness*. In fact, Baudelaire might almost be giving us a demonstrative outline when he describes how make-up transforms a face into the mysterious mask of a priestess, how that mask represents supernatural life, how mascara, *ce cadre noir, rend le regard plus profond... donne à l'œil une apparence... de fenêtre ouverte sur l'infini* [this black outline, makes the gaze more profound... gives the eye an appearance... of a window opened on the infinite].[14] Certain texts in which we find the eyes, such as "A une Passante," may seem very different at first sight, but we can now classify them as permutation groups of the "fascinating light" variants. In that sonnet a glance from a woman encountered by chance on the street—lightning, then night—sets off a mystic dream: the difference, a shift from a gaze-code to a glance-code, is in the frustrating briefness of this illumination. The prose poem "Le Désir de peindre," usually associated by critics with "A une Passante" because of the lightning in the eyes of the female character, belongs, on the contrary, in the main group: among other parallelisms it offers *deux antres où scintille vaguement le mystère* [two caves where mystery gleams vaguely]—note the adverb—a variant of the "fascinating light" structure, complete with translation. This comparative approach also explains why "Les Chats" are inseparable from "Les Hiboux." Both cats and owls stare into darkness, their eyes are phosphorescent, they are philosophic and come to the same moral conclusion as the unmoving Sphinx: happiness is in sedentariness. The two poems are variants of the same structure, and they differ only in style—"Les Hiboux" are like a fable or an apologue.

A description of *Les Fleurs du Mal* based on this method should be an improvement upon the usual enumerations of images arranged by vehicles, that is, according to the codes, to the interchangeable words—these cannot lead anywhere, nor can they account for the variations of meaning in the symbolism of such words—and perhaps there is some justification for this approach to be found in Baudelaire's structuralist definition of the symbol: *la forme moulée sur l'idée* [the form molded to the idea].

---

[14] *Le peintre de la vie moderne*, XI, "Éloge du maquillage" (Pléiade, p. 1185).